Borderland Battles

CONTENTS

TABLES, FIGURES, AND MAPS

Tables

Figures

Maps

ACKNOWLEDGMENTS

This book would not exist without the hundreds of people across the Colombian-Ecuadorian and Colombian-Venezuelan borderlands, and in Bogotá, Caracas, and Quito, who shared their time, knowledge, and experiences with me. I am grateful to them, and especially to the families who welcomed me to their homes and with whom I developed meaningful friendships over the years. Their hospitality and generosity had no limits. They showed me what the social fabric of borderlanders can look like.

There are four women I would like to thank in particular—they know that I mean them. They accompanied me on different parts of my fieldwork journey. Their strength, courage, and leadership do not cease to inspire me. I am confident that with people like them—people who continue to make a difference in their communities, despite the risks that this entails—there is hope for a better, more secure tomorrow in the borderlands. It is my heartfelt desire that one day I will be able to openly thank them and others by name for all they did, and all they continue to do.

The support of many local and international organizations was invaluable for my fieldwork. They made traveling along and across the border so much safer and insightful. I would like to highlight the support by the United Nations High Commissioner for Refugees, the United Nations Office of the High Commissioner for Human Rights, the United Nations Mission Colombia, the United Nations Development Programme, the United Nations Office on Drugs and Crime, the Mission to Support the Peace Process in Colombia of the Organization of American States, the German Development Cooperation GIZ, the Norwegian Refugee Council, CARITAS, the Jesuit Refugee Service, the Colombian National Peace Observatory, the Ecuadorian Border Network for Peace (Red Fronteriza de Paz), and the Venezuelan Fe y Alegría. I also would like to thank Universidad de los Andes Bogotá, FLACSO Quito, and Universidad Central de Caracas for their academic support in Colombia, Ecuador, and

Venezuela, as well as the Colombian High Commission for Reintegration for facilitating access to former combatants.

I have been privileged to be able to work with, and learn from, so many brilliant minds at the University of Oxford. They have informed my thinking during the writing process for this book, especially at the Changing Character of War Centre, the Department of Politics and International Relations, the Department of International Development, the Latin American Centre, Pembroke College, and St Antony's College. I am grateful to the participants at the book workshop at Oxford's Centre for International Studies for their useful feedback, particularly Andrew Hurrell, Robert Johnson, David Keen, Keith Krause, Eduardo Posada Carbó, and Laurence Whitehead. At Oxford, I also would like to thank Alexander Betts, Richard Caplan, Malcolm Deas, Janina Dill, Simón Escoffier Martínez, Jörg Friedrichs, John Gledhill, Halbert Jones, Stathis Kalyvas, Kalypso Nicolaidas, David Preston, Adam Roberts, Diego Sánchez-Ancochea, Felipe Roa Clavijo, Peter Wilson, and Julia Zulver.

I am indebted to Michael Athanson for his excellent mentorship to produce the maps for this book, and I am grateful to Laura Courchesne, Mauricio Portilla, Santiago Rosas, and Andes Zambrano for outstanding research assistance.

Outside Oxford, I would like to thank friends and colleagues at the Drugs, Security, and Democracy Program as partners in crime in embarking and sharing insights on such challenging research, especially Peter Andreas, Desmond Arias, Ana Arjona, Adam Baird, María Clemencia Ramírez, Lucía Dammert, Graham Denyer Willis, Angélica Durán-Martínez, Daniel Esser, Vanda Felbab-Brown, Paul Gootenberg, Thomas Grisaffi, Benjamin Lessing, Eduardo Moncada, Susan Norman, Javier Osorio, Winifred Tate, and Ana Villarreal. I am deeply thankful to Arlene Tickner for her support throughout the process.

This work benefited enormously from inspiring discussions and shared conference panels with conflict scholars and Colombia experts, especially Fernando Cepeda, James Forest, Peter Krause, Romain Malejacq, Théodore McLauchlin, Cecile Mouly, Jenny Pearce, Costantino Pischedda, William Reno, Lee Seymour, Henning Tamm, and Michael Weintraub. My thanks also go to David McBride for his excellent guidance and support at Oxford University Press as well as to the anonymous reviewers for their helpful comments.

I could not have accomplished this work without financial support from the German Academic National Foundation; the Drugs, Security and Democracy Fellowship Program administered by the Social Science Research Council and the Universidad de Los Andes in cooperation with and with funds provided by the Open Society Foundations and the International Development Research Centre, Ottawa, Canada; the Economic and Social Science Research Council Impact Acceleration Award; the UK Higher Education Innovation Funding with the Global Challenges Research Fund; the Santander Award; FLACSO Quito;

and several grants and awards at the University of Oxford, including the Oxford Department of International Development and St Antony's College.

My friends and family accompanied me throughout this process. I cannot thank enough Marthe Achtnich, Chloé Lewis, and Ina Zharkevich for their support. My brother Stefan with Sandra and Mathilda were incredible sources of energy. I am most grateful to my parents, Manuela and Thomas, for their love, patience, and support from the inception to the end of this journey. This book is dedicated to them.

ABBREVIATIONS

ACCU	Autodefensas Campesinas de Córdoba y Urabá (Peasant Self-Defense Forces of Córdoba and Urabá)
ADF	Allied Democratic Forces
AUC	Autodefensas Unidas de Colombia (United Self-Defense Forces of Colombia)
BACRIM	Bandas Criminales Emergentes (Emerging Criminal Bands)
CODHES	Consultoría para los Derechos Humanos y el Desplazamiento (Consulting for Human Rights and Displacement)
COMBIFRON	Comisión Binacional de Frontera (Binational Border Commission)
DRC	Democratic Republic of the Congo
FDLR	Democratic Forces for the Liberation of Rwanda
FDC	Forces de Défense Congolaise
ELN	Ejército de Liberación Nacional (National Liberation Army)
EPL	Ejército Popular de Liberación (Popular Liberation Army)
ERPAC	Ejército Revolucionario Popular Antisubversivo de Colombia (Popular Revolutionary Anti-Terrorist Army of Colombia)
FARC-EP	Fuerzas Armadas Revolucionarias de Colombia—Ejército del Pueblo (Revolutionary Armed Forces of Colombia—People's Army)
FATA	Federally Administered Tribal Areas
FBL	Fuerzas Bolivarianas de Liberación (Bolivarian Forces of Liberation)

M-19	Movimiento 19 de Abril (19th of April Movement)
M-23	Mouvement du 23-Mars (March 23 Movement)
UN	United Nations
US	United States
USD	US dollars

PROLOGUE

Witnessing Insecurity from the Margins

This book is the result of a decade of research in and about the shared borderlands of Colombia, Ecuador, and Venezuela. It presents an alternative narrative of the recent history of the modern world's longest internal armed conflict and its embeddedness in a region where violent crime is entrenched—a history of insecurity witnessed from the margins.[1]

This decade starts on March 1, 2008, when the Colombian armed forces bombed a camp of the Revolutionary Armed Forces of Colombia–People's Army (Fuerzas Armadas Revolucionarias de Colombia–Ejército del Pueblo—FARC). The bombing took place, however, in Angostura, 1.8 kilometer into Ecuadorian territory. Killing the FARC's number two in command, Raúl Reyes, the skirmish marked a turning point in Colombia's internal armed conflict. From the country's center, it was seen as an iron-fisted message of strength from Bogotá to the FARC. Yet the message *to* Bogotá was a different one; furious about the violation of their territorial sovereignty through what they considered an unannounced military incursion, Ecuador cut diplomatic relations with its neighbor. Venezuela did so too, and stationed tanks and troops at its border. At that moment, I decided to carry out field research to explore the spillover potential of Colombia's war to its neighbors in the aftermath of Angostura. I focused my work on the Ecuadorian northern border zone, which was at that time becoming increasingly militarized, securitized, and stigmatized as a result of the attack.[2]

I then decided to widen my lens of analysis to explore all four sides of the Colombian-Ecuadorian and Colombian-Venezuelan borderlands. This way, I was able to witness the developments in Colombia's war from the margins, literally and figuratively. Between 2011 and 2013, my research took me not only to Bogotá, Caracas, and Quito but also to numerous towns, villages, indigenous settlements, and lone farms in the Colombian departments of Nariño and

Putumayo, and the Ecuadorian provinces of Esmeraldas, Carchi, and Sucumbíos at the Colombia-Ecuador border; and in the Colombian departments of Arauca, Norte de Santander, Cesar, and La Guajira, as well as the Venezuelan states of Apure, Táchira, and Zulia at the Colombia-Venezuela border (see appendix C).

This journey was interspersed with historical political landmarks. Shortly after Reyes's death, then FARC leader Manuel Marulanda Vélez died of a heart attack on 26 March.[3] The insurgents were hit hard again when Colombian state forces killed Marulanda's successor, Alfonso Cano, on 4 November 2011.[4] I had just left Tumaco, a border town on the Pacific coast, when I heard the news. Although miles away from where Cano himself was killed (in Suárez, Cauca), that week ten military officials were killed in Tumaco by the FARC in the aftermath of Cano's death, and the people I spoke to voiced their concerns about the recent increase in combat, kidnappings, assaults, and land mines. I then traveled to the remote border department of Putumayo, where locals also felt the violent shockwaves that resulted from Cano's death. Suddenly, my travels became more risky than they had been before—everyone expected acts of retaliation. Cano's killing left the FARC weakened. As some analysts argue, it was this position of weakness that eventually brought them to the negotiation table again,[5] after previous peace talks under then president Andrés Pastrana Arango between 2000 and 2002 had failed.[6]

In August 2012, Colombian president Juan Manuel Santos Calderón announced the beginning of formal peace negotiations between the Colombian government and the FARC rebels. Around that time, my journey took me across the border from Venezuelan Apure to Colombian Arauca, one of the most war-torn regions of the country. While internationally the announcement was met with praise and optimism, in Arauca it resulted in bomb detonations and gunshots. The department registered a spike in the number of attacks and armed clashes between guerrillas and armed forces—after all, no one wants to be seen as starting negotiations from a position of weakness.

In October of the same year, Hugo Chávez Frías was re-elected president of Venezuela, which many interpreted as the beginning of the country's shift toward authoritarianism. Carrying out research in Venezuela's border zone at the time, I joined one of eight Jesuit priests—my hosts—in observing the polling stations in the Venezuelan town of Maracaibo. In this city, the elections not only contributed to the polarization that characterized the rest of the country as well but also fueled fears of a rise in cross-border tensions. Two years later, Chávez would be defeated by cancer, and Nicolás Maduro Moros would become his successor. Since then, Venezuela has been dragged into a downward spiral of economic crisis, political turmoil, and criminal violence.

From the perspective of the Andean margins, the second half of this decade, after 2013, was paradigmatic of a constantly evolving security landscape rather than a linear pathway toward a horizon of peace. In this five-year period, I carried out several follow-up fieldwork trips. In 2014, I returned to the war-torn Catatumbo region, a powder keg where the FARC, the National Liberation Army (Ejército de Liberación Nacional—ELN), and the Popular Liberation Army (Ejército Popular de Liberación—EPL)[7] governed territory and its inhabitants, and liaised with multiple right-wing and trafficking groups to benefit from the lucrative illicit drug trade. I listened to worried people who then still lived under the reign of alias "Megateo," EPL leader and narco-broker. As I discuss in chapter 6, local community members described him as a role model, a "brother" who "understands the people." He was killed by the Colombian armed forces in October 2015. Triggering mass displacements, this lethal military operation greatly concerned locals, yet Bogotá and the international media hailed it as a success in the global war on drugs. The era of the "Warlord of [a] Rural Cocaine Fiefdom," as the New York Times dubbed him, or the "most wanted drug lord," according to the BBC, was over.[8]

While Colombia continued on its journey between war and peace, three humanitarian crises at Colombia's borders with Venezuela and Ecuador overshadowed political developments. First, in 2015, Venezuelan president Maduro mandated the unilateral closure of the Colombia-Venezuela border and started to deport Colombians en masse. More than twenty thousand Colombians who had been living illegally in Venezuela crossed back into Colombia, straining local resources and fueling diplomatic tensions between the two countries.[9] When I returned to the Colombian side in January 2016, it was still formally closed; I was not able to cross over to Venezuela. I then went back to Arauca, where people were not only concerned about how the border closure undermined their livelihoods—to a large extent sustained through legal and illegal cross-border trade—but also about the prospects of "peace" with the FARC. Due to the ELN's dominant position in Arauca, the idea that the FARC might demobilize fueled fears of an increase in violence rather than hope for a better life in the region. The second humanitarian crisis took shape further north, in the department of La Guajira, where I returned to in early 2016. State neglect and severe drought produced a situation in which children, particularly indigenous Wayúu, were dying of malnutrition. Given the immediacy of their needs, for community members, the vision of a peace negotiated in Havana did not translate into a lived reality of peace in their territory. The third crisis affected Ecuador. Shortly after the ELN and the Colombian government announced the beginning of peace talks in Quito in March 2016, a deadly earthquake struck the Ecuadorian border province of Esmeraldas. The resulting humanitarian response became a national priority, stalling mediation efforts until early 2017.

The rest of the year continued to be eventful in Colombia. On June 23, 2016, the FARC and the Colombian government agreed to a bilateral ceasefire. In

August, I was in a meeting with the commander of the Colombian army when he received a call from Cuba where the peace talks were underway; after more than fifty years of armed conflict and four years of negotiations, the Colombian government and the FARC had reached a final peace agreement. Yet while it sparked enthusiasm internationally, within the country skepticism was rife. As a taxi driver in Bogotá put it to me on the morning after the announcement of the deal: how could Colombians be sure that ex-FARC combatants would be able to reintegrate into civilian life after decades in the jungle? Would they not use the demobilization as a pretext to continue life as criminals, fueling insecurity in urban areas? These and other concerns that demonstrated people's mistrust toward peace would go on to contribute to a vote that, while a surprise to many outsiders, was to a certain degree predictable to some of those who were following events closely. Even though on September 26, president Santos and FARC leader Timochenko signed the peace deal, it was rejected in a plebiscite on October 2, 2016. Still, Santos was awarded the Nobel Peace Prize on October 7, 2016, perhaps the Nobel Peace Prize Committee's vote of confidence to the Colombian president.[10] In any case, the results of the plebiscite were telling: having suffered most from continued violence, almost all border areas voted in favor of peace, while in less marginalized regions the "no" vote prevailed.[11]

On November 24, 2016, headlines in Bogotá's newspapers praised Santos and Timochenko for finally signing a revised peace deal, ending more than five decades of armed conflict—this time, supposedly, for real.[12] This revised deal was approved by Congress shortly afterward, paving the way for a new era of peace. The situation on the ground in Colombia's margins, however, did not reflect a straightforward transition from war to peace. At that time, I was back in Tumaco. Locals expressed unease amid uncertainty over who would fill the power vacuums left by the FARC, should they indeed demobilize. They were also worried because of the most recent killings of that month, supposedly triggered by the assassination of a FARC dissident, as I discuss later in the book. Planning my travels for the following day to Catatumbo in the border department of Norte de Santander, I reviewed social media and was sent photos of roads blocked by explosives, an attack by ELN rebels against a police station, EPL pamphlets announcing the continuation of the armed struggle, a burned ambulance marked with EPL graffiti, and farmers fleeing their homes, scared of being caught in the crossfire.

For the international community, the peace deal ended the FARC's armed struggle against a democratically elected government. Yet for many marginalized community members, it also ended their informal protection by the FARC from other armed groups: paramilitary successor groups, Venezuelan gangs, Mexican drug cartels, and ELN rebels. The EPL was another source of fear, as it gained more territory and numbers than the FARC had held in Norte de Santander.[13]

In early 2017, the FARC began to demobilize in designated transition zones across Colombia, and the ELN formally entered peace talks with the Colombian government in Quito. Meanwhile, Venezuela's crisis worsened, producing an overwhelming influx of Venezuelans across the border to Colombia. In Ecuador, former president Rafael Correa Delgado's party secured its legacy by winning the presidential elections held in April 2017. By the time I went to some of the demobilization camps in March and April 2017, where FARC members were laying down their weapons, the Colombian president, ministers, and the international press had already visited, reinforcing the narrative of the peace deal's success to the world. Remarkably, the FARC did complete the process and became a formal political party on September 1, 2017.[14] The country's pathway toward peace seemed to be irreversible now, and gained additional momentum with the ceasefire between the ELN and the government, announced shortly afterward in Quito.

Yet while Bogotá heralded the beginning of a new, more peaceful era, in the borderlands there is still no clear line between war and peace. At the Colombia-Venezuela border, violence continues to be fueled by a brutal war between the ELN and the EPL, the operations of FARC dissidents, and criminals taking advantage of Venezuela's crisis. At the Colombia-Ecuador border, the murders of three Ecuadorian journalists by dissident rebels, Quito's decision to revive militarization of the zone, and the stalling of the ELN talks in Quito (then moved to Havana) also present a sobering critique of the narrative of a "peace era." Across both borders, cocaine production and other illicit businesses are thriving.

Witnessed from the margins, and against the historical backdrop of decades of conflict and crime in the Andean region, perhaps just another decade of insecurity passed by. Yet a perspective from the margins also highlights something else. While the centers have continuously focused their attention on large-scale attacks, as the one with which I started this decade, they have ignored how local communities have been maneuvering multiple kinds of insecurities along and across the border. Listening to their voices and understanding their experiences may not only serve to comprehend why insecurity in the margins has persisted throughout this decade, from 2008 to 2018. Perhaps it can also help change views from the centers, so that in the next decade, peace and security will indeed extend to and across the margins.

BORDERLAND MAPS

Map 0.1 The shared borderlands of Colombia, Ecuador, and Venezuela. Map created by
Author.

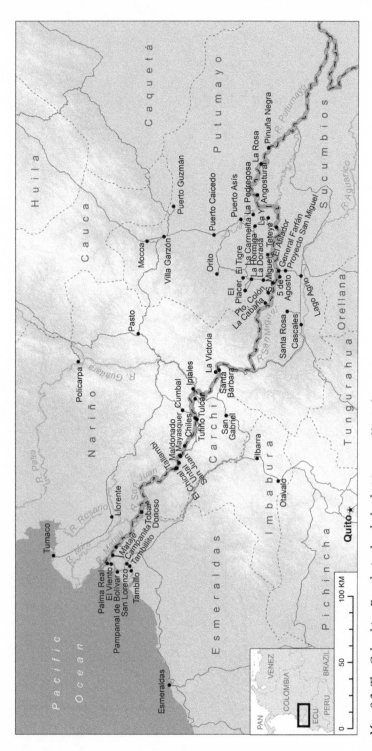

Map 0.2 The Colombian-Ecuadorian borderlands. Map created by Author.

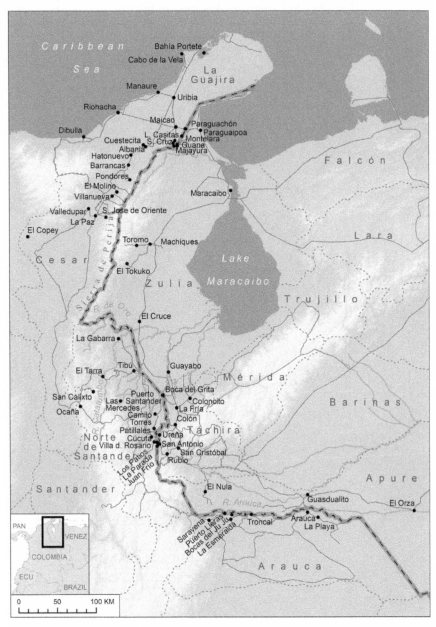

Map 0.3 The Colombian-Venezuelan borderlands. Map created by Author.

Borderland Battles

1

Borderlands

Security through a Magnifying Glass

Paraguaipoa, Venezuela. On 21 May 2012, the Revolutionary Armed Forces of Colombia–People's Army (Fuerzas Armadas Revolucionarias de Colombia–Ejército del Pueblo—FARC) attacked the Colombian army near the remote Majayura village across the border, and then escaped back to the Venezuelan Guana village afterward. They killed twelve Colombian soldiers and injured four. Suspicion and fear prevailed when I visited the Venezuelan village of Paraguaipoa shortly afterward. Who knew the guerrillas' whereabouts? Would paramilitaries strike back in revenge? Those who speak out against either side are targets. An indigenous leader warned me: "They did surveillance on [my friend, a human rights defender]. Both the guerrillas and the paramilitaries attempted to assassinate her. They operate in this zone."[1]

Cúcuta, Colombia. In the same month, some hundred kilometers south in the Colombian bordertown of Cúcuta, an employee of a humanitarian organization commented on the frequent breakdown of fragile alliances among organized criminal groups on the Venezuelan side of the border: "They kill each other in Venezuela and throw the bodies into Colombia. They are not interested in meddling with the national justice system. Instead, the problem should go to Colombia. This is what the paramilitaries did here. They copied them!"[2]

General Farfán, Ecuador. Also in 2012, a farmer from the Colombian-Ecuadorian borderlands criticized: "The Ecuadorian police do nothing regarding security at the border because they fear reprisals by the Colombian guerrillas. The guerrillas run our village. If something bad happens, if a car gets stolen, people go to the other side because they are more efficient than the Ecuadorian police. No one talks about it. Don't talk so that they don't kill you."[3] A few months earlier, a Colombian ex-guerrilla had put this to me clearly: "The Ecuadorians are all friends. If someone is an enemy and doesn't want to collaborate, he pulls himself together, leaves, or is killed. That's how it is. They give us shops, warehouses, houses, or food; they belong to the organization."[4]

Borderlands are like a magnifying glass on the security challenges of the world. They can be plagued with violence, sites of organized crime, and laboratories of governance.

Violence. In frontier areas like Paraguaipoa, mistrust and hostility between fighting parties become death traps to anyone who disobeys the rules of the game. Generating a safe haven for attackers, the borderline facilitates the use of violence. The physical distance from any means of protection augments the proneness to victimization, turning action to effect change into a risk to one's survival. Such fundamental dilemmas related to conflict and cooperation have shaped human interaction throughout history: namely, how to ensure security in the absence of a legitimately perceived authority.

Crime. In border towns like Cúcuta, shared interests in immediate profit from smuggling drugs, arms, and dirty money attract ruthless criminals and conflict actors in search of income to fuel their fighting. Mocking principles of national sovereignty, these violent entrepreneurs cross borders to eliminate defectors and anyone meddling in their illicit business deals. The borderlands' transnationality produces a space of impunity and illegality, leaving witnesses in a limbo of silence and uncertainty. In a diluted, yet expanded fashion, the ease of reaping benefits from the illicit global political economy also lies at the root of a profound change in the world's security landscape today: the transnational and interconnected activities of violent non-state groups, which increasingly stir up a global order still formally dominated by nation-states.

Governance. In peripheral villages like General Farfán, pockets of non-state governance are transformed into transnational regions of illicit authority, penetrating all structures of society. On the margins of both the state and statehood, these forms of order escape the reach of governments. Communities are left to devise their own ways of navigating everyday life, consenting to an existence in the shadows of society. The neglect of fragile borderlands by those in power has consequences that are hardly visible, but very pervasive—and they may foreshadow the state of communities across the globe in the future: an irreparable alienation of the marginalized from central power holders, and a little-registered, but strongly felt, plight of civilians.

Providing unique and exclusive firsthand insights into the war-torn shared borderlands of Colombia, Ecuador, and Venezuela, this book reveals how the myriad and dynamic interactions among rebels, paramilitaries, drug cartels, and other violent non-state groups engender violence, erode the social fabric of communities, and challenge the empirical legitimacy of governments by facilitating alternative forms of governance. It shows how the geography and political economy of borderlands magnify these security repercussions, while concealing them from the outside world.

Such borderland dynamics are particularly pronounced in vulnerable regions, often belonging to the so-called Global South.[5] The physical distance of
border areas from state centers translates into the historical marginalization of
these zones, resulting in weak state governance systems. They lack proper integration into the national economy. Road infrastructure to connect border regions with cities in the central parts of the countries is often absent, whereas
towns across the border offer markets to engage in commercial exchange. Due to
the transnationality, a low-risk/high-opportunity environment characterizes the
political economy of these borderlands: connecting different economic systems,
borderlands are conducive to rent-seeking activities because the decline or increase in the value of various goods at borders makes exchange profitable. These
features turn borderlands into an enabling setting for contraband and smuggling.
Their transnational character, in combination with their distance from power
centers, fuels impunity.

While law enforcement authorities are limited to territorial delineations,
armed non-state actors benefit from the deficient harmonization of two different
security and justice systems at the international border; they are infrequently,
if ever, held accountable for breaking national laws. From a state perspective,
borderlands in vulnerable regions are unruly zones where the borderline as a
marker of territorial sovereignty is the feature most deserving of attention. From
a borderland perspective, non-state forms of governance produce their own
logic of order, in which the pursuit of illicit activities across the border unites
a transnational community in what borderlanders perceive to be legitimate behavior. I consider this the moral economy of borderlands in vulnerable regions.
This tension makes borderlands the "place to be" for an array of different kinds
of violent non-state groups. They compete for territorial control, cooperate in
illegal transnational activities, and jointly undertake huge financially and politically profitable operations. They also impose alternative rules of behavior on
locals, and complement each other in substituting state governance functions,
such as the provision of security, health, or infrastructure.

Complex interactions among violent non-state groups in borderlands occur
across the globe. In Southeast Asia, the terrorist group Jemaah Islamiyah and
the insurgent Free Aceh Movement strengthened their networks in border
regions.[6] In South Asia, the militant group Tehrik-i-Taliban-Pakistan used
Pakistan's Federally Administered Tribal Areas, bordering Afghanistan, as a safe
haven from which to launch attacks on Afghanistan and Pakistan.[7] In Africa's
Great Lake region, the Allied Democratic Forces rebel group benefited from the
strategic location of the Rwenzori borderland shared by Uganda and Congo to
sustain its fighting.[8] In the Horn of Africa, the Islamist Al-Shabaab and Hizbul
Islam organized in Somalia's borderlands to engage in cross-border strikes.[9] In
the Americas, the tri-border area shared by Argentina, Brazil, and Paraguay is a

hub of organized criminal groups and religious extremist groups, allegedly including Hezbollah.[10] The United States (US)-Mexican borderlands are profitable areas for drug cartels and smaller trafficking groups.[11] Even in less fragile
settings in Western Europe this phenomenon is common. The Irish Republican
Army, for example, consolidated its power on the Anglo-Irish border. Also,
more recently, trafficking rings operating around Calais and across borders in
the Mediterranean area fueled conflict while reaping profit by cooperating in
human smuggling.[12]

Borderlands feature a particularly complex security landscape; studying
them helps us comprehend these complexities more broadly. Our world sees
a global trend of proliferation of violent non-state groups, labeled, for example,
terrorists, extremists, rebels, paramilitaries, gangs, or criminals. At the beginning
of the twenty-first century, more than seventy of such groups operate in eastern
Congo, hundreds in Libya, and around six thousand have been counted in Syria.[13]
These groups do not operate in isolation. Tracing their interactions paints a surprisingly diverse picture: they range from brutal fighting over short-lived, unstable arrangements characterized by violent breakdowns, to stable long-term
relationships with low levels of violence. In Africa's Great Lakes region, the M23
rebels and other groups engaged in short-lived business arrangements in the illicit trade of minerals, while fighting each other elsewhere. In Libya, militias engage both in quickly shifting alliances and in relatively stable relations with other
militias, as well as traffickers involved in human smuggling. In Syria, thousands
of different armed groups engage in fragile alliances, violent clashes, and forge
business ties in multiple forms of transnational organized crime that include
antiquities smuggling and arms trafficking.

In unstable regions across the globe where state presence is minimal, we can
observe similar patterns. In the Southeast Asian Golden Triangle, several groups
involved in disputes related to Myanmar's multi-party conflict also engage in
supply chain relationships and other arrangements related to the illicit opium
trade. Groups in Iraq, Sudan, Somalia, Lebanon, and Afghanistan compete and
cooperate in manifold ways over time, and from one region to another. Even
in countries that do not suffer armed conflict, entrepreneurs of violence are involved in arrangements with each other. In El Salvador, Guatemala, Honduras,
and Mexico, drug cartels and gangs forge tactical alliances in some regions, while
in others they fight each other to secure control over supply routes. The activities
of different gangs in Brazilian favelas and South African slums likewise display
elements of conflict and cooperation.[14]

How can we make sense of patterns of behavior among non-state actors that
the state cannot see? We know a good deal about the relationships between states
and violent non-state groups but, despite their increasing global relevance, less
so about the logics of the manifold interactions among various types of violent

non-state groups. Examining the interactions among these groups reveals at least three puzzling behavioral patterns. First, they contradict the widespread view that armed conflict is about monopolistic territorial control. Instead, various armed actors often share territory, regardless of their political motivation, contrary to what one might expect from the civil war literature. Second, they challenge the conventional thinking that ideologically opposed groups fight each other. Insurgents and paramilitaries frequently enter cooperative relationships, even though they are ideological foes. At the same time, some ideologically similar entities, such as two guerrilla groups, fight brutal wars against each other. Third, rent-seeking criminal groups invest costly resources in their disputes, even though one might expect them to reduce costs and maximize profits, for example by communicating intentions via signaling.[15]

Our limited knowledge about these interactions is alarming if we consider their serious impacts on the security of civilians. Conflicts involving numerous violent non-state groups have become the most lethal form of insecurity in the world.[16] They produce severe economic and social hardship, and concurrent flows of refugees. As cases such as El Salvador and Guatemala attest, countries where organized crime is thriving and drug cartels and gangs are operating now have the highest homicide rates worldwide. Typically, "newsworthy" occurrences such as combat between armed groups, clashes with state forces, and mass killings of civilians spark the interest of academics, policymakers, and the wider public. Yet the operations of violent non-state groups also have less visible consequences: they strain people's social ties and alienate local communities from state authorities. Situations with low rates of violence, but high perceptions of insecurity or intense social control imposed by violent non-state groups, have hardly been examined in the context of other, more visibly insecure spaces. We usually avert our eyes once the outbreak of violence is over, although armed actors are still present, and surviving civilians are left in what I describe as a "tense calm."

Which interactions among violent non-state groups result in violence against civilians? When do they fuel perceptions of, rather than observed, insecurity? Why do they matter on a structural level, such as the state-society relationship? The exact way in which interactions among multiple violent non-state groups affect security, and their wider repercussions, remain obscure. Research on security dynamics that arise in the context of violent non-state groups involved in illicit economic activities is limited, perhaps hampered by the inherent danger of the required field research. The lack of knowledge on these issues is most evident at the states' margins. Given the urgency of current crises, opportunities to answer such questions through developing research from persistently fragile settings and protracted conflicts (that have reached or are close to finding a peaceful settlement) are often overlooked.

By immersing myself into the war-torn and crime-ridden Colombian-Ecuadorian and Colombian-Venezuelan borderlands, with this book I do just that.[17] I draw on extensive, challenging fieldwork in four remote border zones belonging to three different countries to explain, through the voices of more than six hundred victims, perpetrators, bystanders, and others, how different forms of interactions among violent non-state groups in these border areas affect citizen security. I use "citizen security" in order not to conflate "security" with "absence of violence," and instead also account for people's social fabric, their perceptions, and the possibility of taking measures to protect oneself.

I argue that interactions among violent non-state groups have distinct impacts on citizen security.[18] Depending on the type of interaction, they create not only physical violence but also less visible forms of insecurity. Three patterns stand out. First, in the absence of an arrangement between groups such as insurgents and paramilitaries, violent clashes between them contribute to civilian deaths and displacements. Notwithstanding their exposure to violence, to maximize chances for survival, people can follow rules that arise from the relatively clear front lines in this situation. Second, unstable short-term arrangements including criminal spot sales (for example, of weapons) and barter agreements (for example, to exchange illicit drugs with gasoline), tactical alliances, and subcontractual relationships, commonly involve selective killings rather than general violence, fueling mistrust and uncertainty in communities embedded in such an environment, which erodes their social fabric. Third, in relatively stable long-term arrangements, namely, supply chain relationships, strategic alliances, pacific coexistence, and preponderance relations, violent non-state groups are more restrained in their use of violence than in the other two patterns. Instead, they are typically the providers of security and other governance functions normally associated with the state. Surrounded by illusory calmness, violent non-state groups can maintain a flourishing illicit economy, a lucrative income source to sustain their fighting elsewhere, and locals can adapt their behavior to this situation. These conditions favor the emergence of what I call "shadow citizenship"—a social contract–like relationship in which armed actors provide public goods and services and define the rules of appropriate behavior while citizens socially recognize their illicit authority—and "shadow citizen security," security provided through such a relationship.

I show that in vulnerable regions, the specific geography of borderlands operates as a magnifying glass, intensifying facets of insecurity which are more diluted elsewhere. This is due to two characteristics of borderlands: first, their transnationality;[19] and second, their distance to state centers. Together, in vulnerable regions such as Colombia's borderlands, they yield a unique political and moral borderland economy and social ramifications:[20] weak state governance, a low-risk/high-opportunity environment, and a propensity for impunity. The confluence of these factors produces a "border effect" that, just as a magnifying glass concentrates rays of light into a powerful beam, concentrates bundles of insecurity: it attracts violent non-state groups and facilitates violence. This confluence also renders it less visible to those outside the borderlands.

International borderlines themselves are directly involved in interactions among violent non-state groups that take place in borderlands. Also, the proximity of violent non-state group operations to the border intensifies the logics of their interactions and related security repercussions. State-centric views ignore or distort these nuances. They also perpetuate urban myths about passive margins. By contrast, research in and on these margins reveals the (nonviolent) everyday battles advanced by the marginalized amid violence, crime, and governance imposed by illicit means. By discussing how this resulting border effect produces a magnified version of insecurities that are present in more-diluted forms elsewhere, I link the analysis of transnational borderlands to debates on relations between three actors relevant for people's security in contexts of armed conflict and organized crime more broadly: people, violent non-state groups, and the state. Adopting a borderland lens as an epistemological approach to understanding security is therefore a means to study wider questions related to violence, crime, and governance that both concentrate on and transcend the state system.

1.1　From Local Security to Non-State Order around the Globe

"You have to be very cautious, always, always cautious. Do your job, but don't risk your life. Because here life isn't worth anything. A Coca-Cola is worth more than life. Life is worth nothing here."[21] This warning from a priest from Colombia's borderlands, one of my interviewees, shaped my fieldwork journeys that lie at the core of this book. I decided to immerse myself in this context to bring to life the experiences of a multitude of different people involved in, or affected by, war and crime in neglected and inaccessible border areas shared by Colombia, Ecuador, and Venezuela.[22] How can research in and on such seemingly desperate spaces help us understand patterns of behavior among violent non-state groups and the distinct impacts of each of these patterns on security?[23] How does it help us critically examine larger questions on order, conflict, and security? Conducting multi-year fieldwork in conflict zones located in remote areas of three countries allowed me to bring to the fore facets of how the world works in very extreme conditions. I learned how life in the borderlands is influenced by the diverse types of interactions that exist among rebels, paramilitaries, criminals, and other armed actors, and I used this understanding to build theory up from the micro level so that it reflects realities in conflict and violent settings in a more grounded way than do narratives written and told from a distance.

Colombia's Borderlands at the Convergence of Armed Conflict and Organized Crime

Colombia's borderlands constitute an extreme case of a complex security landscape. In vulnerable regions, borderlands generally tend to be such extreme cases because of the convergence of weak state governance, high incentives for illicit economic activities, and propensity for impunity in these places. The Andean borderlands constitute an extreme borderland case because, due to their political and socioeconomic context, the security facets that can be observed there are particularly striking. The convergence of the Colombian armed conflict and organized crime in these spaces epitomizes myriad interactions among multiple violent non-state groups that vary with regard to their reputations for how, and motivations for why, they operate and fight. I selected the Colombian-Venezuelan and Colombian-Ecuadorian borderlands rather than Colombia's shared borders with Panama, Brazil, and Peru because these are the most populated borderlands where both legal and illegal economic cross-border activities are thriving.[24]

In 2015, the Spanish newspaper *El País* listed the Colombia-Venezuela border as one of the seven hells on earth that one should never visit—right next to places such as the territory controlled by the so-called Islamic State, northern Nigeria, and Somalia.[25]

While this narrative perhaps seems extreme, there are plenty of reasons for this infamous reputation. And, although less known, the situation is similar at the Colombia-Ecuador border. As I witnessed when carrying out the research for this book, the presence of multiple violent non-state groups, including guerrillas, right-wing groups, and drug cartels, made both border regions difficult places to visit. Conflict actors exert territorial and social control on both sides of the border, cocaine is smuggled in any imaginable way, women and children are kidnapped for human trafficking, and border officials supplement poor salaries with bribes. In some parts, violence is soaring, yet when it comes to crossing the border, the risks are not always visible. There is no fortified wall, like in parts of the US-Mexico border. There is no deep ocean to cross on a life-risking journey, as is the case with the Mediterranean Sea. And there are no robot border guards pointing their guns at people who attempt to cross the borderline, such as at the Korean North-South divide. Yet crossing or moving along these Andean borders in certain parts entails a constant unease and presentiment that something might happen—that one might become a victim. It is tainted with an aura of a perpetual fear that arises from moving from one place to another—inconceivable to me before having experienced it.

Studying these borderlands facilitates exploration of the varying relationships among violent non-state groups and their security impacts across space and time. These border areas constitute geostrategic corridors for transnational organized crime (especially the cocaine business) and unite a civil war with non-conflict, yet violent, settings. This permits us to account for conflict actors in non-conflict territories, which helps us understand contexts in which people suffer insecurity in the absence or aftermath of war, or in which violence is slowly spreading, and we have not (yet) recognized that the situation resembles—or de facto is—a war.

I have been observing, analyzing, and traveling to the borderlands over the course of a decade (2008–2018; see Prologue), but this book reaches further back, to cover mainly the fifteen years from 2003 until 2018. Different conflict and criminal actors have gained and lost significance within this period, with new groups adding to, and others disappearing from, the panorama of armed actors. The year 2003 marked the start of the paramilitary demobilization process. It came shortly after Colombia was described by many as being on the verge of becoming a failed state.[26] The following time span includes the phase of the drug business's most intense fragmentation in decades.[27] It encompasses a period of a full-fledged armed conflict, the beginning of peace negotiations between the FARC (the largest rebel group) and the Colombian government, a unilateral ceasefire, a peace deal between the FARC and the government, the FARC's demobilization, culminating in 2018, with the first presidential elections that included the FARC as a political party (although they did not present a candidate). Yet this period of fifteen years also left a bitter aftertaste: despite high hopes for a peaceful future, multiple violent non-state groups continue their operations. At the time of the elections in 2018, the armed conflict with the National Liberation Army (Ejército de Liberación Nacional—ELN), the second largest rebel group, was still ongoing.[28] FARC dissidents (those who refused to demobilize) and FARC successors (FARC members who formally demobilized, but maintained illegal organizational structures or formed new ones) continue to be involved in illicit businesses. And various other violent non-state groups emerged or strengthened themselves, occupying both their "old" territory, and filling the power voids left behind by the FARC.

To contextualize this latest phase of Colombia's history, I briefly outline the evolution of conflict and crime over the past few decades in the region, and the particular role of the border areas in it. Colombia's borderlands have been exposed to more than fifty years of internal armed conflict, which led to 220,000 people being killed between 1958 and 2016; 81 percent of these were civilians. An additional 60,630 people were "disappeared,"[29] and 7.2 million—almost 17 percent of Colombia's population—were displaced, making it the second largest displacement crisis worldwide after Syria.[30] By 2018, more than 8.3 million people were formally reported as victims of the armed conflict to the government's Victims Unit.[31]

Colombia has a long history of violence. Its most recent iteration, the on-going armed conflict, began in 1948 with "La Violencia," a brutal contestation between the country's conservative and liberal parties, after the Liberal Party presidential candidate Jorge Eliécer Gaitán was assassinated. In the 1960s, dis-satisfaction about unmet social demands led to a conflict between Colombia's government and leftist guerrillas. During the 1970s, Colombia became the world's largest cocaine producer, with an increasing number of armed groups getting involved in the cocaine business. At that time, coca (the plant from which cocaine is produced) was cultivated primarily in Bolivia and Peru, while Colombia was the center of processing and trafficking the illicit drug.[32] With the emergence of two major drug cartels in Medellín and Cali during the 1980s, Colombian traffickers began to dominate the business. This benefited most armed groups, including the paramilitaries that formed in the 1980s to respond to escalating rates of violence.[33] The FARC and the ELN started to levy taxes on traffickers in exchange for protecting illicit cultivation, laboratories, and exports. In the early 1990s, the two major cartels were destroyed, and the cocaine market became more disorganized.[34] Meanwhile, coca cultivation followed the logic of what drug policy experts commonly refer to as the "balloon effect":[35] it declined in Bolivia and Peru, but instead of disappearing, it simply was displaced to and rose in Colombia (see section 3.1). The paramilitaries and the FARC intensified their involvement in the drug business. While the former dominated interna-tional cocaine trafficking, the latter expanded their activities to direct control, production, and domestic distribution.

The paramilitary umbrella organization United Self-Defense Forces of Colombia (Autodefensas Unidas de Colombia—AUC), founded in 1997, added another dimension of violence to the conflict that increasingly muddled the lines between state and non-state actors.[36] In border regions where the state has historically had little presence, this blurring of lines has been particularly evident in the case of *armed* state and non-state actors. Supported by various parts of the Colombian state, the paramilitaries had links with politicians who, in return, actively sought to forge alliances with elements of the AUC to increase their power, a phenomenon that became known as the "para-politics" scandal.[37] Members of the Colombian state forces are also known to have collaborated with paramilitary groups. In some cases, the AUC were in charge of the "dirty tasks," and entered villages to commit massacres.[38] Once this task was completed, the state forces followed. In other cases, members of the armed forces and of the AUC patrolled together without any symbols on their uniforms, meaning that they were indistinguishable from each other.[39]

The Colombian armed conflict also spilled across the country's international borders, and the borderlands themselves soon became principal theaters of war. In 2000, the US Congress approved a counter-insurgency and counter-drug initiative developed by the Colombian government under Andrés Pastrana. With US assistance this initiative, known as Plan Colombia, later became part of then president Álvaro Uribes' Vélez's Democratic Security Policy.[40] Uribe's policies improved security in urban areas and weakened the FARC. They also, however, contributed to moving the conflict's impacts to the periphery and beyond.[41] Colombia's armed forces engaged in intense military operations, which made the rebels retreat to the borderlands and increased refugee flows. Between 2000 and 2009, approximately 300,000 Colombian refugees crossed the border into Ecuador. At that time, almost 85,000 Colombians were reported to already live in the Ecuadorian northern border zone, with 70 percent of them in need of international protection.[42] Similarly, by 2009, around 200,000 refugees crossed over from Colombia to Venezuela. In 2008, the number of Colombians requesting refugee status in Venezuela almost doubled (2,960) compared to 2004 (1,880).[43] From 2003 to 2006, the AUC demobilized, which coincided with the emergence of smaller, paramilitary splinter groups and criminal groups. Some of the best-known ones, which I will hereafter call post-demobilized groups, are the Rastrojos, Águilas Negras, Paisas, and Urabeños (later called "Clan Úsuga"), jointly labeled the BACRIM (*bandas criminales emergentes,* emerging criminal bands) by the Colombian government.[44]

In 2007, the Colombian government initiated Plan Consolidation. Its aim was to substitute coca cultivation with alternative economic development projects and to consolidate state presence, first with a military, and then a civilian focus. Regions with historically high rates of violence, with the presence of armed groups, and with illicit cultivations were prioritized. Of the nine existing "territorial consolidation zones," four (Arauca, Catatumbo in Norte de Santander, Putumayo, and Tumaco in Nariño) included border municipalities.[45] Yet instead of bringing prosperity through development, the fumigations (toxic aerial sprayings to eradicate coca plants) implemented within the scope of Bogotá's counternarcotic policies simply encouraged farmers to grow coca in new areas— and also threatened the health of local farmers. Rather than consolidating a state that fulfills a range of different governance functions, including not only the provision of national security but also health, education, and road infrastructure, the expansion of civilian institutional presence largely remained empty words.

Through Plan Consolidation, in many parts of the border regions the high presence of state forces, yet not of civilian institutions, influenced the relationships between the armed groups and local communities on the Colombian side of the border—and even on the territory of Colombia's neighbors. The rebels had more reason to suspect locals of being state or paramilitary informants. As many farmers expressed in my conversations with them, this often led the rebels to impose stricter behavioral rules on the population.

Bogotá's policies also prompted human rights abuses in Colombian and neighboring territory. Among the most infamous was the case of the "false positives": civilians who were killed by members of the Colombian armed forces—including across the border—and then dressed up and presented as if they had been guerrilla fighters killed in combat. This increased the body count of killed guerrillas and was rewarded with payment from their superiors. The scandal became public toward the end of 2008, when youth who disappeared in Soacha and Ciudad Bolívar in Bogotá were discovered assassinated in the town of Ocaña in the border department of Norte de Santander.[46] Marginalized communities became more alienated from central governments, which in the communities' eyes had lost—or never had—legitimacy, given the weak governance systems they provided, and the shortcomings in border security cooperation that fueled impunity on both sides of all the borders.

This precariousness largely persists in the border regions, even after the signing of the peace deal between the FARC and the Colombian government, which aimed to bring "territorial peace" in the form of development and participatory approaches to the margins of the country. The cocaine business and related forms of organized crime continue to thrive. The border areas still comprise all stages of the illegal cocaine industry: coca cultivation, laboratories to process coca into cocaine, storage locations, and some of the most important starting points of the international trafficking routes. Conflict and criminal actors keep on operating in these regions: the ELN, FARC dissidents, new successor groups of the demobilized FARC, post-demobilized right-wing groups, and criminal groups ranging from youth gangs to the powerful Mexican Sinaloa cartel and the Zetas. Local communities continue to be caught between multiple armed state and non-state actors.

Ethnographic Methods and Multi-Sited Fieldwork

Understanding the nuanced impacts that the operations of conflict and criminal actors have on the security of Colombian, Ecuadorian, and Venezuelan borderlanders requires a multi-sited ethnographic approach.[47] Thomas Schwandt defines ethnographic methods as a "collection of methods of generating and analysing qualitative data that are grounded in a commitment to first-hand experience and examination of some particular social or cultural phenomena."[48] He cites participant observation, interviewing, and the collection of data based on documents, artifacts, and oral histories as part of this approach.[49] Ethnographic methods have become increasingly popular in political science and international relations,[50] but they are still far from mainstream, especially for the analysis of ongoing conflicts. For this study, I coupled ethnographic methods with these disciplines and drew on social sciences more broadly. Identifying variation in the interactions among violent non-state groups and exploring their distinct impacts on security required multi-sited fieldwork, rather than carrying out single-sited fieldwork or fieldwork in several sites as a comparison. George Marcus describes multi-sited fieldwork as follows:

> De facto comparative dimensions develop . . . as a function of the fractured, discontinuous plane of movement and discovery among sites as one maps an object of study and needs to posit logics of relationship, translation, and association among these sites. Thus, in multi-sited ethnography, comparison emerges from putting questions to an emergent object of study.[51]

The comparative dimension in this study develops from a research design that is centered on cases of violent non-state group interactions from across Colombia's borderlands (see appendix A). Marcus supposes that a multi-sited ethnography comprises following people, things, metaphors, plot, life, or conflict, for example, by tracing a person's journey or life.[52] In my study, multi-sitedness arises from mapping these interactions and their influences on security along and across borders, and from tracing how the geography of borderlands affects them. This approach follows Mark-Anthony Falzon's definition of multi-sitedness as "a spatially dispersed field through which the ethnographer [or fieldworker] moves—actually, via sojourns in two or more places, or conceptually, by means of techniques of juxtaposition of data."[53]

Accordingly, during my fieldwork, I moved through a wide range of sub-sites located in the Colombian-Ecuadorian and Colombian-Venezuelan borderlands, my two main fieldwork sites. After a first fieldwork phase to Ecuador in 2009, I conducted the bulk of my fieldwork between August 2011 and May 2013 in four phases, totaling approximately twelve months. My travels took me to the departments of Nariño, Putumayo, Arauca, Norte de Santander, Cesar, and La Guajira in Colombia; the provinces of Esmeraldas, Carchi, and Sucumbíos in Ecuador; and the states of Apure, Táchira, and Zulia in Venezuela, as well as the capital cities Bogotá, Quito, and Caracas.[54] Subsequently, I carried out regular follow-up trips during which I returned to all Colombian border departments and Venezuelan Táchira, as well as Bogotá, to follow the developments of the peace process in the country's power center (see appendix C for the borderland itineraries).

This multi-sited fieldwork across international borders in multiple (borderland) locations helped me capture a broad range of perspectives and variations. As Orin Starn puts it, it provided "a wide-angled view of many faces."[55]

I interviewed more than six hundred stakeholders, including guerrillas, displaced people, indigenous and Afro-Colombian leaders, members of the church, representatives of non-governmental organizations and of local associations, international agency staff, academics, police and military officials, and local government officials. In addition to the interviews in the borderlands, elite interviews in Bogotá, Quito, and Caracas made it possible to contrast these with state-centric views on border security (see Table A.1 for an overview of the interviewees). I also used focus groups to learn from intra-group dynamics, for example, divisions among community leaders.[56]

Finally, I drew on participant observation to complement and overlap with interviews and focus groups. As Schwandt notes, "participant observation is a means whereby the researcher becomes at least partially socialized into the group under study in order to understand the nature, purpose, and meaning of some social action that takes place there."[57] To unpack "participant observation" further, Ray Gold and Buford Junkers divide it into four types of researcher roles, namely "complete participant," "participant-as-observer," "observer-as-participant," and "complete observer."[58] In some instances, I was a complete observer; for example, when I attended meetings between a UN agency and communities in particularly dangerous circumstances due to the guerrilla militia presence and the sensitive issues the UN agency was discussing. In other instances, I was a complete participant: when I cooked, ate, chatted, went shopping, or went dancing with the locals with whom I stayed. Usually, my role shifted between "participant-as-observer"—when I informally chatted with locals about their lives and aspirations—and "observer-as-participant"—when I engaged in more-structured data collection, particularly interviews. While asking interview questions constituted the formal method, I also was careful to observe interviewees' gestures and ways of talking. For example, I took note when people started to whisper and look around uneasily while talking about armed groups. Whenever possible, I lived with families to better understand their way of life. In an ongoing process and thanks to the considerable time I spent with relevant stakeholders in the border areas (see appendix A)— notably, local community members—I learned to access and navigate complex physical spaces and multiple subject groups—most of which are normally too distant or closed to outsiders.

My bottom-up approach gave me a profound understanding of the political (shadow) economy of borderlands and of everyday life at the states' margins. In this sense, it shares elements with an ethnography. "A study becomes ethnographic when the fieldworker is careful to connect the facts that s/he observes with the specific features of the *backdrop* against which these facts occur, which are linked to historical and cultural contingencies," as Isabelle Baszanger and

Nicolas Dodier clarify.[59] My approach indeed permitted me to account for background factors, including the cultural and historical contexts that alter security impacts. I linked non-textual, observable data, such as the color and font of rebel group graffiti, FARC militia presence, or people's fear, observed for example through whispering, to the historical exposure to violent conflict.

Unpredictability, illusoriness, and vulnerability—the themes running through the following chapters—not only characterized my fieldwork journeys but also formed part of my immersion into the subject of this book (see Epilogue). I *sensed* insecurity. Through living in and traveling across the Colombian-Ecuadorian and the Colombian-Venezuelan borderlands, I was able to grasp the differences between insecurity observed from the distance—signaled in the news, in press releases, and government statements, for example, about body counts—and people's perceptions thereof. Learning from victims, perpetrators, and bystanders, combined with my own experiences of tense environments in which death becomes part of everyday life, facilitated nuanced insights into the various forms of insecurity. People from the margins were at the center of my work, or rather, my life, during fieldwork. I listened to them, talked to them, laughed with them, and feared with them.

Of course, there is a caveat to this. Certainly, in addition to engaging with research participants, I also developed lasting friendships, and these more intimate connections provided me with further insights into the emotional aspects of these spaces. Yet despite these insights, I always remained an outsider who immersed into these dynamics and quickly moved out again. By no means do I claim to fully know "what it feels like" to be a borderlander (see Epilogue). Also, researching armed conflict and organized crime is inherently marred by the limited availability of data. Theorizing about how people's lives are affected by trafficking routes, how brokers facilitate cooperation among non-state groups, or when people decide to smuggle cocaine rather than grow cacao is difficult at best, and dangerous at worst. Even an in-depth, grounded approach should therefore not be seen to suggest a full, complete, or "correct" account of the security dynamics in borderlands. Rather, I hope it is taken to shed at least some light on logics that often otherwise remain in the shadows.

Non-State Order and Security

The marginalized nature of the Colombian-Ecuadorian and Colombian-Venezuelan borderlands that I witnessed during my fieldwork, and the relevance of a multitude of violent non-state groups for local security, necessitates a theoretical underpinning that starts from non-state dynamics, rather than from a state-centric approach. The "invisible" nature of security consequences such as omnipresent mistrust and suspicion, fear, and presentiment of danger, requires analytical tools that capture more than "just" physical violence. These tools also need to be receptive to perceptions and relations among people, as well as between people and those who grant protection (or not). I therefore anchor my analysis of security at the edges of Colombia's war in a framework of non-state order and citizen security, which I develop in chapter 2.

I posit that the patterns of behavior among violent non-state groups in a single territory constitute non-state order. Building on our understanding of order in the state system, I conceptualize violent non-state group interactions that give rise to such patterns as falling into three main clusters:[60] the "enmity" cluster, in which violent non-state groups do not have any arrangements with each other; the "rivalry" cluster of unstable short-term arrangements among groups with unpredictable outbreaks of violence; and the "friendship" cluster of relatively stable, nonviolent, long-term inter-group relations. In contexts of illegality where mistrust is endemic, the constant possibility of betrayal makes forging relationships a risky undertaking. While in the "enmity" cluster, inter-group distrust impedes any form of cooperation among violent non-state groups, in the "rivalry" and "friendship" clusters, violent non-state groups draw on distinct mechanisms to reduce distrust between each other. These mechanisms arise from four categories of motivations of cooperation among social actors: interests, personal bonds, values, and power. The motivations "interests" and "personal bonds" operate at the micro level: they reduce distrust on a particular occasion and therefore help explain short-term arrangements between "rivals." The motivations "values" and "power" operate at the macro level: they reduce distrust more generally and hence are conducive to long-term arrangements between "friends."

I develop a typology of violent non-state group interactions with eight distinct types that fall into the three clusters: combat and armed disputes (enmity/ absence of arrangement), spot sales and barter agreements, tactical alliances, subcontractual relationships (rivalry/unstable short-term arrangements), and supply chain relationships, strategic alliances, pacific coexistence, and preponderance relations (friendship/stable long-term arrangements). These types are conceptualized on a continuum to reflect their fluid and dynamic nature. This enables me to systematically demonstrate the distinct implications of these eight types, and the common patterns in the three clusters, as they relate to security of individuals and communities in borderlands, citizen security.

Citizen security describes an ideal-type societal order in which citizenship reduces violence or the threat thereof. If citizenship arises from a mutually reinforcing relationship between a state and its citizenry, then citizen security means that the state provides governance functions and the citizenry adheres to certain rules and norms in return for protection by the state. The citizenry also engages in collective action, rendered possible through a tightly woven social fabric. By drawing on "citizen security," we can explore how actors other than the state, particularly violent non-state groups, substitute such a relationship.

The "citizen security" concept also emphasizes people's agency in the meaning of security. This analytical perspective helps understand why and how, in many places, certain forms of violence persist, and how this violence is perceived: when it fuels fear and when it reassures. Undercurrents of societies, including value systems, inform perceptions of insecurity. They differ from observed insecurity, constructed through the public imagination of it, which, in turn, is predominantly shaped by physical violence and death. Listening to people's accounts of insecurity, watching the communities' everyday practices amid insecurity, and sensing an atmosphere filled with insecurity, as I did during my fieldwork, provides more profound insights into these experiences than do studies from the distance. Such situational awareness puts into perspective how we understand, reproduce, and further develop narratives of insecurity.

The Borderland Lens

Equipped with a theoretical framework built on non-state order and citizen security, I make the case for a borderland lens as a novel epistemological approach to studying security (chapter 3). Considering borderlands a transnational unit, I traveled transnationally during my fieldwork. I crossed the borderlines back and forth, sometimes on my own, sometimes with local community members (see appendix C). Correspondingly, after outlining how state-centric views on borders from outside shape border policies in the region, in the second half of the chapter I sketch the security landscape along and across the 2,219 kilometer-long Colombia-Venezuela border and the 585 kilometer-long Colombia-Ecuador border. To do so, I map a hundred examples of violent non-state group interactions across the border regions (see also appendix B and maps 3.5 and 3.7).[61] Contextualizing these interactions necessitates spatially analyzing transnational illicit supply chains and trafficking routes of multiple forms of transnational organized crime. Together with socioeconomic and cultural conditions that vary along and across the borders, the spatial logic of these flows influence the availability of distrust-reducing mechanisms, which in turn shape group interactions. It shows that a borderland perspective from the margins clashes with views from the power centers impaired by territorial sovereignty as analytical blinders.

The Security Impacts

In chapters 4, 5, and 6 I interweave the borderland perspective from within with a more distanced perspective from outside. I disentangle the myriad types of interactions among guerrillas, paramilitaries, militias, and criminals. Through the voices of my interviewees and my firsthand experience of temporarily living in territories controlled by such groups, I demonstrate how these group configurations matter for people's security, and systematize these magnified dynamics in accordance with the three clusters of violent non-state group interactions. This interplay, rather than simply adopting a singular perspective, demonstrates the tension between observed incidents of physical violence and people's continued devising of survival strategies (chapter 4: Violence and Survival); the focus on drug trafficking and related forms of transnational organized crime and locals' uncertainty when navigating their everyday lives amid armed actors (chapter 5: Crime and Uncertainty); and governance by illicit actors that reduces the outsider's attention and the communities' acceptance to it—either because they do not have any alternative option or because even though illicit, it may be legitimate, in their eyes (chapter 6: Governance and Consent). Each of the eight (i to viii) interaction types has distinct impacts on observed and perceived security. They contribute to violence inflicted on people, to eroding the communities' social fabric, and to undermining a mutually reinforcing relationship between the state and communities. In specific circumstances, they entail shadow citizen security. The availability and efficacy of strategies adopted by civilians to reduce insecurity, or at least to cope with it, are partly contingent on interaction types, as they may indicate what constitutes appropriate behavior to stay safe.

Chapter 4 focuses on the security repercussions of the interaction types where violent non-state groups are "enemies" (i). Embedded in an environment of general mistrust, groups compete for territorial control, triggering violence and hostility, as in the example of Guana near Paraguaipoa that I cited at the opening of this book. Community members experience or expect to experience physical violence, but can adapt behavior to the rules imposed by the opposing parties, for example guerrillas or paramilitaries, to protect themselves. Specific security impacts are related to rural or urban space, combined with the particular phase in the cycle of violence. Three instances stand out. First, in rural areas affected by combat, the lines between hostile parties are relatively clear. Although informants and deserters distort this context, locals are generally able to identify individuals as members of a certain group and can adjust their behavior to the group's rules. Second, in contexts of armed disputes in urban areas, these rules also exist but are less clear, as the lines between group members and bystanders are more diffuse. Third, during periods of tense calm, the anticipation of an outbreak of violence fuels perceptions of insecurity, manifested through fear and anxiety. The transnationality of borderlands makes these spaces prone to impunity, facilitating the victimization of local borderlanders.

Chapter 5 discusses security impacts in the context of the cluster of arrangements in which I view violent non-state groups as "rivals." As the case of Cúcuta, the second example at the beginning of the book, illustrates, various groups cooperate in short-lived illegal activities such as drug trafficking or gasoline smuggling. It is unclear who is involved in these activities and who is not, as well as who is on whose side, and for how long. Analytically distinguishing volatile short-term arrangements from the absence of an arrangement, and from stable long-term arrangements, shows that they cluster in illicit business hubs and at the starting points of international trafficking routes where conflict actors acquire supplies and finances that prolong war. It also shows why mistrust matters not only for cooperation among armed actors but also for the security of local community members; they can become victims of targeted violence if suspected of being informants or collaborators, engendering a constant presentiment of danger. In addition to threatening people's physical security, this incites uncertainty among civilians. In cases of (ii) spot sales and barter agreements, people can adapt their behavior, to a certain extent, to the logics of illicit economies to minimize exposure to violence or employ avoidance strategies. In (iii) tactical alliances, constant group reconfigurations impede such strategies; uncertainty and mistrust prevail. In the context of (iv) subcontractual relationships, group-imposed rules help increase the predictability of violence. Overall, the many different forms of short-term arrangements, including material and financial transactions, barter agreements involving human beings, and remote subcontracting add to this ambiguity. Due to impunity across the border, targeted violence to get rid of betrayers and anyone meddling into illicit business affairs is often invisible.

Chapter 6 discusses long-term arrangements among violent non-state groups, which I term "friendship." The groups establish alternative political orders by assuming governance functions in the territories they control, just as the guerrillas did in General Farfán, in the third vignette I shared earlier. Local communities have reasonable certainty about the prevailing rules. Compared to the other arrangement clusters, physical violence is relatively rare. However, factors such as social control shape perceptions and experiences of security differently from how its representation in the public space outside these territories suggests. When violent non-state groups, rather than the state, exercise governance functions and the local population socially recognizes them, shadow citizenship and shadow citizen security arise. Such a mutually reinforcing relationship between these groups and local communities is particularly likely when three partly overlapping phenomena coalesce: first, violent non-state groups exert political, social, and economic control; second, they constitute an authority because they are perceived to be legitimate "governors"; and third, people feel abandoned by the state.

Through the eyes of the local population, consenting to what is in fact an illicit order means giving up on the idea that the state ought to be the governance provider. It may also imply a lack of belief in such a possibility in the first place. Even if the social fabric within this community is dense, the community is isolated from the rest of the state's citizenry. If shadow citizenship extends across the borderline, the border itself helps disguise the transnational illicit authority of the armed actors. Should the authorities from one side arrive at a remote border region, they can easily escape their reach by crossing over to the other country. The type of long-term arrangement is relevant for the extent to which shadow citizen security exists. In contexts of (v) supply chain relationships, economic opportunities compensate for undemocratic security provision that prevails owing to general mistrust. When violent non-state groups have (vi) strategic alliances, their individual group identities tend to be unclear, making it difficult for locals to be loyal. In (vii) pacific coexistence, violent non-state groups need to secure local support to keep up with the group they coexist with, which constitutes an incentive to be more responsive to citizens. Finally, in (viii) preponderance relations, violent non-state groups provide a variety of governance functions, which can offset undemocratic rules. Individuals perceive rule compliance to be appropriate behavior and internalize or informally accept illicitly imposed norms and practices.

Each type of violent non-state group interaction is significant in its own way. Some are more acutely violent and produce immediate and visible consequences. Those that are not may have invisible consequences, both locally and more broadly. In the long run, such seemingly calm interactions have an impact on citizen security on the structural level—by alienating citizens from the state. Especially in regions where an efficient state apparatus was never present in the first place, people prefer to live under the rule of a non-state actor who establishes "orderly" order.[62] Such situations undermine the empirical legitimacy of central governments because they weaken the states' sovereignty. This slowly leads to, or exacerbates, a perverse status quo of citizenship in which citizens do not trust the state, and the state is unable or unwilling to provide governance functions for the benefit of society. Interpersonal mistrust erodes social fabric and impedes collective action. Scrutinizing the distinct impacts of the group configurations reveals the instances in which violent non-state groups are perceived to be more legitimate security providers than the state. I tie this back to the literature on citizenship and citizen security to show how, due to transnationality, borderlands in vulnerable regions are conducive to shadow citizen security and shadow citizenship. Such borderlands are extreme cases of situations in democracies where the state-society relationship is deficient.[63]

The Border Effect

Chapter 7 zooms out from the regions with specific arrangements among violent non-state groups to take a broader look at the spaces in which I explore them: borderlands. Flows of licit and illicit goods, of people, and of ideas traverse these borders, while law enforcement agents and international organizations are constrained by national sovereignty. This filter mechanism originates in what I term the "border effect": in vulnerable regions, the transnationality of borderlands and their distance from state centers engenders the confluence of weak state governance, a low-risk/high-opportunity environment, and a propensity for impunity. A borderland lens on the security dynamics reveals that, across the borderlands shared by Colombia, Ecuador, and Venezuela, the border effect consistently intensifies the various forms of insecurity that arise from the interactions among armed actors while rendering them less visible from the outside. This happens in spite of the asymmetries in Bogotá, Quito, and Caracas' border security policies and the country-specific historical and cultural contexts in their respective border zones, outlined in chapter 3.

To demonstrate the border effect, I systematically trace how the transnationality of the Colombian-Ecuadorian and Colombian-Venezuelan borderlands and their distance to the state centers influence security in four ways: as facilitator, deterrent, magnet, and disguise (see Table 7.1). First, as facilitator: the transnationality of borderlands facilitates victimization by rendering it less visible, for instance, when crimes are committed across the border. This serves as an incentive for violent non-state groups to resort to violence, as they are less likely to be punished for it. In long-term arrangements, the border effect facilitates the promotion of an illicit economy, which helps foster a consensual relationship between the violent non-state group and the local community. It also facilitates social control conducive to shadow citizen security by making illicit cross-border authority invisible. This is because the reach of law enforcement measures to prohibit such phenomena is only partial; it stops at the borderline. Second, as deterrent: in short-term arrangements, the transnationality of borderlands deters violent non-state groups from trusting their counterparts on the other side of the border. Such heightened inter-group mistrust also makes them suspicious of borderlanders and their allegiances, fueling interpersonal mistrust. Third, as magnet: borderlands attract competition among a large number of violent non-state groups, which often leads them to forge short-lived alliances. The volatile character of these arrangements increases the unpredictability of violence and uncertainty among the local population as to how to ensure security. Fourth, as disguise: due to their historical marginalization and the consequent lack of knowledge of local realities, those who live in the state centers stigmatize the spaces that straddle the borderline as unruly or ungoverned spaces, disguising security challenges that arise from violent non-state group interactions. Such a situation alienates borderlanders from the central governments and facilitates shadow citizenship and shadow citizen security. The generalized image of a violent space tends to be reinforced by the communities who live in the borderlands, where the space "borderland" becomes the scapegoat for all sorts of insecurity. As a result, any nuances in security situations are rendered invisible.

Transcending Categories, Inducing Policy Change

In the concluding chapter, I take stock of the changes that have occurred across Colombia's borderlands over the course of the decade during which I have studied them. I then lay the magnifying glass aside to reflect on the kaleidoscopic, ever-changing configurations among violent non-state groups across the globe. How can we understand their implications for security dynamics more broadly in order to anticipate and ultimately prevent suffering? The findings of my study are derived from an approach that aims to transcend externally imposed categories related to space, time, and agency. Responding to the pressing need for novel theoretical tools to guide evidence-based security policies in rapidly changing violent contexts, they help develop "second-best" policy interventions that target those security challenges arising from violent non-state groups that are mitigated most effectively.

On space, the book suggests that we move beyond studies that categorize states as existing in situations of "armed conflict" or "peace." Focusing on the intersection of conflict and organized crime instead, I explore security dynamics across the borders of a "conflict country" (Colombia) and two "non-conflict countries" (Ecuador and Venezuela). Prioritizing transnational borderlands and not only borders as limits of national sovereignty is essential if policymakers are to enhance people's security, deprive violent non-state groups of illicit authority, and understand and countervail the transnational security threats that arise from violent non-state groups in these spaces.

On time, I break static dichotomies between wartime and peacetime. Instead, I focus on changing security landscapes, as narrated by people who live in the midst of violent non-state group interactions regardless of these paradigms: at the height of the armed conflict, during the peace talks between the FARC and the Colombian government, and after the implementation of the peace agreement. Such a non-politicized understanding of relationships among violent non-state actors can help boost security not only during conflict but also in its aftermath. Transitions from "official" war to "official" peace are prone to a speedy proliferation of multiple violent groups. Post-conflict Central American states have set alarming precedents: they are now plagued by disputes and alliances among gangs. Also, Iraq and Sudan have proven that the complexity of the interactions among violent non-state groups during conflict persists or even increases in its aftermath. Focusing on the reconfiguration of group constellations over time, rather than the trajectory of individual groups that may end with political settlements, sheds light on such complexities.

On agency, I examine the triangle of relations among people, violent non-state groups, and the state to challenge state-centric lenses that presuppose that the state is necessarily among the principal agents in influencing security. Indeed, in remote regions like Colombia's borderlands, it often is the *absence* of the state that matters most for security because it allows for the multiple types of relationships among non-state groups to emerge. When non-state actors behave as if they were the state, while security providers and state actors behave as if they were (illicitly operating) non-state actors, the idealized image of the state as a "solution" to insecurity becomes meaningless. Elucidating the two non-state actors' (people and violent non-state groups) agency in shaping security, among others by contributing to shadow citizen security and shadow citizenship, provides insights for the state: it reveals where it is likely to be easiest for the state to gain empirical legitimacy, which is crucial if it aims to play a part in contributing to security.

I end the book by sketching out three lines of inquiry on which a borderland lens can shed new light: on transnational borderlands (space), on a changing security landscape (time), and on the relations among people, violent non-state groups, and the state (agency).

1.2 Contributions toward a Transformative Goal

With this book, I pursue a transformative goal: to work toward tackling pressing security challenges by "amplify[ing] the voices of those who otherwise go unheard."[64] In this sense, to support "borderland battles" means to unlock critical thinking, transform hardened mindsets, and challenge conventional epistemological and methodological approaches to overcome dominant state-centric, ethnocentric, and androcentric perspectives.

The book's overall contribution, then, arises from critically examining violent non-state groups and security through a borderland lens "endowed" with ethnographic methods that brings together three themes that thus far have been considered separately. These are: borderlands and borders, interactions among violent non-state groups, and how these interactions matter for the security of local communities. The shared borderlands of Colombia, Ecuador, and

Venezuela are ideal spaces to examine the intersection of these three themes using literatures from various disciplines. Nonetheless, they have not yet been studied in their own right. The borderland and border research agendas have mainly been concerned with cases from Europe, Africa, and Asia.[65] In the Americas, while work on the US-Mexican border has been prolific, South American borderlands remain under-researched. Local analyses of the Andean borderlands tend to have a policy focus or have hardly been linked to the broader border studies agenda.[66] The under-researched nature of the Andean borderlands coincides with the bias of state-centric perspectives on armed conflict in the literature on the Colombian conflict. Similar to the urban bias in the civil war literature, most seminal works on the Colombian conflict start from the country's urban centers, draw on data from interviews with elites, and are confined to study the impact of the conflict within its borders.[67] Whether a deliberate choice or a consequence of practical and safety matters, it has shaped our understanding of the conflict.

The presence of armed actors in the Andean border areas has spurred five lines of argument. (i) Scholars such as Angel Rabasa, Peter Chalk, and Carlos Malamud highlight how the Colombian state's deficient territorial sovereignty has jeopardized national security.[68] Accordingly, they focus on the state's military and institutional capabilities to regain control of remote regions seized by the rebels. (ii) The "neighborhood effect" theories emphasize a potential conflict "spillover." Borderlands are considered to be a transit zone from Colombia to neighboring countries, affected by flows of refugees, rebels, and arms, rather than as important unit of analysis themselves. Linked to this, most scholars working on Colombia, Ecuador, or Venezuela consider the impact of the conflict on civilians as constrained to one side of the border.[69] (iii) Scholars including Socorro Ramírez and Ana Bustamante emphasize the implications of borderland disputes for international relations between neighboring states, focusing on national politics rather than trans-regional ones.[70] (iv) Ann Mason and Arlene B. Tickner argue that trans-regional security, including flows of illicit goods, is at stake, without analyzing the micro dynamics of violence.[71] (v) Agencies such as Human Rights Watch see Colombia's borderlands as spaces of humanitarian emergencies, involving mass displacements and other forms of large-scale violence.[72]

While these all provide important insights, they also have reinforced a somewhat distorted image of the border areas, one that is painted from a perspective that starts from the center and exposes the dynamics of only the local or regional level, but not both at the same time. This book seeks to redress these limitations. I further make four contributions that are conducive to supporting "borderland battles," which I outline next.

The Borderland Lens as Epistemological Approach

The first contribution of the book is a call to study borderlands as phenomena in themselves, rather than merely as peripheries that differ from the core of states, *and* to draw on these insights to explore questions related to violence, crime, and governance more broadly. Developing a borderland lens as a novel epistemological approach to studying security thus defies state-centric perspectives that only consider borderlands if they feature violence that challenges the state's territorial sovereignty. It also questions work in border studies that investigates borderlands as fascinating geographical spaces, or as an expression of the margins, but does not link it to wider issues.

It has only been since the 1990s that researchers and policy analysts have acknowledged the value of focusing on borderlands "in their own right," rather than on borderlines.[73] This new emphasis on boundaries as context rather than on boundaries themselves "arose from contemporary interest in pluralistic approaches, the importance of context, and the need to place greater emphasis on localities and on their linkages to other scales of resolution."[74]

Today, borderlands and borders are at the core of a growing multidisciplinary research agenda, but these disciplinary strands do not necessarily engage with each other. I integrate various strands to ensure that the borderland lens I develop rests on a comprehensive understanding of borderlands. As a starting point, I follow political scientists and geographers to adopt a territorial conceptualization of borderlands. This perspective analyzes the geographical space of borderlands and the political economy that arises due to the specific location of these spaces, that is: "what happens where the state ends."[75] The field of conflict studies, for instance, considers the relevance of borderlands for national security issues, for example, as sanctuaries for rebels.[76] Further to this, I add anthropological insights on questions of how boundaries constructed through social discourse define power relations between both sides of the border,[77] and of where the state's margins are.[78] Finally, I engage with sociological work focused on the social, economic, and political links across borders, expressed in the term "transnationalism."[79] This enables me to disclose the divergence of views from the centers and local perceptions in borderlands, bring to the fore the moral economy of borderlands where cross-border activities may be illegal yet perceived as legitimate, and reveal the sense of belonging to a transnational border community that emerges under these circumstances.

Equipped with a more comprehensive understanding of borderlands in their own right, I show that violent non-state groups benefit from concentrating their activities in borderlands in vulnerable regions to consolidate their power. The geography of these spaces reinforces the security dynamics that arise in the context of the various interactions among such groups. Both facilitating and concealing the use of violence, the transnationality of borderlands produces a discrepancy between experiences on the ground and how they are observed from a distance. Many of the resulting security impacts impinge directly on the lives of thousands of civilians, yet, invisible from outside these spaces, they remain unnoticed. The conventional view on borderlands in vulnerable regions is one of so-called ungoverned spaces: they evoke the image of distant, violent regions in which lawlessness and hostility prevail. However, the center's political awareness of borderlands tends to be one of misperception or generalization. Large swaths of border territory in fact constitute illicitly governed spaces, a phenomenon that is relevant far beyond the local level. Borderlands are safe havens for terrorists and business hubs for transnational organized crime, constituting a threat not only to local but also to international peace and security.[80] Many of the transnational illicit flows that originate in the involvement of violent non-state groups in illegal cross-border activities penetrate societies across the globe.

Ethnographic Methods for Global Security Questions

A second contribution that arises from the borderland lens is a methodological approach that intellectually bridges these local and global phenomena. The starting point for this is the case selection based on social rather than spatial configurations: violent non-state group interactions serve as cases (see appendix A). Such an approach helps understand not only the Andean region. It can also be applied to any setting where various violent non-state groups operate to grasp the multiple security impacts on communities who live under such conditions. It challenges both what could be called the "staying local tendency" in anthropological and development studies and the "macro-level bias" that prevails in security studies and related disciplines. Employing ethnographic methods across multiple field sites, I grasp micro processes and local conditions, but also explore questions relevant to wider security affairs with which these dynamics are intermeshed.[81]

Fieldwork is not limited to borderlands; the data collection sites also comprise power centers. The disconnect between the two is startling. There is a knowledge gap between the realities of "subjugated" borderlanders and the imaginaries of the power holders in capital cities. As outlined above, through my travels across fragile border areas, I gained access to unique accounts of a multi-faceted security landscape, including people's agency in informing it.[82] Engaging with ministers, ambassadors, generals, and other senior officials in Bogotá, Caracas, and Quito, as well as elites outside the region, discloses that these nuanced understandings of the security contexts in the borderlands are invisible to those at the centers of the state.

Existing work on the intersection of armed conflict and organized crime tends to assume macro-level approaches that privilege quantitative studies. If qualitative fieldwork is included, it mostly reinforces the "urban bias."[83] Researchers gather data in state or regional capitals and via elite interviews rather than by interacting with farmers and others in remote, rural regions where violent non-state group relationships are most pronounced. They focus on text and numbers, ignoring oral data and nonverbal expressions such as visual clues or emotions. Instead of simplifying complexities on the ground, the resulting narratives have distorted them.

I chose ethnographic methods because original qualitative research was necessary to obtain analyzable textual, oral, and visual data. The scarce literature that is available on some of these borderland areas mainly draws on center-based perceptions rather than original *in situ* research. Much of this work is self-referential, entailing reproduction rather than critical engagement or complementary studies.

Moreover, much of the existing work on the region provides descriptions of borderland life yet fails to engage in theorizing.[84] Listening to hundreds of individuals who influence and are influenced by security dynamics across various border areas shows that the interactions of violent non-state groups manifest repeating behavioral patterns that can be organized into a clearly defined typology. Combining an inductive and deductive approach between manifestations of insecurity on the ground and these interaction types allows for systematization of the impacts these interactions have on citizen security, and for theorizing about the influence of the geography of borderlands on them. Through this approach, I translate my empirical findings obtained from the bottom up into more abstract theoretical insights relevant to larger debates on global security.

Theorizing Non-state Order

As a third contribution to working toward the goal of supporting (nonviolent) borderland battles, I offer a nuanced theoretical understanding of dynamic behavioral patterns among violent non-state groups. Integrating work on state order, alliance formation in civil war, cooperation among social actors, and mistrust in contexts of illegality, I theorize violent non-state group interactions as various forms of non-state order. My framework constructed around distrust and various motives for cooperation among social actors highlights the relevance of illicit business interests alongside explanations, such as ideology, for the formation of group interactions to elucidate the nuances between them. Integrating original empirical research with this conceptualization yields a novel

typology of group interactions, nested into clusters. Drawing on both the literature on armed conflict and on organized crime, I address multiple types of violent non-state groups to acknowledge the complexity of the violent contexts in
which they are embedded. This includes occasions in which guerrillas join forces
with paramilitary groups in the cocaine business; others where criminal gangs,
drug cartels, and left-wing groups establish tacit agreements of non-aggression;
and instances in which various rebel groups fight each other. Unpacking these
arrangements illuminates the fluid and dynamic nature of such relationships.
Changes do not necessarily occur in a continuous way; rather, they evolve from
one into another, blurring the distinctions between different arrangements.

The manifold violent non-state group interactions constitute analytical blind
spots to conventional approaches that adopt a state-centric perspective, or that
follow a world politics paradigm that takes the state as a starting point.[85] Given
the increasing relevance for global security dynamics, debates across disciplines
begin to explore behavioral patterns among violent non-state groups. In civil
war contexts, this includes understanding group interactions through variation
in territorial control,[86] and how relationships that are contrary to, or fall outside,
typical conflict cleavages change and prolong wars.[87] Scholarship on organized
crime has revealed the undermining impact of cooperation among criminals
and cartels for the security of people in US suburbs, Southern Italy, or Mexico,
for instance.[88] This work, however, only partly explains the multilayered nature
of interactions among violent non-state groups in unstable settings where conflict and crime overlap. On the one hand, the debates in conflict research have
illuminated the motives, characteristics, and consequences of single types of
relationships among violent non-state groups. This led to the categorization
of conflicts, for example, into those characterized by fluid alignments, transnational alliances, fragmentation, or stable alliances.[89] Such categorizations
ignore that settings with multiple violent non-state groups typically manifest various kinds of interactions concurrently, and that single groups do not
necessarily operate homogenously across space. On the other hand, scholars
studying organized criminal groups have reduced interactions to a dichotomy
between conflict and cooperation or economic relationships.[90] Phil Williams's
work on Iraq and Daniel Pécaut's on Colombia account for conflict and cooperation among various armed actors yet stay within this dichotomy.[91]
Furthermore, there is a tendency to study single categories of violent non-
state groups, namely, the mafia,[92] criminals,[93] or criminalized legacies,[94] drug
cartels,[95] warlords,[96] terrorists,[97] and civil war actors,[98] particularly rebels.[99] In
brief, we either learn about few interaction types between different categories
of violent non-state groups, or about different interaction types within a single
category of groups.

Still, there are clear benefits to integrating the debates on civil war and on organized crime to explain the puzzling variation in group interactions.[100] The civil war literature on the motives of violent non-state actors to forge alliances with other conflict actors, for example, helps explain why and how organized criminals maintain and expand their networks and interact with other groups. Insights into the role of trust for cooperation among criminals provide lessons for the security of local communities in civil wars.[101]

Rethinking Security

Finally, as a fourth contribution, the book depicts the distinct impacts of interactions among various violent non-state groups on citizen security. This is different to existing work that typically captures how the *presence* of violent non-state groups impinges on security. Typically, there is little dialogue between proponents of security approaches focusing on observed factors related to insecurity, and those focusing on perceived insecurity. Drawing on the concept of citizen security allows us to make connections between these two approaches. To do so, I build on perspectives on security and violence from political science, sociology, anthropology, economics, and psychology. Violent non-state groups use repertoires of violence that result in diverse patterns of insecurity.[102] Scholars have argued that the intensity and type of violence is related to the group type and levels of territorial control.[103] Political science approaches to these phenomena, as well as those of international organizations, governments, and advocacy groups, have mostly focused on "observable" violence, measuring insecurity, for example, with homicide, displacement, disappearance, rape, and torture rates.[104] Yet insecurity is more than physical violence. Less-tangible security impacts, including fear and resulting behavioral adaptations, affect communities as well. Insecurity also arises from the sheer exposure to the presence of armed actors, from being vulnerable to violence and crime.[105] At the same time, the normalization of violence as a means of responding to it can reduce perceived insecurity, even if observed rates of violence remain the same.[106] Psychological, criminological, and economic approaches thus highlight fear and uncertainty, while anthropologists point to the moral economies of war and violence to comprehend the underlying narratives and structural conditions supportive of the conduct of violence.[107]

Addressing the less-tangible consequences of violent non-state group interactions is a matter of urgency. Where armed groups engage in quickly shifting alliances, the response tends to be a militarized one. This however does little to establish "sustainable peace of mind:" in countries suffering crises, enduring psychological distress detrimentally shapes entire future generations.[108]

Such a failure has been evident in places like the Colombian towns discussed in this book, and entire countries like Libya and Syria. Identifying clusters where violent non-state groups do not have any arrangement, of short-term arrangements, and of long-term arrangements provides insights into how each cluster influences the security of communities in distinct ways, including levels of violence and its predictability. This is the case across wartime and peacetime, and in contexts where civil war, criminal, and terrorist violence is blurred. Each qualitatively different security outcome therefore requires a distinct policy response.

In the following chapters, I start by outlining the theoretical framework and then demonstrate the logics of the security dynamics along and across the Colombia-Ecuador and Colombia-Venezuela borders. The role of borderlands in these dynamics is striking: they magnify security challenges. Yet it is also this very intensified version of multiple insecurities that raises questions about how we can and ought to understand them in a global context. The study presented in this book is therefore not conclusive. Rather, as I discuss in the last chapter, it aims to plant a seed of change when it comes to researching security more broadly, using a borderland lens.

2

Non-State Order and Security

There is insecurity. But this is the feeling of insecurity that something
might happen if I did something [. . .]. We Venezuelans are afraid because we don't understand the [conflict's] dynamics. We think that the
population could be attacked at any moment.

Humanitarian organization employee, Machiques, Venezuela, 2012[1]

The situation described by this Venezuelan borderlander suggests an absent
or dormant Leviathan. It also hints at the local population's ignorance about
any kind of regular pattern that could provide protection amid violence. The
dilemmas of such situations of ubiquitous insecurity, and the attempts to escape
them, have been at the core of scholarship concerned with social order domesti-
cally, and in the international system.[2] This includes relations among states, the
state's relations with its own people, and its relations with non-state actors. Such
work largely ignores, however, settings where order emerges from the relations
that *various* violent non-state groups have with each other, as is the case in many
multi-party conflicts, and where criminal and conflict dynamics converge. This
is the case in the state-neglected Venezuelan border area.

What happens in these realms that the state does not see? Borderlands in vulnerable regions are the places where such non-state dynamics are particularly
evident. They are, however, also the places where these dynamics are perhaps
least legible from the state's point of view because they do not conform to the
systems created by the state, most notably, international borderlines.[3] In the next
chapters, I unpack these dynamics by assuming a borderland perspective instead.
Here, I first aim to demonstrate why so-called non-state order in these and other
spaces is key to comprehending insecurity and to identifying ways to escape it.

In many fragile regions across the world, including border regions, violent non-state groups are present in overlapping territory and concurrently
engage in various kinds of interactions with each other. They may fight each
other but also engage in cooperative arrangements. Our understanding of
social order and security dynamics is only partial if we neglect the behavioral patterns of non-state actors out of the state's sight. In such situations,

31

security dynamics like those the Machiques resident referred to above are shaped more forcefully by how violent non-state groups interact with each other than by how they interact with state forces. And yet we know very little about these dynamics.

To address this blind spot, I develop a theoretical framework that puts violent non-state groups at the center of attention and *then* factors the state in.[4] I first theorize non-state order as three clusters of violent non-state group interactions: the "enmity," "rivalry," and "friendship" clusters. I then offer a typology of violent non-state group interactions that reflects how these forms of non-state order take shape empirically. Subsequently, I theorize the influence of these group interactions on the security of the communities in whose territory they operate. Table 2.1 provides a detailed overview of the theoretical framework. The security influences of the group interactions can be summarized in the following way:

"Enmity" cluster   →   violence, but relatively clear rules of behavior
"Rivalry" cluster   →   selective violence and uncertainty
"Friendship" cluster   →   shadow citizen security and shadow citizenship

Just as frameworks of international order offer explanations for war and other security outcomes internationally, the concept of non-state order sheds light on violence and other security outcomes in places where state governance is absent or insufficient. As detailed in Table 2.1, it brings to the fore relations among violent non-state groups, relations between these groups and communities, and relations between non-state actors (communities and violent non-state groups) and the state. Putting emphasis on people's perceptions and experiences of— and agency toward—their relations with the state and violent non-state groups, this approach therefore allows for an exploration of "the feeling of insecurity," as the Venezuelan borderlander put it.

I define violent non-state groups as a set of at least three individuals who are i) "willing and capable to use violence for pursuing their objectives"; ii) thereby directly or indirectly challenging the state's legitimate monopoly on the use of violence by using or threatening to use violence illegally; and iii) "shaped through an organisational relationship or structure that exists over a specific period of time."[5] I further adopt two assumptions about these groups. First, their behavior follows instrumental rationality that hinges on "a prior context of power, expectations, values, and conventions, which affects how interests are determined as well as what calculations, given interests, are made."[6] Second, longer-term relationships among violent non-state groups will become more institutionalized.[7] For the purpose of this study, I refer to groups with political or economic motivations, or a mix of the two.

Acknowledging the challenge of empirically distinguishing between "state" and "non-state," I use "non-state" (in "violent non-state groups") as an analytical category that refers to behavior rather than formal identity or affiliation. It includes everything fully outside the state, but also non-state (informal) behavior of state actors if, through their behavior, they question the legitimate monopoly of violence of the state, or disobey the law. This is the case, for example, when military officers form or participate in a trafficking ring. I use "violent" rather than "armed" (as in similar terms such as "non-state armed group") to include non-armed violence, for example, non-armed sexual violence, and to highlight the challenge these groups pose to the state's legitimate monopoly of violence.[8] We do not normally refer to state forces as "violent" groups, as long as their use of violence is perceived to be legitimate by the people. Furthermore, a group or an individual can be armed, but this does not necessarily mean that they are perceived to be violent; for example, the police in many Western European countries, a group of bodyguards, or rangers. Rather, these armed actors may *become* violent actors.[9]

Overall, the term "violent non-state groups" encompasses a wide range of different types of groups ranging from those labeled rebels, paramilitaries, and militias, to criminals, drug cartels, and gangs. It is a useful umbrella term to analytically shift attention from the groups' *raison d'être* and their motivations to *exist* (e.g., political or economic goals) to the motivations of a variety of different kinds of groups to *cooperate* with each other.[10] The motives for groups to exist can change over time and the borders between different kinds of such motives are often muddied, entailing fluid group identities rather than clear-cut distinctions.[11] Outsiders' perceptions of the groups can change as well. Therefore, externally imposed categories of violent non-state groups reflect only a certain viewpoint of a specific moment in time.[12] As we see below, the motivations of groups to *cooperate* display commonalities regardless of what motivates their *existence*, of how these change, or of the changes in the labels applied to them. Of course, I still account for variation in their agendas, modes of operation, and further attributes throughout the analysis where this is necessary to understand security dynamics, for example for the relations the groups have with local communities. For the rest of this book, if known, I draw on the names with which these groups identify themselves or with which local communities describe them. For illustrative purposes, rather than making a value judgment, I also use terms such as "guerrillas," "paramilitaries," or "post-demobilized groups."

2.1 Non-State Order

*The heat on this border not only has to do with the presence of the guerrillas
but also of various criminal groups that move around this border area.*
Local resident, Riohacha, Colombia, 2016

I posit that in territories with multiple violent non-state groups, like the one described by this Riohacha resident, their interactions constitute non-state order, defined as patterns of behavior among violent non-state groups.[13] This definition is built on our understanding of social order, which, broadly speaking, is viewed either as stable, predictable patterns of human behavior, or as a value that facilitates a certain goal, like cooperation.[14] I use the former, sociological meaning of social order that includes both conflictual and cooperative patterns of behavior.[15] It reflects settings where violent non-state groups fight each other and where they engage in cooperative arrangements.

I conceptualize non-state order as falling into three mutually exclusive and exhaustive clusters, described as "enmity," "rivalry," and "friendship" clusters. They are characterized by variation in the quality and durability of the violent non-state group interactions they comprise, which, in turn, are informed by the ways in which the groups reduce distrust between each other: as "enemies," violent non-state groups distrust each other, they fight and aim to eliminate each other; as self-interested "rivals," they reduce distrust on particular occasions, which allows them to engage in unstable short-term arrangements with each other that can include unpredictable outbreaks of violence because general distrust persists; as "friends," they reduce distrust generally, and engage in relatively stable, nonviolent long-term arrangements with each other.

In this sense, non-state order is somewhat similar to international order because the three clusters are analogous to certain qualities of the three structures of anarchy according to which international order can be understood.[16] The debates associated with the traditions of thought include whether, when, and why interactions among states are regulated by war in a zero-sum game fashion ("Hobbesian" enmity); by cooperation based on shared interests and behavior as self-limited, rational rivals ("Lockean" rivalry); or as a family of nations with shared moral obligations that coexist peacefully ("Kantian" friendship).[17] Each gives rise to distinct security outcomes.

In what follows, in a first step, I explain the role of distrust for interactions among violent non-state groups and present four motives for cooperation among social actors, which serve as sources of distrust-reducing mechanisms. In a second step, I outline the three clusters of violent non-state group interactions to explain how these mechanisms influence the various forms of non-state order. As I discuss in the second part of the chapter, inter-group distrust influences not only the interactions between these groups but also the relations between violent non-state groups and the communities in whose territories they operate, and therefore, people's security.

The Role of Distrust in Non-state Order

Similar to states, violent non-state groups operate under anarchy, understood as the absence of a central authority that governs interactions among them.[18] In such contexts, "cheating and deception are endemic."[19] Distrust prevails. Therefore, in order to engage in cooperation, they need to overcome the problem of distrust.[20] States can establish rules (formalized in domestic or international law), and regimes to overcome distrust. In the case of violent non-state groups, however, the activities at the core of their cooperation are illegal. Illegality enhances economic benefits because it confers high value on a good or activity, but the risks attached to it are also high. Since arrangements about illegal issues are not legally binding, the possibility of betrayal and treachery is omnipresent. "People who are untrustworthy are also more likely to think that others are untrustworthy," argues Diego Gambetta.[21]

Furthermore, by definition, their modus operandi involve violence. As Peter Andreas and Angélica Durán-Martínez state, "participants in illicit trade do not have recourse to the law to enforce contracts and thus business disputes are more likely to be dealt with by shooting rather than suing."[22] Violent non-state groups can draw on enforcement methods with some form of (violent) punishment for noncompliance, which override any nonviolent mechanisms to facilitate cooperation.[23] Yet violent enforcement is not sufficiently able to overcome the problem of inter-group distrust, unless there is a considerable power imbalance between the actors involved. Gambetta notes:

> [w]hat [punishment] does not do is to increase the credibility of the promises of the tough guy. Being violent does not make one *generally* credible. If anything it has the opposite effect, as people fear that someone who uses force to protect himself from cheating will also use force to protect himself when *he* cheats.[24]

Gambetta refers to individuals, but his reasoning also applies to groups; the threat of violence is not sufficient for violent non-state groups to deter other groups from cheating. This increases the fear of being cheated and contributes to the dilemmas these groups face when consenting to engage in arrangements in the absence of the other party's trustworthiness.[25]

In the absence of trust, violent non-state groups draw on distrust-reducing mechanisms that facilitate cooperation and allow them to be "rivals" or "friends," instead of "enemies." In light of the context of illegality and violence, I thus emphasize the need to *reduce distrust* rather than to *build trust*. I define distrust as the absence of Gambetta's understanding of trust, "a particular level of the subjective probability with which an agent assesses that another agent or group of agents will perform a particular action, both *before* he can monitor such action [. . .] *and* in a context in which it affects *his own* action."[26] Trust arises in a "relationship with people who are to some extent free [and which] itself must be one of *limited freedom* [. . .] it must be possible [. . .] to refrain from action."[27] Karen S. Cook et al. show that cooperation can be successful without trust across a variety of different social actors, ranging from interpersonal relations over institutional structures to entire societies and states. Instead of drawing on trust, these actors draw on different mechanisms to ensure cooperation.[28]

When violent non-state groups share motivations for cooperation, they are able to reduce distrust, and thus to engage in certain forms of cooperation. Game theory work on cooperation among social actors typically focuses on strategic interactions between rational actors.[29] Accordingly, based on their preferences, social actors, including states and violent non-state groups, develop strategies to make cooperation feasible.[30] Once cooperation is established, the actors' interdependence can help maintain it. According to Bernard Williams, "a situation in which two agents cooperate necessarily involves at least one of them *depending on* the other, or being [. . .] a *dependent party*."[31] In some situations, "everyone in them is under the immediate control of everyone."[32] This interdependence produces "incentives for cooperation so that cooperation would be rewarded over the long run, and defection punished," note Robert Axelrod and Robert Keohane.[33] By moving one step back and widening the focus from strategies, preferences, and the context of ongoing cooperation to include *motivations* of cooperation, we can account for the prior context of expectations and other considerations that shape the behavior of social actors.[34] After all, "preferences are expressions of actual psychological attitudes, notably of dispositions," as B. Williams reminds us.[35]

Broadly speaking, there are four motives for cooperation among social actors: interests, personal bonds, values, and power.[36] Interests include economic interests; personal bonds refer to sympathies with an individual rather than at the group level; values comprise a "moral or ethical disposition, such as the recognition of a general duty of fidelity," arising from shared political, cultural, or religious beliefs;[37] power refers to the credible threat of coercion. It is compulsory power according to which relationships between actors "allow one to shape directly the circumstances or actions of another."[38] I follow B. Williams, who considers interests and personal bonds *micro* motivations because they are motives "to cooperate, on a given occasion or occasions, which does not imply any general motive to cooperate as such." Values and power are *macro* motivations—they are general dispositions to cooperate.[39]

When two or more violent non-state groups share the same motivations to cooperate, these motivations operate as distrust-reducing mechanisms and permit the groups to cooperate. These mechanisms are "interest convergence" for interests, "mutual sympathies" for personal bonds,[40] "shared values" for values, and "power asymmetries" for power. Just as the groups are either motivated to cooperate on a given occasion only (in the case of interests and personal bonds) or have general dispositions to cooperate (in the case of values and power), the distrust-reducing mechanisms that arise when motivations are mutual reduce distrust either only on a particular occasion (in the case of "interest convergence" and "mutual sympathies") or in a more general manner (in the case of "shared values" and "power asymmetries"). The motivations are enabling factors that enhance the chances for cooperation to arise, but they do not rule out a fallback into a situation where distrust overrides any form of cooperation.[41]

As I outline next, variation in the presence of these motivations influences what kind of interaction among violent non-state groups exists,[42] and thus what form of non-state order arises: "enmity" between violent non-state groups that do no cooperate at all; "rivalry," characterized by unstable short-term arrangements among violent non-state groups; or "friendship," characterized by relatively stable long-term arrangements among violent non-state groups.

The Three Clusters of Non-state Order

The "Enmity" Cluster: Absence of an Arrangement

In the "enmity" cluster, violent non-state groups have no motivation to cooperate: distrust prevails. The groups do not have any arrangement with each other, thus "enmity" shapes their interactions. Analogous to Carl Schmitt's and other scholars' conceptualization of enmity, violent non-state groups do not recognize each other's right to exist and are willing to engage in unlimited violence against each other.[43] Suspecting that any other group threatens their own existence, the groups aim to eliminate others from the territory in which they operate and into which they expand, or from the (illegal) economic activities in which they are involved to enhance their own economic, social, and/or political power. Enmity and unlimited warfare do not mean that there is *always* total warfare.[44] In the case of states, as Hedley Bull notes, the state "does not find its energies so absorbed in the pursuit of security that the life of its members is that of mere brutes."[45] Similarly, fighting between violent non-state groups is temporally limited because the groups have to invest material, financial, and human resources to sustain it. Armed clashes constitute episodes of violence within longer periods of tense calm, the phase in the cycle of violence before or after the outbreak of violence.[46] The relationship of enmity nonetheless persists in these periods, just as the state continues to assume a posture of war even in the absence of fighting. Therefore, during periods of tense calm, violence has the potential to erupt at any time.

The "Rivalry" Cluster: Unstable Short-Term Arrangements

In the "rivalry" cluster, violent non-state groups are self-interested rivals who distrust each other. Their only motivations to cooperate with each other are interests and/or personal bonds. When their interests converge, or when they have mutual sympathies, they reduce inter-group distrust.[47] This is conducive to unstable short-term arrangements. The convergence of interests reduces inter-group distrust on a particular occasion, for example a business deal, through strategies like what Cook et al. call hostage-taking:[48] shared information on illegal business deals between the groups involved renders them hostages of each other.[49] In settings with only two actors, iterated deals make cooperation more stable.[50] Against this, where multiple groups compete to maximize profit, general distrust persists, which makes group interactions more volatile; cooperative arrangements are of a short-lived nature only. Inter-group distrust is reduced in the context of one such arrangement, but not necessarily a second one. When Group A and Group B have engaged in a business deal and then a third Group C arrives, Group B may decide to forge the next deal with Group C, if they also share the same interests. Group B and Group C may even decide to fight Group A together to reduce competition.

Mutual sympathies between individual members of each group reduce distrust only in the context of specific shared personal or private goals of these individuals, typically group leaders. These individuals do not necessarily resemble "egoist rationalists."[51] Rather, private goals on which mutual sympathies are based involve emotions such as pride, anger, or humiliation, and hence can trigger unpredictable breakdowns of the arrangement between the groups. They therefore can also override the economic calculus in the service of the group's well-being.[52] Both motivations—interests and personal bonds—are used as strategies of individual incentives on a particular occasion or with regard to an individual.[53]

Violent non-state groups maintain the status quo as long as it suits them, including by cooperating with other groups. Without the overriding goal of eliminating another group in a totalitarian way, they do not engage in unlimited warfare against each other like enemies do. Still, they fight if necessary, including over the control of people, trafficking routes, or illicit markets. The groups use targeted violence against betrayers as pre-emptive measures, in deterrence or to settle disputes.[54] In the absence of a central authority or law that governs group interactions, it is up to the groups and their members to judge when to resort to such violence and to what extent to constrain its use. The limitation of violence is contingent on their instrumental reasoning,[55] yet their reasoning is grounded in prior experiences and expectations unknown to the other groups. Therefore, suspicion and misjudgment can easily lead to violent escalation.

The "Friendship" Cluster: Stable Long-Term Arrangements

In the "friendship" cluster, violent non-state groups are motivated by values and power to engage in cooperation. Shared values or power asymmetries enable them to reduce inter-group distrust in a general manner, which makes stable, relatively nonviolent, long-term arrangements possible. Values can be shared between groups directly, or with a third party. In both cases, shared values make groups (or the groups and third parties) appreciate each other over time.[56] When there are clear power asymmetries between groups, behavioral rules imposed by the more powerful group facilitate the reduction of distrust. The more powerful group subordinates the less powerful one(s) without eliminating it (or them).

Despite the underlying anarchy in non-state order and the context of illegality, both shared values and power asymmetries allow for mutual credibility over long periods of time. The groups respect each other and largely refrain from using violence against each other. Instead, violent non-state groups forge a "bond of mutual non-aggression,"[57] and may even support each other in the case of an outside threat.[58] I call this behavior "friendship" between violent non-state groups. To be sure, this friendship is not an idealized one. It is not akin to a case where friends love each for their own sake. Especially in the case of power asymmetries, it resembles more what Aristotle has termed the "friendship of utility," in which "men love their friend for their own good . . . and not as being the person loved, but as useful or agreeable."[59] Yet given the groups' general disposition to cooperate, this friendship is still a comparatively stable and durable relationship; it is qualitatively distinct from rivalry and enmity.

A Typology of Violent Non-State Group Interactions

The clusters described above take shape in myriad ways. Borderlands as extreme cases of complex security landscapes in particular host many different violent non-state group interaction types, each of them falling into one of the clusters. My empirical data from the Andean borderlands therefore provides particularly clear insights into what the three clusters look like on the ground. Based on the data and the relevant literature, I have identified eight types of interactions

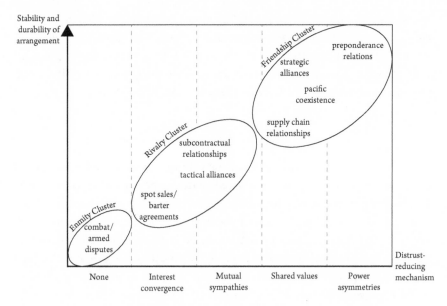

Figure 2.1 The continuum of clusters of violent non-state group interactions

among violent non-state groups. Based on the quality and stability of these interactions—that are the outcomes of the availability of distrust-reducing mechanisms to the violent non-state groups—each of the eight types can be allocated to one of the three clusters, as shown in Figure 2.1: (i) combat and armed disputes (enmity); (ii) spot sales and barter agreements, (iii) tactical alliances, and (iv) subcontractual relationships (rivalry); and (v) supply chain relationships, (vi) strategic alliances, (vii) pacific coexistence, and (viii) preponderance relations (friendship). A list of a hundred observations of these interaction types can be found in appendix B. Those dated between 2011 and 2013 are marked with numbers on Maps 3.5 and 3.7.

To build this typology, I borrow from business network theory and related scholarship on cooperation among criminals. Phil Williams, for example, postulates that interactions among criminal groups can be conceived of as "arrangements of convenience," or varied linkages to pursue specific interests, which can range from conflict and competition to coordination and cooperation.[60] These links resemble those in the legal business world: "the collaboration may take diverse forms ranging from strategic alliances and joint ventures at the most ambitious level through tactical alliances, contract relationships, supplier customer relations, to spot sales at the most basic level."[61] To enhance mutual benefit and spread risks, groups form adaptable, resilient, and expandable networks. Such business links have become increasingly important to illegal economic cross-border activities, as Manuel Castell notes:

[The] internationalization of criminal activities induces organized crime from different countries to establish strategic alliances to cooperate, rather than fight, on each other's turf, through subcontracting arrangements, and joint ventures, whose business practice closely follows the organizational logic of what I identified as "the network enterprise."[62]

While P. Williams's and Castells's business models account for economic considerations only, I address interactions among various types of violent non-state groups that include, but are not limited to, business relationships as the motives for cooperation—or the lack thereof—discussed above. Similar to long-term relationships in the business world, high levels of interdependence (e.g., as a result of low levels of distrust) are conducive to stable cooperation that benefits all parties involved.[63]

Enmity: Absence of an Arrangement

Combat and Armed Disputes

When violent non-state groups have no arrangement with each other, the political situation of the country or region in which the groups operate (armed conflict or non-conflict), geography (especially urban or rural spaces), and the group type influence the specific form in which the groups interact: in combat or in armed disputes. The distinction between these two forms is often blurred.

I define combat as overt military clashes between violent non-state groups. It includes, but is not limited to, "fighting between armed forces";[64] that is, the conduct of hostilities between parties to an international armed conflict or a non-international armed conflict as understood in international humanitarian law. In intra-state conflicts, combat includes military clashes between civil war actors, including rebel versus paramilitary groups,[65] rebel group versus rebel group,[66] and the state versus rebel group.[67] Combat occurs in countries in a situation of armed conflict. The definition however goes beyond these settings to include combat in a non-conflict country when foreign conflict actors fight each other in that country's territory. It also refers to clashes between violent non-state groups that are not considered conflict actors, for instance drug cartels, gangs, or militias. Combat features highly visible, and "spectacular,"[68] violence that typically attracts media and government attention beyond the territory in which it takes place.[69]

I define armed disputes as situations where contesting groups selectively use or threaten to use violence against each other's members or wider support networks. Their contestation rests on armed violence but is not fought in open military clashes.

In combat, the groups involved are public about (some of) their intentions, for example by publicly declaring war on others, denominating the "enemy" as a military objective, and identifying themselves through uniforms or armbands with emblems. In armed disputes, the activities of the violent non-state groups are more covert. These can include clandestine operations and the killings of informants and messengers rather than of immediately identifiable group members. Armed disputes take place in both conflict and non-conflict settings. In conflict settings, urban militias—the civilian branches of rebel or paramilitary groups—are examples of groups that can be involved in armed disputes.[70] In non-conflict settings, criminals, gangs, drug cartels, and mafia groups may interact this way.[71] Armed disputes constitute a convenient *modus operandi* for violent non-state groups with few military capabilities, meaning that they can maintain a low profile (which is important in settings where they coexist with state actors).[72]

While combat is predominant in rural regions, armed disputes prevail in urban areas.[73] In cities and towns, violent non-state groups benefit from muddied distinctions between civilians and those involved in fighting, allowing them to conceal their identity more readily than in remote regions. Armed disputes take place in contexts in which conflict and non-conflict dynamics are blurred, as is the case in border areas. From the perspective of the conflict side of the border, armed disputes typically attract little attention since they do not fall under "combat activities" that are followed by analysts, governments, and international organizations interested in the dynamics of the armed conflict. From the perspective of the non-conflict side, a potential escalation and evolution into combat is often put down to the spillover effects of the neighboring conflict, as opposed to finding a more appropriate local explanation.

Since violent non-state groups must invest material, financial, and human resources in order to sustain their fights, combat and targeted rivalry are temporally limited.[74] Referring to the dynamics between the state and rebels, Paul Staniland's description of "non-cooperation," including "guerrilla disorder" (both parties are in the same territory) and "clashing monopolies" (the groups try to seize control over the other's territory), illustrates the cyclical nature of this violence:

> Sometimes non-cooperation is a brief burst of extreme unrestrained violence amidst a longer pattern of bargaining or the endgame of clashing armies after a long process of escalation. More rarely, it characterizes the entire nature of the conflict. This relationship can also result from the breakdown of more cooperative wartime political orders into a spiral of escalatory violence. Political interests shape how capacity is deployed, but given the lack of political cooperation, outcomes in these orders are substantially a function of military power.[75]

Combat and armed disputes are episodes of violence within longer periods of tense calm during which violence can erupt at any time.

Rivalry: Short-Term Arrangements

Spot Sales and Barter Agreements

Spot sales and barter agreements are one-time financial or material transactions that arise from the convergence of interests in a specific transaction. Even if the groups do not perceive each other to be generally trustworthy or credible, they reduce distrust in this particular instance. The deals may concern commodities, for example illegal drugs or weapons purchased "on the spot," either on a cash basis or as a barter agreement (for example, arms-for-drugs deals). The commodities can be destined for the internal market or for export. Spot sales occur on different scales, ranging from small amounts of goods to business deals that require large financial commitments. Groups involved are hardly interdependent. Minimal regulation characterizes these arrangements. At the time of switching products or paying cash for goods, however, all parties involved have to agree on the terms of the deal because they depend on each other for the deal to be successful. This guarantee and restraint for both parties can be increased through enforcement methods.[76] The business deals can materialize spontaneously. Leaders of hostile groups may undertake a deal one day because it brings mutual benefits, but go back to fighting each other the next day.

Tactical Alliances

Tactical alliances between violent non-state groups are motivated by shared interests and/or personal bonds between groups, and generate immediate and temporary benefits. Devoid of initial expectations of long-term commitment,[77] tactical alliances are fragile and minimally institutionalized.[78] The groups are interdependent to a limited extent because they engage in a relation with each other, but can still easily abandon the arrangement. Tactical alliances can exist in any territory where groups share an interest in balancing the power of a third party. Joining forces with two or more actors brings benefits vis-à-vis other actors. Thus, tactical alliances also serve to trump another group.[79]

Territories where conflict dynamics coincide with the functions of illicit supply chains, in which the economic interests of these groups converge, however, provide a particularly fertile ground for such alliances, which often contradict the wider conflict cleavages. Violent non-state groups form tactical alliances by sharing intelligence to circumvent law enforcement measures, using the same docks or transport routes to ship their illegal goods, or purchasing equipment, such as ammunition and weapons, or cocaine from the same brokers. Personal bonds influence and, at times, supersede shared interests in reducing distrust. Sympathies between group leaders can be based on emotions tied to private goals, such as the desire for revenge or jealousy toward the leader of a third group, conferring on the alliances an incalculable and volatile character. Alliances break, for instance, if a leader feels humiliated by the actions of a member of the other group, if an alliance with a different group promises greater benefits, or if someone is suspected of being a traitor.

For tactical alliances to be reasonably stable, some central control is necessary. Groups with a network structure of independent cells or nodes led by relatively independent mid-level bosses are fragmented. They face dilemmas that are more relevant than in hierarchically organized groups. The alliances based on the personal bonds of their leaders produce volatility, which can tear the intra-group social fabric. How can one be loyal to superiors if they might have switched allegiances? How can one rely on the support of fellow group members if they might be willing to betray the group to maximize their personal benefit? Scholars have explained how intra-group fragmentation leads to infighting.[80] From a "cooperation perspective," newly formed sub-groups forge tactical alliances to infight other subgroups, for example if they are not strong enough to outpower each other individually.

Subcontractual Relationships

As with spot sales, barter agreements, and tactical alliances, shared interests and/or personal bonds reduce distrust in subcontractual relationships between violent non-state groups. In subcontractual relationships, one group accepts an offer from another group to provide services, such as security using modern mercenaries, or a one-time service such as a contract killing, over a defined period.[81] The groups involved are more interdependent than in spot sales and barter agreements; this is usually also the case in relation to tactical alliances. Such interdependence contributes to the stability and durability of the arrangement.

Whereas in tactical alliances all parties act simultaneously, subcontractual relationships involve staggered action that requires some regulation. First, one party contracts the other(s), then the service is provided, and after that (or before that) this service is rewarded. Both parties have more incentive to abide by the arrangement. Quitting the arrangement before service provision (or before the service provided has been paid) would entail financial loss or punishment for reneging. In tactical alliances and spot sales or barter agreements, both groups lose if one of them quits.

In some cases of subcontractual relationships, particularly in contract killings, an intermediary is placed between the two parties. This broker is an additional guarantee to reduce distrust: the contracted party does not know the contractors' identity, making cheating less feasible. A broker also serves to spread the risk and increase impunity as it is more difficult for law enforcement officials to trace the crime's initiator as opposed to the perpetrator of a direct crime.

Subcontractual relationships can emerge from simple favors, a practice common among mafia structures:[82] a gang boss helps someone and then subcontracts this person to provide a service. Such favors are also feasible between groups, often arising from personal bonds between group leaders.

Generally, both parties in subcontractual relationships benefit. Yet the line between mutual convenience and dependency is thin. In an asymmetric power constellation, the subcontractual relationship can turn into a preponderance relation in which the weaker group complies due to fear of punishment rather than due to mutual benefits arising from shared economic interests. Subcontracted groups can also turn against the contractors to gain power.

Friendship: Long-Term Arrangements

Supply Chain Relationships

In supply chain relationships, shared values with a broker reduce distrust, enhancing the stability and durability of the relation and diminishing the likelihood of violent clashes. In such relationships, violent non-state groups participate in transactions along a supply chain, for instance the cocaine supply chain. The groups involved typically respect the territorial limits of influence within which each group exerts economic, social, and/or political control.[83] Territorial segmentation arises from the division of labor along the supply chain in which each group assumes one or several functions.[84] This specialization maximizes profits from the different stages. The groups cooperate through financial or material transactions between each stage, facilitated by intermediaries. In the absence of trust, these transactions require some form of regulation and enforcement.[85] Toward the later stages of the supply chain, therefore, a third party broker reduces distrust through shared values with the groups to enable such relations.[86] These values can be *perceived,* rather than *de facto,* shared values. The broker knows how to convince the groups that he or she is like one of them by adapting to different group cultures or norms in order to appear to share their values. The broker negotiates and mediates between the parties involved in the arrangement, developing a high level of interdependence between him/her and the groups. The groups do not interact directly with each other.

The broker also facilitates the high institutionalization of supply chain relationships.[87] Cooperation with the broker is "stabilized" through the duty of fidelity on both sides. He or she builds up a reputation of trustworthiness, or at least of being as good as his or her word, when it comes to these illicit business deals. The groups value the broker as a reliable and credible business partner and in return honor their side of the deal. As an intermediary, that is, by bridging the "trust gap" between the groups, the broker contributes to the longevity of supply chain relationships, particularly if the groups have differing political motivations.[88]

Supply chain relationships constitute an anomaly within the typology of arrangements among violent non-state groups because shared values (and "friendship") with a broker, rather than with another group, function as distrust-reducing mechanism in a general manner while inter-group distrust persists. Even though all groups benefit from the broker's ability to reduce distrust, they also depend on the broker to purchase, sell, or ship the illegal product. As the glue that holds together the supply chain relationships, the broker has the parties involved at his/her mercy.

Strategic Alliances

Strategic alliances are informed by shared values between violent non-state groups. Political beliefs function as shared values that give rise to a duty of fidelity. If the groups share the same values, they are more likely to also be concerned by the same external constraints such as aggressive or non-aggressive government policies against violent non-state groups. Taken in combination with shared external circumstances, for instance an unfavorable geopolitical situation, values are therefore particularly solid mechanisms for reducing distrust.

Political motivations are the most readily available shared values in settings with politically and economically motivated violent non-state groups, but not the only ones. Shared values also include moral obligations that derive from cultural beliefs, for instance. As values are shaped over a long period and do not change as quickly as emotions or economic considerations, violent non-state groups are not able to simply adapt their values to another group's values. Shared political beliefs—in their function as shared values—may reduce distrust sufficiently for the groups to be willing to give up individual identifiers, even though it makes them more vulnerable to mutual abuse.[89] Accordingly, in strategic alliances, the groups share information, revenue, and/or expenses, and operate jointly in the same territory over extended periods, in order to exercise economic, social, and/or political control over that territory. The groups adhere to rules of nonviolence and mutual aid in the case of a common external threat. They may engage, for example, in "war pacts" to fight jointly against a third group.[90] Strategic alliances are therefore characterized by high interdependence entailing institutionalization that can take shape in written memoranda that formalize (but not enforce) the arrangement between the groups.

Pacific Coexistence

As with strategic alliances, in pacific coexistence violent non-state groups share values that facilitate the reduction of distrust. Thanks to these shared values, over time the groups involved perceive each other to be credible. Contrary to strategic alliances and other long-term arrangements however, the violent non-state groups are less interdependent. They share territory but operate in parallel, with each of them exercising economic, social, and/or political control in their zones of dominance. Therefore, mutual credibility is more important to avoid noncompliance by either of the parties than is the case, for example, in interdependent strategic alliances. Without joint operations, which would involve sharing information, the groups have fewer constraints to defect. Contrary to tense calm, that is, in times where the absence of distrust-reducing mechanisms means that violent combat or armed disputes can break out at any time, in pacific coexistence, violent non-state groups have tacit agreements of non-aggression and non-interference in each other's affairs.[91] Cooperation thus consists of adhering to such tacit agreements of non-aggression: that is, the rule of nonviolence without mutual aid (whereas this is the case with strategic alliances).

Preponderance Relations

Power asymmetries between groups gives rise to stable long-term arrangements as long as the more powerful group refrains from absorbing or defeating the others. In such situations, the preponderant group exercises economic, political, and social control over a given territory, and other groups adhere to the rules imposed by this group. The less-powerful actors have an exit option: to flee the territory controlled by the powerful actors. As long as they accept their role as members of the subordinate group and consider the power constellation constitutive of their own security, the inter-group relations fall into the "friendship" cluster of long-term arrangements.[92] Preponderance relations therefore differ from a Hobbesian domestic situation with a Leviathan, in which people cooperate out of fear from punishment because there is no individual Leviathan: the preponderant party is a group, and members of the subordinated groups could decide to defect and join the preponderant one. Preponderance relations also differ from an international setting with states, where weaker states may have no other option than to adhere to the rules of the more powerful states, as in so-called bandwagoning arrangements, making distrust irrelevant.

The Fuzzy Continuum of Clusters of Violent Non-state Group Interactions

Having conceptualized non-state order and established the typology of violent non-state group interactions, I place these eight types of interactions included in the "enmity," "rivalry," and "friendship" clusters on a "fuzzy continuum."

This depicts, first, the fluid nature of these interactions; second, the multiple directions in which they can change; third, their spatial variations; and fourth, the sometimes muddied identities of the violent non-state groups involved (see Figure 2.1).

First, even though the three clusters are bound by the respective group motivations and the ways in which distrust is reduced, the interactions themselves are dynamic. They can evolve from one into another, and the differences between them are sometimes blurred. The continuum illustrates this: a relationship based on a single distrust-reducing mechanism can take shape in different ways. A tactical alliance can last, for example, for only five days or for ten days, depending on the group leaders' personalities, the local context, third parties, and so on. Hence, the arrangement's exact location within each cluster may vary.

Second, change in violent non-state group interactions is multidirectional: tactical alliances, for example, may mutate directly into armed disputes or into a strategic alliance. This means that movement between the three clusters is also nonlinear: violent non-state groups that engage in "friendly" long-term arrangements, or see each other as rivals in short-term arrangements, can fall back into situations of combat or armed disputes.

Third, violent non-state group interactions can vary across regions and overlap on the same territory (see Maps 3.5 and 3.7). Violent non-state groups are seldom monolithic, and their organizational structure matters. Group members can disagree on how to engage with other groups, especially if the group is structured as a network rather than a hierarchy. Therefore, single groups do not necessarily operate homogeneously across space; they may engage in various interaction types simultaneously.[93] Different arrangements can even be embedded into each other, and form spatial enclaves. For example, a barter agreement may be embedded in a supply chain relationship.

Finally, the groups' identities are not always clear. Some operate in the name of others, and subgroups operate separately under the same name, which can make it difficult, for instance, to distinguish between the preponderance of one group and the pacific coexistence of several ones who use the same "label."

The three clusters help us make sense of the complex interactions that exist among violent non-state groups. Yet it is this very fuzziness that affects people's everyday lives by fueling ambiguity and uncertainty and hence needs to be accounted for if we are to comprehend how non-state order influences both the tangible and intangible elements of people's security. The change, or the potential for change from one type to another type of interaction, for example, can fuel perceptions of insecurity, even if this change occurs nonviolently. It is this relationship between non-state order and people's security to which I turn next.

2.2 Security

Fear is in people's minds. It won't leave you. For the armed groups, it's better to instil fear than to cause damage. [...] Honestly, there isn't really anything good to say about security here.

Resident of Maracaibo, Venezuela, 2012

Social order is as much about the pattern in the relations between the various social actors that constitute such order as it is about the result understood as a particular security outcome. Much of the existing scholarship on security outcomes in the context of violent non-state groups has focused on violence, not least because the regulation of violence is one of the most fundamental problems of order. Yet people's security consists of more than the absence of physical violence. It also concerns freedom from fear, the ability to trust others, and the availability of rules for appropriate behavior that allow for self-protection.

The concept of non-state order sheds light on how violent non-state group interactions matter for such a comprehensive understanding of people's security. The territories in which violent non-state groups operate may be abandoned by the state, but they are home to the communities who reside in them. The logics of each cluster influence the security of these communities in distinct ways. It is important to communities whether violent non-state groups generally distrust each other, reduce distrust only on particular occasions, or reduce distrust in a more general way. These varying levels of inter-group distrust also shape the levels of distrust the groups display towards the communities. Furthermore, communities pay attention to whether violent non-state groups see each other as enemies, rivals, or friends because they can adapt their behavior accordingly. Finally, the specific characteristics of individual violent non-state group interaction types likewise influence whether and how people embedded in such dynamics can make sense of, and adapt to, the dynamics of non-state order in which they live.

In order to grasp these multifaceted aspects of security, I use a people-centered approach to these phenomena: the concept of citizen security. It conceptually links the absence of physical violence and fear, the social fabric of communities, and the ways through which consenting to an authority helps communities enhance their security.

Citizen Security

Security is an "essentially contested concept."[94] It matters "who gets to decide what security means, what issues make it onto security agendas, how those issues should be dealt with, and, crucially, what happens when different visions of security collide."[95] Understanding security dynamics from the bottom up in the margins, in line with a critical security studies approach, emphasizes that security is about threats against people, rather than threats considered through a state lens.[96] This "non-traditionalist" thinking is reflected in the "deepening" of actors: the referent object is not only the state but also the regions, communities, individuals, and individuals in their relationship with a larger group, such as citizens who belong to a polity.[97] From this perspective, both observable "damage" as well as what is "in people's minds," including fear, shapes the meaning of security, as the Maracaibo resident above notes. Analyzing the security repercussions of the various types of violent non-state group interactions thus requires going beyond studying violence; it also requires making sense of "societies of fear."[98]

The concept of "citizen security" reinforces this approach. It takes citizens as the referent object of security. The "issues that make it onto security agendas," as noted above, concern individuals, the community, and institutions.[99] The individual level pertains to the absence of physical violence and fear; the community level to the density of social fabric;[100] and the institutional level to the norms and rules that arise from the relationship between a governance agent and a citizenry. Security can thus be considered an outcome of a particular pattern in which social or political order is organized. This means that we can understand non-state order not just with regard to how it shapes "crude" physical security, but also in relation to the social fabric of communities and the legitimacy of the governance agent, most notably, the state and violent non-state actors as its substitute.

I conceptualize citizen security as a societal order in which citizenship reduces violence and fear (see Figure 2.2). Following John Bailey, I limit the violence component in this concept to "actual physical violence or the overt threat of violence intentionally inflicted by one person or persons on another or others" in the public sphere.[101] I further draw on Charles Tilly, who defines citizenship as:

> a relation between 1) governmental agents acting uniquely as such and 2) whole categories of persons identified uniquely by their connection with the government in question. The relation includes transactions among the parties, of course, but those transactions cluster around mutual rights and obligations.[102]

Where the governance agent (what Tilly calls "governmental agents" or "government") refers to the state, citizenship—and hence citizen security—arises from the mutually reinforcing state-society relationship. In this case, as citizenship invokes fundamental human rights, including the right to life and personal integrity, that lie at the heart of democracy,[103] threats to democracy and human rights constitute a security issue. According to this conceptualization of citizen security, protection responsibilities are reciprocal. In the case of "state-based" citizen security, the state has a duty to protect its citizens; citizens have the right and responsibility to participate in ensuring security. The state is a legitimate security provider; citizens consent to its authority, which involves legitimatizing it. This mutually reinforcing state-society relationship is a function of state capacity and responsiveness, on the one hand, and social fabric and the participatory approach of citizens to security policies, on the other. Capacity refers to the state's ability to exercise governance functions: to provide basic services, public goods (including security and justice), and an enabling environment for the economy.[104] State capacity helps reduce violence when citizens receive these services and goods by nonviolent means. Responsiveness requires taking into consideration citizens' interests, facilitating their participation in designing (security) policies, accountability, and the ability to manage conflictive situations.

Social fabric is a web of relationships that holds society together. Just as clothing fabric is woven with fibers, social fabric is woven with social capital.[105] The latter is based on interpersonal trust that leads to a sense of community and civic cooperation.[106] This is conducive to citizen security because "good citizens are those who learn to behave with civility towards each other," as Laurence Whitehead explains.[107] Or, in Robin Collingwood's words, "where it refers to a man's relations with his fellow men [being civil] indicates abstention from the use of force."[108]

Since social capital facilitates cooperation and stabilizes democratic institutions,[109] a tightly woven social fabric strengthens a mutually reinforcing state-society relationship. Social fabric fosters considerate behavior with respect to other citizens' rights. It thus is a prerequisite for the active participation of civil society in governing violence through the design of social and public policies that protect citizens, including civic infrastructure to reduce insecurity.[110] This includes, for example, citizen security councils, education, youth programs, and alternative mechanisms for conflict resolution.[111] It is only if citizens have agency by articulating their opinion on how to reduce threats of violence that the state can be truly responsive.

Citizenship itself can reinforce considerate behavior that reduces insecurity. This is because it is not only a social status that emerges from the relation between the governance agent and citizens, it also guides people's action by defining legitimate meanings and behaviors through shared "values, norms, interests, identities and beliefs," as James G. March and Johan P. Olsen note.[112] In these authors' terms, it contributes to a "logic of appropriateness."[113] Accordingly, action "is seen as driven by rules of appropriate or exemplary behaviour, organized into institutions,"[114] namely, the shared set of norms including those that reduce insecurity.

Whitehead notes that:

> for the great majority of acts by individual citizens the rule of law is
> only enforced to the extent that groups and individuals practise appro-
> priate forms of self-limitation. The rights and restraints of citizenship
> are thus internalized rather than imposed.[115]

In an ideal-type "state-based" citizenship, upholding these (internalized) norms
consolidates social fabric among the citizenry and loyalty toward the state in exchange for capacity and responsiveness. People identify themselves as members
of this polity; they develop a sense of belonging.[116] They play by the rules that
they have agreed upon together with the state; that is, they exercise rights and
duties both internalized as norms and codified into laws.

From a people-centered perspective, citizens must have a say in what they
consider "security."[117] Its scope differs from one society to another. Security can
mean the protection of citizens from threats as diverse as domestic violence, social violence, common crime, organized crime, and corruption. In line with this,
citizen security takes account of people's agency. It distinguishes between objective and subjective security.[118] *Objective* citizen security is tied to the state's
capacity and responsiveness. It includes observable factors such as homicides,
as well as the extent to which citizens participate in reducing insecurity through
establishing an appropriate civic infrastructure. *Subjective* citizen security refers
to the socially constructed concept of security. It addresses people's perceptions,
including fear and uncertainty. Perceptions of security are contingent, inter alia,
on the local context and past experiences, including a state's history of violence.
Lucía Dammert notes that perceptions of insecurity have "a deep social, cultural,

Figure 2.2 Citizen security

and economic impact and may even contribute to defining (or redefining) the very structures of the State."[119] They impair interpersonal trust, eroding the social fabric necessary to exercise agency as citizens.[120] Similarly, Koonings and Krujit note that "fear is the institutional, cultural and psychological repercussion of violence. Fear is a response to institutional destabilization, social exclusion, individual ambiguity and uncertainty."[121] Thus, "a society that is characterized by fear, as well as by the constant perception of threat and risk has serious limitations to consolidate active citizenship and a strong civil society."[122]

Objective and subjective citizen security do not always coincide. A society may have low homicide rates, and yet people may *feel* less secure than those of other societies with higher homicide rates, for example. The levels of subjective and objective citizen security also vary across societal groups. Caroline Moser and Cathy McIlwaine, for instance, note that in their case studies in Colombia and Guatemala, youth and young men were likely to experience physical violence, whereas women, children, and the elderly were vulnerable to fear and uncertainty, which limited their mobility.[123] Despite its relevance for notions of security more broadly, we still lack understanding of this discrepancy between objective and subjective citizen security.[124]

Even though citizen security has specific, and often differing meanings for individual societies, it is always a necessary component of the universal objective of human security. In its broadest interpretation, as outlined by the 1994 Human Development Report, human security comprises seven dimensions: economic, food, health, environmental, personal, community, and political security.[125] Personal security refers to protection of individuals from physical violence;[126] "[community security] emphasizes the needs of the community and the importance of bringing together different groups to design common approaches to common problems."[127] The more recent view on human security, as adopted in a United Nations General Assembly Resolution in 2012, subsumes those various dimensions into three components:[128] freedom from fear, freedom from want, and the right to live in dignity.[129] Citizen security as defined above involves freedom from fear and it implies that security includes the consolidation of institutions that protect people in a participatory and sustainable way.[130]

Importantly, when operationalizing citizen security as a component of wider human security in vulnerable regions, it is the very notion of the state coming in as the "solution" to security challenges that needs to be problematized. Such contexts feature deficient versions of the ideal-type state-based concepts of "citizenship" and "citizen security" that I have outlined here. Furthermore, at times, they also feature different "kinds" of citizenship and citizen security altogether because the governance agent is a violent non-state group, rather than the state. This is the larger point that I make toward the end of the next section, in which I theorize how non-state order influences people's security, that is, citizen security.

Security amid Non-state Order

Each cluster of non-state order and the interactions within each cluster have distinct influences on the security situation of the communities where violent non-state groups operate.[131] Employing "citizen security" as an analytical tool to trace these influences reveals distinct security outcomes. Understood in relation to an ideal-type citizen security situation, these influences concern the absence of violence and fear, the density of social fabric, the mutually reinforcing relationship between a governance agent and the citizenry, the availability of rules of appropriate behavior, and the agency of people in enhancing their perceived and/or de facto security through coping mechanisms and protection strategies.

Before continuing with the last two points—appropriate behavior and what can be subsumed under security-enhancing practices—require further clarification. Above, I briefly discuss how behavioral rules and norms embodied in citizenship contribute to citizen security. In contexts where the state is not sufficiently capable or responsive, norms associated with what I refer to as "state-based" citizenship become elusive. Often, this is the result of the state's institutional flaws. Moreover, in contexts where violent non-state groups operate, external influences such as groups seeking a weak state as a base for their operation may further erode the principles of such state-based citizenship.[132] When multiple violent non-state groups are present and state governance, and with it state-provided security, cannot be taken for granted, the particular pattern of non-state order influences what kind of behavior is appropriate to enhance security. By following and, at times, influencing, these rules, community members can therefore minimize insecurity. Community members also develop security-enhancing practices themselves. These include strategies to protect themselves from physical violence, as well as practices that influence their perceived security and that can operate as coping mechanisms. Across the three clusters, the latter, for example, take shape in the normalization of violence and victim blaming. Each cluster also favors distinct practices, as I show later. Together, accounting for the availability of rules of appropriate behavior, and for people's own actions to reduce *perceived* insecurity, shifts attention to what it means to be a *potential* victim, in addition to the experience of being victimized.

A situation of "enmity" then, in which violent non-state groups do not have any arrangement with each other, contributes to people's exposure to violence, but also to the availability of relatively clear rules of behavior for the community. In contexts of unstable short-term arrangements among violent non-state groups that I label "rivalry," violence is typically more selective, but the fragile character of the arrangements contributes to the erosion of the communities' social fabric. The communities also face more uncertainty in terms of what constitutes appropriate behavior to enhance their security. In contexts where non-state order takes shape in what I term "friendship," civilians experience comparatively little violence. As I discuss below, they can rely on rules of behavior arising from "shadow citizenship" to enhance their security, that is, "shadow citizen security."

In addition to summarizing the conceptualization of non-state order, Table 2.1 provides an overview of how each cluster of violent non-state group interaction influences these various citizen security components. In the remainder of this section, I explain these influences in more detail. Later, in chapters 4 to 6, I unpack them empirically, and further trace how specific characteristics of individual interaction types influence the security situation of local communities. Ultimately, this framework demonstrates the disconnect between how power centers *observe* (in)security and how those whose everyday lives are affected by violent non-state group interactions experience (in)security (see also Epilogue). Applied to borderland areas, it uncovers the crumbling of the state's perceived legitimacy at its edges.

The "Enmity" Cluster: Violence and Survival

In the context of combat and armed disputes, community members suffer violence, especially when they are caught in the crossfire of armed clashes between violent non-state groups in which they engage as enemies. In such situations of general mistrust, community members can also become direct victims of violence against civilians.[133] In addition to physical harm, violent clashes affect people's minds. Violence can both undermine and reconstitute social capital,[134] and hence both tear and tighten social fabric.

Enmity does not only begin when armed clashes start, nor is it over when they stop. It can precede outbreaks of violence and continue afterward. The general inter-group distrust that translates into mistrust toward the population likewise persists.[135] During tense calm, even though there is no violence, people still *feel* insecure because they are embedded in a context of general mistrust. Everyone knows that violence could break out at any moment because the violent non-state groups still aim to eliminate each other. In these cases, community members know that they might still become victims of direct violence.

In circumstances where the state is absent or may be complicit with one of the groups and "behave" as a non-state actor, people are unable to rely on the state as a protector. Even if a community's social fabric is dense and, for example, its members support each other to protect themselves, abiding by rules and norms that emerge from citizenship is unlikely to enhance one's security. Indeed, these norms are void, undermining the (absent) state's authority. Instead, communities draw on a more basic set of rules of appropriate behavior that emerges from the pattern of non-state order in which they are embedded— even in the context of tense calm where violence is (temporarily) absent. This is

Table 2.1 **Non-State Order and Citizen Security**

		"Enmity" Cluster	"Rivalry" Cluster	"Friendship" Cluster
Context	**Motive for cooperation**	none	interests, personal bonds	values, power
	Distrust-reducing mechanism	none	interest convergence, mutual sympathies	shared values, power asymmetries
	Inter-group distrust	general distrust	distrust reduced on a particular occasion	generally reduced distrust
Violent Non-state Group Interactions	**Quality and durability of arrangement**	none	unstable, short-term	stable, long-term
	Inter-group violence	unlimited violence	selective	none
	Types	combat/armed disputes	spot sales/barter agreements subcontractual relationships tactical alliances	supply chain relationships strategic alliances pacific coexistence preponderance relations
Citizen Security	**Absence of violence and fear**	exposure to general violence	exposure to selective violence	relatively little exposure to violence
	Dense social fabric	varying	erosion of social fabric	dense intra-community social fabric
	Governance agent–citizenry relationship	dysfunctional	dysfunctional	shadow citizenship
	Appropriate behavior	rules emerging from enmity	uncertainty	rules emerging from shadow citizenship
	Security-enhancing practices	just-world thinking	avoidance	rule of silence towards outsiders

because violent non-state groups know each other's intentions. They know that they *cannot* trust each other, that they are enemies. To a certain extent, they predict behavior based on each other's military capabilities and support among the local population. Albeit to a lesser extent, similar knowledge is available to local community members who can use this knowledge to at least aim to behave "appropriately" to maximize chances for survival. In this case, appropriate behavior to protect oneself arises from the assumption that the various violent non-state groups fight each other in combat, armed disputes, or have a posture of fighting each other during episodes of tense calm. In this regard, understanding combat and armed disputes as manifestations of "enmity" explains why in the absence of any arrangement between groups there are clearer rules of behavior than when we see forms of cooperation such as short-lived alliances.

These assumptions also play into the mechanisms that individuals use to make sense of or cope with these circumstances. The notion of the Other as the enemy is reflected in a just-world thinking according to which the "bad ones" belong to the Other and hence deserve death whereas the "good ones" survive.

The "Rivalry" Cluster: Crime and Uncertainty

In settings where violent non-state groups engage in unstable short-term arrangements as self-interested rivals, criminal groups do not shy away from lethal violence to enhance profit.[136] So too do conflict actors who use criminal activities as an income source. As the armed actors engage in targeted killings of group members who might cheat or who constitute an obstacle to profit maximization, community members are exposed to selective, rather than general, violence. In such contexts of illegality, suspicion rules. The groups only reduce distrust to cooperate on specific occasions while general inter-group distrust persists. Distrust between groups, but also between groups and community members, is high because anyone might harm their business. The environment of mistrust, in addition to profit maximization, fuels more violence: selective violence to deter whistle-blowers who harm the business contributes to physical insecurity. The groups and their members themselves judge whether, and to what extent, to constrain the use of violence, not only against other groups (see section 2.1) but also against potential betrayers among the local community members. This gives their operations and potential outbreaks of violence an unpredictable character. Living in the midst of rivaling violent non-state groups puts civilians in a situation in which the possibility of a descent into all-out fighting, and hence of being caught in the crossfire of violence, is ever present.

Yet there is more to this general mistrust than the body count. The volatility of their operations (see section 2.1) and the involvement of local community members in the groups' criminal activities produces ambiguity about who is on whose side, and for how long. Combined with the uncertainty due to the unpredictability of violent breakdowns of the groups' arrangements, this ambiguity deprives people of rules of behavior with which to protect themselves. "Uncertainty refers to the state of an organism that lacks information about whether, where, when, how, or why an event has occurred or will occur," note Yoav Bar-Anan et al.[137] Information about the intentions of violent actors in their territory would allow people to predict and, in some instances, control their environment, making it possible to adapt their behavior to their advantage. When such adaptation is not an option, the resulting uncertainty means that community members have a largely negative perception of their personal security situation.[138] In violent settings, this uncertainty can become lethal. Constant uncertainty, translating into pervasive fear, indifference, or paranoia adds to the distrust between groups, and between groups and community members, eroding the social fabric.

Like in the context of the "enmity" cluster, persisting selective violence committed by violent non-state groups suggests that the state has failed to fulfill its protection responsibilities. At the same time, the community's eroded social fabric prevents it from engaging in collective action to protect itself. Since it is not possible for community members to adapt behavior to any identifiable patterns, like who is an enemy and who not, in the "rivalry" cluster, avoidance strategies emerge as a dominant behavior to reduce insecurity amid uncertainty.

The "Friendship" Cluster: Governance and Consent

When violent non-state groups reduce distrust in a general manner and refrain from using violence against each other, community members do not end up caught in the crossfire. Since the groups have no intention to eliminate the other group (as in the "enmity" cluster) and have less reason to suspect the other groups of being cheaters (as in the "rivalry" cluster), they are also able to approach local communities with less mistrust. The risk of community members supporting the other group(s) and inflicting damage on them through this support is low, compared to the other two clusters. This reduces the need for violence against community members.

Relatively stable long-term arrangements among violent non-state actors are typically attached to a given territory. This is different to interactions driven by the goal of eliminating other groups through violence, or to arrangements motivated by economic interests or short-lived personal bonds. The groups rely on governing that territory or on being given "permission to stay" by those who govern it. This governance benefits from the reduced distrust toward the community and from the absence of the state. When operating on overlapping territory, violent non-state groups can complement each other by providing governance functions otherwise provided by the state.[139]

In many conflicts around the world, conflict actors, rather than the state, assume governance functions and establish "orderly" order.[140] Outside conflict settings, criminal structures likewise "govern" urban areas, like in the case of Brazilian favelas.[141] Both in conflict and non-conflict settings, in order to control territory, violent non-state groups rely on the local population's support, at least in situations where power through violence alone is too costly.[142] Rodney Hall and Thomas Biersteker refer to such control exercised by violent non-state groups as "illicit authority":

> The claim to authority of private illicit actors in the international system rests upon their capacity to provide public goods and their private control of the means of violence that competes with, or supersedes, the capacity of public authority. The social recognition of illicit authority is also essential to its emergence as private authority, not simply its possession of power.[143]

At first glance, in such illicitly governed spaces, the security outcome involves primarily one thing: the absence of violence. A closer look at whose agency makes this illicit governance possible demonstrates that it is contingent on the local communities' consent by legitimatizing the illicit governance agent's authority *and* their active participation in the mutually reinforcing relationship between them and the governance agent.

Shadow Citizenship

In illicitly governed spaces that exist when non-state order takes shape in the "friendship" cluster, citizens not only consent to an (illicit) authority, they may also have a say in their relationship with it. This is reflected in what I call shadow citizenship. Shadow citizenship is a form of citizenship in which the governance agent is a violent non-state group. An ideal-type shadow citizenship hinges on a recursive relationship in which violent non-state groups provide public goods and services—including the provision of security—and define the rules of appropriate behavior while people socially recognize the illicit authority, consent to these rules, and participate in shaping them. Put differently, shadow citizenship is a cluster of illegal institutionalized organizational structures that guide behavior in illicitly controlled territory.[144] What constitutes appropriate behavior is defined through the rules imposed by the groups, yet also influenced by people, as well as through shared norms internalized by the people who participate in this relationship. These norms and rules thus govern the community these people belong to—a shadow community, as I call it.

In contrast to concepts such as Zachariah Mampilly's "insurgent governance,"[145] or Hall and Biersteker's "illicit authority,"[146] shadow citizenship focuses on the reciprocity of the relationship between the governance agent—here the violent non-state group—*and* citizens, that is, the people, with a particular analytical emphasis on people's agency.

Based on a governance agent that is not the state, shadow citizenship also differs from what Tilly considers thin citizenship, in which case "transactions, rights and obligations sustained by state agents and people living under their jurisdiction" are not fully exercised,[147] and from what Guillermo O'Donnell calls "low-intensity citizenship."[148] In this case, local populations have access to few (if any) effective government institutions but can nonetheless be empowered "in terms consistent with democratic legality" to transform this into "full, democratic and liberal, citizenship."[149] Shadow citizenship further differs from James Holston's notion of "insurgent citizenship" that emphasizes the agency of citizens as a "new urban citizenship," and where the marginalized claim their citizenship rights through auto-construction.[150] Rather, shadow citizenship is an "alternative citizenship" similar to Barbara Oomen's,[151] which is oriented toward non-state actors (yet not *violent* non-state actors) instead of the state.

In the context of shadow citizenship, the provision of governance enhances the violent non-state groups' perceived legitimacy among local communities.[152] I refer here to empirical legitimacy that is contingent on perceptions, "a belief of subjects."[153] The kinds of governance functions that violent non-state groups fulfill, as well as the prioritization of these functions, influence their empirical legitimacy and hence the quality of shadow citizenship. These issues depend, among other things, on the specific type of violent non-state group interaction in the "friendship" cluster, that is, supply chain relationships, strategic alliances, pacific coexistence, or preponderance relations. They are also related to the type of violent non-state groups, their organizational structure, their raison d'être, and the influence of transnational actors.[154] People's demands, as well as their perceptions of the armed actors' motives and performance in exerting governance functions, matter too. The balance between the two is contingent on context. For example, a community under threat of physical violence is likely to be willing to accept and follow the rules of the actor who is able to protect it against such threats, irrespective of how much or how little the community identifies with this actor and its motives.[155]

Paramilitary and right-wing groups often provide only security and justice, hence their empirical legitimacy is based on their ability to protect the population.[156] Urban citizens affected by high crime rates may also prioritize security provision.[157] In contrast, in many rural areas, insurgents win a social base because, in line with their propaganda against the government, they provide public goods such as road infrastructure. As a result, rural communities may tolerate strict rules and undemocratic practices.[158] Groups with primarily economic interests, such as drug trafficking or mafia groups, control the supply of protection in return for charging protection money.[159] This makes social recognition harder to achieve. While insurgents offer economic opportunities in the cultivation and first stages of drug processing, criminal groups including trafficking rings typically provide jobs as messengers, informants, drug mules, or contract killers. This group-dependent variation indicates how their relationship with the local community and their social recognition differ as well, even in the same context. Hence, empirically, ideal-type shadow citizenship may not always arise. Rather, it is likely to see an imperfect (in the conceptual sense) shadow citizenship.

Shadow Citizen Security

When violent non-state groups in the "friendship" cluster govern territory illicitly, they refrain from employing violence against communities as a means of deterrence or punishment for supporting another group. They also stop others from employing violence in the territory they control. In other words: they provide security. If people have a say in this particular governance provision, then violence and fear is reduced through shadow citizen security. Building on my definition of citizen security provided above, shadow citizen security, then, is a societal order in which shadow citizenship reduces violence and fear, and where shadow citizenship refers to the mutually reinforcing relationship between the violent non-state group as governance agent and the community as citizenry.[160]

Shadow citizen security indicates that, in the respective territory, the violent non-state groups' control over the means of violence supersedes, and effectively replaces, the state's capacity. Yet shadow citizen security is not just about the armed actor's ability to assume protection functions; people's perceptions matter, too. The classical Weberian approach to thinking about the state views coercion as central source of a state's legitimacy;[161] the legitimate monopoly of violence is considered a core feature of statehood. Generally, when the state judicial system is absent or inefficient, people settle disputes among themselves or set up institutions to do so. Insufficient state protection prompts people to employ self-defense mechanisms such as creating surveillance committees, engaging in vigilante justice, or arming themselves.[162] When violent non-state groups have the monopoly on violence over a territory in stable long-term arrangements, these groups take over such protection functions. When the groups are also *perceived* to be the legitimate holders of this monopoly, people turn to the groups. Communities, for example, may consider the groups' parallel justice more efficient than the state's; the groups punish delinquents immediately, whereas the state justice system is absent or protracted and sometimes never reaches a verdict.[163]

In an ideal-type shadow citizenship, the community members' physical security is rarely undermined, provided they play by the rules that emerge from shadow citizenship.[164] If physical violence does occur, community members perceive it to be a legitimate means of coercion, for example in the case of non-compliance with the rules imposed by the violent non-state groups. The threat of violence—rather than violence itself—then is an effective means of coercion that contributes to security.[165]

The quality of shadow citizen security is contingent on whether the behavioral rules are sufficiently clear to be followed in order to stay safe and on whether there is room to negotiate the rules if citizens disagree with them. When acceptance of these rules rests on fear only, people's subjective citizen security is undermined, even if they are physically safe. The more there is room for communities to have a say in how behavioral rules that facilitate protection are designed, the more shadow citizen security resembles "ideal-type" citizen security—albeit with a violent non-state actor operating in illegality rather than the state as governance agent.

Of course, the notion of the logic of appropriateness suggests that de facto security can be undermined without citizens perceiving it this way. For example, people who have been living under illicit rule over generations in the absence of the state may perceive shadow citizen security, that is, security provided by violent non-state actors, as the preferable choice. Consent to the violent non-state actor then is appropriate to ensure security, even if resistance is more beneficial in the long run.

Shadow citizenship and shadow citizen security have consequences for security and citizenship more broadly. Communities consent to the monopoly on violence of violent non-state groups in a certain territory and develop a sense of belonging to this "shadow community," rather than to a national polity. Within this community, the social fabric is likely to be dense, especially if people have internalized shared norms of appropriate behavior, instead of simply following the rules imposed by the groups. They tend, however, to be isolated from the "outside world." The social fabric between them and those beyond their community is torn apart.[166]

The sense of belonging to a relatively non-violent community, yet out of the purview of the state, is also reflected in a strategy often adopted by communities to further enhance their security: the rule of silence toward outsiders. Not speaking out to those who do not form part of their shadow community reinforces the stark contrast between the community's dense intra-community social fabric and those who they consider "outsiders."[167]

2.3 The Role of the State and the Regional Context

Studying non-state order with a "citizen security" tool zooms in on the triangle of relations among three types of actors: people, violent non-state groups, and the state (or its absence). These relations include, first, the relationship between the state and these communities; second, the relationship between violent non-state groups and local communities; third, relations among community members; and fourth, the relationship between the state and violent non-state groups.[168]

Certainly, grasping the influence of non-state order on security presupposes acknowledging that the state and its various entities is often just one of many possible actors that communities engage with. It is not necessarily the most important one. For people living in fragile settings, as is the case in many border areas in vulnerable regions, the interactions among various non-state groups can shape their everyday lives in an equal or more decisive way than do combat or alliances between non-state and state forces. Similarly, where state governance is absent or insufficient, the relationship of a violent non-state group with the (absent) state—for example whether it fights it as insurgents, colludes with it as paramilitaries, or sidelines it as criminals—may matter little for people on the ground. It is more relevant for people's security that the armed actors operating in the territory "behave like a state" by providing governance functions, including security, than whether they are a rebel, paramilitary, or criminal group.

Nonetheless, as the "people, violent non-state group, state" triangle epitomizes, a focus on (violent) non-state relations rather than state (or international) relations does not imply ignoring the state. The concept of non-state order and its influence on security benefits from various theoretical perspectives on the state—most importantly, those on citizenship and citizen security—especially when they see the state as the principal governance agent. At the same time, our understanding of the state benefits from insights on non-state dynamics.

As seen in the subsequent chapters, I also include the state as an actor that matters throughout the analysis. For example, there are instances where a government's support for a violent non-state group reinforces the group's dominance, or where foreign state forces allow (tacitly or directly) such a group to operate in their territory, reinforcing the impunity that is prevalent in borderland spaces. Furthermore, violent non-state groups engage in relationships with state entities such as armed forces, local authorities, and national governments.[169] Finally, it is the state's very failure to intervene to protect its citizens, despite its formal obligation to do so, that increases insecurity.

Before moving on to the spaces where everyday life is shaped by non-state dynamics—the Andean borderlands—I historically contextualize my approach within Latin America. This further justifies the choice of citizen security as the analytical tool I apply to the three clusters of non-state order.

Much of Latin America was under authoritarian regimes throughout most of the twentieth century. Security policies centered on maintaining law and order through repressive and punitive means, in accordance with a national security doctrine thinking.[170] The focus of Latin American states was on public security, according to which state institutions have the responsibility to protect persons and property from physical violence. This protection can be double-edged because "governments are in the business of selling protection . . . whether people want it or not."[171] Indeed, although governments claimed to protect their citizens from internal and external threats, these very threats often arose from the governments themselves.

The concept of citizen security gained traction in the early 1980s when, with a "third wave of democratisation,"[172] democracy became the prevalent political system in Latin America. The debate shifted from public order and repression to a normative thinking grounded in the creation of an "environment conducive to peaceful coexistence" and "activities to prevent and control the factors that generate violence and insecurity."[173] It was considered the state's task, through its public and social institutions, to contribute to maintaining and promoting peaceful coexistence and human rights within the wider framework of law and culture.

Working toward the ideal-type societal order of citizen security with the state as governance agent could not be more pressing in Latin America than today. Contemporary Latin America is the region with the world's highest homicide rates; violence, crime, and fear have been cited consistently as the most serious challenges to security. Andean citizens including Colombians, Venezuelans, and Ecuadorians cite crime and citizen insecurity as their countries' biggest problem.[174] With a conviction rate of only twenty-four per 100 victims of intentional homicide in the Americas,[175] high rates of impunity and corruption add to this sobering security panorama. They may explain ongoing public dissatisfaction with insufficient government commitment and distrust toward state institutions.[176]

Citizen security therefore remains at the core of public policy in the region. Governments, think tanks, and international organizations have developed tools, including surveys with indicators, to measure citizen security.[177] The Inter-American Development Bank, for example, established twenty-two indicators, including administrative records of homicides, firearm deaths, and theft rates, as well as survey data on perceived insecurity, risk, and fear.[178] The United Nations

Development Programme even made citizen security the topic of its 2013–2014 Human Development Report for Latin America.[179]

As is the case with security and conflict research more broadly,[180] the concept of citizen security has been typically applied to mostly Latin American urban centers. The incipient literature on fear and citizen security concentrates on crime in cities, especially in metropolises, reflecting a strong urban bias.[181] Policymakers also prioritize urban centers rather than peripheries when designing surveys. Data hardly exist for remote borderlands. If they do exist, the high incidence of unreported cases in rural areas and the misrepresentation of perceptions of security in victimization surveys due to dynamics of fear in communities controlled by violence, distort such security indicators. Scared by the presence of armed groups, people prefer not to tell the truth.[182]

Moving the concept "citizen security" to the peripheries reveals how the referent object "citizen" is particularly vulnerable to the harmful repercussions of non-state order on security in transnational borderlands. These are the geographical peripheries of the state, but they are also social spaces at the margins of statehood. In the next chapter, I integrate work on geographical state boundaries into anthropological views on statehood to explore the tension between the concept of state borders and life across the margins. This is necessary to explain dynamics that transcend state territory, including the transnational illicit flows and violent non-state group interactions that I map in that chapter. It further prepares us for the subsequent analysis that challenges conventional thinking on these issues, namely: of behavioral patterns of non-state actors rather than of states; of people's security rather than national security; and of transnational borderland dynamics in their own right rather than of borders as state limits.

3

The Borderland Lens

As we are in a border zone, they ignore us more. We are invisible to the rest
of society and the rest of the world. Just because we live near the border.
Resident of San Lorenzo, Ecuador, 2012[1]

The words of this borderland resident capture the resentment I witnessed
across the Colombian-Ecuadorian and the Colombian-Venezuelan borderlands.
People are invisible. At best forgotten, at worst banished, from the rest of society,
as a result of the fear of the unknown, the bizarre, that exceeds one's imagination:

> [T]he borderland is a site of extreme anxiety for the modern state. The
> state's partially obscured view of borderland activities, the gap between
> people's understandings of what they are doing versus the state's, incon-
> sistent notions of illegality, and the presence of other legalities across
> the border, all make, for the state, the borderland an area where by defi-
> nition criminality is rife and sovereignty under constant threat.[2]

It is this gap between the state-centric view on borders and the transnational
realities at the margins, which, in vulnerable areas like the Andean region,
makes borderlands extreme cases of complex security dynamics that magnify
challenges of violence, crime, and governance. And it is also in these spaces
where various forms of non-state order, as outlined in the previous chapter,
rather than state order only, determine people's security. State presence is often
nonexistent or temporary, and is considered a nuisance or intervening factor
that alters, yet is not decisive for security. If the state's view on borderlands from
the center is obscured and renders residents invisible, then a borderland perspective sheds light on what the state cannot see. This alternative perspective
transcends the category "state" and challenges thinking in spatially bounded
concepts more broadly. Commencing from the margins demonstrates the possibility of transforming this "extreme anxiety" noted above into grounded understanding by "making the invisible visible, bringing the margin to the center,
[and] rendering the trivial important," as is called for in critical scholarship.[3]

Assuming this alternative perspective, I now put the multiple forms of non-state order and their myriad influences on people's security into the context where their contours are particularly distinct: borderlands. Viewing these security dynamics through a borderland lens reveals the underlying logics that create them in the first place. Historical state neglect across the borders is the basic condition that gives rise to non-state order. The geostrategic relevance of border areas, especially those that serve as mobility corridors and safe havens in the non-conflict territory for those who fight in the armed conflict, is a key factor for the emergence of the "enmity" cluster of violent non-state group interactions. A spatial analysis of the interconnected illicit flows—most notably of cocaine—reveals how topographic and geographic features of border areas are conducive to the existence of certain forms of non-state order in some regions, but not in others.

For example, the presence of fluvial systems to transport illicit goods, of mangroves to hide cocaine in places where the location of the exact borderline is ambiguous, or of natural harbors used as starting points for international trafficking routes, matters for whether armed actors have economic interests to cooperate with each other in such regions. Yet features such as the existence of informal border bridges through which to funnel weapons in exchange for drugs, climatic conditions that favor coca cultivation, and cultural traits such as the binational character of some indigenous people whose constant border-crossing facilitates smuggling practices also inform the logics of violent non-state group interactions and hence security on the ground. A borderland lens shows that none of these driving forces of multiple forms of non-state order—weak governance systems, geostrategic relevance, and transnational illicit flows facilitated by topographic, geographic, and cultural features—stops at the borderline. Rather, they rest on the very transnationality of borderlands and on their distance from the central states.

After outlining the conventional views on the borders, I apply this borderland lens to map the violent non-state group interactions whose influences on security I examine in the following chapters (see also appendix B).

In chapter 7, I return to the geography of borderlands to demonstrate its striking effect on these security outcomes: the intensification of the insecurities and vulnerabilities that locals are exposed to, and the strengthening of the sense of belonging to what I call a transnational shadow community, which ultimately questions the notion of the territorial state altogether.

3.1 Borders Viewed from the Centers

According to state-centric perspectives, global dynamics shape state centers and these centers affect the peripheries.[4] The power centers expand, militarize their borders in defense, or make agreements on cross-border trade, all of which result

in repercussions for the borderlands.[5] Indeed, the world has been shaped by political border drawing. Inter-state conflicts aimed at territorial conquest and the
importance of borders in deterring military incursions characterize the state
system's history.[6] Hence, realists emphasize the traditional military function of
borders as "strategic lines to be militarily defended or breached."[7] Despite the
decline of inter-state conflict, power politics and boundary disputes still matter.[8]
Not only states but also other geographical spaces are commonly conceptualized
as bordered entities and thus evolving borders produce larger repercussions on
local, regional, and global orders. For example, changes of borders, such as the
fall of the Iron Curtain and the founding of the European Union, entailed global
and regional political, economic, and social developments.[9] Boundaries defined
by religious, cultural, and ethnic identities dominate world politics in the post-
9/11 era.[10] More recently, strengthened nationalism, economically promoted
regionalism, and the reclaiming of identities and culture have reinforced existing
boundaries while simultaneously creating new ones.

State-centric or otherwise bounded perspectives undervalue what transcends
borders: transnational flows. As Itty Abraham and Willem van Schendel note:

> The contemporary social sciences are ill equipped to make sense of
> transnational flows due to their symbiotic history with the modern state
> and its interests. Most social science is expressly and unconsciously
> bound by state boundaries, categories that are reproduced within insti-
> tutionally sanctioned academic specializations.[11]

Meanwhile, those who draw attention to borders by focusing on their absence,
such as globalists, do not capture what is in between: the transnational dynamics
that shape the world's security landscape.[12] Yet it is the tension between these
transnational flows and the prevailing state-centric paradigm that produces the
complex security dynamics with which we grapple in today's globalized world.
Moreover, if these flows belong to the so-called underworld, or move across the
underworld and the "upper world," this tension engenders security threats, such
as the ones I discuss in the subsequent chapters.

Illicit flows call into question the function of borders as delimiters or barriers,[13]
but they also exist due to the very persistence of these same borders. Anne Clunan
and Harold Trinkunas emphasize that "'asymmetries' in states' taxation and regulation in a world of globalized demand create the incentives for engaging in
'jurisdictional arbitrage' in the form of smuggling and trafficking."[14] Such illegal
economic cross-border dynamics are historic.[15] As Manuel Castells put it, "crime
is as old as humankind. Indeed, in the biblical account of our origins, our plight
began with the illegal traffic of apples."[16] Yet the scope of the activities is new, due
to the "de-bordering" process of globalization.[17] Globalists argue that growing

global interdependence has made borders progressively less relevant due to a continuing deterritorialization.[18] Ken'ichi Ōmae even suggests that we live in a "borderless world."[19] However, borders are still relevant, albeit in a different way. Or, as Peter Andreas states, "geopolitics is transformed, not transcended."[20] Economic liberalization, financial mobility, and new communication and transportation technologies—broadly speaking, globalization—have transformed borders into "bridges for commercial transactions rather than economic barriers and fortified military lines."[21] These very transformations come along with changes in the activities that belong to the "Other Side of Globalization":[22] local smugglers are being superseded by global networks, common criminals join transnational terrorists, and chains of illegal drug, human, or weapons trafficking expand beyond regional boundaries, crossing continents and reaching into cyberspace.[23]

State regulation, law enforcement, and political awareness of illegal economic cross-border activities have changed as well, contributing further to the transformed meaning of borders.[24] New technologies did not reduce the importance of borders, but brought them to the center of policy concerns. While border controls have become stricter through sophisticated intelligence and surveillance technologies, these same technologies enable those who evade the law to circumvent controls and adapt to changing market conditions such as demand and competition. This in turn generates even more sophisticated law enforcement strategies, leading to a never-ending "border game."[25] More border control to curb such activities may be counterproductive: the greater the risk associated with the illegal enterprise, the higher the profits and hence the incentives to engage in it.[26] Therefore, as Andreas notes, "the economic importance of smuggling demonstrates that there is not just a formal, aboveground dimension of regional and global interdependence but an informal, underground dimension as well."[27] By using increasingly astute strategies to cross borders, those who evade the law by doing so endorse these very borders—without them their activities would vanish.[28]

State Policies toward Andean Borders

In the Andean region, the borders' military function has lost significance. The last border war—between Ecuador and Peru—was settled in 1998. To be sure, some inter-state tensions persist. Colombia and Venezuela, for example, dispute their maritime boundary and ownership of the Los Monjes islands, and diplomatic squabbles have led to demonstrations of Venezuelan tanks at the shared land border.[29] Continued weapons purchases have fueled these dynamics to some extent.[30] However, they are not necessarily directly linked to borders. They should also be seen as the muscle-flexing logics of deterrence, as the shadow of the Cold War still looms over what the United States used to consider—or continues to consider—its backyard. The role of cultural, religious, and ethnic boundaries is not dividing either, at least not between the Andean states.[31] Having shared Simón Bolívar's struggle for independence against the Spanish, and formed Gran Colombia, the modern-day states of Colombia, Ecuador, and Venezuela preserve cultural, religious, and linguistic ties. Intraregional migration, energy cooperation, and economic integration have ensured that the countries are largely connected across borders and with their Andean neighbors.[32]

Yet the importance of borders in the Andes is evident in their significance for centers to ensure territorial sovereignty, consolidate the state project, and enhance democratic governance. In this sense, it is an inward-looking meaning. In several instances over the last decade, academic and policy commentators have warned of an "Andean Crisis," "a profound crisis of authority, governance, democratic legitimacy, and territorial security," or a "crisis of democracy."[33] All five Andean states (Bolivia, Colombia, Ecuador, Peru, and Venezuela) have suffered internal turmoil, rooted in issues such as horizontal inequalities, struggles over land and natural resources, poverty, and exclusion. Constitutional and legislative changes during this time suggest the neglect of such structural problems, and a tendency toward hyper-presidentialism rather than a commitment to redressing institutional flaws. Promoting authority, legitimacy, and security then starts in the power centers and reaches outward to the margins, with the former being prioritized over the latter.

In this context, state borders are where state governance is least consolidated. They are the frontiers, as their socioeconomic marginalization and "unruliness" reflect. In the three countries discussed in this book (Colombia, Ecuador, and Venezuela), the border areas are among the regions with the countries' lowest development rates, highest poverty rates, and a notorious absence of well-functioning state institutions. They are also extremely violent places, if compared to central regions. The Colombian, Ecuadorian, and Venezuelan border areas are home to comparatively high homicide rates. Kidnappings, forced disappearances, forced displacement, violent threats, extortion, armed robbery, and sexual violence are further factors that contribute to insecurity. Levels of impunity are also high. Colombia's border departments are among the regions with the highest impunity rates in the country. In Venezuela, all three border states (Apure, Táchira, and Zulia) have higher impunity rates than the national average, according to police figures.[34] Regarding the Ecuadorian northern border zone, a 2012 citizen security analysis carried out for the Association of Ecuadorian Municipalities explains high rates of lethal violence as the effect of low police presence (2.9 for every 1,000 inhabitants in the Canton of Sucumbíos) and the inefficient justice system. This was reaffirmed by the Ombudsman's

Office in Lago Agrio.[35] According to the United Nations Special Rapporteur on Extrajudicial, Summary, or Arbitrary Executions, Philip Alston, as of 2011, only about one out of every three or four killings in Sucumbíos was reported to the police.[36]

Surveys on people's perceptions of security paint a similarly sobering picture, yet also produce some seeming inconsistencies. In a study carried out from 2012 to 2013, perceptions of insecurity were higher in Colombia's capital city of Bogotá than in the border town of Cúcuta, where homicide rates soared.[37] A 2008 study published by the Ecuadorian National Citizen Security Plan states that the national average of perceived insecurity was higher (44.4%) than in the border provinces of Esmeraldas (38.8%) and Carchi (42.3%), even though Esmeraldas was one of the most crisis-ridden and violence-torn regions of the country.[38] Finally, a 2010 Venezuelan National Statistics Institute survey about security disaggregated data between border and non-border respondents. In both cases, between 60 and 63 percent of the respondents described their situation of personal security to be "very bad" (62.4% of border respondents and 60.5% of non-border respondents),[39] thus providing little insight into the differing security dynamics.

Overall, such views from the center toward the peripheries display the inequality between the two—literally, the marginalization of the margins. Yet this inequality is just the tip of the iceberg. These views are also problematic in several other regards. First, they create an image of a generally violent frontier, neglecting the nuances. As Figure 3.1 demonstrates, homicide rates in the Ecuadorian province of Carchi, for example, are lower than the Ecuadorian national average—which is partly explained by strong social control that armed groups exert across the border, as discussed in chapter 7. Second, the results of perception surveys are distorted because many respondents do not report out of fear. Third, such results can lack proper interpretation by not accounting for the normalization of violence over time. People do not feel insecure because they are used to feeling this way, rather than due to objectively low levels of violence. Finally, views on security from the center tend to stop at the national borderline, ignoring that similar dynamics continue across the border. Visualizing homicide rates clustered *across* the borders, rather than only by contrasting centers and peripheries, depicts that, in many cases, variation between regions in the same country is often higher than across the border. For example, homicide rates in Ecuadorian Esmeraldas resemble more those in Colombian Nariño than those in neighboring Carchi. Similarly, homicide rates in Venezuelan Táchira resemble more those in Colombian Norte de Santander than those in neighboring Apure (see Figure 3.1). This suggests that security dynamics are shaped by logics that transcend borders and hence cannot only be considered in relation to the states'

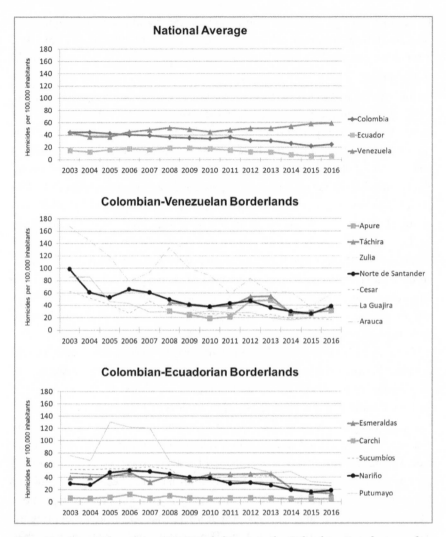

Figure 3.1 Homicide rates per 100,000 inhabitants in the Colombian-Ecuadorian and Colombian-Venezuelan borderlands. Source: Data based on various sources including the United Nations Office on Drugs and Crime, Colombia's National Institute of Legal Medicine and Forensic Sciences, Ecuador's Ministry of the Interior, and Venezuela's Observatory of Violence.

centers. These dynamics emerge because of the very transnationality of these spaces, as we see in the subsequent chapters.

Before discussing the transnational dimension in depth, it is helpful to look at the borderlines themselves more closely to comprehend how Bogotá, Caracas, and Quito's policies toward their respective border zones have coincided, merged, and diverged at these lines. Analytically, this

follows lenses such as Oscar Martínez's model on alienated, coexistent, interdependent, and integrated border regions. It considers each border zone
a unit to examine the relationships between both sides of the border.[40]
Departing from a state-centric perspective, such a view on border zones
reveals the differences in security repercussions in each border zone arising
from the state policies and actors tied to, and contained within, the territorial
limits of each bordering state.

Colombia-Ecuador Border

Ecuador and Colombia share a 585 kilometer border. As historically friendly
neighbors, the two countries have had few border tensions. In 1979, they established binational border control instruments, and in 1996, they created the
Binational Border Commission (COMBIFRON). During Uribe's presidency in
Colombia, these bilateral relations progressively deteriorated. Ecuador rejected
Plan Colombia and responded with its own "Plan Ecuador," a peace plan based
on development, and centered on human beings rather than territory, in response
to Colombia's war offensive. The toxic fumigations to eradicate coca cultivation
employed by Colombia with support from the United States affected crops and
the population's health in Ecuador's border zone.[41] In 2006, Ecuador reached
an agreement with Colombia to refrain from spraying within ten kilometers of
the border. In 2013, this was reduced to 5 and later up to 2 kilometers from the
border.[42]

Colombia and Ecuador also disagreed on border security responsibilities.
For Colombia, border control meant employing active interdiction measures. For Ecuador, border security consisted of ensuring Ecuador's sovereignty without actively fighting Colombian violent non-state groups to avoid
interference in Colombia's internal affairs. While Colombia did not recognize
Ecuador's border control efforts, Ecuador downplayed the threat of armed
groups' presence to its own territorial integrity. An unannounced Colombian
military incursion on Ecuadorian soil in Angostura on March 1, 2008 that
killed the leader of the Revolutionary Armed Forces of Colombia–People's
Army (Fuerzas Armadas Revolucionarias de Colombia–Ejército del Pueblo—
FARC), Raúl Reyes, sparked the rupture of diplomatic relations and the suspension of COMBIFRON.[43] Border security cooperation improved again with
COMBIFRON's reactivation in November 2009 and led to increased intelligence sharing.[44] In 2012, Colombia and Ecuador agreed on further border cooperation instruments. Yet the border also saw an increase in militarization and
securitization, along with abuses of the local population and the stigmatization
of Colombian refugees.[45]

Colombia-Venezuela Border

The Colombia-Venezuela border extends 2,219 kilometers. According to Carlos Malamud,[46] "of all Colombia's borders with its neighbours, the one it shares with Venezuela is the most active and troublesome." From the 1980s to the mid-1990s, Venezuela engaged in hot-pursuit operations across the border to curb violence emanating from Colombian armed groups in Venezuelan territory. The perceived threat of violence led to the creation of the Colombian-Venezuelan Neighborhood Commission in 1989, complemented in 1994 by the Binational Border Commission (COMBIFRON), established to exchange intelligence. This perception changed after 1999 when Chávez was elected president of Venezuela. While Venezuela regarded the guerrillas as a Colombian problem, Colombia accused Venezuela of complicity with the FARC and the National Liberation Army (Ejército de Liberación Nacional—ELN), leading to the suspension of most border cooperation agreements including COMBIFRON.[47] After Uribe became president of Colombia in 2002, tensions between Venezuela and Colombia heightened; yet some border cooperation mechanisms such as the Presidential Commissions on Integration and Border Issues remained in place.[48] Cooperation gradually diminished. In 2009, the only bilateral security cooperation still in force was between the Colombian National Police and the Venezuelan Border States' police forces,[49] a situation that deteriorated in 2010 when Venezuela broke off diplomatic relations over Colombia's allegations that Venezuela was actively permitting armed groups to operate on its soil.[50] Diplomatic relations were re-established and improved after Juan Manuel Santos assumed the presidency of Colombia in August 2010, and later again, under Chávez's successor Nicolás Maduro. The controversy over the FARC's presence in the Venezuelan border zone, however, continued. When I asked a humanitarian organization employee in Maicao about this in 2012, he insisted that FARC presence in Venezuela helped protect it from a US invasion:

> I will tell you the truth. If the US [. . .] invades Venezuela, they invade via Colombia and Zulia. Who do we need at the border as the first line of resistance? The FARC! [. . .] We need the FARC at the border; we allow them to be at the border because they will protect us. Because the Venezuelan soldier, as soon as he hears the first shot, runs away. Now we are already better prepared, but previously we have never been at war. Colombia has always been at war [. . .]. We need the FARC at the border due to our fear, but also due to the paramilitaries. You know there was an incursion.

This was not an isolated testimony. Many other Venezuelans I interviewed echoed these sentiments. As these accounts show, at least in the public discourse and people's imaginations, the controversy was not just considered a bilateral quarrel, but one that spanned the American continent, notably to include the United States.

In the case of both the Colombia-Ecuador border and the Colombia-Venezuela border, state policies did not stop illicit trafficking flows and other cross-border phenomena that undermine security in the region. According to internal information from the Colombian and Ecuadorian police and military, in 2015, the Colombia-Ecuador border featured at least fifty-two informal border crossings, as opposed to only two with official migratory control: the Rumichaca bridge between Ipiales and Tulcán, and the bridge between San Miguel and Lago Agrio (see Map 3.1).[51] Similarly, the Colombia-Venezuela border features numerous informal border crossings, but only three have migratory control (see Map 3.2). Violent non-state groups use these border crossings to traffic drugs, arms, ammunition, gasoline, equipment, and humans.

As this brief overview demonstrates, viewed from the center, state policies can only partially address the exposure of the Colombia-Ecuador and the Colombia-Venezuela borders to the Colombian internal armed conflict, the global cocaine business, and other forms of transnational organized crime. Indeed, the confluence of these phenomena has many more far-reaching consequences than such a cursory glimpse of the margins can elucidate. The remainder of this chapter therefore delves more directly into these dynamics and adopts a view of the borderlands from the margins, that is, from within these very spaces.

3.2 Borderlands Viewed from the Margins

Adopting a borderland lens sheds light on local realities at the interface of the contemporary state-centric security paradigm that dictates both thinking and action on peripheries and transnational security threats. According to statist perspectives, borderlands "are usually defined, 'nationalized' and symbolized by the power located in the heartland at the centres."[52] Willem van Schendel therefore concludes that "we know much more about how states dealt with borderlands than how borderlands dealt with states."[53] A borderland lens transforms our knowledge into a more holistic one. It is revealing at the micro level: starting from within the borderlands sheds light on how the activities of violent non-state groups give rise to various forms of non-state order across borders, while state policies are largely limited to national boundaries. This is essential to grasp the security situation of people like the borderland resident cited at the beginning of this chapter.

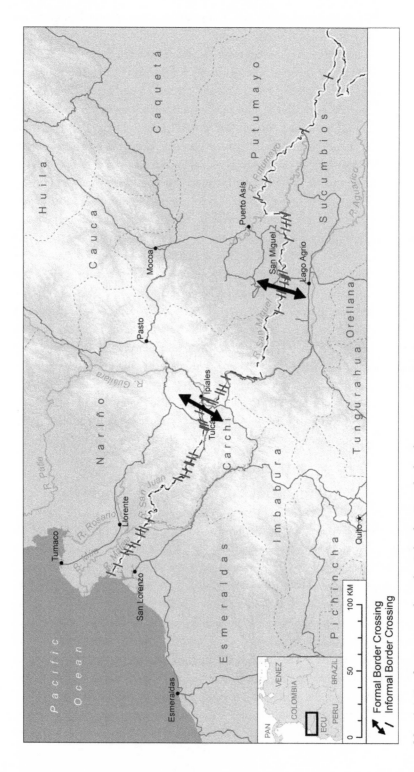

Map 3.1 Border crossings along the Colombia-Ecuador border. Map created by Author.

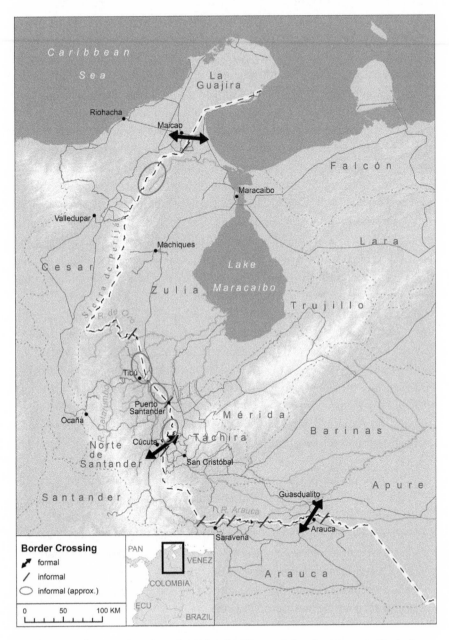

Map 3.2 Border crossings along the Colombia-Venezuela border. Map created by Author.

Assuming a center-based view on the borderlands neglects these dynamics. A borderland lens is also enlightening at the macro level: Benedikt Korf and Timothy Raeymakers argue that borderland dynamics "radiate" outward to the regions in which they are embedded.[54] This "radiation" can extend to the state's power centers: borderland dynamics shape state policies relevant to territorial sovereignty, national identity, and the state's embeddedness in the regional context. Accordingly, van Schendel posits that "many states stand or fall by how their borderlands handle them."[55] Finally, a borderland lens links the micro with the macro level; the concomitance of national and transnational influences on security prevails across the globe yet is particularly evident in borderlands. As the remainder of this chapter shows, borderlands magnify security dynamics that exist in other spaces as well— we can better understand security in the world by studying this extreme case.

Borderlands manifest distinct social, political, and economic structures shaped by their geographic location.[56] Niles Hansen defines borderlands as "sub-national areas whose economic and social life is directly and significantly affected by proximity to an international boundary."[57] Heikki Eskelinen, Ilkka Liikanen, and Jukka Oksa suggest that understanding borderland dynamics requires analyzing how the border affects the life of borderlanders.[58] Arguing that borderlands constitute "a transition zone within which a boundary lies," John Prescott's definition emphasizes the transnationality of borderlands.[59] Jonathan Goodhand calls the zone a "region," implying people also reside permanently in these zones.[60] I adopt a definition that combines these characterizations: borderlands are "regions situated on the edges of states which straddle an international border,"[61] "whose economic and social life is directly and significantly affected by proximity to an international boundary."[62] This definition reflects the border's influence on phenomena in these spaces, including the transactional character of borderlands, which Barbara Morehouse et al. allegorize as follows:

> Where boundaries slice and glue, borderlands airbrush differences, mix things up. Fundamentally, a borderland is an area through which a boundary line runs, but the most important key to understanding borders and borderlands, i.e. the territorial spaces along the boundary, lies in recognizing their transactional nature. Borderlands acquire their basic identity from interactions with the boundary and its rules, and from transactions that take place across the boundary, between inhabitants of the borderland territory.[63]

Borderlands are a universal concept. Across the world, they are traversed and influenced by an international border, and they are physically distant from state centers.[64] Due to their transnationality, borders "divide and unite, bind the interior and link with the exterior, [as] barriers and junctions, walls and doors, organs of defense and attack."[65] Korf and Raeymaekers contend that "border-land dynamics [have to be considered] not just as outcomes of diffusing state-hood or globalization, but also as actual political units that generate their own actions and outcomes."[66]

Overcoming the obstacle of considering the state as one analytical unit, I take borderlands and borderlanders, rather than heartlands, as a starting point.[67] Accordingly, while border zones adjoin the borderline from one side, borderlands comprise both sides of the border. Such a borderland perspective that considers the area of both sides as one spatial unit facilitates an analysis of how borderlands are interconnected horizontally through the flow of goods, people, and ideas, although they are separated vertically by official state borders.[68] It reveals how the political and cultural systems of both sides overlap in the borderlands.[69] Borderland communities develop commercial, cultural, and social cross-border ties that entail a sense of belonging to a transnational community rather than to (or in addition to) the national state. Their identities and experiences differ from those who live further away from the border. Such an approach necessitates acknowledging the dynamic nature of borderlands regarding the spatial dimensions, and of the border's influence on borderland life. Correspondingly, the breadth of borderlands is conditioned by the local context. According to Goodhand,

> where the borderland periphery ends and the state-controlled centre begins may be conceptualised as a mobile, semi-permeable, internal frontier—a zone of transition from low to high administrative intensity.[70]

As van Schendel notes, "there is nothing passive about borders; in borderlands, the spatiality of social relations is forever taking on new shapes."[71] William Zartman posits that "borderlands need to be understood, not as places or even events, but as social processes."[72] They all imply the agency of borders to shape the social, political, and economic phenomena in borderlands. Identities such as border guards, smugglers, or refugees would not exist without the agency of borders.[73]

Non-State Order across Andean Borderlands

I now map the various clusters of violent non-state group interactions across the Colombian-Ecuadorian and Colombian-Venezuelan borderlands. Grasping these interactions and, as we see in subsequent chapters, their implications for citizen security, requires a transnational approach because they are driven by factors that transcend state boundaries. Consider Abraham and van Schendel's point on how borderlanders and other actors relying on the border understand these transnational spaces:

> If we want to understand how they "scale" the world, we must start from their cognitive maps—their organized representations of their spatial environment and their own place in it. Since these maps are rarely stored externally (in the form of a physical map), an essential part of studying the changing geographies of borderlands is to access cognitive "maps in minds."[74]

The cognitive maps in minds of borderlanders do not stop at the borderline. They include both sides and, instead, may stop at the limit between borderlands and heartlands due to the perceived disconnect between the two. The borderland perspective starts from these maps. It contextualizes the availability of distrust-reducing mechanisms that facilitate cooperation between violent non-state groups and give rise to the various clusters (see chapter 2). In vulnerable regions, this availability responds to the logics of the cross-border nature of people's everyday lives in the absence of efficient state governance systems, and of the confluence of the dynamics of the armed conflict and transnational illicit flows. Such a spatial analysis of the clusters and their socioeconomic, geographical, and cultural contexts across borders reveals how these are at odds with the state policies outlined above.

From a developmental perspective, asymmetries in socioeconomic dynamics that arise due to varying levels of state governance across the border provide fertile ground for single violent non-state groups involved in Colombia's armed internal conflict to consolidate their power position and establish preponderance, one of the eight types of violent non-state group interactions I present in chapter 2. Weak state governance across borders is also conducive to stable long-term arrangements among *various* groups; they are able to complement each other by providing governance functions, taking advantage of local grievances toward the absent or inefficient state.

From a geostrategic perspective on the conflict dynamics, the discrepancy of the neighboring states' border policies concerning security, justice, and economics, for instance, makes borderlands convenient sites of retreat, reorganization, and operation of the major conflict actors. Until its demobilization in 2017, the FARC's financing fronts operated in the border areas: in the Colombian-Ecuadorian borderlands the mobile column Daniel Aldana, and in the Colombian-Venezuelan borderlands Front 33. FARC dissidents and successor groups filled this space afterward. Likewise, the ELN operates across the border in Colombia, Ecuador, and Venezuela. Being in border zones facilitates crossing over to deal with logistics and supplies, including arms, ammunition, uniforms, food, and medicine—essential elements to sustain one's armed struggle. The regions also comprise mobility corridors, facilitating access to safe havens across borders, as confirmed to me by interviewees across border zones and across stakeholder groups (see Table A.3). The strategic value of these corridors explains why at times they have been settings of combat and armed disputes among various conflict actors, the interaction types that fall into the "enmity" cluster of my non-state order framework (see chapter 2).

From a topographic and geographic view on illicit supply chain networks, the borderlands are pivotal for the interconnectedness of multiple forms of transnational organized crime. The United Nations Office on Drugs and Crime estimates that transnational organized crime generates 870 billion USD annually.[75] Many of these global supply chain networks that contribute to this massive profit originate in territories across the Colombia-Ecuador and Colombia-Venezuela border, through the presence of coca cultivation and the physical infrastructure required to process coca leaves into cocaine. Violent entrepreneurs sustain supply chain activities at this local borderland level by connecting them with related illicit flows, for example of weapons or gasoline used to produce cocaine. While locally this is conducive to stable long-term arrangements among violent non-state groups (in particular, supply chain relationships), internationally it ensures stable profits from the various illicit businesses, as these networks are embedded in the global illicit economy.

In 2015, around 400 tons of cocaine were estimated to be produced in Colombia, resulting from an overall area of 96,000 hectares of coca cultivation, compared to 20,200 hectares in Bolivia and 40,300 hectares in Peru.[76] In 2016, the area of cultivation increased to 146,000 hectares, with 63 percent of it concentrated in the Colombian border departments of Nariño, Norte de Santander, and Putumayo (see Figure 3.2 and Map 3.3)[77]. Areas of coca cultivation also

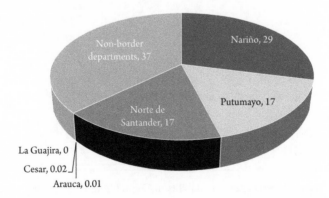

Figure 3.2 Percentage of coca cultivation in Colombian border departments, 2016. Source: Data based on United Nations Office on Drugs and Crime and Government of Colombia. "Colombia. Monitoreo de Cultivos de Coca 2017," Bogotá: United Nations Office on Drugs and Crime, Government of Colombia, 2017, 25.

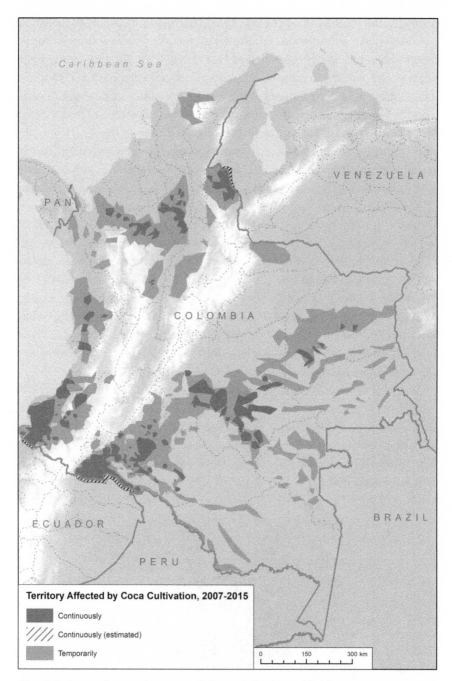

Territory Affected by Coca Cultivation, 2007-2015

   Continuously

   Continuously (estimated)

   Temporarily

0   150   300 km

Map 3.3 Regional coca cultivation stability in Colombia and border zones, 2007–2015.
Source: Data based on United Nations Office on Drugs and Crime and Government of Colombia.
"Colombia. Monitoreo de Cultivos de Coca 2016," Bogotá: United Nations Office on Drugs and
Crime, Government of Colombia, 2016. Credit: Map created by Author.

exist in the border zones of Ecuador, Brazil, Panama, and Venezuela, often near processing laboratories.

Mapping cocaine supply chain networks that originate in the cultivation regions, as well as the interlinked illicit flows, demonstrates that clusters of short-term arrangements among violent non-state groups coincide with the nodes where these flows coalesce and networks intersect. The strategic transit points and logistical hubs at border crossings, towns, roads, and rivers where the trafficking routes of cocaine and other goods converge, as well as the starting points of international trafficking routes at maritime borders, promise particularly high economic benefits. The interests of the numerous violent non-state groups (ranging from guerrillas and paramilitaries to Mexican cartels) involved in drug trafficking, as outlined in chapter 1, thus converge in these points. This interest convergence serves as a distrust-reducing mechanism that facilitates cooperation on a particular occasion—short-term arrangements—even if the groups fight each other elsewhere (see chapter 2).

The transnational flows linked to the cocaine business pervade the entire Andean region. All Andean states are transit or starting points of drug trafficking routes to markets in Europe and the United States. The most important ones start at the western extreme of the Colombia-Ecuador border, the Pacific coast, and at the northern extreme of the Colombia-Venezuela border, the Caribbean coast (Map 3.4). Thriving on the illicit drug trade (but not the legal economy), the Andean border regions are also hubs for related forms of transnational organized crime. Among other reasons, this is because services connected to the cocaine business are provided throughout the region. Ecuador is used for money laundering and to provide chemicals; Venezuela offers cheap, subsidized gasoline. Chemicals and gasoline are required to process coca leaves into cocaine. Cocaine is also exchanged for arms or ammunition that are trafficked via Colombia's neighbors into the country, and Colombian rebels and paramilitaries acquire supplies such as food, medicine, or clothes from across the border.[78] In such contexts, the drug industry influences the local economy through jobs in coca cultivation, processing laboratories, the smuggling of chemical precursors, money laundering, and other related economic activities.[79] What complicates the matter is that the lines between legal and illegal cross-border activities are blurred, veiling much of these dirty businesses. The smuggling of products ranging from household goods and food, to gasoline and chemical precursors for the drug business, arms, ammunition, human beings, and, of course, cocaine, occurs in parallel with legal cross-border trade, partly on the same routes.

In what follows, I sketch how the logics of the armed conflict and illicit transnational flows inform the spatial and temporal variation of non-state order, that is, the clusters of violent non-state group interactions, as outlined in chapter 2. These logics, in turn, are influenced by topographic and climatic diversity,

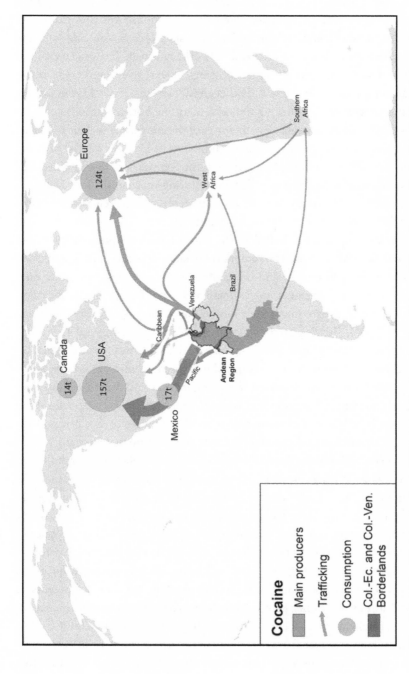

Map 3.4 Main global cocaine flows, 2009. Source: Data based on United Nations Office on Drugs and Crime. "World Drug Report 2011," Vienna: United Nations Office on Drugs and Crime, 2011. Credit: Map created by Author.

rural-urban divides,[80] and distinct historical and cultural contexts along the two borders.[81] One factor is common to all the regions: the deficiency of efficient, inclusive state governance systems focused on people. Starting from east to west at the Colombia-Ecuador border, and then from south to north at the Colombia-Venezuela border, I map the various violent non-state group interactions and how they have been evolving over time. I present one hundred of these here— the most dominant ones (see appendix B). Those dated between 2011 and 2013 are illustrated on maps 3.5 and 3.7. Of course, given their fluidity and constantly changing nature, this is only a partial portrayal of the dynamic reality.

Colombian-Ecuadorian Borderlands

The Colombian-Ecuadorian borderlands comprise two Colombian departments and three Ecuadorian provinces. They extend from the Amazonian Putumayo (Colombia) and Sucumbíos (Ecuador) to the highlands of Carchi (Ecuador) together with the eastern part of Nariño, to the coastal area shared by Nariño (Colombia) and Esmeraldas (Ecuador). Overlaying a borderland lens across the international borderline reveals that dynamics across the border resemble each other more than those of their respective state centers. Map 3.5 demonstrates the presence and interactions of the violent non-state groups across the border.

Putumayo—Sucumbíos

Putumayo and Sucumbíos, both part of the Amazon basin, are among the border regions where state neglect is most entrenched, creating ideal conditions for violent non-state groups to consolidate power, become preponderant, and forge stable long-term arrangements. They are among the regions where Plan Colombia's influence on the conflict dynamics was particularly intense. The hostility between paramilitaries and insurgents inflicted brutal violence on civilians. As a major coca production area, the structure of the illicit economy in the region explains the presence of supply chain relationships, as well as of short-term arrangements among those interested in the drug business. These are embedded in the supply chain relationships, particularly at important nodes and transit points of the illicit flows.

The departments—and the Amazon region more widely—have historically been seen as little more than "a destination for people displaced from other parts of Colombia. This [. . .] is key to the sense of marginalization and abandonment that drives the discourse of the region's people when they refer to the central state," as María Clemencia Ramírez notes.[82] When I was walking through the streets of Putumayo's capital Mocoa for the first time in 2011, I noticed an overall condition of marginalization. With a poverty rate of 52.6 percent,[83] it felt

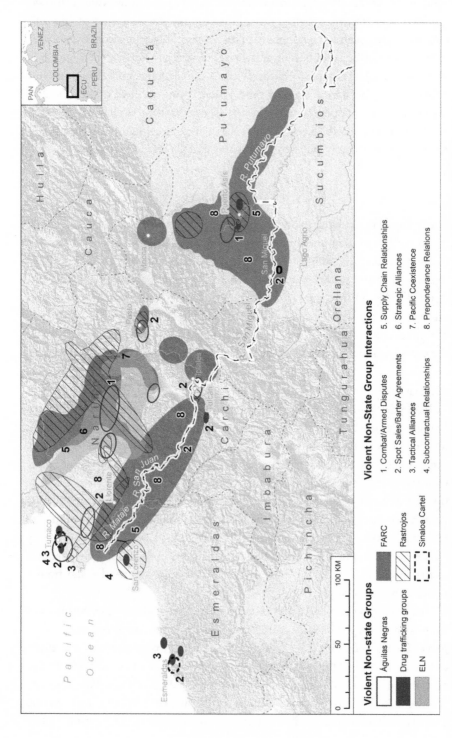

Map 3.5 Violent non-state group interactions along the Colombia-Ecuador border (2011–2013). Map created by Author.

Figure 3.3 *Plaza* of Mocoa, Colombia, 2011. Photo by Author.

more like a remote jungle town than a departmental capital (see Figure 3.3). This impression was reaffirmed during one of my more recent trips to Putumayo in 2017. I departed from the region just half a day before a devastating landslide in Mocoa left more than three hundred people dead. Many lives were lost due to inappropriate housing; the difficulties in the emergency response highlighted the persistent lack of essential infrastructure and building standards. The Putumayo department is home to fourteen local ethnic groups, producing a striking cultural diversity. Those from outside the region, however, often categorize Putumayo's population as guerrilla collaborators: indigenous people in particular suffer from discrimination.[84] Putumayo attracted considerable state attention when, with substantial assistance from the United States, it became a focus area of the government's Plan Colombia in the early 2000s, and after 2006 one of Consolidation Plan's target zones (see chapter 1).[85] Yet this attention was of military rather than civilian nature. The extractive industry also increasingly mattered for this "non-people-centered" attention. In 2011, Putumayo was declared a "Special Mining District."[86] Locals claim that Putumayo's increasing militarization in recent years has served to protect the extractive industry rather than the communities. It reflects the problematic relationship between residents of Putumayo and the Colombian state.[87]

Across the border in Ecuadorian Sucumbíos, the situation is similar. Established as a province in 1989, Sucumbíos is a rural Amazon region, separated from neighboring Colombia by the wide Putumayo River (see Figure 3.4). Indigenous people

Figure 3.4 Border river between Colombian Putumayo and Ecuadorian Sucumbíos, 2011. Photo by Author.

used to live in the region in relative isolation until not long ago; Quito only really started to take note of its existence in 1967 when the first oil well was drilled. Since then, the oil industry has dominated the region and triggered an influx of migrants who came to work in the sector, particularly in Sucumbíos's capital Nueva Loja, commonly called Lago Agrio.[88] This produced social problems, including prostitution offered in mobile brothels where young women are brought to their clients. In my field notes on conversations with people in Bajo Putumayo and in General Farfán, I captured their sobering descriptions of this phenomenon:

> There is prostitution for the oil workers, soldiers, *guerrilleros*. They say they are girls from the interior of the country, but the majority are from Putumayo. The girls go for one weekend to sell magazines or clothes from a catalogue but, in reality, they go to prostitute themselves. Sometimes they never go back because they have seen things and are therefore killed.

Long-term arrangements, especially preponderance relations facilitated by the FARC's and their successor groups' power position, dominate in the region.[89] Putumayo has historically been a guerrilla stronghold. Given the absence of governance provisions by the state, insurgents were able to take over some of the functions—by their own means—and, through this, develop a relatively close relationship with local populations. Between 1980 and 1982, the insurgent group 19th of April Movement (Movimiento 19 de Abril—M-19) prevailed in much of the region and, between 1984 and 1991, the Popular Liberation Army (Ejército Popular de Liberación—EPL) controlled certain areas. The M-19 demobilized in 1990, and EPL members in Putumayo in 1991. Yet the FARC, which entered the department in the 1980s,[90] persisted until its demobilization in 2017. Its successors and others who filled the power vacuum remain in the region until the present day.

Putumayo's strategic location in the dynamics of the Colombian armed conflict as a principal target of Plan Colombia contributed to it (and, to some extent, Sucumbíos) becoming a main theater of combat. Toward the end of the 1980s, paramilitary structures linked to illegal drug business arrived in the area, triggering a shift from relatively nonviolent preponderance to violent non-state groups interactions characterized by "enmity" between insurgents and paramilitaries. In 1987, the first paramilitary base was reported in El Azul (now Puerto Asís), Putumayo. In the mid-1990s, the United Self-Defense Forces of Colombia (Autodefensas Unidas de Colombia—AUC) appeared.[91] This included the paramilitary Central Bolívar Bloc's Southern Front, whose violent incursion into Putumayo in the 1990s came along with massacres of local communities, including in El Tigre and El Placer.[92] The presence of this new powerful actor in the region destabilized the insurgents' preponderance for some years, giving rise to brutal combat between the paramilitaries and the FARC. This was of course in addition to—or some analysts would say intertwined with—the combat between the insurgents and state forces who, in the 2000s, implemented Plan Colombia in Putumayo. On March 1, 2006, 504 paramilitary South Front members demobilized as an outcome of the Colombian government's peace talks with the AUC.[93] After that, direct combat between paramilitaries and guerrillas became rare.

With open hostilities between the guerrillas and the paramilitaries effectively disappearing, non-state order mainly fell back into the cluster of relatively stable long-term arrangements. Even though weakened, the FARC expanded their territorial control again.[94] They re-established—or continued—preponderance in many rural areas. The FARC's Front 48 reportedly included two hundred troops in 2012[95] and controlled most of the border zone toward the east of Putumayo. They were in charge of finances and the trafficking of arms that enter Colombia from Peru via Ecuador.[96] Toward the west, the FARC's Front 32 was present with another two hundred troops, and the mobile column Daniel Aldana dominated the area that borders with Nariño.[97] Taking advantage of Quito's neglect in the region, the Colombian guerrillas could easily extend their preponderance to Ecuadorian Sucumbíos. They were viewed as controlling the Ecuadorian border village of General Farfán and surrounding areas, and had recuperation and reorganization camps in more remote Ecuadorian regions.

The logics of the cocaine supply chain and related forms of transnational organized crime influenced the FARC's interactions with other violent non-state groups, in addition to their "enmity" with the paramilitaries. As a result

of the fumigations carried out in the context of Plan Colombia, coca cultivation decreased in Putumayo and moved elsewhere, especially to neighboring
Nariño.[98] The cocaine supply chain networks that connect Putumayo and
Sucumbíos with regions further west through brokers who, as I explain in
chapter 6, connect the various supply chain links, thus were significant to those
who did not want to lose access to drug money and influence.

In most parts of Putumayo, cocaine supply chain relationships concentrated
around the first production stages: coca cultivation and the processing of coca
leaves into coca paste.[99] Putumayo has hardly any road infrastructure to connect it with other parts of the country: it has one precarious road to Pasto (the
capital city of the neighboring department of Nariño) and one road to the
Cauca department. Generally, road and communication infrastructure (as well
as electricity, education, and health services) on the Ecuadorian side is more
developed and more easily accessible than in Colombia.[100] I experienced this
myself when travelling between the Colombian southern border departments.
The road between Pasto and Mocoa involves a six-to-eight-hour drive through
mountainous rainforest along a winding road strewn with memorial marks dedicated to those who died in landslides or accidents (see Figure 3.5). It is the only
road connecting these two towns, and frequently closed due to landslides.[101]

Given these deficiencies on the Colombian side, the river system, as well as
roads across the border in Ecuador, have been important in connecting these
first stages of the cocaine supply chain with the subsequent ones, that is, to
move illicit goods from Putumayo toward the Pacific coast. Many of these first
processing laboratories were near the San Miguel River, via which traffickers
transported chemical precursors. Local farmers told me that those involved in
the illicit business took the coca paste via Jardines de Sucumbíos to Estrella or
La Victoria in Nariño, where others processed it into cocaine and took it to the
Pacific coast.[102]

Mapping the illicit cocaine supply chain and other transnational illicit
flows linked to the cocaine business demonstrates why these relatively stable

Figure 3.5 Road between Pasto and Mocoa, Colombia, 2011. Photos by Author.

long-term arrangements between the FARC and other actors in rural regions are interspersed with clusters of short-term arrangements in urban areas along the major trafficking routes across Putumayo and Sucumbíos. These are hubs in which various flows intersect, or strategic transit points through which the multiple groups involved in the business deals need to pass.

Even though the rebels were dominant again, the AUC's demobilization gave rise to the appearance of new actors—or old ones with new labels. One of these was the Rastrojos who, in 2006, started to consolidate their presence in Putumayo. The Rastrojos and other groups engaged in such deals along the main road that connects Putumayo with Ecuador. In particular, they were involved in spot sales and barter agreements, one of the three types of short-term arrangements I present in chapter 2. The groups' economic interests in the drug industry and in other illicit cross-border activities converged with the FARC's, who required income to sustain their fighting and to ensure the supply of weapons, ammunition, and other equipment. According to the Colombian Ombudsman's Office, the income of most violent non-state groups in the region stemmed from trafficking illegal drugs, chemical precursors, arms, and ammunition, from contraband of oil derivatives (required to process coca into cocaine), and from extortion.[103] Being close to the border helped them to acquire cheap arms, supplies, and gasoline from Ecuador.

The trafficking route from northern parts of Colombia via Putumayo to Sucumbíos and Quito connects three places: Puerto Guzmán, Puerto Caicedo, and Puerto Asís. Around 2012, the FARC dominated rural areas and the area surrounding Puerto Guzmán. The Rastrojos and other violent non-state groups, including the Urabeños, were primarily present in urban areas. They did not wear uniforms, emblems, or show off their weapons, and yet they still had a firm grip on the local population. As I learned through my observation and conversations with community members, subtle features that "outsiders" are blind to (such as a particular haircut, a certain clothing style, or jewelry) make them visible to—and often feared by—locals. The Rastrojos dominated Puerto Caicedo, a critical transit point for drugs and arms. If groups such as the FARC passed their illicit goods through the village, the Rastrojos charged "taxes" or took a share of the cocaine. Thanks to this arrangement, the FARC were able to pursue their function within the supply chain without being attacked by the Rastrojos, who profited financially or materially. Various groups (including FARC militias) controlled Puerto Asís, with the Rastrojos being the most powerful group.[104] The FARC's Front 48 was also involved in barter agreements, notably drugs-for-arms deals, with Ecuadorian traffickers near the San Miguel border bridge (see Figure 3.6).[105] Based on micro motivations through which distrust is reduced on particular occasions only rather than in a generalized manner (see section 2.1), these fragile arrangements broke down easily. Accordingly, non-state order

Figure 3.6 Border bridge San Miguel between Putumayo (Colombia) and Sucumbíos (Ecuador), 2012. Photo by Author.

at times "slid down" on the continuum into the cluster comprising combat and armed disputes. In 2009, for example, the FARC and the Rastrojos fought each other in the Puerto Caicedo municipality.[106] In the same year, the Águilas Negras threatened locals they accused of being FARC collaborators in Putumayo.[107]

Nariño and Carchi—Esmeraldas

The border area of the Colombian department of Nariño and the Ecuadorian provinces of Carchi and Esmeraldas features all three clusters of interactions among a wide array of different violent non-state groups, making the situation particularly complex. This complexity is akin to the diversity of the region's geographic, socioeconomic, and cultural features, as well as its peculiar role in the conflict dynamics. Mapping illicit flows and studying local contexts gives insights into where certain patterns of interactions prevail.

Four factors stand out. First, although it became a central theater of the Colombian armed conflict more recently than other regions, Nariño is home to crucial mobility corridors. Second, with poverty and state neglect being characteristic of the area on both sides of the border, especially at the coast, economic opportunities linked to vast areas of coca cultivation have led to a relatively stable illicit political borderland economy across the borderline. Third, the fluvial system and remote trails link the precarious road infrastructure. This opens key trafficking routes from the interior of both countries to the sea, and it enables groups to stay removed from law enforcement authorities. Fourth, the coastline comprises the starting points of essential routes toward Central America and the United States. Compared to the Putumayo-Sucumbíos border area, this geostrategically significant location in the global illicit economy means that the stakes involved in the various

interconnected illicit flows are particularly high, attracting economically interested groups, in addition to conflict actors who are attracted by the region's
geostrategic value.

Compared to the other border regions, the shared border area of Nariño,
Carchi, and Esmeraldas stands out in its topographic, climatic, and demographic
diversity. The Andean Cordillera traverses Ecuadorian Carchi and the eastern
parts of Nariño. In these mountainous zones, indigenous people including the
Otavaleños and the Pastos have spent generations surviving in a harsh and cold
climate. Only a few hundred kilometers to the west, the region turns into tropical jungle and then dips down into the hot coastal parts at the Pacific. Mestizo
farmers, indigenous people such as the Awá, and Afro-Colombian and Afro-
Ecuadorian populations inhabit both sides of the border.

Nariño's place in the dynamics of the Colombian conflict differs from neighboring Putumayo's because it became a central theater only later, mostly after,
and indeed because of Plan Colombia's impact in Putumayo. Owing to intense
aerial fumigations and the state forces' military operations, both coca cultivations
and armed groups shifted westward to Nariño. On July 30, 2005, the paramilitary Liberators of the South Bloc demobilized in Nariño.[108] Between 2005 and
2006, the Águilas Negras and the Autodefensas Gaitanistas, another right-wing
group, gained strength, yet were afterward widely co-opted by the Rastrojos,
who started to invade Nariño in 2007 and expanded their presence in subsequent years.[109] In 2008, a Colombian think tank estimated that 2,300 members
of at least six different groups operated in the department, with the Rastrojos
being the most numerous.[110] In 2012, the Urabeños became their main rival in
the entire country, including in Nariño; and the Paisas, yet another right-wing
group, also expanded their presence.

Despite the paramilitary incursion and subsequent operations of right-wing
groups, both the FARC and the ELN maintained a strong presence in the area. As
they faced the same external threats (i.e., the state forces and right-wing groups,
including Rastrojos and Águilas Negras) and shared ideological values (at least
in general terms), the guerrillas forged long-term arrangements, including strategic alliances and pacific coexistence in the region. At times, however, they
also fought each other due to issues related to securing mobility corridors. The
FARC had three main structures in the region. One of them, the mobile column
Mariscal Sucre, operated in the eastern mountains. Another one, the Front 29,
operated in the municipalities of Magüí Payán, Roberto Payán, the northern
parts of Barbacoas, El Charco, Cumbitara, Policarpa, and Leiva to control the
exit to the Pacific.[111] Additionally, structures from Cauca (FARC Front 60) and
Putumayo (FARC Front 48) occasionally entered the department of Nariño
to secure mobility corridors. Mapping ELN presence during the same period
shows that the two rebel groups partly occupied the same territory. Its Fronts

Héroes de Barbacoas, Mártires de Barbacoas, and Comuneros del Sur operated in Barbacoas.[112] The latter was also active in the municipalities of Samaniego, La Llanada, Guachavez, and Leiva. In some of these regions, the FARC and the ELN engaged in a strategic alliance and, in others, they operated in pacific co-existence to share mobility corridors, as this was considered strategic for their wider operations in Colombia.

When group members at the subnational level decide to act independently from their central command and stop operating in line with the strategic goal of the organization, such mutually beneficial long-term arrangements can crumble locally. The ELN is less centralized than the FARC, which may explain why the strategic alliance between these rebel groups broke down in Nariño in 2006. According to an ex-FARC member, at the local level, the ELN did not honor the arrangement whereby each could pass through the territory freely. As he explained to me indignantly, the rebels would have started to charge taxes, leading to the breakdown of the alliance:

> They took some of our drugs, part of other things. They even took money from us. [. . .] And this was when the fights started . . . because, why would I let them rob me? It lasted around three years during which they brutally clashed with each other. When I demobilized, the FARC and the ELN fought hard, there were many deaths.[113]

In 2010, armed clashes between the ELN and the FARC continued to be registered, for example in the Barbacoas municipality in 2010.[114] Later in the same year, however, the two guerrillas stopped fighting each other as part of their nationwide decision to end combat each other. Around 2011, the guerrillas coexisted in the mobility corridors that connect the Andean zone with the coastal foothills; they had a pact of nonaggression and to some extent operated jointly in the municipalities of Santa Cruz, Samaniego, Cumbitara, La Llanada, and Los Andes.[115] In the municipality of Roberto Payán, they engaged in joint armed activities and, as the Ombudsman's Office reported, they also jointly placed antipersonnel landmines on roads and trails.[116] In 2011, when clashes between the FARC, the Águilas Negras, and the Rastrojos struck the region, a government official from Pasto revealed to me how the mutually supportive strategic alliance between the FARC and the ELN in Nariño was linked to the conflict dynamics:

> They fight together against the army, against the Rastrojos, nowadays. Two years ago, this would have been impossible. They have joint guerrilla plans. For example, the ELN looks after the FARC's rear guard and, in this entire sector, the FARC look after the ELN.[117]

An ex-FARC member confirmed this, highlighting the role of corridors used to move troops and drugs:

EX-COMBATANT: They make an agreement. They talk, or rather, the two commanders sit together to negotiate: "Ok, let's negotiate. I want you to collaborate with me!" For example, [the territory] from here to there is ELN, from there to over there is FARC. If the army meddles here, the ELN comes and helps me. Now they are united like this, therefore they support each other.

ME: *Was there similar support between the FARC and the Rastrojos?*

EX-COMBATANT: I don't know. While I was there I never saw that. Who knows, because I demobilized four years ago [. . .]. Everyone has their way of negotiating. They have their routes to move their drugs. I can pass freely. If the *elenos* pass through my area, they can transit freely.[118] For example, if an *eleno* comes through I don't have to say: "You're passing through my zone. You have to pay me this amount as a tax!" No. Neither the ELN nor the FARC. Previously yes. When you passed through ELN areas previously, they would tie you up and take everything you had.[119]

While the conflict dynamics influenced the logics of armed clashes and stable arrangements to outpower the enemy, state neglect and profitable illicit economic opportunities allowed the armed actors to consolidate their power in the region. A borderland lens demonstrates that these developments are largely "a-national." They take shape across, and partly exist due to, the very borderline, just as the local communities' livelihoods extend across both sides of the border. The numerous informal border crossings that cluster at border villages (see Figure 3.7 and Map 3.1) depict how borderlanders' everyday lives extend beyond the borderline. They are used to exchanging goods, going shopping, participating in binational soccer matches, going to school, or visiting relatives across the border. Borderland dynamics in such peripheral regions are inherently transnational, while state policies stop at the borderline—or do not even reach it. The account of a civil society representative from Colombian Pasto illustrates this:

There are two ways to see the border: first, the border's edge, the line. People enter Ecuador from here to there with cars from Ecuador, merchandise from Ecuador [. . .]. People look badly on the Colombians. They check your documents, you can't enter with a vehicle, and merchandise only flows under suspicion [. . .]. But the entire department is a border department. The dynamics of Ecuador influence the dynamics in Colombia. When they broke diplomatic relations, it affected many people in Colombia, for example in Tallambí, Mayasquer,

Figure 3.7 Informal border crossing between Tufiño (Ecuador) and Mayasquer (Colombia), 2012. Photo by Author.

Jardines de Sucumbíos, La Victoria.[120] It affected the bridges built by the community, not by the state. These are illegal bridges. The military even say the guerrillas built them, but no, the community built them. Without them, they would not be able to access anything. People access Ecuadorian health centers to have vaccinations. They also go to Ecuador and try to obtain dual nationality.[121]

Regardless of who built the bridges, they facilitate movement across the border both for local communities and for violent non-state groups. This was an important modus operandi for the FARC's mobile column Daniel Aldana, the third main FARC structure in the region. As of 2011, this column was preponderant in municipalities near the border: Cumbal, Cuaspud, Carlosama, Ricaurte, and Tumaco. The FARC's presence extended beyond the borderline to Ecuadorian Esmeraldas and Carchi. When I visited the Ecuadorian villages of Chical, Tufiño, and Maldonado in 2012—the "twin border villages" of Tallambí and Mayasquer mentioned by the civil society representative above—I was able to confirm through interviews that the FARC exerted cross-border authority in these remote areas of Carchi province.[122]

A government official in Nariño described the infrastructural asymmetries between the Ecuadorian and the Colombian sides of the border to explain how the lack of infrastructure in Colombia facilitated the armed actors' preponderance:[123]

There is an issue with the border, which is the unequal development. Consider the border bridge of Rumichaca on the Pan-American Highway. If you leave the Pan-American Highway from here on the Ecuadorian side toward the Pacific coast, there is road infrastructure. If you take the Highway on the Colombian side, via Ipiales, you only get to Cumbal. From there onward, there is nothing. There is no connectivity at all. Further down, there also isn't any electricity, any communication, nothing. This is also why the Ecuadorian state has been much more successful in stopping the war from reaching the country's interior because it has infrastructure to confront it. By contrast, in Colombia, this doesn't exist. Even for the army it's difficult to reach the border. From the Pan-American Highway, it takes them five days on foot to reach the remote border zone [. . .] and the groups use this situation to their advantage.[124]

The account of an ex-member of the FARC's financing front points to an additional comparative advantage: the easy access to a safe haven across the border. It is in those jungle areas that lack infrastructure where the insurgents used to cross the border, for example, to bring their injured members to Ecuador to receive medical treatment:

EX-GUERRILLA: I was in Tumaco around six years ago [. . .]. We went there to transport a sick [comrade] who was going to be taken to Ecuador. [. . .] We went in a jeep to Tumaco and there we handed him over. [. . .] He was a [fellow FARC member]. [. . .] They treated him in Ecuador, I don't know where exactly. In any case, they took him with them.
ME: *Who attended to him, the organization [FARC]?*
EX-GUERRILLA: No, I don't know. Ecuadorian doctors do the treatment.[125]

As was the case in Putumayo, preponderance in remote and hardly accessible regions with a strong social base allowed the FARC to benefit from controlling areas of coca cultivation. At the same time, they were able to engage with other groups in stable supply chain relationships. Coca cultivation increased (to 42,627 hectares), so that, in 2016, Nariño continued to have the largest area of coca cultivation of all the Colombian departments, favored by propitious climatic and geographic conditions. The territory is also used to process coca leaves into coca paste and to crystallize this paste into cocaine. In total, 753 cocaine-base laboratories and 67 hydrochloride cocaine laboratories were destroyed in 2016.[126] Further laboratories have been detected but not destroyed; presumably more have not been detected.

Fluvial systems in the region have been pivotal for keeping the illicit cocaine supply chains going. To bring drugs and other illicit products to the Pacific coast, the armed actors use, for instance, the border River San Juan that separates Colombia from Ecuador. Also, the River Mira is a route along which coca is processed into cocaine, which is then transported toward the Pacific coast.[127] Rather than ad hoc cooperation, some stages of this supply chain require a certain level of stability and institutionalization, for example the regular buying and processing of coca leaves. In these cases, the various groups involved rely on financiers and brokers to overcome distrust. In 2012, along the River Mira, the FARC's mobile column Daniel Aldana controlled Bajo Mira, including the river's upper and the middle part, where they protected the cultivation and the first processing stages. Brokers bought the coca paste to sell it to a group that transported it to the laboratories in Alto Mira and Frontera. According to local reports, in 2011, the Rastrojos, who were in charge of further processing and transporting, dominated these lower parts of the river that lead to the ocean. In 2014, the FARC gained more control over the river's lower reaches. The ELN's Front Héroes de Sindagua, also present in Pizarro, reportedly also participated in cocaine supply chain relationships. Other brokers then negotiated with criminal organizations such as the Mexican Zetas or the Sinaloa cartel, who bought cocaine to ship it to the United States.

As mentioned above, the cocaine supply chain does not exist in isolation. It is just one of many overlapping networks that links different forms of transnational organized crime through interconnected flows. Nariño is strategic for the supplies of major conflict actors, and such interconnectedness is thus pronounced in this border region, as Map 3.6 illustrates. The nodes where these various flows intersect, not infrequently determined by critical infrastructure including informal border bridges, typically comprise clusters of short-term arrangements of convenience among a variety of different groups whose economic interests converge.

At the formal border crossing between Colombian Ipiales and its Ecuadorian twin town Tulcán, the capital of Carchi, barter agreements, spot sales, and financial transactions are commonplace.[128] The towns lie on the Pan-American Highway and are therefore strategic points for the flows of resources between Ecuador and Colombia. Arms, precursors, and gasoline enter Colombia, and money flows are channeled through Ipiales to enter Ecuador's dollarized economy via money-laundering processes. Ipiales features relatively strong (civilian) state presence. Hence, violent non-state groups involved in such illicit transactions manage financial flows with a low profile to avoid interdiction by the authorities. Tulcán is a major trade hub of legal and contraband merchandise. The Colombian violent non-state groups have little permanent presence in Tulcán except for informants

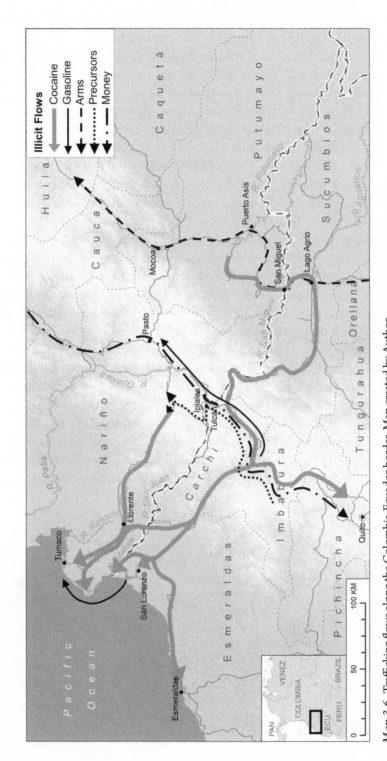

Map 3.6 Trafficking flows along the Colombia-Ecuador border. Map created by Author.

and militias. Instead, they send their people on short trips to Tulcán to negotiate the business deals with Ecuadorian traffickers (see chapter 5).

In the remote Ecuadorian border villages I visited in 2012, including Maldonado, Chical, and Tufiño, the FARC not only exerted illicit authority. Their members also engaged in spot sales and barter agreements to buy medicine, arms, food, and uniforms.[129] At that time, the FARC, for instance, were said to engage in arms trafficking with Otavaleño trafficking groups from the Ecuadorian province of Imbabura via Carchi to Nariño, and even connected with various trafficking groups in Nariño's capital city, Pasto. The goods are transported, for example, on a 102-kilometer long road that connects Chical with Tulcán (see Figure 3.8), and another one that connects Tulcán via Ibarra with San Lorenzo, twin town of Tumaco.

In addition to the border crossings, strategic locations both for the conflict dynamics and for the illicit economy concentrate short-term arrangements. Llorente, a village on the road that connects Pasto in the Andean region with the harbor town of Tumaco at the Pacific, is a case in point. After guerrilla preponderance in the early 2000s, followed by combat between guerrillas and the AUC until their demobilization, non-state order shifted to the "rivalry" cluster of violent non-state group interactions, most notably spot sales and barter agreements, involving groups such as the Águilas Negras, Mano Negra, Nueva Generación, Rastrojos, and the FARC, around 2007. Armed actors met to negotiate shipments of drugs and precursors and made payments to access trafficking routes or purchase illegal goods (see section 5.1). Even though, by 2011, the Rastrojos became largely preponderant, they also continued to be involved in spot sales with FARC militias. Llorente has since continued to serve as "business center" of spot sales and barter agreements. This is due to the village's strategic

Figure 3.8 Road between Chical and Tulcán, Ecuador, 2012. Photo by Author.

position on the road where the activities and economic interests of multiple violent non-state groups and of the armed forces converge. The road limits the presence of state and non-state armed groups and is used to transport illicit goods to Tumaco—including by means of bribing one's way through the checkpoints, as a local government official pointed out:

OFFICIAL: The road is fundamental because it's the central axis where the groups have limits [. . .] parallel to the road. There is a sector of the road between Mayama, Piedra Ancha, and Tumaco, but more between Mayama and Llorente, a sub-municipality of Tumaco. In this sector—we are talking about more or less 120 kilometers—[. . .], the groups have their crossing corridors. They communicate with each other. For example, they place a bus or a car with explosives across the road [. . .] in the middle of this sector so that they can pass. It always happens there. One knows that, in some way, the groups are on the move.

ME: *When the groups want to cross over to the other side of the road?*

OFFICIAL: Yes, they put obstacles so that state forces cannot advance.

ME: *Who controls these corridors?*

OFFICIAL: Currently, the state forces control the road. If you go from Tumaco to Pasto [. . .], I think it's the world's most militarized road. How many checkpoints did you count [when you traveled from Tumaco to Pasto]?

ME: *Maybe seven or eight. . . .*

OFFICIAL: Counting the police stations in the urban centers, there are eighteen checkpoints!

ME: *How can these groups maintain these crossing points?*

OFFICIAL: That's the thing! They would have to put a policeman, a soldier, every fifty meters to control it. No single army would be able to do that. It's difficult. The zone's topography, a mountainous zone, pure jungle, benefits the groups. [. . .]

ME: *What occurs on the other side? Is there presence [of armed actors] as well?*

OFFICIAL: Yes, they look after themselves due to the diplomatic issue [. . .]. They know that, if they are visible, it's not the same to be in a Colombian zone and confront the Colombian army as to generate an international conflict between states. All groups protect themselves from this.

ME: *Also the [Colombian] army?*

OFFICIAL: They are more cautious. Since they are the state, they have to. They know that this is very serious.

ME: *The groups benefit from this?*

OFFICIAL: Yes, as well. There are zones, this zone of Tumaco [. . .]. If one group has to bring arms from Ecuador, let's say from Guayaquil. Do they have to control it? Passing them through the entire jungle and bringing them into

Colombia and to [Nariño] is much more expensive than bringing them in a container via Ipiales. This is a matter of rationality of resources. The [...] logistics and the movement of resources are much cheaper via the Pan-American Highway than a journey of one month to reach a certain point.[130]

The final defining features of the distribution of clusters of violent non-state groups are the starting points of international trafficking routes. Comprising a maritime border with the Pacific Ocean in addition to the Colombia-Ecuador land border, the region of Nariño, Esmeraldas, and Carchi contains several such starting points. Along the coast, cocaine is loaded, for example, on to partially submersible vessels (semi-submarines) to be then transported with fast speed boats via the Galápagos Islands to Central America, or via Mexico to the United States. The city of Tumaco, Colombia's second most important port on the Pacific coast after Buenaventura, is the starting point of such a key route. Particularly weak state governance that distinguishes the city from other border towns like Ipiales means that violent entrepreneurs interested in the lucrative drug business hardly face reprisals by law enforcement authorities. According to interviews with locals, in 2011, the Águilas Negras, the Rastrojos, the FARC militias of the mobile column Daniel Aldana (while other units operated in rural areas), the Mexican Sinaloa cartel, and other criminal groups were to different degrees involved in short-term arrangements. These included tactical alliances (e.g., between the Águilas Negras and the Rastrojos) and subcontractual relationships, reportedly between the Sinaloa cartel and Águilas Negras to provide security services.[131]

Imposing a transnational borderland perspective on Tumaco and its Ecuadorian twin town San Lorenzo sheds light on the strategic significance of the location. Like Tumaco in Colombia, San Lorenzo is one of Ecuador's poorest and least developed towns, and yet the opulent design of some of the buildings suggest that some citizens have access to unexpected wealth, likely linked to the illicit economy (see Figure 3.9).

San Lorenzo has direct access to the open Pacific Ocean and is only twenty-four boat hours away from the Panama Canal, making it a strategic point for international trafficking routes. Numerous small islands, many inhabited, characterize the coastal areas near San Lorenzo. Residents of San Lorenzo and of the islands of Pampanal, Palma Real, and El Viento that I visited—the last points before crossing over to Tumaco on the waterway (see Figures 3.10 and 3.11)—voiced concerns about pirates who steal motors for fast-speed boats to transport the drugs. Indeed, the islands' large mangroves are used as hiding places for cocaine to be shipped abroad. Both the FARC and post-demobilized groups, that is, the AUC's successors, supposedly the Popular Revolutionary Anti-Terrorist Army of Colombia (Ejercito Revolucionario Popular Antiterrorista

Figure 3.9 San Lorenzo, Ecuador, 2012. Photos by Author.

Figure 3.10 Harbor of El Viento, Ecuador, 2012. Photo by Author.

Figure 3.11 Palma Real, Ecuador, 2012. Photos by Author.

Colombiano—ERPAC) and the Águilas Negras, have been present in the region, and have subcontracted youth gangs across the border in San Lorenzo to provide security services.

A five-hour bus ride south along the coast leads to Esmeraldas, the provincial capital, and another major starting point of illegal drug routes. Knowledge of this illegal activity became public through media coverage in 2012, due to the involvement of the head of police in a major trafficking ring. In partnership with a non-governmental organization of Spanish residents in Ecuador, the traffickers shipped goods to poor children in Africa: a strategy used to traffic hidden cocaine via West Africa to Europe.[132] Several Colombian post-demobilized groups were also present in Esmeraldas. They were involved in tactical alliances, spot sales, and barter agreements, reconfirming that the logics of the interactions of these groups extend beyond the borderline.

Colombian-Venezuelan Borderlands

The Colombian-Venezuelan borderlands comprise seven Colombian departments and four Venezuelan states.[133] At the southern end, the borderlands extend to remote jungle regions: the departments of Vichada and Guainia, which adjoin Venezuela's Amazonas. These are followed by Colombian Arauca and a small part of Boyacá, which together border the state of Apure. Further north, the metropolitan area of Cúcuta, Norte de Santander's capital, meets the urbanized areas of Venezuelan Táchira, and the Catatumbo region meets with southern Zulia. The Colombian department of Cesar adjoins the mountainous lower parts of Zulia. In the northern extreme, Colombian La Guajira and Venezuelan Zulia share the arid Guajira Peninsula. Map 3.7 illustrates the presence and interactions of the multiple violent non-state groups across the border.

Arauca—Apure

In the borderlands of Colombian Arauca and Venezuelan Apure, weak state governance systems have contributed to the ELN's power position, influencing the security dynamics differently from those in many other regions where the FARC were the only dominant insurgent group in the conflict's recent history. The relationship between the two guerrillas oscillated between "enmity" and "friendship" and was further complicated through interactions with a third left-wing group, the Venezuelan Bolivarian Forces of Liberation (Fuerzas Bolivarianas de Liberación—FBL). The logics of the mining industry present in the region have shaped economic incentives differently than has the cocaine industry elsewhere. Nonetheless, this industry exists in parallel with the border's porosity, which has facilitated other illicit flows related to gasoline smuggling

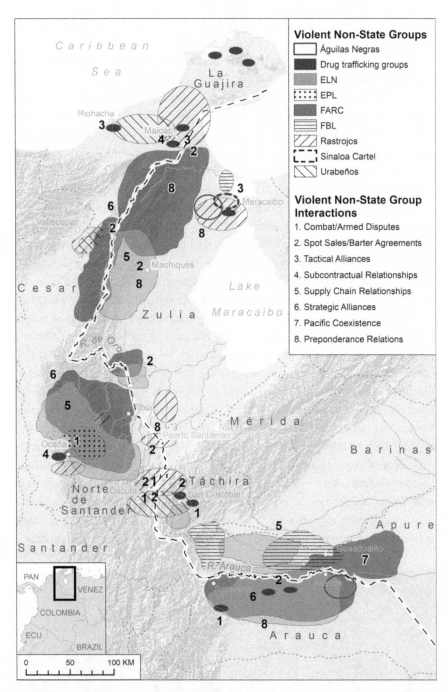

Map 3.7 Violent non-state group interactions along the Colombia-Venezuela border (2011–2013). Map created by Author.

and drug trafficking for example, making the border area attractive to multiple armed actors.

Weak state governance systems and deficient road and communication infrastructure leave Arauca isolated from more central and even neighboring regions, a convenient condition for guerrillas, particularly the ELN, to turn the department into one of their strongholds. Like in the Putumayo-Sucumbíos border region, in order to travel by land between the two departmental capital cities Cúcuta and Arauca, it is quicker to cross over into Venezuela and take the road on the Venezuelan side. When I first visited Arauca, I arrived in Venezuelan San Cristóbal, traveled down to Guasdualito, and crossed the border to Arauca, rather than crossing over at Cúcuta. Similarly, when the border was closed in 2015 and 2016 (see Figure 3.12), people were facing twelve-hour drives on Colombian roads, rather than six-hour drives via Venezuela. These conditions of neglect sharply contrast with Arauca's importance for Colombia's economy: the discovery of oil in the department in 1983 gave rise to an oil boom. "Saudi Arauca," as the region was often dubbed, attracted government investment and national and international oil companies, as well as armed actors, aiming to reap benefits from the mining industry.[134] Yet similar to Putumayo, the Colombian government has emphasized its focus on the mining industry, rather than Arauca's population. Indeed, the claims of locals that 80 percent of the fifteen thousand state troops based in Arauca as part of the government's Consolidation Plan protect infrastructure rather than the population resemble the tales of neglect in Putumayo. Even a nonexpert observer would be able to confirm such an impression. When I accompanied an international organization in Arauca in 2012, we passed through the highly militarized zone of the Caño Limón pipeline where vehicles have to strictly maintain a speed of 60 km/h in order to reduce the risk of terrorist attacks. Meanwhile, many of the inhabitants of remote border villages are left without protection from threats by multiple armed actors. State neglect is also evident in other governance areas, including

Figure 3.12 Border closure at Arauca (Colombia) and Apure (Venezuela) , 2016. Photos by Author.

(a lack of) basic services. Such neglect, despite the region's richness in oil, provokes bitterness among the population. The example that a woman in a border village in Arauca shared with me puts it in a nutshell: "The only day on which you can get sick is Thursday." There are no other days when a doctor is present.

The region has seen an oscillating evolution of non-state order, starting with the prevalence of the "friendship" cluster in the 1960s, then moving to "enmity" from the late 1990s until 2010, and since then reverting back to the far-right corner of the continuum of clusters of violent non-state group interactions, to preponderance relations (see figure 2.1). There have been enclaves of the "rivalry" cluster as well, but to a lesser extent than in other border areas.

Even though it has only been involved in armed guerrilla activities since the 1980s, the ELN entered the region that today is the department of Arauca as early as 1966. This permitted the group to build a strong social base, gain economic and political power, and consolidate its preponderance. The FARC expanded their presence to Arauca in the late 1970s and early 1980s. Both groups coexisted in the territory and extended their presence to Venezuelan Alto Apure (and Táchira, discussed below) as a zone of rest, recreation, and recovery. In the 1990s, Apure, and in particular Páez municipality (with high levels of poverty that fueled grievances of the population), became a zone of political influence and source of collaborators and supporters.[135] At that time, the ELN "mentored" the FBL (hence the FBL's activities to acquire income now resemble those of the Colombian group) while remaining preponderant.

This relative equilibrium among the leftist non-state actors changed when, toward the end of the 1990s, the paramilitary Conquerors Bloc of Arauca entered the region, producing a shift from the "friendship" to the "enmity" cluster in which the right-wing paramilitaries, together with a strong state military offensive starting in 2002, fought the guerrillas. The paramilitaries demobilized between 2005 and 2007. Rather than moving back to the previous equilibrium, however, "enmity" persisted, but this time in a different group constellation: in 2006, the FARC and the ELN started a brutal guerrilla war with each other in Arauca and Apure that endured until 2010 (see section 4.1).

Viewing the conflict dynamics through a borderland lens rather than from a state-centric perspective that starts from Bogotá reveals how "bordered" counterinsurgency operations in Arauca clashed with the transnational logics of the interactions between the FARC, the ELN, and the FBL. After years of combat between the FARC and the ELN, beginning in March 2006, on both sides of the border stable long-term arrangements shaped non-state order again. The guerrilla war took up considerable resources on both sides;[136] it ended in November 2010.[137] In 2011, the following structures were present in Arauca: the ELN companies of Rafael Villamizar, Camilo Cienfuegos, Ernesto Che Guevara, Barquiley, Compañero Tomás, Omaira Montoya Henao, Martha Elena Barón, and Domingo Laín; and FARC Fronts 10, 28, and 45, as well as the mobile column Alfonso Castellanos and the mobile company Reinal Méndez. The two guerrillas established a nonaggression pact with each other and engaged in a strategic alliance in Arauca. In 2011, this alliance encompassed joint attacks against state forces or infrastructure, the recognition of the mistakes committed by both groups, the return of displaced civilians, respect for the territorial dominion of both groups, the rejection of coca cultivation, and refraining from imposing taxes on their social bases. Notably, the arrangement also comprised sharing territory in Venezuela without engaging in armed activities that could bother the Venezuelan government, and clarity on the same enemy: "the empire," that is, the United States.[138] The alliance, which strengthened their position vis-à-vis the Colombian state, therefore directly benefited from Venezuelan Apure as a safe haven.

The pacific coexistence on the Venezuelan side of the border also included the FBL, adding complexity to the relationship between the FARC and the ELN. In 2012, the three left-wing groups' pacific coexistence involved the division of territory in the following different sectors: the southeast side, especially El Orza, was FARC territory; and the sector toward Táchira, particularly the area near El Nula (a village in Alto Apure), belonged to the ELN and the FBL. Guasdualito (the capital of Apure) featured all three groups.

The FBL and the ELN had already fallen into dispute in 2003, and some analysts even argue that the FBL had a strategic alliance with the FARC, through which they would have opposed the ELN together.[139] After 2010, FBL resistance to ELN presence became noticeable in a few developments, albeit in a concealed manner. In September 2011, a protest march against the ELN took place in El Nula. Organized by farmers' movements, it was supposedly initiated by the FBL. Rather than opposing the Colombian guerrillas on Venezuelan territory with violence, the FBL tried to rally public support behind them.[140] With an interest in former president Chávez's re-election in September 2012, all three groups maintained a low profile to avoid any media attention that could have cited high rates of violence to accuse Chávez of mishandling the situation in the border zone.

Regarding socioeconomic influences, at the Arauca-Apure border the oil industry particularly stands out in informing non-state order, while coca cultivation and processing have lost significance. This contrasts with the previously discussed Colombia-Ecuador border, where socioeconomic, topographic, and climatic conditions favor the cocaine industry that shapes the logics of relatively stable supply chain relationships among multiple violent entrepreneurs. The illicit drug business hinges on direct or indirect cooperation along the supply chain and linked forms of organized crime; the division of labor based on comparative advantages of each group maximizes profit. These activities require coordination or business deals between various armed actors. In the borderlands of Arauca and Apure, both rebel groups shared economic interests in the oil revenue, but in the context of Arauca's mining industry this does not necessarily result in the convergence of interests in a division of labor along a supply chain. Rather, expanding territorial control, the social base, and co-opting the political elite have been advantageous activities. Illicit income streams linked to the oil industry result from diverting royalties from the local authorities to the guerrillas' coffers, necessitating the penetration of local institutions, or collusion with, local political actors. Profit further stems from extracting money from oil companies through bribes and threats, that is, by charging protection money. Finally, it also involves lucrative deals in the concession of public contracts related to the mining enterprise. According to information from Colombian authorities, the ELN alone diverted an estimated 17 percent of Arauca's oil royalties in the 1990s and early 2000s.[141]

The conflict dynamics shaped by Venezuela's connivance, and the region's economy characterized by Arauca's oil focus, inform the interactions between the guerrillas, and between the guerrillas and paramilitaries. Identifying and mapping major illicit flows complements the picture because it points to locations where the economic interests of rivaling violent non-state groups converge, giving rise to short-lived arrangements of convenience: at strategic border crossings and in the few urban areas of the region. Like in other border areas, armed groups in Arauca acquire supplies from across the border. While coca cultivation and the number of processing laboratories decreased in Arauca, it increasingly became a transit zone for drugs, gasoline, cattle, and other goods, fueling another illicit business: the extortion of smugglers. To curb gasoline smuggling, in March 2012, the Venezuelan government introduced a "chip" to regulate the amount of gasoline that each vehicle could transport across the border from the Venezuelan states that border Colombia. It made gasoline smuggling in the region more difficult. In Puerto Lleras, for example, 500 to 600 barrels used to be smuggled per night. In April 2012, it was only 100. In La Playa, where a smuggler had previously earned 200,000 pesos (about 105 USD) in one week, in April 2012, he only earned 20,000 (about 11 USD) in the same period.[142] Yet while this affected individual smugglers, large-scale business deals between organized criminal groups continued. After the AUC's demobilization, urban areas featured right-wing groups including the Águilas Negras, ERPAC, and a group called "Vencedores," with many of them entering the department via Casanare.[143] Residents of the city of Arauca confirmed the Águilas Negras' presence between 2011 and 2012; in Tame, the presence of the Vencedores had been reported.[144] To what extent post-demobilized groups operated in Alto Apure is less clear. People claimed to have seen pamphlets with death threats in Guasdualito, the capital of Apure, yet some argued these pamphlets had been brought from Arauca where they were originally distributed. Given that these regions are not closely located to major international trafficking routes, as are the Pacific and the Caribbean coast, clusters of short-term arrangements have been less pronounced than in other regions.

Norte de Santander—Táchira and Southern Zulia

The border region comprising Colombian Norte de Santander and Venezuelan Táchira, as well as southern Zulia, has been an epicenter of political violence and a hub of illicit cross-border activities for decades. Similar to the Nariño-Esmeraldas/Carchi region, various factors that shape violent non-state interactions coalesce in the region. First, weak state governance allowed armed actors to turn the region into their stronghold. Second, climatic conditions conducive to the cultivation of coca, and the geostrategic location that connects mobility corridors and trafficking routes from Colombia's interior across the border to Venezuela, and to the north toward the Caribbean, have facilitated the presence of almost all stages of the cocaine business. This attracted a wide range of different violent non-state groups involved in supply chain relationships. Third, the presence of strategic border crossings and other crucial nodes at these routes gave rise to short-term arrangements. Fourth, comprising the border's only metropolitan area around the border twin towns of Colombian Cúcuta and Venezuelan San Antonio de Táchira, it includes an illicit business hub where violent entrepreneurs meet to strike deals. As a result, all three clusters of violent non-state group interactions, that is, "enmity," "rivalry," and "friendship," have shaped non-state order in the region not only across time but also concurrently across space.

In rural regions of these borderlands, non-state order shifted from being dominated by the cluster of stable long-term arrangements to "enmity," and back to stable long-term arrangements. The ease with which multiple violent non-state groups were able to establish roots in these zones relates to how the power centers have dealt—and are still dealing—with the region. Colombian governments have historically neglected Norte de Santander's rural areas— disregarding military attention. Like in Colombia's other border regions, road infrastructure is insufficient, and the basic services situation is extremely precarious: many villages do not have electricity, schools, or health centers. As a farmer from the Catatumbo region pointed out with frustration, recruitment of minors is particularly prevalent in those villages where no school bus passes by.[145] Other farmers complained that, in the absence of electricity, they lacked fridges to preserve products such as vegetables or eggs; hence, cultivating coca was a more stable and feasible livelihood strategy.[146] This is a fertile breeding ground for insurgencies to consolidate power and subordinate smaller non-state groups.

The first armed confrontations in Norte de Santander's recent history were rooted in grievances of farmers during "La Violencia," followed by clashes between state forces and guerrillas in the 1970s.[147] The FARC, the ELN, and a section of the EPL, preponderant in rural areas with militias in urban centers, positioned themselves and expanded their activities to border areas.[148] Para-state groups—that is, armed civilians, supported by landowners, traffickers, and the state—had already been operating violently from 1982 onward.[149] In the mid-1990s, however, the officially constituted paramilitaries conducted brutal massacres to fight the guerrillas while pursuing the drug business. From 2000 to 2002, after the Peasant Self-Defense Forces of Córdoba and Urabá (Autodefensas Campesinas de Córdoba y Urabá—ACCU) evolved into the AUC, the AUC's paramilitary Border Bloc and the Catatumbo Bloc consolidated their presence in Norte de Santander, leading to a spike in violence in the region.[150] The conflict dynamics of Colombia extended across the border to Venezuelan Táchira. After the paramilitaries entered Norte de Santander in May 1999, the ELN, the EPL, and the FARC withdrew to and across the border. Soon the paramilitaries followed. Meanwhile, the FBL maintained its presence in Venezuela's Fernández Feo municipality.[151] In 2006, when the AUC demobilized in Norte de Santander, the Águilas Negras appeared. When the Águilas Negras's leader died in 2007, the right-wing Paisas and Urabeños started to dispute the Águilas Negras's preponderance between 2007 and 2008. Reportedly comprising farmers, youth from marginalized neighborhoods, recruited children, and demobilized AUC members, they came mainly from Córdoba, Urabá, Antioquia, and the Atlantic Coast.[152]

After the paramilitary demobilization, the "friendship" cluster became more prominent. Certainly, violence had been continuing in the form of armed disputes between right-wing groups and of persistent guerrilla attacks against state forces, especially in the Catatumbo region. Research trips in 2011 and 2012 took me to extremely remote villages like El Tarra, Filogringo, and Tibú, where guerrilla graffiti, craters near the road left by explosives, burned-out houses, and tanks on dirt trails were testimony to the ongoing insurgency and the state's violent responses. Still, long-term arrangements formed another layer of violent non-state group interactions in the region. Some of them were located in strategic conflict corridors that connect Norte de Santander with the "heartlands" of Colombia. These includes for example, from 2006 onward, the preponderance relations of guerrillas in the village of Las Mercedes and neighboring villages in the municipality of Sardinata on the road that connects Cúcuta with Ocaña.[153] Others reached across the border to Venezuelan southern Zulia. With arguably three left-wing guerrillas (the FARC, the ELN, and the EPL) present in the region, the operations of the state forces as a common threat and the highly militarized context brought their shared ideological values that allow reducing mistrust to the fore. Around 2011, the FARC's Front 41 Cacique Upar and Front 33 Mariscal Antonio José de Sucre were operating in a strategic alliance with the ELN's Front Camilo Torres Restrepo in Catatumbo.[154] This alliance emerged from the two groups' strategy "Unity Action in Border Zones" that envisaged joint activities in border areas. It was rooted in the FARC's "Re-Born Plan," published in 2008, in which the FARC laid out their new emphasis on guerrilla warfare rather than a war between two large armies.[155] The joint strategy meant that the groups' commitment went beyond a particular occasion to also hold more generally. This diminished the possibility that one of both groups walked away or cheated on the other.

Similar to the situation in Nariño, it was not only conflict cleavages but also the logics of illicit economies that determined non-state order in these borderlands. In the Catatumbo region, these logics concerned the cocaine business and interlinked forms of transnational organized crime, giving rise to supply chain relationships. By the early 1990s, coca cultivation had already become common in Medio and Bajo Catatumbo in the River Catatumbo Basin.[156] Catatumbo's geostrategic location at the beginning of the international trafficking route via Venezuela, and its easy access to the Colombian Caribbean coast in the north, incentivized the establishment of laboratories in the same region for cocaine production, since the product could be easily transported further. I spotted separate ELN graffiti and FARC graffiti during my research trips to remote coca-growing regions, signaling their control of this first stage of the supply chain; interviewees confirmed this.[157] Tracing supply chain relationships reveals the division of labor even among ideologically opposed groups. Relying on a third party, a broker, as a distrust-reducing mechanism explains why they were not directly fighting each other in the rural areas (see section 2.1). Local reports also mention pacific coexistence of the FARC and the Águilas Negras in late 2007 and early 2008 in Norte de Santander,[158] but the two groups were likely to be involved in different stages in the same supply chain without directly interacting. In 2009, the Rastrojos expanded their presence to and within Norte de Santander.[159] Around 2011 and 2012, the FARC and the Rastrojos operated in supply chain relationships, suggesting that the Rastrojos replaced the Águilas Negras in their function in the chain, while the FARC's function and relation with the broker(s) persisted.

The interconnectedness of cocaine supply chains with networks of other forms of transnational organized crime, including arms and gasoline smuggling, as well as money laundering,[160] gives rise to the "rivalry" cluster as a further form of non-state order in the region. Mapping the various routes of networked illicit flows that link the Catatumbo region with the heartlands of Colombia, as well as the starting points of international trafficking routes in the Caribbean and across the border in Venezuela, reveals key transit nodes where several flows intersect.

Of strategic significance for mobility corridors in the conflict and for the income sources of various violent non-state groups, these nodes attract multiple groups with converging interests.

One of these nodes is the town of Ocaña, the second largest city of Norte de Santander, a four-hour drive northwest of Cúcuta. Ocaña's function as a prime transit point for the trafficking routes from the heartlands of Colombia toward the border with Venezuela, Catatumbo, and the Caribbean shapes dynamics in the area and hence justifies considering it a borderland town.[161] In Ocaña, between 2011 and 2012, powerful post-demobilized groups allegedly subcontracted youth gangs to control neighborhoods, while what I describe as tense calm (falling into the "enmity" cluster) characterized the relations among these various powerful groups (see section 2.1).

Further strategic locations are border crossings, such as the village of Puerto Santander, at the border with Venezuela (Map 3.8). When I visited the village in 2012, a local government official alluded to Puerto Santander's function as key point on the trafficking route for cocaine and gasoline: "This is not the *puerto* (port); this is the *portón* (huge port)." In 2012, the Rastrojos were preponderant in Puerto Santander. Since they controlled the gasoline-drug business, there were few violent disputes, as a community leader from Cúcuta explained:

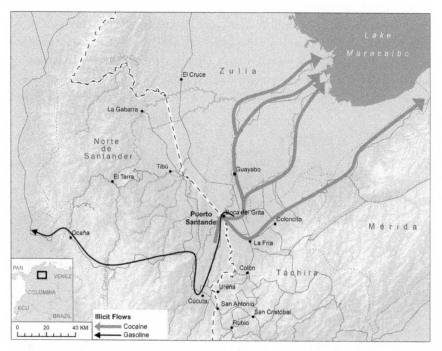

Map 3.8 Trafficking routes through Puerto Santander, Colombia. Map created by Author.

On this side, the blood of the dead doesn't flow as much as it flows in
the zones of La Parada, Cúcuta, or Ureña. There isn't much blood flow
because the only things that flow are dollars, coca[ine], and gasoline.

While cocaine leaves Colombia through the "gateway" Puerto Santander,
Venezuelan gasoline, used to process coca paste into cocaine in laboratories in
Colombia, enters the country through the same route, often via the river that
separates Puerto Santander from the Venezuelan town of Boca del Grita that I also
visited during my trips in 2011 and 2012 (see Figure 3.13). Various trafficking
groups engaged in barter agreements and spot sales with the Rastrojos to benefit
from the business during that time. The gasoline station from where the groups
smuggled gasoline across the border via Puerto Santander southward is only
few kilometers away. The two forms of organized crime are interconnected,
and the groups' involvement in these supply chain networks can only be fully
comprehended when tracing them across the border. After all, the groups' interests
in controlling strategic sections of the trafficking route reinforced their expansion
into Venezuelan territory. The northern parts of Venezuelan Colón municipality,
particularly the village of Coloncito, are crucial for this purpose: Coloncito lies on
the Pan-American Highway, used to transport drugs toward the Venezuelan coast,
from where they are sent via the Caribbean islands to the United States or Europe.

Finally, in addition to essential transit nodes and border crossings, hubs for
illicit business deals are critical. The cross-border area of Colombian Cúcuta
and Venezuelan San Antonio de Táchira is a critical hub for illicit business deals
struck to channel illicit flows across the Colombia-Venezuela border. As the only
metropolitan zone along the border, it also is a major gateway toward Venezuela,
attracting multiple groups. Therefore, Cúcuta has continuously featured enclaves

Figure 3.13 Border post Boca del Grita, Venezuela, and international border bridge
between Puerto Santander (Colombia) and Boca del Grita (Venezuela), 2012. Photos by
Author.

of fragile, economically motivated arrangements of convenience. In 2009, the Rastrojos positioned themselves in the urban border areas of Cúcuta, Villa del Rosario, and Los Patios to control the international trafficking routes.[162] Others subordinated to the Rastrojos and, for a while, they even became the only group present in some territories. Preponderance relations end if the weaker group's members defect to the preponderant group, as demonstrated by the case of the Rastrojos and the Paisas. When I asked whether these groups joined forces, a community leader explained to me:

> One group absorbed the other one. It already happened this way with the Águilas Negras. Men who used to work with them were offered: "Look, this is the new boss, now we're changing our name, ok? Before, Macaco ruled us, now Loco Barrera tells us that we are going to call ourselves Rastrojos, therefore now we are Rastrojos." "Ah ok, sure." And they continue with the same work.[163]

As an enclave in this long-term arrangement, the Rastrojos used the shopping center "Alejandría" in Cúcuta for financial transactions of spot sales and barter agreements with other violent non-state groups (see section 5.1).

Given the strategically significant location of Cúcuta for international trafficking, short-term arrangements can easily be overshadowed by, or change into, armed disputes. This was the case in 2011 and 2012, between the Rastrojos and the Urabeños. As a high-ranking police official in Cúcuta explained, the Urabeños tried to oust the Rastrojos to control the drug route, that is, the logistics linked to the physical space where the drug is transported:

> [The Urabeños] have to dominate territory to handle the business, the routes, the logistics chain. When we talk about these things, you often hear [. . .] that the criminals even sell a "route." [. . .] In the criminal arena, when they say the Rastrojos sell a route, they sell the entire logistics chain: [. . .] the know-how, how they do it and who is there [. . .]. They say: "Look, I know [. . .] who has the coca production sites. I know how they bring the precursors into this sector and I have the contact. I know where the laboratories are and who can process the coca leaves first into coca paste and then coca paste into cocaine. I know about the entire process and where we can stockpile [cocaine]. I know with whom and where we can get it out [of the country] and what to transport it in and who will receive it abroad, in Spain, in the United States, or in export countries. I know how to transport the money because I have the contacts." This is a route.[164]

With the strategic value of such routes originating in their transnationality, the logics of group interactions are of transnational character too. Post-demobilized groups operated not only in Cúcuta but also on the Venezuelan side of the border, in urban areas near Cúcuta and the Pedro María Ureña and Bolívar municipalities. In 2011 and 2012, the Rastrojos and the Urabeños extended their armed disputes across the border to Ureña and San Antonio de Táchira. Similarly, around the same time, paramilitary successors and the ELN were involved in armed disputes in the Venezuelan village of Rubio. My interviewees considered San Cristóbal, the capital of the Venezuelan state of Táchira, the logistics center where violent non-state groups meet with a low profile to avoid attention and violent clashes (see section 5.1). Subcontractual relationships were also used for this purpose: in 2009, post-demobilized groups subcontracted local criminal groups to conduct illicit activities, such as extortion, for them and thus became an important "employer" in a region with high unemployment rates (see section 5.3).[165]

Cesar and La Guajira—Zulia

In the Colombian border regions of Putumayo, Arauca, and Catatumbo, the guerrillas' preponderance in many territories has considerably shaped non-state order. In Cesar and La Guajira, however, the paramilitaries' influence, and their links with other stakeholders in the armed conflict, has significantly informed the logics of group interactions. Non-state order first shifted from being dominated by relatively stable guerrilla preponderance to the cluster of "enmity" between insurgents and paramilitaries. It evolved into stable long-term arrangements between guerrillas in the southern parts of La Guajira and Zulia, and clusters of "rivalry" in strategic transit zones and at border crossings. This can be explained by the region's location. The area comprises strategic corridors, partly based on existing road infrastructure, that connect the cocaine production zone further south with the starting points of international trafficking routes in the northern part of the Guajira Peninsula, and with the "exit" to Venezuela, where gasoline smuggling shapes the logics of illicit flows as much as the drug trade. While macro conflict cleavages influenced the southern parts more directly, in the northern parts across the Colombia-Venezuela border where trafficking routes toward the United States and Europe begin, local interests—both of economic, and of political nature—informed the logics of group interactions, particularly short-lived ones.

In the 1970s, the FARC and the ELN used the borderland region of Cesar and La Guajira mainly to rest and recover. They then stepped up their political work, for example through community meetings during which they explained their political goals, and sustained their power in the region with kidnappings.[166] This way, in the early 1980s, the FARC's Front 4 from Magdalena Medio and the ELN consolidated their presence first in the Sierra Nevada, and then in the Sierra de Perijá.[167]

When the paramilitaries invaded Cesar in 1995, they decimated the guerrillas locally.[168] Attempting to control the entire Caribbean coast between the Gulf of Urabá and La Guajira, they engaged in a second wave of violence after 1999, backed by an alliance between the paramilitary North Bloc and the local political elite with the open complicity of the state forces.[169] Also in La Guajira, further north, the stable arrangements that became most known were those established between state and non-state actors. When entering the department, the AUC forged ties with the local political elite of La Guajira, influencing elections and other aspects of public life. On March 8 and 10, 2006, the paramilitary Northern Bloc demobilized in Chimila (El Copey) and in La Mesa (Valledupar) in Cesar; the alliances between paramilitaries and politicians, including congressmen, became public as the "para-politics" scandal. Nonetheless, and as the 2013 capture of Juan Francisco "Kiko" Gómez, the governor of La Guajira, exemplifies, similar alliances continued with paramilitary successor groups.[170] Members of state forces were also complicit, or turned a blind eye to the violent non-state groups' illegal economic activities in order to profit from them. Some considered this a form of compensation for being based there. Given La Guajira's extreme marginalization in Colombia, even in comparison to other border regions, representing the state forces in that territory was considered unattractive. This is illustrated by the graffiti next to a police station in Castilletes, in the north of the Guajira Peninsula, as seen in Figure 3.14. It translates to: "Never compare this paradise with a punishment. 'Enjoy it!'" As with the case of Cesar, in only focusing on the state-/non-state dyad or the collusion between the two, one can easily miss that the state forces are just "another armed group" as many interviewees put it, and

Figure 3.14 Border police station Castilletes, La Guajira, Colombia, 2012. Photos by Author.

that right-wing groups also forged strategic alliances with other non-state actors. They did so, for example, with Wayúu families via marriages—a special case of shared values with a long-term commitment (see section 6.2).

Despite having lost its power in La Guajira, around 2011, the FARC's Fronts 59, 41, and 19 dominated Sierra del Perijá's rural areas and so did the ELN's "Mixed Commission."[171] In these regions, interaction types characteristic of the "friendship" cluster, particularly strategic alliances and preponderance, influenced non-state order. In 2011, the FARC were present in Cesar with the Fronts 59, 41, and 33, and the ELN with the Front Camilo Torres Restrepo. The FARC's Front 59 and the ELN operated in a strategic alliance in the region where Cesar and La Guajira adjoin Zulia. The various groups engaged in stable long-term arrangements, especially preponderance relations, pacific coexistence, and strategic alliances on the other side of the border, in Venezuelan Zulia, as well. Also supply chain relationships, with guerrillas and other groups involved, extended from the Colombian side of the border over to Zulia, especially near Machiques. Around the same time, the FARC were present in all seven border municipalities of Zulia, the ELN in five out of these seven, and the FBL in one (Mara municipality). In towns such as Guayabo, post-demobilized groups prevailed.

The geographic features of the region shape the conflict dynamics, as they provide reliable mobility corridors.[172] They also guide the logics of the various illicit flows and, thus, the convergence of economic interests in crucial nodes where such flows intersect, including at border crossings. This in return motivates group interactions belonging to the "rivalry" cluster that emerges at such locations. The Cesar department, whose economy relies heavily on coal, connects with the departments of Bolívar, Magdalena, La Guajira, and Norte de Santander. It is a transit zone for cocaine that is produced further south and that then is transported to the starting points of international trafficking routes in the north. The Sierra de Perijá separates it from neighboring Venezuelan Zulia. Indigenous people who live in this mountainous region move back and forth between the two countries and violent non-state groups use the mountains as a zone of protection. For the wider population, however, cross-border interactions are more difficult than further south or further north at the border.[173] One such location in the south is La Paz municipality, near the department's capital, Valledupar (see section 5.1). The Rastrojos, the Urabeños, and the Paisas were among the groups that engaged in spot sales and barter agreements involving both gasoline and drugs across the border at this "node." Meanwhile, on the Venezuelan side of the border near Machiques in Zulia, a somewhat different form of spot sale persisted around 2011 and 2012: the guerrillas and criminal groups engaged in spot sales of human beings (see section 5.1).

Further north in La Guajira, Maicao, Dibulla, and Riohacha, the urban centers closest to relevant starting points of trafficking routes at the Guajira Peninsula's coast, have strategic "business" functions. Around 2011 and 2012, the Rastrojos, the Urabeños, the Paisas, the group Alta Guajira, and several private Wayúu armies operated there, engaging in rapidly changing tactical alliances,[174] based on the convergence of interest in profit. Shared economic interests also gave rise to barter agreements between various groups, including the FARC across the border and in Venezuelan Zulia. For example, they would exchange cocaine for arms, as the cocaine is shipped on trafficking routes that start near Lake of Maracaibo and continue through West Africa to Western Europe. More generally, and similar to the Colombia-Ecuador border's extreme at the Pacific coast, non-state order on the Venezuelan side has been more of an extension of it in Colombia, rather than a distinct phenomenon. This reflects geography: the region constitutes one Peninsula, despite the technically dividing borderline. Indeed, the presence of Colombian violent non-state groups in Zulia is not new. Both the Colombian Norte del Valle cartel and the Cali cartel had been operating in Zulia since 1997, and it later became the base of the Rastrojos and the Urabeños.[175] When I visited the Venezuelan town of Maracaibo in 2012, various criminal and post-demobilized groups were engaging in tactical alliances there and the Mexican Zeta cartel allied with the Rastrojos in wider Zulia.[176] The local population referred to the post-demobilized groups as the Águilas Negras, and groups operating under this label have also been reported in all municipalities.[177]

Attempting to grasp the logics of illicit flows at the Colombia-Venezuela border without a borderland lens would ignore one of the most decisive factors that influences non-state order in the region. The main starting points of (drug) trafficking routes via the Caribbean and Central America to the United States, or, via Venezuela and West Africa, to Europe are located on the desertic Guajira Peninsula, shared by Colombian La Guajira and Venezuelan Zulia. As neither the Colombian nor the Venezuelan state has had strong regulatory presence there, illicit cross-border activities have thrived and attracted multiple violent non-state groups. 48 percent of La Guajira's and 8 percent of Zulia's population are indigenous Wayúu who have been living in Colombian and Venezuelan territory in the Guajira Peninsula since before the border existed.[178] Indeed, they are a nomadic people who have historically moved around the territory. The lines between the legal and the illegal are particularly diffuse due to the region's cultural and historical context. Trade in contraband as a prevalent economic activity dates back to the sixteenth century,[179] and hence the Wayúu perceive contraband, including gasoline smuggling—although illegal—to be legitimate. They have decentralized political and judicial systems that solve disputes between clans, with punishment and enforcement measures based on violence. These internal disputes became a matter of contestation between various different violent non-state groups that soon resembled what can be understood as the "enmity" cluster between the second half of the 1970s and the first half of the

1980s. At that time, La Guajira experienced a marijuana boom.[180] As a consequence, the Wayúu's private armies were co-opted by external violent non-state
groups that started armed disputes over the control of territory.[181]

When the cocaine business became more lucrative than the marijuana boom,
non-state order evolved into the "rivalry" cluster between various violent non-
state groups. At the end of the 1990s, the paramilitaries and, after their demobilization in 2006, their successors, allied with Wayúu clans to access trafficking routes,
given the Wayúu's control over arms trafficking and private armies in the region.[182]
These included also strategic alliances, for example, between paramilitaries under
alias "Pablo" and Wayúu groups around 2004, and later, around 2009, between the
Paisas and certain Wayúu groups. These were made possible through marriage (see
section 6.2). Wayúu clans were not only co-opted. Many of them "learned," and
sought to forge these tactical alliances with paramilitaries, their successors, and
reportedly members of the state forces to maximize their own benefits. Referring
to the late 2000s, a Wayúu leader explained to me that "the army accompanied
groups such as the paramilitaries that never demobilized, drug-traffickers, and indigenous groups, who also dedicated themselves to wrongdoing."[183] Some Wayúu
groups themselves became—at least from an analytical point of view—violent
non-state groups. Even according to some Wayúus' perceptions, certain clans act
like an armed group. A Wayúu interviewee in Venezuelan Zulia conceded:

> I have to admit that we Wayúu are somewhat peculiar; I say we Wayúu,
> because I'm Wayúu. Sometimes our compatriots are driven by interests.
> Money, they like money, expensive whisky, clothes, cars. People en-
> trust themselves to these organizations [violent non-state groups], put
> themselves in their hands. That's why what happened in Bahía Portete
> actually happened: there was an alliance between paramilitaries and
> families from the harbor.[184]

In the extreme north, in the desert zones of the Guajira Peninsula, some Wayúu
groups control the remote, hardly accessible natural harbors used as starting
points of the drug routes, or defend them against rivals. Not only the harbors,
but the coastline itself became disputed terrain, given the lucrative business.
According to an international agency staff member in the Venezuelan town of
San Cristóbal, the capital of the Táchira state, one mode of trafficking, for example, was for planes to drop drug shipments over the Atlantic Ocean near the
coast and for small boats to pick them up to take them to Trinidad and Tobago
and other Caribbean islands from where they are shipped to the market in the
United States or Europe (see Map 3.4).[185]

To close here, these multiple forms of non-state order at the local level cannot
be understood without zooming out to see the global context. They are also

shaped by the global illicit economy, as the drug flows from La Guajira attest, and by geopolitical influences, as shown by the role of the US-promoted Plan Colombia in Putumayo, the region with which I began this mapping of violent non-state group interactions across the Andean borderlands. A borderland lens therefore not only permits insights into transnational local phenomena that go beyond the state's reach. It also puts non-state order into the context of global order as an overarching backdrop against which to understand these "glocal" security dynamics.

3.3 Conclusion

The borderland lens reveals the tension that arises from the coexistence of transnational dynamics and those tied to state territory. The very discrepancy between nationally constrained security policies and transnational operations of armed actors intensifies the logics of the insecurities that result from their illicit activities in borderlands (see chapter 7). Bringing three states—Colombia, Ecuador, and Venezuela—into the sphere of analysis reveals three security asymmetries: the first arises from extremely high rates of insecurity in the peripheries when compared to the countries' centers; the second stems from higher observed rates of insecurity on the Colombian side of the border and lower ones on the Ecuadorian and Venezuelan sides; and, as the following chapters demonstrate, the third originates from high perceptions of insecurity on the Ecuadorian and Venezuelan sides, as opposed to the normalization of violence in Colombia.

A view from the power centers of Colombia, Ecuador, and Venezuela focuses attention on Bogotá, Quito, and Caracas's policies to tackle insecurity close to their shared borders. Over the past decade, Colombia mainly assumed a hard-line, confrontational approach to violent non-state groups in its border zones (if present at all), while civilian institutions remained deficient. Ecuador's policies changed from passivity to heavier militarization combined with investment in development. In Venezuela, connivance seemed to most aptly describe state action toward Colombian violent non-state groups on Venezuelan territory. Yet viewed from the margins, it becomes evident that state policies on each side of the border coexist with transnational processes, including violent non-state interactions, which shape local security dynamics. Korf and Raeymaekers highlight the co-presence of several systems with state practices and rules and norms arising from such transnational processes.[186] This confluence in the margins produces dynamics that characterize how the periphery and the center are linked: these systems can be complementary, parallel, or competing. The confluence also adds to the characteristics of borderlands as an extreme case of complex security landscapes that arise from the very gap between a state-centric paradigm and the transnational illicit flows to which I allude at the beginning of this chapter. Anchoring the analysis in the margins is a starting point from which to begin to narrow this gap.

4

Violence and Survival

You always have to be careful because talking openly about the paramilitaries or the guerrillas produces risks. It's not that we don't talk about this, but only with caution and certain norms because we are in a conflict zone.

Lago Agrio resident, Ecuador, 2012[1]

Now it's calm. Well, there are deaths in the villages, but this is between them or it's social leaders, activists . . .

Farmer from Samaniego, Colombia, 2012[2]

Growing up during an armed conflict without any memories of peacetime makes people tough. It is as if they develop a sixth sense that tells them how to behave and what to say without risking their lives. In the Andean region, such risks know no borders, as the cautionary note of the Ecuadorian citizen above attests. Yet, in some instances, these risks are more obvious and strategies to reduce security threats are more effective than in others. Viewing these security dynamics through the borderlands' magnifying glass highlights nuances in the security situation that are blurred in other contexts. To demonstrate the variation in threats that arise when several violent non-state groups operate in the same territory in the "enmity" cluster of violent non-state group interactions, I draw on cases located along the Colombia-Ecuador and Colombia-Venezuela borders.

The border directly impacts security dynamics in some of these cases, even if this is not visible from the outside. As I demonstrate in the previous chapter by adopting a borderland lens, the guerrilla war between the National Liberation Army (Ejército de Liberación Nacional—ELN) and the Revolutionary Armed Forces of Colombia—People's Army (Fuerzas Armadas Revolucionarias de Colombia—Ejército del Pueblo—FARC), for instance, took place not only on Colombian soil, in Arauca, but also extended across the border to Venezuela. Both rebel groups took advantage of cross-border impunity to cover up their activities and escape the Colombian authorities' reach. They also benefited from intra-borderland displacements, which concealed the suffering inflicted on civilians (see section 7.1). In other cases discussed in this chapter, the proximity of the border intensified the logics of the group interactions and related citizen insecurities. In the example of fighting between paramilitaries and guerrillas in Putumayo, the border department's marginalization and state neglect facilitated the presence of these groups and their use of violence (see section 3.2). In the cases of armed disputes in Venezuelan Táchira and Colombian Cúcuta across the border, the border's low-risk/high-opportunity environment and its propensity to provide impunity turn the region into a strategic hub for transnational organized crime, a reason for multiple groups to fight for its control. Similarly, in Colombian Ocaña, the influence of the border makes it a useful case to comprehend how the "enmity" cluster matters for people's security. This area is a crucial transit zone for the trafficking routes between Colombia's heartlands and Venezuela. The stakes in controlling parts of the region are high for paramilitaries, rebels, and drug cartels alike, attracting their presence and increasing the difficulties in reducing mistrust among them.

When violent non-state groups do not have any arrangement with each other, like in the examples discussed here, the situation can be understood as falling into the "enmity" cluster, in the bottom-left corner of the continuum (see Figure 2.1). In this cluster, distrust-reducing mechanisms are absent, diminishing both mutual accountability and restraints on fighting each other. Depending upon variations in space and time, the cluster takes the form of combat, armed disputes, or tense calm. In addition to physical violence, impacts on security include fear and erosion of the social fabric necessary for citizens to jointly participate in designing security policies. As the state does not fulfill its protection responsibilities, the state-society relationship is dysfunctional. During combat situations, community members typically know how to behave to reduce insecurity because the frontlines are relatively clear. However, this is not the case under short-term arrangements that form part of the "rivalry" cluster presented in chapter 5. In long-term arrangements contained in the "friendship" cluster, citizens can follow certain rules to ensure their security, as I discuss in chapter 6. Together, these three chapters show that differentiating between distinct relationships among violent non-state groups enhances understandings of security. It reveals the manifold ways in which both objective and subjective security can be undermined and the strategies that citizens use to cope with, or reduce feelings of, insecurity.

4.1 Combat

The most prominently cited impact of violent non-state groups in combat on civilians is the infliction of (lethal) violence.[3] There may be few clear rules regarding the type of violence used against civilians,[4] yet there are rules civilians can follow, even amid violence. As outlined in chapter 2, if two or more violent non-state groups in the same territory have continually-conflicting interests and aim to eliminate each other, the community in this territory is usually aware of this "enmity." People know who is on which side, at least regarding the combatants.[5] They can decide to defect or facilitate information as collaborators.[6] Despite the risk of being detected, this helps increase protection by those with whom information is shared. Often, people do not have a choice; they may be forced to support one of the groups. Nevertheless, they know the respective group's expectations and can behave accordingly. These rules enhance certainty, or at least perceived security, and reduce mistrust among community members. With that said, people can still be affected by violence, for instance if they get caught in the crossfire, or if the group to whose rules they do not adhere punishes them. Furthermore, these rules do not protect people from long-term repercussions— the gradual disintegration of the social fabric of a society that has to cope with extreme psychological stress and trauma for decades afterward.[7]

Terror Warfare and Behavioral Rules

Combat between paramilitaries and guerrillas in Putumayo, and between the FARC and the ELN in Arauca and Apure, demonstrates how high levels of violence coincide with relatively clear behavioral rules. This can impact people psychologically and emotionally, with detrimental impacts on mental health, critical to citizen security.[8] While the logic of "enmity" of combat between paramilitaries and guerrillas provides for at least some rules of behavior, in a war between guerrillas people follow rules of behavior in a more "mechanical" way, as these rules contradict the logics of the conflict cleavages.

Counterinsurgency in Putumayo

As contextualized in the previous chapter, Putumayo faced soaring violence in the 2000s, with fighting between guerrillas and paramilitaries who supported the state's counterinsurgency. A displaced woman from Bajo Putumayo, who I met in Mocoa in 2011, recounted with horror the daily exposure to death:

> When they initiated fumigations in 2000, the first paramilitaries arrived. Oh my god, what can I tell you, the river didn't carry water anymore, but blood. They killed the poor. They killed the farmers, ordinary people. [. . .] When we lived in the countryside, the soldiers [paramilitaries] attacked the guerrillas because there were a lot of them. There were bombs—boom, boom—from one side and from the other side. They came at night and took people with them. Afterward, we thought we would have to leave the area because otherwise we would be lost. They entered houses and took people with them saying: "You have to show us

the way because we are lost. We reached this point, but we don't know where we are and you know the area!" They pulled them out of the door and the guerrillas took them with them. These were the guerrillas. On the other side, there were the soldiers. After a moment, the soldiers came: "These guys passed by and you know about this, tell us where they went!" I was scared. It is not good to live in the countryside. I told my husband that we should live in the village. Sometimes we passed by the gas pipes and they exploded. We were stuck and couldn't go to the village.[9]

Communities followed whatever rules either insurgents or paramilitaries imposed to reduce insecurity. The lines between the two contesting parties and their respective rules entailed a "logic of appropriateness" (see section 2.2). In the Colombian conflict, obeying rules does not necessarily represent ideological affinity, but rather an instrument to ensure protection.[10] The displaced woman continued: "The guerrillas already controlled the village. People did what they told them to do. Back then, there was no law [state authority]."[11] The same applied to territories where paramilitaries were prevalent.

Even though the imposition of rules by armed actors has been a constant feature of the armed conflict over decades, the situation in the 2000s still differed from the 1990s when the guerrillas were the only "authority." At that time they imposed rules, but also respected, and were at times responsive to, some of the people's concerns regarding their governance style.[12] According to the displaced woman, in the 2000s, the local community members' protests seemed to fall on deaf ears:

You found dead people everywhere. You found one here, over there you found another one. They killed each other. We thought they sent the other ones for that reason, because they were fiercer. The [guerrillas] respected us at least. I don't want to justify this because this was a thing for which there is no justification, but I remember that the guerrillas killed [state forces]. Those who didn't like them simply didn't like them. The paramilitaries were different. Back then, the paramilitaries arrived and took a house in San Miguel. They entered the house, people say a man lived there. They caught him in the village and took him to the other side of the river and there they slaughtered him. [. . .] They also caught people in broad daylight. These people didn't wait until it got dark, no, they caught them in broad daylight when the entire village community was there. On a Sunday, they caught some people and took them with them. Everyone said: "No, don't do that!," and a woman shouted: "Please, don't kill my husband!" "You also have to come with us, you are an accomplice! You know about this!" They took her with them. [. . .] Don Miguel who lived on the other side of the river [. . .] said: "Please, don't kill me, please, please!" After that, these people switched on their chainsaws and they cut him up like this and this and this! A woman screamed: "For god's sake, don't kill me! Help, help!" The man had already died because he drowned in the river. Some people picked him up, he didn't move. [. . .]

In some instances, the armed actors would change their behavior after a while, for example from throwing dead bodies into the river to letting people dig their own graves to reduce the contamination of the water. Yet it is questionable whether this is an act of response to the communities' concerns or a self-interested decision based on the groups' own need for drinking water. The continuation of the woman's account illustrates this:

For each dead person they paid 800,000 pesos (around 400 USD in 2011). The more they killed, the more money they made.[13] They threw the first ones into the river. Since in [the village] where we live the river is the only water source because there is no aqueduct—there is nothing—the police inspector said "No!" He called the paramilitaries and the entire village community joined. "What do you want?" "We would like to ask you a favor. You know our only water source is the river . . . We can't consume this water because you kill people and throw them into the river." "What do we do with the dead then?" "You shouldn't kill," a woman said. He took out the gun and killed her. These were the paramilitaries. They told us no one would give them orders whether to kill or not: "If it's my turn to kill my mother, I kill her. No one gives me orders." After that, they started to disappear people and did not throw them into the river anymore. They made them dig a hole. Then they killed them and threw them into the hole. Then they filled it in [. . .]. They killed them very terribly. They killed a man called Danilo. They killed and disappeared him. "Come with us or we kill you." Why should it be the mums' fault if their sons decide to take that path? They caught a mother: "Where are these snitchers? Where are your sons?" "I don't know." They killed her and left her. At night her sons came back.[14]

In brief, even though community members had certain rules to which to adapt their behavior in order to increase chances for survival, these rules did not emerge from a mutually reinforcing relationship between the violent non-state groups and the community (which would give rise to shadow citizenship, as I explain in chapter 2), but from the pattern of "enmity" between the two hostile sides. It is a very crude set of behavioral rules. What is more, the groups typically were not even responsive to the requests of their own group members, a measure to harden them toward their enemy. The woman's memories also point to such group-internal behavior:

> There was one paramilitary who deserted. He arrived at our door at night. "Who are you?" "I escaped from the paramilitaries, open the door!" "What happened?" "I left them, I don't want to be a paramilitary. They already made me kill two guys, I had to kill two guys! The paramilitaries were like animals! They killed them and took out pieces of meat of the leg. They opened it like this and said, you have to eat it! But I said no, I don't want to eat it. But the guy cut the meat with a knife."

At the time of the interview, in 2011, post-demobilized groups and guerrillas were still hostile to each other, but in a less deadly way. Homicide rates in Putumayo had fallen from 130.3 per 100,000 inhabitants in 2005, to 53.7 per 100,000 in 2011 (see Figure 3.1). However, the groups' cruelty in the 1990s has long-term consequences arising from what Carolyn Nordstrom calls terror warfare:

> Terror warfare is about destroying, not people, but [. . .] humanity. This form of terror is not directed at the destruction of life and limb, but against all sense of a reasonable and humane world. The strategy here is not to control people through fear of force, but through the horror of it.[15]

People's psychological state less than a decade after the atrocities still reflected the horror they experienced. Recalling information such as names, the woman's memories were marked by witnessing brutal violence inflicted on community members during fighting between paramilitaries and guerrillas. As the report of the National Commission of Reparation and Reconciliation (CNRR) on the 1999 massacre of El Tigre, Putumayo, confirms, perceived insecurity accompanied by a permanent state of fear, sadness, and nightmares due to trauma continued to be high.[16] Reducing the analysis of security during combat between armed groups to body counts and acts of displacement distorts brutal memories. Listening to the narratives of these community members gives a more holistic picture of the security impacts that outlasts dead bodies and erodes the social fabric in the long run.[17]

The need to identify behavioral rules for survival amid terror extended across the borderline to Ecuador. This country's function as a place where the ideologically opposed groups organized retaliation reinforced the notion of a clear front line between them. Yet Ecuador was more than a safe haven; it increasingly became a war theater as well. Therefore, Ecuadorians perceived Ecuador to be "contaminated" by the Colombian conflict.[18] When I spoke to a well-informed employee of a local media outlet in Sucumbíos, she explained how people had to choose between supporting one side or the other—or to flee the territory. Her account reaffirmed that community members follow the logics of "enmity" arising from the conflict cleavages—even on non-conflict territory:

> From 2001, when Plan Colombia started to operate [. . .], the province's social situation changed due to the presence of [. . .] the Colombian conflict's jurisdiction. When [. . .] the Colombian government intensified the war with the illegal groups, we felt how the conflict started to be displaced to Ecuador. In the medium term, we rarely noted the groups' movements here. They came to our country and organized acts of revenge. They confronted each other. It became a scene of violence because Colombia had always been reported as a country with many assassinations, but everything indicated that these were the groups that fled Colombia and came here. This contaminated our population and affected the peaceful coexistence which previously prevailed in this area.
>
> The Colombian conflict's expansion into our country brought many consequences. Extended violence increased and, gradually, the civilian population in the border zone ended up between a rock and a hard place: on one side the regular forces, [on the other side] the irregular forces. The civilian population that doesn't participate in this conflict ends up in between and is pressured from both sides. People start to flee or to leave their farms, their towns, or their provinces. They don't want to become involved in the conflict. There is nothing good about it. People have to change their way of life and leave their towns or farms [. . .]. Until 2006, the situation was critical, then the intensity decreased [. . .], but the issue is still latent. It's not that it disappeared and everything became normal again. The issue continues to be latent.[19]

Like in Putumayo, the long-term impacts of people's exposure to violence were evident. These included the interruption and subsequent change of people's lifestyle, and the continued fear that violence may flare up again since enmity continued to be "latent," as the interviewee described. Yet, in Ecuador, it had the additional impact of fueling xenophobia within communities because

Colombians were perceived to "contaminate" the previously "peaceful" coexistence of Ecuadorians. In these border villages, the presence of Colombians is widespread, as a result of family and commercial ties across the border. Animosity against Colombians, manifested for example in accusations of being part of one side or the other of the conflict cleavage, also eroded the social fabric of these communities, meaning that they were not able to engage collectively in activities to support each other.

Guerrilla War in Arauca and Apure

While combat activities between paramilitaries and guerrillas have received substantial scholarly attention, fewer have studied the repercussions of fighting among rebels, as was the case from 2006 to 2010 between the FARC and the ELN in Colombian Arauca and Venezuelan Apure.[20] This type of combat is less predictable, often occurring in spite of previous periods of mutual respect or collaboration. Such "contradictory combat" inflicts violence on local communities and influences citizen security on a more structural level. It overturns what until then had been a logic of appropriateness of behavioral rules that resulted from "enmity" between left-wing and right-wing groups, and from "friendship" among various left-wing groups as well as the Venezuelan leftist government. The guerrilla war unhinges people's view of such a familiar world in which combat occurs between "enemies," rather than between those who have been "friends." It also voids shared values between the two groups, values that otherwise would have reduced distrust and suspicion between them and vis-à-vis the local population. These ramifications add to the severe psychological consequences that ensue from violence.

During the first half of the 2000s, then president Uribe's Democratic Security Policy strengthened the state forces in Arauca, while the paramilitary Conquerors Bloc of Arauca weakened the guerrillas' social base. They seized control over land used for coca cultivation, over strategic parts of cocaine trafficking routes, and over financial flows, including claims for the royalties granted by the state to the local administration (see section 3.2).[21]

At that time, the population of Arauca and Apure was used to "enmity" between guerrillas and the Colombian government, and between guerrillas and paramilitaries. In this context, survival rather than ideological affinity explained people's obedience to the rebels' or paramilitaries' rules. The war itself was explained by decade-old enmity, contributing to the normalization of violence between these two fronts—even on the Venezuelan side of the border. After an incident in 2004 for example, that left six Venezuelan soldiers and an employee of a Venezuelan oil company dead, the FARC distributed propaganda pamphlets, dated September 21, 2004, among the border population. The pamphlet pointed to "paramilitaries sponsored by the Colombian government" as "provocative elements of the extreme right in the region, dedicated to destabilize the revolutionary process led by President Hugo Rafael Chávez in Venezuela" (see Figure 4.1).[22] In the case of another pamphlet, dated September 30, 2004, the FARC accused local Venezuelan authorities of abusing the population of

FUERZAS ARMADAS REVOLUCIONARIAS DE COLOMBIA - EJÉRCITO DEL PUEBLO FARC–EP.

COMUNICADO DEL DÉCIMO FRENTE A LA OPINION PÚBLICA COLOMBO-VENEZOLANA

El Estado Mayor del Décimo Frente. Hace saber a la opinión pública Colombo-Venezolana:

1. Que realizada la correspondiente investigación a nivel de todas las unidades de nuestra organización se ha podido constatar que no hubo participación de ninguna de nuestras tropas (guerrillas o milicias), en los hechos ocurridos el día viernes 17 de Septiembre en cercanías de caserío de Mate caña, donde fueron masacrados 6 soldados del ejército venezolano y una ingeniera de la compañía PDVSA los cuales se desplazaban en una canoa por el río Sarare.

2. Que en ningún momento hemos considerado a las autoridades civiles y militares de la República Bolivariana de Venezuela como nuestros enemigos, por tal motivo no son considerados objetivos militares de nuestra organización revolucionaria.

3. Se ha podido establecer por medio de informes de inteligencia la presencia de elementos provocadores de extrema derecha en el área, dedicados a desestabilizar el proceso revolucionario liderado por el presidente Hugo Rafael Chávez en Venezuela.

4. Hacemos un llamado a las comunidades del área fronteriza Colombo-Venezolana a mantener la vigilancia en los pueblos y caseríos con el fin de evitar la infiltración de los grupos paramilitares patrocinados por el gobierno colombiano y por los sectores de oposición venezolanos, que solo buscan crear el caos y la confusión entre la población.

Frontera Colombo-Venezolana, septiembre 21 del 2004

ESTADO MAYOR DEL DÉCIMO FRENTE
"GUADALUPE SALCEDO"
BLOQUE ORIENTAL FARC-EP.

CON BOLIVAR POR LA PAZ Y LA SOBERANIA NACIONAL

Figure 4.1 FARC pamphlet, September 21, 2004. Photo by Author.

FARC-controlled border territory by charging taxes to community members, "even for laughing," by assaulting farmers, and criticized operating in complicity with Colombian intelligence services "in paramilitary style."[23] Ignoring state borders, the pamphlet invited the "Colombian-Venezuelan population" to continue to support the FARC's political and military structures (see Figure 4.2).[24] While these accusations already suggested a change in the FARC's attitude—because the critique was directed toward the leftist Venezuelan authorities—the shared ideological values between the FARC and the ELN—and the Venezuelan Bolivarian Forces of Liberation's (Fuerzas Bolivarianas de Liberación-FBL)— seemed to hold and reduce distrust between the two and vis-à-vis their respective supporters, as mentioned earlier.

By the time the United Self-Defense Forces of Colombia (Autodefensas Unidas de Colombia—AUC) demobilized between 2005 and 2007, however, the two guerrillas were left with less territory, income sources, and local support, at least in Colombian Arauca. In response, they sought to co-opt new parts of the population and regain territory, leading to disputes between them.[25] With the demobilization of the AUC, the two guerrillas faced a less powerful common external threat that otherwise would have made them bond over their shared values, reducing distrust and facilitating cooperation. This development further incited inter-guerrilla dissonances.

In March 2006, the assassination of the FARC's finance boss, alias "Che" by the ELN's alias "Queca" triggered the war between the FARC and the ELN.[26] According to the FARC, the ELN's alias "La Ñeca" and "Culebro" "cowardly killed him from behind" on December 12, 2005 (see Figure 4.3).[27] As a result, the FARC criticized the crumbling of the shared values between the FARC and the ELN: "The ELN's activities against our process have no revolutionary principles and arise from the infiltration that the enemy maintains in this organization," their pamphlet read.[28] On the same document, they reiterated their commitment to those communities who support organizations that want real social change, thereby fueling divides between communities under FARC and ELN control, respectively.

When the guerrilla war was at its height toward the end of 2006 and in 2007, FARC pamphlets described ELN commanders as "dressed up as revolutionaries" or as "thugs" and encouraged the cross-border population to question the ELN's behavior (see Figures 4.4 and 4.5).[29] They also called upon people to denounce ELN misbehavior, further deepening the chasm between both sides, which aggravated mistrust and suspicion:

> The confrontation between the FARC-EP and the ELN is rooted in ideological principles. Such principles cannot be sold, but the ELN nonetheless acts as if it is a paramilitary organization. [...] We

**FUERZAS ARMADAS REVOLUCIONARIAS DE
COLOMBIA - EJERCITO DEL PUEBLO
F A R C - E P**

COMUNICADO A LA OPINIÓN PÚBLICA

Ya son más de las 450 personas que han tenido que desplazarse hacia otro lugar de la geografía nacional victimas del atropello que a diario reciben de la fuerza pública en el departamento de Arauca en cabeza del gobernador Julio Acosta Bernal, la XVIII brigada del ejercito, la policía y los grupos paramilitares instalados en esta zona por ellos mismos. A la frontera venezolana han llegado una cifra aproximada de 340 personas provenientes de los municipios de Tame, Arauquita, Fortul y Saravena que no encontraron otra salida, sino la de abandonar sus tierras y propiedades para proteger sus vidas y la de sus familias. La política de "Tierra arrasada" implantada por el fascista presidente Uribe Vélez y llevada a la práctica por los organismos de seguridad del estado, no es otra cosa más que otro experimento de los cuales han realizado en esta región del país. El ejército colombiano quiere asegurar la ejecución y la implantación del nefasto proyecto del ALCA, y para eso ha desarrollado la más implacable persecución a los dirigentes populares, al campesinado Araucano y en especial a aquellos que viven sobre la vía Arauca - Pueblo Nuevo - Tame, la cual la convirtieron en el centro de operaciones de la política de exterminio a sangre y fuego. Muchas de estas familias campesinas han abandonado sus tierras en busca de protección, otros se han incorporado a la lucha contra ese estado que les quiere arrebatar lo que con mucho sacrificio han logrado formar y muchos de ellos se encuentran en la otra trinchera esperando a que muy pronto se dé una solución definitiva al conflicto que por muchos años se viene desarrollando en nuestro país.

El otro problema lo encontramos con las autoridades venezolanas que operan en la frontera, quienes se empeñan en cobrar impuestos hasta por reírse en el área donde mantienen su influencia. En varias ocasiones han hecho incursiones militares en distintos sectores del área y en especial a los de caño Trónqueras, los Bancos, Cutufí y

Figure 4.2 FARC pamphlet, September 30, 2004. Photo by Author.

Mata de Balso; donde le dan plan sin compasión a los campesinos, saquean las fincas, roban gallinas, animales, electrodomésticos, dineros y en algunas oportunidades le echan plomo a las personas que consideran sospechosas, como lo ocurrido el día 10 de septiembre, cuando una patrulla al mando del teniente Medina Zambrano afanado por que no le habían cancelado la cuota semanal que cobra por dejar trabajar a los comerciantes de la gasolina, abrió fuego de fusiles desde el barranco frente a Puerto Contreras contra una canoa en la que viajaban civiles hiriendo a los señores Albeiro Téllez con un tiro en el pecho el cual le perforo un pulmón y al señor Duber Armando Vargas con un tiro en la pierna derecha.

En las poblaciones del Nula y el piñal los agentes de la DISIP, el DIM y PTJ, en complicidad con el DAS colombiano y escoltados por el ejercito venezolano, se han convertido en los grupos de exterminio al estilo paraco, pues ya en repetidas ocasiones han desaparecido a más de 25 personas sin dar explicación del los hechos o acusaciones, convirtiéndose en la amenaza más latente en el área fronteriza. Hechos como estos se cometen en un país donde se supone existe un gobierno amigo del pueblo y en el cual se desarrolla un proceso revolucionario encaminado al bienestar de sus habitantes y donde deberían ser las autoridades militares quienes tomaran las riendas de la consolidación de dicho proceso y ponerse al lado del pueblo, pero ocurre todo lo contrario; El pueblo repudia y rechaza a estas autoridades y prefieren nuestras orientaciones que están enfocadas al bienestar colectivo sin represión ni atropellos y al crecimiento del socialismo y la unión latinoamericana. Invitamos a toda la población colombo-venezolana a seguir apoyando nuestras estructuras políticas y militares. Nosotros seguiremos adelante con esta lucha en beneficio del pueblo y al lado del pueblo.

Septiembre 30 del 2004, frontera colombo-venezolana

ESTADO MAYOR DEL DECIMO FRENTE
"GUADALUPE SALCEDO" BLOQUE ORIENTAL
FARC-EP.

CON BOLÍVAR POR LA PAZ Y LA SOBERANÍA NACIONAL

Figure 4.2 Continued

**FUERZAS ARMADAS REVOLUCIONARIAS
DE COLOMBIA – EJÉRCITO DEL PUEBLO
F A R C - E P**

COMUNICADO A LA OPINIÓN PÚBLICA

La Columna Móvil Julio Mario Tavera del Décimo Frente de las FARC – EP, informa a los habitantes del Departamento de Arauca y la zona de frontera Colombo Venezolana lo siguiente:

1. Que los hechos que han venido aconteciendo con el ELN hacen parte de un plan de esta organización de acabar con los líderes y colaboradores de nuestro Movimiento Revolucionario.
2. Como resultado de este plan tenemos las bajas que estos han venido en forma selectiva ocasionando tanto a la militancia como a guerrilleros y milicianos de las FARC, con la modalidad de capturarlos, torturarlos y luego desaparecerlos; en algunas oportunidades no se han encontrado los cuerpos de estas victimas, como los casos de Eliécer, Rambo y Jhon, tratando de culpar a las autoridades venezolanas y al paramilitarismo.
3. Que el día 12 de Diciembre, mandos del ELN alias la Ñeca y Culebro, citaron a dialogar al Comandante Che del 45 Frente en el sitio conocido como el cruce del rió Cusay Puerto Nidia – Botalón y en el momento de despedirse de estos lo asesinaron de forma cobarde por la espalda.
4. En el caso de la zona de frontera, cuando han ocurrido estos casos hemos dado respuesta acatando las conclusiones de la Octava Conferencia Guerrillera, donde nos habla que "de acuerdo al trato que nos den, daremos."
5. Informamos y aclaramos a la población civil del Departamento de Arauca y la zona de frontera, que el accionar del ELN contra nuestro proceso no tiene principios revolucionarios y obedece al infiltramiento que el enemigo mantiene en esta organización.
6. Ratificamos nuestro compromiso con el proceso revolucionario y con el pueblo colombiano, respetando las bases de las organizaciones de izquierda que se perfilan hacia el verdadero cambio social que requiere nuestra patria.

Montañas y Sabanas de Arauca, Diciembre 20 del 2005

**COMANDO DE DIRECCION
COLUMNA MOVIL "JULIO MARIO TAVERA"
DÉCIMO FRENTE "GUADALUPE SALCEDO"**

CON BOLIVAR POR LA PAZ Y **LA SOBERANIA NACIONAL**

Figure 4.3 FARC pamphlet, December 20, 2005. Photo by Author.

**FUERZAS ARMADAS REVOLUCIONARIAS
DE COLOMBIA – EJÉRCITO DEL PUEBLO
FARC - EP**

COMUNICADO A LA OPINION PÚBLICA

La Columna Móvil Julio Mario Tavera del Décimo Frente de las FARC-EP informa a la opinión pública del área de frontera Colombo-Venezolana, lo siguiente:

1. Nos complace enormemente el contundente triunfo que nuevamente ha logrado el bravo pueblo venezolano en beneficio del proceso revolucionario que debe ser extendido a toda América. Una vez más ha quedado demostrado que el sentir de las mayorías se enrumba hacia un verdadero cambio social nutrido de bienestar a la población menos favorecida y que había sido negada mezquinamente por los gobiernos oligárquicos e imperialistas durante siglos.

2. Aunque decir que todo esta en orden seria desconocer la realidad; Esos planes diseñados por el imperialismo norteamericano de sabotear y acabar con el proceso revolucionario Bolivariano no terminan aún y han encontrado dos (2) fuertes aliados que le hacen juego a tan criminales pretensiones. Por un lado el Estado Colombiano con su más fiel servidor Uribe Vélez, quien de forma constante han enfilado sus engendros

Figure 4.4 FARC pamphlet, December 2006. Photo by Author.

paramilitares hacia Venezuela con el propósito de crear el terror, la zozobra y 'el desplazamiento en bastos sectores de la zona de frontera especialmente en los Estados de Zulia y Táchira. El cobro de vacunas, la extorsión, el chantaje y el secuestro de venezolanos ha sido su principal mecanismo de desestabilizar el proceso revolucionario y a la vez se ha convertido en su principal fuente de obtener recursos para fortalecer su aparato de guerra y narcocriminal.

3. Otro factor que ha ocasionado la incertidumbre ha sido los múltiples asesinatos que se han presentado en los últimos tiempos en sectores como los Bancos, Mate Balso, Tres Esquinas, El Nula, entre otros; protagonizados por el sicariato organizado obedeciendo órdenes de algunos mandos del Ejército de Liberación Nacional (ELN), disfrazados de revolucionarios. A estos hechos alzamos nuestra voz de protesta y aclaramos a la población que rechazamos estas acciones que solo obedecen al alto grado de infiltración por parte de los enemigos del proceso revolucionario que carcome a dicha organización.

4. Invitamos a todas las organizaciones coopetivas y comunales a fortalecer los mecanismos de fiscalización y veeduría ciudadana con el fin de evitar el desvió o despilfarro de los recursos provenientes del Estado en beneficio de las obras de desarrollo e infraestructura, ya que existen funcionarios inescrupulosos y corruptos que causan el más grave daño y desprestigio al proceso revolucionario Bolivariano.

5. Nuestro compromiso es de combatir todos estos elementos que ocasionan lesivos daños al proceso revolucionario, por eso estaremos atentos y a la ofensiva para que no solo en Venezuela, sino en toda América se pueda consolidar los cambios sociales y el bienestar del pueblo negado por los gobiernos mezquinos y corruptos.

6. Por último nos queda desearles a todo el pueblo de la frontera Colombo-Venezolana una Feliz Navidad y un Prospero Año 2007 lleno de alegría, justicia social y lucha; recordando que "En Bolívar nos encontramos todos".

COLUMNA MÓVIL "JULIO MARIO TAVERA"
DÉCIMO FRENTE "GUADALUPE SALCEDO"

LA SOBERANIA NACIONAL

Figure 4.4 Continued

invite the Colombian-Venezuelan population to determine if this behavior corresponds to a revolutionary organization and also to denounce the abuses repeatedly committed by this supposedly revolutionary organization against the Colombian-Venezuelan people [see Figure 4.4].

**FUERZAS ARMADAS REVOLUCIONARIAS
DE COLOMBIA EJERCITO DEL PUEBLO
FARC - EP**

Abril 30 del 2007

COMUNICADO A LA OPINIÓN PÚBLICA
NACIONAL E INTERNACIONAL

La Columna Movil Julio Mario Tavera del Décimo Frente de las **FARC - EP** hacemos saber a toda la opinón pública colombo venezolana lo siguiente:

1. Que no tenemos nada que ver con los hechos acontecidos el día Domingo 29 de Abril del 2007 en la población del Nula, donde resultaron heridas dos personas y tres (3) muertos entre ellos un niño de tan sola 14 años de edad, el cual se dedicaba a sus estudios.

2. Por el contrario repudiamos estos hechos realizados por los matohes del ELN que hacen presencia en esta localidad.

3. reiteramos una vez más, que la confrontación entre las FARC - EP. y el ELN es por principios ideológicos, pues estos no se venden y el ELN con sus actuaciones pareciera ser una organización paramilitar.

4. Invitamos a la población colombo venezolana a que haga un analisis, si estas actuaciones son de una organización revolucionaria y de igual forma denunciar los atropellos que reiteradamente ha venido realizando esta organizacion supestamente revolucionaria en contra del pueblo colombo venezolano.

EL PRESENTE ES DE LUCHA Y
EL FUTURO SERÁ NUESTRO

Y LA SOBERANIA NACIONAL.

Figure 4.5 FARC pamphlet, April 30, 2007. Photo by Author.

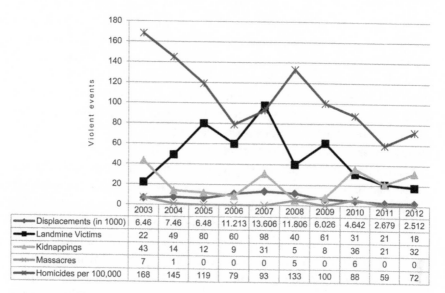

	2003	2004	2005	2006	2007	2008	2009	2010	2011	2012
Displacements (in 1000)	6.46	7.46	6.48	11.213	13.606	11.806	6.026	4.642	2.679	2.512
Landmine Victims	22	49	80	60	98	40	61	31	21	18
Kidnappings	43	14	12	9	31	5	8	36	21	32
Massacres	7	1	0	0	0	5	0	6	0	0
Homicides per 100,000	168	145	119	79	93	133	100	88	59	72

Figure 4.6 Violent events, Arauca, Colombia, 2003–2012. Source: Data based on Sistema de Alertas Tempranas 2009, 4; Observación y Solidaridad con Arauca OBSAR 2011, 12–13; and Vicepresidencia 2008.

As these pamphlets addressed to the cross-border population attest, the FARC-ELN war did not stop at the border. The rebels also fought each other on the Venezuelan side of River Arauca, in Apure, where FBL presence made the disputes among these armed groups even more complex (see section 3.2). The longevity of the guerrilla war can be partly attributed to the role of the two neighboring governments.[30] After 2007, the ELN strengthened its presence by collaborating with the Colombian state forces in Arauca.[31] Allegedly, they also colluded with the Venezuelan local and national authorities to counter the militarily superior FARC.[32] By 2009, the ELN had partly ousted the FARC in Apure.[33]

The guerrilla war that lasted until 2010 sparked a humanitarian crisis.[34] As Figure 4.6 shows, the numbers of displacements, land mine victims, and kidnappings in Arauca increased when the FARC and the ELN went to war and decreased only in 2010, once hostilities were over. When adding the killings that occurred as a result of what could be described as the extended guerrilla war on the Venezuelan side of the border, the crisis assumes even more concerning dimensions. The numbers suggest that massacres declined due to the paramilitaries' demobilization. Between 2006 and 2010, more people were displaced than between 2001 and 2003, the most brutal years of the paramilitary incursion in Arauca.[35]

People's memories of violence during that time add sobering color to these dark statistics. My interviewees referred to the period between 2007 and

2009 as the most violent years they had ever experienced.[36] In Venezuelan Guasdualito, for instance, six to eight people were supposedly killed per day in violent disputes, "even in front of the police station," as one of my interviewees recalled.[37] According to Guasdualito residents who lived in the area between 2007 and 2009, the victims were seldom locals; they mostly came from "outside."[38] This is in line with reports from the Colombian Ombudsman's Office, which state that many Colombians who fled to the Venezuelan side were killed there because the deadly disputes extended to that side.[39]

Notwithstanding the devastating violence arising from the guerrilla war, people had some guidance on how to behave in order to fulfill the rebels' expectations. The two groups established zones of influence, conducted censuses, and exerted social control.[40] As was the case during the fighting between the FARC and the paramilitaries in Putumayo, living in a FARC-influenced zone meant abiding by their rules and becoming their supporters. Living in an ELN-influenced zone meant doing the same for the ELN. Due to the guerrillas' presence in Arauca over decades, the communities internalized *their* rules rather than state-imposed ones as the norm. In 2012, residents of a remote village in Arauca that I could only access via the border river told me that guerrillas usually came and ask for favors, such as water. In this case, the villagers had to provide them with water.[41] In another village, a farmer explained: "If you respect them, they respect you."[42] Many residents of Arauca's border zone stated they were safe "as long as we behave well."[43]

One might conclude that following rebel-imposed behavioral rules was a better way to maximize chances for survival than to wait for the state to fulfill its protection responsibilities. Although the activities of the guerrillas led to the region's militarization, help from the state to alleviate the communities' suffering in some areas never materialized, and was insufficient in others. Between 2006 and 2011, the Colombian Ombudsman's Office issued four risk reports that were converted into Early Warnings,[44] more than in any other region in the same period, and yet violence continued.[45] In fact, the government's more-or-less tacit siding with the ELN fueled violence and abuse against the local population,[46] provoking the communities' mistrust of state institutions, their isolation from the state, and even stronger alignment with non-state actors.

Even though it was possible to follow rules of behavior, the guerrilla war upset the logic of what I term "friendship" among rebels (see chapter 2). The similar ideological values shared by the FARC and the ELN no longer yielded a stable long-term arrangement between the two groups. In such cases, as I discuss in chapter 6, the armed groups and communities may develop a mutually reinforcing relationship, giving rise to "shadow citizenship," which provides community members with rules of behavior they can adapt to—and even negotiate at times. In the context of the guerrilla war, despite the persistence of certain shared values between the rebels, these rules were no longer available. This unusual situation gave further reason for mistrust, suspicion, and paranoia.

The guerrilla war ended in 2010,[47] but violence, poverty, and institutional deficiencies persisted. Fumigations and manual eradication of coca plantations also continued to negatively affect the livelihoods of local farmers.[48] In June and July 2012, the FARC increased attacks in Arauca. I spoke to locals about the hostile activities during my visit to the region in the following months of 2012. They argued that the FARC thought this would place them in a position of strength when entering the peace talks in October 2012. At the time of my return to Arauca in 2016, it continued to be among the three Colombian departments with the highest homicide rates.[49] The civilian population was still affected by kidnappings, recruitment of minors, anti-personnel mines, and forced displacement.[50]

Likewise, the psychological impacts of the war persisted. Indeed, these impacts may have endured even more intensely than in the context of armed combat between left-wing and right-wing groups. As mentioned above, in addition to physical harm, this form of inter-group violence calls into question the established norms and values that informed people's logic of appropriate behavior to ensure survival in war previously. Nordstrom argues that "identity, self, and personhood, as well as physical bodies, are strategic targets of war."[51] In the aftermath of violence, community members often suffer post-traumatic stress disorder. According to a study by Doctors without Borders in Colombia, these people have a higher risk of committing suicide due to the psycho-emotional consequences of the trauma they have witnessed and experienced.[52] Even after the guerrilla war was over (but armed conflict continued), Arauca was the Colombian department with the fourth highest suicide rate, at 5.6 suicides per 100,000 inhabitants in 2011, well over the national rate of 4.1. This included a disproportionately high rate among adolescents.[53] Over the course of a single week that I spent in Arauca in 2012, for example, there were three suicides and another attempted suicide, two of which were committed by minors.[54] These high suicide rates appear to be related to the violence of the guerrilla war these minors witnessed.[55] In Nordstrom's words, these young personhoods were destroyed by the terror they endured, terror that had no explanation based on previous conceptions of norms of survival and the defined enemy.

Exploring post-guerrilla war perceptions of security suggests that, when frontlines are less clear, the rules disappear, and with them the logic of appropriateness on which the rules are based. This increases uncertainty, which in return reduces perceived security as it constitutes a negatively perceived state of affairs (see section 2.2). Locals were unable to identify which actors were present: the same groups operated under changing labels in Arauca's urban spaces, including as Águilas Negras.[56] In a small village in the Arauquita municipality of Arauca, for example, the lines between the two contesting groups were clear during the guerrilla war. In 2012, unknown post-demobilized groups fueled uncertainty. When I met with about twenty women from the village in 2012, they lamented that little had changed in the village since 2007. The women were convinced that public order was the same, if not worse. This perception contradicts "observables" of security: homicide rates in Arauquita were 61 per 100,000 in 2007 and 38 per 100,000 in 2011.[57] The women had not heard a gunfight for a while; only the insurgent's bombs targeted against the electricity towers, which seemed to worry them little. Similarly, combat between guerrillas and the state forces was a form of risk that people had learned to live with. When I accompanied a humanitarian mission to meet communities located along the River Arauca that marks the border with Venezuela, people told us that lately they had not been bothered very much by fighting between the state forces and the guerrillas. This perception persisted, despite the fact that half an hour later there was a clash between the Colombian military and the rebels in the neighboring village.

Rather than killings or clashes with state forces, changes in the presence of violent non-state groups shaped the women's perception of worsening public order. They explained with concern that strangers had recently come to the village and intimidated them. Another group of women shared this worry with me independently as well. They also stated that unknown armed men dressed as civilians had entered the village and threatened adults and the youth.[58] Reportedly, the armed men declared they disliked seeing people in public spaces after sunset. Shops closed at six in the evening because people were scared. Anonymous threatening pamphlets were seen in the streets. When I asked what they had done about this, the women replied: "We don't get involved!" This is different from statements referring to how people adapted to the rebels' rule in earlier years, such as "behaving well" or "showing respect." The unease arising from the post-demobilized groups' presence was also obvious in the graffiti that spread in Arauca. The guerrillas marked their territory, a silent, yet omnipresent reminder of the constant fear that I felt myself there (see Figure 4.7). According to locals, graffiti had not been that widespread in earlier years.

There were some rules on what *not* to do that arose due to the mistrust between guerrillas and these new groups. For example, in the city of Arauca, I went to buy rubber boots because we were going to take a boat trip that would be preceded by an hour's walk on foot through a jungle area to visit rural communities without access roads. I was going to pick black boots, the only available color in my size, but my contact told me not to buy them—guerrilla militias wear black boots. Had I worn them, people might have identified me as guerrilla collaborator.

Figure 4.7 Guerrilla graffiti in Arauca, Colombia, 2012. Photos by Author.

Besides such minor points regarding taboo behavior, from 2012, when the new groups' identities and expectations were not clear, it was difficult to know how to behave appropriately or show respect. The women sadly accepted they lacked previously available protection. The guerrilla militias who used to protect farms supposedly fled to Venezuela to reorganize against the new groups. The nature of the security threats and the strategies to avoid them were less obvious than during the guerrilla war, and therefore, the only applicable rule was not to be associated with anyone's side—not to get involved. As I discuss in more detail in chapter 5, such an avoidance strategy that people resort to when behavioral rules are ambiguous further contributes to general mistrust, undermining collective action based on solidarity.

Inevitable Death and Coping

Where violence inflicts suffering on local communities, people adopt coping strategies. This is particularly evident in the context of the "enmity" cluster. Coping strategies help deal with repercussions on subjective citizen security under rule noncompliance *and* under compliance because they mitigate fear and (perceptions of) insecurity when death is perceived to be inevitable. Murder victims in the Saravena municipality in Arauca, for example, were said to be ELN or FARC collaborators, killed to eliminate the enemy's social base.[59] It does not matter whether or not these victims complied with rules. Rather, one distances oneself from such murders by convincing oneself to be different to the victim, in this case, by not collaborating with the groups.

The logics of enmity in the context of combat activities of armed groups are conducive to just-world thinking to cope with, or make sense of, the violence that surrounds people. According to psychologist Melvin Lerner, we try to tell ourselves that those who do wrong will pay for it at some point while good deeds will be rewarded.[60] Hannah Arendt imagines what bystanders must have thought about the events that took place during the Holocaust: "What crimes must these people have committed that such things were done to them!"[61] Similarly, in Putumayo, the displaced woman, about whom I write above, justified extreme violence in the 2000s during fighting between paramilitaries and guerrillas with the victim's viciousness:

> There were bad people. I will tell you about a woman and her children. They were all killed because she was very bad. But we realized this only now, we didn't know what sort of people we were living with, with very bad people. Someone told us that she had workers with her, to work for her, and she made them work very hard. Afterward, she didn't pay them. She took them away and killed them. Behind her house she had a huge graveyard with all the dead workers . . . when these people came, they started to investigate and when they found out about it, they killed her sons, one by one. She saved herself because she left, but this shows that there are heartless people, bad people. They also killed another woman. They dragged her body right through the village, but this was also because they investigated her life and found out that she was a very bad person. Therefore they took her. Now of course these women were bad, but there are also examples of good people who were killed.[62]

The bad-people-versus-good-people dichotomy, which stood out in many of my interviews in Putumayo and Arauca, reflects the process of Othering that warring parties themselves engage in when they see each other as enemies, as in the "enmity" cluster. Being constantly exposed to these enmity logics and having to internalize them in order to survive makes such thinking plausible for understanding violence and death among civilians as well—not just for justifying one's own involvement in the elimination of the Other. "'Just world thinking' may become more tempting as the world [. . .] become[s] more arbitrary," notes David Keen, due to "the allure of certainty in uncertain times."[63] The killings of the mother and all her children indeed appear to be arbitrary. They seem to be more tolerable when victims are "bad people." The normalization of brutality can make it appear to be deserved.[64] Just-world thinking therefore helps people cope with the situation: it reduces fear and perceptions of insecurity because being "good" reduces the likelihood of being killed. This behavior is also a form of "lifeboat ethics." Like Nancy Scheper-Hughes's description of Brazilian women who do not let themselves feel any affection for their dying children because they have high expectations that the child may die in infancy,[65] in these communities people detach themselves by thinking their neighbors, acquaintances, or others who are killed were doomed to die. People do not feel pity for them.

Violent non-state groups can adopt a similar just-world rationale, or Othering, to justify the killings of members belonging to specific societal groups. While this can make people outside the specific societal group feel more secure, it undermines the security of that group. In his reflections on Oedipus, René Girard notes that societies living in violence identify a scapegoat responsible for any ill they experience.[66] Violent non-state groups seek scapegoats for harm inflicted against them and hence punish marginalized groups, for instance, for collaborating with the enemy, as the following example of the indigenous Awá in Nariño shows.

The year 2007 was one of extreme hostility between the FARC and the ELN in Nariño, displacing more than 35,000 people.[67] While the guerrilla war ended in 2009 in Nariño, subsequent fighting broke out between insurgents and post-demobilized groups.[68] In 2011, the FARC massacred Awá indigenous people in the Ricaurte municipality, who were painted as collaborators with the FARC's adversaries.[69] At the same time, the Awá repeatedly pointed to disappearances and abuses committed by the post-demobilized groups, who accused the Awá of being guerrilla collaborators. According to an Awá leader from Pasto:

[the Awá] go to the village and on the way they meet [the BACRIM]. Then they start to accuse them. Just because you have long hair and walk around with boots you are already considered a guerrilla member. This kind of stigmatization is common among the [Awá] communities and families.[70]

The singling out of societal groups as scapegoats makes these groups vulnerable and contributes to the fragmentation of society: the contesting groups and their respective supporters, as well as further marginalized groups such as indigenous people, all distrust each other. As I show in the following chapter, this is different from cases with short-term arrangements where mistrust *omnium contra omnes* erodes the social fabric even within groups, leading to the isolation of individuals rather than of groups.

I identified another coping strategy applicable in situations of indiscriminate, unavoidable violence. It is similar to what Caroline Moser and Cathy McIlwaine call a conciliation strategy through religion, by praying for victimizers or victims.[71] Adhering to rules imposed by the armed groups facilitates a perception of being able to protect oneself, but when violence occurs it is often ascribed to God's plan or to fate. Trusting in God is a common "security measure," as plenty of anecdotal evidence shows. When I told an interviewee that I was not comfortable crossing one of the border bridges between Venezuela and Colombia alone after sunset as he suggested, he replied: "You won't be alone, God will be with you!"[72] Or, as an interviewee in Puerto Asís, Putumayo, put it when I asked if it would not be too risky to visit a combat zone: "If it happens, it happens anyway!"[73] Indeed, violence may happen anytime, and to anyone. For example, reports by the Ombudsman's Office on Arauca in 2009 list the killings of a father with his son, several children, and an underage girl who was four months pregnant as victims of the armed conflict.[74] Putting faith in a divine external locus of control allows an individual the relief of not being accountable for his or her own actions, particularly when death and violence can be random and indiscriminate. When there are no actions that can guarantee safety, people turn to the only thing that seems constant: a deity who protects.

4.2 Armed Disputes

In Colombia and in the border zones of Ecuador and Venezuela influenced by conflict in Colombia, armed disputes spread after the AUC's demobilization. With the reconfiguration of new illegal armed structures, the groups modified their dispute strategies to a more covert way of operating in urban areas. This enabled them to enhance efficiency in exerting social control, dominate illegal activities, and interfere in politics.[75] Contrary to large-scale violence such as massacres in combat, in urban areas violent non-state groups use selective violence against their adversaries. In civil war settings, civilians are not always easily distinguishable from combatants, for example when civilians are informants and collaborators of the conflict parties.[76] In areas with armed disputes, the dividing lines between bystanders and violent non-state groups are even more blurred, making uncertainty more pervasive than in combat. Situations of armed disputes resonate with Mary Kaldor's "new wars," where the distinctions between "legitimate bearer of arms and the non-combatant" break down because "the monopoly of organized violence is eroded from below by privatization."[77] Without knowing who is trustworthy, people perceive themselves to be "potential victims."[78]

Ambiguity amid Enmity

Similar to combat that prevails in rural areas, in armed disputes more prevalent in urban environments people can distinguish between different violent non-state groups, but the lines between the groups and bystanders are more diffuse (see section 2.1). This fuels mistrust and uncertainty among the local population, as the case of the Venezuelan village of Rubio in Táchira demonstrates. Because it is a strategic transit point for the drug trafficking route from Colombia to the ports of Valencia and La Guajira, multiple violent non-state groups have an interest in controlling the village.[79] Both post-demobilized groups and the ELN were present and made their identities explicitly known to the local community. In 2008 for example, the post-demobilized groups distributed pamphlets in the village, calling on the residents of Rubio to stick to their rules, including a curfew. As a consequence, no one left their house at night for over two weeks, as if the curfew had been officially imposed.[80] As for the guerrillas, in Rubio between 1 P.M. and 4 P.M. everyone listened on 96.7 FM to "Antorcha Stereo," the ELN's radio station, through which the group informed locals about acceptable behavior.[81]

The ELN and paramilitary successors employed selective violence in Rubio to attack each other and to enforce the population's compliance. The following account of a Rubio resident in 2012 illustrates how members of the ELN, of the paramilitary successors, and bystanders became intertwined, fueling mistrust:

> In Rubio three taxi drivers were killed within one month. From the way in which they were killed, they had to be [supporters of the] paramilitaries.[82] [The ELN] had a meeting in the mountainous zone in Venezuela and gathered the presidents of the taxi companies. They told them that they knew there were taxi drivers who transported the *paracos* to collect extortion money [. . .].[83] They told them to remove these people from here because otherwise . . . And that, if things continued like this, they shouldn't pay extortion money because this would strengthen [the paramilitaries]. The ELN gave them a deadline of three months. After these three months, they came down [from the mountains] and the president of this particular [taxi] company [. . .] was so frightened that he didn't say anything to them. The other taxi companies indeed were "purified." Since [. . .] the ELN was not the owner of the cars, they told him: "You are suspended and you are not allowed to take out the car!" The man got scared and, indeed, three taxi drivers were killed within one month. It was the ELN. They killed those who supported the paramilitaries. These taxi drivers supported the paramilitaries and therefore the ELN came down [from the mountains] and tried to weaken them.[84]

Some taxi drivers were drawn into the conflict by aiding the paramilitary successors. Had they refused to do so, they could have killed them. Taxi drivers were also used to gather intelligence.[85] When getting into a taxi, people did not know whether they were dealing with a supporter of the paramilitary successors and, if so, whether this support was voluntary or forced. In these armed disputes in Rubio, the identities of the two antagonists were clear, allowing people to adhere to certain rules, as is the case in combat in rural zones.

Yet the uncertainty regarding who among the civilian population was involved in their activities and who was not muddied these rules. This example resonates with Edelberto Torres-Rivas's account of life under military dictatorships in Latin America, which demonstrates that uncertainty is strong for individuals experiencing the arbitrariness of violence:

> In the life of those whose daily life is far from politics [. . .] it is trau-
> matic to have to accustom oneself to living with extraordinary and ab-
> normal conditions of pain and fear, insecurity and lack of confidence.
> It is what O'Donnell has called the "normalization of the abnormal"
> and appears in those conditions where a climate of generalized uncer-
> tainty prevails: in other words, a climate that affects all levels of society.
> [. . .] The rules of the game are not known or, when they are known, are
> ignored by the officials of public order.[86]

Impeding Bystanding and Blaming the Victim

Situations in which one violent non-state group disputes another's preponder-ance contribute to general mistrust among the population because the lines between bystanders and participants are not clear. Ongoing armed disputes have a similar influence, but in these situations, exposure to violence is less evi-dent. Referring to civil war contexts, Stathis Kalyvas contends that the form of violence—discriminate or selective—depends on the extent to which groups control contested territory.[87] Citizens are more severely affected by indiscrim-inate violence when one group starts to dispute the preponderance of another than when both groups are in a continuing disagreement.[88] Francisco Gutiérrez Sanín made similar points, illustrating them with the case of the Colombian paramilitaries. Other scholars have specifically studied the operations of Colombian post-demobilized groups in urban areas, where a similar logic ap-plied.[89] I complement these scholars' arguments mostly focused on "hard" se-curity to also draw attention to the repercussions of these situations on people's perceptions of security. Where a dispute has just broken out, people face more uncertainty regarding appropriate behavior. It is unclear whether defection from the first group is advisable because the new balance of power has not yet been established. The first group might prevail over the intruder. Furthermore, since the intruder's presence is recent, it may not yet have communicated its rules, producing uncertainty among community members and fear of not meeting the group's expectations.

The case of Cúcuta illustrates this point. Uncertainty surrounded Cúcuta in 2011 when the Urabeños began to dispute the Rastrojos' preponderance in the town. According to a high-ranking police official in Cúcuta, the Rastrojos had "virtually achieved the imposition of their hegemony, their law, in Cúcuta because they penetrated many sectors through corruption."[90] Yet in 2010, they were increasingly weakened by the capture of some of their leaders. The Urabeños used this window of opportunity. In 2011, they re-entered Cúcuta to dispute the Rastrojos' preponderance in this town and across the border in Ureña and San Antonio de Táchira. The police official provided a startling description of the constellation of groups in Cúcuta:

> Normally, [the Rastrojos and Urabeños] don't form alliances. Initially, they negotiate for money, to sell the territory the way it had been done before, or they fight for it by fire and sword. What happens here is a territorial dispute [. . .]. Here, we have the Rastrojos. This is a reality that is impossible to hide. They maintained hegemony more or less until last year. They managed to establish themselves [. . .]. Until May last year, they were in charge. They were the only ones and had the complete monopoly of everything: drugs, micro-extortion, homicides [. . .]. When we started to hit the Rastrojos, to capture the leaders, and to expose the leaders, some very important operations led to some of them going to prison. This produced a breakdown of their structure [. . .]. The Urabeños took advantage of this situation. They don't come to negotiate or to micro-distribute. They [. . .] try to take over the business because the others resist them. When the Rastrojos became even weaker and the leaders were captured, the [Rastrojos members] remained a long time without payment. They didn't pay them because they lost the capacity to pay the "grass root criminals." Many of those who were unpaid defected to the Urabeños because another boss came who told them: "I'll pay you, come and work with me!" This caused a big dispute. Here, they don't divide the business between themselves. With the pure drug business they do [. . .].[91] This does not happen here. Here, territorial disputes occur, and each one wants to stay in their space to stay active in the irregular activities.[92]

He continued, claiming that the Rastrojos and the Urabeños

> are generators of violence because one of the most evident forms in which the dispute in Cúcuta takes shape is murder. This phenomenon stemming from organized crime, from criminal groups, and from drug traffickers affects security.[93]

Sixty-eight homicides were recorded between January and April 2012. As many occurred in public spaces, everyone felt like a potential victim. During my stays in Cúcuta in 2011 and 2012, several people were killed on the much-used international bridge that connects Colombia to Venezuela, which I crossed several times. Other murders were committed at the popular Malecón, a promenade along the river where many Cucuteños spend their evenings or weekends. In places like this, anyone can get caught in the crossfire.

Since in urban areas armed actors operate in plain clothes rather than in uniform, and sometimes task community members with doing work for them, it is hard to know whether one is dealing with people related to violent non-state groups or not, fueling general mistrust. Striving for territorial and social control, the Urabeños killed the Rastrojos' informants and messengers who were hardly distinguishable from innocent bystanders. As a civil society leader from Cúcuta explained, these killings served to impose their own informant network:

> For the last two months [as of October 2011], the Rastrojos have permanently controlled the Hill of the Cross.[94] But [the Urabeños] are coming. The week before last week they killed three security guards, people who keep watch in the zone. These killings were related to a common phenomenon here; the armed groups have always had their great allies at night. They are young boys who go out with a whistle on the streets and signal to let people know that there is someone watching. Usually those in this zone belong to the Rastrojos, and now they eliminated the boys. They killed them. The Urabeños killed them; the Urabeños are already coming in. They are already transforming the conflict in these sectors.[95]

Soaring homicide rates produce fear, disintegrating intra-community relations and the state-society relationship. Referring to the Guatemalan context, Linda Green notes:

> Fear destabilizes social relations by driving a wedge of distrust within families, between neighbors, among friends. Fear divides communities through suspicion and apprehension not only of strangers but of each other. Fear thrives on ambiguities. Denunciations, gossip, innuendos, and rumors of death lists create a climate of suspicion. No one can be sure who is who.[96]

Cucuteños faced uncertainty regarding the groups' modus operandi in their territory. Before 2011, the Rastrojos dominated Cúcuta. During that time, I carried out over forty interviews in Cúcuta. Interviewees belonged to different stake-holder groups such as displaced people, priests, community leaders, academics, and local authorities, including the police.[97] They all knew about the Rastrojos' presence and power in the city, not least because the local newspaper regularly reported incidents involving the Rastrojos. When the Urabeños attempted to gain control, the situation became confusing for Cucuteños because it was not clear which group would prevail and hence whose rules should be followed. Both the previously preponderant and the newly present group extorted money from locals, creating a dilemma of who to pay. If people paid both, one of the groups could have punished them for having paid the other one. If they only paid one group, the other group could have punished them for not having paid. Generally, the groups charged small amounts of money, 1,000 pesos (0.50 USD in 2011) per *pimpina* (gasoline canister), but this charge was levied on a large number of people. This micro-extortion amounts to substantial profit each day, given the quantity of gasoline that crossed the border. Between Táchira and Norte de Santander, an estimated 1.2 to 2.7 million liters, and along the entire border an estimated 4.1 million liters, were smuggled every day.[98]

This is not unique to Cúcuta. In Maicao in La Guajira, the Rastrojos disputed the Urabeños' preponderance in 2010. They killed the Urabeño leader in charge of extortion. The victims of extortion feared revenge from the Urabeños on all those who were reluctant to pay extortion, as this could have been interpreted as collaborating with the Rastrojos.[99]

Situations like these are very fluid. It takes time for the power constellation to become apparent. People do not know whether the situation will evolve into full "enmity," or whether the previously preponderant group or the newly pre-sent group will prevail, making it difficult to assess whose rules to adhere to so as to reduce insecurity. The dispute between the Rastrojos and the Urabeños was also advantageous for third groups that entered the territory to pursue their own interests, increasing fear among the local population who did not yet know what to expect from these groups. The continuation of the interview with the high-ranking police official in Cúcuta illustrates this:

> When the Rastrojos began to lose strength, the Urabeños arrived. We, the police,[...] have managed to trace them since they arrived. Last year [...] we inflicted an important blow on the Urabeños with Operation Safari. Again, we weakened them [. . .]. This is when the other organi-zations emerged, the Nueva Generación and the Bloque de Fronteras. Why do they emerge? Because there is a large unemployed workforce, but a workforce qualified to commit crimes, not to do other things. These organizations then engaged in territorial disputes with each other [. . .]. After the blow on the Urabeños, this group decided to leave, but

those who brought the Urabeños here are a bunch of ex-paramilitaries in prison. These ex-paramilitaries don't want to leave because they are from this territory and therefore want to stay, even though they came united with the Urabeños. The Urabeños say: "No, we lost this battle, this is very difficult. We leave as a group!," but the others say: "No, how can you go and leave us alone?" These ones stay and say: "We will use another name, Autodefensas de Norte de Santander." [. . .] The other group called Bloque de Fronteras that I mentioned before emerged from all the "orphans" of the two groups: of the Rastrojos and the Urabeños. They simply thought, "Okay, our bosses left, we are going to join forces and continue to commit crimes." In the end, they don't know anything else but to commit crimes.[100]

As the police official argued, it was also unclear whether local gangs would evolve into more serious violent non-state groups:

[Besides the right-wing groups,] some drug-traffickers dare to establish themselves on their own. They say: "We are going to send drugs directly. We are going to use the route through Venezuela. [. . .] We won't tell anyone about it. We think we don't need anyone. We are capable of doing this on our own. We don't have to coordinate with anyone." Given that they are criminals, [. . .] they know very well how to do this business. However, when other traffickers steal their drugs, they easily end up being killed because they haven't told the [post-demobilized] groups about it who otherwise would protect them. If they are drug traffickers from here, the [post-demobilized groups] extort money from them. They pressure them in order to get a share of the deal.[101]

Most people in the community know members of such local groups: a son, cousin, friend, or neighbor. Some decide to support them because they are close to them, while others distance themselves, even from relatives, because they are aware of the potential retaliation by the post-demobilized groups. This erodes the social fabric. It isolates people from each other, preventing a sense of community.

The absence of clear rules for people due to the uncertainty about the evolving power structures of old and new violent non-state groups helps explain why the phenomenon of victim blaming is a means to make sense of such a situation, and helps increase people's *perceived* security.[102] People create their own behavioral rule: not to get involved. Becoming a victim must be the victim's fault because he or she did not stick to this rule. This is similar to just-world thinking that I have identified in contexts of combat where victims are also seen to deserve death or punishment. However, while in combat situations people are seen to deserve death due to their Otherness, following the logics of the enmity between the armed actors, in situations of disputes over preponderance these logics become void. Inculpating the victim helps reaffirm the self-imposed rule of not getting involved, and thus increases certainty by pointing out that the victim did not comply with the rules. People are not considered to be genuinely "bad" like in combat situations, but to have done something incorrectly, not following the rules. It creates the sense of reducing one's own vulnerability to being victimized because one can comply with the rule to ensure security.[103] To some extent, this is a fallacy, of course. As I mention above, even passive bystanders can easily become targeted because the lines between them and those involved are blurred. It is for this reason that victim blaming can be seen as a coping mechanism to enhance perceived security, rather than constituting a strategy to increase the level of people's de facto, or observed, security.

My interviews in Cúcuta, for example, revealed how victim blaming served to cope with muddied lines between armed actors and bystanders. People tended to attribute victimization to the victim's involvement in illicit activities. The police official's account succinctly captures these views:

ME: *Do homicides only occur among the groups?*

POLICE OFFICIAL: This is what people tend to say. You can ask whoever you want . . . it's normal to associate homicides with the armed groups . . . of course, people also know about homicides due to quarrels or an assault, but these types of killings are seen to be the minority. Usually, people immediately connect them with the armed actors. . . It's not that they tolerate homicides, but they say: "He was involved in stories!" Most of [the homicides] are the product of the BACRIM.[104] I don't justify these deaths. I just say that many of the homicides—a big percentage—85 percent in Cúcuta, are related to confrontations between BACRIM.

In circumstances where the behavioral rules of "enmity" fade away, and neither the state nor a non-state actor provide rules that people might follow to stay safe, victim blaming makes people feel more secure. It helps people distance themselves from acts of victimization by dismissing them as something internal to the illicit groups. In people's eyes, this in turn increases control over their own destiny by not getting involved, which ultimately serves as a mechanism to cope with ambiguity and uncertainty.

4.3 Tense Calm

Instead of constant bloodshed, as conflict is often portrayed by the media, the kinds of violence I encountered while in the field were sporadic and short-lived, interspersed with long periods of what people described as tense calm. This tense calm is particularly impactful when forming part of the cycle of conflict dynamics that exists when armed groups operate as "enemies." Periods of tense calm are less violent than phases of combat or armed disputes, but violence may erupt again at any time.

Nordstrom and Robben call this the "uncertainty of violent events." As I experienced myself as a fieldworker, the unpredictability of violence spreads an alarming sense of unease that is impossible to capture in observable measures of security (see Epilogue).[105]

In Cúcuta, the periods of tense calm between the killings generated by the dispute between the Urabeños and the Rastrojos in 2011 and 2012 lasted only a few days. There was a wave of violence in June and July 2011: in less than three weeks, sixteen people were killed. After this wave of killings, the city was calm. It was a tense calm, though: state forces had not defeated the groups, nor was there a truce between them.[106] The armed groups were still present, devoid of any arrangement, manifested by graffiti with written threats against each other in several locations of Cúcuta. For Cucuteños, violence could erupt again anytime and anywhere. The situation was similar when I visited Cúcuta in October 2011. A member of the church therefore whispered to me ominously: "We expect a bloodbath, Anita."[107]

The Premonition of Violence

In Ocaña, the tense calm lasted from January until April 2012. Historically a zone of transit and a clandestine operation center for the FARC, the ELN, the EPL, the paramilitaries, and later the Rastrojos, the Urabeños, and the Paisas, Ocaña has been exposed to conflict dynamics for decades. When I talked to a senior local government official in Ocaña in April 2012, he confirmed that no homicide had been reported since January 2012. During our conversation, he tried to convince me that four months without homicides was an indicator of an improvement in Ocaña's security situation. Given the number of times he looked out of the window of his small office absorbed in thought, I wonder if he was in fact trying to convince himself rather than me. According to him, the fact that people were still afraid to go out in public would be related to culture and a problem of public order, that is, common crime—not to the illicit drugs business or the armed conflict. However, he did not trust the calmness:

OFFICIAL: [The state forces] say that in Ocaña there is complete calmness. As you can see, this is true: [...] since 1 January, and we are talking today on 25 April, in a region where we have a conflict, we don't have any deaths caused by homicide [...] in the Ocaña municipality. Both in the urban and in the rural sector [...]. Last year by this time we already had thirteen. We have tried to demand a lot from the public forces regarding their operations, their strategies, the way they search people, they ask for their documents to identify the suspects. All of this has contributed to reducing criminality [...]. We haven't had homicides again [...]. Four months without homicides, this has been a big achievement for us. [...] But it also leaves a feeling of ... I mean, if there are criminal bands, why would they suddenly be respectful of the authorities...? There also could be some kind of nonaggression pact, or they don't want to damage the municipality because it is a strategic point for movements—it serves them ... I have a couple of hypotheses in mind. One doesn't know if there is presence [of groups] or if there isn't, or if this is complete calmness. ... Sometimes it worries me that I don't know at what moment this all might explode and that I don't know what is all going on underneath the surface. The perception that we have is that something complex might happen. [...] It is a *tense calm* because one doesn't know ... with much tranquillity, and thanks to God, it is quiet ... there aren't deaths ... but this is a *tense calm*. We really hope it is true that things are getting better.

ME: *Is it true that people stay home at night [...]?*

OFFICIAL: [...] In this region we have always lived in conflict [...]. There haven't been any homicides, but people look after themselves [...]. They avoid going out at night. This is not a town with nightlife. It also isn't our culture [...]. Here, people come home, watch the news, their favorite program, and then they go to sleep to get up early to go to work [...]. This is a cultural issue and there is also the issue of public order. One has to take certain precautions.[108]

Green calls this tense calm in the Guatemalan civil war context an "eerie calm": "an unease that lies just below the surface of everyday life."[109] This is expressed in a personal experience the above government official shared with me: "114 days without homicides in the town, but there is an anxiety. [...] Every day I receive messages on my mobile phone: 'Prepare yourselves, they will arrive!'"[110]

Other residents of Ocaña expressed similar feelings of unease about this calm. In fact, a human rights defender stated even more directly that people suspected something bad was going to happen:

> The [illicit] drug business has contributed to a relative calm in this zone here, but those people who act against the business interests have to leave the region. Many of them have been killed [...]. Many of us speak

out against this, but they always silence us with threats. Yes, we also had deaths, but in the last three years, they haven't killed any of our leaders. Nevertheless, we are scared because, lately, the police have taken their job of providing us protection [due to the death threats] much more seriously than usually. But they don't tell us why. We suspect that something is happening . . . Another strange thing happened: I received a note of a supposed complaint that I made against these [armed] groups. In this note, they respond to this supposed complaint that I never made—we [human rights defenders] would never complain to the groups directly ourselves. It seems like someone leaked information [. . .]. I have talked to all the social leaders in Ocaña and the police have doubled the security for all of them. They are hatching a plan.[111]

The news from Ocaña in the weeks after my fieldwork trip to the town confirmed this suspicion. From the beginning of May 2012, pamphlets appeared in Ocaña in which an anonymous group threatened social cleansing—that is, the killing of undesired people—and ordered a curfew at 11 P.M. (see Figure 4.8).[112] It included a list of twenty-seven people with whom they were going to start the cleansing. On May 6, 2012, three people who were on the street after the curfew were killed: a baker, a woman who sold "minutes" for phone calls, and another one who sold mobile phones.[113] This suggests that the tense calm was a temporary lull before an outburst of violence, by means of which one of the groups attempted to impose its dominance in the town. Ocaña's residents had experienced similar strategies implemented by the paramilitaries before

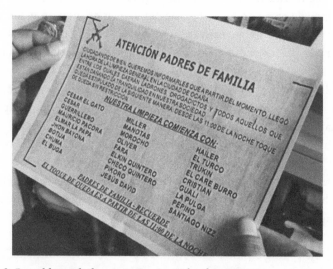

Figure 4.8 Pamphlet with threats in Ocaña, Colombia, 2012. Source: La Opinión. "Panfletos amenazantes en Ocaña." *La Opinión*, 3 May 2012.

their demobilization. Given that they had lived a similar experience before and knowing about the atrocities committed once the calm was over, in 2012, they relived this fear. Their sense of foreboding tragically materialized.[114]

Levels of violence are comparatively low in periods of tense calm, but the anticipation of insecurity undermines *subjective* security. The premonition that violence is imminent, without knowing when, how, and where it will break out, erodes the community's social fabric. It fuels uncertainty and distrust toward those outside the circle of friends or family.[115] Any stranger in town, any unusual occurrence, could be a trigger of violence. As it may happen at any time and people are most vulnerable in public places, they prefer to stay at home, isolating themselves, rather than enjoying a sense of community.

4.4 Conclusion

When violent non-state groups lack distrust-reducing mechanisms and instead operate as mistrusting "enemies," community members in rural areas can adapt their behavior to rules arising from two opposing fronts. Yet the groups are not responsive to the community members. The rules they impose are rooted in brutal coercion, which produces long-term psychological consequences. In urban contexts of armed disputes, particularly when preponderance relations are being disputed, the lines between group members and bystanders are obscured. It is therefore harder to identify rules of behavior. During periods of tense calm before or after the outbreak of violence, such rules are virtually absent. This uncertainty fuels anxiety, fear, and distrust among people, which thwarts a sense of community and erodes social fabric. The state-society relationship is dysfunctional: the state does not protect its citizens. What is more, as the cases of combat at the beginning of this chapter demonstrate, the state sometimes even contributes to violence by supporting one of the conflicting parties, in these cases the paramilitaries in Putumayo and the ELN in Arauca.

In all instances of the "enmity" cluster of violent non-state group interactions, people draw on coping mechanisms to make sense of violence and to enhance perceived security: just-world thinking, expressed in victim blaming, and conciliation strategies involving religion or fate. Yet while they may help people to cope, such behavior also disintegrates the social fabric even further: instead of showing solidarity with the victims and taking collective action to respect and protect them, people distance and isolate themselves.

These security impacts differ from those of the other clusters of violent non-state group interactions. In particular, the prevalence of violence in conjunction with the availability of behavioral rules distinguishes security dynamics in contexts of combat activities between violent non-state groups from other security outcomes. As the discussion of armed disputes, and to some extent tense calm, has shown however, even in the "enmity" cluster, the availability of rules of behavior can be distorted because identities may not be clear. In these cases, the security repercussions resemble those of unstable short-term arrangements among violent non-state groups, especially tactical alliances.

As I argue in the next chapter, in contexts where violent non-state groups engage in such short-term arrangements that I include in the "rivalry" cluster, community members are exposed to violence, but can hardly draw on any rules of appropriate behavior. In settings of stable long-term arrangements among violent non-state groups, there is comparatively little violence, but community members are able to adapt their behavior to the rules the groups impose in order to enhance their security.

5

Crime and Uncertainty

> The armed actor damages the morality of society [...]. They slowly
> beat, break the pearl, the pearl of the Pacific. The pearl is of a very hard
> and beautiful material, it is already scratched, almost subtly fractured,
> but it starts to be really fractured.
>
> Resident of Tumaco, Colombia, 2011[1]

Organized crime in conflict zones is a ruthless business. Brutal murders are its
most glaring immediate consequences, inflicting great suffering on communities.
But the uncertainty and fear that arise in such contexts inconspicuously fracture
society in the long run, as the Tumaco resident explains about his town, "the
pearl of the Pacific." "Fear is elusive as a concept; yet you know it when it has
you in its grip," notes Linda Green.[2] Uncertainty does not necessarily increase
body counts. It does, however, fuel perceptions of insecurity, preventing collective action and citizens' agency in designing security policies. It alienates citizens from a state that does not protect them, inhibiting the mutually reinforcing
state-society relationship that underpins citizen security.

Perceptions of insecurity characterize everyday life in the context of short-
term arrangements among violent non-state groups, included in the second
cluster on the continuum illustrated in chapter 2 (see Figure 2.1). This "rivalry"
cluster comprises three arrangement types: spot sales and barter agreements,
tactical alliances, and subcontractual relationships. As in the previous chapter,
I examine these security dynamics through the magnifying glass of borderlands,
providing enhanced analytical clarity. In all the examples, the border powerfully
intensifies relations and insecurities. In some of the short-term arrangements, the
borderline itself gives rise to the arrangement. This includes gasoline trafficking
as well as spot sales of human beings across the Colombia-Venezuela border, and
spot sales of arms across the Colombia-Ecuador border (see section 5.1). In addition, the border effect exacerbates the security situation of local communities in
a particularly serious way. First, the borderlanders suffer more stigmatization (see
also section 7.4); second, those who are themselves involved in the illicit cross-
border business are more alienated from the state, undermining the state-society

relationship; and third, cross-border impunity makes them particularly exposed to victimization and abuse (see also section 7.1).

In the other examples of short-term arrangements discussed in this chapter, the proximity of the border accentuates security impacts. This is because it epitomizes the intersection of economic and political agendas, a phenomenon that lies at the core of short-term arrangements where conflict actors engage in illicit business deals. Criminal and political violence coalesce.

As I outline in chapter 3, the lucrative nature of the business in places like Tumaco, due to its geostrategic location, attracts numerous politically and economically motivated groups. It enhances the fragility of their alliances so that the effects on security are more intense than they would be in other places (see section 7.3). Tumaco's location at the double border with Ecuador and the Pacific coast, featuring some of the most important starting points of international cocaine trafficking routes, makes it attractive to those who want access to these routes. The geostrategic location facilitates disappearing people across the border in the sea and offers Ecuador as a safe haven for armed actors, which can reinforce criminal dynamics (see section 7.1). Like Tumaco, La Guajira department, at the double border with Venezuela and the Caribbean coast, provides the starting points for international trafficking routes. Violent non-state groups face fewer constraints when victimizing civilians here than elsewhere; intra-borderland displacements and cross-border killings render violence and terror less visible (see section 7.1).

Finally, in still other cases, including the examples of the illicit logistics and business hubs in Cúcuta, Llorente, and San Cristóbal that I discuss below, the very reliance on, and influence of, illicit transactions across the border incentivizes violent non-state groups to engage in arrangements with each other. This further intensifies negative impacts on citizen security.

In settings with short-term arrangements, the erosion of the local population's social fabric and the distortion of the state-society relationship are particularly pronounced. As we see in the previous chapter, alienation from the state also exists in the absence of arrangements among violent non-state groups. In the "rivalry" cluster—especially in tactical alliances—the arrangement's short-lived nature can reinforce this alienation. This is because under combat, people can demand state protection against the group not supported by the state. In tactical alliances, (corrupt) state officials change sides as quickly as members of non-state groups do. This makes distancing oneself from the state the safest option. Due to the one-off nature of short-term arrangements, it is unclear whom to support and what to do to ensure one's security. Trust relationships and solidarity prevail only in small circles, such as the core family.

When civil war actors intermingle with civilians, uncertainty and identification problems arise. Therefore, these actors employ violence to impede defection of civilians to the hostile competing side. Accordingly, civilians either decide to obey these rules to avoid violence, or to defect.[3] However, as the cases of Tumaco and La Guajira show, this is unfeasible when conflict and criminal violence converge, and multiple parties ally or compete with each other in unpredictable ways. The blurred lines between community members and violent non-state groups, and victims and perpetrators, increase disorientation and uncertainty. Survival comes down to devising the best self-protection mechanisms or avoidance strategies as rules of behavior.

Outside observers often misunderstand short-lived arrangements among violent non-state groups. They sometimes ignore them because they only play out at the local level, as in the cases of the village of Llorente and the shopping center "Alejandría," which I discuss below. In other cases, outsiders focus on their violent breakdowns, conflating them with territorial contestation and conflict cleavages, which would presuppose the elimination of the other group as these actors' goal, at least if they behave as "enemies." Yet the intensified logics of these arrangements in border areas make it clear that the security challenges that communities face when exposed to such dynamics are qualitatively different from those in situations of combat, armed disputes, or tense calm. The "rules of the game" are less clear and uncertainty paralyzes civic action.

5.1 Spot Sales and Barter Agreements

Spot sales and barter agreements are interactions among violent non-state groups with a particularly strong potential for fueling uncertainty among local populations. Featuring low group interdependence, spot sales and barter agreements are largely not institutionalized, hence no clear rules of behavior emerge for people in such circumstances. If they occur on an iterated basis, these interactions can develop a regular pattern, which helps the groups involved reduce distrust between each other.

How do community members know whether the armed groups have decided to continue business as usual, have disagreed over prices and deliveries, or have cheated on each other, for example by taking all of the profit arising from lucrative drug deals instead of sharing it? Deals can be struck behind closed doors, in places such as remote jungle areas, or they can be hidden in other ways, for example by intertwining them with licit transactions. The groups themselves sometimes find out about cheaters only after the deal, as a Revolutionary Armed Forces of Colombia–People's Army (Fuerzas Armadas Revolucionarias de Colombia–Ejército del Pueblo—FARC) ex-combatant working in their "finance section" reported (see section 7.2). Community members have a hard time adapting their behavior to such ambiguous circumstances. Lack of clarity over behavioral rules also arises because violent non-state groups fail to establish a consensual relationship with the local population. Except for material transactions that require infrastructure and a labor force, the armed actors do not need the local population's support. Interactions with locals are therefore less relevant for the groups than in other arrangements. Finally, general mistrust fuels uncertainty. The groups reduce distrust between each other through interest convergence on a particular occasion—the business deal—which is typically conducted among a few group members only. More generally, however, suspicion prevails. This is particularly the case in one-off deals that do not have a long-term horizon which would make violence costly. If groups know they only need their business partner once because they can turn to a new one for the next business deal, they might as well draw on violent enforcement methods to deter any undesired activities the other group may engage in. Such situations thus can easily inflict violence on other groups and innocent community members alike.

There is an upside to this type of arrangements for the security of local communities though. Based on interest convergence, spot sales and barter agreements are limited in time and space. Behavioral rules are therefore less essential than in other arrangements that last longer, are more extensive, and involve more stakeholders. Rather than having to identify behavioral rules to ensure survival, as in the case of the "enmity" cluster discussed in the previous chapter, avoidance strategies are more feasible options to eschew insecurity and level out uncertainty at times.

Avoidance Strategies amid Terror

Spot sales with financial transactions among violent non-state groups do not directly involve locals but still expose them to violence. Instead of trusting fellow community members and the state as a protector, or demanding protection from the state, locals develop self-protection mechanisms to avoid becoming victims.[4] They are agents in ensuring citizen security yet remain limited in their mobility.

Alejandría, the Illegal Business Palace

Alejandría, called "San Andresito," is a shopping center in the heart of Cúcuta. It is home to many shops that sell products, including counterfeit and smuggled goods, cheaply.[5] As I witnessed, during the day it is frequented by ordinary shoppers, but later in the day it becomes a hub of illicit business activities. In some parts of Cúcuta, the nights are calm and safe enough to walk alone. In contrast, the area where Alejandría is located is busy and hectic. A community leader in Cúcuta told me that merchants would start to whisper to each other: "Listen, I'm going to buy strawberries!" Someone else would answer: "No, buy mango!" He explained that these are codes used to distract attention from Alejandría's hidden function as a "business palace" for illegal activities.[6]

In 2012, this shopping center was supposedly the "economic and intelligence headquarters" of the Rastrojos, whose office was in the basement, protected by an intelligence network. Street hawkers surrounding the area watched every movement. Akin to "security rings," these street hawkers reported to the Rastrojos and infiltrated other groups who did illicit business with them at San Andresito. The community leader further shed light on these perplexing dynamics:

> Until recently, Pedro [managed the office of the Rastrojos in Alejandría], but these guys change quickly. They keep the enterprise but change the management. They use this modus operandi because they have learned that you cannot allow anyone to be visibly involved. They say: "This is the office. Go and see whoever attends you in the office!" They don't negotiate over this. This place is small. It's only two blocks and, yet, any illegal economy that you can imagine is moving in there. Deals for any military machine that you can imagine are negotiated there, and for any illicit drugs as well. But of course, the illicit goods themselves are not there. There, you hardly find anything. You turn everything upside down, but you don't find anything, not even the Rastrojos themselves. They go to San Cristóbal [to escape the Colombian law enforcement's reach].[7]

Compliance with the deals is violently enforced. In October 2011 for example, a man was killed in Alejandría's parking area. A member of the Urabeños, also involved in business deals, purportedly "punished" him for having invaded the groups' economic space.[8]

Alejandría represents what Veena Das calls the "mutual absorption of the violent and the ordinary."[9] Referring to post-Partition India, she speaks of people's "descent into the ordinary" by focusing on small things in everyday life, such as going shopping to *recover* from violence.[10] In Cúcuta, people attend to the ordinary to *withstand* violence by continuing to shop at Alejandría as usual. They engage in ordinary things, such as frequenting the shopping center while violence continues—and they are aware of it. Given the extensive media coverage, most Cucuteños know about the lethal nighttime disputes in Alejandría between the Rastrojos and Urabeños.[11] They therefore stay away when it is dark, but they do not shun the place altogether—they do not let violence take away their everyday routines. This avoidance strategy influences how people think about murders in the area. It is the other side of the victim blaming coin: violence does not affect them because they avoid dangerous places. Killings in Alejandría are considered the victim's fault because, instead of avoiding the venue, he or she has obviously exposed him or herself to danger.

When spot sales with financial transactions operate in limited space, citizens change their mobility patterns to stay safe. They avoid spaces where these

transactions take place.[12] Locals are expected to be their own advocate in reducing the risk of physical violence, by shying away from dangerous places when
the state fails to protect them. This increases the stigmatization of those who
do become victims, does not hold authorities accountable for investigating the
case, and leaves areas like Alejandría at the mercy of groups like the Rastrojos.
These dynamics suggest that the norms and principles that guide everyday life
are produced through a self-help system rather than through citizenship. Such
self-help systems ensure security to some extent, but not *citizen* security where
the mechanisms to provide for security are based on a mutually reinforcing
state-society relationship.

Llorente and San Cristóbal: the Narco Hubs

Violent entrepreneurs do not necessarily limit themselves to hidden subterra-
nean places to strike illicit deals, like in the example from Cúcuta. They also engage in spot sales and barter agreements in less pre-determined locations across
towns. In such cases, it is unfeasible for people to adopt a spatial avoidance
strategy, as people's homes tend to be located within the area. Instead, they have
to change their entire lifestyle to stay safe. The case of the village of Llorente in
Nariño, on the road from Pasto to Tumaco, illustrates this. Llorente opens up
two strategic paths on the drug trafficking routes: on one side, the River Rosario,
which flows toward Tumaco and the ocean, and on the other side, the River Mira
(see section 3.2).[13]

Llorente is a center for cocaine supply and the movement of illegal merchandise to Tumaco (see Map 5.1). As a Nariño resident explained, in the 1990s,
Llorente was made up of only three houses, one made of concrete and two made
of wood.[14] When the coca boom started in Nariño in the early 2000s, people
started to move to Llorente. They "suddenly started to build houses made of
brick and cement," and migrants from Caquetá in the east arrived, she added.[15]
The village quickly acquired supermarkets. Money arrived and, with the money,
prostitutes, as is typical with most places with a thriving narco-economy.
Llorente became a town.[16]

The anecdote of a human rights defender from Pasto illustrates how, in 2002
and 2003, the paramilitaries tried to oust the guerrillas who had dominated the
region:

> Several men arrived at a house in Llorente where a man was painting
> a wall. They asked him to take them to the park and he replied that he
> wanted to finish the part he was painting. They said they needed him
> now. He answered: "Ok, I'm coming; you know that I always collab-
> orate!" "What do you mean, son of a bitch, you always collaborate?"

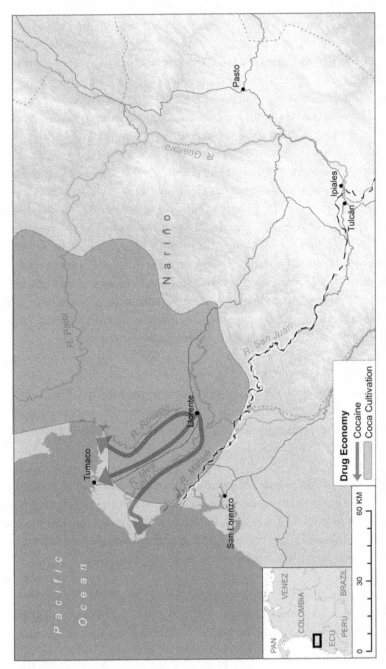

Map 5.1 Drug trafficking routes that start in Llorente, Nariño, Colombia. Map created by Author.

They hit him. They were not from the guerrillas who used to be present in the territory, but paramilitaries who had newly arrived in the village. As a punishment for being guerrilla collaborator, they tortured him in public and tore his body into pieces. They left the pieces on the street and no one could touch them. [...] How do you think people felt after that? The paramilitaries' message was unequivocal: "Here, we are the rulers. Look what happens to people who collaborate with the others!" This is horrific terror, politics of terror, of terrorizing people. It means that I can't say anything. If they ask me to do something, I don't even think about it, and just say: "Yes, of course, yes, yes, yes!"[17]

In subsequent years, after the demobilization of the United Self-Defense Forces of Colombia (Autodefensas Unidas de Colombia—AUC) in Nariño, the paramilitaries reorganized into new groups, using names like Águilas Negras, Mano Negra, and Nueva Generación. They also recruited more young men.[18] Throughout the process of fragmentation and proliferation of these groups, Llorente developed into a hub for illicit business deals. The human rights defender described Llorente as a "commercial zone" in which multiple armed groups were present. Accordingly, the armed actors' attitude toward each other was: "We are all here, but we give way to each other. We are not at war. We give way to each other."[19] An international agency employee confirmed:

Not only *narcos* go there to do business, also the FARC and the paramilitaries, both groups [. . .]. Everyone goes there for business. Those who go expose themselves to an imminent risk, but they know how to move about in these risks, they know how to sail through troubled waters.[20]

As in the case of Alejandría, the groups enforced compliance via intimidation and violence, but on a larger scale. In 2006 alone, the Rastrojos were accused of being responsible for 270 homicides in the area.[21] In 2007, Llorente's peak year as a "narco-business hub,"[22] the Human Rights and International Humanitarian Law Commission of Nariño received the following complaint:[23]

In Llorente, there are sixty armed guys dressed as civilians. During the day, they sell women's underwear, and at night, they drive around in pairs on motorbikes, heavily armed, despite the presence of the state forces.[24]

In 2007, it was common to see dead bodies by the roadside. Fearing retaliation by the murderer for showing compassion for the victim, no one dared to pick them up. Veena Das and Arthur Kleinman call such behavior "unlearning" normal reactions because "the old maps and charts that guided people in their relation to the ordinary have disappeared."[25] No rules applied. Unlike the delimited area of the shopping mall in Cúcuta, terror reigned in the entire town of Llorente.

Even though in Llorente, homicide rates in the context of spot sales and barter agreements in 2007 were as high as those during combat situations in 2003,[26] the form of violence and the security outcomes were qualitatively different. From a community perspective, the security impacts in 2007 were twofold. On the one hand, violence was selectively directed toward those involved in business deals. It was not employed indiscriminately against civilians. There was a sensation of terror, but no "terror warfare,"[27] as in the case of the painter described above, when the guerrillas and paramilitaries were fighting each other. On the other hand, in contexts of general mistrust, the error rate of selective violence is high, and "just in case" killings to preempt whistle-blowers inflate murder rates further. Anyone was a potential victim, which increased perceptions of insecurity. The mix of perpetrators and bystanders in the same space reinforced fear, interpersonal mistrust, and uncertainty. The only avoidance strategy was what Ana Villarreal describes as a form of "logistics of fear": avoiding insecurity by isolating oneself and staying home.[28] People self-imposed the "rule of silence";[29] as it was difficult to know who to trust, people preferred to interact only with people they knew well.

Comparing Llorente with Venezuelan San Cristóbal in Táchira with a similar "business hub" function, one also finds that silence prevails as a self-imposed behavioral rule. While towns closer to the border were mostly Rastrojos- or Urabeños-controlled, San Cristóbal featured—and still features—many different groups, allegedly including Mexican cartel members who are there to engage in business deals. Many residents know that Colombian armed actors visit San Cristóbal to do business, but they keep quiet instead of reporting to the police. The reason for this is simple, as a humanitarian organization employee explained to me in San Cristóbal: "If you say something, they kill you [. . .]. 'Silenced by death' is a topic no one touches."[30] Colombian groups kill mercilessly to deter others from interrupting their illegal business deals. According to another interviewee from San Cristóbal, if someone is considered *sapo* (an informant), they murder them, cut out their tongue, and put it on their body like a tie.[31] Such symbolism is a strategy of terror to demonstrate what happens to people who speak out against violent non-state groups.

The generalized mistrust that invokes silence has consequences for the community's social fabric:[32] it is strengthened at the micro level among close friends and the nuclear family, but eroded at the community level. Describing Guatemala's civil war, Green notes that "silence can operate as a survival strategy, yet silencing is a powerful mechanism of control enforced through fear."[33] In Llorente and San Cristóbal, this control mechanism is diffuse. It does not originate from fear of one specific group, but rather from the dynamics of mistrust and suspicion against anyone who might harm someone's illegal business. Blaming the victims as a strategy to reduce perceived vulnerability to violence is less feasible than in the case of Alejandría. If there is no particular place to avoid, no victim can be blamed for not having done so. Instead, people adopt a more general attitude toward blame: those who became victims must have somehow been involved.

People from other parts of Colombia and from the Ecuadorian northern border zone stigmatized Llorente's residents as collaborators. Blaming them for participating in the illegal business, they denied the innocence of victims.[34] They distanced themselves from the occurrences in Llorente both mentally and physically. The village became a "no-go area." This isolation undermined not only the residents' livelihoods based on commerce but also their sense of being citizens of a wider community.

In 2011, the Rastrojos controlled Llorente;[35] rates of violence decreased. Sometimes FARC militia entered the village to do business and left again, but did so "undercover" because they were in conflict with the Rastrojos in the region at that time. The stigma of belonging to the illicit and violent business that was associated with Llorente's residents seemed to have been overcome. While in 2007, people avoided stopping in Llorente when traveling from Tumaco to Pasto and vice versa, they took fewer precautions in 2011. In fact, I had lunch in Llorente in October 2011 when traveling with a diplomatic mission this very route. What attracted my attention were the many hardware shops in the village, apparently supplying armed groups with equipment, a visible remnant of Llorente's era as a "narco-business center."

The evolution of non-state order in Llorente from (i) guerrilla preponderance to (ii) combat between guerrillas and paramilitaries, to (iii) spot sales and barter agreements among both parties, and finally to (iv) the Rastrojos' preponderance demonstrates how the security situation in the context of spot sales differs from those of other arrangements. Under preponderance, people orient their behavior to the rules of the dominant group to avoid violence. By contrast, combat triggers the need to identify front lines to survive "terror warfare." In the context of spot sales and other illicit one-off business deals, people face unpredictable, selective violence, fueling uncertainty. While Cucuteños can stay away from Alejandría because it is a designated and delimited shopping area, the residents of Llorente and San Cristóbal are constantly exposed to violent enforcement methods, even if they do not collaborate with any group.

Violent Abuse and Alienation from the State

When spot sales and barter agreements involve material transactions, the repercussions on citizen security are more immediate than in financial transactions. This is because, in addition to living in the territories where these take place, community members are implicated in the transactions or related activities themselves. Unless they take place in unpopulated areas, barter agreements rely on the communities in which the armed actors operate, especially if the arrangement is repeated and involves goods of a large volume. People are stigmatized as, or become, collaborators—voluntarily or otherwise—to ensure their income. As a result, the distance between the state and its people grows; people refrain from raising their voices against the insecurity generated by armed groups due to their own (alleged) involvement. Given the general mistrust that persists in the context of interest convergence between groups on the one hand, and the illegality of the activities from the state's point of view on the other, communities neither draw on illicitly granted protection from violent non-state groups, nor turn to the state to seek protection. The repercussions on citizen security therefore comprise uncertainty and alienation from the state. This happens to varying degrees, depending on the specific context, as the following examples show. The first illustrates how people are vulnerable to becoming victims in cases where the groups need infrastructure to stockpile or sell goods and require community members to act as a labor force. To achieve the population's compliance, violent non-state groups provide financial incentives paired with selective violence or threats thereof. This differs from financial spot sales, in which there are fewer reasons for the groups to target the population directly. The second example epitomizes the virtual impossibility for borderland communities to avoid the economic activities related to armed groups, due to the interconnected nature of other forms of cross-border trade. The third example outlines the most immediate impact, when people themselves become the subject of transaction. While these examples manifest diminishing levels of direct exposure to violence, alienation from the state and general uncertainty persist throughout.

Gasoline Trafficking in La Paz

The example of gasoline trafficking and gasoline-drugs barter agreements in La Paz at the Colombia-Venezuela border reveals the parasitic character of the relationship between violent non-state groups and communities.[36] In these situations, even though people may gain some economic benefit, they are extremely vulnerable to violent forms of coercion.

The indigenous Wayúu have traditionally controlled gasoline smuggling between Colombian La Guajira and Venezuelan Zulia (see section 3.1). When the AUC's Northern Bloc under their leader Jorge 40 entered the region in the 1990s, various high-ranking paramilitary members contested the control of business. After the AUC's demobilization in Cesar in 2006, post-demobilized groups did the same.[37] This business is lucrative. In 2011, the value of the gasoline increased more than fifty-two times between Zulia and Bogotá (see Map 5.2). Most gasoline is smuggled for regional distribution, but it also serves to process coca leaves into cocaine.[38]

In the La Paz municipality near Valledupar, community members started to smuggle gasoline in 1995. Two families who traveled frequently from La Paz to Maicao in La Guajira to trade goods brought cheap gasoline from Maicao to La Paz to sell it at a profit.[39] Seeing the benefits, more families began to drive north to Maicao and bring gasoline back south to La Paz.

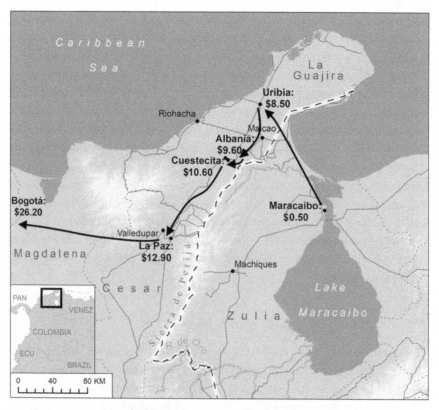

Map 5.2 Gasoline price in USD per container (21 liters) at the Colombia-Venezuela border in 2011. Source: Data based on El Heraldo (2011) and Unidad de Planeación Minero Energética (2012). Credit: Map created by Author.

However, from 2011 onward, public officials denounced the involvement of the Rastrojos and the Urabeños in gasoline smuggling in La Paz, often in the form of barter agreements for cocaine.[40] These and other violent entrepreneurs transported gasoline in trucks from Venezuela via La Guajira to La Paz. They then used the empty trucks to transport cocaine from municipalities in central Cesar via La Guajira to the Colombia-Venezuela border. There, they handed over the cocaine to trafficking groups operating in Venezuela, including Mexican cartels.

The post-demobilized groups' involvement in gasoline smuggling and barter agreements with cocaine contributed to the stigmatization of locals as traffickers, thus increasing their vulnerability. The groups forced people to sell their properties, including shops and private homes, to stockpile the gasoline they received in return for drugs. They pressured locals to launder money originating from gasoline or drug spot sales, and offered money to residents to invest in the purchase of gasoline and of gasoline tanks.[41] Compliance was typically violently enforced: those who rejected the offer or refused to pay back the money faced threats or actual violence.[42] According to Colombia's Ombudsman's Office, in March 2011, for example, the Urabeños threatened a La Paz resident's life so that the individual would pay back what they had lent him.[43]

According to a human rights defender from Valledupar, most murders affected people linked to the illegal economy or local armed structures.[44] Notably, his reasoning followed the just-world logic of other interviewees. Yet despite his view, these murdered people include locals who were involved against their will. Leaders of violent non-state groups reduce distrust through interest convergence in the business deal (see section 2.1). Striving to be credible, they therefore may refrain from violent punishment among themselves. However, general mistrust prevails.[45] Therefore, at the grassroots level, violent non-state groups deter defection with violence.

The violent non-state groups' direct interaction, and the fact that they depended on locals as labor force only to a limited extent, makes this situation similar to those of long-term arrangements among violent non-state groups, especially in regions of coca cultivation under preponderance relations. Under these circumstances, even though coca farmers suffer social control, confinement, and stigmatization because they are labeled guerrilla collaborators, they are still provided basic governance functions, such as conflict resolution. Violent non-state groups provide these functions in return for social recognition, allowing them to continue their activities undisturbed and to count on local "shadow citizens" as a labor force (see section 6.4).[46] In iterated material barter agreements and spot sales as in the example of La Paz, violent non-state groups offer economic opportunities but do not assume other governance functions. They further do

Figure 5.1 Queue at gasoline station near San Antonio de Táchira, Venezuela, 2012.
Photo by Author.

not strive for social recognition through responsiveness because, where inter-group distrust prevails and locals are suspected of collaborating with the other group, violence is a more reliable enforcement method than social control.

The proximity of these dynamics to the border intensifies the harmful effects. Gasoline-for-drugs deals are not isolated activities in specific locations where the groups draw on locals in a parasitic relationship only. Rather, these interactions are just one of many forms of illicit cross-border trade, a common state of affairs in border areas in vulnerable regions (see section 3.2).

At the Colombia-Venezuela border specifically, various forms of gasoline smuggling occur. Although illegal, local communities consider it a legitimate practice because it constitutes their livelihood strategy.[47] In Cúcuta, where people sell gasoline bought in Venezuelan San Antonio (Figure 5.1), the high-ranking police official confirmed that residents consider contraband, particularly smuggled gasoline, legitimate:

> People in Cúcuta engage in illegal activities because it is a border zone. [. . .] There are no alternatives. This is the best option they have. Unfortunately, people have suffered under the guerrillas, the paramilitaries, and the BACRIM. They also consolidated this culture of illegality. People therefore come to believe that contraband is normal. This contraband is the origin of many fictitious economies. [. . .] People end up accepting these things [. . .].[48]

Indeed, anyone crossing the border can see that smuggling is an open secret. While in Colombia, I observed the movement of vehicles and people at the border crossings of Paraguaipoa-Paraguachón (Maicao), Puerto Santander-Boca

Figure 5.2 Typical car used for gasoline smuggling, Zulia, Venezuela, 2012. Photo by Author.

Figure 5.3 *Pimpinas* stall at the Colombia-Venezuela border, 2012. Photo by Author.

del Grita, Cúcuta-Ureña, and Cúcuta-San Antonio. At all of these crossings, it was common to see LTD, Maverick, Ford Forlaine, or Malibu cars and trucks—vehicles with big tanks, convenient for the smuggling of large quantities of gasoline (see Figure 5.2).

There are three types of gasoline smuggling. The first is the only one that directly involves drug trafficking controlled by armed groups: large-scale smuggling in tankers that transport between 12,000 and 16,000 liters.[49] Supposedly, these tankers increasingly serve gasoline-for-drugs-deals. Most gasoline smugglers, however, fall into a second and third category: medium-sized smuggling, using modified Renault 18s or Mazda 626s, and small-scale smuggling, involving *pimpineros*, people who sell gasoline on the street in *pimpinas* (see Figure 5.3). Despite usually only engaging in this third level of activity, typically because they are poor and lack alternative options, gasoline smugglers have been stigmatized as drug traffickers and collaborators with these armed groups. This ends up restricting their daily activities.

Even if locals are engaged in this more "innocent" form of gasoline smuggling (i.e., in small quantities), the concurrent large-scale, illicit gasoline business, which includes a multiplicity of armed actors ranging from Colombian rebels to Venezuelan traffickers, casts a shadow over the region and paints them as collaborators, increasing their vulnerability to abuse by both state and non-state armed actors.

The stigmatization of gasoline smugglers has two important consequences for the mutually reinforcing state-society relationship that lies at the root of citizen security. One concerns citizen participation in ensuring security and the other concerns the state's duty to protect its citizens (see section 2.2). Stigmatization increases the smugglers and their families' vulnerability vis-à-vis state institutions and the illicit groups.[50] They refrain from reporting abuse or extortion to the police because it would reveal their own involvement in illegal activities. Many consider extortion an unavoidable deduction from their income, akin to taxes—a payment to receive protection from law enforcement and criminals.[51] Who knows whether the police officer they might report abuse to would act in his capacity as police officer, that is, a representative of the state? What if, in his "nighttime job," this same police officer is a member or collaborator of the very non-state group that the smuggler is reporting for abuse? In a context of mistrust with few economic opportunities, and where the overriding shared interest is maximizing profit, such a scenario is plausible. The capacity of violent non-state groups to act as both tormentors and protectors contributes to their leverage over the borderland population. They manipulate borderlanders to make them behave in a way that promotes their interests (that is, the group's), while shielding themselves from the state's influence and the risk of punishment.

The empirical legitimacy of borderlanders' illegal activities alienates these communities from the state while drawing them closer to the illegal groups. Benedikt Korf and Timothy Raeymakers note that such a "tendency toward transgression" also questions the state's perceived legitimacy.[52] The state may turn into a greater threat to the borderlanders' livelihoods than the non-state groups. For borderlanders, the borderline represents the state because any other expression of it is absent.[53] Operating in illegality themselves, people consider customs, police, and military officials threats to their livelihoods. As Peter Andreas highlights, "smuggling is defined by and depends on the state's exercising its metapolitical authority to criminalize without the full capacity or willingness to enforce its laws."[54] The space opened up for smuggling, through the gap between the state's laws and its enforcement of these laws, creates a limbo: borderlanders benefit from this gap but are also damaged by it.

Arms Trafficking along the Colombia-Ecuador Border

Comparing the citizen security impacts of gasoline-for-drugs deals along the Colombia-Venezuela border with those of arms spot sales along the Colombia-Ecuador border supports the argument that such material transactions across borders increase the vulnerability of local communities to violence and abuse, further undermining the state-society relationship. The previous example demonstrated how the presence of various *scales* of illicit cross-border trade intensified people's vulnerability, especially as small-scale smugglers were tarred with the same brush as large-scale criminals. The case of arms spot sales at the Colombia-Ecuador border shows how the presence of multiple *forms* of illicit economic activities across borders increases insecurity.

Arms trafficking represents just one illegal flow that operates alongside many legal forms of cross-border trade. Given that armed groups are involved as trade partners in both illicit and licit flows, however, speaking out against illicit activities can undermine the legal business too, placing a veil of silence over these border areas. Weapons and ammunition entering Colombia from Ecuador were sold to the FARC and to other violent non-state groups on informal markets. According to El Comercio, Geoffrey Ramsey, and interviews with military officials, most arms originated in Peru, diverted from the Peruvian military to the black market.[55] According to interviews, and confirmed by local media reports, the FARC's Front 48 in Putumayo had drugs-for-arms deals with Ecuadorian traffickers near the border crossing of San Miguel between Sucumbíos and Putumayo. The Ecuadorians transported cocaine along the border to Ibarra and from there to Quito. On the other side of the border, the arms were (and are) transported via Mocoa to the departments of Caquetá and Meta, where the FARC had their strongholds. Paramilitaries and post-demobilized groups have also been involved. I learned about the mechanics of carrying out such deals from a woman I interviewed in Nariño. She was a FARC member but fell in love with a paramilitary and, in 2002, therefore joined the paramilitary Bloc "Liberators of the South," from which she demobilized in 2005. As she explained, the arms-for-drugs deals were conducted between Colombian armed groups and criminal groups in Ecuador, using (and paying) "ordinary people" from Ecuador as traffickers:

EX-COMBATANT: They gave us the arms [in Ecuador] and from there we brought them here. [. . .] I don't know who they were because these were ordinary people who arrived [at the deal site] and we didn't follow them anywhere else. The commander was the only one who knew them. We did not have contact with them prior to that. He simply told us, "Here is what you need, take the money" and we carried it with us. [. . .] Only the commander [. . .] and the higher-ranking members [knew them].

ME: *Were [the traffickers] Ecuadorians?*

EX-COMBATANT: Yes, Ecuadorians. There were no Colombians. [. . .]

ME: *Was this in Tulcán [in the Ecuadorian province of Carchi]?*

EX-COMBATANT: No, we followed some trails that are like shortcuts that go through other parts. We had to cross dangerous places. If you fall down the ravine, no one notices. People don't even remember you. We took these routes far away from [Tulcán] because the police were there. [. . .] We went by car to Tulcán. From there onward, they took us in their cars, therefore I have no idea where exactly we went [. . .]. After that, we had to walk maybe six hours to where we received the stuff. From there we had to walk until we reached Colombia. [. . .] Not on a trail of course, otherwise . . . Then we walked [. . .] until we reached Putumayo [. . .]. There were many of us. We didn't buy guns or other small things. We brought bigger weapons that were worth it.

ME: *Did you have any problems with the army?*

EX-COMBATANT: No. When we do a maneuver like this, generally there is always someone who does the logistics beforehand and investigates where to go, how to go, which route to leave by, and whether the army is there. If the army is there, obviously, we don't do anything. We stay quiet until we can do what we need to do. [. . .] The commander always makes sure that there is no danger [. . .] so that we can do these things.[56]

Like the gasoline-for-drugs deals at the Colombia-Venezuela border, locals were thus to some degree involved in deals. In cases like this example of arms trafficking though, it is more feasible for locals to avoid exposure to violence because the deals do not have to take place in one specific location, like in La Paz, and do not require a specific physical infrastructure. The armed actors' general presence, rather than their specific involvement in arms sales, fueled people's fear, as the continuation of her explanation suggests:

ME: *What were relations like with people in Ecuador and Colombia?*

EX-COMBATANT: In Ecuador, we only [. . .] got what we had to receive and left. Here in Colombia—at least from what I perceived—people were scared of me. Obviously this is because in our case [of the paramilitaries] we don't represent something good, but something bad. We represent something people are scared of. They don't have respect, but fear. When I told them to do stuff, many people did it out of fear, not out of respect. This is the relationship we had with them.

ME: *Where was the mafia from [with whom you had arms deals]?*

EX-COMBATANT: In the FARC, I met people from other countries, from Saudi Arabia, from El Salvador [. . .]. With the paramilitaries, we had deals with people from Medellín, Cali, and the Atlantic coast [. . .].

ME: *Did you change arms for drugs or money?*
EX-COMBATANT: I didn't see drugs, only money. The exchange was always for a
lot of money [. . .]. We went to certain places, exchanged, paid, and we left.
Sometimes we paid extra for training, they trained us how to handle and clean
the arms.[57]

Between Carchi and Nariño, arms spot sales influenced the security of local
residents more directly because the business was localized. A resident of Carchi
commented to me in a low voice:

> The armed groups have infiltrated here. Also, there are those who
> help, people who provide [the armed actors] with food, with med-
> icine. We also have problems with arms trafficking. People traffic
> many arms [. . .]. They pass them from here over there [to Colombia].
> I don't know where the arms come from. When I came back from [the
> border village], I saw a person selling blackberries [. . .],[58] but it's just
> logical that blackberries don't grow here. [. . .] Tomorrow is market
> day in [the other village]. [. . .] You should go to the market and then
> you can see people who buy 12 kilograms of this, ten kilograms of
> that, six kilograms of the other . . . per family! [. . .] There they sell
> arms as well.[59]

The (illegal) economic opportunities were more diverse than in La Paz. The interviewee above refers to the fact that Ecuadorians sold arms and gunpowder,
hidden underneath berries. They also sold ammunition and uniforms to the
guerrillas, mostly the FARC Front 29. Being involved in such illicit spot sales
alienated people in a similar way to those involved in gasoline smuggling at the
Colombia-Venezuela border.

Yet if people did not wish to engage in arms sales, they could participate in
other economic activities, while still benefiting from the FARC as clients. This
was the case with the market dynamics in one of the Ecuadorian border villages
that I visited where FARC members regularly crossed the border as civilians
to buy supplies.[60] These dynamics explain the many kilos of goods bought by
individuals. This diversity of economic options reduces the threats of violence
to the population because they can choose to engage in a less risky economic
activity, like selling food. At the same time however, these dynamics also conceal illegal activities, increase people's vulnerability and stigmatization, and alienate locals further from the state. Those not involved in arms trafficking do not
report it. They also stay silent about FARC presence more generally. Speaking
out could jeopardize their own livelihood—legally selling goods to guerrillas in
plain clothes.

Stigmatization as a citizen security repercussion is particularly strong if it concerns a minority group and has implications for the wider state-society relationship. The indigenous people from Otavalo in Ecuador's Imbabura province are a case in point. The media regularly singled out the Otavaleños as arms traffickers.[61] Locals also perceive the Otavaleños as major traffickers and, as such, another violent non-state group. The Carchi resident continued:

> It's the Otavaleños who bring the arms. They sell them. They are the arms traffickers, the indigenous people of Otavalo. There is a sector in Otavalo, Peguche, that's where they produce artisanal baskets. I told you I saw an indigenous person with a basket selling blackberries when I came up the hill. They are from various parts near Peguche. They were arrested with arms and gunpowder, but everything here is arms trafficking. It's normal, normal!

Indigenous Otavaleños were arrested for trafficking arms, camouflaged among other products, like in the example of the blackberries, or hidden elsewhere. As the Ecuadorian newspaper *El Comercio* reported, in 2009 for example, two indigenous women were paid 25,000 USD by the FARC to smuggle twenty-three grenades attached to their bodies and twenty-two sticks of explosives hidden in a doll.[62] While such individual cases are not unusual, the labeling of the Otaveleños per se as an arms trafficking group, as practiced by the local media and among the local population, is rooted in a stereotype: in Ecuador, indigenous people are often seen as poor, inferior, and badly educated, and hence as prone to engage in illegal activities to sustain their livelihoods.[63]

The stigmatization of the Otavaleños is characteristic of their alienation from other society members and from the Ecuadorian state. Since some of them engage in illegal activities with the FARC, the line between such specific societal groups and the armed groups is blurred. In cases like gasoline-for-drugs deals, the members of the armed groups originate from other regions and "invade" a territory, thereby changing the rules through which community members become collaborators. In the cases mentioned here, locals themselves become, or are perceived to become, illicit groups, rather than individual collaborators. If part of the state's citizenry "exits" the state-society relationship by becoming a violent non-state group, the state has failed to be responsive to this societal group. If this portion of the citizenry is *perceived* to be an illicit group, there is a "tear" in the social fabric that holds society together. In such cases, the entire group, rather than individuals, are excluded from society. In Robert Putnam's words, there is a lack of "bridging social capital" within society because there is a gap between those citizens perceived to be an illicit group and the rest.[64]

Comparing the Otavaleños' stigmatization in the context of the arms sales at the Carchi-Nariño border with the other cases of spot sales and barter agreements reveals differences in the wider state-society relationship. In La Paz and other places, the stigmatization of *individuals* contributes to their alienation from the state and general mistrust *erodes* the social fabric. People do not take collective action, or isolate themselves to avoid being targeted as traitors. The *group* stigmatization of the Otavaleños *fragments* the social fabric. The Otavaleños have strong intra-group ties, but there is no sense of community between other borderlands and the Otavaleños.

Spot Sales of Human Beings in Machiques

In some spot sales, the traded goods are people. These spot sales are part of human trafficking or of kidnapping. Certainly, these crimes occur in non-border regions as well, but the proximity to the border—especially the cases where spot sales occur *across* borders—increases the likelihood that groups from different nationalities are involved and that potential traces of the crime can be covered up more easily. The practice of spot sales of human beings has been widespread in the municipality of Machiques in Venezuelan Zulia. In 2009 alone, eighty-six people were reportedly kidnapped in Zulia, of a total of 589 kidnappings in all of Venezuela that year.[65]

As a common practice, the Colombian guerrillas kidnap wealthy ranchers and businessmen near the Machiques highway leading to El Tokuko, hide them in the Sierra de Perijá, and sell them to criminal groups, often Venezuelans from the interior of the country. These groups then demand ransom from their families who are normally expected to pay hefty sums of money. This practice also exists the other way: criminal bands kidnap people in Caracas and sell them to guerrillas in the Colombian-Venezuelan borderlands. Either way, the victims are held in captivity until the guerrillas and the criminal groups reach an agreement, or another bidder offers a higher price. The groups may kill the victim if they do not consider it worthwhile to keep him or her, for example, if they feel the offered price was too low. While the guerrillas are thought to respect their hostages, purely economically motivated criminal groups are less "professional." They are more likely to kill their victims if it is in their economic interest to do so, or if there is a risk of prosecution by law enforcement agents. Thus, as opposed to kidnappings by a guerrilla group only, the involvement of criminal groups in the form of spot sales magnifies the risks for victims.

The practice affects the entire community. Those who know that they are "kidnappable" because the violent non-state groups favor their profile live in constant fear of being kidnapped.[66] In Machiques therefore, many left the region and paid farmers to manage their ranches in their absence. Those who were not "kidnappable" were also afraid because people had been confused with wealthy ranchers and kidnapped by mistake. Generally, the phenomenon limits people's mobility, as lone roads are avoided to minimize one's own exposure. For people from outside the region, the risk of becoming the subject of spot sales is also high, as those who travel from other places to the region are viewed to promise high ransoms too. I experienced the fear arising from being "kidnappable" myself when traveling on my own between Machiques and Maracaibo (see Epilogue). Even in these situations, alienation from the state can be the consequence. When people seek protection from the authorities, violent non-state groups have more reason to believe that the "good for sale" promises high profits. Poor farmers would not have any reasons to take such a step. Yet approaching the authorities for protection in this region can be risky for wealthy ranchers because officials themselves may be involved in the business. Therefore, the "kidnappable" people often prefer to take care of their own protection measures, distancing themselves from the state as the supposed security provider.[67]

5.2 Tactical Alliances

In tactical alliances, the border is not involved directly. The proximity of these arrangements to the border, however, reinforces their volatile character and with it the contexts of uncertainty in which locals find themselves. Tactical alliances are typical in multi-party conflicts where conflict actors switch sides or join forces temporarily to compete with a third group, as the example provided by a government official in Pasto, capital of Nariño, illustrates. As he explained to me in 2011, even though they normally operate independently, the Rastrojos engaged in a tactical alliance with the Águilas Negras in Tumaco. Their joint goal was to fight the FARC and to defend themselves against the state forces. This alliance only lasted a few months. Once the threat decreased, they operated separately again.[68]

Such dynamics fuel uncertainty and mistrust among the local population because of the unpredictable changes, especially if they contradict the wider conflict cleavages. Adding economic agendas reinforces the volatility of these arrangements even further. This is particularly evident at the starting points of international trafficking routes, where economic benefits in illicit businesses are high, as the cases of Tumaco on the Pacific coast and La Guajira on the Caribbean coast attest.

Most of the cocaine produced in southern Colombia is transported to Tumaco because the harbor town comprises the starting point of the principal drug trafficking route from South America via Central America or Mexico to the United States (see section 3.2). Tumaco's key function in the cocaine supply chain is partly owed to its unique geography. The harbor town is made up of three islands. The biggest one, El Morro, hosts the local airport and is connected to the other two by a 300-meter long viaduct. These, in turn, are linked to the mainland via a single bridge, making control over the viaduct and the bridge a key asset for anyone involved in transporting cocaine or other goods from other parts of the country to Tumaco's many shores.

As production and transport routes converge in Tumaco, the town attracts numerous violent non-state groups who aim to benefit from the lucrative cocaine business or other forms of organized crime. These groups share interests in protecting their operations from law enforcement measures, including cocaine seizures. The opportunity costs of losing shipments at the starting point of a trafficking route are higher than at the production or processing stage, as the final product—cocaine—has accumulated more value (see section 7.3). Joining forces on specific occasions to evade law enforcement measures is therefore of mutual benefit to the groups involved, even if usually they are "rivals." An international agency employee in Tumaco explained:

> In one part of the River Mira, various actors process coca into cocaine, not only the FARC. Each of them has their own production site and often they join forces to send the quantity of cocaine that is required. This ensures their security: the more united they are, the more likely it is that the Colombian state will not catch them or their products. They all have different informants and intelligence on the state's operations, this is what unites them.[69]

Counternarcotic operations are not the only reason for "rivaling" groups to team up. They also forge alliances based on their shared interests in reducing competition in the drug business, as in the example provided by a civil society leader from Tumaco:

> You and I, we are partners. I'm a guerrilla member and you are a member of a criminal group [...]. Between us, we have a pact, an agreement, and we want to eliminate the competition. What do we do? We look for strategies to jointly eliminate this competition. We tidy up, and we become much stronger. How do we tidy up? The first thing that they think in Colombia is: that's easy, contract someone to kill him [the leader of the competition] and we solve the problem. What do we do with the other group members? The same: we kill them. You take the bull by the horns.[70]

Unpredictable Violence

In cases like the tactical alliances described above, violent non-state groups are not interested in eliminating the other group(s) per se, as is the case in the "enmity" cluster. Violence is related to general inter-group distrust, reduced only to engage in a specific arrangement. Cheating and betrayal are constant risks, contributing to an environment of suspicion and uncertainty in which violence is unpredictable—both for the groups involved and for local communities. The continuation of the narrative provided by the international agency employee about groups who forge alliances to transport cocaine together is one of many accounts that confirm this:

> They don't have a territorial dispute. When they kill each other, it's for retaliation because they lost a cocaine shipment or someone important has been killed or arrested by the state forces, and they think this is to take someone out of the market. [. . .] Soon afterward they come to terms with each other again. They come back and talk to each other, do something to calm down, and things continue as usual.[71]

Since the danger of treachery is omnipresent,[72] preemptive killings constitute a "rational" option for violent non-state groups. The armed actors' inhibition threshold for engaging in violence is low due to the environment of impunity; it is less costly to kill someone by mistake than *not* to kill someone who could jeopardize one's business or life. As Diego Gambetta notes, "if one can ensure that the threat of punishment is credible, would-be offenders think twice."[73]

An anecdote narrated by a civil society leader from Tumaco about a rural area in the Tumaco municipality illustrates the logic of such preemptive killings:

> The military found and dismantled a cocaine laboratory. This generated fear [for possible acts of retaliation against suspected informants], therefore some community members started to flee. Their departure aroused the suspicion of the other [group] who thought those who fled had provided information to the military. They searched for them— first, to see if it was true; and second, to send a signal to potential state informants. Even if it is not true, it is better to kill a displaced person and say: "Look, he was a *sapo* [informant], but we pursued him and we killed him!" [. . .] Even if he never had said anything [. . .]! This way the rest of the population is already sufficiently terrified to never say anything. Community members are almost forced to become informants of the illegal armed actor.[74]

Violent non-state groups not only engage in killings as a means of preemption but also for revenge. If a member of one of two allied groups breaks the rules and escapes with the money that was supposed to be shared between both groups, he or she will face revenge at some point. The account of a civil society leader from Tumaco illustrates this:

> People say: "Okay, he was lucky, but sooner or later they will find him!" Therefore there are crimes where they say: "If the person was not in- volved in anything, we ignore him." But if a long time ago, he "twisted himself" [became involved in criminal activities], they will come back at him. This is how far the respect goes: if he manages to get away with breaking the agreement, fine, but at some point they will get back at him.[75]

As these breakdowns are difficult to predict, the foreboding of danger is om- nipresent and lasting. People can be killed even years later. Likewise, family members or friends without knowledge of the individual's illicit activities in the past can be threatened or killed in an act of revenge against that individual. Revenge is not always targeted at the group that broke the alliance, but also at informants, broadening the circle of those who fear retaliation. This may explain high homicide rates in locations that feature tactical alliances, but no combat, and where relatively few community members belong to illicit groups.

The rapid reconfigurations of tactical alliances also make violence less pre- dictable than in other arrangements. Generally, tacit rules imposed by various armed actors regulate everyday life in Tumaco. The Pasto government official I mention above had been working in and on Tumaco extensively, in particular on the conflict dynamics, and thus expounded to me how this works in practice:

> It is not necessary for a group to say: "The territory from here to here is mine and from there to there is yours!" People know [the rules] due to how they operate [...] and because these groups lead communica- tion networks, developed among shopkeepers, shops, and traders. All businesses have them. One of the first things that [the groups] provide is security. [...] Some men watch, they will make sure you can pursue your commercial activity safely, but you have to pay for it. They are protecting you from their own group. This is only a form of collecting resources to sustain the group [...], to finance themselves rather than to control the population. [...] But as you know, at the same time, it also entails social control. In a way, it is inherent in their approach because sustaining a group also requires a process of control, of maintaining the zone.[76]

These tacit rules stand on shaky grounds though. Sooner or later, fragile alliances among the groups break down. The neighborhoods at the shore—of which there are many, given that Tumaco is made up of three islands—are particularly prone to sudden breakdowns. These neighborhoods are key elements of the trafficking routes for cocaine, chemical precursors, gasoline, and weapons.[77] The government official from Pasto outlined the route like this to me:

> There is a drug trafficking route that first passes [next to the airport] and then reaches an isolated zone over there, despite the presence of the military. [. . .] They all [corrupt military officials] belong to the business. This group, the Águilas Negras, has to send the drugs this way, but there is another neighborhood, controlled by the Rastrojos [. . .]. The groups make an agreement of mutual respect so that [the drug] flows. The same applies vice versa: if the Rastrojos require a drug trafficking route and they have to pass through the zone where the Águilas Negras are present, they make an agreement.[78]

Multiple groups continuously replace each other in arrangements to secure access to these routes, rather than striving to gain territorial control. The presence of one unknown person in such a neighborhood can be reason enough for a tactical alliance to break down because it could be a sign of infiltration, facilitated by one of the allied groups, behind the other group's back.[79]

Suddenly, then, the residents' protection is no longer guaranteed. Behavioral rules become void, for example, when communication networks are infiltrated as well. Shop owners, traders, and other residents no longer know to whom to pay the extortion money or whether the extorting group still has the capacity to protect them.[80] Due to quickly changing dynamics, community members lack guidance on whose rules to adhere to, making self-protection from violence harder than in combat where people can comply with the respective group's rules. In such situations, virtually everyone is a potential victim because murders are committed based on suspicion, and stray bullets kill innocent people.[81] When I visited Tumaco in 2011, the neighborhood of Viento Libre was particularly badly affected by such violence. According to a local religious organization, state institutions could not even enter this neighborhood.[82]

Tactical alliances and their breakdowns have led to intra-urban displacement as a widespread reaction by the local population. Contrary to long-term arrangements in which violent non-state groups control large parts of a territory, or the absence of an arrangement where dispute occurs across entire municipalities, tactical alliances are very localized.[83] While the alliances are ongoing, intra-urban displacement can serve as a preventative measure: a mother in Tumaco told me in 2011 that she went with her son to live with relatives in another neighborhood to protect him from being recruited by armed groups.[84] When alliances break down, people flee to another island or neighborhood, controlled by another group, to escape violence.

Between May and August 2012, for example, more than three hundred people were displaced within Tumaco from a neighborhood called Brisas de los Ángeles due to localized disputes.[85] In subsequent years, the situation deteriorated when the FARC consolidated themselves in Tumaco, which produced more intra-urban displacements.[86] When I returned to Tumaco in November 2016, a wave of homicides shattered certain neighborhoods, resulting again in displacements. As locals commented, these murders seemed to be the result of the breakdowns of a number of drugs-related arrangements because four days before my arrival powerful FARC dissident "Don Ye," in control of critical cocaine routes in the region, had been killed.[87]

Throughout those years, intra-urban displacements often were—and continue to be—the only way for people to escape threats, given limited resources that prevent them from going further away. It is, however, a very questionable means of self-protection; the armed actors can easily follow those who have fled. Moreover, intra-urban displacement attracts less attention from the government or international agencies than mass displacements in rural areas do. This obscures the actual magnitude of violence resulting from tactical alliances—neither the state nor international agencies take adequate action. Hence, notwithstanding the changes in Colombia's wider security landscape throughout these years, in Tumaco, precariousness remained a constant.

The Loss of Civility

The impacts to citizen security that arise in the context of tactical alliances also distinguish themselves from those of other violent non-state group interaction types through the way in which they affect the referent object of security: the "citizen."

Being a good citizen implies behaving with civility toward other citizens (see chapter 2). At a minimum, this means respecting fellow citizens' lives; behaving "civilly" therefore contributes to citizen security.[88] I refer here to the "intimate dimension of civility," a form of interpersonal behavior.[89] It speaks to what Teresa Bejan calls "mere civility," which she associates with the seventeenth-century thinker Roger Williams. Accordingly, "unmurderous coexistence" is based on "a minimal, occasionally contemptuous adherence to culturally contingent rules of respectful behavior."[90]

Being in a context where others engage in violent behavior, that is, where certain people do not respect other people's lives, does not mean that those exposed to these dynamics necessarily engage in the same behavior, which would undermine civility. The exposure to quickly shifting alliances among violent non-state groups, however, does catalyze the loss of civility because of the unique ways in which it influences people's behavior. Such contexts blur the distinction between nonviolent bystander and violent accomplice, contributing to an environment of extreme mistrust. This, in turn, promotes the disintegration of a community's social fabric. These dynamics need to be understood against the backdrop of the context which gives rise to these behavioral patterns among violent non-state groups in the first place: the clash of the *plata fácil*, the "easy money" as locals call it, to be made at strategic locations of the cocaine business, with the lack of licit economic alternatives and of other opportunities such as education to enhance one's quality of life. It fosters a culture of indifference, even among family members and close friends, and the normalization of violence. These violent everyday life dynamics are not what could be described as culturally contingent, as is perhaps the case in the violent inter-clan disputes of the indigenous Wayúu, which I discuss below. Such disputes do not contradict civility if they comply with what the Wayúu consider accepted behavior. These dynamics also do not constitute a form of violent behavior against an enemy, following the logic of enmity, as discussed in chapter 4. Rather, they are the product of the complete absence of rules of behavior: a constant ambiguity that entails a decline in, if not loss of, civility.

Blurred lines between ordinary citizens and members of violent non-state groups fuel uncertainty in armed disputes and material spot sales or barter agreements, where community members become collaborators or entire social groups are perceived to be violent non-state groups (see section 4.2 and above). In tactical alliances, these distinctions become even less discernible. Given the dynamics of suspicion and revenge, even against individuals who belong to one's own group, community members are involved in many different ways. This goes beyond people simply being pulled to support one side (as in the absence of an arrangement) or forced into compliance to ensure illegal business activities (as in material spot sales and barter agreements). It is unclear who is armed legitimately, who is armed illegitimately, and who is not armed, as Mary Kaldor notes, *and* who is fighting on whose side for how long.[91] This situation produces a spiral of uncertainty and mistrust: general mistrust gives reason for groups to engage in preemptive and retaliatory killings. In turn, the uncertainty of not knowing when to expect violence and from whom to expect it fuels interpersonal distrust even further. This tears the social fabric and impedes collective action, both of which are essential for citizen security.

Community members of any age or sex become involved in the activities of violent non-state groups, voluntarily or otherwise. For example, the groups use community members as messengers to deliver messages to other group members or to an allied group. Since distrust is high even between allied groups, this is safer than direct interaction with them, which could lure them in a trap. Children often act as messengers or carriers. In Tumaco, violent non-state groups paid children 2 USD to make them transport arms in their school bags.[92] Other community members are used as informants to gather intelligence on who enters and leaves the neighborhood, what meetings are held in which places, and what events are occurring. It is for this reason that, for example, across multiple sites of my fieldwork, I noticed how the same men on motorbikes were riding around public places where I met with interviewees. Similarly, taxi drivers cruising for passengers, owners of the small booth selling mobile phone "minutes," or old men reading newspapers on park benches might be informants. The simple act of talking to them without knowing which group they are currently working for can make a person vulnerable to the other group's accusations. Also, these informants risk punishment if their information falls into the wrong hands, as the anecdote of one of my interviewees illustrates. The person in question bought juice every morning from an old woman on the corner, opposite the police station in Tumaco. One day, the woman was not there anymore; she was later found with her throat slit in her house. Apparently, one of the groups killed her because she reported information on the movements of police officers to another group, putting the first group at a disadvantage.[93]

Community members also become involved as contract killers. Violent non-state groups hire them to execute preemptive and retaliatory killings. An international agency staff member in Tumaco explained why youth are particularly popular "employees," insisting that young people have few options:

STAFF MEMBER: For the Rastrojos, it is easier [to carry out assassinations] by paying for another actor's service, including youth. Teenagers are [. . .] cheaper and less suspicious. It is easier for them to get to the potential victim. [. . .] They use teenagers as contract killers [. . .].

ME: *How do they recruit them?*

STAFF MEMBER: [. . .] For underage people it is always forced recruitment, independently of whether they pay or offer them something else. If the adolescent to whom they offer a job decides not to do it, he or she already falls into disgrace. The person is marked. Either he does the job or he does the job. He has to do it if he received money for it, but even if he doesn't receive money he knows that he has to do it anyway. You can't refuse to do it. If he is selected to kill someone, he has to do it. There is no other way. If he doesn't do it he has to leave, disappear, flee, but if he does it he receives money and this money constitutes an income for him. He also will have a group of friends who will always help him if he gets into trouble. This is part of the rewards of working for an armed group: they will never be short of anything, they won't be short of food, drinks, a place to sleep, clothes. They will always have money, can wallow in vice, be it prostitutes, drugs, alcohol, it's the best job. They always have free time. They provide one or two services and the rest of the time things are calm.[94]

Joining a violent group is seen as bringing opportunities.[95] Male teenagers are particularly prone to this behavior, as owning a gun is viewed as reaffirming their masculinity.[96] In Colombia, a society characterized by *machismo*, this is particularly true. James Gilligan notes that violence is committed "to ward off or eliminate the feeling of shame and humiliation" and achieve respect, pride, and dignity.[97]

Many teenagers adapt their behavior to the Machiavellian logic of their bosses, that is, their immediate superiors or the group leaders, to enhance their achievements and receive recognition for what they are doing. In the absence of economic opportunities, this compensates for the lack of recognition they would otherwise receive for example at their workplace or via education. A civil society leader from Tumaco was outraged when he described this behavior to me:

> These gang leaders, who do they use [as contract killers]? Children! Children who are eleven, twelve, thirteen years old. They attract them with guns, playing war. I have met children in cities like Quito where they meet at a corner, talking about their lives and drinking beer, but these ones don't. They talk about other things: "I will do more than my boss. When I have the opportunity, I will achieve more than him; I will have more money, I will ship more drugs. I will show my boss that I can do this. Boss, do you want to see that I'm capable of killing these people who sit over there?" "Let's see, show it to me." Boom, boom, they kill them! "Okay, I can do it, now I want to have a share of this *gramaje* [illegal tax]." This is not normal! This is not normal in human behavior![98]

What the civil society leader considered abnormal behavior can perhaps be explained in part by these children's lack of self-esteem. They typically live in marginalized poor and violent neighborhoods. It is plausible that some of them engage in such violence to overcome their shame for not having achieved much in life, according to their perceptions. Hannah Arendt's remark that "impotence breeds violence" applies to these children whose gun-handling skills are seen by them as their only means to be heard in society.[99] Referring to war in Sierra Leone, David Keen notes that "the gun itself commanded 'respect.'"[100] This has also been observed in other conflicts.[101] The motivations to engage in violence are therefore not necessarily solely economic, but can also include moral ones. As Keen further notes, "our most immoral actions may stem precisely from our moral impulses, since without these we would have no sense of shame in the first place."[102]

In the case of these young people, the immoral act of killing may be driven by their view that they ought to achieve something in life in order to be a "good" father who can sustain his family's livelihoods, a "good" boyfriend who has something to offer to his girlfriend, or a "good" son who financially supports his mother and of whom she is proud. When chatting to male teenagers at Tumaco's harbor about life in the town and their aspirations for the future, I learned that these were issues that mattered to them. "Working" for one of the groups can be a means (but not the only one) to achieve these aspirations. These value systems are also reinforced by the very people the youth aim to be "good" to. This is illustrated by the reflections of a woman in her mid-thirties who I interviewed in one of Caracas's marginalized neighborhoods, ridden by similarly volatile inter-armed groups dynamics as Tumaco. In a convinced fashion, she asserted that she would rather have her son die by the age of twenty-five as a famous gang leader than see him grow old, unemployed, and without respect from the community.[103]

Many of the responses of Tumaco's residents to violence, fear, and uncertainty amid the unpredictability of killings reinforce the loss of civility influenced by the breakdown of the distinctions between perpetrators and victims. Indifference, victim blaming, and the normalization of violence are among these responses. Respect for life has been lost or is under threat in many vulnerable regions of the world, including in parts of Colombia, Ecuador, and Venezuela. In the context of tactical alliances in Tumaco, this phenomenon penetrates even close relationships, to which must be added the indifference among bystanders. This affects not just very aspirational versions of civility, it further directly contributes to the decline of civility understood as respecting other people's lives. Put differently, some of Tumaco's residents are complete strangers to Putnam's "virtuous citizens," who "are helpful, respectful, and trustful towards one another, even when they differ on matters of substance."[104]

As in the case of spot sales and armed disputes, people adapt to the situation.[105] Changing their daily habits to minimize risks, they meet at friends' houses instead of in public spaces to avoid stray bullets, for example, and adhere to the rule of silence. As noted earlier, such self-protection alienates them from the state, but can tighten social fabric at the micro level. Yet in the case of Tumaco, I found examples where the social fabric was eroded even at this level, where family members or close friends would fail to support each other due to pervasive mistrust. These people deliberately did not show an interest in their friends' situation. It is an extreme response to the blurred lines, an extreme measure to protect themselves. A resident of Tumaco explained:

> Between friends or neighbors one doesn't know what illicit activity they are involved in, but you notice it if someone arrives with a luxury car, for example. Nevertheless, I don't care if he bought it with money or with drugs or if he won it in the lottery. I don't care. And I'd better not ask.[106]

Green contends that terror-imposed silence fosters social consensus because the community is jointly silenced in the face of an external threat.[107] This can strengthen community-level social fabric because, in solidarity, community members are more likely to cope with the threat. In settings of tactical alliances, terror emerges from within society: people's indifference in Tumaco impedes social consensus and caring even between friends, questioning any "civility."

Victim blaming also reinforces the loss of "civility" because it justifies killings as a result of noncompliance with rules, even if no rules exist. When discussing the armed disputes of preponderance as part of the "enmity" cluster of violent non-state group interactions in chapter 4, I show how people blame victims who do not stick to the rule of "not getting involved." In the context of spot sales, people blame those who do not avoid certain places. In settings of tactical alliances, a similar logic applies; yet it seems even harder to not get involved or to avoid certain places, due to the unpredictable nature of the killings and other forms of violence people might be victim of. In Tumaco, I witnessed victim blaming when I took a *mototaxi* (motorbike taxi) from one interview to the next one. We passed by a completely destroyed shop with people gathered outside. I asked the *mototaxi* driver what had happened. He replied that a grenade had been thrown into the shop only minutes before, destroying it. My driver felt it was the shop owners' fault because he had not paid the protection money. The owner had not complied with the rules and was therefore punished.

The problem with this simplistic explanation is that, most of the time, under quickly changing short-term arrangements, rules are not clear. Victims get involved without knowing it. Nevertheless, as the following extract from an interview with a civil society leader from Tumaco illustrates, people blame them regardless of whether they could have avoided being involved. Such victim blaming helps people increase certainty about their own security:

ME: *How is the population affected [by the breakdown of tactical alliances]? [...]*
LEADER: Indiscriminate assassinations do not exist. They only occur if someone is killed by a stray bullet. Normally, assassinations occur due to two specific actions. First, they occur because people are human rights defenders and,

with their discourse [. . .], they affect [the groups'] operations because they put corruption on the agenda; or they speak out against those involved in the illicit drug business. They publicly denounce crimes and criminals. These civil society members become targets to be eliminated [. . .]. Second, the person who is mixed up with them [is "killable"]. This is someone who [. . .] did something he/she shouldn't have done and therefore is assassinated. Many *mototaxistas* (motorbike taxi drivers) died here. Assassinated.

ME: *Why were they assassinated?*

LEADER: [. . .] We know little about the assassinations of the ten dead *mototaxistas* in the last three or four months. Which one was a good person, an honest citizen, and which a criminal? However, the public perception is that they must have had something to do with [the armed actors]. Either they did not get along well, or they got something wrong, or they did not want to do a certain thing, which could be used in evidence against the armed actor. Therefore, the best thing for [the armed group] to do always is to clean up.

ME: *Does this happen at night or only in certain neighborhoods?*

LEADER: Anywhere, at any time. It depends on the crime's seriousness, on the urgency of committing the murder, on the extent to which the citizen who is going to be assassinated is protected, on his/her lifestyle. It can be more difficult to kill him quickly, therefore either they have to take their time or they have to wait for a suitable moment. In the end, whether it's day or night doesn't matter here. Most murders in Tumaco occur during the day.[108]

People commented that the *mototaxistas* were killed for a reason even though "not getting involved" is virtually impossible. This is especially the case for young men, as they are vulnerable to being selected by violent non-state groups to do jobs for them. It was also reflected in local media articles on killings, which highlighted whether the murdered person had a criminal record, suggesting that he or she must have been involved in something bad. The implicit notion that these people deserved to be killed was used to justify these killings.[109] This reinforces the point I make in the previous chapter, whereby, rather than constituting a strategy to reduce the actual possibility of being physically victimized, victim blaming serves as a protection mechanism, or a coping strategy, to increase *perceived* security by distancing oneself from the person who was killed.

Another response to violence that thwarts civility in the context of tactical alliances is the normalization of violence.[110] According to Philippe Bourgois, normalized violence renders violence invisible to those within and outside the community and generates social indifference.[111] The understatement "it's a bit complicated" was a frequent answer to my inquiries about the situation. When I asked the civil society leader mentioned above about how people think about the frequent killings in Tumaco, he responded that "there is often fear, but the next day the fear disappears. One could almost say fear disappears completely with the individual's funeral. They bury the person and anxiety ends."[112] I watched the funeral procession of what seemed to be a young man, accompanied by his football team (see Figure 5.4). Most likely, he was one of those who "got involved," as the person next to me commented in that moment. The next moment, he was already talking about something else.

Everyday life is interjected by horrific spectacles of brutality; yet people normalize them and fall back into their daily routines, despite these interruptions. According to Carolyn Nordstrom's research in Mozambique, locals continued their daily lives amid war—"they defied the assault on the present to construct their own future."[113] Similarly, people's return to normal life after the funeral of a murdered person can be considered their way of coping with, or defying, the violence they are surrounded by.

Figure 5.4 Funeral procession in Tumaco, Colombia, 2011. Photo by Author.

The normalization of violence also occurs under other arrangement types, but in the context of tactical alliances it is particularly important as a coping mechanism, that is, to improve perceived security—at the expense of civility. Killings are not always "spectacles," like the example of the tongue used as a tie to deter people from interfering in spot sales,[114] or as brutal as the example of paramilitaries in combat who killed people with chainsaws (see chapter 4). Sometimes, they simply happen. Respect for life disappears because violent death is nothing out of the ordinary. In Tumaco, this normalization has led to a situation in which, after a weekend, people chat in a way that perpetuates the "banality of violence," as Daniel Pécaut calls it,[115] and obscures terror. A typical conversation that one can overhear on a Monday morning in one of the small shops, for example, goes like this:

> "Hey, how many deaths took place between Friday and Saturday?" "In the Ciudadela they snuffed out four, in the Morro two more, let me see, in total, ten, fifteen!"[116]

Although adapting daily habits reduces physical insecurity, and victim blaming as well as the normalizing of violence serve to reduce perceptions of insecurity, uncertainty persists. Going back to the situation after a killed person's funeral, the civil society leader I interviewed explained that, in general, the community continues life as usual once a murdered person has been buried. Yet he also elaborated further on the effect it has on the people close to the victim:

> The close family and close friends continue to be scared because they don't know where this might lead. The killed person's close friends are most scared—more than the family—because the family generally is not involved in the crime, only one family member. This person, however, has friends. Friends are most scared because often they are involved as well. Even if the friends are not involved themselves, the armed actors believe that they know something and assassinate them, only because of their friendship [with the person who was killed].

Given the widespread nature of killings though, such a situation is not an exception either. As a result, there is a constant tension between what appears to be the continuation of ordinary life at the surface, and permeating fear below.

Ultimately, quickly changing allegiances impede rule formation, making life a constant struggle of mistrust not only of the unknown but also the known. Das and Kleinman describe such "loss of context" the following way:

> As faith in trusted categories disappears, there is a feeling of extreme contingency and vulnerability in carrying out everyday activities [. . .].

Everyday life is then something that has to be recovered in the face of a skepticism that surrounds it like a ditch. One is not safe simply because one never left home.[117]

In the absence of an arrangement, everyday activities may help life continue. Under tactical alliances, however, the absence of rules entails constant skepticism and mistrust, even toward the known. When, in such contexts, uncertainty degrades collective action and makes respect for life crumble, civility is in decline.

The Gray Zone

The Guajira Peninsula is the border area in the Andean region that perhaps lies most at the margins of the periphery. It is an extreme case of the "rivalry" cluster because both interests and personal bonds as micro motivations for violent non-state groups to engage in short-lived arrangements influence the security situation (see section 2.1). Interest convergence among a large number of violent non-state groups *and* mutual sympathies between individuals of different groups facilitate cooperation on particular occasions. The layered nature of these two distrust-reducing mechanisms complicates security. Through the context of short-lived tactical alliances involving indigenous Wayúu, local drug-traffickers, and powerful post-demobilized groups, life in La Guajira converted into a gray zone.[118] Primo Levi describes an extreme "gray zone."[119] He discusses the Third Reich's concentration camps, in which the victims themselves sometimes became victimizers. Furthermore, these were spaces where the moral judgment of outsiders can be considered unwarranted:

> The enemy was all around but also inside, the "we" lost its limits, the contenders were not two, one could not discern a single frontier but rather many confused, perhaps innumerable frontiers, which stretched between each of us.[120]

While the context of La Guajira is not akin to the horrors Levi described, there are elements with "gray zone traits": the limits between victims and victimizers, between right and wrong, and between good and evil have been constantly redefined and are often void.

After the AUC's demobilization in 2006, newly emerging groups engaged in numerous short-lived alliances with other violent non-state groups (see Figure 5.5). The paramilitary Northern Bloc's Counterinsurgent Front Wayúu, later called Alta Guajira, did not demobilize and consolidated its

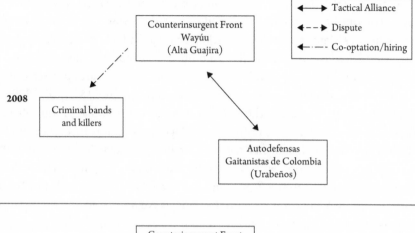

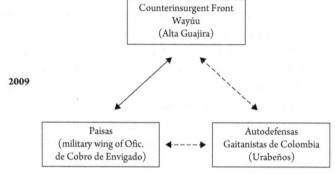

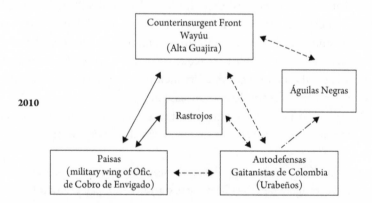

Figure 5.5 Shifting violent non-state group alliances in La Guajira.

presence in the region.[121] Other groups emerged to benefit from illegal economic activities. In 2008, forty men were seen patrolling the town of Uribia, wearing army uniforms and carrying long-range weapons. They supposedly belonged to the Alta Guajira.[122] Alias "Pablo," the paramilitary

Counterinsurgent Front Wayúu's leader, established alliances with other illegal structures and subcontracted and co-opted networks of criminal bands
and killers in Maicao, Dibulla, and Riohacha. He had a tactical alliance with
the Autodefensas Gaitanistas de Colombia, who consolidated themselves
in La Guajira after the paramilitary demobilization. This group, later called
the Urabeños, declined after its leader was captured on 15 April 2009.[123]
Simultaneously, the Paisas, the military wing of the criminal group Oficina
de Cobro de Envigado, came from the Magdalena region to La Guajira.[124]
Alias "Pablo" broke the alliance with the Urabeños (Gaitanistas) in mid-2009
to establish another one with the Paisas, provoking a dispute between Alta
Guajira in alliance with the Paisas, and the Urabeños.[125] Reportedly, in 2010,
Alta Guajira also had disputes with the Águilas Negras. However, the Águilas
Negras presumably were, or worked for, the Urabeños.[126] In the same year, the
Paisas specialized in contract killings, and the militarily powerful Rastrojos
maintained a tactical alliance in Cesar and in La Guajira to jointly fight the
Urabeños. Later the Rastrojos absorbed the Paisas. Alias "Pablo" was captured
in 2010 and extradited to the United States in 2012,[127] after which Alta Guajira
was dismantled. In the same moment that the Paisas had virtually disappeared
and the Urabeños were weakened, the Rastrojos began to enter La Guajira.[128]

As Figure 5.5 demonstrates, these quickly shifting tactical alliances in
La Guajira produce a volatile, if not erratic, pattern of non-state order that
perpetuates uncertainty. To some extent, this situation is akin to the situation described by the high-ranking police official from Cúcuta in the previous
chapter. In that case, new groups arrived, others left, and still others simply
assumed new labels. But there is one crucial difference—in Cúcuta, two main
parties were hostile to each other: the Rastrojos and the Urabeños. In the same
way that, as a researcher, I was able to make sense of this situation by identifying
who was hostile to whom, local community members were also able to identify
the groups with power. This was less so the case in La Guajira.

In 2012, I talked to a civil society representative from Riohacha. Despite following the groups closely, she was not sure who was allied with whom:

> They started to distribute pamphlets [advising about social cleansings]
> about two years ago when the Gaitanistas started to appear. I remember
> that, in May, [the groups] were mixed up, and they always organized
> marches and whatever. Around this time of the year, two or three years
> ago, [the Gaitanistas] even threatened the *personero* (municipal om-
> budsman) and the Ombudsman's Office [...]. One year later, the armed
> groups started to forge these alliances with each other, again many
> killings occurred among themselves. They also started to attack and co-
> opt the demobilized ones, including those who didn't want to take up

arms. Many dead bodies appeared [. . .]. I'm not sure who allied with whom, but nowadays we hear about Urabeños, Rastrojos, and Águilas Negras.[129] Recently, a Wayúu family said the Águilas Negras were threatening them near the border, but in the city center of Riohacha, in all the city centers of the municipality, there are the Urabeños and the Rastrojos.[130]

Not only were the differences between groups hard to distinguish, also confusion regarding the boundaries between perpetrators and victims made life in La Guajira indecipherable. Juan Carlos Gamboa Martínez divides the violent non-state groups' blurring modus operandi into two broad streams.[131] First, they maintained coercion networks through controlling micro-trafficking and illegal drugs distribution in the internal market. They further engaged in micro-extortion, selective killings, intimidation, and social control. To sustain these networks, they hired individuals as informants, contract killers, and messengers, as they did in Tumaco.

Second, the groups engaged in more sophisticated operations related to transporting, stocking, monitoring and shipping cocaine, money laundering, and managing the logistics of these activities. To camouflage these operations, they established networks of civilian straw-men, that is, intermediaries, across the region. When a tactical alliance breaks down, those who have worked for one group or the other no longer know whom to obey, who will pay their salary, and whom to trust. Some youth groups started to work independently. They used the name of a more powerful group, such as the Águilas Negras, a practice common in other conflict contexts as well,[132] which adds to confusion, uncertainty, and insecurity.

Just like the cases along the Ecuadorian northern border, these phenomena did not stop at the borderline. Venezuelans argued that violence had been "exported" from Colombia. A journalist from Maracaibo, for instance, asserted that, in May and July 2012, grenades were launched against a municipal institution building and the local newspaper in Maracaibo, and that these attacks were linked to rivalries between some of the criminal and post-demobilized groups. To be sure, the presence of violent entrepreneurs who engage in tactical alliances to enhance profit from illicit businesses is nothing new in Maracaibo (see section 3.2). The high-profile violence they were using, however, indeed was a relatively new modus operandi in Maracaibo, whereas it had been common practice in Riohacha in Colombia. His conclusion was that those who staged such attacks in Riohacha had crossed the border to expand their area of operation.[133]

The local context of the Guajira Peninsula, influenced by the Wayúu's culture and their status as binational people (see section 3.2), fortified the negative impacts on citizen security in two ways: first, by aggrandizing the role of violence;

and second, by shoring up the fragile character of inter-group alliances—and with them the vulnerability of community members—through the relevance of personal bonds.

First, the resort to violence is catalyzed by the Wayúu's frequent inter-clan disputes, which they deal with in their own decentralized political and judicial systems. These cultural institutions include violent punishment and enforcement measures. In the early 1990s, drug traffickers took advantage of existing disputes among Wayúu clans by co-opting or engaging in short-lived alliances with one of the clans, but not the others.[134] The drug traffickers implicated the clans in order to expand their own control, producing a shift away from the Wayúu's traditional parallel dispute management systems, and toward a violent strategy of pursuing their and their allies' interests. Paramilitaries and later their successor groups employed similar methods. Taking advantage of historic intra-ethnic rivalries, they drew certain Wayúu clans over to their side to help them fight others.[135] At the same time, Wayúu leaders exploited the external groups' interests to further their own goals. In 2009, for example, when alias "Pablo" broke the agreement with the Urabeños, more locals gradually became involved in subsequent disputes. This was because the Wayúu saw an opportunity to oust alias "Pablo"'s group and return the territory to the indigenous community. Some of them took revenge. According to one account, the Wayúu accused alias "Pablo"'s group of promoting the persecution of the Wayúu by the armed forces and therefore engaged in retaliatory actions.[136] According to another account, a Wayúu group calling themselves Águilas Negras, had previously worked with alias "Pablo," lost a cocaine shipment, and was excluded by him from further business deals. They took revenge because of the exclusion.

Second, the heightened speed of changes in dispute cleavages is related to the prevalence of personal bonds, the second micro motivation next to "shared interests" that is conducive to short-term arrangements. Bonds between group leaders are motives for cooperation related to personal issues on particular occasions (see section 2.1). These issues include private goals such as revenge, defending one's honor, or dignity. Because of this, the motive for cooperation disappears as soon as the goal is achieved. In many Latin American societies, where *machismo* is entrenched, ensuring "possession" of the most beautiful girl-friend in town, or taking revenge for humiliation by another man are among the reasons for forging short-lived alliances between two groups.[137] Examples like these were cited by several locals in Tumaco.[138]

In La Guajira, the cultural context of the Wayúu reinforces the volatility of personal bonds in tactical alliances. A case in point is the alliance between two drug trafficking groups, one of which was mainly made up of Wayúu. The alliance was forged between the two group leaders. They had a good relationship with each other because of a previous deal that should have given one of them access to enough money to have surgery to remove a facial scar that identified him to state forces. The following anecdote, related to me by a Wayúu leader in Maicao in 2012, demonstrates how the private goals of the group leaders triggered violence and engendered fear that affected the entire Wayúu communities. These goals provoked one Wayúu community's involvement in the violent activities and another one's victimization and eventual displacement:

> The story with the FARC's involvement [in alliances with other groups in La Guajira] is very funny. This was due to a well-known leader sought by the DAS [Colombia's former security service agency] and the state forces [. . .]. He was from La Guajira. The man was rebellious, he had a similar story to the man they captured in Venezuela a while ago, alias "Loco Barrera" [. . .].[139] After belonging to the military, he joined the paramilitaries and then he escaped [. . .], went back into the army [. . .], escaped again with arms and uniforms, and joined the FARC. When he was going to escape from the FARC, he ended up getting injured, acquiring an ugly scar in his face. . . . He practically ended up being obliged to stay with the FARC. Supposedly, this was his destiny, but the man was obsessed with getting rid of the scar because it [identified him to] state forces. They looked for him everywhere, but he [. . .] made fun of them [. . .]. They tried to find his face, they were after him, close on his heels, but never caught him. Never. Until he tried to have surgery [. . .], but never did it [. . .]. A drug trafficker found out that he was looking for money to get rid of the scar. Therefore, [the drug trafficker], with a group of traffickers, contacted him and offered him 30 million pesos [15,000 USD in 2011] [to do a job for them]. This was how he entered our community and the other displaced community. This was how he meddled there. [. . .] He came with forty, forty-five men [. . .]. Fifteen of the men were his own, but all the others who suffered most violence in the dispute [were Wayúu]. His brother, who was the group's sub-commander, died. [. . .] He ended up disabled [. . .] and some of his men were killed, but he forced these Wayúu to get involved. The situation was going to be complicated for the drug trafficker who had sent them because [the man with the scar] was going to tell the community who sent him to their *ranchería* [farm]. [. . .] In the end, I think he died [. . .] with an almost rotten body [. . .]. He never managed to have surgery on his face.[140]

Another example involves an alliance between a drug trafficking group and a Wayúu clan who wanted to take revenge on a member of a hostile clan. It demonstrates how personal goals can quickly supersede the relevance of economic interests, escalating situations that otherwise may be kept under control. When we were sitting in front of a shed on a *ranchería* on the outskirts of a rural town, a Wayúu leader explained to me her view on the situation. After appropriating part of the clans' territory in the 1990s, the drug trafficking group supported by another clan was looking to gain even more territorial control, due to the area's strategic location on the trafficking route from Valledupar to Maicao:

> Jairo, the person who invaded our territory, was [. . .] not only a drug trafficker but also had huge economic influence. [. . .][141] Basically, we left him a large part of our territory. [. . .] Jairo had a group of drug-traffickers with their own armed and uniformed men. They were heavily armed, handled their own people, financed their own people. [. . .] They wanted to appropriate the land, but [. . .] we didn't let them. [. . .] But this friction always remained; this appetite for more, for a conflict with our family [. . .].
>
> Unfortunately, in that particular year, something unexpected occurred. My uncle killed a man in self-defense, Carlos, a drug trafficker [Carlos was Jairo's nephew].[142] This is how this war started. [Being close to the leaders of another Wayúu clan with whom we have disputes,] Jairo joined forces with them to take revenge.
>
> [. . .] It was always a conflict in which one party was affected more than the other one. The two parties were two very different clans: our clan, we knew what we had and what we wanted. But the other clan, which allied with Jairo's men, obviously used their power. We would always be inferior to them. [. . .] We tried to settle the dispute and sent a messenger, [. . .] who was a cousin of the other clan, of the affected people, but it didn't change anything.
>
> This was when Jairo demanded my uncle's surrender. My family was opposed to this because, initially, Jairo said the perpetrator [the uncle] had to surrender himself so that they could hand him over to the army. However, since we knew about [Jairo's] influence on the army [. . .], we could hardly have done what he demanded. It would have been a sign of cowardice to hand over our blood to that clan [in alliance with Jairo's group] instead of dealing with this issue in another way, for example, through reparation. But he never talked about reparation. He always talked about two options. One was that the perpetrator surrendered and the other one that we would [. . .] go to war. We decided to go to war.
>
> We insisted we could pay him for his missing nephew Carlos, the person who was killed. We could pay him for the death of his nephew, but he never wanted that. A year later, [. . .] Jairo's people, together with the other clan, opted to exterminate our family. They picked on my

uncle first, who is wealthy, and the son of a well-known person from
La Guajira. They suddenly were scared that, if they started to kill us,
my uncle would [take revenge]. Jairo first wanted to have this uncle
killed. They sent a group of some thirty to fifty people. But our clan
resisted. They found the uncle alone and injured him. A bullet hit him
in his head. Nevertheless, he escaped. Jairo's group, together with the
other clan, were after him in the whole of La Guajira [. . .]. They were
after the uncle [. . .] until we found a strategy to conceal the fact that he
had survived. We said he had died. This was an internal strategy so that
these people wouldn't wipe us out.[143]

The clan's strategy of averting a full-blown inter-clan war revealed that (personal) rivalry based on revenge for Carlos, the nephew, rather than enmity,
characterized the situation.[144] This rivalry based on personal issues inflicted violence on the Wayúu population. Additionally, it created ambiguity regarding
who is on whose side because the drug trafficker's group allied with one of the
clans based on personal contacts, and in order to pursue private goal, revenge.
Clear conflict cleavages disappeared, fueling uncertainty among the local population. With the removal of the private goal (through the supposed death of the
uncle) rather than a victory (over the entire clan), violence may flare up whenever new personal issues become a matter of contestation.

   The Wayúu have been among the most affected victims of the conflict and
criminal dynamics in La Guajira. They have suffered stigmatization, displacement, targeted killings, and massacres.[145] This can partly be ascribed to their
direct involvement in, or exposure to, the violent non-state group interactions.
Nonetheless, the Wayúu's culture reduces the visibility of these security impacts.
Many displacements of Wayúu families within La Guajira to urban centers like
Maicao and Riohacha, and across the border to Venezuela, have never been recorded (see also section 7.1). When I visited Maicao the first time in 2012, a
humanitarian organization employee explained:

Here you can't distinguish the illegal from the legal actor, the state, because here is no state. When you talk about the state, you also talk about
citizens. State actors do not represent the state. They belong to the state
apparatus, but [. . .] most of their activities are illegal. Example: contraband. They don't confiscate the contraband. They only confiscate it
when it suits them. In other cases, they exact payment like any armed
actor. Another example: the army's activities. Here, especially in La
Guajira, you have to have clarity on the legal and the legitimate. These
two terms have to be addressed. For the Wayúu it is legitimate, for us

who are not Wayúu it is illegal. For example, trade. For us, it is illegitimate, for the *wuachaco* [smuggler] it's simply contraband. [. . .] They
[. . .] don't use the term "binational," instead they are one nation, like
one people, the nation Wayúu. [. . .] They say, "we are the same people."
When you cross [the border] from here to there, it's the same people,
the Wayúu, they are neighbors. When you are in Cúcuta and cross over
to San Antonio, it's the same people. Equally, when you go to Arauca
and cross to Apure, it's the same people. I know Arauca and I know
Norte de Santander. [In these regions,] when you go to the other side
of the border, it's the same. The same crops, the same customs. . .[146]

Wayúu families do not always denounce displacements to Colombian state
authorities because they have their own community institutions for support.[147]
Violent deaths of Wayúu often go unnoticed because, according to Wayúu
traditions, non-Wayúu are not allowed to touch the dead body. Instead, the body
is brought as quickly as possible to the family cemetery to be buried according
to their customs.[148]

One particularly emblematic case of security repercussions received widespread attention: the massacre in Bahía Portete from April 18 to 20, 2004. This
atrocity left six Wayúu dead and displaced six hundred more. It was the result of
a tactical alliance between the paramilitary Counterinsurgency Front Wayúu led
by alias "Jorge 40," and a Wayúu group led by alias "Chema Bala" (see section
3.1).[149] This Wayúu group intended to use the alliance with the paramilitaries
to resolve an inter-clan territorial dispute on Bahía Portete, a rural bay strategically located for contraband. The arrangement with the paramilitaries turned
this intra-ethnic dispute into a brutal contestation that did not bear any resem-
blance to previous confrontations. During the massacre, several Wayúu women
were tortured and killed, even though women normally receive respect in the
Wayúu's matrilineal society.

In 2016, I spoke to one of "Chema Bala's" relatives in Riohacha.[150] She
explained that "Chema Bala" and many other family members had been legally sentenced or were being sought. She lamented: "There was pain on their
side, there is also pain on our side. In the end, we will realize that we were all
victims." This view contributes to the powerful notion that the Guajira Peninsula
represents a "gray zone." The paramilitaries made the Wayúu allies to further economic interests, but they further encouraged behavior that involved
disrespecting Wayúu women's lives, thereby going against one of their most sacred principles.

In the case of Tumaco, the loss of civility arose from the locals' indifference
toward other people's suffering. In the case of La Guajira, in certain ways, the

loss of civility is even greater. Here, the active subversion of ethics, of what is normally viewed as morally repugnant, contributes to its gray zone character, in which people's marginalization from the rest of society turns everyday life into a constant struggle.

5.3   Subcontractual Relationships

Like spot sales and barter agreements, subcontractual relationships are based on shared interests. Yet while in the former, violent non-state groups strive for material or financial benefit, in subcontractual relationships the aim itself is often social control. This leads to more direct security impacts, but also entails the trivialization of insecurity because it can be attributed to local gangs, rather than powerful paramilitaries. The high levels of group interdependence due to the staggered nature of subcontractual relationships matters for security. Given the presence of intermediaries (subcontracted group) between the victim and the intellectual perpetrator (contractor), it is difficult to identify who the latter really is. Uncertainty over who imposes rules, and when they change, increases people's vulnerability; the contractor can decide to subcontract another party, or the subcontracted group can decide to work for another contractor. They may impose new rules, and random actors may claim to be the new contractor or subcontracted party.

The Trivialization of Insecurity

Violent non-state groups subcontract local groups when they are not familiar with the local context. Both parties benefit from their comparative advantages. For example, in 2011, the Mexican Sinaloa cartel supposedly subcontracted the Águilas Negras, who knew the area well in Tumaco, to gain access to this strategic port. Working with the Sinaloa cartel put the Águilas Negras at an advantage vis-à-vis other rivaling groups and increased their profits. Both groups, even though usually competing over drug money, shared an interest in this type of arrangement. Subcontracting youth gangs also benefits violent non-state groups because, as we have already seen in the case of hiring young people in Tumaco, youth are particularly prone to giving in to material incentives. A civil society representative from Valledupar explained the case of the subcontractual relationships between the Rastrojos and Urabeños on the one hand, and youth gangs in Maicao on the other:

> In Maicao, it is obvious that they [Rastrojos and Urabeños] contract gangs. The typical case is the young boys who can't study. They give

them motorbikes and say: work for us as *mototaxistas,* but you inform us via radio of movements in the city, and when we need you
for certain jobs, you do them for us. This way they contracted the
gang of young people. At a certain time *mototaxismo* was a strategy
of these structures to do intelligence work. The *mototaxistas* collected the extortion money. They also contracted them in specific
neighborhoods of Maicao to provide security, but not security for
the neighborhood; security for the houses where they planned their
operations [. . .].[151]

The youth gangs receive material rewards and benefit from the post-demobilized
groups' protection from law enforcement measures. The post-demobilized
groups benefit from the intelligence provided by the young people and from
being able to distance themselves from activities like extortion. An outside observer might see a gang of young people running an extortion racket, which
does not look like an activity that severely undermines the community's security. Yet local community members know that there are powerful players behind
the scenes, and that there are potentially lethal consequences if they refuse to
pay. If arrested, underage people receive less severe sentences, reducing the likelihood that they will cooperate with law enforcement agents against the post-
demobilized groups.[152]

Post-demobilized groups also subcontracted youth gangs in Ocaña in
Norte de Santander. Although the town is two hundred kilometers away from
the border by road, the border's influence remains strong. Many locals are involved in smuggling gasoline and supplies, especially food. Ocaña is a strategic
trafficking transit point that connects central Colombia, especially the south of
Bolívar, with the Caribbean and the border to Venezuela. Multiple groups were
present. As Map 5.3 illustrates, the precursors to process coca leaves into cocaine
in the laboratories in Catatumbo pass through Ocaña.

In Ocaña, large-scale gasoline smuggling and the drug business controlled by
the FARC, the National Liberation Army (Ejército de Liberación National—
ELN), the Popular Liberation Army (Ejército Popular de Liberación—EPL),
and post-demobilized groups overshadowed small-scale contraband. Gasoline
is smuggled under the auspices of organized groups, supposedly controlled by
narco-broker alias "Megateo" until his death in 2015. Corrupt police and military officials may facilitate the business. Locals reported that, despite multiple
checkpoints between Cúcuta and Ocaña, officials did not stop the flows of
smuggled goods and gasoline, nor check trucks for illegal drugs.

As a human rights defender in Ocaña explained to me, subcontracting youth
gangs allows the armed actors to maintain power and minimize attention:

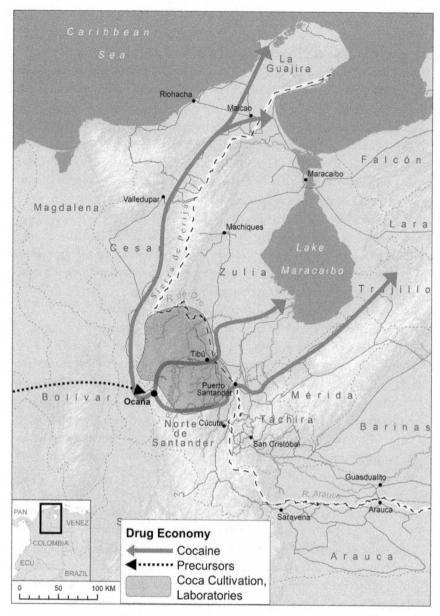

Map 5.3 Strategic location of Ocaña (Colombia) for drug trafficking routes. Map created by Author.

ME: *How is the population affected by these groups?*

HUMAN RIGHTS DEFENDER: Above all, the population is affected by uncertainty. These armed groups have dedicated themselves to a new wrongdoing here in Ocaña: youth gangs. They have started to give them money, drugs, and arms to fuel anxiety in the communes, and to control the population of Ocaña. This is happening in the whole province, in all of Catatumbo.

ME: *What is the relation between the youth gangs and the BACRIM?*

HUMAN RIGHTS DEFENDER: The paramilitaries have links with youth gangs. This is a way of destabilizing the harmony that exists, and of disguising the selective deaths that they carry out. They simply say they are carried out by gangs operating in the zone. Put differently, the gangs are an offshoot of the illegal groups [. . .] used to do the jobs of threats, pamphlets, assassinations, and contract killing. The illegal groups finance them [. . .]. They are an extension created to disguise the deaths because we have many violent deaths and all of them are related to drug trafficking, or at least most of them.

ME: *Have there been any deaths recently?*

HUMAN RIGHTS DEFENDER: Lately there were only a few deaths, but there still were some. Everything is related to the precursors, and the payment of *gramaje* [taxes on cocaine] or of *peaje* [road tolls] to pass the drugs. Most violent deaths in the region are related to drug trafficking.

ME: *People who are not involved in drug trafficking are not affected?*

HUMAN RIGHTS DEFENDER: This is the most interesting part: the gangs don't argue among themselves. They created these gangs, but this is a farce. Yes, it is true that there was a conflict among young people, but they were students from one high school, fighting with those from another high school. Conversely, the gangs are armed. These are gangs from peripheral neighborhoods, from settlements of victims of violence, forced displacement, disappearances, rapes. These neighborhoods are breeding grounds for violent groups. [. . .] These gangs don't fight among each other. They exist in every neighborhood to exert control over certain people [. . .].

ME: *Are there only deaths when someone doesn't pay?*

HUMAN RIGHTS DEFENDER: Exactly, because they don't fight with each other. [. . .] The gangs are divided in different zones of territorial control, but the Autodefensas [post-demobilized groups] have the overall control, therefore problems like in cities such as Cali when someone crosses a border do not exist. Here they coexist with the guerrillas. They all negotiate now with the drug traffickers. Everything revolves around the drug business.[153]

Subcontractual relationships obfuscate the ways in which violence originates from post-demobilized groups: insecurity in Ocaña is perceived to be a *local* problem. Trivializing insecurity by attributing it to youth gangs means that powerful groups can operate without meeting countermeasures from the state. If the state acts against a youth gang, the groups subcontract another one to exert control. Community members are intimidated by these dynamics. To protect themselves, they spread the narrative that youth gangs constitute the problem, even if they know that more powerful actors are behind it. Alternatively, they do not comment at all on these dynamics when asked about them by outsiders, adhering to the rule of silence. Added to this is people's distrust of state authorities, due to their involvement in illegal cross-border activities and police officials' links with violent non-state groups. These factors distance community members from the state and prevent them from participating in activities that contribute to citizen security, such as forming citizen security councils, or initiating education programs to raise awareness among youth about alternatives to illicit activities (see section 2.2).

The human rights defender revealed another role of the youth gangs:

> The climate of Ocaña is pleasant, people are nice. Therefore, what do the big leaders [of the post-demobilized groups] do? They bring their families [...] to live and study in Ocaña because we have good schools. This is another function of the youth gangs: protect the families of these gentlemen who live in Ocaña. [...] The worst thing about this is the acceptance of the community that doesn't have anything to do with drug trafficking. They accept that these persons do harm to this region yet welcome them as if they formed part of their family.

People fail to engage in collective action against post-demobilized groups and the drug business because they consider insecurity to be related to youth gangs. They also fear retaliation ordered by post-demobilized groups and acted out by youth gangs. This reinforces the image that youth gangs are the main problem. Subcontractual relationships between powerful groups and these gangs distort the population's perception of violence in their communities, obscure root causes of violence, and endanger those who speak out against them.

The ambiguity that often surrounds subcontractual relationships is striking as a citizen security impact, particularly when comparing these contexts with the modus operandi of groups in the context of tactical alliances where they subcontract *individuals*, like in Tumaco. Certainly, when groups rather than individuals are subcontracted it is easier for people not to get involved by staying away from youth gangs. However, subcontracting groups rather than individuals also distracts more attention from the intellectual mastermind behind the illicit deed, with two immediate effects: from the outside, insecurity may look less severe because "only" local groups fuel it, and local groups may claim to work for more-powerful groups to increase their status (even if this is not the case), contributing to further uncertainty.

When subcontracting is more remote, ambiguity intensifies. In Venezuelan Maracaibo and other cities, *pranes,* criminal leaders who control prisons, for example, remotely subcontract criminal groups from within the prisons to extort or kill for them. In the cases of cross-border subcontractual relationships, which I discuss in section 7.2, the border effect reinforces this ambiguity even further. In such contexts of subcontracted groups, it is difficult for locals to identify a logic of appropriateness, fueling uncertainty, and hence perceptions of insecurity.

5.4 Conclusion

Violent non-state group interactions that fall into the "rivalry" cluster negatively influence people's ability to ensure their physical security in the territories in which these interactions take place. Interpersonal mistrust that erodes the social fabric further stalls such attempts. In *spot sales and barter agreements*, people can partially adapt their behavior to the violent non-state groups' economic interests. In financial spot sales, they can avoid the space where these take place (like in Alejandría) to ensure their security. In material spot sales and barter agreements, the groups need community members as a labor force and access infrastructure, which generates violence if people do not comply with the groups' demands. It is basically unfeasible for people to protect themselves through avoidance strategies. The constant reconfigurations of *tactical alliances* produce ambiguity as to whose rules to comply with to protect oneself. Violent non-state group members and bystanders are intertwined, fueling mistrust and provoking victim blaming and the normalization of violence. Civility, a core element of citizen security, gets lost. In *subcontractual relationships*, citizens can protect themselves by following group-imposed rules. The rules however can be unclear if the contractor is not known. Subcontractual relationships between a powerful group and a youth gang contribute to the trivialization of insecurity, with severe consequences for local communities. Despite imposing social control, the powerful contractor is not visible and hence not accountable, making people particularly vulnerable to physical violence.

In the long run, the security impacts of contexts with "rivalry" clusters of violent non-state group interactions, particularly of tactical alliances, negatively influence all components of what I presented as an ideal-type citizenship (see section 2.2). This includes civility in human interaction, the notion of mutual responsibilities both by the citizenry and the state, and the sense of belonging to one community, fostered by wide-ranging participation. Given the lack of opportunities and the ubiquity of suspicion in contexts of unstable short-term arrangements among violent non-state groups, illicit activities and violence become common ways to earn money and solve problems. As a civil society leader from Tumaco put it:

Here it is possible to contract people for any kind of services: "I want
you to kill that guy because I owe him money. I'll give you some money,
he dies, and I don't have to pay him back!"[154]

Human life is sometimes worth as little as twenty to fifty USD (the cost for
contract killers in San Lorenzo).[155] In Tumaco, civil society leaders organized
protest marches to attract the state's attention to the situation. These activities
produced some, but not sufficient, change. The decline of respect for life reduces
the possibilities for collective action.

In contexts of desperation, it is hard to draw clear lines between victimizers
and victims, between those who undermine security and those whose security
is undermined. This is most evident in the cases of Tumaco and La Guajira. It
also derives from analyzing subcontractual relationships: are subcontracted
youth gangs those who undermine security or those whose security is being
undermined?

As I note earlier, committing violence can enhance feelings of pride. Yet as
we know from studies on armies, rebels, terrorists, and other violent non-state
groups across the globe, being killed while defending one's groups' interests can
also be a source of pride for the person who is killed and their family members.
The same is true for localized gangs. In such cases, understanding why group
members accept exposure to violence has to be considered in light of subjectivity, "the felt interior experience of the person that includes his or her positions
in a field of relational power." Each individual experiences violence differently.[156]
Many of my interviewees said they did not fear death. Having lived in a war
context for decades, violent death becomes part of everyday life, lowering the
threshold to become a member of such groups.[157] For those *forced* to engage in
or suffer violence however, the interior experience mentioned above seems not
to count.

Unlike situations in which violent non-state groups are "enemies" and thus
a certain form of order emerges from the availability of rules to ensure security
reduces distrust (see chapter 4), in the context of short-term arrangements interpersonal distrust and uncertainty disintegrate the social fabric at the community level and across regions. This impedes the collective action necessary for
citizens to participate in designing citizen security policies. Even if people trust
each other at the micro level, such as within the immediate family, joint action
beyond this is difficult. Entire communities are stigmatized by those outside the
communities—particularly the state's centers—just because homicide rates are
high and youth are involved in acts of violence. Ultimately, these communities
become isolated from the rest of the citizenry and the state.

The security repercussions in settings of subcontractual relationships
are most similar to those in contexts of stable long-term arrangements,

the third cluster of violent non-state group interactions which I discuss in the next chapter. These relationships are also situated most closely to long-term arrangements on the continuum (see Figure 2.1). In contexts of subcontractual relationships, violence can be less pervasive than in other short-term arrangements and disassociated from the perpetrator. Locals may not speak out against the social control they are subject to, such as extortion rackets, because they fear retribution by the person behind the control. This creates a stark contrast between the outside impression of security— a perception of security influenced by small criminal gangs only—and the actual strong pressure local communities live in due to the powerful groups behind the smaller gangs. As we see in the next chapter, under long-term arrangements, violence is typically even less prominent, but social control remains strong. Security as a provided governance function is not the result of an absence of armed actors, as it may seem at first glance, but in fact the product of a socially imposed behavior.

The case of Llorente shows that "enmity" and "rivalry" clusters may feature similar homicide rates, but that the form of violence is likely to be different: selective killings in the former, and combat or armed disputes in the latter. Generalized mistrust in the "rivalry" cluster of short-term arrangements erodes the social fabric of a society more directly than less generalized levels of mistrust in the context of long-term arrangements between violent non-state groups. As the final chapter concludes, these qualitatively different security outcomes require distinct policy responses.

6

Governance and Consent

When two neighbors have a dispute, they don't say: "I'll call the po-
lice!" They say: "I'll call the guerrillas!," or "I'll call the paramilitaries!"
This is how people threaten each other.
Civil society representative from Valledupar, Colombia, 2012[1]

They even decide on couple problems. The woman doesn't go to the
prefect []. Instead she goes to the guerrilla commander to tell him that
her husband beat her. If a boy has problems with a teacher at school, he
goes to the commander so that he calls the teacher.
Resident of the Venezuelan border zone, 2012[2]

Illicit governance is not just about armed conflict. It also is about the ordinary
things in life that matter regardless of war or peace. In the absence of a functioning
state, concepts such as "police" and "prefect," cited above in Colombia *and* in
Venezuela, have little meaning. In territories where the state lacks empirical
legitimacy among local communities and violent non-state groups engage in
stable, relatively non-violent, long-term arrangements with each other, people
turn to another authority rather than rebelling against the state.[3] Yet consenting
to the imposer of such an order is both shield and exposure at once: it ensures
protection from the ruler, but it also makes people more vulnerable to outside
rejection. Such dynamics are rife in Colombia's borderlands.

The border effect brings to the fore the distinct security implications of long-
term arrangements that fall into the "friendship" cluster of violent non-state
group interactions, particularly of supply chain relationships (see section 2.1). In
borderlands, violent non-state groups benefit from the enhanced stability of the
illicit economy, facilitated by the border's "filter mechanism": non-state actors
can easily operate transnationally while law enforcement agents and state forces
are more constrained by national boundaries (see section 7.1). This facilitates
supply chain relationships and the illicit economic opportunities arising from
them. Examining borderland cases also sheds light on other types of long-term
arrangements and their bearing on people's security. In effect, marginalization
and state neglect turn the states' peripheries into convenient drug corridors,

amplifying the contrast between state absence and the non-state provision of illicit livelihood options. As a result, people are more inclined to consent to such illicit opportunities while putting up with violent acts. As long as borderlands are stigmatized as generally dangerous places and the disconnect between the countries' capital cities and their margins persists, illusorily calm, but illicitly governed, spaces go unnoticed. Violent non-state groups can forge stable long-term arrangements, deciding on the rules of behavior in these forgotten communities, without central governments even realizing (see section 7.4).

The "friendship" cluster of violent non-state group interactions that comprises stable long-term arrangements is located in the continuum's upper-right corner. The location indicates the arrangements' long-term durability and stability compared to other forms of non-state order. This is possible thanks to what I term a very basic, perhaps utilitarian, version of "friendship" in which the groups refrain from using violence against each other, or against a broker. Largely informed by shared values or power asymmetries as mechanisms to reduce distrust between the groups, the arrangements comprise supply chain relationships, strategic alliances, pacific coexistence, and preponderance relations (see section 2.1). Compared to other types of relationships, the groups that engage in long-term arrangements reduce mistrust among each other in a more general way; incidents of physical violence are comparatively rare. Instead, armed actors exert social control, define the rules of behavior, and typically complement each other in fulfilling governance functions. In state-neglected spaces, communities orient their behavior toward rules imposed by these groups, as opposed to a state-oriented citizenry in regions where the state overrides, or competes with, another actor's authority. This mutuality fosters a sense of belonging to the local community while alienating its members further from the state. When communities normalize the presence and practices of these "shadow governors," it is hard to comprehend what is going on for anyone outside the community. These dynamics facilitate shadow citizenship and shadow citizen security.

6.1 Supply Chain Relationships

In supply chain relationships, the violent non-state groups' mistrust toward the community makes shadow citizen security hard to attain. The groups' unresponsiveness and the communities' fear of punishment for noncompliance with the imposed rules hamper the armed actors' legitimacy, especially when punishment is perceived to be arbitrary. None of Weber's three inner justifications upon which domination rests—traditional, charismatic, or legal domination—applies when this domination is based on power alone rather than on authority.[4] Yet armed actors can counterbalance this trend by providing (illegal) economic opportunities that increase the communities' tolerance margin vis-à-vis undemocratic rules.

Mistrust *Omnium contra Omnes*

Inter-group distrust sets supply chain relationships apart from other long-term arrangements and aligns them with short-term arrangements characterized by mistrust *omnium contra omnes*. Violent non-state groups in supply chain relationships do not necessarily share values with each other nor is their relationship based on power asymmetries between a preponderant group and the others, which would help reduce distrust between them. Third parties, brokers, contribute to the relatively stable and durable character of these arrangements, and to lower levels of inter-group violence, even between ideologically opposed groups. Shared values materialize between groups and brokers, especially at the higher ends of the supply chain. The groups therefore are able to reduce distrust in a general manner with the broker, but not among themselves.

The following examples demonstrate how inter-group distrust translates into distrust toward local communities. The prevalence of an environment of general mistrust and suspicion was a recurrent theme in a large number of interviews; here I have picked the ones that confirm its relevance from a variety of different perspectives, reflected in the breadth of my interlocutors. The first one, from the perspective of a former paramilitary member, illustrates inter-group distrust. The second one, explained by an ex-rebel, shows how this leads to distrust among their own ranks when the enemy might have infiltrated. The third one demonstrates how such conditions fuel mistrust among local communities because of the lack of clarity over the identity of those whose rules they are supposed to obey. This and the subsequent two examples further reveal the varying security implications, depending on the "type of civilian" concerned. Those who speak out openly, namely human rights defenders, are least tolerated. Outsiders, such as international organizations, are potential whistle-blowers, especially if they are not known to the groups, and hence may constitute a threat against the groups' business affairs. Known, local organizations are tolerated as long as their activities do not meddle in the groups' affairs. The final example, of a local priest, shows how paranoia arises in such circumstances through which even the most trusted members of society are viewed as potential enemies or whistle-blowers that need to be silenced, in this case, members of the Church.

In the Colombian-Ecuadorian borderlands, distrust persisted between the Revolutionary Armed Forces of Colombia–People's Army (Fuerzas Armadas Revolucionarias de Colombia–Ejército del Pueblo—FARC) and paramilitaries or post-demobilized groups, even though they partook in the same illicit supply chain. Around 2011 and 2012, one of these chains, for example, included the FARC's mobile column Daniel Aldana in Bajo Mira, the Rastrojos in Alto Mira and Frontera, and other post-demobilized groups along the River Mira in Colombian Nariño, and Ecuadorian Esmeraldas and Carchi (see map 3.7). Such distinct groups are linked in the cocaine supply chain via a broker. This was corroborated by my conversation with the female ex-combatant I mention in the previous chapter who was first a member of the FARC, then a paramilitary member, and also worked along the Colombia-Ecuador border (see section 5.1). She called such a broker "mafia" or "drug-trafficker." Different to Felbab-Brown's argument, referring to Peru in the 1990s, that the relationship between armed groups and these brokers "falls apart just as easily as it comes together,"[5] evidence from Colombia's margins in the 2010s suggests that it is a relatively stable business "agreement":

ME: *How was the relationship between paras and the FARC [. . .]?*

EX-COMBATANT: As far as I was concerned and according to how they treated us, the only relationship that existed was the one between my husband and me because he was *paraco* and I was *guerrillera*. I had already left the [FARC] when I met him. [. . .] The rest did not have any relationships. As the FARC operate on the basis that they are against the army and against the paramilitaries, the paramilitaries cannot meet with the *guerrilleros* or else they die.

ME: *How about the drug business?*

EX-COMBATANT: This is like parasitism. The FARC protect, but the paramilitaries take over. There can be combats, but the paramilitaries take the profits. Because the paramilitaries have better access to the cities, they are less persecuted, less bothered, whereas the *guerrilleros* are bothered a lot. There is a difference. The *guerrilleros* have to hide. The paramilitary doesn't. [. . .] The paramilitary simply doesn't reveal his identity.

ME: *Were there links, for example, that they handed over paste or [. . .] cocaine [. . .]?*

EX-COMBATANT: From what I understand: no. There was no relationship, neither links in the drug business nor arms. What we acquired here, we acquired it through us, through our commanders, but I never heard or noticed them saying, "Okay, we have an agreement with this FARC Front so that they let us pass," no.

ME: *With the mafia?*

EX-COMBATANT: Yes. [. . .] The *paras* have contact with the drug traffickers, with whom they make [. . .] agreements in arms and drugs. Regarding sales, they usually don't go lower than paste. The FARC process the leaves, they always process them. But who generally makes profit is who gets hold of the rest, the paste. They do the marketing [. . .]. The FARC always sow, process, and pass on. Each one, each group has its contacts and its ways and means, and generally a laboratory. The paramilitaries found the laboratory so the FARC had to run away and they left it there fully operational [. . .]. The army or the paramilitaries take some of the drug and burn the rest to let everyone know that they burned everything, but they take the paste. [. . .] It also depends on the commanders, not all of them are corrupt. Some maintain their ethics, their standards, a kind of transparency, and others don't.

ME: *Were there cases in which the FARC sold arms or drugs to the mafiosi and then the paramilitaries bought them from the mafia?*

EX-COMBATANT: Possibly [. . .]. I noticed that we dealt with people from the mafia or with people specialized in selling arms.[6]

While in other long-term arrangements in fragile settings violent non-state groups are mostly concerned about state infiltration, in supply chain relationships informants from hostile groups constitute an additional threat. As the interview extract shows, from a rebel perspective, the collusion between elements of the army and the paramilitaries means that there is not much difference between these two for them. From a civilian perspective however, avoiding retaliation by the rebels is yet another reason to keep a distance from the army, the state's most prominent representative in these war-torn peripheries. In fact, this is not the only layer of distorted conflict cleavages of which civilians have to make sense of. This account suggests that, at least at the tactical level, hostility between the state and insurgents is more likely to be defined by who has control over a valuable product—in this case, the coca paste—than by whether one defends the nation or a revolutionary cause. Talking to an ex-FARC couple, I noted how this mistrust bred suspicion. In 2006, the man was the supervisor in a cocaine laboratory for the first processing stages in La Victoria, Nariño:

ME: *Who was in charge of [the laboratories]?*

EX-GUERRILLA HUSBAND: The guerrillas, but inside there were civilian workers. I was with them for two years as a supervisor. [. . .] We were there to support them. Sometimes people came; therefore we protected them with arms. [. . .] The laboratories are practically theirs [FARC's], because they use them to finance themselves [. . .].

ME: *What did they do with the cocaine after the laboratories?*

EX-GUERRILLA WIFE: They pass it on to other countries. There are people in charge of this [. . .]. This was in 2006, our kid was two and a half years old.

EX-GUERRILLA HUSBAND: We were working in a laboratory [. . .]. There were infiltrators [among the civilians who worked in the *cocina*]. Infiltrators always tried to join. We noticed that there were two guys. . .

EX-GUERRILLA WIFE: [interrupts] They had only spent two months there, no more!

EX-GUERRILLA HUSBAND: . . . they belonged to the paramilitaries and later they [the FARC] realized it and they killed them.

ME: *So they were. . .*

EX-GUERRILLA HUSBAND: Civilian workers! Around one month later, they
    burned the laboratories, they burned everything.
ME: *The paramilitaries?*
EX-GUERRILLA WIFE: The army.
EX-GUERRILLA HUSBAND: Through them [the paramilitaries]. They arrived
    straight away. It was a hidden place that no one could find, but they came
    straight there. After that I decided to leave. Through my brother, because the
    truth is [...]: if you kill someone they kill you. [...] Therefore we left. There
    were also civilians in the *cocina*. There were around six civilians at the en-
    trance and six of the organization and three with radios inside. [...][7]

Supply chain relationships between various armed groups do not take place
in isolation. Local community members are involved as workers in processing
laboratories, as this account attests. During my interviews on the Ecuadorian
side of the border, in the province of Esmeraldas, locals also explained that
young men from Nariño and from Esmeraldas across the border were lured
by high salaries to work in cocaine laboratories. Often they were not allowed
to go back to their community afterward because of their knowledge of the
process and the people involved. Nonetheless, many were ignorant of these
consequences when accepting the work.[8] From a community perspective,
being embedded in such cocaine supply chain dynamics shapes people's way
of life just as distinctively as open combat. The workers' lives may find an ab-
rupt end while working in the laboratories through an attack by the military,
or through assassination by the guerrillas or paramilitaries. The cocaine supply
chain dynamics also shape the lives of the workers' families who have to cope
with their relatives' disappearance after they go off to work in the laboratories,
not knowing whether their loved ones are still alive. In addition to this,
communities are affected more broadly, given the fear that their children might
be lured into the business. Yet while the local population can sense this constant unease through and through, these repercussions are hardly visible from
the outside. Their plight goes unnoticed.

    Borderlanders are often caught in a limbo situation of ensuring their
livelihoods through illicit, yet legitimately perceived, economic opportunities
that arise in the context of cocaine supply chain networks, while being vulnerable to abuse by armed actors. Trusting no one in such settings becomes a survival strategy. This reflects Daniel Pécaut's statement that "even in the absence of
any disputes between armed protagonists [...], it is possible for banal, everyday
violence to be transformed into terror" and that, "having become used to the
rule of silence, the population at large learns to trust no one."[9] What is more,
supply chain relationships facilitated by brokers produce a paradoxical situation
in which the very possibility of nonviolent inter-group relations undermines

the local communities' citizen security. This might not be in observable terms, for instance, captured in numbers of mass displacements and massacres, but in perceived terms, noticeable in unease and anxiety. The simultaneous existence of the conflict cleavage along ideological lines and the groups' cooperation due to shared interests in the illicit economy, in addition to the shared values with the broker who makes the cooperation possible, means that community members lack clarity on appropriate behavior. Neither strategies typically applied during conflict, such as collaborating with the more powerful group, nor strategies applied in the contexts of illicit economies, such as offering labor to both groups, ensures survival. The local population knows about agreements between groups in general. However, since these are made through third parties, brokers, they are not necessarily aware of the identities of those who impose the rules of local behavior. In this context of non-confrontational yet persistent mistrust, threats or killings of relatives or community members—rather than members of the other group—are common. A human rights defender from Norte de Santander explained these dynamics to me:

HUMAN RIGHTS DEFENDER: Nowadays, the calamity is worse because there is a Machiavellian agreement between the guerrillas and the narco-terrorist groups, as the government calls them [laughter]. The guerrillas produce and the groups that previously were the *paras* and are now the illicit groups market. There is a pact between them. This situation is more diabolical for the civilian population than it used to be. In the long run, it severely affects the population in this zone of Catatumbo. If they do not agree with the drug commercialization, they have to flee. As of January 2012, 12,500 people were displaced in the municipality [. . .]. It is worse [if there is a pact] because people don't know who they are dealing with. Previously, when the guerrillas or the paramilitaries were there, they knew how to work with them. Now, anyone arrives in an area and identifies him or herself simply as the boss. The other groups who are the sellers retaliate against people because they say those who arrived didn't have permission. This is worse for the population because they don't know who they are currently living with in the area.

ME: *Do the groups identify themselves? [. . .]*

HUMAN RIGHTS DEFENDER: They say they are in charge and that's it. [. . .] They don't have a clearly defined political identity anymore, as existed earlier when there was a rightist or extreme-rightist political identity. [. . .] Nowadays, the mid-level officials who stayed free of the self-defense groups' peace process of 2005 do business themselves [. . .]. They make and break their deals, now that they live with the guerrillas.

ME: *How do they make these agreements? Do they negotiate?*

HUMAN RIGHTS DEFENDER: Yes, the hardest part is that, in addition to the guerrillas and the illicit groups, Catatumbo's law itself (state forces) plays a role. The law knows the routes, how to get the precursors. They bribe with money and belong to the same game. Those who do not agree not only with any of the *two*, but of the *three* groups, leave the region or die. This is what is most unfortunate about the situation in Catatumbo.[10]

The role of "Catatumbo's law" mentioned by the human rights defender corroborates an important point: from a local perspective, distrust among various violent non-state groups—and state actors such as "Catatumbo's law" behaving as if they were violent non-state actors—contributes to general mistrust and unease in contexts of illicit supply chain relationships. These dynamics can shape everyday life more forcefully than, or add to, "enmity" between state forces and insurgents. As the continuation of our conversation shows, speaking out jeopardizes one's life; the work of human rights defenders in particular risks becoming a silent scream:

ME: *Are there many threats?*

HUMAN RIGHTS DEFENDER: Many threats, many, many threats. Human rights defenders, leaders, everyone, there is no one who has not been threatened. We are all threatened. This has been serious. It is difficult because the Ministry does not give guarantees to exert civilian control over the armed actors in the region, which is what we do in defense of human rights.

ME: *What type of threats?*

HUMAN RIGHTS DEFENDER: Text messages, calls, and in person, they approach you and talk tough to you.

ME: *Do they tell you who they are?*

HUMAN RIGHTS DEFENDER: No, they show you their weapon and then you don't ask. The most difficult part is when you report it to the public prosecutor. Anyone, that is, a leader or an ordinary person, who wishes to make a complaint, first has to report to the public prosecutor or to the National Police. They ask you: "Against whom, tell me against whom?" Or they ask you what the person was wearing . . . You say the guy had a gun and that you don't know because in that particular moment you only see the weapon, nothing else. You don't see the face or the name.

ME: *Are there other cases in which they want people to know who they are?*

HUMAN RIGHTS DEFENDER: No [. . .]. Here, they only care about the illicit drug business.[11]

Mistrust is not directed only toward locals. It also affects outsiders who enter the territory where the illicit business is thriving. The consequences are twofold: either one enters and obeys the local rules, as in the following example, or one stays out (see section 7.4). When I accompanied a diplomatic mission in one of the borderlands, I witnessed how, in regions with cocaine supply chain relationships, as an outsider one can be easily caught amid tension in a seemingly harmless situation. I captured this situation in my field notes:

> We traveled to [the farm near the international border] to talk to the community council's president. Upon arrival, we first went to see the river and the beautiful landscape. At that moment, several canoes hastily took off from the riverside near us and crossed the river to the other side. We then met the council president and other people outside his house next to the border river. When we were talking to the council president, some people started to move cattle across the path to the river. My colleague and I stood up to watch them. The president reacted harshly: "Don't take pictures!" We had not even taken out our cameras and all we could see was seemingly peaceful countryside. When a woman complained to the president, "But the other guy is taking pictures as well!," another man who was taking pictures quickly put his camera away.

I discussed this incident with locals who were familiar with the conflict and crime dynamics in the region. Independently from each other, several of my contacts were convinced that these people were guerrillas or guerrilla collaborators involved in supply chain relationships who used canoes to traffic merchandise. I made two observations in particular that suggest the plausibility of this hypothesis: first, there was a hierarchy. The way in which the woman behaved toward and looked at the president suggested he was her superior. Second, the farm was located in a strategic zone for illegal cross-border activities. The cattle were probably stolen on one side of the border and smuggled to the other, but, given the rapid departure of the canoes, they were trying to hide something else, likely cocaine trafficking. Presumably, they were concerned that we would gather intelligence that could be used against them in one way or another. Where dynamics of armed conflict and illicit supply chain relationships converge, anyone may be hand in glove with the enemy, hence suspicion and mistrust toward outsiders is a justified reaction.

Certainly, there are valid objections to these examples: human rights defenders and international organizations are perhaps the most extreme cases in which mistrust suggests itself, and therefore scrutinizing less likely cases is necessary to avoid bias. Indeed, local humanitarian organizations, for instance, can operate in these territories without being threatened—insofar as they stick to the rules. If they do, they are still embedded in dynamics of general mistrust, which makes the validity of these rules less certain than in other circumstances. Even if not targeted directly, such mistrust *omnium contra omnes* produces what Taussig, referring to Colombia in the 1980s, calls "situations of terror as usual":[12] contradictory and inexplicable factors that fuel fear of the unknown.

An anecdote of an incident during one of my borderland trips in the Venezuelan border zone illustrates this. On that trip, two friends working for a humanitarian organization accompanied me from Machiques, Zulia, to a village further toward the mountainous border area. The illicit supply chain networks originating on the Colombian side of the border extend to this region. Therefore, armed actors engage in supply chain relationships in this area of the Venezuelan side of the border too. On our way, we were stopped by uniformed armed men, which, according to my friends, was unusual on that route. When they saw the decal of the humanitarian organization on our car and one of my friends showed his employee identity card, they let us pass. My friends were not sure which group they belonged to. The men did not identify themselves and did not seem to trust us until they saw the decal on the car. The illicit checkpoint was terror as usual.

Even members of the Church were met with distrust. Some years ago, a priest explained to me that the FARC Front that ran the area of the Ecuadorian border zone in which he lived had gathered eighty photographs showing him in numerous locations during different activities over a period of six months, the time he had been living there. They claimed to have 1,120 pictures of a colleague who had been living in the region for longer.

PRIEST: They had pictures of me in [City A] when I was in the supermarket eating ice cream with two friends. They had pictures of me in [City B] and [City C]. I asked them: "Are you going to print a journal with this or what? Give me a copy because I don't have these pictures!" They said, "We can't." Pictures during a service in [City D], during a service in [City E].
ME: *Why did they show you the pictures?*
PRIEST: To tell us that we are marked, that they gathered intelligence on us . . . and I was scared . . . this is a way of terrifying people, too, isn't it?[13]

Mistrust places constant pressure on people's lives and induces paranoia by all against all. These were just two examples of pervasive manifestations of suspicion and paranoia: the council president's paranoia that the international organization staff and I would take pictures of them, and the priest's paranoia due to the pictures taken of him. Such low levels of trust correlate with high levels of fear,[14] and fear surfaces in aggressive mindsets, dreams, and chronic illness.[15] Although harder to quantify than physical violence,[16] the costs of constant fear for society are high, if translated, for example, into costs for the public (mental) health budget or the damage it does to citizen participation.[17] The population responds to this fear-generating mistrust with apathetic silence rather than collective action. This is to avoid suspicion since one wrong word to the wrong person might be deadly: "Everything is handled in silence," the priest explained.[18] As in the context of the "rivalry" cluster of violent non-state group interactions, it is a deliberately chosen means of self-protection.[19]

Behavioral rules dictated by mistrust produce some kind of security: the rules create order, including the absence of theft, rape, and other crimes because potential victimizers fear punishment by the guerrillas. As the priest told me, after an incident of rape in their community, he and a colleague tried to convince the local FARC leaders not to kill the rapist. The FARC, however, argued that such behavior was unforgivable. According to rumors, some days later they killed the rapist by firing a rifle in his anus.

In a study on Putumayo of the early twentieth century, Taussig states: "*Narratives are in themselves evidence of the process whereby a culture of terror was created and sustained* [italics in the original]."[20] These rumors fueled such a culture of terror in the borderlands. This also applies to other regions. A resident of Tufiño, an Ecuadorian border village in Carchi province, pointed to the effectiveness of rules dictated by mistrust: "Across the border, you don't see any problems, either of rape or of something getting lost. You can leave a bag of money on the street, it wouldn't get lost."[21] While, at times, community members approve of the guerrillas' substitution of state functions, on other occasions they do not have any choice other than to accept it, highlighting the undemocratic nature of their governance.

Vulnerability amid Illicit Opportunities

Cocaine supply chain relationships entail economic opportunities for the local population, compensating for shortcomings in other governance areas and widening the margin for accepting violent measures. Vulnerability to abuse can be traced back to the function of small brokers, so-called *financieros*, at the first stages of the supply chain. This phenomenon is not unique to geographical peripheries. What I call the moral economy of borderlands at the convergence of conflict and crime, which emerges in border areas of vulnerable regions, however, makes it particularly evident. The term "moral economy" refers to an alternative way of understanding exchange that is not (only) shaped by neoliberalist market logics but also informed by deeper societal and cultural processes.[22] In the context of Colombia's borderlands that concentrate the first stages of the cocaine supply chain, the social processes in which the cocaine economy is embedded are intertwined with illicit cross-border flows and the logics of the armed conflict. In such a context, communities share in their belief that illicit activities across the border constitute a legitimate means to making a living. This intensifies the contrast between the absence of licit livelihood options and the prevalence of opportunities at the margins, or outside the realm, of legality.

Financieros are brokers who buy the farmers' coca leaves and coca paste, and sell it to violent non-state groups who further process or traffic the product. Coca farmers cannot choose their clients; they have to sell their product to certain *financieros*. A farmer from Putumayo confirmed: "They only sell to them. To no one else. If you sell to another person, they will punish you, punish you, punish you!"[23] Whether they cultivate coca at all is the farmers' choice. As an international agency staff member put it, "the communities are not forced [to cultivate], but they are told: 'Okay, if you cultivate, you have to sell to me, I'm your only client and, whoever wants to, can sell to this client.'"[24] Given the profits and the absence of comparatively lucrative alternatives, many see it as the only viable option to sustain their families. The *financieros* pay the farmers, but do not protect them. On the way from their plots to the village where the *financieros* buy the coca paste, the farmers sometimes have to pass numerous police or military checkpoints with the illicit goods. In 2011, a displaced woman who used to cultivate coca in Bajo Putumayo explained to me the temptation of the money, despite the risks:

> You sell [the coca paste], you go to the village and the buyers come to the village. [. . .] Every weekend, they come. For example, during one week everyone harvested. [. . .] On Sunday, everyone went to the village and there were the people, and the money from Cali arrived [. . .] big burlap bags . . . they found the ways to get the money to the village. [. . .] Every Sunday we took [coca paste] to the village. The women, not the men, took out coca paste from the farms because the police were there. When they showed up, they searched the men but not the women, and we stuck the paste here onto our body and kept it here until the village. Then we took it out and sold it in the village. One gram of merchandise costs 1,000 pesos [around 0.52 USD in 2011]. . . it was a thousand grams, one kilo is a thousand grams, right? This is a lot of money [. . .]. Of course [. . .], we helped, but the men did the work, it was very hard work. The women, we sowed the coca and we took the coca paste off from the farm because there were always checkpoints with soldiers and policemen, and they always searched the men.[25]

Less powerful than those brokers who operate at the later stages of the cocaine supply chain, *financieros* change frequently through being killed or caught, with consequences for the communities. These consequences include persecution and death. First, when *financieros* are caught, the farmers who sold coca to them can be accused of being collaborators. Second, new *financieros* tend to implement new rules, sometimes without coca farmers being aware of what new rules apply, of the product's price, and of when and where they can sell it. Third, confusion about the *financieros'* identity causes harm. As my conversations with farmers and representatives of the Ombudsman's Office in Putumayo and Nariño revealed, in some cases, people came to a village pretending to be *financieros* sent by a bona fide group. Farmers sold them the paste and once the "real" *financiero* arrived, they were punished for selling it to the others.[26] The function of the *financieros* makes rules of behavior for the communities less legible while increasing people's exposure to abuse, undermining both perceived and objective citizen security.

Economic opportunities provided by violent non-state groups in the supply chain narrow the legitimization gap arising from mistrust *omnium contra omnes* and increased vulnerabilities. In a way, the armed actors themselves impede alternative licit livelihood strategies. This enables them to present themselves as saviors for people in need of income—just as in other contexts they provide protection from insecurity produced by themselves. The presence of armed groups impedes licit economic opportunities because it deters companies from investing in such regions. Even if investors are present, community members have difficulties in securing the sought-after jobs. In Putumayo, for instance, where the oil industry attracts investors, few employees are locals because they are branded as collaborators of the guerrillas who attack mining infrastructure.[27] Yet the state itself is also indirectly or directly responsible for the fact that the armed actors achieve such a status: indirectly, when due to its very absence no alternative options are available; and directly, when state officials are (perceived to be) complicit in the promotion of the illicit economy.

In many contexts of shadow economies, state capacities are deficient and the state does not provide alternative livelihoods.[28] Colombia's borderlands are no exception. In Bajo Putumayo, civilian state institutions have never been widely present and the road infrastructure is poor, which has allowed the guerrillas to promote a coca economy.[29] Many villages lack connections to nearby towns. Rather than growing cacao or bananas, goods that have to be transported to markets, farmers prefer to grow coca and to engage in the basic processing from coca leaves into paste and base that the *financieros* pick up and pay for in nearby villages.[30] According to a 2012 study of the United Nations Office on Drugs and Crime (UNODC), in Putumayo 64 percent of the coca growers sold coca leaf, and 36 percent processed the leaf themselves into the basic paste, the second highest percentage region in Colombia after the Meta-Guaivare. A farmer expounded the process:

We all work in it. We don't work in anything else. I plant coca with my husband. We also work in the laboratories. We had a small house where we always processed the coca leaves we harvested into paste. After that, we took it to the laboratory where they turn it into powder. To make the paste, we cut it up, then we added cement, salt, soda, gasoline, and all of that, stomped on it, and then stirred it with a stick. The treatment took up to two hours. After two hours we got oil that looks like coffee. Then we refined it and what remained was the paste. We all lived on that.[31]

Working in the coca(ine) industry increases people's income, allowing them to look after their families, as another farmer confirmed at a community meeting in Bajo Putumayo in March 2012. I gathered similar accounts in all border regions where the climate is favorable to coca cultivation.

People taking risks for jobs the guerrillas offered also reflects how economic opportunities widen the tolerance margin to being vulnerable to abuse. An international organization employee put it bluntly, when she imitated the farmers' narratives: "There are cases of multiple executions [...]. These only happen if you don't comply with the rules. I live under pressure, but I can live here [...]!"[32] In January 2012, a Colombian female farmer in Ecuadorian Sucumbíos explained to me that farmers cultivate coca, despite the modest profits, security problems, and health issues because they lack alternative options:

No one will tell you what I'm telling you now. [...] The guerrillas go to the farms and pick up the fixed merchandise (coca paste). They don't let it be brought here [to Ecuador] anymore; therefore it is scarce on this side. [...] The guerrillas oblige people to sell [...] and people have to pay vacuna (extortion money) to them. Those who go there to sell [...] have to pay the guerrillas [...]. For these villages it has always been like this. Sometimes they postpone for a while, maybe because they don't receive the money [...]. They come to pick up the merchandise during the harvest, but our village has been calm. One time they attacked the police and killed lots of them. My husband said many of these guys had passed by and that they were going to do something. [...] We have the hardest time and we earn little. In order to cultivate we have to fumigate the plants and the soil. Then we have to scrape, then chop. Then, in the laboratory, they make the first coca paste. It smells a lot of the chemicals. That's why I say my husband is skinny because he always had to deal with the chemicals. Then we go and sell [the coca paste] to those who take it and crystallize it. But people from here also do the crystallizing. If you want to get some crystallized [coca paste], you can get it from them. But it is a lot more expensive. The paste costs at least 1,200,000 pesos [636 USD]. The base costs 2,500,000 [1,236 USD], and the cocaine that they sell further down is four million [2,121 USD] because it's been crystallized [. . .]. They already have all the contacts. They sell it abroad, to Quito, to anywhere you can think of.[33]

Her numbers resemble those of UNODC, according to which, for Putumayo in 2011, the average price of coca paste was 1,659,000 Colombian pesos per kilo (880 USD), for cocaine base it was 2,500,000 (1,326 USD), and for cocaine hydrochloride 4,500,000 (2,386 USD).[34]

She then shared with me her and her fellow borderlanders' frustration with the government, rather than the guerrillas. As a matter of course, such frustrations diminish the prospects for a mutually reinforcing state-society relationship. From her perspective, not only did the government fail to provide viable alternative options, it also actively contributed to the cocaine business and coca cultivation in particular. This view was echoed in many other interviews, and concurs with findings of other studies:[35]

To be honest, the government can say what it likes but what brings money is coca. [. . .] Look, the cacao is currently very cheap [. . .]. One pound is worth forty cents. This will never happen to coca [. . .]. Here, there isn't much coca, but further down there is a lot and people harvest 1,000 or 2,000 *arrobas*.[36] The thing is that it is not convenient for the government to eliminate the coca. They live off it. Their work depends on it, they come to eradicate it. But they never eradicate everything, why should they? They leave some seeds so that in four or five years it grows again. They don't want to finish it off because [it]'s their own business [. . .]. Even soldiers, the military: if there wasn't so much coca in Colombia, what would they need such large armed forces for? [. . .] It wouldn't be convenient for them because they would lose their jobs. If there was no problem anymore, they would need neither the army nor the police force [. . .]. It's also the government's fault because [. . .] they gave us some poor seeds of corn and some fish [. . .]. They thought we would live on this and that's it. But the seeds didn't even grow [. . .]. If they gave us something that works, even if it is cacao, if they gave us a credit at low interest rates, then people would perhaps stop growing coca. However, if they don't give us anything, there is nothing we can do. [. . .] Imagine, this is not a town, this is all countryside. You don't have money, you don't have anything. They come and give you some poor corn seeds which won't grow. This is going to help us? It will never help anyone, it doesn't help![37]

The mistrust *omnium contra omnes* and the increased vulnerabilities of farmers who depend on *financieros* suggest that it is difficult for the groups to achieve social support and that therefore shadow citizen security is hardly attainable. Yet as this section has shown, the constellation of the provided goods matters. Whether economic opportunities provide enough weight to bring about shadow citizen security is contingent on perceptions and experiences: borderlanders who have experienced violence in the past may find the required behavior "normal" and accept violent non-state groups as legitimate governance agents. Others for whom violence is new often reject the groups because their perceptions of insecurity outweigh the legitimizing effect of the economic opportunities.

Exposure to Sporadic Violence

Mistrust *omnium contra omnes* and the vulnerability to abuse that communities experience in contexts of supply chain relationships undermine citizen security in a relatively constant way, especially at the lower stages of the supply chains. In regions that host later stages of the supply chain, violent non-state groups rely on powerful brokers to overcome the trust problem when engaging in relationships with each other. This adds another, more punctual, element unique to this type of group interaction that increases the precariousness of the security situation. As long as the broker fulfills his function,[38] the inter-group relations are stable and relatively nonviolent, even if inter-group distrust persists. The capture or killing of a powerful broker, however, can trigger power struggles over succession or revenge,[39] resulting in sporadic waves of violence. These violent struggles rarely target the general public directly; they nonetheless put the population's security at risk. The unpredictability of such incidents engenders fear. Lack of clarity over who fills the power void and when incidents might occur fuels anxiety, making it hard for local communities to adapt their behavior in a way that would enhance their security.

The case of broker alias "Megateo" illustrates the stabilizing effect of his function on the supply chain relationships between the FARC, the National Liberation Army (Ejército de Liberación Nacional—ELN), the Popular Liberation Army (Ejército Popular de Liberación—EPL), and various right-wing groups in Colombia's war-torn Catatumbo region. It also shows the lack thereof, after the Colombian military had killed him in October 2015.

As of 2011 and 2012, "Megateo" contributed to maintaining an equilibrium in the supply chain relationships in the region.[40] Performing an intermediary role, he engaged in business deals with the FARC and the ELN and was connected with regional politicians and the economic elite. With a sphere of influence that reached across the Venezuelan border, he was the puppetmaster of cocaine and related deals in the region. He also helped ensure the division of labor within the illicit drug business over many years.[41] A former leading member of the Maoist guerrillas EPL, his ideological affinity with the FARC facilitated reducing distrust vis-à-vis the rebels. He was a modern form of Eric Hobsbawm's "social bandit."[42] Like a warlord,[43] he used his influence on local communities to be perceived as serving the peasantry, in line with the guerrillas' political beliefs.[44] A community leader from Cúcuta explained to me in 2011:

LEADER: "Megateo" is a man from San Calixto, a farmer, who talks and understands the rural issue ideologically. He became the region's leader. Everyone appreciates him, including the FARC and the ELN. People appreciate him because they know the region. [...] People say he controls transit [of drugs] and brokering. He is the boss of brokering, he has an intermediary role.

ME: *How do they keep the limits?*

LEADER: The one who creates respect is "Megateo;" he imposes order.

ME: *How can he have so much power?*

LEADER: I personally attribute it to his leadership. He is a man who used to be an ordinary citizen. The farmers from Teorama say he is a man who understands the people and talks to them in their own language. He is a brother. He has become a role model.[45]

"Megateo" also drew on shared values to reduce distrust with right-wing groups such as the Rastrojos. For them, his influence on state actors increased his credibility as a mediator because these contacts helped avoid state interference that could undermine the deals. As a high-ranking police official from the region put it when I interviewed him, "'Megateo' made everyone talk to each other: guerrillas, narcos, criminal groups, the authorities. This grand man achieved to fuse the business, and he became a patron." "Values" reduced distrust between the broker and the groups. He was "trustworthy to all of them," as the police official added.[46]

After "Megateo"'s death in October 2015, power struggles on his succession flared up in the region. When I interviewed local community members a year later, in November 2016, several of "Megateo"'s close men had attempted to tread into his footsteps, but none endured for very long. Also, outsiders and high-ranking members of the other armed groups had tried to assume his position, but with none of them possessing "Megateo"'s reliable, trustworthy, and well-networked profile, these attempts had produced clashes and assassinations both in the rural Catatumbo region as well as in the urban center of Cúcuta, the closest town.[47]

"Megateo" was among the most powerful brokers, but by no means the only one. Other figures with influence along and across the Colombia-Venezuela and Colombia-Ecuador border in recent years have included the Colombians "Marquito" Figueroa, "El Pulpo", and Loco Barrera; Venezuelan broker Walid Makled; and Ecuadorian broker Jefferson Ostaiza. As these examples show, brokers do not all consider themselves necessarily as "warlord-ish, quasi–Robin Hoods," as "Megateo" did. In fact, the boundaries between politicians, businesspersons, and shadowy figures involved in the illegal drug trade are highly blurred with some brokers operating more visibly in the political sphere, others in the business world, and only some primarily in the under-world. Marcos "Marquito" Figueroa García, captured in 2014 among other crimes due to his role as a broker, was among those with political ambitions. Closely linked to La Guajira's regional government, he was well known to the local population. He also coordinated much of the regional drug and gaso-line trafficking in La Guajira and Cesar. According to locals, his removal was noticeable on the regional level in La Guajira, where rivaling Wayúu clans as well as local traffickers clashed in competition for the power position.[48] The broker with alias "El Pulpo" had his focus of operation on the business side of things. El Pulpo was shot dead in a popular restaurant in Cúcuta in April 2012. Maintaining the façade of a successful businessman, he was respected by diverse sectors of society while supposedly a narco-broker. When I visited Cúcuta the week after he was shot, many locals talked about the good deeds he did for the poor in a "Pablo Escobar-like" fashion, and lit candles in front of his house. Cúcuta suffered two bomb blasts in central areas within the week I was there. Locals assumed that the blasts were connected to the death of El Pulpo; they speculated that an escalation of violence would ensue.[49] Similar problems arose after Loco Barrera's capture in Venezuelan San Cristóbal, Táchira, on September 18, 2012.[50] He controlled around 40 percent of the cocaine sent to market from Colombia.[51] Allegedly, he had his base in the Colombian Eastern Plains but operated throughout Colombia and beyond, and he was an appreciated mediator between various groups. He negotiated the purchase of the coca paste from areas under FARC control and had deals with the Popular Revolutionary Anti-Terrorist Army of Colombia (Ejército Revolucionario Popular Antiterrorista Colombiano—ERPAC), the Rastrojos, and inter-national trafficking groups to coordinate cocaine sales to Western Europe.[52] He supposedly had links with the Mexican Sinaola and Zeta cartels,[53] and controlled some of the clandestine airstrips in Apure, used for cocaine flights to the Caribbean and Central America—with the connivance or assistance of Venezuelan state forces.

Loco Barrera's capture triggered disputes over who would inherit his cocaine reign. In 2011, the Venezuelan broker Walid Makled's capture provoked struggles between violent non-state groups and state officials. Makled's links with high-ranking military officials allowed him to use Puerto Cabello, the port close to Caracas, as a starting point for international trafficking routes.[54] These ties helped him gain the trust of those who wanted their illegal goods to be shipped abroad and of international buyers. Given the wide-ranging network of actors involved, those with voluntary or involuntary knowledge of this network feared retaliation. Finally, Jefferson Ostaiza, captured in Ecuador in 2009, was an influential broker who moved between the underworld and public world in Ecuador. He had links to the FARC Fronts 29, 30, 32, and 48, as well as Ecuadorian, Colombian, Mexican, and Nicaraguan traffickers, the Ecuadorian then Under Secretary of Government José Ignacio Chauvin, and other politicians. His capture left a power vacuum that triggered conflicts over who would take over his position.[55]

In brief, at first glance, the captures and killings of brokers are the business of intelligence services or rivaling violent entrepreneurs, occurring far down in the underworld, removed from people's everyday lives. In practice however, the repercussions are felt across sectors of society. To a certain extent, these impacts are akin to the well-documented effects of the elimination of mafia bosses in Russia, Sicily, the United States, and other places.[56] In the context of armed conflict, its destabilizing influence on the relationships between ideologically opposed groups adds another dimension of insecurity the local population has to cope with.

6.2 Strategic Alliances

In strategic alliances, violent non-state groups share certain values. This reduces distrust between the groups in a general matter, permitting them to actively support each other and share intelligence so that they become symmetrically interdependent (see section 2.1). This, in turn, minimizes distrust toward community members because each group has less reason to suspect them of being collaborators of the other group. At the same time, communities need to be less concerned about accusations of collaborating with the other group than in the context of short-term arrangements or of supply chain relations where general mistrust persists. Nonetheless, an obstacle absent in other long-term arrangements hampers the violent non-state groups' social recognition by local community members: the provider of rules being composed of two allied groups obscures each group's individual identity. Under the authority of a single group, people can develop a sense of belonging to this "shadow community" and, if the group is accepted as the illicit authority or even perceived to be legitimate, be loyal to it. In strategic alliances, people cannot establish the identity of the armed person they interact with as easily as in settings of pacific coexistence or preponderance relations, the arrangements I discuss below. It is not clear whom exactly locals should be loyal to, making it difficult for the two (or more) violent non-state groups to establish a mutually reinforcing relationship with the local community.

The consequences of muddied group identities for citizen security are twofold. On the one hand, civic consent is not as important for violent non-state groups to maintain control as in pacific coexistence: information sharing between both groups (which is not the case in pacific coexistence) lowers the risk that community members will side with one group to the disadvantage of the other. The absence of mistrust also reduces violence. On the other hand, without knowing the specific identity of their "shadow governors," the community is less likely to feel represented by them and remain loyal if another actor—including the state—enters the scene. These obstacles to a fully mutually reinforcing relationship between citizens and the violent non-state group encumber ideal-type shadow citizenship and shadow citizen security. Cases in point are the strategic alliance between FARC's Front 41 Cacique Upar and Front 33 Mariscal Antonio José de Sucre with the ELN's Front Camilo Torres Restrepo in Catatumbo; and, in 2011, the strategic alliance between FARC's Front 59 and the ELN in the region where Cesar and La Guajira adjoin Zulia (see section 3.2). The FARC's and the ELN's strategic alliance in Arauca is another example.

Blurred Identities

The FARC and the ELN share values on which they based their joint strategy related to how to confront state forces.[57] Considering the strategic alliance between the FARC and the ELN, Núñez argues that these two guerrillas combined the FARC's military capacity with the ELN's social influence. Joint commissions comprising members of both organizations would have discussed how to make best use of these comparative advantages.[58] This strategy, possible thanks to reduced levels of inter-group distrust, empowered the guerrillas vis-à-vis the state forces. It also made the guerrillas highly interdependent. As visual clues and the reactions of local community members to FARC and ELN presence in the regions of Cesar and Catatumbo suggest, this interdependence constituted an obstacle to shadow citizenship. Three examples confirm this. First, while in other regions I observed graffiti from either group on house walls, locals reported that in rural areas near Tibú in Catatumbo there were graffiti of the two group names on house walls, painted in the same colors and the same style, suggesting that a single person drew it.[59] People from Tibú, La Gabarra, Filo de Gringo, and Cúcuta argued in 2012 that, if either of the two insurgent groups had objected to the graffiti, they would have removed them. Yet, they noted that it was unclear who *really* imposed the rules of behavior there now, and whom to obey.[60] Second, according to local sources, guerrilla members were patrolling streets without emblems of either the FARC or the ELN, leading to confusion over which group they belonged to. Therefore, people did not know whom to turn to when these specific individuals were not around.[61] Finally, locals commented they had seen FARC soldiers near the road passing through the El Molino and Villanueva municipalities in southern La Guajira. However, as a source close to the FARC countered, these were ELN members, supposedly of the Fronts Luciano Ariza and Gustavo Palmesano Ojeda.[62]

Such confusions demonstrate the difficulties of establishing ties with one particular group, even if they respect the communities. Without knowing which group the uniformed people who impose order belong to people have difficulties showing loyalty, depriving the groups of their social base and, in the long run, their perceived legitimacy. Certainly, physical security improved over the years. In the 1990s, Cesar featured extremely high kidnapping rates, and in the 2000s, civilians were the primary victims of murders, displacements, and massacres in the region. In 2000, when the Central Bolívar Bloc consolidated, massacres in Cesar soared, with 103 victims counted among nineteen massacres.[63] After the paramilitary demobilization and during the strategic alliance between the FARC and the ELN, the levels of violence against civilians were more moderate again, but neither citizen security nor shadow citizen security, which both go beyond mere physical security, could be achieved.

The guerrillas assumed governance functions by providing justice and security. Without being perceived as a legitimate (illicit) authority, however, they could not establish shadow citizenship and shadow citizen security, which would allow them to substitute "state-based" citizenship. The communities were in limbo: the state failed to monopolize violence legitimately and to provide services and therefore was not perceived to be a legitimate authority in the territory. The rebels, despite exercising governance functions, failed to make their individual identities clear. Neither a sense of belonging to the central state, nor a sense of belonging to a "shadow community" was likely. In such situations, local (nonviolent) authorities or community leaders may have a chance to achieve greater acceptance and recognition than elsewhere, but this would require the armed actors to let this local leadership emerge, which I could not detect in Cesar.[64]

Societal Groups as Allies

In some cases, violent non-state groups have strategic alliances with societal groups that themselves become such groups. The lines between these groups and the local population, rather than those between two violent non-state groups, become blurred. This can promote the rapprochement between armed actors and the local community, if the latter is aligned, rather than hostile, to the "societal group-turned armed actor." Such a rapprochement, in turn, increases the distance that the communities feel vis-à-vis the state.

As discussed in chapters 3 and 5, in the Guajira Península, some indigenous Wayúu clans fit the definition of violent non-state groups under certain circumstances. Motivated by shared economic interests and mutual sympathies between group leaders, they have forged tactical alliances with paramilitary and their successor groups. There have also been instances of durable strategic alliances between these groups. In these cases, marriage between members of Wayúu and paramilitary groups facilitated cooperation. The Paisas, for example, paid a Wayúu family so that one of their men could marry a Wayúu woman.[65] Another case is paramilitary leader alias "Pablo" who, while frequently switching alliances with several right-wing groups, is married to a female Wayúu, the sister of Wayúu leader alias "Chema Bala" extradited to the United States for drug trafficking (see section 5.2).[66] Ruling dynasties in Europe have been using royal intermarriages since the medieval times to prevent war, to fight a third party, or to aggrandize their power. A similar logic applies to marriages between right-wing groups and Wayúu clans in the Guajira Peninsula. I consider marriage a "shared value" here because both parties share in their appreciation of the institution of "marriage." They are morally obliged to adhere to this bond. Respected by both sides, such an institutional tie serves as a distrust-reducing mechanism in a general manner; it thwarts suspicions of cheating. Although creating ties of kinship, marriage is therefore different to personal bonds that motivate short-term arrangements. First, through ethnicity, it links the entire Wayúu family to the arrangement. Second, marriage is a more durable and more institutionalized commitment than personal bonds between two group leaders and hence more conducive to reducing distrust more generally.[67]

As an outcome of strategic alliances via marriage, the paramilitary or post-demobilized groups were able to aggrandize their power while the Wayúu received protection. This is comparable to alliances between the FARC and the ELN, which brought together the FARC's military capabilities and the ELN's strong social base, as noted above.[68] Since the Wayúu are a matrilineal society, such marriages constitute an entry point for paramilitary or post-demobilized groups to social networks of the family, a useful means to improve the group's image among Wayúu communities. It allows them to enhance their perceived legitimacy among locals. It also gives access to the clan's knowledge about the natural harbors at the Caribbean coast that are of strategic significance for the drug trade, but normally only accessible by the Wayúu. As of 2010, 30 percent of Colombia's cocaine and heroin was said to leave the country from the shores of the Guajira Peninsula, controlled at that time by alias "Pablo."[69] However, bringing in the military capabilities of the right-wing group can improve the communities' sense of security: through the strategic alliance, the Wayúu woman's family can guarantee protection to other clan members more credibly. The family can use this as a means to enhance its own status.

Strategic alliances between the Wayúu group and paramilitaries are less prone to the identity problems that exist in the case of alliances between the FARC and the ELN. The allied Wayúu group is embedded locally; community members know their members. After all, the allied family is part of the community themselves. Also, the Wayúu differ from members of paramilitaries coming from other parts of the country in terms of their behavior shaped by their culture, and physical appearance including facial traits and clothing. Therefore, locals are likely to recognize the two individual groups, despite their allied character. Overall, strategic alliances facilitated by marriages influence the relationship between armed actors and local communities by contributing to a proximity between the two. If this occurs, it increases the local communities' perceived distance, or even hostility, toward other parts of society—including hostile clans in the case of the Wayúu—and the state. The phenomenon of transnationality intensifies this logic: as a binational people, the Wayúu are an indigenous group that is particularly removed from a state-centric citizenry and has developed a strong nonstatist sense of belonging to a local cross-border community. These dynamics facilitate forging a mutually reinforcing relationship between Wayúu clans and paramilitaries in such special cases of inter-group marriage even further.

6.3 Pacific Coexistence

Situations of pacific coexistence among several violent non-state groups are more likely to approximate shadow citizen security than those of supply chain relationships and strategic alliances. As with strategic alliances, the reduction of inter-group distrust between the coexisting groups through shared values lowers the groups' suspicion vis-à-vis the local population. However, usually coexisting groups do not share information; they are less interdependent. Pacific coexistence requires the groups to be responsive to local community members to balance interests and the empirical legitimacy of all groups involved. Stathis Kalyvas argues that "typically, insurgent rule is based on a variable mix of consent and coercion."[70] In pacific coexistence, consent can outweigh coercion. The community's consent matters more for each group than in strategic alliances because the lack of social recognition toward one group can be exploited by another group to drive deeper roots, and gain a comparative advantage.

When violent non-state groups operate in pacific coexistence, three aspects characterize their relationship with the community. First, for groups operating in pacific coexistence, it is particularly important to deal with matters of everyday life. This is different to what I observed in the context of other long-term arrangements in which violent non-state groups achieve civic consent mostly through efficiency in security and job provision. Second, the capacity to deal with matters in a variety of circumstances, and the armed groups' responsiveness to the concerns of the local population, increase their perceived legitimacy locally. In the absence of state services, violent non-state groups assume the role of "all-round" governance providers. Third, and contrary to settings with strategic alliances, their individual identities are typically clear to the local population. Having to secure social recognition, the groups have an interest in being identifiable to the local community. This alienates the community from the state and fosters their relationship with the armed actor. Community members can adapt their behavior to certain rules to ensure security. Such a relationship is (partly) based on mutual respect. Combined, these aspects facilitate the establishment of shadow citizenship and shadow citizen security.

Everyday Life in the Shadow

In Venezuelan Alto Apure, the Bolivarian Forces of Liberation (Fuerzas Bolivarianas de Liberación—FBL), the FARC, and the ELN had been operating in pacific coexistence since 2010. The quest for social recognition explains the ELN's provision of justice to communities for issues ranging from conflict between neighbors to thefts and property damage. In a study on the Colombian Justice System, Elvira Restrepo highlights how systems of justice have a legitimizing effect: "The legitimacy of state authority rests on the ability to support and uphold just institutions."[71] The same applies to violent non-state groups. As a priest explained to me when I was carrying out fieldwork in Apure, the population of El Nula resorted to the rebels in all kinds of conflict situations: "If a cow gets lost, people run to the guerrillas. They always run to the guerrillas!" He further commented on the guerrillas: "They intervene to provide even Solomonic solutions."[72]

The insurgents respected (some of) the local community members' decisions. In return, the rules that the insurgents imposed were mostly met with approval.[73] In 2012, a female farmer from Alto Apure shared with me her views on the rules imposed by the left-wing groups:

FARMER: The other day they called a meeting and asked people to come. Many people went. I didn't go, because I never go to these meetings.

ME: *They don't say anything if you don't go?*

FARMER: No, no. Everyone can decide whether to go. No, I never go, I went to one meeting, but this was because the communal council invited us and we thought the communal council was holding the meeting. But it was them. The entire community went to the meeting, but this was because of them. When we arrived, one of them held the meeting.

ME: *Do you know who they are?*

FARMER: Of course.

ME: *Is the council linked to them?*

FARMER: No, they wanted to call this meeting to set some limits, some rules of coexistence (*"leyes de convivencia"*) and some other issues. [. . .] Rules of coexistence are, for example, the usage of marked ways; or if you leave animals outside, you have to pay. If there is an animal on the farm track, you have to pay a fee to them, and another one to the owner of the corral where they keep it; to keep the farm tracks clean. [. . .] These are the rules of coexistence.

ME: *And if someone does not comply with these rules?*

FARMER: They make you pay a fine . . . For example, if you leave an animal outside on the farm track you have to pay thirty bolívares: ten to the corral's owner and twenty to the organization. Better you don't leave your animal outside!

ME: *Do you think these rules are good or bad [. . .]?*

FARMER: I think good because, look, sometimes one has to struggle a lot because [. . .] these farm tracks get overgrown. I think the rules are good because people have already got used to the idea that this is what they are obliged to do. No-one would do it on one's own behalf. They have to say: "Look, you have to clean. If you don't clean . . ." People have already got used to it. They have already adapted to it.

ME: *Don't you think that people should be more aware about doing this themselves?*

FARMER: They should be aware, but they aren't. They aren't because where I live, where I have my plot, the farm track is full of undergrowth from side to side . . . The farm owner should clean it, but he doesn't [. . .].[74]

The guerrillas' regulatory role in this example has a dual function. Rules of coexistence help achieve civic consent rather than sheer territorial dominion, as attained by imposing order through social cleansing, for instance. They help farmers handle everyday concerns without restricting their freedom. Fines—rather than violence or humiliation—as punishment command respect instead of fear. A similar modus operandi can exist in preponderance relations, especially if groups aim to keep costs of violence low and widen their social base, as I discuss below. Also, both in pacific coexistence and in preponderance

relations, a region's history of coercion and violence may reinforce the implic-
itness of illicit authority and relative absence of violent punishment. Given
people's memories of the groups' violent measures in the past, the armed actors
do not have to resort to violence to gain the population's acquiescence. Groups
draw on violence to establish their power position but, once it is achieved, they
typically refrain from it. Yet in the case of pacific coexistence, refraining from
violence and dealing with everyday matters further helps maintain a balance of
support among the local population in relation to the coexisting groups. The
farmer later told me that before 2010, when the groups were still in conflict,
rather than aiming for social recognition they induced the population's compliance by coercion:

ME: *Do they tell you what time to be home?*
FARMER: Before, one couldn't go out at night. During some months, one had to
  be home by nine. Today it is different.[75]

The continuation suggests that the guerrillas were indeed considered a legitimate authority, the second aspect of the relationship between armed groups and
communities:

ME: *Have there also been rules which you didn't like?*
FARMER: [. . .] The issue of cutting wood . . . We are not allowed to cut green
  wood. I don't think that this is good because where are we then going to sow
  seeds? If we live in the countryside and we cannot sow seeds . . . What are we
  going to eat [. . .]?
ME: *Did they explain to you why they imposed this rule?*
FARMER: Yes, they said we could fell three hectares of trees. More than that
  would be bad.[76]

The woman criticized the type of rule, but she did not question that it was the
guerrillas who imposed it by illicit means. She had internalized the guerrillas'
role as governance provider as a norm and thus respected them, which occurs
in situations of citizenship, in this case, shadow citizenship (see section 2.2).
Furthermore, she referred to the rebels by the neutral term "organization," also
used by the insurgents themselves. This attitude relates to their penetration of
local governance bodies, for example the communal councils and apparently
the mayor's office of Guasdualito. Guerrilla presence was omnipresent and
normalized.

Another account of this farmer reveals the processes through which the armed
actors' responsiveness further contributes to their mutually reinforcing relationship with the community. Maintaining the pacific coexistence constituted

an incentive for the insurgents to ensure social recognition and consent. As the farmers' community was affected by recruitment of minors, she asked members of the ELN not to recruit at her fourteen-year-old son's school.[77] They accepted her request and, as of September 2012, had not attempted recruitment in that school. Having to equilibrate their position vis-à-vis another independent group in the same territory, they would have risked losing legitimacy by comparison had they rejected the request. Such accommodating gestures are unusual under other long-term arrangements, especially supply chain relationships, characterized by a tension between people's beliefs in the guerrillas' efficiency and varying cruel punishments for noncompliance.

Competition for Consent

The farmer's account also sheds light on the distinct identities of the violent non-state groups—the third aspect that shapes the relationship between armed actors and communities, and hence citizen security, in settings of pacific coexistence. The community members' ability to identify who controls their territory allows for a stronger relationship between the local community and individual violent non-state groups in pacific coexistence, if compared to settings of strategic alliances or supply chain relationships. The farmer was clear about who imposed rules in her community:

ME: *Who imposed this rule [of the curfew]?*
FARMER: The *boliches*, these were the *boliches*.[78]
ME: *And the rules on cutting wood and on the farm tracks?*
FARMER: These were the *elenos*, although the *boliches* do similar things.[79]

Identities are not blurred as in strategic alliances and not as obscured as is often the case in supply chain relationships due to the broker arrangements and persisting mistrust.

The clear group identities mean that factors other than capacity and responsiveness influence social recognition. These factors include whose territory they operate in and the groups' image more generally. According to the farmer from Alto Apure, the ELN and the FBL imposed similar rules, but the FBL were less respected than the ELN, despite the ELN being a foreign group in Venezuela:

ME: *Do the boliches learn from or imitate the ELN?*
FARMER: They imitate, they imitate. And moreover, they have many children [in their ranks]. They have many young people [. . .]. They have many children; their rifles on their backs reach the floor. They have so many young, inexperienced boys. . .[80]

The ELN had a competitive advantage over the FBL, which can unbalance their relationship. However, the latter was "at home" while the former was in violation of Venezuelan national sovereignty. Both knew that, even if more powerful, the ELN relied on the FBL's connivance for both groups to operate in the territory. These overlapping interests contributed to a balance in the pacific coexistence, although the local population may have respected the ELN more than the FBL.

All the points on pacific coexistence discussed so far suggest that this arrangement type is conducive to shadow citizenship and shadow citizen security devoid of violence, similar to preponderance relations, as we see in the next section. Nevertheless, there is a bitter aftertaste that sets pacific coexistence apart from preponderance. The low interdependence of violent non-state groups who coexist in the same territory can be reason for concern that such an arrangement can break down very unexpectedly, and give rise to intergroup disputes instead. The possibility of groups turning against each other is more latent than in other circumstances and can therefore fuel unease among the local population. In strategic alliances, a common joint threat (e.g., the state forces) and clear mutual commitments (e.g., joint strategies) constitute hindrances that do not exist in the case of pacific coexistence where for example the change in external circumstances can more easily yield a breakdown of the tacit arrangement of non-aggression. Without sharing information, it is also difficult for coexisting groups to adapt their strategies in a concerted manner to a changing context. Up to March 2008 when Colombia bombed the FARC camp in Angostura, Colombian violent non-state groups coexisted in Ecuador's border zone. Afterward, Ecuador militarized its northern border, increasing the number of military operations from twenty-two in 2007 to 248 in 2009 (see section 3.1).[81] This reduced the space for Colombian armed actors to stay undisturbed.[82] Several groups started to violently subordinate less-powerful groups.[83] Pacific coexistence did not hold. Precedents like the post-Angostura situation are reasons for unease among communities, in the midst of pacific coexistence among various groups.

6.4 Preponderance Relations

Of all violent non-state group interaction types, those that feature significant power asymmetries according to which one violent non-state group prevails over all others are most conducive to shadow citizenship and shadow citizen security. The preponderant armed actors exert governance functions and the local community respects and supports them. The preponderant group's authority and identity are clear. This is typically least visible outside the community controlled by the group. In the examples I have studied, when circumstances external to the arrangement changed, the preponderance relations typically remained stable because others followed the preponderant group's decisions. In the case of the FARC and the ELN, preponderance in the absence of other groups, rather than preponderance *relations*, were/is also common because, in line with their own security and justice systems, they typically did/do not tolerate other violent groups in their territory.[84]

Shadow Citizenship and Shadow Citizen Security

People socially recognize and actively support violent non-state groups, if, for example, due to grievances toward the state, they are committed emotionally and morally to do so.[85] Such grievances are reflected in the statement of a teacher in Putumayo at a community meeting in 2012, when the FARC had lost influence but were still preponderant in important areas: "We are in a war against the state . . . The state has abandoned us." This feeling of abandonment was echoed by others, who complained about the lack of road infrastructure, schools, electricity, and drinking water while the only state actor present was the military (see Figure 6.1). They had more confidence in the guerrillas than in the state. "At least we had our land, our farm, and they helped us feed our families," commented another farmer in Bajo Putumayo on the FARC's sole authority during the 1990s.[86] According to a displaced farmer, "the guerrillas reigned: they were the kings there."[87] The FARC consolidated their

Figure 6.1 Poor road infrastructure in Bajo Putumayo, Colombia, 2012. Photo by Author.

preponderant position in Putumayo constituting a "state,"[88] openly patrolling the villages and demonstrating authority without fearing resistance. Filling the void in state governance, the FARC won the communities' respect.[89] They helped build health centers and arranged the construction of roads. Many locals believed that the FARC, viewed as effective at getting things done, took care of those who assisted them, which partly helped the FARC secure legitimizing consent to their authority.[90] In some cases, the relationship was mutual and, since the FARC were patrolling the streets, included providing security. The result was shadow citizen security, security provision based on a consensual relationship between the guerrillas and the local community, rather than the state and the community.

Preponderant violent non-state groups are interested in being perceived as legitimate in maintaining their authority in the long run without having to invest too many resources in violent action. Yet while in pacific coexistence, the need to counterbalance the other group's endeavor to obtain the population's support partly drives them, in preponderance relations, incentives are determined less exogenously. Counterintuitively, rather than thinking that they do not have to care about civic consent since they are sufficiently powerful to impose their will, they often strive to be considered responsive to avoid costly enforcement methods, among other reasons. One method seen to be responsive is organizing or infiltrating community meetings. Many of my respondents explained that, in the early 2010s, this was the case in the municipality of Tumaco in Nariño where the FARC Front 29 exerted preponderance that also reached across the border to parts of Esmeraldas in Ecuador.[91] Similarly, during my fieldwork trips between 2011 and 2012, I learned about the existence of this practice by the FARC's mobile column Daniel Aldana in the municipality of Ricaurte in Nariño, where it exerted preponderance that extended across the border to the Ecuadorian villages of Chical, Tufiño, and Maldonado.[92] At the Venezuelan border, community meetings organized or infiltrated by the ELN in Arauca similarly demonstrate responsiveness (see Figure 6.2)—as long as the armed actors attend them to listen and understand the community's concerns rather than to only dictate rules. Across both border areas, locals confirmed to me that at these gatherings, they were indeed encouraged to raise concerns. Even so, of course, this responsiveness can be a charade. The groups may still decide what is negotiable and what not. Another related way to ensure support is refraining from violence. In functioning democracies, citizens can constrain the enforcers of law and order. Also, the dominant group's activities can be curtailed. In preponderance relations, there are no clear ways for the powerless to prevent abuses by the powerful, hence only self-imposed constraints on its use of force maintain the legitimacy of violent non-state groups.[93]

Figure 6.2 Community meeting in Arauca, Colombia, 2012. Photo by Author.

Social Control between Fear and Respect

The preponderant group induces the community's compliance without violence through social control. This takes the form of silencing people, imposing rules of behavior, as well as penetrating and controlling public life and local state institutions. On the non-conflict side of the borders, the rule of silence is particularly striking. Ecuador's and Venezuela's limited recognition of the presence of violent non-state groups obscures its security impacts. Borderlanders can hardly call upon state institutions, such as Colombia's Early Warning System, to alert the state to act.[94] The example of the priest who had been photographed eighty times (see section 6.1) demonstrates that the result is "absolute silence," as he called it. He lived on the Ecuadorian side and only occasionally crossed over to Colombia, but the intimidation of the guerrillas did not stop at the border. While they engaged in supply chain relationships with other groups in Colombia, they also operated in preponderance on the Ecuadorian side. The resident warned: "Tranquility is a bad sign in this zone. This is like a person, a friend, who never talks, who always keeps quiet. This is not good!"[95] A resident of Ecuadorian Lago Agrio expressed similar concerns:

If I open my mouth and say who is here, they kill me because "a closed mouth catches no flies." This is an adage that we have here. They tell you that, if you don't say anything, nothing happens to you, but if you speak out, they kill you right away. This is our fear and due to this fear many things that occur are not reported. There were rapes, kidnappings, deaths, threats, but we never reported them because of the fear. Due to this fear we can't make any progress.[96]

While in Colombia, state *absence* has fostered the guerrillas' preponderance, in countries where violent non-state groups do not have an anti-state discourse, the state's *connivance or collaboration* with these groups veils complex security dynamics and helps the armed actors consolidate their preponderance. A human rights defender from Paraguaipoa explained how the Venezuelan government's supposed involvement in northern Zulia made it difficult for locals to take action against FARC control in these territories:

HUMAN RIGHTS DEFENDER: They even recruit young Venezuelans to enter the FARC's ranks. They seduce them. The guerrillas always have their area. Each has their function and, of course, there is an ideologist who brainwashes them. [...] Examples abound. [...] I have heard of young people who have recruited among themselves. I have a nephew who carries a weapon, but for me he isn't a guerrilla fighter, he is my nephew. He told me that they don't let him go out, they monitor him. They gave him a phone. I'm sure that the phone has GPS so they can locate him. They have technology. They finance him. If he wants a motorbike, they buy him one. [...] He is a boy, he is nineteen years old. He doesn't consider the consequences.
ME: *Do people talk about [the consequences] in their families or at school [...]?*
HUMAN RIGHTS DEFENDER: No, because this is delicate. It is delicate because they have ears everywhere. Furthermore, they have the army's, the government's support. As long as the state does not make a statement saying that they are here, they are not here. The government is not stupid. They manage this diplomatic discourse between states, but they know it [...]. Everyone knows what the other one is doing.[97]

The human rights defender did not dare to say "FARC" aloud, suggesting the pervasiveness of that social control far beyond people's homes and at school:

HUMAN RIGHTS DEFENDER: There is a discourse of order; they come here with motorbikes. They are militias. They come here [...].
ME: *Aren't there any BACRIM?*
HUMAN RIGHTS DEFENDER: No, here is only *their* dominion, *they* have control.

ME: *Elenos?*

HUMAN RIGHTS DEFENDER: No, no, only *them* [. . .].

ME: *Are people afraid of them?*

HUMAN RIGHTS DEFENDER: [. . .] This is simple: no one says anything, no one sees anything, and therefore people live peacefully. [. . .] Do people look for help? From them. They ask for their help. People believe that, if you want [to establish] a shop, ask the guerrillas. If you want to set up something, ask the guerrillas. They will give you money. They acquire the money through the *vacuna*. One shop has to pay 5,000 bolívares [around 1,200 USD in 2012] or five million pesos [around 2,200 USD in 2012]. [. . .] This protects them. No one would steal their cattle, but anyway, they have already established order in this zone. No one steals. There was a man who stole animals and they eliminated him. They arrive at a house early in the morning and ask how things are [. . .].[98]

With the guerrillas controlling behavior and discourse, citizens are virtually unable to state their preferences, raise their voice, and attract public attention. Solidarity from outsiders is scarce. As these communities are isolated from the rest of a state's citizenry, mistrust and the guerrillas' rule remain unnoticed. These communities tend to be stigmatized as guerrilla collaborators and do not receive the state protection necessary to ensure citizen security. Scholars have pointed to the interrelation between violent conflict and the erosion of social cohesion.[99] Nonviolent social control by violent non-state groups also has profound consequences for a society's social fabric because it leads to a fragmentation through which society as such loses its meaning. It is no longer based on a joint sense of belonging. Even if shadow community members mingle spatially with "the others," there is an estrangement: in Zulia, some inhabitants of Machiques claimed that the guerrillas came down from the Sierra de Perijá to their village from time to time. However, several sources argued that these were Colombian refugees, alienated from the state and from other citizens.[100] In the Sierra de Perijá, these Colombians lived under illicit control. Yet since they adhered to the rule of silence and many Machiques residents were prejudiced against them, the Colombians and the population of Machiques did not bond with each other.

A second common way of ensuring social control is via imposing rules of behavior, as in the case of pacific coexistence. Different to that case, however, where the need to counterbalance support of the other group partly shapes the constraint regarding the type of rules and of punishment for noncompliance, in preponderance relations it is up to the group itself. The group type (e.g., guerrilla or paramilitary) and personalities of leaders therefore matter and determine the degree of leniency vis-à-vis the local population.[101] It is not always clear to what extent citizens in a territory with a preponderant violent non-state group socially recognize the group or comply with their rules to protect themselves. Yet, and contrary to the "rivalry" cluster of violent non-state group interactions, they know the rules and their enforcers, making violence more predictable. As in other arrangements, obeying the actors' rules helps increase one's security. Yet under preponderance, the rules are much clearer than under short-term arrangements and there are fewer risks of experiencing violence in spite of compliance, as in the context of the "enmity" cluster. This makes compliance and hence security more feasible.

In Cumbal municipality in Nariño, for example, as of 2007, the FARC asked businesspersons and traders to pay taxes and farmers to sow, collect, and process coca and latex for heroin.[102] In other areas, they told farmers not to lend their animals as pack mules to the army and distributed pamphlets to warn communities of lethal repercussions should they be in contact with state forces. Further behavioral rules include curfews or restrictions on the population's access to goods and their mobility, for instance by laying anti-personnel mines, as was the case in Samaniego municipality in Nariño. Education is regulated as well: a teacher in a border village in Ecuador told me that the syllabus had to contain certain elements and should not mention guerrilla presence. Anecdotes that demonstrate the dangers of noncompliance abound. Community leaders, medical staff, and teachers were killed due to alleged collaboration with the Colombian army. The Rastrojos killed and dismembered young men in defiance of locally imposed rules in 2010.[103] In the village of Las Mercedes in the Sardinata municipality in Norte de Santander, two community leaders were killed in 2007 after they had started the initiative "Friends of Peace," which aimed to declare the village neutral without rules imposed by armed actors.[104] I experienced the threat of lethal consequences for noncompliance of the armed actors' rules myself when I accompanied a humanitarian mission. In a pamphlet in March 2012, FARC advised that "in conflict zones vehicles of the media and of humanitarian agencies must transit with perfectly visible decals and minimum speed" to avoid becoming "military targets" (see Figure 6.3).

Since violence is virtually absent, situations like Colombian Bajo Putumayo in the 1990s, Ecuadorian Carchi in the early 2010s, and, as I discuss below, Venezuelan Guayabo in 2012, may appear peaceful. In reality, this is because the violent non-state groups exert social control and replace the state in the provision of goods and services. Furthermore, violent non-state groups also employ strategies of charming people to make their social control invisible. They camouflage coercive power to make their relationship with the local community more "amicable." Using accommodating language is a form of charm: the guerrillas typically ask the population to "collaborate" financially with them, while in fact they extorted money from them.[105] As I cite at the opening of the book in the first chapter, a Colombian ex-guerrilla who used to work in

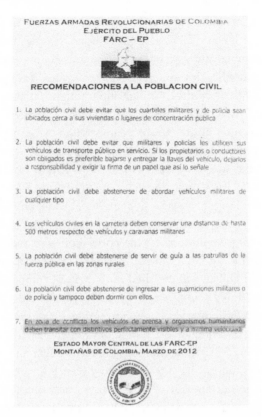

Figure 6.3 FARC pamphlet with warning against humanitarian agencies. Source: anonymous.

Ecuadorian Sucumbíos described his relationship with the local population as friendship. People who refused to be "friends" would have to be killed (see chapter 1). The firmness with which he explained the consequences of such refusal when I asked further, revealed the lethal undertone of a seemingly harmless language:

ME: *Were there people who didn't want to be friends with the guerrillas?*
EX-GUERRILLA: [. . .] They get lost [killed] because the measures over there are: or they pull themselves together or death penalty. We kill these people. [. . .] I dealt with people who resisted collaborating with the group, so I told them: "I give you half an hour. Either you leave or . . ." This is a thing of fury, of anger. I lived in regions with such people. [. . .] We killed them. We peeled them [he laughed]. To peel means to kill.
ME: *You had to do this?*
EX-GUERRILLA: Well, sometimes we had to. . .[106]

Another way of consolidating social control is by means of penetrating and controlling public life and local state institutions. This has been found across regions in Colombia and has been a common modus operandi by both guerrillas and paramilitaries in neighboring countries. The guerrillas, for example, enhanced their control through infiltrating local state institutions in Apure, while the paramilitaries used this approach to achieve greater control in selected towns and villages. This is demonstrated by the Venezuelan village Guayabo. The paramilitaries started to seize control of Guayabo, a strategic point in the trafficking route from Norte de Santander toward the Lake of Maracaibo, in 2005. They disseminated a "death list" and killed selectively—at first, one or two killings per week—it could hit anyone: one week a baker, another week a mechanic, another week a businessman. The lack of a pattern of chosen victims spread panic among the population who had not experienced such violence before. In 2012, when the paramilitaries supposedly controlled Guayabo, rates of violence diminished noticeably in comparison to previous years.[107] In early 2012, a colonel stationed in Guayabo told the paramilitaries to leave the village. Within one week, he was promoted and moved to a post elsewhere. According to a humanitarian organization employee from Machiques, most people believed the paramilitaries were responsible for his promotion.[108] The armed actors did not have to resort to violence to remain undisturbed; they used their power position to make others obey. People buying into this and hence attributing overwhelming power to the paramilitary group shows that the paramilitaries were accepted as ruling the territory. They established shadow citizen security.

In addition to the paramilitary's pervasive control without resorting to violence, this example elucidates a further aspect relevant to preponderance relations. The paramilitaries achieved that position after having drawn on considerable violence. Given the community's prior experience thereof, this obedience can be explained as a result of these memories. The case of Puerto Asís in Bajo Putumayo illustrates this well on Colombian territory. Traditionally a guerrilla stronghold, it became a strategic control point for post-demobilized groups in the late 2000s. Besides leaflets, graffiti, and threatening phone calls, post-demobilized groups have been using social networks to intimidate Puerto Asís's population. In August 2010, a group—allegedly Rastrojos—posted a list of names of young people in Puerto Asís on Facebook, spread further by email, in which they told them to leave the area within three days or face assassination. On August 15, two were shot; another one some days later. They expanded the list to sixty-nine names.[109] Counting friends and families of those listed, such measures affect virtually everyone, spreading fear and terror. When I visited Puerto Asís in 2012, things had calmed down somewhat. The group had become preponderant.

According to Francisco Gutiérrez Sanín, paramilitaries, when entering a new zone in a first phase, conduct indiscriminate massacres.[110] In a second phase, violence tends to be more selective. By then, power is based on extortion networks and social control. Indeed, I found many examples that confirmed this variation in the use of violence over time. Preponderance relations typically feature low rates of violence against local communities. When the groups are still in the process of establishing their preponderance, however, the "newcomers" implement threats to achieve credibility, particularly in regions with a history of violence caused by other violent non-state groups.[111] These variations over time can turn the continuum of clusters of violent non-state group interactions into a cycle: a group's preponderance can be disputed by another one, drawing them both into the "enmity" cluster (see section 4.1). This in turn can lead to the other group's preponderance if it defeats and subordinates, rather than eliminates, the first one. Non-state order is constantly in flux.

6.5 Conclusion

All four types of stable long-term arrangements that together form the "friendship" cluster of violent non-state group interactions influence people's objective security in relatively minor ways, if compared to the "enmity" and "rivalry" clusters. Across the four arrangements, the low levels of inter-group violence also make the exposure of local community members to violence less likely. However, the specific ways in which the armed actors reduce distrust between each other influence other aspects of citizen security in distinct ways.

Examining *supply chain relationships* demonstrates the relevance of brokers for the security of communities who live along cocaine supply chains. In particular, unpacking the mechanisms—including *financieros* and brokers—that make the cocaine supply chain work serves to detect less-tangible security impacts such as mistrust, fear, and the lack of guidance for appropriate behavior. Since the groups reduce distrust via a broker rather than directly, they still bear mistrust against communities. These communities also experience uncertainty over the prevailing rules in illicitly controlled territory and they are exposed to sporadic waves of violence. The communities' acceptance of the groups' illicit authority is often based on fear rather than respect. The provision of illegal, yet legitimately perceived economic opportunities by the armed actors can, however, countervail these sentiments because it augments people's tolerance margin vis-à-vis abuse and violence. These dynamics are part of the moral economy of borderlands where conflict and crime converge. Such an environment contributes to shadow citizen security: it incentivizes the local population's support toward, and acceptance of, the groups' illicit authority, which in turn undermines people's sense of belonging to a national citizenry. In *strategic alliances* and *pacific coexist-ence*, shared values reduce distrust between groups, allowing for a more respon-sive relationship with local communities. While in strategic alliances the groups' blurred identities hamper social recognition, in pacific coexistence it is impor-tant for the armed actors to be perceived as the legitimate authority. In *prepon-derance relations*, mutual clarity on the ability of one party to enforce compliance by the other party reduces distrust. This asymmetric power constellation with one group dominating all others is most conducive to shadow citizenship and shadow citizen security.[112] From the community's perspective, the preponderant violent non-state group is legitimized and the state delegitimized due to the opportunities, goods, and services the group provides. Therefore, preponder-ance relations have probably the least visible, but most systemic, repercussions on security.

Having demonstrated how violent non-state group interactions influence se-curity across the "enmity," "rivalry," and "friendship" clusters during the course of the previous three chapters, one important remark is in order before I move on to demonstrate what I call the "border effect" in the next chapter. Of course, these distinct security impacts are more blurred on the ground as it may seem from this analysis. While I demonstrate here the distinct influences of the var-ious forms of non-state order on security, empirically, several interaction types often overlap and so people's security may be affected by this very overlap as well. Non-state order is dynamic and ever changing, resulting in fuzzy distinctions within each cluster of violent non-state group interactions. The interactions do not belong to static categories—except the three overarching clusters—and it is for this reason that I conceptualize non-state order on a continuum (see chapter 2). It is this very fuzziness and the fluidity that complicates life in such settings. It is also why major changes, such as the demobilization of one group, fuel uncertainty.

A spatial analysis demonstrates the overlaps, firstly, among various stable long-term arrangements and, secondly, between stable long-term and unstable short-term arrangements.[113] First, the lines between various long-term arrangements are blurred, for example between supply chain relationships and preponder-ance. When a group forges transactional relationships at the margins of the ter-ritory in which it is present, regulation by the broker prevents other groups from disputing them. This favors the group's preponderance at the heart of the terri-tory in which it is present. For citizen security, this means that at the fringes of a territory with preponderance, mistrust starts to creep in, and the population's consent to the illicit authority may be based more on fear than on respect. Also, pacific coexistence among various armed groups can evolve into preponderance of each group in smaller enclaves next to each other. In such cases, it is no longer necessary for armed actors to strive for more social recognition than the other groups because they are sufficiently isolated from them.

Second, many territories with long-term arrangements feature enclaves of short-term arrangements within the same territory. For example, the FARC were preponderant in Putumayo but, along strategic roads within the territory that the FARC dominated, other groups engaged in short-term business deals. Likewise, supply chain relationships overlap with barter agreements and spot sales at the fringes. In both cases, community members may benefit from economic opportunities, but not from any other governance functions. Without a clear spatial separation, it may make people involved even more vulnerable to the volatile nature of arrangements that form part of the "rivalry" cluster and that interferes with the relative stability of supply chain relationships. Consider the example where people are paid as drug mules to traffic cocaine across a border. The cocaine is produced by one armed group and is sold to another group that will ship it internationally. At the Colombia-Venezuela border shared by Norte de Santander and southern Zulia, for example, cocaine has been smuggled hidden in tires, children's toys, dogs' stomachs, women's breast implants, and inside the bodies of dead babies passed off as being asleep. People who serve as mules in these ways between the links of the supply chain are exposed to punishment or harassment by law enforcement officials and of course risk their lives when they smuggle cocaine inside parts of their own body. Given people's gratitude for the "job opportunity," however, they often view violence or death as the mules' mistake. Another case where the overlap of various interaction types influences people's security is the overlap of pacific coexistence with unstable short-term arrangements. Here, the rules that community members need to follow to enhance their security become elusive. According to residents of southern Zulia, in the Venezuelan village of El Cruce in that region, pacific coexistence and tactical alliances between insurgents and paramilitaries co-occurred. In other situations of pacific coexistence, locals know the rules relatively well and negotiate them; in El Cruce, uncertainty abounded. The influence these dynamics had on citizen security was less akin to the one in settings of pacific coexistence discussed above with certain room for people to negotiate rules. Instead, silence and the attitude of "not getting involved" prevailed. A humanitarian organization employee summarized this effect on people's lives the following way: "As long as you don't bother them, tranquillity prevails in El Cruce. Then there is no problem."[114]

In borderlands that appear to be calmest, security can be most affected. Regions where violent non-state groups engage in relatively stable long-term arrangements may feature few observable factors of insecurity. These regions hardly attract government, media, or public attention. This differs from situations of the "enmity" cluster of violent non-state group interactions with soaring homicide and displacement rates. It also differs from contexts of short-term arrangements where selective violence produces the deaths of innocents. Yet this calmness is deceptive and distracts from structural impacts shaping the state-society relationship and the communities' social fabric. Borderlanders may not necessarily voice their concerns regarding insecurity outside their community due to the social control that violent non-state groups exert. Or, perhaps, they do not feel insecure because of a consensual relationship between the community and the group that provides protection. Although a consensual relationship between violent non-state actors and the community may indeed be more conducive to physical security than a dysfunctional social contract with the state, such security is shadow citizen security, security based on illicit means. This is problematic across all types of long-term arrangements. Ultimately, it is up to the group to decide whether they are responsive, as they cannot be held accountable for their actions.

The type of group, the personality of the local leader, and other factors play into such decisions, rather than the rule of law. Church members in Colombian Nariño in a region of supply chain relationships, for example, told the guerrillas that they did not agree with graffiti of guerrilla leaders on the church walls. They repainted the walls in white.[115] In this case, the insurgents decided to comply with their request, while in many others, for example in the case of the punishment of the rapist, they did not (see section 6.1). Similarly, in places like Puerto Asís, or Guasdualito where non-state order is shaped by pacific coexistence among various violent non-state groups, delinquency is virtually absent, but this is because the groups would kill any delinquents.[116] The illusory tranquility that emanates from shadow citizen security thus is sometimes blended with subjective citizen insecurity: when the group's authority is based on a mix of fear and respect. Such a relationship increases the communities' alienation from the state: insecurity is ignored externally due to the very mechanisms that undermine the communities' security. As a result, shadow citizen security questions democratic governance at the most basic level: the state's perceived legitimacy.

As we see in the next chapter, border areas are particularly prone to illusory calmness. The distance to the state centers and the resulting state neglect, which are a constant undercurrent to the existence of the long-term arrangements discussed here in the first place, play a crucial role in this. The transnationality of borderlands adds another layer of complexity, giving rise to a border effect that intensifies various insecurities.

7

The Border Effect

There is a clash between concepts. For example, the concept of the border. What do the Wayúu understand by border? What do we understand by border? [...] For them the border is an imaginary line.
Resident of Maicao, Colombia, 2012[1]

The clash between concepts, or indeed, worldviews, epitomizes the function of borderlands as magnifying glasses on the security challenges of the world. Both violent non-state groups and local communities operate and live across markers of national sovereignty. Yet they are met by historical, cultural, and political influences tied to individual countries and by government policies designed in the states' power centers. The very tensions arising from state-centric views that attach importance to the borderline, and the dynamics that cross it, contribute to the border effect: the confluence of weak state governance, a low-risk/high-opportunity environment, and a propensity for impunity, which arises from the transnationality of borderlands in vulnerable regions and their distance to state centers. The border effect consistently intensifies the logics of violent non-state group interactions and, with them, non-state order, making borderlands an extreme case of a complex security landscape. This is influenced by the fact that these three characteristics mirror the factors that facilitate the emergence of the distinct clusters of violent non-state group interactions in the first place: weak state governance as the outcome of state neglect; the low-risk/high-opportunity environment as an integral component that drives the illicit economy; and a propensity for impunity that allows the conflict dynamics to take their course without restraints (see section 3.2).

In the previous chapters, I demonstrate how the borderland lens sheds light on transnational border regions: it magnifies the distinct security repercussions that arise in the context of intensified logics of non-state order and that exist in more-diluted forms elsewhere. In what follows, I focus on the border effect itself. I trace the processes through which it influences violent non-state group interactions and intensifies insecurity by negatively affecting distinct elements of citizen security across the four border zones of the three states (Colombia, Ecuador, and Venezuela). Table 7.1 illustrates

Table 7.1 **Border Effect on Violent Non-State Group Interactions and Citizen Security**

Border Effect		Citizen Security			
				Governance Agent - Citizenry Relationship	
		Absence of Violence and Fear	Dense Social Fabric	Authority	Consent
Transnationality (cross-border dynamics)	**Facilitator**	Concealing victimization (1–4): increases exposure to general violence		Obscuring social control (6–8): facilitates illicit authority	Promoting illegal economies (5): widens tolerance margins for abuse
	Deterrent	Reducing predictability (4): increases exposure to selective violence	Fueling inter-group distrust (2): intensifies interpersonal distrust		
Distance from Center (proximity to border)	**Magnet**		Boosting profits (2–4): reduces civility and respect		Thwarting countermeasures (5–8): consolidates consent to illicit authority
	Disguise	Generalizing unruliness (1–4): trivializes violence		Reinforcing stigmatization (6–8): disguises illicit authority	Deepening the disconnect (5–8): alienates communities from the state

Interaction Types

1. combat/armed disputes
2. spot sales/barter agreements
3. tactical alliances
4. subcontractual relationships
5. supply chain relationships
6. strategic alliances
7. pacific coexistence
8. preponderance relations

how the border effect takes shape in four mechanisms: as facilitator, deterrent, magnet, and disguise. As underlined in the cells of the table, it influences violent non-state group interactions, marked with 1–8. These influences, in turn, have consequences for citizen security. Depending on which of the four mechanisms is at work, they affect the various elements of ideal-type citizen security, namely the absence of violence and fear, dense social fabric, and the mutually reinforcing relationship between the governance agent and the citizenry. Some concern all violent non-state group interaction types (1–8) and others only a few of them.[2]

The border's effect as a facilitator derives from the borderline itself, which, despite being a social construct, creates a chasm between two differing security and justice systems. Its effect as a deterrent is the result of regions being cross-border spaces where two different state territories with different national features shaped by culture, history, and state policies meet. Its effect as a magnet originates in the border zones' proximity to the borderline, which attracts multiple groups due to the high opportunities on offer there, while risks are relatively low. Finally, the border's effect as a disguise emerges from the distance to state centers, which turns border zones into stigmatized spaces.

7.1 The Border as Facilitator

The transnationality of borderlands facilitates three phenomena that intensify the various ways in which violent non-state group interactions undermine citizen security. First, by operating across borders, armed actors can conceal acts of victimization, attracting less attention from the state and others. This lowers the inhibition threshold to engage in such crimes. Second, the transnationality of border spaces is conducive to promoting illicit economies across borders, which helps armed actors evade law enforcement measures and garner support from locals who benefit from illicit economic opportunities. Third, it obscures social control and therefore facilitates illicit cross-border authority, alienating local communities further from the state and contributing to the emergence of shadow citizenship (see Table 7.1).

"Landscapes, history and daily life generally 'spill over' state boundaries," note Paul Nugent and Anthony Asiwaju, as do those evading the law, while state agents do not.[3] Drawing on Ratzel's organismic analogy,[4] Morehouse et al. consider the border a filter or a membrane: it permits some actors and resources to flow across the border while restricting others.[5] Violent non-state groups cross the border and commit crimes on the other side, but state forces and prosecutors whose job is to be "fully in control right up to, but also not across, that red dotted line" cannot cross it.[6]

Concealing Victimization

Victimization across the borderline is often not reported nor prosecuted. This lack of accountability facilitates committing crimes. Without being registered, these crimes are not subjected to government action or the public's attention. The border effect conceals three main forms of victimization: cross-border killings, cross-border disappearances, and cross-border displacements within borderlands. They are most common in the context of the "enmity" cluster of violent non-state group interactions where arrangements among violent non-state groups are absent, in the context of spot sales or barter agreements, of tactical alliances, and of subcontractual relationships.

Cross-border Killings

The border region of Putumayo and Sucumbíos exemplifies how intra-state and cross-border impunity mask civilian suffering during combat between violent non-state groups. The Ecuadorian Ombudsman's Office in Lago Agrio documented cases in which Colombian paramilitary and post-demobilized groups killed civilians in Ecuadorian Sucumbíos. These groups followed the guerrillas across the border into Ecuador, asked the population whether they had seen them, and threatened or killed people whom they suspected of being guerrilla collaborators, especially if these people had been in Colombia before.[7] On September 28, 2009, for example, post-demobilized groups assassinated two Ecuadorians and four Colombians, including a human rights defender, in the Ecuadorian border village of Barranca Bermeja and afterward escaped to Colombia.[8] Portrayed by the authorities and the media as settling scores, such homicides were seldom followed up by Quito or Bogotá due to a lack of political will or the downplaying of cross-border movements of armed groups.[9]

Quito made more efforts to address impunity in the case of Ecuadorian victims on Colombian territory. In 2007, the bodies of eight Ecuadorians were found in Putumayo in a mass grave dug by paramilitaries. The Ecuadorian foreign minister demanded Ecuador's participation in the judicial proceedings and the identification of bodies in other mass graves along the border in Putumayo, which could also include Ecuadorians.[10] Yet most commonly, the victims' or the perpetrators' tracks faded once they crossed the border, making them unidentifiable.[11]

At the Colombia-Venezuela border, cross-border killings also amplify the vulnerability of communities to becoming victims. In Norte de Santander and Táchira, the border's filter mechanism enhanced incentives for the Rastrojos and the Urabeños to resort to violence while fighting each other, exposing community members to insecurity. Although both groups originate in Colombia, the leaders operated in Venezuela to evade Colombian authorities.[12] They carried out assassinations of each other's leaders in Venezuela, attracting less attention from Colombia, whose government imposed stricter law enforcement measures than its Venezuelan neighbor. A humanitarian organization employee in Cúcuta explained to me that the Urabeños lured Rastrojos leaders into traps in Ureña, a Venezuelan border town on the other side of Cúcuta:

> [The Rastrojos] established a group at the border, which is like a small combo of paramilitaries. [The] guy who heads them [. . .] is called "Carevieja" [. . .]. The Urabeños are after him because the guy escaped them. This was in Ureña, around November. They called him to a meeting. He sent a trusted man [. . .]. They entered Ureña with a car and murdered him. In the end, [Carevieja] saved himself, but they had already assassinated Pecueca in Ureña, another finance boss of the Rastrojos.[13]

Since the Venezuelan authorities' response to such crimes was deficient, the killings spread fear and terror among the local population, silenced through social control and *vacunas,* the protection money that community members have to pay to the groups. Committing murders across the border from the non-conflict territory to the Colombian territory to conceal victimization also became common practice, as the third vignette at the opening of this book illustrates.

Violent non-state groups take advantage of cross-border impunity to commit murders. Phil Williams notes that transnationality in their economic activities enhances profits.[14] Yet national sovereignty is their protection. As an interviewee from Tumaco complained, Colombian violent non-state groups in the Colombian border zone had been using Ecuador as a safe haven:

> [The border] is no longer a protection. The perception is that in Ecuador's northern border zone there are the same illegal groups. They don't have as much presence [as in Colombia], but people believe that there are small groups [. . .]. Hence, [crossing the border] is safer for the guerrillas and other illegal armed actors; it becomes a protective environment for them. Why? Because the armed actor assassinates without any problems. [. . .] The military forces cannot assassinate anyone they want to. [. . .] They assassinate, but sometimes they find the perpetrator, or they find out that it was a false positive [. . .]. The illegal

armed actor simply assassinates the victim and says it was the Rastrojos or whatever. Impunity is relatively high. Therefore, the citizens of this zone where these activities exist are persecuted by the illegal actor [...]. Previously, the border was a protective factor. The armed actor did not cross. Nowadays, he crosses the border.[15]

This is just one of many illustrations in which violent non-state groups benefited from cross-border impunity. The guerrillas in particular have used it to consolidate their preponderance over other groups and their power position vis-à-vis the state. At the Colombia-Ecuador border for example, in September 2010, the FARC launched grenades from Ecuadorian territory on Puerto Colón in Colombia.[16] When I talked to a police official in Puerto Asís in 2012, he confirmed that the FARC used the same tactic to strike an attack against Teteyé (also in Colombia) that year. The official also explained that, in February 2012, the FARC killed three police officers in Puerto Colón in Bajo Putumayo and escaped to Ecuador immediately after the attack.[17] At the Colombia-Venezuela border, examples include attacks initiated from the Venezuelan side of the river that hit the police station of the city of Arauca in 2012.[18]

Cross-border impunity resulting from the constraints that international borders pose to the authorities' activities not only facilitates violence but also increases mistrust toward anyone not known to the community, contributing to its isolation. In Venezuelan Zulia, outsiders were suspected of providing intelligence to the Colombian army among other groups, due to the FARC's strategy of attacking the Colombian army from across the Venezuelan border and escaping back into Venezuela afterward. When I visited Zulia shortly after the FARC's cross-border strike from Venezuelan Guana on Colombian Majayura, for example, as illustrated at the opening of this book, a local human rights defender warned me:

> If you go to Guana, if they see a little face like yours, they don't know if you are someone from the CIA [...]. Therefore, [the human rights defender] María[19] asked me who you are, where you come from, and why. Because they did surveillance on María [...]. [Some time ago], both groups attempted to assassinate her, both the guerrillas and the paramilitaries. They operate in this zone.[20]

This suspicion enables the guerrillas to foster shadow citizenship in the Venezuelan territory they control (as part of the "preponderance relations" interaction type). At the same time, it increases stigmatization of these communities as guerrilla collaborators, especially from the Colombian point of view.

Cross-border Disappearances

Latin America has a dark history of enforced disappearances, typically associated with the state.[21] In the Colombian conflict, this phenomenon has been used by all conflict parties as well as criminal actors and typically ends in the disappeared person's death. Torres-Rivas notes that disappearances generate

> insecurity and pain in the greatest degree [. . .]. The fear and insecurity produced by this phenomenon lead to lasting reactions, perhaps passive or neurotic adaptations, in response to the permanent presence of death.[22]

If people are disappeared across borders, such pain can be even greater because violence is less obvious and excluded from national statistics, especially at maritime borders. According to interviewees in Tumaco, various armed groups used to throw bodies into rivers that flow into the Pacific. Floating into the open sea, these bodies were never identified.[23] A total of 216 people were reported to have been killed in Tumaco in 2013, and another three were disappeared. The latter number is likely much lower than the reality, but disappearances are typically not reported.[24]

Along the Colombia-Venezuela border, cross-border disappearances can be explained as a consequence of the United Self-Defense Forces of Colombia's (Autodefensas Unidas de Colombia—AUC) incursion in the 1990s. In the first decade of the twenty-first century alone, 16,000 people were killed and 1,800 disappeared in the borderlands of Norte de Santander and Táchira.[25] Between 1999 and 2001, the AUC buried bodies in mass graves, cemeteries, or threw them into the river to eliminate traces. Since 2001, the paramilitary leaders Salvatore Mancuso and Carlos Castaño ordered the incineration of bodies in various locations in Norte de Santander including Cúcuta, Villa del Rosario, and Puerto de Santander to lower official homicide rates and to avoid the attention of human rights organizations.[26] Violence skyrocketed in Norte de Santander's Catatumbo region, and especially in its Tibú municipality. Between 2000 and 2004, an average of three to five murders per week occurred in Tibú municipality.[27] Tibú also accounted for almost 68 percent of the cases of disappearances (346, of which 233 were registered as enforced disappearances) in Norte de Santander between 2000 and 2009.[28] 245 of these victims were registered in the village of La Gabarra in the Tibú municipality that I visited. El Tarra municipality, another site I went to, registered twenty-seven enforced disappearances during this period.[29]

In 2003, the paramilitary Catatumbo Bloc's Border Front started to employ cross-border disappearances: the victims were killed in Colombia and buried in

Venezuela, or both killed and dumped in Venezuela. Between March and April 2003, the bodies of more than fifty Colombians were dumped in Venezuela near the village of Juan Frío. Leaving the bodies in unpopulated areas near the border, the perpetrators were hardly accountable.[30] Since the AUC's demobilization, post-demobilized groups have continued with these cross-border disappearances.

Cross-border disappearances blur the differences between two types of violence in borderlands: Colombian civil war violence and Venezuelan common crime. To camouflage the crimes, the perpetrators generally no longer kill their victims as brutally as they used to in Colombia, for example by dismembering them.[31] They make the dead bodies look like victims of street crime, which has been rising in Venezuela in recent years.[32] The unclear origin of lethal violence reduces accountability. Over the last nine years, an estimated three hundred bodies—supposedly, murdered Colombians—were buried as "unknowns" in the cemetery of San Cristóbal.[33] In the end of 2009 alone, twenty-three unidentified bodies were thrown into a mass grave.[34] I mainly retrieved specific information about cross-border disappearances from reports by local, or specialized, human rights organizations and via interviews. To the general public outside the border region, such dynamics typically remain invisible. Only large-scale cross-border crimes appear in the national, and even international, media, for example the "massacre of the football players" in Fernández Feo municipality in Táchira on 11 October 2009, in which nine Colombians were kidnapped and disappeared as reported by the Ecuadorian newspaper *Hoy*.[35]

It is harder for the victims' relatives to obtain information on their loved ones' whereabouts across the border than within the national territory. Identified dead Colombians in Venezuela are issued a Venezuelan death certificate which is invalid in Colombia. Therefore considered officially alive, these people do not figure into homicide statistics and relatives cannot claim benefits as victims of the conflict.[36] Repatriating the corpse is complicated and expensive.[37] The cross-border nature of these disappearances reinforces the fear that Rivas-Torres notes for "ordinary" disappearances:

> The modality of the "disappeared" is even more cruel than public assassination, since it raises the perception of danger by placing it in an imaginary world, unsure but probable, created by the possibility that the disappeared person is alive. While one suspects that the disappeared person may be dead, nobody knows the truth. Doubt, prolonged over time, is a highly productive way of sowing fear. Fear has come to stay.[38]

According to the human rights NGO Fundación Progresar, based in Cúcuta, Venezuela's systematic failure to investigate crimes is due to the lack of a coherent strategy, infrastructure, and culture.[39] It also relates to the time lag in facing these crimes on such a large scale. In Venezuela, this started in the 2000s, whereas Colombia has experienced disappearances for a much longer time.

The degree of impunity depends on the interests of governments in particular border areas and on changes in their bilateral relations.[40] The ups and downs in Colombia's diplomatic relations with its neighbors have conditioned border cooperation. For example, the communication channels between the Forensic Institute of Táchira (part of the Venezuelan Ministry of People's Power for Internal Relations and Justice) and the Colombian authorities was obstructed due to diplomatic tensions for the first half of the 2000s, which made cross-border judicial cooperation more difficult.[41]

Cross-border Displacements within Borderlands

Cross-border displacements within borderlands (as opposed to displacements to the recipient country's interior) obfuscate victimization. During the war between various guerrillas in Arauca between 2006 and 2010, Colombian borderlanders sought refuge in Apure, their cross-border community.[42] Starting a new life in a familiar environment is easier than in another region without support systems, and being near relatives who stay behind is comforting. Between 2002 and June 2010, 4,230 Colombians sought refugee status in Apure.[43] Many more, however, did not seek this status because they were staying with relatives or friends and thus did not consider themselves refugees.[44] These people neither registered as internally displaced persons in Colombia, nor as refugees in Venezuela, which rendered their displacement invisible. Only in 2015, when Venezuela decided to shut the border and deport thousands of Colombians who were illegally living on the Venezuelan side of the border, did this situation begin to attract attention.

Cross-border intra-borderland displacements of bi-national indigenous people are particularly invisible outside the community due to the borderlands' transnationality combined with their nomadic way of life. A case in point is the displacement of Wayúu in La Guajira and Zulia, within the border zone. Geographical mobility is part of their lifestyle,[45] and they hardly report displacements to state institutions because they have their own legal system. It is therefore challenging to distinguish the movements of this indigenous group from forced displacements.[46]

Similarly, in Nariño, during the FARC's combat against paramilitaries in the early 2000s, and post-demobilized groups including the Rastrojos in the 2010s, many indigenous Awá in Nariño and Carchi fled massacres. An Awá leader explained the invisibility of the displacements:

> The Awá family lives in another country because [the borderline] is an imaginary line that does not exist. [Our country] is a territory like the Colombian and the Ecuadorian one [. . .]. Many of the armed actors have used this side of the border corridor like a strategic zone, a site for refuge and trafficking of drugs and arms. This drug trafficking conflict has affected us here in the border corridor. [. . .] Some of our families were obliged to migrate to Ecuador or to other places. The families know that this is one territory, though another country, but they continue to live as if they were in Colombia. We have had a problem with this because the families are displaced from here. They cross the border and one never realizes that so many people were displaced to another country. The same way as they belong to the same family, they leave and take refuge, successively, at their uncle's place, their cousin's, their grandparents'. . . This problem is invisible because one hardly realizes that it happens. Only when you start to investigate do you know that they left due to [. . .] the armed conflict [. . .]. For the international community and for the Colombian or Ecuadorian government it is invisible [. . .]. Many families who lived in Colombia and cross over to Ecuador [. . .] are Colombians [. . .]. Sometimes they haven't been granted the rights included in the [Ecuadorian] Constitution because for [the Ecuadorian authorities] they are foreigners, but according to our vision they are not. Many families are sometimes threatened in the Colombian Awá territory and the only option they have to protect themselves is cross over to the other country because their family lives there. [. . .] Some of them stay there and others return after a while. This type of displacement is not visible to the national and international community [. . .]. [They think that] maybe they just went on holiday or to visit their family, but in reality they had to flee threats or something else related to the Colombian armed conflict.[47]

While Colombian refugees in Ecuador and Venezuela receive official assistance, Ecuadorians and Venezuelans who face "intra-border zone displacement" or who are displaced from the border zone to the interior of their country tend to be overlooked. Bogotá adapted its policies to the long history of violence. Even if implemented imperfectly, since 2011 it has committed itself to assist victims of the armed conflict with the Victims Law.[48] Also, Colombian legislation concerning the protection of indigenous people and Afro-Colombians is more advanced than its Venezuelan or Ecuadorian counterparts because, in Colombia, these ethnic groups have been historically disproportionally affected by the armed conflict and subject to systematic targeting by various groups.[49]

The border's filter mechanism makes victimization less obvious, fuels violence among violent non-state groups, and at times increases people's exposure to it. Proximity to the border has been intentionally (ab-)used to camouflage homicides. Because of deficient official border cooperation, exacerbated by diplomatic tensions, the perpetrators of violence are rarely held accountable so that the de facto security situation is often more precarious than reflected in media coverage or homicide statistics. With cross-border impunity facilitating engagement in violence, the sense of being a potential victim is particularly palpable in such border areas.

Promoting Illegal Economies

The proximity to an international border allows evasion of law enforcement measures aimed at destroying drug business infrastructure. Those involved in the illicit business move laboratories to crystallize coca paste into cocaine across the border, change storage areas for the cocaine ready for international shipment from mangroves or harbors on one side of the border to the other, and rebuild airstrips to ship cocaine abroad across the border. This stabilizes the income of communities who work along the cocaine supply chain for the various violent non-state groups: provided they are reasonably mobile, workers in laboratories do not lose their jobs, and suppliers of products such as coca paste can continue to sell their products. It helps foster the groups' legitimacy in these people's eyes and increases the tolerance margin for abuse and violence committed by them. That is, it enhances shadow citizen security.

In the Colombian-Ecuadorian borderlands, as of 2011, mobile laboratories existed in both Sucumbíos and Putumayo because the guerrillas used to move laboratories to the Ecuadorian border zone to avoid military pressure. According to the Ecuadorian Ministry of the Interior, in 2010, five cocaine laboratories were detected and destroyed and 3,870 coca plants eradicated in the Ecuadorian border zone.[50] In Norte de Santander and Zulia, mobile laboratories were detected near the road that links Cúcuta with Puerto Santander, for example near the areas of Camilo Torres and Patillales. Around 2012, approximately 75 percent of the gasoline smuggled from Venezuela to Norte de Santander to be used for cocaine processing entered the country in this region with little state presence and was transported to the laboratories. A community leader from Cúcuta noted that, as of 2011, the Rastrojos managed the laboratories and moved them across the border when the army entered the zone.[51]

The borderline is not always a distinct feature, such as a river. Often, there is ambiguity regarding the side on which violent non-state groups operate. One such case exists, for example, north of the River Oro, where the border runs through an inaccessible mountainous area, the northern part of Sierra de Perijá shared by Cesar and Zulia. When I interviewed a humanitarian organization employee and his friend in Zulia in 2012, not too far away from this case, they described how the armed actors take advantage of this ambiguity to promote the illicit economy:

EMPLOYEE: People say there are laboratories in this zone. [. . .] Three years ago, the National Guard detained [an indigenous Barí], accusing him of transporting drugs down the mountains from a laboratory, but the Barí said he did not transport drugs, that he was not involved [. . .]. The place that the National Guard mentions is not Venezuela, it is Colombia. They went into Colombia without permission from the Colombians. In the end, the Barí was sentenced to fifteen years. [. . .] According to the government, they have dismantled laboratories [in Venezuela], too.

FRIEND: They also found a laboratory in Jesús María Semprún municipality [. . .].

EMPLOYEE: In the mountainous zone that can be reached by going up from [the village], there are places where they process the drug. This is done on the Venezuelan side. The drug business is thriving in this zone! We visited people in the zone who have pictures of the drug presses, but we don't know who they are and how they bring the drug down [to the village] [. . .]. The guerrillas are in charge of it. Since the place is near the Colombian side, people say they go to the Colombian Sierra de Codazzi, where the coca is. They harvest the coca and bring it here to process it. [. . .] This is a zone of difficult access; normally there are only the indigenous people.[52]

In order to distribute the drug business's different supply chain stages to both sides of a poorly defined border, the guerrillas rely on the locals' support to carry the drugs down to the road to be transported onward, while locals rely on this income. The Barí's involvement in transporting drugs is plausible, given the difficult access to legal economic opportunities due to stigmatization as guerrilla collaborators.

In Nariño and Esmeraldas on the Pacific coast, cocaine destined for international trafficking by sea is stocked in harbors and mangroves (see Figure 7.1). The groups involved in the drugs business move cocaine stocks across the border to evade law enforcement measures, enhancing income stability for the community members involved.

Figure 7.1 Cocaine hideout: Mangroves on the Pacific Coast, 2012. Photo by Author.

An estimated 216.3 tons of cocaine is shipped every year from the Pacific coast via the Galápagos Islands, Central America, or Mexico to the United States.[53] Borderlanders work as boatmen, informants, messengers, or providers of motors and gasoline. When the Colombian government intensified interdiction measures in Tumaco to stop boats ranging from fast lane boats to semi-submarines, traffickers simply diversified their routes to use starting points in Ecuador as well. Within Ecuador, the criminals kept the routes flexible, which made their networks more resilient. Although Guayaquil and Esmeraldas had been the most known starting points of international trafficking routes for decades,[54] locations near the border with Colombia were used for large-scale illicit cocaine deals, as cases of seizures revealed. On September 15, 2008, the Operation Huracán de la Frontera led to the confiscation of 4.7 tons of cocaine in 4,415 packages, hidden in La Campanita, an area in Esmeraldas province only 20 meters away from the Border River Mataje. Each package was marked with Nike, Apache, or Águila, signs used by FARC Fronts 29 and 32,[55] and to be shipped in submarines to Acapulco, Mexico.[56]

Violent non-state groups also benefit from movement across the border at the starting points of air routes. Arauca used to be an important starting point of cocaine flights toward the Caribbean and the United States. However, in 2005, the Colombians (with US assistance) imposed stricter control of their airspace, and Hugo Chávez stopped cooperation with the US Drug Enforcement Administration.[57] The clandestine airstrips were relocated to Apure. According to the White House Office of National Drug Control Policy, in 2010, South America "exported" around 850 tons of cocaine. More than 200 tons went through Venezuela, and, of those, more than 100 tons were shipped from Apure.[58] Map 7.1 depicts 121 tracks of what are thought to be cocaine flights in 2010. The data suggest that 113 of them departed from Apure. This illustrates the effect of the border as facilitator: as violent entrepreneurs were able to move air routes across the border, the illicit drug business continued to flourish, despite stricter interdiction measures in Colombia.

Income stability in regions that lack state-provided economic opportunities enhances the social recognition of violent non-state groups as job providers, preventing the state from easily (re-)gaining legitimacy. Shadow citizen security and shadow citizenship become more worthwhile than citizenship oriented toward the state. Paradoxically, by diminishing the risk of interdiction measures, transnationality also reduces the population's risk of insecurity because, when cocaine shipments are confiscated, or laboratories destroyed, violent non-state groups tend to compensate for the loss with an increase in extortion or kidnappings to generate alternative income. Therefore, one could argue that it is in the population's best interest *not* to inform the authorities about any illegal economic activities, even if they occur under repressive conditions. Illegality becomes a means of protection.

Obscuring Social Control

"What happens at borders exerts a powerful, but too rarely recognized, influence on processes of state and nation formation," notes Willem van Schendel.[59] The transnationality of borderlands obscures social control imposed by violent non-state groups, including across the border. Mats Berdal, Rohan Gunaratna, and organizations such as the United Nations Office on Drugs and Crime (UNODC) highlight the transnationality of the activities of such groups (e.g., transnational organized crime) or of their organizational structure (e.g., transnational terrorist networks), yet it also concerns their authority.[60] Wolfgang Zeller notes:

> borderlands are always zones of regulatory ambiguity, and during open conflict the opportunity to make up and enforce different (formal and nonformal) regimes of regulation is particularly prevalent.[61]

Violent non-state groups enhance their cross-border authority while state authorities are limited to one side. If borderland communities do not feel part of a

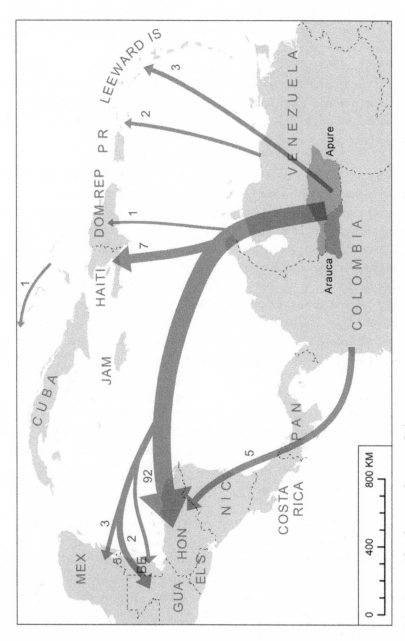

Map 7.1 Tracks of supposed cocaine flights in 2010. Source: Based on radar data made available by the US Joint Interagency Task Force South. Credit: Map created by Author.

national citizenry, they may "exit" the deficient, if not imaginary, state-society re-lationship and enter a mutually reinforcing relationship with a violent non-state group instead.[62] According to a staff member of an international agency based in Mocoa, Putumayo, for example, deals with guerrillas and post-demobilized groups were more efficient and safer than asking the state for help. Therefore, the communities would prefer silence vis-à-vis the state:

> People put up with the situation because they know that the state out-side does not offer them anything. It is often better to settle on a deal with [the groups], to dialogue, and to mediate to reach agreements in-stead of having to leave.[63]

Such shadow citizenship can also arise in non-border regions. However, in the case of communities with a sense of belonging to a transnational community— a product of their everyday lives taking place across the border—illicit cross-border authority can yield a particularly strong version of shadow citizenship. The resulting institutional pluralism contradicts conceptions of borderlands as ungoverned or ungovernable spaces;[64] borderlands transform into illicitly governed spaces.[65] These processes question the very notion of territoriality. In John Ruggie's terms, in such borderlands, the "unbundling of territoriality" is a constant reality.[66] In this sense, analyzing how the borderlands' transnationality obscures social control serves to do what Benedikt Korf and Timothy Raeymaekers suggest when asking where the state ends geographically:

> to visualize the often fragmented geographies of sovereignty that characterize state-society encounters at the physical margins of the state, and which often involve important processes of bordering and boundary-drawing between what is categorically termed as distinctions between state and society, formal, and to informal or public and private systems of rule.[67]

Carchi is usually cited as the least violent and most secure northern Ecuadorian border province.[68] Many interviewees in Quito interpreted its low homicide rates as the absence of violent non-state groups. However, interviews I carried out in 2012 in remote border zones including Chical, Maldonado, and Tufiño pointed to dynamics indiscernible from outside the region. Accordingly, the FARC had supply chain relationships with the Rastrojos on the Colombian border side, and the FARC's Front 29 sustained and extended their preponderance in Colombia to Ecuador through cross-border social control, enhanced through psychological pressure and strict rules without a visible presence. This can lead to long-term psychological trauma and has repercussions on the state-society relationship. Whispering, a local resident in the Ecuadorian northern border zone told me that the guerrillas sometimes crossed over to Carchi:

> The guerrillas convene many meetings, last week they called four or five meetings. The problem is that when they arrive, no one can enter or leave anymore, they control everything because there could be informants.[69]

The threat of violence is usually sufficient to enforce the borderlanders' silence. Knowing about the violent punishments imposed on their Colombian neighbors, Ecuadorians adhered to the FARC's rules and the FARC continued their activities undisturbed. The groups' control over public discourse enshrouded this manifestation of non-state order in rural Carchi. It hardly received attention from the state or media. Social control stopped community members from speaking out, as they did not expect support. It masked cases where silence resulted from the Ecuadorians' social recognition of the Front 29's authority, rather than from fear. Local residents argued that coca leaves were cultivated and processed in Colombia only.[70] When I enquired further, I found that Ecuadorians crossed over to Colombia to work in coca plantations, suggesting that the silence was also predicated on the known involvement of Ecuadorians. Some perceived the FARC to be a legitimate authority because, while violence and combat between insurgents and state forces were limited to Colombia, job opportunities arising from the cocaine business were open to Colombians and Ecuadorians alike. Ecuadorians could work and go back to the comparative safety of home in Ecuador.[71] I experienced this attitude myself when stepping onto the border bridge pictured in Figure 7.2 on the Ecuadorian side and beginning to walk across. Once I approached the center, my Ecuadorian friends told me to return because otherwise I would enter FARC territory. The spiral of silence and neglect is tragic: the rule of silence distances people from the state; they are less likely to contribute to citizen security themselves by demanding accountability and denouncing crimes, contributing to impunity. State neglect fuels resentment against the state, making popular support of the armed actors more likely, which contributes to silence over events in return.

Keeping quiet about the locals' complicity is an important protection mechanism in a context where communities suffer extreme vulnerability. The local resident mentioned above continued:

> Here, absolute silence reigns. You will never get anything out of anyone. [. . .] People won't tell you anything. People know who is helping [the guerrilla] with medicine, who facilitates support, which authorities are involved in these things. But they won't tell you [. . .]. Of course

Figure 7.2 Unofficial border bridge between Carchi (Ecuador) and Nariño (Colombia), 2012. Photo by Author.

other foreigners like you come here, it's just that [. . .] be careful when choosing the people you talk to because you could say what everyone's doing. This is why I'm telling you: watch out![72]

Silence vis-à-vis outsiders, yet solidarity among community members to conceal their involvement, suggests that the "bonding social capital" among those from the same cross-border community is high and hence social fabric dense, whereas the "bridging social capital" with those outside the group is low.[73] Being a *cross-border* community rather than a marginalized group within a single state produces an even deeper tear in the social fabric between the community and the rest of the citizenry, one that is more difficult to repair. As these cross-border communities do not feel that they belong to either of the two bordering states, the fabric comes away at the edges rather than being damaged from within, without the state even noticing.

A politician from Tulcán commented on the northern border zone as follows: "From the perspective of other regions one could think that the issue of security is delicate, but if you visit the border you don't find problems. They are not visible to the naked eye!"[74] The public discourse in Ecuador conveys a generalized image of the border zone. Visiting the region gives an impression of calmness, usually confirmed by locals. Yet this illusory calm results from the

FARC's remote cross-border social control. The Ecuadorian authorities do not have evidence against the FARC, as they are not physically present. If they are present, it is as civilian militias, often with an Ecuadorian passport, as a member of the Church explained:

> There isn't warlike violence on this side, but there is another form of violence. This region isn't declared a zone of extension, but it is a zone of extension. The problem is that many from [Colombia], including *guerrilleros*, have dual citizenship.[75]

In coastal areas such as Esmeraldas (Ecuador) and Tumaco (Colombia), the financial benefits of growing coca surpass those of licit activities, and many locals consider them legitimate. In 2009, a fisherman in the Ecuadorian village of San Lorenzo earned 50 USD per week. If he opted to work in Colombia as a *raspachín*, a person who scrapes the coca leaves to harvest them, he earned between 600 and 800 USD per week. His family could live in relative safety of San Lorenzo, compared to the more dangerous Colombian twin town of Tumaco.[76]

In Sucumbíos, near the border crossing between San Miguel and General Farfán, the FARC Front 48 exerted illicit transnational authority,[77] inducing shadow citizenship. The guerrillas influenced all kinds of aspects of local life on both sides of the border, ranging from the local economy and people's participation in community initiatives to health and the education system. As of 2012, they regularly called Ecuadorian farmers to attend meetings in Colombia to inform them about the *vacuna* rate to be paid in Ecuador and about what to cultivate at their farms in Colombia. As coca cultivation exists to a limited extent on the Ecuadorian side, Ecuadorian farmers from Sucumbíos crossed the border to Putumayo to work during the week on coca plantations and in rudimentary laboratories where coca leaves are processed into paste. This is more profitable than working within the border zone where they reside and where they are unable to earn enough to sustain their families.[78] A Colombian woman who lived in Sucumbíos, but worked on a coca farm in Putumayo, described the benefits of working in the cocaine business:

> The guerrillas don't sell [cocaine]. It's those from the other side of the border [Ecuador], but people from here are obviously Ecuadorians. Those who buy [cocaine] transport it to sell it in Quito [...] for consumption. I know people who carry only a little bit. They take 100 or 200 grams and sell it in a village. This is how they make a living. They sell retail. Others take two or three kilos and transport [the cocaine] abroad. There they add stuff to it [...] to increase the quantity

and make profit from it [. . .]. Here, those who work in the cocaine business are Colombians, Ecuadorians, everyone. Even for the labor force, the *raspachines,* they use Ecuadorians. The *raspa* [coca leaf picking] is good because [. . .] on a normal working day in the field, the *raspachines* earn at least 15,000 pesos [7.80 USD in 2011]. If they harvest seven to eight *arrobas,* they make forty, fifty, or even 60,000 pesos [21 to 31 USD in 2011]. So how should they not like this? [. . .] In this work, they pay you piece rates, not per day. Therefore, of course everyone does it![79]

She felt safer on the Ecuadorian side:

On the Colombian side, there are always many armed groups and the police. I lived on a farm on the other side [in Putumayo] and they always bothered you: "Where do you come from?" They always harass you [. . .]: "Have you seen the army?" This is uncomfortable for the population. Why? Because you can't be there, they grab your wrist and ask questions. [. . .] In my opinion there is lots of terrorism [. . .] because terrorism is when they frighten you, right? When they do things to scare the population. At any time, the armed groups put bombs, pipe-bombs. They shoot at the police. [. . .] They frighten the residents. This is terrorism for me [. . .]. Here [in Ecuador], this is not the case. Personally, I feel supported. I feel safe on this side because [. . .] you never hear shootings here, or people asking, "Who could that be?" [. . .].[80]

The bad image of state forces, often perceived as yet another dangerous group, further contributed to the guerrillas' illicit cross-border authority. A resident of Lago Agrio stated that "along the entire border there is danger because there are the FARC, paramilitaries, and Colombian militaries." Yet while the state was considered ineffective, the guerrillas were respected and feared.

State neglect on each side of the border facilitates illicit authority across the border. It helps violent non-state groups to be perceived as a legitimate authority and fosters shadow citizenship transnationally. As in Ecuador, residents of the Venezuelan border zone felt abandoned by the state, as a 2009 citizen security survey of the Venezuelan National Statistics Institute confirms.[81] Of those surveyed, 85 percent believed state presence was weak or very weak. This feeling was also high among the rest of the population (79 percent).[82] However, this could be explained by distorted perceptions: what borderlanders perceive to be strong state presence tends to be weak for the rest of the population. Borderlanders are not even used to a minimal presence. Therefore a limited state presence is already considered an improvement over previous levels. Furthermore, corrupt authorities in borderlands reduced the borderlanders' confidence in the state. Among respondents in the border states of Amazonas, Apure, Táchira, and Zulia, 7.6 percent identified the police as the major source of crime, as opposed to 4.6 percent of non-borderland respondents.[83] Such mistrust allows violent non-state groups to lure borderlanders from state-led security-provision to shadow citizen security. Consider the South of the Sierra de Perijá, which stretches down to Catatumbo, where the Río de Oro forms the border between Colombia and Venezuela. Even though they had to flee to Venezuela, many Colombians decided to live next to the river to work in coca cultivations in Colombia during the day. These dynamics contributed to an increased distance between the Venezuelan state and the borderlanders while promoting a consensual relationship with the guerrillas.

7.2 The Border as Deterrent

Violent non-state groups defy the functions of international borders, but they do not completely override them. Indeed, contrary to conventional views according to which borders are void for these illicit actors, the border can deter violent non-state groups from reducing distrust between each other. As discussed in chapter 2, this, however, is essential for them to engage in any kind of arrangement with each other. Where there is mistrust only, arrangements between violent non-state groups do not exist (see figure 2.1).

In cases where the border has such a deterring effect the groups are also likely to display more mistrust vis-à-vis the local population. The border effect reduces the predictability of breakdowns of violent non-state group interactions and negatively influences people's exposure to selective violence (see Table 7.1). The ramifications for the local population are, however, often overlooked due to the asymmetry of insecurity caused by physical violence across borders. Levels of physical violence were generally reported to be lower on the non-conflict sides of the border, that is in Ecuador and Venezuela (see section 3.2), than on the Colombian side. Furthermore, widening the perspective from physical violence to other elements of citizen security, in particular, the local communities' social fabric, demonstrates how the inter-group distrust also intensifies interpersonal mistrust among community members (see Table 7.1). This thwarts a sense of unity in border communities that comprise nationals from both sides of the borderline.

Fueling Mistrust

Security analysts highlight that violent non-state groups are *not* bound by state borders and therefore benefit from (illegal) cross-border activities, such as trans-national organized crime,[84] or from cross-border impunity due to the border's filter mechanism, as discussed above. Michael Miklaucic and Jacqueline Brewer note that

> criminal and terrorist entities are mobile and increasingly migratory actors capable of shifting both their locations and their vocations in order to exploit geographic, political, enforcement, and regulatory vulnerabilities. They do not view state borders as impenetrable "castle walls."[85]

Although they do not see them as "castle walls," violent non-state groups do inter-pret borders as obstacles, particularly when it comes to intangible elements such as inter-group trust. In the case of cross-border spot sales and barter agreements, members of one of the groups must cross the border to meet members of another group. The constraints on the local violent non-state group to cheat the foreign one are typically lower than for the foreign group because the former is more familiar with the environment. As a result, the foreign group has at least three disadvantages. Firstly, as they do not normally operate in that territory (e.g., be-cause the local group is dominant), it is more difficult for group members to bribe or infiltrate the state forces of that country to acquire information on their operations. Secondly, as foreigners, they have weaker ties with the local popula-tion. Finally, they are vulnerable to cheating by the local group. The latter group can more easily avoid retaliation from the foreign group, unless there is a signifi-cant power imbalance in favor of the foreign group. In brief, across a border, the convergence of economic interests as distrust-reducing mechanism to engage in the specific business deal, as explained in chapter 2, is set against the backdrop of these additional mistrust-fueling factors. As I demonstrate below, this increased distrust among violent non-state group also negatively influences interpersonal trust among local community members in that territory.[86]

A Colombian ex-guerrilla fighter who used to work in the finance section of one of the FARC fronts explained to me how these cross-border barter agreements and spot sales worked in practice:

EX-GUERRILLA: In [Village A] I was part of [. . .] finances. We entered Ecuador to negotiate with people from there. Our business was supplies, for example military equipment. We met with Ecuadorians who sell stuff, or we arrived at the border and arranged a meeting with these people and then they came to see us [...]. They sold everything: armaments, ammunition, military clothes, medicine, provisions [...].

ME: *Were you in plain clothes?*

EX-GUERRILLA: Of course [...].

ME: *In [Village B] as well?*

EX-GUERRILLA: In plain clothes. [...]

ME: *How did you cross the border [...]?*

EX-GUERRILLA: [...] They got me a fake ID [...]. We stayed in [Village A] around four, five, or eight days. This is quick because once we made the deal we left again.

ME: *Did the deal involve armaments or medicine or...?*

EX-GUERRILLA: It was a bit of everything. You strike a deal and afterward in another area, they hand over what you have ordered and you pay them. Camouflage clothes cost that much, a sweatshirt costs that much, this drug costs that much, a rifle costs that much, ammunition costs that much... They set the price and then you start to negotiate. Let's say a rifle costs 10 million, then I say: "I will give you that much and it's a deal [...]." Then other FARC members pick up the merchandise. They transport it via [Village C], from here to there to hand it over to the boss [...].

ME: *How did they bring the merchandise to Colombia, via [Village D]?*

EX-GUERRILLA: No, they have their own trails. [...] I don't know these routes, but by the time one finds out they're already there with the stuff. They call us and say: "Here is your stuff, come." [...] For example, they tell you: "The commander has requested this and that!" Then I make him a list. You have to memorize everything; you can't take a paper with you because of the checkpoints [...]. You arrive and you go to a house or to a hotel and you shut yourself up and ready. Let's negotiate [...]. "How many days will it take?" "We need it quicker!" It takes that long because there are many checkpoints on the way. It takes at least a month, up to one and a half months.[87]

As our conversation progressed, the former rebel revealed the profound inter-group distrust in the context of illicit cross-border business deals. Of course, problems of credible commitment arise in other contexts as well, and criminals and others use a variety of strategies such as hostage-taking, as outlined in chapter 2, and issue-linkage to mitigate these.[88] Across international borders, however, the exposure to potential cheating is particularly high:

ME: *[...] Did you already know how to negotiate?*

EX-GUERRILLA: No, they give us instructions [...]. Let's say I bring the material I want to sell. The commander does not let himself be seen. Instead, he tells someone to go and negotiate: "For a grenade pay that much!" If he says,

"Pay up to that amount," then don't go higher, don't go lower than that [. . .].
He doesn't let himself be seen by those who come because you never know,
something might happen. [. . .] So he tells you if you can [pay the price] or
not, or to tell them to lower [it] a bit more. This is a long process [. . .]. It's very
complicated! These arms traffickers are very greedy. Once, when we bought
200 grenades from them, fifteen had no primers. A month later we found out,
a guy in charge of maintenance found out. He took off the grenade's lid and,
of course, there wasn't any primer. They had filled it with dirt. This was really
bad for me. The person who was told off was me because I negotiated and was
supposed to check everything really well.

ME: *Aren't these traffickers trusted people?*

EX-GUERRILLA: No [. . .], some of them are trusted people, but others are not.
Since we want to have things cheaper, I have to buy from them and they realize that they can cheat us . . . and we have to go to Ecuador to meet them and
this is where they lure us into a trap.[89]

There are at least three ramifications for the citizen security situation of local
border communities in such contexts.

First, locals are exposed to potential threats by the foreign armed actors if
they are suspected of aiding the local actors. If cross-border deals are carried
out in populated areas, local communities are embedded in a context of suspicion in which the armed actors mistrust them.[90] Community members can be
suspected of aiding one of the groups to cheat the other, or of being whistle-
blowers. Negotiating the deal in a closed space such as a house or a hotel, as the
ex-combatant explained, reduces the possibilities for saboteurs to meddle into
the deals, but does not rule out this possibility completely. For the population to
stay safe, the rule is to feign ignorance about these deals. Possessing knowledge
bears the risk of being killed, as the options for violent non-state groups to deter
whistle-blowers with social control are limited. When I asked a local employee
of an international organization whether community members are aware of
Colombians crossing over to Ecuador to engage in such deals, he replied: "Most
people don't say anything, or you decide not to ask because it is difficult." The
borderlanders reduce their vulnerability by keeping quiet. Yet silence to avoid
being suspected of sabotaging the deal actually contributes to people's isolation
from each other.

Second, relationships among the border population are marred by interpersonal mistrust. Profound inter-group distrust has an undermining effect
on the social fabric of border communities, especially if they mix recipient
and displaced populations. As of 2009, around 85,000 Colombians lived
in the Ecuadorian northern border zone, with 70 percent of them in need of

international protection.[91] Xenophobia against Colombian refugees has been a general problem in Ecuador, where stereotypes of Colombian male *sicarios* and female prostitutes, as well as stories of rebels and paramilitaries masked as refugees, regularly featured in the media and public discourse. In border regions where locals are aware of cross-border deals between Ecuadorian trafficking groups and Colombian armed actors in civilian clothes, suspicion against Colombians is further reinforced. Ecuadorians suspect them of being dealers who come to Ecuador incognito to do business. This increases xenophobia and thwarts a sense of unity in such communities.[92]

Third, given high levels of inter-group distrust, locals are used as "buffers" to implement deals or become negotiating counterparts themselves. The violent non-state groups involved in cross-border deals take advantage of locals to circumvent potential cheating. As the ex-guerrilla's account demonstrates, it was his responsibility to avoid cheating (which he failed to do) and he also had to avoid being lured into a trap. It is common that lower-ranking members of armed groups are tasked with these risky endeavors. If a deal falls through they can be more easily dispensed with—either by being moved to a different front for example, or by being killed—than senior members. Military superiority is therefore not necessarily an insurance against betrayal. The ex-rebel's organization, the FARC, was more powerful than the Ecuadorian trafficking group. Even so, he had to bear the risk as an individual when physically crossing the border. However, while group members negotiate the deal, locals are often used to physically collect or carry items across the border. In these cases, violent non-state groups reduce risks of cheating by drawing on locals as drug mules, gasoline smugglers, or messengers, for instance (see section 6.1). Consequently, these people are exposed to harm and abuse exerted by one group to deter cheating, to cheat on, or to retaliate against the other one.

Some borderland community members are themselves involved in cross-border deals with armed actors. This means that foreign groups avoid potential cheating altogether. Dealing with individuals rather than an armed group keeps the power imbalance in their favor, even on foreign territory. While these deals are difficult to implement with illicit goods such as drugs and weapons, they are more feasible with licit ones, including money and gasoline. People engaged, for instance, in cross-border money laundering, which is particularly lucrative along the Colombia-Ecuador border because Ecuador is dollarized. Members of Colombian violent non-state groups cross the border to engage in these deals as in the account discussed above. However, since they only interact with vulnerable locals who further benefit from this practice, cheating and betrayal is of lesser concern. In Esmeraldas province, an international organization employee commented:

Those from the [Colombian] side of the border come with fifty- or one-hundred-dollar notes. Since no one in the country receives a note of such a high value, they demand: "Change this one-hundred-dollar note!" People say: "I don't have so many ten-dollar notes," "Don't worry, I'll give you hundred and you give me fifty in return!" Then you go to San Lorenzo and deposit it at the bank. These are dollars, no counterfeit money, these are real dollars. People began to get involved in this practice as a business. They told me the guerrillas camp at night in this zone. They come to rest and, in some cases, people make friends with them. Due to this money relationship, they make more and more friends. People say: "I give you hundred and you give me fifty in return. That's a deal! I don't work, but gain fifty dollars from time to time."[93]

Most of the time, ambiguity is people's protection. Consider the following story told during the same interview:

One day I was talking to a man in [a village] at a gasoline station [...]. We were promoting agriculture so that people would stop being involved in something illicit and dedicate themselves to legal activities. One of the men sitting with us stood up and left. [...] They told me that he smuggles gasoline all the time. They told me that they made 1,000 USD every day by smuggling gasoline and that they knew that this gasoline would go to Colombia to process cocaine. There is this link between drug trafficking, the guerrillas, and people from this side who participate in the business.[94]

People's silence disguises their involvement. Given the circumstances, it is possible that a Colombian armed group member had negotiated the deal and price with the man at the gasoline station. Yet the man could also be unaware of the guerrillas' involvement and their use of the gasoline for processing coca into cocaine (e.g., if middlemen were involved). To some extent, this ambiguity plays into the man's favor. It is to even greater benefit, however, to the armed group, who can conceal any such deals if they involve locals rather than violent non-state groups from across the border.

In cases like this, silence about the presence of Colombian armed groups in Ecuador is in the borderlanders' interest. Those who are not involved keep quiet to avoid being suspected of whistle-blowing. The rule of silence applies of course in many situations in which violent non-state groups are present. In the case of these cross-border arrangements, however, the Colombian groups must keep a low profile to use foreign territory for supplies and money laundering. They have more reason to mistrust Ecuadorian borderlanders who may report their presence to the authorities, which could provoke higher state military presence.[95]

Reducing Interdependence

The border's characteristic of deterring trust between violent non-state groups increases people's exposure to selective violence in the context of cross-border subcontractual relationships. Despite being in a "staggered" relationship (see section 2.1), when groups are contracted across the border, they are more independent than within the boundaries of a state. This is particularly evident when the contracting group has a differing position vis-à-vis the respective government on each side of the border. A conflict actor may be willing to punish a subcontracted group with violence on conflict territory where its reputation is that of an established violent actor. In this case, the group is likely to deter the subcontracted group from breaking their relationship, for example by threatening to kill subcontracted group members. Yet on neighboring territory, it may prefer to keep a lower profile to avoid attention from that state in order to be able to use the territory as a safe haven and space for acquiring material supply and finances. Therefore, if counting on the local community's support, the subcontracted group has more scope to operate independently. This group constellation across the border gives armed actors more reason to distrust each other than would be the case within the territory of a single state. It makes the group's expectations of the community members' behavior less predictable. Memories shared by residents of the Ecuadorian northern border zone about an Ecuadorian group subcontracted by powerful Colombian groups illustrate this. A Tumaco government official described Ecuadorian San Lorenzo at the Pacific as an extension of Tumaco.[96] Most residents of San Lorenzo have family links or commercial relations with this Colombian town. Certain practices in Tumaco are "exported" to San Lorenzo. They include trends among youth, like the type of clothes they wear, but also those related to violent non-state groups such as contract killing, participation in drug trafficking, extortion, and social control through imposing behavioral rules. Contract killings have been widespread in Colombia since at least the 1990s. In Ecuador, they only became common in the early 2000s, when "contract killing schools" were established in Esmeraldas.[97] In 2008, an Ecuadorian youth gang, called the Sons of San Lorenzo, conducted social cleansing in San Lorenzo.[98] According to local accounts, Colombian post-demobilized groups from Tumaco had contracted them from across the border.[99] This way, the Colombian group was able to exert control over the population of San Lorenzo while maintaining a low profile.

This intensified insecurity in various ways. In general, being exposed to the "rule" of a subcontracted violent non-state group rather than an independently operating group increases uncertainty over whether and when the subcontracted group might change the rules of the game. As this decision is taken by the distant contractor rather than by the group community members that they interact with, it is hard for the community to anticipate any changes, for example through changes in the group's behavior. The reduced interdependence of the local group that arises in *cross-border* subcontractual relationships makes sudden changes even less predictable, and exposes locals to violent abuse.

Indeed, when I interviewed local residents of San Lorenzo, they explained that the Sons of San Lorenzo started to ask community members for protection money (extortion), which seemed to allow them to act independently from, if not directly against, the Colombian group.[100] These residents insisted that *locals* should protect San Lorenzo from being overtaken by violent entrepreneurs. Many blamed Colombia for insecurity in their village; xenophobia was on the rise.[101] They suggested keeping Colombians out. Yet at the same time, it was not entirely clear whether the Sons of San Lorenzo's decision to charge protection money was their own. Several community members suspected that some of these young people were still complicit with the Colombian group. This fueled uncertainty as to how behave toward Colombians. It also entailed more interpersonal mistrust among community members whose allegiances were not clear.[102]

Both the strategy of Colombian armed groups and the attitude of the residents of San Lorenzo changed after 2008. As of February 2012, the Ecuadorian state, via San Lorenzo's police, was still not able to ensure security. The police explained that this was due to deficient human and material resources.[103] A Colombian post-demobilized group reportedly was present in San Lorenzo to establish "order," apparently no longer concerned about maintaining a low profile. Direct presence replaced the strategy of subcontracting locals. Many residents approved, as they felt safer then. This demonstrates how Colombian presence had become normalized in Ecuador, too, and how Daniel Pécaut's argument that order and violence are considered intertwined in Colombia had expanded to Ecuador.[104]

7.3 The Border as Magnet

The border's effect as a magnet in the proximity of (rather than across) international borders in vulnerable regions arises from two factors. First, governments display relative restraint in adopting countermeasures against violent non-state groups and the illicit economy that sustains them, as these may cause a diplo-matic uproar in the neighboring country. This consolidates the local community's consent to the armed actor as their "governor." Second, the prospects of profits from illicit economic exchange in a low-risk/high-opportunity environment near borders are particularly high. The large number and particularly entrenched presence of violent non-state groups that these dynamics entail intensify the exposure of communities to arbitrary rules of behavior and to selective violence. This, in turn, negatively influences civility and, more broadly, respectful behav-ior among community members.

Thwarting Countermeasures

Near borders, state policies that target violent non-state groups and illicit economies can have an adverse impact that the neighboring countries across the borderline do not agree with. In the case of Colombia's borderlands, these policies include military operations and counternarcotic measures. The diplo-matic crisis between Colombia and Ecuador, and Colombia and Venezuela, trig-gered by the bombing of the FARC camp in Ecuadorian Angostura in 2008 (see section 3.1), is a case in point. Also, military operations close to, rather than across, the border are easily misinterpreted. Particularly in regions where the exact location of the borderline is unclear, such operations can trigger tensions between the two countries, especially if security cooperation along the border is deficient. From the perspective of the armed actors, the relative constraints of governments to carry out counterinsurgency and other military operations in borderlands is convenient. It plays out to their advantage, as an ex-FARC couple explained to me:

EX-GUERRILLA HUSBAND: If you behave well, if you are nice to the Ecuadorian army, everything is fine. They hardly cooperate with the Colombian army.
ME: *Where did you live better?*
EX-GUERRILLA WIFE: We lived better on the Ecuadorian side because we did not fear the Ecuadorian army. [. . .]
EX-GUERRILLA HUSBAND: When I was there, we conversed, we talked, they caught many guys, but normally this doesn't happen [. . .].
ME: *Is it better to be in the organization (the FARC) near the border?*
EX-GUERRILLA WIFE: Of course! In any other region, there could be a bombard-ment. Near the border it is safer [. . .] because, in Colombia, if there is a bom-bardment, you don't know what might happen if it is the army. [Our friend] was killed two years ago [. . .]. Who killed him? We don't know, he only turned up dead. These things happen. . .[105]

Certain restraint concerning state military operations implies less exposure to violent clashes between state forces and insurgents for the local population. It also means that violent non-state actors can more freely decide on their own treatment of locals, including governing the area, which leaves the population more vulnerable to the armed actors' rules (see chapter 6).

Diplomatic considerations related to specific issues also thwart counter-measures against the violent non-state groups' illicit activities in border regions. The controversial toxic sprayings to eradicate coca cultivations exemplify how violent non-state groups take advantage of such situations. Armed actors involved in the cocaine industry benefited from the prohibition of these fumigations within ten kilometers of the Colombia-Ecuador border. Quito requested these due to the serious health problems that they caused on the Ecuadorian side of the border (see section 3.1). As the UNODC's Integrated Illicit Crops Monitoring System's (SIMCI) mapping of territory with coca cultivation reveals, these are the areas where coca cultivation persisted (see Map 7.2), thus constituting a less risky income source than in other places where one would have to fear eradication. For local populations, it reinforces the security ramifications that exist in regions where violent non-state groups offer illicit economic opportunities in the context of supply chain relationships (see section 6.1): the stable provision of income through the illicit economy widens people's tolerance margins vis-à-vis other governance areas even further.

Boosting Profits

The potential for high profits makes proximity to international borders attractive to violent non-state groups. Border regions, especially coastal ones, comprise the starting points of international trafficking routes, promising particularly lucrative economic benefits. They also feature strategic transit points and logistical hubs where the trafficking routes of cocaine and other goods converge, as the cocaine business is interlinked with illicit services provided in neighboring countries. This spatial concentration of economic exchange and other business opportunities near borders appeals to a large number of groups with shared economic interests, providing the motive for groups to engage in short-lived arrangements of convenience (see section 3.2). The large number of groups and the rapid changes fuel mistrust among the local population. This disintegrates the communities' social fabric (see chapter 5), and it further erodes civility and respectful behavior.

Near Colombia's international borders, especially maritime borders from where cocaine is shipped abroad, the illegal drug's value is typically higher than elsewhere, as it has already passed through various stages of the supply chain.

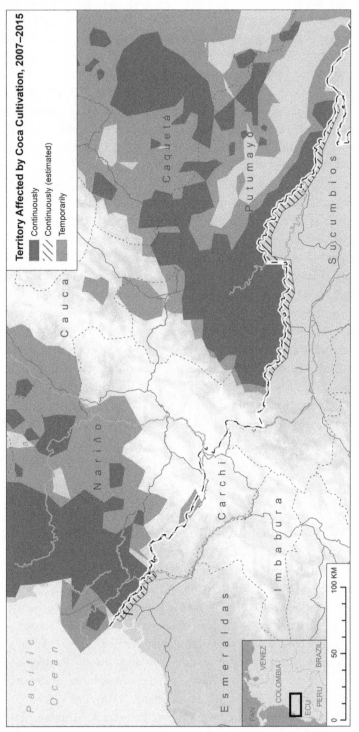

Map 7.2 Persistence of coca cultivation along the Colombia-Ecuador border, 2007–2015. Source: Data based on United Nations Office on Drugs and Crime and Government of Colombia. "Colombia. Monitoreo de Cultivos de Coca 2016," Bogotá: United Nations Office on Drugs and Crime, Government of Colombia, 2016. Credit: Map created by Author.

Each time illegal products cross the border their value increases, and thus many actors engage in drug deals across the border, especially at the starting points of trafficking routes.[106] According to 2015 figures from the Colombian National Police, the price of cocaine at Colombian ports is more than three times higher than in Colombia's interior: a kilogram of cocaine costs 2,200 USD in the interior as opposed to 5,500 USD to 7,000 USD at ports.[107] Drawing on SIMCI data and the UN World Drug Reports, the UNODC provides similar figures. Accordingly, one kilogram of cocaine hydrochloride (80 percent purity) costs 2,521 USD in the Colombian production zone, around 2,800 USD at Colombian ports, between 10,000 USD and 15,000 USD in Central America, 17,000 USD in Mexico, and between 20,000 USD and 25,000 USD in the United States. On Asian or Australian markets, it can reach more than 150,000 USD.[108] This enormous profit margin stands in stark contrast to the lack of legal economic opportunities in these regions. Unemployed youth are therefore often available as cheap recruits, and local gangs are available as "junior business partners."[109] The attractiveness of starting points of international trafficking routes for multiple violent non-state groups to engage in ad hoc cooperation, together with the easy availability of new recruits, reduces constraints to cheat on business partners; they are easily replaced. Group members are prepared to take risks and switch allegiances to enhance profits. This contributes to the fragility and volatility of short-term arrangements, especially tactical alliances, in these locations. Uncertainty about the commitment of groups to the arrangement reaffirms skepticisms between them, leading to a mutually reinforcing spiral of distrust and breakdown of arrangements.[110]

Tracing the arrangements between the Rastrojos and other groups in the Colombian harbor town of Tumaco, a case I discuss in chapter 5, illustrates the mechanisms of this border effect. A government official from Pasto explained to me:

> From 2006, the Rastrojos had been controlling the Tumaco-Junín-Barbacoas axis and Ricaurte. The Águilas Negras controlled some rural parts and the city of Tumaco. What did the Rastrojos decide in 2009? To penetrate the urban center of Tumaco! The Águilas Negras resisted and therefore, in 2009, there were massacres on the road because the Rastrojos took the Águilas Negras' men to the road to assassinate them. In 2010, the Rastrojos won the fight and entered the city of Tumaco, but the Águilas Negras were still there. [There were] a number of drug trafficking groups, all armed, and they submitted to the Rastrojos. Yet some of them whom [the Rastrojos] did not manage to defeat stayed in Tumaco, so they made an agreement: "Okay, you can be in Tumaco, take some sectors and we will have the others!" This is what happens nowadays [. . .]. A situation of direct, armed confrontation is

not sustainable for a long time [. . .]. They use messengers and have agreements of mutual territorial respect. Armed confrontation only occurs if these agreements are violated because armed people protect the territories.[111]

As of 2012, the Rastrojos controlled cocaine transport from other parts of Nariño to Tumaco, the starting point of the trafficking route to the United States. They achieved nearly hegemonic control over the route, including in areas such as Leiva, Policarpa, and Cumbitara, after defeating the Nueva Generación. While the Rastrojos were a consolidated group with a well-organized, unified command structure and high military capabilities, the Águilas Negras, who operated in Tumaco (in addition to FARC militias), functioned as small groups of drug traffickers with a cellular structure. According to an interviewee from Pasto, they consisted of a loose coalition of autonomous local organized criminal groups, but were financially accountable to the Águilas Negras' leadership. Other analysts claim that there was no single leadership and that the term "Águilas Negras" referred to various local groups. Both interpretations explain why, when the Rastrojos tried to take over power in Tumaco in 2009, they faced many small groups rather than a unified one. Some of these groups fought against the Rastrojos, but others forged tactical alliances with their junior partners to ship cocaine abroad.

The border geography attracted many different powerful armed actors from other regions; multiple junior partners were available as well. These arrangements were compromised by defection and retaliation from all sides, contributing to the frequent breakdowns of alliances (see section 5.2). Even though less militarily powerful than the Rastrojos, as locally embedded groups, the Águilas Negras possessed more local knowledge about Tumaco. They also benefited from access to information about state interdiction operations that was less accessible to the external traffickers.[112] Akin to the "prisoner's dilemma,"[113] these comparative advantages should have been conducive to cooperative arrangements of convenience. If the powerful group defects, they lose profits. If the junior partners defect, they lose profits and fear retaliation from the powerful group. However, the Rastrojos did not rely on one particular group to repeat the deal. In other contexts, defection can be averted by the shadow of the future, to use Robert Axelrod and Robert O. Keohane's words in their discussion of cooperation among states.[114] In borderlands at the starting points of international trafficking routes, each deal is a one-shot rather than an iterated game, due to the large supply of groups willing to make a deal. Consider the situation in which one group was engaged in an alliance with one Águilas Negras (sub-)group. Another group offered better intelligence or a more useful place to stock cocaine than the Águilas Negras (sub-)group to the group. The group therefore switched business partners. Typically, the junior partner should have an interest both in maintaining the alliance in the future and in avoiding retaliation. But in Tumaco, other powerful groups such as the Urabeños and, later, FARC militias emerged, and threatened to take the Rastrojos' place by inciting the Águilas Negras to break the alliance with the Rastrojos and forge one with them instead. Prospects for protection provided by a newly arriving group such as the Urabeños reduced fear of retaliation. Similarly, strategies to "lengthen the shadow of the future" that make cooperation more likely were barely available in this borderland scenario.[115]

Tactics of decomposition over time help reduce distrust in spot sales or barter agreements.[116] This could look like exchanging the first portion of drugs for weapons at one time and the second portion later, for example. However, in tactical alliances, both groups have to employ their capabilities simultaneously (for example, military capabilities to avoid interference by other groups and local knowledge to avoid interference by state forces) to ensure a successful deal. Likewise, strategies of issue linkages are difficult in contexts of quick turnover of alliances due to ongoing newly emerging actors.[117] Two groups allying to increase profits (due to shared economic interests) and to fight state forces can be regarded as issue linkage: if one group breaks the economic alliance, the other one will stop collaborating against the state forces. Yet as this would constitute a negative payoff for both rather than one of them, such issue linkage does not necessarily deter defection.

The large number of groups attracted by high profits also reduces their constraints to use violence against each other.[118] Following the logics of criminal cooperation, one would expect violent non-state groups involved in illicit business deals to try to reduce costly violence. We know from Gambetta, for example, that criminals use signals to communicate because "the tough guy will scare people who deal with him but may also scare them off."[119] The groups rely on each other for their business deals and to assert themselves against other parties. Yet contrary to contexts in which a limited number of people are considered suitable to become business partners, the high supply of groups and recruits make it easy to find another business partner: if the first one shies away due to the groups' cruel reputation.

The border effect takes shape via boosting profits from illicit cross-border activities. Through the large number of groups attracted by this, their relationships become even more volatile. As a consequence, it is particularly difficult for local community members to know who is on whose side and for how long. This influences citizen security dynamics by reducing respectful behavior and civility among community members even further.

7.4 The Border as Disguise

The border effect's fourth mechanism—the border as disguise—derives from the distance of borderlands to the state's power centers. It results from state-centric views. As I discuss in chapter 3, according to these views, borders are seen not just as geographical margins, but coincide with the imagined margins of the state, and of statehood. Paradoxically, state centrism is so deeply rooted that it is replicated in the very periphery. Borderlanders themselves internalize state-centric views and normalize their marginalized existence. Marginalized spaces exist across state territories. Yet it is this unique congruence of geographical and social marginalization that reinforces stigma and disguises the violent non-state groups' role in contributing to insecurity, as the latter is attributed to general unruliness. I view this situation as an intensified version of the disconnect between power centers and those at the margins more generally.

Let me go back to the state-centric view on borders, which I introduced before I mapped the multiple forms of non-state order across the shared borders of Colombia, Ecuador, and Venezuela (see chapter 3) and demonstrated how they influence citizen security in distinct ways (see chapters 4 to 6). Such state-centric views ignore, misunderstand, and indeed distort the security dynamics that I unpacked, using the bottom-up perspective and a borderland lens. Perspectives both from the centers and from the borderlands contribute to the stigmatization of these spaces as generally violent. They generalize unruliness, which contributes to the trivialization of violence among community members. This conceals the distinct security dynamics linked to the presence of violent non-state groups, particularly less violent ones (such as social control) that foster shadow citizenship. The generalization reinforces stigmatization of borderlanders, which disguises illicit authority. Finally, the border effect deepens the disconnect between communities and the state. Shadow citizenship in isolated borderlands contributes to nationwide "fragmented citizenship," since different forms of citizenship exist at the national level (see Table 7.1).[120]

Generalizing Unruliness

"From the perspective of the state, both frontiers and borderlands are unruly spaces," note Korf and Raeymaekers.[121] Due to their distance from the state centers and state governance, borderlands are considered dangerous and disconnected spaces.[122] Ignorant about the micro dynamics of borderlands, the center imagines a constant threat to be emanating from the margins. Homicide and displacement rates dominate the databases of governments, international organizations, and human rights organizations, as well as the writings of academics and security analysts. Of course, these are valid security concerns across Colombia's borders, but they are not the only ones, and they do not take shape in the same way across the region. Perceived security and repercussions concerning community's social fabric as well as the state-society relationship play a role too. Even victimization surveys do not reflect perceptions of security. They are conducted without understanding people's fear in answering them, arising, for example, due to threats by the armed actors (see section 3.1). Such surveys therefore not only present a distorted image of (physical) victimization, they also miss a crucial issue that shapes people's every life security: social control. Given the image of generalized violence in the border areas by those in the state centers, staying away from the periphery is a logical consequence, yet also one that reinforces this view even further. In 2007 in Ipiales, for example, government researchers commissioned to report on the population's security situation surveyed only 50 percent of the population to ensure their (the researchers') own security.[123] The reluctance of "outsiders" to engage with these communities contributes to the ignorance of local security dynamics and the dissonance between these communities and the state.

The disengagement does not stop with powerful elites. Citizens in the heartlands do not feel connected with those in the peripheries due to a lack of interest or information on the regions, which are perceived as "other spaces" that do not fit the images they have of their country. In Bogotá, most people know the war in the borderlands only from television, and call it "a different Colombia." Some have even denied the existence of a war—which has had perhaps its most severe consequences in the periphery.[124] In non-conflict countries, the threat of spreading violence and conflict contagion is considered to "radiate" from the borderlands into the heartlands, contributing to the stigmatization of borderlands.[125] In the case of Ecuador and Venezuela, guerrillas, paramilitaries, and criminal groups are seen as exporting violence from Colombia (see section 4.1). In Quito, the northern border zone is dismissed as a dangerous place, infected by "the Colombian problem";[126] in Caracas, the border with Colombia is considered the "Wild West," as distant as any Hollywood movie people watch in their living rooms.[127]

Paradoxically, borderlanders themselves reinforce the stigma of borderlands as violent spaces. They generalize these violent dynamics to other borderlands across the world. Rather than taking action to address the presence of violent non-state groups in their territory or demand state involvement to enhance citizen security, they assume insecurity in their territory is due to geography—to being located in borderlands rather than in heartlands. This makes violence in border spaces appear inevitable. Borrowing Girard's surrogate victim theory again (see chapter 4), the "borderlands" space itself becomes the scapegoat for any violence inflicted on borderlanders.[128] In Maicao, a humanitarian organization employee stated:

> Arms smuggling, drug trafficking, contraband, deaths, kidnapping— people get scared when talking about the border dynamics of La Guajira, but these things happen at almost all borders of the world. The Mexican[-US] border, for example, is the most heavily guarded one, I don't know with how many soldiers and cameras and still, they smuggle arms from the United States [to Mexico]. It is the same with Colombia.[129]

Similar points were raised in Venezuela, for instance by the head of a humanitarian organization:

> You have to realize that all border towns are tense. There is no single border town that isn't tense because the border in itself implies contraband, trafficking of persons, from the very beginning it bears certain risks. Here, one has to add drugs, which is very serious.[130]

Attributing violence to general insecurity in borderlands rather than to violent non-state groups further contributes to the stigmatization of borderlands as violent spaces. As the following example illustrates, borderlanders actively concealed the origin of insecurity in the presence of armed groups to protect themselves. In March 2012, flyers stating that "Ecuador is for Ecuadorians, not the criminals of the FARC" were distributed in General Farfán (see Figure 7.3). The employee of a local human rights organization I interviewed immediately

Figure 7.3 Pamphlet against the "Criminals of the FARC," 2012. Source: Anonymous interviewee.

rejected the statement to avoid taking sides against the FARC, which could have provoked retaliation against the population. The employee emphasized the organization's opposition to any type of violence and its appeal to the government to protect the borderlanders.[131] This rejection could be interpreted as supporting the FARC, increasing suspicion among right-wing groups about locals. It demonstrates the borderlanders' dilemma: if they raise their voice against a specific armed group, they fear retaliation. If they demand protection without specifying the source of insecurity, they receive less attention because insecurity originating in the settling of scores or disputes among neighbors are considered inherent to borderlands.

Borderlanders reinforce the image of geographical margins characterized by generalized unruliness. They contribute to it by trivializing violence. When asking an indigenous leader in Mocoa in 2012 about the security situation in La Hormiga, a small village in Bajo Putumayo, she replied: "Things are fine, nothing happened. There was only one combat this week."[132] On the other side of the border, in General Farfán, a civil society leader commented with sarcasm on the combat explosions that he saw over on the Colombian side: "It's so nice when they celebrate these kind of parties with fireworks ... or they have a birthday over there and celebrate it!"[133] Such sarcastic humor can be seen as a way of coping with these events. "Atrocity [is] a poor way to explain yourself; and humor [is] a good way to survive," notes David Keen.[134] Yet this behavior also trivializes, turning insecurity in borderlands into part of everyday life. It reaffirms the narrative that borderlands are inherently dangerous. Such trivialization exists in non-borderlands as well. However, the borderlands' distance to the state centers makes trivialization particularly plausible, perpetuating the stigmatization of borderlands.

The disproportionately strong focus on the unruliness of borderlands viewed from the states' centers means that the distinct forms of non-state order and resulting security facets are neglected. Violence in unruly frontier zones is seen as a threat to the states' legitimate monopoly on the use of force. State centers do pay attention to it—however, not to understand, but to suppress it. State forces come in to "pacify" such unruly regions. With the state as reference point, emphasis in the public imagination of such situations lies on security dynamics between state and non-state actors while non-state dynamics that the state cannot see remain obscure (see section 2.1). When state forces are affected by violence in the periphery, it attracts attention from the heartlands. The media and the government spread narratives of a powerful state through taking pride in the killing of guerrillas by state forces and/or mourning the deaths of soldiers and police. In 2012 in Nariño, twelve policemen died; in Putumayo only seven. Homicide rates that also include the killings of ordinary community members were 80 percent higher in Putumayo than in Nariño.[135] Bombardments, patrolling of armed groups, mined zones, and several guerrilla-imposed "armed strikes" also characterized community life in Putumayo.[136] Despite this, the media reported more widely on violent clashes in Nariño that involved state forces.[137] To cite another example, in October and November 2009, post-demobilized groups ordered all shop owners of Venezuelan San Antonio de Táchira, opposite border twin town Cúcuta, to close their shops for several days. Despite threats against the population, the authorities did not react. When these groups killed two Venezuelan National Guard members (belonging to the armed forces), the international border bridge Simón Bolívar was shut,[138] attracting international media coverage.[139]

The various forms of non-state order receive less attention, especially in regions where stable long-term arrangements among violent non-state groups prevail. Such relatively nonviolent regions do not fit the category of unruly spaces. When violent non-state groups fight each other and community members are caught in the crossfire or have to flee, those outside the communities typically remain unaware, especially if violence does not occur on a large scale. So-called drop-by-drop displacements (as opposed to mass displacements) receive even less attention from authorities and humanitarian organizations. They are often the product of short-term arrangements, or of confinements in regions where armed actors engage in stable long-term arrangements. Situations in which the security of borderlanders is undermined on a more structural level, for example, when their social fabric is eroded or when they suffer social control under an illicit authority, remain invisible to the centers. As a result, state centers typically ignore the fact that a substantial part of their citizenry in borderlands lives under another authority.

The disregard by the center of the various forms of non-state order tends to come in the form of "neglect by design" in the way security dynamics are measured and analyzed from a state-centric viewpoint. Consider the previously cited citizen security survey of the Venezuelan National Statistics Institute.[140] It distinguished between border and non-border residents, and hence between those affected by the dynamics of the Colombian armed conflict in the Venezuelan border zone and Venezuelan security dynamics more widely. However, its state-centric survey design focused on tangible, visible elements of security that reflect general unruliness, but not the distinct security dynamics that exist in the border area, next to a country in armed conflict. The respondents, divided into those residing in the border states and those in all other states, were asked whether common criminals, guerrillas/paramilitaries, organized criminal groups, the police, the National Guard, or the police, together with common criminals, committed most crimes, including violent ones like murder.[141] Of these, 5 percent of borderland respondents and 1 percent of respondents of non-border municipalities cited guerrillas/paramilitaries as the most dangerous.[142]

This result is revealing on several levels. First, the difference is only 4 percent, even though the guerrillas and paramilitaries have strong presence in the border municipalities and low presence in the rest of Venezuela.[143] This suggests that respondents were reluctant to name guerrillas and paramilitaries due to fear of retaliation, or that they do not think of these groups' activities as "committing crimes." This would be the case, for example, when they exert little violence, but strong social control, as in Apure and Machiques.

The responses to another question that asks respondents who they think is the main group that commits crime, support this interpretation: 3.1 percent cited paramilitaries from Colombia, 9.2 percent paramilitaries from Venezuela, 6.83 percent the FARC, 0.88 percent the ELN, and 0.67 percent the Bolivarian Forces of Liberation (Fuerzas Bolivarianas de Liberación—FBL).[144] This is consistent with the fact that, while paramilitaries (post-demobilized groups were also called criminal groups) operated in short-term arrangements that generated violence, the FARC, the ELN, and the FBL engaged in long-term arrangements in Apure, and the FARC and the ELN in Zulia. In these situations, social control prevailed over violence.

Graphic representations of security also reflect the partial, if not distorted, view from the centers. According to an international organization's 2010 map of displacements in Nariño on the Pacific coast (in eight municipalities), eighteen displacements comprising 991 families took place.[145] The map of displacements (Map 7.3) suggests that things were calm in the municipalities that border Carchi. However, this is where the FARC's mobile column Daniel Aldana regularly crossed over to Ecuador to acquire supplies and effectively exerted cross-border control. As the map of confinements illustrates (Map 7.4), in 2011, communities were confined in Alto Mira (Tumaco), Barbacoas (Barbacoas), Nulpes (Ricaurte), Mayasquer and Miraflores (Cumbal), and La Victoria and Jardines de Sucumbíos (Ipiales), as well as in five other municipalities.[146] In several of these zones, humanitarian access to the communities was restricted, yet such situations remain hidden with the focus on unruliness.[147]

Reinforcing Stigmatization

The distorted picture and resulting stigma of borderlands is reinforced from within these spaces. As a result of the restrictions imposed by armed actors, the borderlanders themselves limit the outflow of information that may reveal the security dynamics on the ground to outsiders. Violent non-state groups control the communities' discourse and influence the outside world's perception of the same community, allowing them to maintain their authority without intervention from any third parties, such as the central government or humanitarian agencies. For example, in rural parts of the Ipiales municipality bordering

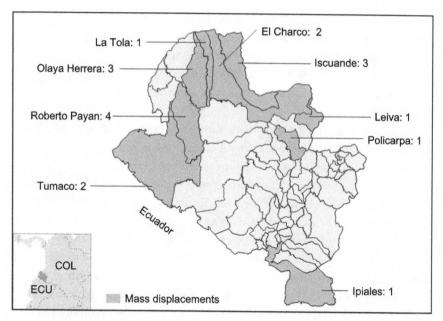

Map 7.3 Displacements in Nariño (Colombia) in 2010. Source: Based on data made available by the United Nations High Commissioner for Refugees, Colombia, 2011. Credit: Map created by Author.

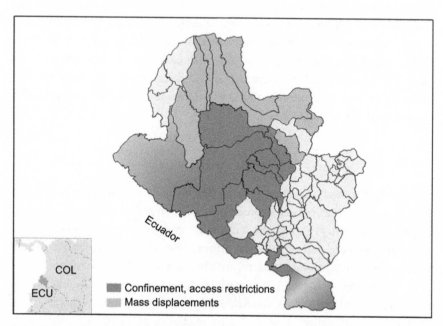

Map 7.4 Confinement in Nariño (Colombia) in 2010 and 2011. Source: Based on data made available by the United Nations High Commissioner for Refugees, Colombia, 2011. Credit: Map created by Author.

Ecuador in 2012, the FARC used to conduct obligatory regular meetings with all community members and told them not to mention human rights violations when talking to international agencies; otherwise they would be punished. Similarly, the guerrillas told community leaders only to let "outsiders" enter the territory, if they did not address human rights, and otherwise to completely deny them access.[148]

When I accompanied a diplomatic mission in Bajo Putumayo in 2012, we were going to visit the village of Puerto Colón. One day before the visit, the local contact person did not answer his phone or reply to text messages. Without further explanation, the morning of the planned visit we received a call advising us that no one would have time to meet us. According to the diplomatic mission's staff, this was the FARC's way of refusing us access. Similar to the regions in Nariño, a resident of Puerto Caicedo explained in 2012 that most villages from San Miguel to La Cabaña—all located along the borderline, close to the formal border bridge—were confined.[149] Neither the Ombudsman's Office nor the United Nations (UN) High Commissioner for Refugees was allowed to enter these villages. With these institutions unable to access the communities, little information on the security situation of the local communities was available. In the non-conflict border zones, such citizen security dynamics were even less visible because they are typically a phenomenon of situations of armed conflicts. Many communities in Ecuador's and Venezuela's border zones were confined as well; however, the resources to respond to such crises were limited. Defined as a war crime under international humanitarian law, unlawful confinement "formally" only takes place in war situations (like Colombia).[150] Humanitarian organizations such as the UN Office for the Coordination of Humanitarian Affairs were not present in Venezuela and Ecuador, although their border zones also experienced humanitarian crises.

Deepening the Disconnect

Ultimately, the marginalization of borderlands accelerates the divides between periphery and center, between borderlanders and their government, leading to a fragmented citizenry in which the sense of belonging to a transnational community supersedes one that would emerge from a mutually reinforcing state-society relationship. It makes borderlanders "invisible," as the San Lorenzo resident, cited at the beginning of chapter 3, lamented. Hastings Donnan and Thomas Wilson and Michel Baud and Willem van Schendel point to relationships characterized by the transnationality of borderlands: relationships of borderlanders with borderlanders from the other border zones, with heartlanders, the state, and borderland elites.[151] Indeed, borderland communities comprise, or are influenced by, people from both sides of the border, rather than only those from the same state. While enriching the borderlanders' identities, this can also undermine the sense of solidarity of heartlanders with borderlanders. It can engender fluid identities. This is particularly true if people find themselves at the disadvantaged end of asymmetries across the border.

Oscar Martínez highlights that, within borderlands, some people are more influenced by the border than others.[152] Those whose livelihoods depend on the border because they are engaged in cross-border trade or work as customs officials, and those whose family lives on both sides, have a stronger border experience. They differ more from heartlanders than from others who are little engaged in cross-border activities.

In the context of asymmetries across the border, the entire community has such a strong border experience. This creates an even starker schism between heartlanders and those at the margin. In Bogotá, the asymmetry of institutional presence, communication, and road infrastructure in favor of the Ecuadorian, rather than the Colombian, side of the border is typically ignored.[153] And yet, this is a crucial condition that has contributed to the protracted nature of the Colombian armed conflict (see section 3.2). Exposure to the discrepancies in how neighboring states treat their citizens versus how Bogotá treats them has various repercussions. First of all, the way that Colombians strive to benefit from neighboring, more advanced, development policies promotes a sense of belonging to a cross-border community rather than to the national citizenry (for example, when Colombians access healthcare in Ecuador and send their children to schools in the Ecuadorian border zone).[154] It also fuels resentments among peripheral communities against the Colombian state that is perceived to neglect them while the neighboring, especially Ecuadorian, state delivers. Many Colombians told me that Colombian villages are in the dark, whereas Ecuadorian villages are "on the bright side"—illuminated by electric street lamps. This in turn provides armed actors present in the community with a credible discourse about a more valuable alternative, which consolidates their illicit cross-border authority and shadow citizenship. Through the existence, yet the state's neglect, of these cross-border shadow communities, the state "loses" part of its citizenry, thwarting the formation of a nation that includes all citizens up to the borderline. It questions the state's role as the legitimate governance provider across its territory. Unless the state engages in bilateral cooperation with its neighbor to jointly provide governance functions, including transnational security and justice, cross-border communities voluntarily or involuntarily adopt shadow citizenship provided by violent non-state groups or any other non-state citizenship.

7.5 Conclusion

The border effect reinforces citizen insecurity. It cuts across all forms of non-state order, the various interactions among violent non-state groups. In all types of group interactions that inflict violence on civilians, most notably where armed actors are involved in combat or armed disputes, the border works as a facilitator for violent non-state groups because it renders victimization invisible. This is an incentive for the groups to resort to violence, as they are less likely to be punished for it. The border facilitates the promotion of an illicit economy, which helps foster a consensual relationship between the violent non-state group and the local community. This is particularly relevant in supply chain relationships in which illicit economic opportunities help offset shortcomings in other governance areas. It also obscures social control in the context of long-term arrangements, facilitating illicit cross-border authority that is conducive to shadow citizen security. Especially in situations in which people live on one side of the border while working along the cocaine supply chain on the other side, the transnationality contributes to the groups' perceived legitimacy as job providers because it helps people stay safe, despite their direct engagement with the armed actors. In cross-border spot sales and barter agreements as well as subcontractual relationships, the border effect deters the groups from reducing distrust between each other and vis-à-vis the local population, fueling interpersonal mistrust. The border further functions as a magnet for violent non-state actors, attracting a large number of groups, promoting rivalry among them, and with that, the fragility of tactical alliances and other short-lived arrangements. This increases uncertainty among the local population as to how to ensure security. Finally, the border disguises the distinct ways in which violent non-state groups fuel insecurity in these spaces, due to the general stigma of borderlands as unruly spaces from without and from within. This permits these groups to promote shadow citizenship while alienating borderlanders from the states (see Table 7.1 for an overview of these dynamics).

In brief, and referring back to the continuum of clusters of violent non-state group interactions (see section 2.1), interactions that form part of the "rivalry" cluster become less stable through the border effect. They move left and down on the continuum, toward the absence of an arrangement. Violent non-state group interactions included in the "friendship" cluster move in the opposite direction toward the upper-right corner of the continuum. The border effect is conducive to greater stability and durability of these arrangements.

Borderlanders and violent non-state groups know better than the state how to benefit from the geography of borderlands to influence the security dynamics described above. The state's legitimizing authority in borderlands is curbed by its absence. Violent non-state groups have the "skill to redirect state institutions, undermine state territoriality, and rescale states."[155] Benefiting from cross-border impunity, they can conceal their operations in borderlands from the state and others outside the community. This imperceptibility impinges on citizen security: it renders violent non-state groups less accountable for exercising violence, changing rules, and imposing social control.

Borderlanders have agency in shaping these borderland dynamics, too. Their local knowledge and utility as laborers allow them to influence the rules imposed by violent non-state groups to ensure their security. In short-term arrangements among violent non-state groups such rules are elusive. In the absence of arrangements, borderlanders have hardly any agency in changing rules, but can follow existing ones to increase security. In long-term arrangements, they can influence them, facilitating shadow citizen security. Although vulnerable to the unlawful actions of the armed actors, borderlanders affirm their independence from the state through their agency. By constantly transgressing the border between states, the legal and the illegal, and a national citizenry and a cross-border community, they contest state sovereignty and challenge the state-society relationship, calling into question the concept of citizen security and, as such, an unequal practice of democratic governance. Therefore, as Korf and Raeymaekers note, borderlands "are not just reflective of power relations at the 'center', but they are also *constitutive* of them."[156]

Global Borderlands

Security through a Kaleidoscope

Majayura, Colombia. In January 2016, almost four years after I witnessed the repercussions of the FARC's cross-border attack on the Venezuelan communities living close to the incident, as described in the opening of this book, I returned to the region. This time I visited the scene of the lethal incident on the Colombian side of the border. I sensed tension and mistrust. A community member murmured: "The guerrillas often sojourn in the village. It's hard to know who is who. You recognize people's faces, but you never know who they really are."[1] On this trip, unlike the previous one, people reported that violence was committed more widely on the Venezuelan side, where guerrillas openly transited with arms, and members of the Venezuelan military clashed with non-state groups involved in illicit activities. Another community member insisted: "[The presence of armed groups in Venezuela] has increased. Thieves only steal twice because the third time they don't appear alive anymore."[2]

San Cristóbal, Venezuela. Fourteen months later, in March 2017, I returned to another border region to visit the Venezuelan town of San Cristóbal. The words of a local resident resonated with what the humanitarian worker, quoted on the first page of this book, had said to me five years earlier on the Colombian side of that border area: that the groups in Táchira had no interest in an armed struggle against the government, but were prepared to resort to whatever means were necessary to defend their illicit cross-border deals.[3] Fearful mentions of the Rastrojos and the Urabeños were replaced by references to the Autodefensas Gaitanistas and the Clan del Golfo. It had become more common to hear Mexican accents, supposedly due to the expanded presence of the Zeta cartel. While labels and accents had changed, the ongoing fear of locals had not.

River Putumayo, Colombia. When I returned to the Colombia-Ecuador border in 2017, where in 2012 the guerrillas' illicit authority had reached across the border to Ecuadorian General Farfán, as also stated at the opening of the book, these dynamics were mirrored. At least formally, the FARC were no longer seen to be in *charge. Communities in Bajo Putumayo commented on other groups—or labels—to me, including the so-called Comuneros, supposedly active on the Ecuadorian side but exerting social control across the border in Colombian Putumayo. Used to the FARC's visible presence and known identity as the provider of shadow citizen security in their communities, now the Colombian farmers faced more uncertainty: "Previously, there was combat between [the guerrillas] and the armed forces, but at least there was security."*[4]

Like a kaleidoscope, constellations of violent non-state groups are continuously changing, but they repeat themselves over time. Groups substitute each other just as shards of one color replace pieces of another. Sooner or later, however, they fall into places that yield newly tinted, yet eminently recognizable, patterns of non-state order: the eight types of interactions, subsumed into three clusters, which I have unpacked in this book. These interactions among violent non-state groups produce distinct forms of insecurity. Paradoxically, in borderlands the insecurities resulting from these interactions are more intense, but also less discernible to outsiders.

As the three vignettes above show, I returned to the three borderland regions with which I opened the book several years later. In each case, I went to the opposite side of the border zone that I had visited on the first occasion to explore how the evolving political, social, and economic context shaped by factors including the Colombian peace process and Venezuela's political crisis may have influenced the "border effect." This effect includes the ways in which the transnationality and distance from state centers of borderlands intensify the logics of violent non-state group interactions and the respective insecurities that result from them (see chapter 7).

Increased Exposure to Violence. In the region comprising Colombian Majayura and Venezuelan Paraguaipoa in the northern part of the Colombia-Venezuela border, the border effect persisted over time. The armed actors adapted the border's safe haven function to the changes in the political context, particularly to the advanced peace negotiations between the FARC and the Colombian government, and the border closure imposed by Venezuelan president Nicolás Maduro. In 2012, communities on the Colombian side were exposed to violence resulting from the armed groups' high-profile attacks, while Venezuelans feared that paramilitary groups would retaliate against the guerrillas' actions or that either of the groups would resort to targeted killings to silence potential whistle-blowers on Venezuelan soil. They were also afraid that the Majayura attack would attract more attention by Colombian or Venezuelan authorities (see Figure 8.1). They feared that this would trigger increased presence of law enforcement officials and hence prevent community members from smuggling gasoline and contraband, their means to make a living.

In 2016, the context of the peace negotiations meant that the situation flipped around across the border, but the overall influence of violent non-state group interactions and the border effect on security remained similar. With a unilateral ceasefire announced and implemented by the FARC in 2015,[5] armed activities were largely reported by locals on the Venezuelan side, whereas in Colombia the FARC and the ELN demonstrated their presence through collecting "taxes" and social control. The ceasefire changed the group's attitude vis-à-vis the Colombian state; a low profile was now preferable. They avoided Bogotá's attention while benefiting from the Venezuelan officials' passivity (or complicity). Venezuela's deepening socioeconomic and political crisis, together with the state of turmoil in the region due to the border closure, made violence a convenient means to expand control and fight other groups on Venezuelan territory. This resulted in the FARC shifting a greater proportion of their operations to the Venezuelan side, which was useful for those combatants who wanted to circumvent a potential demobilization on the Colombian side.[6]

Under these circumstances, while Venezuelan communities had to understand what new rules they needed to adhere to in order to escape violence, Colombian communities received "protection" from the FARC and the National Liberation Army (Ejército de Liberación Nacional—ELN) in Baja Guajira as long as the community members paid "taxes" and kept quiet. Colombians were granted shadow citizen security, yet with an undercurrent of uncertainty due to the often unknown identity of the one who governed.

The border closure had the perverse effect of making illicit cross-border activities even more lucrative. Contrary to the porosity of the border a few years earlier, in 2016 the border was shut, officially. The only three formal border crossings along the more than 2,200 km long borderline were closed, which intensified scarcity of goods on the Venezuelan side of the border.[7] The increased presence of state officials, particularly of Venezuelan officials, made legal cross-border interactions difficult and led to numerous abuses of local community members.[8] Yet violent non-state groups continued to cross the border on informal trails. Thus, despite increased risks near the formal border crossings—if not because of them—illicit cross-border trade was thriving.[9]

The border closure further led to diplomatic tensions between Bogotá and Caracas. The two differed in their views on how to deal with the humanitarian crisis at the border.[10] The heightened diplomatic sensitivities and the decay of bilateral cross-border cooperation fueled impunity: violating the other country's national sovereignty to track down armed groups might have had disastrous consequences for law enforcement agents. Overall, the gap widened between the states' limitations through the borderline and the transnationality of the armed actors' operations and illicit flows. The border's filter mechanism, as discussed in chapter 7, was in full swing.

Figure 8.1 Bullet holes after the FARC's attack on the Colombian army, near Majayura, Colombia, 2016. Photo by Author.

Heightened Vulnerability amid Crime. At the border crossing between Colombian Cúcuta and Venezuelan San Antonio de Táchira and San Cristóbal— the only metropolitan border area that Colombia shares with a neighbor—the changed political contexts in Venezuela and Colombia in 2017 reinforced the border effect, compared to how I observed it during my previous trips to the region. My travels to Venezuelan Táchira took place just a few days before what was labeled an "auto-coup" in March 2017.[11] This was followed by further political action that hardened the authoritarian traits of Maduro's regime in subsequent months.[12] Hastings Donnan and Thomas Wilson's description of borderlines as "places of divergence and convergence" could not be more fitting to this new context.[13] By then, the border region had become a uniting space as it had been reopened for pedestrians after almost two years of closure. Yet this space also hosted a border that had become a dividing line of—at least on the surface— clashing realities with which only a few other borders can compare, for example the US-Mexico one. On one side of the border, Venezuela was trapped at that moment in a downward spiral that, in a worst-case scenario, could end in state collapse. On the other side, Colombia was trying to create a reputation as an up-and-coming regional leader, internationally promoting as an export good its success in signing peace.

The stark contrast bolstered the border effect in two ways. First, it catalyzed the economic differences across the border, turning the borderlands into even more profitable environments for transnational organized crime. Venezuela's hyperinflation, unemployment, and food shortages made it easier for violent groups to attract young recruits.[14] The crisis increased the lucrativeness of smuggling and other illicit cross-border activities, including the prostitution of Venezuelan women and girls in Colombian Cúcuta, other border towns, and indeed throughout the country.[15] Second, the positions of both governments contributed to cross-border impunity, facilitating the obfuscation of violent acts. On the one hand, perhaps trying not to disillusion people's hope for a peace dividend, the Colombian government seemed to downplay power struggles among the groups that aimed to take the FARC's place. This included the expansion of the Popular Liberation Army (Ejército Popular de Liberación— EPL) (then called "Pelusos" by the Colombian government) near and across the border with Venezuela through the distribution of pamphlets, recruitment, attacks, and acts of terror.[16] Even though strongly felt by communities on the ground, the continuation of large-scale violence was somewhat ignored beyond the local level. On the other hand, Venezuelan authorities were accused of covering up killings behind the smokescreen of general unrest.[17] While the ELN's presence in Venezuelan territory hardly received any media attention in the country, armed clashes between the Colombian right-wing Gaitanista group and Venezuelan state forces were reported in the news.[18] In earlier years, such open confrontations between non-state actors and state forces were normally made public when they occurred on Colombian soil, but not when they happened in Venezuela. Overall, this partial reporting masked the numerous violent groups that continued to forge short-term arrangements on both sides of the border in this strategic transit zone for cocaine, gasoline, and other products. People still had to navigate everyday uncertainty, fuelled by violent breakdowns of short-lived alliances. The changed situation heightened the vulnerability of borderlanders. Amid the blurring of criminal and political violence, locals reported that they faced more difficulties in speaking out in a context of general mistrust.[19]

Enhanced Illicit Governance. At the border between Ecuadorian Sucumbíos and Colombian Putumayo, historically a FARC stronghold, the border effect also continued to intensify insecurities. Just as in previous decades, the cross-border region's distance from the power centers manifested itself in the region's extreme marginalization, which alienated the local population from the central states.

The FARC's demobilization had led analysts to speculate over who would fill the power vacuum left behind by the guerrillas and what kind of non-state order would emerge in the absence of the rebels.[20] This is because the transnational border space continues to be a convenient site for anyone interested in exerting social control across the border to benefit, among other things, from the cocaine business.

Rather than suffering violent power struggles among armed actors trying to fill the power void, the region saw a subtle, but firm reaccommodation of groups—or group labels. The so-called Comuneros, for instance, reportedly operating in rural areas, were said to comprise ex-FARC members of Ecuadorian nationality who remained outside of the demobilization process.[21] In Putumayo's small towns, by 2017, a group labeled "Constru" had replaced the labels "Rastrojos" or "Águilas Negras" in the local newspapers' headlines about extortion, displacement, homicides, or social cleansings.[22] By March 2017, around 450 FARC members had gathered in the demobilization camp in "La Carmelita," near Puerto Asís.[23] However, numerous militias as well as combat FARC members of the three FARC Fronts that operated in the area continue to be present in the region outside the camp. Estimates by local analysts referred to 50 percent of the overall number of FARC members who used to operate in the region before the demobilization process began.[24]

Regarding the cocaine business, after the revised peace deal was signed in November 2016, there were a few months of disequilibrium in the cocaine supply chain, during which time farmers complained that they were not able to sell their coca leaves. The links in the chain had to be reconnected. Apart from this short period of recalibration, to all intents and purposes the cocaine supply chain remained intact.[25]

As throughout the armed conflict between the FARC and the government, communities waited with varying levels of patience for the arrival of civilian state institutions. Amid uncertainty over whether this would happen at all, communities who previously lived under shadow citizenship with the FARC started to organize themselves into conciliation committees and other structures to manage their everyday lives and resolve disputes themselves. In some cases, they did so under the guidance of the FARC. Others adhered to the rules of behavior imposed by new illicit actors in return for protection.[26]

One thing changed, however, in the Putumayo-Sucumbíos case: armed clashes between the FARC and state forces, or paramilitaries, that had inflicted suffering on the regions so many times in previous decades (see section 3.2) became a phenomenon of the past. A return from the "friendship" cluster of stable long-term arrangements among violent non-state groups to the "enmity" cluster, in which various violent non-state groups are prepared to engage in unlimited warfare against each other (see chapter 4), has become extremely unlikely. In the context of combat, civilians suffered violence but could follow a certain logic of appropriateness in their behavior. The guerrillas' demobilization reduced the possibility of people's exposure to large-scale violence, but it has also

concealed security dynamics in the region even further. From the perspective of
the state centers, the absence of such large-scale violence means there is no need
to bother about these border areas. Illicit cross-border authority is ignored, and
so is the loss of the state's perceived legitimacy in these regions. The demobilization also diminished the availability of rules of behavior that existed during
combat, or during the preponderance of one single powerful actor, the FARC.
Maybe this is why one farmer I met in Putumayo remarked, "we are worried that
this peace will become another battlefield."[27]

The passage of time became a litmus test for my findings, not just in these three
paradigmatic examples, but also in the other border areas to which I returned.
Once it became clearer that Colombia would see a historic change in its security
landscape due to the culmination of the peace talks, I decided to visit all border
departments again. I examined how the arrangements among violent non-state
groups and their security impacts had changed over the years. In January 2016,
when the peace talks were still ongoing, I returned to Arauca and La Guajira.
This was followed by travels to Nariño and Norte de Santander later in the year,
after the first peace accord had been rejected in the plebiscite, producing a limbo
situation between war and peace. Finally, in early 2017, after the FARC's demobilization process had begun, I returned to Putumayo, Cesar, and again to
La Guajira. I also conducted targeted trips to and conversed with my contacts
from the Venezuelan and Ecuadorian sides of the borders to follow up on the
changes in the neighboring countries. As I confirmed over the years through
my repeated field trips, similar patterns of arrangements among violent non-
state groups persisted across the borderlands shared by Colombia, Ecuador, and
Venezuela; and so did the repercussions on local communities. This was the case
throughout the evolving context from the height of the armed conflict, over the
peace negotiations, the unilateral and then bilateral ceasefire, the signing of the
peace deal, its rejection, the signing of the revised version, and during the first
months of the challenging task of implementing the peace accords. It mattered
little for people's perceived and observed security on the ground whether the
region was in war or peacetime, conflict or non-conflict territory. In the end, the
distinct security impacts continued to influence people's everyday lives.

8.1 Borderland Battles for Positive Change

Throughout the evolving contexts, the borderland lens to the security dynamics
in the Andean peripheries provided clear insights into factors influencing security that are bundled in these transnational spaces, albeit existing in a more
diluted fashion elsewhere. Coupling the borderland lens with a bottom-up approach added to the depth and richness of the findings. It demonstrated how

the varied interactions among violent non-state groups give rise to distinct forms of order and disorder, uncertainties, and insecurities. At the macro level, conceptualizing non-state order as three clusters of violent non-state group interactions brought to the fore the larger patterns and the differences between them: the "enmity" cluster, in which violent non-state groups do not have any arrangement with each other; the "rivalry" cluster, in which these groups forge fragile, short-lived arrangements; and the "friendship" cluster, which comprises relatively stable long-term arrangements among violent non-state groups. At the micro level, it helped untangle the complex interactions among these groups and identify the distinct impacts on the perceived and observed security of local communities. Conceptualizing the arrangements on a continuum highlighted their fluid nature (see Figure 2.1), the dynamism within, and the fuzziness at the margins of, each cluster.

The borderland lens—that considers borderlands as one transnational unit yet accounts for differences in each border zone (on each side of the border)— had practical implications: it required carrying out multi-sited fieldwork on *both* sides of the conflict-ridden borders of Colombia with Venezuela and Ecuador, respectively. I found cases of all interaction types in all four border zones and was able to analyze each of the three countries individually, and also jointly as a region.

This approach revealed the triple asymmetries in the security dynamics across the Andean border region, which I foreshadow in chapter 3. A view from the center highlights the asymmetry of the typically higher rates of violence in the margins compared to the more central parts of each country. A view from the margins through a transnational borderland lens gives insights into the other two asymmetries that are less well understood. The second asymmetry consists in higher levels of observed, or objective, insecurity on the Colombian side of the border than on the Ecuadorian or Venezuelan side (see Figure 3.1), even in the presence of the same violent non-state groups. This security gap arises in situations where differing state policies influence the way in which a single type of violent non-state group interaction affects citizen security on each side of the border—provided that the state is not just a nominal entity in whose territory the groups operate, but also has some tangible presence.[28] A case in point is the guerrillas' preponderance across some parts of the Colombia-Ecuador border where, on the Ecuadorian side, the guerrillas were more restrained in resorting to violence and instead reinforced social control as a means to maintain their preponderance (see sections 6.4 and 7.1). Maintaining such a lower profile is possible due to Ecuadorian government policies that formally reject, but do not aggressively fight, the insurgents. Different levels of state responsiveness and capacity further contribute to variation in security outcomes. Transnational borderlands magnify this variation because they provide a contrasting view on pronounced differences that lie geographically very close together—the differences arising from the fact that borderlands span two (or more) sovereign states.[29]

The transnational, locally grounded perspective from the peripheries also reveals a third asymmetry, an asymmetry in reverse: perceived, or subjective, security is sometimes higher on the Colombian side than on the non-Colombian side of the border. This demonstrates the importance of understanding local perceptions, informed by the respective historical and cultural contexts, including the normalization of violence. It further highlights the need to consider people's agency in deciding what constitutes a threat to their security (see section 2.2). Christian Lund notes that "what is legitimate varies between and within cultures and over time, and is continuously (re-)established through conflict and negotiation."[30] The historical, political, and cultural context of a community, including their prior experiences, informs their perception of what is normal, of legitimacy, and of security. It shapes the borderlanders' agency and responses to violent non-state group interactions, among others, their coping mechanisms, avoidance strategies, and disposition to resistance. This is most evident when the perception of security in two border zones that form part of the same borderlands differs, even if residents are affected by the same arrangement. In 2003, for example, homicide rates in Norte de Santander were 98.7 per 100,000 inhabitants, but only 31.3 in Zulia, where they subsequently rose (see Figure 3.1). Despite these numbers, given Norte de Santander's history of violence, locals in Norte de Santander's Catatumbo region adapted their lifestyle to the presence of violent non-state groups. In this region, people commented that things had been calm in the last two years; they went out during the weekends and life continued as usual.[31] This was even though, in 2010, homicide rates were still between one and two per month.[32] In Jesús María Semprún and Catatumbo municipalities in southern Zulia bordering this region, Colombian groups started to operate with a relatively high profile only in the mid-2000s. Less used to their operations than Colombian communities across the border, Venezuelans felt extremely insecure due to the groups' activities, although the observable security impacts were more pronounced in Colombia.[33]

Due to the long history of armed conflict in their country, Colombian borderlanders have been exposed to a narrative of violence and, in many cases, lived under the authority of violent non-state groups over various generations. In Ecuadorian and Venezuelan border regions, the explicit presence of such groups is a newer phenomenon, or a localized one that is not as widely reflected in the government discourse and wider debates as it is in Colombia.

The three asymmetries can shift over time. They can become stronger or even out, or they can evolve into the reverse constellation, influenced, for instance, by changes in state policies, local perceptions, and external shocks. For example, the militarization of Ecuador's northern border zone after Colombia's incursion into Ecuador in 2008 increased pressure on multiple violent non-state groups, complicating their operations in that region and increasing the local community's exposure to violence in certain parts of the border zone.

Understanding these evolving asymmetries is essential for grasping the striking peculiarity of security dynamics in borderlands, on which I focus in chapter 7. Regardless of variations in state policies, observed security, and perceived security, the border effect consistently intensifies the distinct forms of insecurity that arise in the context of the various interaction types while rendering the dynamics less visible. Paradoxically, it both transcends and is influenced by states. Just as the same relationships among violent non-state groups extend across the borderline, the border effect works on both national territories. Across all border zones, the nearby presence of the border in these vulnerable regions intensifies the logics built into the arrangements. And across the region, the borderlands serve as magnifying glasses for examining such dynamics because the transnationality of these spaces, as well as their distance from the economic and political centers, translates into the confluence of weak state governance, a low-risk/high-opportunity environment arising from the clash of two different economic systems, and the propensity for impunity.

These findings could be the beginning of a larger scholarly endeavor, one that views global security through a borderland lens. Referring to James Scott's work on how states had to make their people "legible" in order to have control over them, Andrew Hurrell notes that "it became, and has remained, extremely difficult to avoid seeing the world except through the eyes of the state."[34] Scott explains that

> the premodern state was, in many crucial respects, partially blind; it knew precious little about its subjects, their wealth, their landholdings and yields, their location, their very identity. It lacked anything like a detailed "map" of its terrain and its people. It lacked, for the most part, a measure, a metric, that would allow it to translate what it knew into a common standard necessary for a synoptic view. As a result, its interventions were often crude and self-defeating.[35]

In a similar vein today, states hardly know their hinterlands, their margins. It is in starting from the margins, by "sensing through" borderlands rather than "seeing like a state," that we may better understand the world as it really is.

This brings me back to the transformative goal I stated at the beginning of this book: to bring the margins and the marginalized to the center of power holders' attention and thereby transcend the dominant frameworks that shape current thinking on security issues. After all, this book would be incomplete if it only told a story about violence, crime, and governance at the edges of Colombia's war. It must also support the borderland battles for more secure lives—not the ones fought with blood and bullets, but those advanced with words, thoughts, and community action. In this last section, I therefore discuss how the findings of this book depict ways to design policies that support such battles for positive change. I also outline a research programme consisting of three avenues for further research that emerge from applying a borderland lens to security dynamics more broadly. They concern transnational borderlands (space), the changing security landscape (time), and the balance in relations among people, violent non-state groups, and the state (agency).

On Transnational Borderlands

To transcend conventional categories related to "space," I have focused on "the transnational" that challenges the dichotomy between conflict and non-conflict countries. A transnational approach demonstrates how policies overly determined by states as spatial units are ill-equipped to address security dynamics that know borders as malleable, porous, and subjective, rather than as fixed, impervious limits. Such ideas of fixed limits of states need to be transformed if governments are to tackle the transnational security threats that arise from violent non-state groups. This is not to say that state policies do not matter. After all, the asymmetries recapped above are manifestations of their relevance. Rather, incorporating three different states in this study has demonstrated that the transnational realities of borderlanders—and of violent non-state groups in borderlands—are out of sync with the wider national approaches and identities of all three states.

In the shared border areas of Colombia, Ecuador, and Venezuela, the same larger theme is the undercurrent to the various nuanced security dynamics influenced by specific state policies, group interactions, and other factors: state neglect. Bogotá, Caracas, and Quito have had different relationships with their respective citizenry (see sections 2.3 and 3.1). Many Latin American countries, including Ecuador, have undergone a change from oppressive military dictatorships to democracies toward the end of the last century, entailing a shift of emphasis from public order to citizen security. Meanwhile, Venezuela has been moving toward a more authoritarian regime in recent years. The government's openly oppressive measures did not impede, but rather fueled, violent resistance. And finally, the case of Colombia constitutes a particularly noteworthy outlier in the political landscape of Latin America. On the one hand, it is singled out as the country with the longest-standing democracy in the region. On the other hand, Colombia has faced a more than five-decade-long armed conflict in which repressive measures against its own population—sometimes overt, sometimes covert—took shape in links between paramilitaries and state agents as well as in scandals such as the "false positives" (see section 1.1).

Despite these diverging political trajectories, across the three countries state neglect at the margins meant that a large proportion of the borderlanders resorted to pragmatism to ensure survival rather than fighting for democratic values. For those who have never lived a life in which the state fulfills its governance functions, the option of shadow citizenship, a mutually reinforcing relationship between a violent non-state group and communities, rather than a "social contract" between the state and society, becomes the least disadvantageous one. This is especially the case in the presence of multiple armed groups in which guarantees of self-protection are hardly feasible.

Placing the analysis of citizen security at the intersection of several states by focusing on the shared transnational borderlands of Colombia, Ecuador, and Venezuela thus provides insights not only into *the* state and its relation to citizens. It also elucidates the differences between the relations that various states have with their respective citizenry—and the *absence* of such differences from a borderland point of view. Certainly, there are important nuances that shape people's perceptions of security and their responses across the border in distinct ways, as discussed earlier. People living on the Colombian side of the border generally reported stronger state neglect and abandonment than did their Ecuadorian and Venezuelan counterparts. This feeling of abandonment can be a reason for these Colombians to be less critical toward violent non-state groups that aim to foster a sense of belonging to a shadow community than in the neighboring countries. Overall, however, everyday life on the margins is shaped by *transnational* dynamics including influences from across the border that range from listening to the same radio channels, sending children to the same schools, or visiting the same food markets—that is, by rather than by *national* markers of identity. The sense of belonging to a transnational borderland community is therefore often stronger than to a national polity.

Viewing borderlands as dynamic spaces rather than lines is a precondition for recognizing that violent non-state groups operate across these spaces. National boundaries are social constructs that help states make dynamics on the ground "legible": they provide limits on how to think, plan, and act on behalf of a population. Yet it is by transcending these boundaries that we may be able to detect misinterpretations and tackle threats against these very populations that are otherwise ignored. Bogotá, Caracas, and Quito need to prioritize social development in their borderlands, not only national sovereignty delineated by borderlines. Colombia's security policies during the 2000s pushed the conflict toward the country's margins, contributing to making the Andean borderlands hot spots of diverse interactions among violent non-state groups. The impact that this shift has had on the security of local communities extends across the borders and therefore necessitates bilateral or regional responses, made in co-operation with Ecuador and Venezuela. Colombian conflict actors have inflicted suffering on communities in Ecuador's and Venezuela's border zones, and soci-oeconomic dynamics in these spaces have fueled conflict in Colombia. In the aftermath of Colombia's peace deal with the FARC, violent entrepreneurs con-tinue to fuel instability across the border.

The First Avenue for Further Research

The relevance of transnationality in the Andean case opens up an important avenue for research: studying security and violent non-state groups in other transnational border areas where the state is weak and illegality thriving. This includes exploring how the nature of the border itself shapes the border effect. Do colonially drawn borders intensify insecurities in a similar or stronger way than borders constructed differently? It also involves comparing the border effect across contexts: the confluence of weak state governance, a low-risk/high-opportunity environment, and the propensity for impunity may have distinct impacts, depending on the type of organized crime, or the role that religion, ethnicity, and ideology play in the interactions among violent non-state groups and in their treatment of local communities. How does the type of organized crime matter, when comparing the involvement of rebels in the cocaine industry in Colombia with the involvement of militias in human smuggling in Libya, or of terrorist groups in antiquities trafficking in Syria? What difference does it make at which stage of the supply chain the relationships emerge? While in Myanmar the interactions among violent non-state groups are part of the pro-duction stage of illicit drugs, at the Kenya-Somalia border they are embedded in an emerging transit region. These differences may well yield distinct results in the nuances of the security outcomes. Only a quick glance at borderland dy-namics across continents, however, reveals surprisingly familiar patterns with Colombia's borderlands in the Americas. Take the Great Lakes region in Africa and the Afghan-Pakistani border area in Asia. Both are regions in which, like in the Andean region, armed conflict and organized crime converge and have attracted multiple different violent non-state groups.

Africa's Great Lakes Border Region

Despite very different historical, cultural, and geographical contexts, overlaying a transnational borderland lens on Africa's Great Lakes region depicts security elements that have much in common with the Andean case discussed in this book. Since the early 1990s, armed conflict has plagued the eastern parts of the Democratic Republic of the Congo (DRC), which has led to the deaths of perhaps up to 5.4 million people.[36] While in the Andean context, political and economic motivations are the main determinants in group formation, in Africa's Great Lakes region, ethnicity is an additional factor that influences the complex panorama of violent non-state groups. In 2015, at least seventy different violent non-state groups reportedly operated in eastern Congo. Membership in these groups is largely in line with their participants' ethnic identity.[37]

Despite these differences, as Lindsay Scorgie-Porter and I have shown in a brief, exploratory comparative study on the Colombia-Ecuador and the DRC-Uganda borders, a borderland perspective highlights significant commonalities in the two regions' sociopolitical and economic dynamics that influence the respective security situations.[38] Among other factors, the country's natural resources have fueled the Congolese wars: mining and the illicit trade of minerals constitute lucrative income sources for the numerous Congolese and foreign violent non-state groups involved, somewhat similar to the cocaine business in the Andean region. As the 2011 report of the United Nations Office on Drugs and Crime (UNODC) notes, "the illicit trade in Congolese gold alone is worth an estimated 120 million USD, about ten times the value of the country's licit gold exports and about twice the value of coffee, its largest agricultural export."[39]

Other forms of transnational organized crime include smuggling of illicit timber, ivory, cannabis, coltan, tantalum, tin, and other minerals. Many of these trafficking flows cross the DRC-Uganda border. In both the Colombia-Ecuador and the DRC-Uganda case, conflict actors have benefited from illicit cross-border trade to sustain their fighting and were able to draw on the support of local (transnational) communities, alienated by the respective states. At the DRC-Uganda border, the rebel group Allied Democratic Forces (ADF) was involved in gold mining and other illicit businesses, especially between 2003 and 2013. These activities were favored by a somewhat mutually reinforcing relationship between the armed group and the locals. The rebels collected taxes from the mines, and locals benefited from economic opportunities in illicit cross-border activities.[40] The gold industry was not monopolized by the ADF but lent itself to territorially segmented supply chain relationships among various groups. The rebels Democratic Forces for the Liberation of Rwanda (FDLR), who also operate in Eastern Congo, cooperated with smaller Mayi-Mayi groups. They mined gold near Kasugho in North Kivu, which was then traded in Butembo, and afterward across the border in Ugandan Kampala.

Transnational ties unite people living on both sides of the border. The ethnic Lugbara, for example, live both in northwestern Uganda and in northeastern Congo.[41] Such long-lasting ties are convenient for the multiple violent non-state groups engaged in illicit cross-border activities: they can use the border population and their knowledge of the local context to smuggle the goods across the border. Decades-old smuggling networks to traffic gold and other minerals as well as ivory from DRC to Uganda and further abroad provided a solid basis for such endeavors.[42] Furthermore, the ADF took advantage of the borderlands' propensity for impunity and used the Congolese border area as a safe haven to stage attacks against Uganda—comparable to the FARC's modus operandi in Ecuador and Venezuela against the Colombian state forces. The lack of state presence in the region enabled the rebels to consolidate their own presence across the border, a process that stretches back to the colonial era.[43]

As in the Andean case, the interactions that the ADF and other armed groups in the region have had with each other might well be understood as various forms of non-state order, and thus could be studied with regard to their distinct influences on security. The "enmity" cluster with armed clashes and attacks among groups attracts most international media attention. Examples of this include the 2012 armed clashes and attacks in Walikale and Masisi territories between the Mayi-Mayi Raïa Mutomboki, Mayi-Mayi Kifuafua, and the Forces de Défense Congolaise (FDC) on one side, and FDLR and Mayi-Mayi Nyatura on the other side. These and similar violent clashes led to killings, torture, sexual violence, and mass displacements of local communities. Between January and September 2012 alone, 767,000 people were displaced in North Kivu and South Kivu.[44]

The region has also featured numerous quickly shifting short-term arrangements that fall into the "rivalry" cluster, driven by economic interests in the illicit cross-border trade or tactical considerations in the armed conflict. The ADF, for example, was involved in arrangements with other violent non-state groups through illicit business ventures as well as alliances to attack third parties.[45] Other examples include the rebels of the 23rd March Movement (Mouvement du 23-Mars—M23), by far the largest armed group in the region that surrendered in November 2013. In that same year, it forged tactical alliances with the Union of Congolese Patriots, a loose coalition of a number of smaller groups and defectors of the Congolese state forces, and with the Union pour la Réhabilitation de la Démocratie du Congo (known as Mayi-Mayi Hilaire), another smaller militia group.[46] The M23 engaged in barter agreements and spot sales involving weapons, ammunition, gold, and ivory with these groups. Similar short-term arrangements could be observed among these smaller militias and between them and other violent non-state groups.[47] The frequent shifts in control of territory and the blurred lines between stable and contested areas had severe impacts on the local communities. The volatility impeded locals from negotiating protection; they were not able to follow clear rules of behavior.[48]

Finally, the long-term arrangements of the "friendship" cluster can also be observed. The M23 were reported to have a strategic alliance with the Local Defence Forces Busumba and the FDLR/Mandevu while operating in pacific coexistence with other groups (Mayi-Mayi Simba and the FDLR/RUG).[49] In the latter case, the groups tolerated each other. This may have reduced the levels of violence between the groups, but it did not necessarily alleviate the anxiety of the local population, who had to fear an increase in violence as soon as the tolerance was over. In South Kivu, local militia groups consolidated their preponderance through social ties with local communities, who stated that it was easier to nego-tiate protection with these groups than with the armed forces since these were either not present or considered ineffective, suggesting shadow citizen security.[50]

Contrary to the Andean case, however, where such shadow citizenship and shadow citizen security may be considered by and large the product of state ne-glect of the margins, in the Congolese case, ethnic lines add to this fragmentation of belonging. A community's resentment toward, or fear of, a specific section of the armed forces of a different ethnicity is a catalyst of the mutually reinforcing relationship between local armed groups and the community.[51]

Even this cursory overview suggests an important additional factor that influences security in this border region: in a similar fashion to the Andean case, the border effect intensifies insecurities. In the interaction types that in-volve the border directly, such as barter agreements and the illicit mineral trade for example, the border's relevance surfaces very clearly. It makes locals more vulnerable. Also in other arrangement types, the borderlands' propensity for impunity facilitates victimization, which raises questions about the nuances of the different forms of insecurity that may emerge (as in cross-border killings, cross-border disappearances, and intra-borderland displacements in the Andean case). Finally, people's sense of belonging to a transnational border community rather than a national polity suggests that social control can be easily extended across the border, posing questions on how armed actors have benefited from this to consolidate "crude" power or, indeed, established shadow citizenship.

The Afghan-Pakistani Border Region

Another example of a case where the borderland lens could prove useful for analysis is the border region shared by Afghanistan and Pakistan. In this re-gion, tribal governance structures overlap with shadow citizenship promoted by violent non-state groups, and various forms of transnational organized crime penetrate the local economy. As these borderlands comprise a semi-au-tonomous region, the Federally Administered Tribal Areas (FATA) of north-west Pakistan, bordering Afghanistan, the notion of "transnational" needs to be revisited altogether. As armed conflict and organized crime converge in this border region, it features violent non-state group interactions from across the continuum of arrangements. For example, the Afghan Taliban engaged in short-lived arrangements, with occasional tactical alliances formed with both Al-Qaeda and Hizb-i-Islami Gulbuddin groups;[52] the Tehrik-i-Taliban jointly planned attacks with Al-Qaeda and received funding as well as training from them, suggesting a strategic alliance between the two groups;[53] other groups such as the Lashkar-e-Taiba and the Jamaat al Dawa al Quran compete with them for territorial control; and yet other groups, especially local criminal gangs, are subcontracted to collect extortion fees.[54] In order to explore how these and other group interactions influence local security dynamics, they need to be analyzed against the backdrop of the meaning of the border and state formation in this particular context.

In the FATA region the local sense of belonging is particularly powerful. In this remote border area, Pakistan's most underdeveloped region, local tribal leaders exert governance functions.[55] Understanding local non-violent governance structures, in addition to the role of central governments, is therefore key for exploring how violent non-state groups have come to change or substitute these, and how this has influenced the perceived and observed security of local communities.[56] The mountainous FATA have been a safe haven for a number of different violent non-state groups, including Al-Qaeda, the Afghan Taliban, and other Islamist groups.[57] These groups benefit from local governance structures, as they can complement or co-opt them and, given the populations' distance to the central state, garner support among locals. In the absence of a strong sense of a nation-state identity, shadow citizenship may easily overlap with, or complement, these local forms of governance. These forms are neither necessarily based on violence, nor form part of the state's formal governance system. Conflict resolution mechanisms and the regulation of property rights are among the "services" provided by local structures— both violent and non-violent. For example, the Pakistani Taliban offered dispute resolution via sharia court systems and other justice mechanisms to achieve local support.[58] As the Andean case shows, when two violent non-state groups operate in pacific coexistence, each strives for the social recognition of the local population in order not to be out-ruled by the other. In the Afghan-Pakistani borderlands, violent non-state groups attempted to achieve greater support through supplying public services normally provided by the tribes and clans.[59]

The convergence of conflict and organized crime further complicates the complex landscape of violent and non-violent non-state actors in the region. Similar to the Andean case, at the Afghan-Pakistani border legal economic opportunities are scarce and smuggling is a lucrative income source. An estimated 45 percent of illicit opiates in Afghanistan are trafficked across the border to Pakistan.[60] To this adds the smuggling of arms, timber, gemstones, and chemical precursors for the production of heroin, taxed by groups such as the Hizb-e-Islami Gulbuddin in Kunar and Nuristan.[61] Being based in borderlands thus not only offers protection from state action but also helps increase income to sustain the fighting. Furthermore, it enables the groups to offer economic opportunities in the illicit trade to local communities, which serves to improve the armed actors' rapport with them, a precondition to establishing shadow citizenship. From the Andes, we know that the border effect facilitates promoting an illicit economy while rendering victimization less visible. Studying the border effect in the FATA more closely could reveal how the unique character of the border in this region influences local security and economic dynamics differently.

This brief discussion suggests that in all three cases—Colombia's borderlands, the Great Lakes region, and along the Afghanistan-Pakistan border—the confluence of conflict and organized crime gives rise to similar patterns of relationships among violent non-state groups and of the security impacts that follow from them. Likewise, in all three cases the geography of the borderlands makes it easier for violent non-state groups to get away unpunished when they increase the levels of violence, which disguises insecurity.

Notwithstanding these commonalities, there are important influencing dimensions that require further attention. I have pointed to "ethnicity" in the African case, and to the meaning of the border in the Asian case, as possible aspects to explore in more depth with future studies. Focusing on "vulnerable regions" rather than the Global South permits the inclusion of other regions that suffer less from a perhaps Western-biased, ethnocentric view on these dynamics. It shows that these borderland dynamics are present across the North and the South. Henry Patterson, for example, documented cases at the Irish-British border where terrorists crossed the border to commit murders and crossed back to safety, taking advantage of the impunity in borderlands that fuels violence and crime.[62] In brief, despite historical, cultural, and geographical differences across borderland cases, unpacking the activities of violent non-state groups and conceptualizing them as clusters on a continuum suggests itself as a useful approach to better understanding how people's security is compromised by these groups.

On the Changing Security Landscape

To transcend conventional categories related to "time," this book has explored fluid, changing patterns of violent non-state group interactions that challenge static views on security and fixed categories of war and peace. The dynamic nature of the group interactions impacts on perceived security. As the discussion of the "rivalry" cluster in which groups engage in volatile short-term arrangements has shown (see chapter 5), uncertainty amid shifting alliances contributes to the presentiment of danger, the unpredictability of violence, and people's feeling of being a potential victim. Suspicion and general mistrust are indicators of this. It is this uncertainty in the face of change that also fuels perceptions of insecurity in broader terms. In any form of arrangement, if one group terminates it, previously established rules suddenly cease to apply or reduce insecurity only to a limited extent. People are likely to feel insecure because they do not (yet) know how to protect themselves. They have to select behavior according to the demands of either group to ensure their security. Depending on how closely the groups had been collaborating beforehand, deciding which group to obey may be challenging. Under preponderance relations, citizens can follow relatively clear rules imposed by the preponderant group to remain safe. Yet when another group starts to dispute this preponderance, they must decide whether to stick to the erstwhile preponderant group's rules or whether to adapt to the new group's rules. In strategic alliances, group identities are blurred. Therefore, ascertaining who is on which side once the alliance breaks down can be difficult. Two antagonistic groups may emerge, but the breakdown can also result in a complete reconfiguration of group constellations. New groups benefit from power vacuums, as some members form splinter groups and others defect from one group to join another. In rapidly changing constellations, perceptions of insecurity prevail.

Change not only plays a role while violent conflict is ongoing. It is particularly crucial in transitions from armed conflict to a post-agreement period. The changes in group constellations brought about by the demobilization of the FARC are paradigmatic for the impact of such developments on the security of communities that live in territories where the arrangements among several groups are changing. Once the demobilization process had started, uncertainty regarding the armed actors who entered their territory fueled mistrust, suspicion, and fear in many parts of Colombia's borderlands, as the vignettes at the beginning of this chapter attest.

Categories of "war" and "peace" then coexist in tension with experiences on the ground. Exploring the security impacts of violent non-state group interactions, regardless of whether during armed conflict or in peacetime, helps constantly re-evaluate whether these concepts and norms are still "fit for purpose" because it brings these tensions to the surface. A nation may be at war, but not every nation's member's security is affected by it. Citizen security can be undermined by "warlike" drug violence, even though the nation lives in peace. Perceived insecurity may worsen during transitions from war to peace due to higher levels of uncertainty, while observed security improves, if measured in battle deaths.

The framework on non-state order does not rely on either war or peace contexts. It is a reflection of the state of security across time and hence helps understand violence, crime, and governance, as well as perceptions thereof more broadly. It is also a tool to design strategies targeted to specific arrangements, even if the groups themselves change, as in transition and post-conflict strategies. Despite demobilization processes, transitions from conflict to peace tend to feature reconfigurations of violent non-state groups rather than their disappearance. In Colombia, the FARC gained strength over the course of the peace talks, but the different types of arrangements continued to exist. Rather than mutating into new forms, the arrangements shifted to the right on the continuum (see Figure 2.1). They evolved into more stable, long-term arrangements between various violent non-state groups because, in many regions, the FARC became preponderant again. This includes areas such as Catatumbo and Nariño where they had been in conflict or in short-term arrangements with other violent non-state groups around 2012.

After the peace accord, another reshuffling of arrangements took place, suggesting a shift toward the "rivalry" cluster, yet the continuum's validity remained intact. The FARC were the group that figured most prominently in the "friendship" cluster: as preponderant group, as strategic ally, as pacific "coexister," and as a crucial player in cocaine supply chain networks. Their withdrawal not only led to power struggles over who would fill the power void, triggering a (temporary) return to the "enmity" cluster in several regions. Even in cases that reached a new equilibrium, it became a more fragile one. Most of the groups that attempted to fill the void are less powerful than the FARC, making a similar preponderance unlikely. Since they are primarily right-wing or criminally motivated groups, forging stable relations with the ELN (as the FARC did) is more difficult. They would have to draw on shared values via institutional mechanisms such as marriages (see chapter 6), rather than similar ideology. Durable relations between violent non-state groups in post-FARC Colombia are most feasible in the context of illicit supply chains, where trusted brokers can stabilize the links. While we can perhaps optimistically hope that, in many regions, a return into a "enmity" cluster is unlikely, it is these durable relations along illicit supply chains that may challenge people's perceived and observed security most pervasively in the long term.

The Second Avenue for Further Research

Transcending time-bound categories such as "war" and "peace" by applying the framework of non-state order across the globe to focus on changes in security landscapes is the second avenue of research.

Not just in the Andes, but across the world, violent entrepreneurs concentrate their presence in transnational borderland "hubs." Yet in today's interconnected world, in which illicit economies that fuel conflict span continents, the arrangements that these groups form impact on security internationally—in border and non-border areas.

Despite the relevance of all forms of non-state order for people's security, most analyses of security focus on just one of them (if focusing on non-state, rather than state-non-state, dynamics at all); the "enmity" cluster, in which violent non-state actors do not have any arrangement with each other. This is the case at the local level, such as in armed disputes between Mexican drug cartels; the national level, such as rebel infighting in Darfur; or the transnational level, such as combat activities between various militias across the Syrian-Iraqi border. Yet consider this last case through the lens of the three clusters of violent non-state group interactions. In addition to the horrendous killings and displacements of civilians produced by violent clashes between armed groups, in many parts of Syria those civilians who cannot flee also have to navigate the constant uncertainty and unpredictability of violence as a product of the quickly shifting alliances among numerous armed actors. Such intangible repercussions, the mistrust they fuel, and the erosion of social fabric that they produce, become evident when focusing on short-term arrangements and their breakdowns. The constant changes in group constellations shape people's everyday experience of insecurity as much as violent clashes—in some regions even more.

Zooming in on long-term arrangements among various violent non-state groups when exploring changing security landscapes also offers new insights that remain hidden when drawing on fixed notions of wartime and peacetime. From the Taliban in Afghanistan and Hezbollah in Lebanon to the Maoists in India, non-state groups illicitly govern spaces, substituting the state-society relationship with shadow citizenship. The preponderance of one group is receiving increasing attention among scholars and policymakers. However, it is those cases where *various* groups exert complementary governance,[63] or relate to each other in other types of long-term arrangements, that are particularly relevant across war and peace. In ongoing conflict, differentiating between cases where groups share territory in pacific coexistence, and cases where they actively exchange intelligence and join forces against third parties in strategic alliances, sheds light on people's security in these regions, as I suggest below. Beyond that, in transitions from war to peace, accounting for these long-term arrangements helps comprehend who may govern territory, and how, after a peace deal. Colombia is just one of many contemporary cases of multi-party conflicts. In such cases, a peace agreement between the government and one of the groups does not stop the armed conflict between the government and another or several others (as with the ELN in Colombia). It also does not stop the operations of criminal groups. Negotiating peace deals in protracted conflicts, such as in Myanmar or the Philippines, with one or only some groups means that non-signatory groups are likely to continue to uphold a certain form of shadow citizenship. And in conflicts where criminal dynamics are ripe, as in Mali, peace deals with a few groups may even lead to the strengthening of some others.

This book's framework on non-state order and citizen security is also applicable to global security trends more broadly. Three trends in the world's security landscape make studying dynamic violent non-state group interactions, rather than static group categories, increasingly relevant. First, the recent proliferation of these groups; second, the growing ease with which violent non-state groups operate transnationally, thanks to advances in the transportation and communication infrastructures that came along with the process of globalization; and third, the increasingly sophisticated use of information technology by these groups, which facilitates interactions and the evasion of law enforcement measures. I allude to some of these global arrangements in various chapters; they were the side scenes of this book: the relations of Colombian rebels with Mexican cartels, of Venezuelan gangs with West African smugglers, and of Ecuadorian criminals with Spanish trafficking rings. Unpacking the multilayered networks of group relations across regions and continents promises to elucidate security repercussions that may not be as direct as in Colombia's borderlands but are likely to shape security trends in the world in the longer run.

On People, Violent Non-State Groups, and the State

To transcend conventional approaches in global affairs related to "agency," which regard the state to be one of the principal security agents by default, I have explored a triangle of relations with an explicit focus on communities and violent non-state groups, yet implicit ramifications for their respective relationships with the state. By analyzing those who are *not* the state and those who strive to be state-like, we better understand the state through their lens—and how state interventions may be best aligned with realities on the ground. Focusing on relations via a bottom-up approach challenges the connotations attached to these categories, if viewed from a state perspective: that violent non-state groups are the "bad guys," that local communities are "the victims," and that the state holds the "solution." Instead, according to local narratives, rebels often hold the solution, state forces are considered the bad guys or "yet another" armed group, and those people who were victimized sometimes come to be viewed as "bad guys" as well. State interventions need to account for these perceptions in order to be successful. Starting from these perceptions, how and where can the state replace violent non-state groups in their relationship with communities in a way that is conducive to a mutually reinforcing state-society relationship that reduces fear, physical violence, and the threats thereof? Understanding the difference between communities' support to the violent non-state group out of fear or out of respect, as well as the impact of arbitrary versus predictable coercion, helps identify entry points for "second-best" interventions, that is, policy solutions that may not yield perfect results, but that are most appropriate, given difficult circumstances.

As I allude to in the first chapter of this book, the dilemma that communities face in contexts of shadow citizen security is not too different from dilemmas that arise from the state's use of coercion. Violent non-state groups base their empirical legitimacy partly on coercion; community members respect them for providing shadow citizen security and respect their monopoly of violence. Yet violent non-state groups also use coercive means to pursue ends that go beyond providing security. Similarly, Charles Tilly notes that governments (of certain regime types) may use coercive means "to seize other people's assets, settle scores with old enemies, extract sexual services, collect protection fees, purvey government resources, or sell confiscated property."[64] In this case, the question of how to distinguish legitimate force from illegitimate violence arises as well. In both cases, arbitrariness matters.

When are violent non-state groups providers of shadow citizen security based (at least to some extent) on the community's consent, and when do they impose order based on crude power? The groups' ways of solving problems can be more efficient than state-provided justice but, aiming to maintain what they consider "order," violent non-state groups provide security "in their way." They decide who is a threat to society, inform people about behavior they consider undesirable, and threaten, or apply violence against, those who do not comply. If people influence and agree with these decisions and play by the rules, as in the example of some regions in Venezuela that I discuss in chapter 6, shadow citizen security arises. Yet if people do not agree and the groups are unwilling to change, it turns into crude power that instils fear, at least among some of the community members. The armed actors may decide who is undesired in society, for example thieves. While some community members may see this as conducive to their own security since they no longer have to be afraid of theft, the thieves themselves may fear becoming a target of "being removed" from society, as in the case of San Lorenzo discussed in chapter 5. In such cases, one person's desired and respected security may be another person's feared social cleansing.

If the provision of security is not only against the will of part of the community but also occurs arbitrarily, shadow citizen security becomes unattainable. The groups no longer possess an illicit, yet legitimately perceived monopoly of violence. Violent punishment for noncompliance, for instance, may be considered a valid source of legitimacy. Arbitrary violence, however, fuels fear. Where people play by the rules and nonetheless are subject to violence, or where there are no rules available to respect in the first place, consent becomes problematic: there is no rule to which to consent. In these circumstances, the state can most easily establish a mutually reinforcing relationship—both as protector from arbitrary violence and as credible provider of security more generally.

The distinction between arbitrary coercion and shadow citizen security, and the implications for the state, are particularly revealing in territories with multiple violent non-state groups (as opposed to territories with a single holder of the monopoly of violence). In such cases, shadow citizen security is hard to establish. Consider arbitrary coercion in the "rivalry" cluster of violent non-state group interactions. Violent non-state groups may hold the monopoly on violence, but they are not necessarily perceived to be the *legitimate* holders of this monopoly. Quick changes in group constellations and frequent breakdowns of alliances make rules unpredictable and shadow citizen security unobtainable; punishment or other forms of coercion become arbitrary. This is what contributes to constant fear of coercion rather than respect of an authority. In the "friendship" cluster, violent non-state groups fulfill different state functions in varying ways, depending on the specific type of arrangement and the distrust-reducing mechanisms, giving rise to three main constellations. First, in cases where shared values between groups and a third party reduce distrust between these two actors as in the context of supply chain relationships, a consensual relationship between violent non-state groups and the local community is hard to establish because general mistrust prevails. The groups' empirical legitimacy mainly rests on their ability to provide economic opportunities. Second, if shared values between groups reduce general mistrust and the groups are highly interdependent, as in a strategic alliance, they are likely to be less concerned with social recognition because, due to shared information, it is unlikely that one group will establish deeper roots in the community to the other's disadvantage. Third, if violent non-state groups are less interdependent because they coexist pacifically, they are more likely to establish a consensual relationship with the local community than in the case of the other arrangements that form part of the "friendship" cluster. Similarly, if one of the groups is preponderant, such a relationship can reduce the costs of coercion. Hence, shadow citizen security and shadow citizenship are easier to attain.

Transforming State Interventions

The variation in the relationships between communities and violent non-state groups contingent on the group interactions provides insights into what the state ought to do to (re-)gain legitimacy, if this is desired. In the near future, democratic states will, even if inadequately and to varying degrees, be the actors most capable of providing citizen security in the Andean region. Where Latin American states have implemented institutional reforms and adjusted their security policies democratically in the past few years, citizen security has been strengthened.[65] This is in line with people's perceptions: according to the public opinion survey Latinobarómetro, 93 percent of Venezuelans, 81 percent of Ecuadorians, and 75 percent of Colombians in 2013 thought that democracy may have problems, but that it was overall the best form of government.[66]

Ensuring citizen security more broadly, and particularly in marginalized regions, requires rethinking what kind of structures help people best govern their everyday lives. Empirical legitimacy is contingent on prior experiences and local contexts. Violent non-state groups perceived to be legitimate providers of security by local communities can be an indication that the state in such contexts cannot compete with the capacities of non-state groups. However, it can also be the result of the absence of a prior experience in which the state was a "better" option. From a community perspective, historic state absence thus raises the question of whether it is preferable to consent to a governance structure imposed by illicit means, or to fight for state-provided governance that may never materialize. Above, I note that such pragmatism to ensure survival makes people strive for shadow citizenship, rather than a state-based citizenship. If the prospect of state presence is not a credible one because of unmet expectations in the past, *and* if people have perhaps also had bad experiences with the state, for example through suffering inflicted by state forces, the relationship between violent non-state groups and communities is likely to endure, even if it is based on fear.

In order to transform such perceptions, the state needs to prioritize its resources according to how to improve its relations with communities most effectively, rather than assuming it will be seen as the solution across varying contexts. This suggests that designing security policies only according to levels of violence is unsuccessful because it ignores the foundation of "state-based" citizen security: a mutually reinforcing state-society relationship. In addition to drawing on homicide and displacement rates as security indicators, employing legitimacy indicators might ensure a more targeted, and thus more successful, approach to transforming insecurity or shadow citizen security into citizen security in regions with the presence of violent non-state groups. Consider, for instance, the cases where community members complained that the state provides coffee crops, but did not construct roads to transport products to the market as in Putumayo, or provided seeds that did not grow as in Sucumbíos, or where citizens agreed with the groups imposing rules because otherwise there was disorder due to state absence as in Apure. In such cases, the state's empirical legitimacy is low and needs to be enhanced for any state policies to be successful. In cases like Putumayo, there need not only to be acts of "legitimacy" but also recognition of having abandoned communities in the past, that is, of having left them to the armed actors. Here, the first task in fact may be to convince people that the state is indeed acting in good faith. Yet in other regions like Cesar, local residents pretended to have seen guerrillas on their streets to make the authorities act (see chapter 6). Here, the government can implement policies with the community's support and design citizen security policies based on a mutually reinforcing state-society relationship without having to invest heavily in gaining legitimacy beforehand. A state is only likely to win (back) the hearts and minds of shadow community members with adequate provision of public goods and services if it is responsive to people's needs.

In multi-party conflicts or fragile settings complicated by criminal agendas as in Colombia, the three clusters of arrangements should help prioritize state interventions, including violence reduction and enhancing credibility and empirical legitimacy. In regions where arrangements among violent non-state groups are absent, reparation for displacement and for loss of relatives is not sufficient. Terror and fear affect these communities over generations, as does the adaptation to actors who base their rule on violence. Victims' compensation needs to include psychological assistance to these communities to facilitate healing and reconciliation if future generations are to live not only in peace among people but also of mind.

Where violent non-state groups predominantly interact in short-term arrangements, the ready supply of groups and recruits that lack alternative life opportunities facilitates the formation of new alliances while violence as a means to an end becomes more normal. A purely militaristic approach in such contexts is unsustainable. Providing alternative livelihood strategies and demonstrating that security can be achieved through a functioning justice system makes recruitment more difficult. Programs to foster these communities' social fabric, eroded by interpersonal mistrust and constant uncertainty due to quickly shifting alliances, can give these citizens a voice in security policies and foster the state-society relationship through a participatory approach.

In long-term arrangements, many violent non-state groups strive to be the providers of services, goods, and opportunities in order to be socially recognized by the community, which helps minimize costly violence and avoid being trumped by other groups or the state. Everyday life in such territories can be less dominated by fear than in contexts of short-term or no arrangements among violent non-state groups, allowing for denser social fabric and hence more possibilities for collective action and mutual support within the community. By identifying distinct long-term relationships among violent non-state groups, we know where gaining state credibility and legitimacy and thus reducing the risk of shadow citizen security is likely to be easiest: in regions where several groups are engaged in strategic alliances. In such cases, the groups have a harder time winning social recognition than where they coexist pacifically or are preponderant. In strategic alliances, the individual groups are not clearly identifiable, which complicates the prospects of these groups to be perceived as legitimate, making it more feasible for the state to enter as a "legitimate governor."

Tracing relations rather than analyzing fixed categories of actors also shifts attention to the agency of those who otherwise remain in the background. The analysis on how groups interact along cocaine supply chains has revealed a change of control from two monopolies (the Medellín and Cali cartels) and the fragmentation of groups after the AUC's demobilization to a "multi-monopoly model" that comprises several powerful narco-brokers who serve as enablers of supply chains in certain regions. Understanding the agency of these brokers who operate as bridges between different violent non-state groups helps rethink the intersection between—or convergence of—organized crime and conflict, and criminal and political violence. Powerful brokers are difficult to replace because they need to be seen as trustworthy by wide-reaching network of supporting actors in multiple sectors of society. Brokers have to build a long-standing reputation of being honest with their clients, whereas violent non-state groups only require the trust of intermediate business partners. Manipulating trust relationships among different groups via the broker could therefore be an option to address the illegal drug problem. Analyzing brokers as agents needs to start at the beginning of the supply chain. Understanding the role of *financieros,* the small-scale brokers at the lower stages of the cocaine supply chain, could help find entry points to reduce uncertainty among rural communities who do not always know which violent non-state group is behind the *financieros* and thus cannot adapt behavior to their rules. This is important in reducing interpersonal mistrust and strengthening the communities' social fabric. Targeting the groups involved in the drug trade hardens the trend of the drug business's constant adaptation and reconfiguration that has produced rapidly changing, unpredictable arrangements that have undermined security in Colombia's borderlands and elsewhere. In the long run, addressing the mechanisms that connect the links in the cocaine supply chain promises to be a more effective approach than current drug policies that focus on individual links, such as coca cultivation, in isolation. In addition to constituting a step toward mitigating the illicit drug problem, it provides opportunities for enhancing security along the cocaine supply chain.

The Third Avenue for Further Research

The avenue of research that arises from considering the triangle of relations between people, violent non-state groups, and the state is to deepen thinking on borderlands as an extreme case that offers insights into security issues more broadly. This study focuses on security dynamics in Colombia's borderlands, with facets of borders and borderlands magnifying the insecurity that results from specific types of relationships among violent non-state groups. It proffers insight into these intensified dynamics, but it also enhances understanding of how relationships would play out and affect insecurity farther inland from Colombia's borders. This yields more questions on how the security dynamics emerging from the relations among people, violent non-state groups, and the state in borderlands take shape in the wider region. The margins of a society tell us a lot about the society as a whole. Similarly, studying the various agents of security in Colombia's borderlands is telling for relations between those agents more widely. How is this triangle reproduced in other parts of Colombia, for example in internal borderlands such as slums, and how is it different at the national level? This includes tracing where the categories "people," "violent non-state group," and "state" start and end, which raises questions such as: who constitutes the social base ("people") if the violent non-state groups and social groups, such as indigenous clans, are allies (see chapter 6)? Given the entanglement of community and armed group members, how can one draw the line between violent non-state groups and community members, and determine whose security is affected? Analyzing differing local contexts might shed light on the role of ambiguity regarding identity in such arrangements and on how it influences citizen security. Another important question that follows from this approach concerns the difference between "state" and "non-state." What can we learn about non-state actors behaving like states and vice versa in a society more broadly, not just at its margins? And finally, what does the state's (nonexistent) relationship with borderland communities tell us about how it treats its citizenry more broadly?

Advancing borderland battles for positive change requires understanding those who are engaged in them. "Heartland policymakers" need to respect and protect borderlanders as citizens in the same way as nationals from non-borderland regions. In this book, I therefore emphasize contextually shaped perceptions in the margins and disclose the top-down misperceptions from distant centers. Typically, the view from the center focuses attention on the visible incidences of physical violence. Seemingly calm situations with the presence of violent non-state groups and less tangible security impacts—including the erosion of social fabric, the uncertainty that arises when the lines between victims and perpetrators are blurred, and pervasive fear—tend to be neglected. These are structures on which it is hard to build a prosperous society, that is, a citizenry that contributes to a mutually reinforcing state-society relationship. And yet, crucially, these are the undercurrents that inform perceptions in the margins.

To be sure, in the Andean case, there is some newfound openness toward such security components, as is evident in programs to provide symbolic reparations, mental health services, or efforts to promote reconciliation. A focus on the relations between people at the margins and the wider society—and the implications of this for the state-society relationship—is one that may not only yield important insights on the role of social fabric, indeed of solidarity, across society more widely but also help to take this openness further.

8.2　Putting the Marginalized Center Stage

Let me conclude by putting the marginalized at the center of our attention to show how engaging in these borderland battles can indeed induce change. In 2016, I visited the region in Tumaco where the FARC gathered before moving to the zones in which they would lay down their weapons. They had been ruling in that area for decades, a fact facilitated by the state's historical absence. Numerous banners put up by the FARC's column Daniel Aldana promoted peace—or their version of it (see Figure 8.2). When asked about what he thought was most important for the local community once the guerrillas had demobilized, a FARC member in this marginalized zone insisted: "They need a state. We are their father, their family. They are sad because when we leave they have no one who will take care of them."[67] The guerrillas' way of "taking care" of a community is questionable, but so too was the absence of any peace sign or banner put up by the Colombian state. In this setting, it seemed that peace was only determined by the FARC and their relationship with the locals, rather than by a mutually reinforcing state-society relationship. This sort of relationship would include the citizens' adherence to democratic rules and civility, but also the state's responsibility to care for its citizens.

　　I was reminded of this rebel's words in 2017, when I returned to another border area where a farmer commented: "War is more than armed conflict."[68] Indeed, the FARC's armed battles against state forces were over (while those of the ELN and other violent non-state groups continued), yet the battles of the marginalized for basic services, security, justice, and legal economic opportunities continued. Borderlanders influence the relationships among violent non-state groups as

Figure 8.2　FARC peace banner in Nariño, Colombia, 2016. Photo by Author.

(non-)collaborators in the absence of an arrangement, as informants, messengers, or providers of infrastructure in short-term arrangements, and as a labor force or social base in long-term arrangement. In brief, they consistently co-shape security dynamics. Yet it is also through these actions that they transform these dynamics.

Such borderland battles for positive change started long ago. I witnessed them, for example, in 2012 in Colombian Arauca. At that time, when the conflict was at its height in this department, a woman told me that life at the border is in some ways more sustainable than elsewhere because one can live from contraband. Indeed, for many borderlanders, borders constitute "a resource rather than an obstacle, providing livelihoods and political status and serving as a sanctuary against mutual incursions,"[69] in a situation of neglect and marginalization. In such circumstances, interdiction against violent non-state groups curbs not only their activities but also undermines the borderlanders' perception of social justice.[70] Rather than implementing measures such as the recent closure of the Colombia-Venezuela border, governments should support the borderlanders' eagerness to engage in cross-border trade and foster licit means for them to do so.

In the same region, on the way from Arauca to Saravena, I passed through several villages, all of them with guerrilla graffiti on the house walls. In one village, Troncal, all houses were newly painted and decorated with paintings of cacao plants—to cover graffiti, as I was told (see Figure 8.3). The sense of community

Figure 8.3 House with cacao plant painting in Arauca, Colombia, 2012. Photo by Author.

and dense social fabric, reinforced through these paintings, reaffirmed the villagers' say in what citizen security should look like. Namely, it should be based in united efforts to transform the actions of the armed actors into creative rather than violent exploits. I saw the cacao plants as a symbol of an alternative liveli-hood strategy to the cocaine industry. And I considered the paintings as a re-minder that the state must play its part to allow for such strategies to bear fruit and foster a mutually reinforcing state-society relationship in borderlands—the groundwork of citizen security.

EPILOGUE

Experiencing Insecurity in the Margins

This story about violence, crime, and governance at the edges of Colombia's war is rooted in experiences of insecurity in the margins. During my fieldwork, I learned about these experiences through the narratives of those at the margins, and through my own observations and experiences. Telling such a story requires taking the notion of reflexivity seriously.[1] It goes without saying that awareness about my own subjectivity in the field was necessary in order to address the ethical and practical challenges that arose from studying such a sensitive topic in a violent setting across borders, and thus to complete the study in a responsible and safe manner. Perhaps less self-evidently, but equally importantly, making sense of my own experiences in relation to those of others surrounding me also shaped my data analysis, and hence the findings of this research. Indeed, it directly influenced my thinking about the subject and the way I decided to write about it. Therefore, in this Epilogue, I elucidate this process of making sense of experiences of insecurity to make the story complete.

Separating the private from the public self is a difficult, if not impossible task during fieldwork informed by ethnographic methods.[2] My "self" as a private person was mostly superseded by my "researcher self." It is this intertwining of "experiencing" and "researching" that informed my perspective on security in the borderlands. As became clear during my fieldwork journeys, unpredictability, illusoriness, and vulnerability characterize many of the experiences of insecurity. These themes not only became central to how I navigated challenging fieldwork situations but also came to shape the central concepts of this book: non-state order, citizen security, and borderlands.

Unpredictability and Non-state Order

Various forms of non-state order influence people's everyday lives at the margins. Rules of appropriate behavior emerge from understanding how violent non-state groups operate, rather than from relying on the state as protector. Learning about such rules was part of my fieldwork process and thus revealed their crucial importance in violent settings. Often, however, these rules cease to exist, not least because the various forms of non-state order are dynamic. This makes the risks and threats that one is exposed to unpredictable.

During the research, I had to make sure not to breach any of these often implicit rules as well as to maintain my academic integrity and neutrality. I learned about the importance of perceptions. In contexts of non-state order, it often matters less what one's actual intentions are, and more how others *perceive* them. The following examples serve to illustrate this. First, in insecure spaces such as Colombia's borderlands, one has to learn what issues one can talk about. I normally preferred to conduct interviews with local stakeholders in public spaces, such as restaurants, yet in contexts of constant suspicion people are not usually predisposed to talk about sensitive issues outside their homes. "They," namely the guerrilla militias and informants of post-demobilized groups, "have ears everywhere," as I was told several times. Accordingly, there was a constant worry that they might misinterpret the interview process.

People living in the context of non-state order also need to understand how being perceived to belong to one side rather than the other, especially in situations of combat or armed disputes, puts one at risk. In one border area, for instance, I followed an interviewee to the headquarters of his farmer organization. Afterward, I learned that the organization was seen as a guerrilla militia "branch." My trusted local contacts told me I should refrain from going back because I had been observed by members of other groups. In this situation, they might have thought that I supported the rebels.

In another instance, an informant offered to arrange an interview with the local boss of a post-demobilized group. Together with my informant, I visited the boss's girlfriend. If she liked me, I would get permission to talk to her partner. After the visit, I received the green light and my informant offered to accompany me to a place where I would be able to interview this boss. In the end I decided not to go. The rival groups in town might have perceived me to be on the other one's side, which could have jeopardized my security.

A major challenge in insecure settings like the Andean borderlands is that non-state order is not fixed. The fluidity and dynamic nature of the various types of violent non-state group interactions, reflected in my conceptualization on a fuzzy continuum, means that there are limits to the benefits of understanding patterns of non-state order. The possibility of change is ubiquitous, which undermines the reliability of any rules. Acknowledging rapid changes in conflict dynamics matters both for collecting and analyzing data. As Carolyn Nordstrom and Antonius Robben note:

the complexity of violence extends to the fieldworkers and their
theories as well. Understandings of violence should undergo a process
of change and reassessment in the course of fieldwork and writing because it is not only unrealistic but dangerous as well to go to the field
with ready-made explanations of violence so as to "find truths" to support our theories.[3]

Unpredictable conflict dynamics thus affect the fieldworker "who becomes
suddenly enveloped in a situation of violence for which he or she was not prepared," as Nordstrom and Robben further add.[4] This is similar for the people
residing in these contexts.

External "shocks" to a given pattern of non-state order may easily undermine
otherwise stable rules. I experienced a situation like this when I aimed to visit
a small village in Bajo Putumayo in 2011. At that time, the situation was stable,
as the FARC had a stronghold in this area near the Ecuadorian border. Despite
the FARC's preponderance, as I call it, the otherwise clear rules of behavior in
this situation no longer applied. This was because the Colombian state forces
had just killed then FARC leader Alfonso Cano in the Cauca department (see
Prologue). I had planned to travel to the village in FARC-held territory together
with an indigenous leader a few days later. We complied with the implicit rule
of announcing our visit to the village community, and a community member
reassured us that we would be fine. Even though far removed from the lethal
incident, and despite the fact that the situation was relatively calm in the village
at that moment, locals suddenly were no longer confident about the stability
of their area. The chances for retaliation acts were high across Colombia, the
rules of access suddenly no longer applied. I decided to postpone the visit. This
demonstrates that it is not sufficient to know the local context. Grasping wider
conflict dynamics is a crucial prerequisite for staying safe.

Importantly and paradoxically, the unpredictability of violence in the context
of non-state order often derives from the very state itself. The previous example
demonstrated the potential repercussions of state action for people's exposure to
violence. The following one illustrates how rules of appropriate behavior become
void in a more direct way, and how the effect magnifies across borders. When
visiting Ecuador's border province of Esmeraldas, I took a boat trip with two
local Afro-Ecuadorian staff members of a human rights organization to Palma
Real, a town on a small island between San Lorenzo and the Colombian city of
Tumaco (see Figure 3.11). I was going to speak to Ecuadorian soldiers and community members. While I was talking to the highest-ranking military official,
a helicopter appeared above us. At first, I did not pay much attention, but the
nervous gazes of the official and his subordinates started to worry me. It was a
Colombian military helicopter in Ecuadorian airspace. Instantly, I remembered

that some years ago, a Colombian military helicopter had bombed the village, as it was suspected to be a guerrilla hideout. Normally, people live in the village relatively calmly. By respecting the rules of the armed actors without meddling in their affairs, people can ensure their security. Yet suddenly this situation changed. The two staff members of the human rights organization looked at me in panic. One of them grabbed my hand. We ran to the shore, jumped into our boat, and went back to San Lorenzo. Given that San Lorenzo has one of Ecuador's highest homicide rates, I had not felt safe in the town earlier. On returning from Palma Real, however, I was relieved to be back. No bombing took place this time, but who knew whether it would again one day. The feeling that Palma Real might be struck by lethal violence in any moment—in this case, violence by a state against a non-state actor—remained.

Incidents like these are particularly disturbing in border regions. The Colombian helicopter's mere transgression of territorial sovereignty is something out of the ordinary, producing even further uncertainty regarding its intentions. The memories of violence linked to a similar event in the past multiply the possible negative futures, a complexity of violent options that make the outcome unpredictable. Suddenly, playing by the rules no longer guarantees security.

Illusoriness and Citizen Security

Another theme that shaped my data collection as well as the findings of my research is the illusoriness of situations where insecurity is not easily observable. It brought to the fore how certain types of violent non-state group interactions result in shadow citizenship and shadow citizen security rather than large-scale violence, and how fear and perceived insecurity affect people, even if physical violence does not materialize.

Tranquility may be an illusion. I could have visited many of the regions discussed in this book and left again, taking with me the impression of an idyllic hinterland. On one occasion, for example, I joined a diplomatic mission to a community meeting in a war-torn border area. The people in this region told us how the situation had improved and that clashes between the state forces and the guerrillas had not occurred for a long time. Later I learned that half an hour after we had left there was a clash between the Colombian military and the guerrillas next to the village where we had our meeting. Rather than tranquility, the region in fact experienced tense calm, where the threat of violence was always present. If one only captures "snapshots" during fieldwork, the data collected may be distorted representations of security.

The horror often also lurked under the surface, not visible to the casual observer, but crystal-clear to those whose lives are enmeshed in it. It requires carefully analyzing any clues that may indicate risk. In sites where violent non-state groups impose social control on the population, I could have put others into danger by asking sensitive questions and thus I preferred not to conduct interviews. I had to adapt my research strategy accordingly, for example by engaging in observation instead. Knowing when such a situation exists is not always self-evident. It requires attentive studying of gestures, mimics, and other tacit signals rather than waiting for explicit verbal requests to refrain from asking questions.

As they are limited in their mobility, local interlocutors are in particular need of protection when talking about sensitive issues.[5] Yet they hardly receive any and hence resort to the "rule of silence." This "rule of silence" also limited the ways in which I was able to conduct research. As John King summarizes Amy Ross's argument, "penetrating fear-based psychological barriers to speaking about the unspeakable is almost impossible in countries that have lost the security of the person."[6] It is not only impossible but also undesirable. After all, "for traumatized individuals and groups, silence may be a coping, not just a survival, strategy."[7] It is an ethical obligation not to re-traumatize these individuals by asking them to talk about issues about which they prefer to remain silent.[8]

In interviews, I often asked broad questions about life in the borderlands, and about how previous years differed from the present. I learned to be a good listener. People's stories about matters important to them provided me indirectly with the responses I was curious about. People would tell me about security issues because it was part of their daily concerns. In one instance, an interviewee told me at the beginning of the interview that he would speak about anything except security. We started chatting about other things. Toward the end, it seemed that I had gained his trust enough for him to mention security issues, albeit framed in a different way. When discussing life in his village, he observed that, due to murders and fear, the quality of life was low.

I further learned about the difference between illusory calmness and tranquility rooted in citizen security through people's speech modes. Their way of talking was an indicator of how comfortable they felt when speaking about certain issues, regardless of whether any immediate risk was observable or not. Some interviewees whispered when referring to the guerrillas or paramilitaries, even when we met in their homes where it was unlikely that anyone would overhear them. Whether people were willing to touch upon sensitive issues or not partly indicated the tension in their lives—their *perceived* security.

Vulnerability and Borderlands

The third theme related to experiences of insecurity that influenced my work is vulnerability. The transnationality of borderlands and their marginalization makes it a theme that resonates particularly strongly with these spaces. Traveling among multiple research sites across and along borders, I was constantly reminded of my own and of other people's vulnerability—as well as the differences between these two forms of vulnerability. Hastings Donnan and Dieter Haller remark that "research on state borders requires a doubling of effort."[9] In my case, it required knowing three countries and the four sides of two borders. Planning multi-sited fieldwork across borders involves establishing contacts, identifying accommodation, booking flights, or working out backup plans for each new site.[10] Local institutions or contact people would offer their support, accompany me, and even invite me to stay in their homes, but I typically had little time to find out details about them. And they seldom work across borders. Every time I crossed the border, I had to find new support networks. I often had to rely on recommendations from previous interviewees as my only reference.

Being on the move across the border, but also more generally in marginalized spaces, is linked to a threat of the constant exposure to danger. I usually traveled alone and was aware that I physically stood out as being a foreigner. Through this, on a number of occasions, I experienced the fear of being a potential victim. In one case, when traveling in the region, it was the fear of being "kidnappable." I was forced to make choices between "the worst" and "the least bad" options, a potentially life-threatening situation in which many borderland communities find themselves on a regular basis. An extract from my field notes illustrates this dilemma:

> It is around 6.30 P.M. The sun is setting. I arrive at the Maracaibo bus station after a trip to Machiques. I look forward to seeing my friend who was going to pick me up. I get off the van but he was not there. I'll wait some minutes, he should be here soon. He is not. He calls. He seriously tells me he is at the other Maracaibo bus station; there are two! Given the traffic and the distance, it would take him an hour to arrive. Panic slowly spreads in me. It is already seven and dark. This is the bus station everyone has warned me about. Don't go there at night. Don't be by yourself, a white, blonde woman. That's why we arranged for my friend to pick me up. Who could have known that there are two bus stations?! A well-dressed woman in her early forties watches me while I tell my friend on the phone: "No problem, I'll wait for you!," thinking, "What

shall I do, all these guys are watching me and it's dark already!" Should I talk to the taxi driver with whom I drove here, the only familiar, but not trustworthy face around me? But he is a man. He left as well, as did all the other passengers. The woman says: "Are you alright? Is no one picking you up?" "Yes, my friend. I just have to wait a bit." "You can't wait here. That's too dangerous. It's dark already! Let's go, come with me, I'm scared here too. Come with me, don't stay here with these men!"

I follow her. What should I do? Everyone had warned me of this bus station, only men around me, she is the only woman, the only well-dressed person I see. "Where are we going?" "Just come with me, we can't stay here. Here is my car, get in the car, we can wait for your friend in the car...." I get in her car, an expensive-looking jeep. I start to feel hot and cold. I have just got into a stranger's car in the dark at the Maracaibo bus station, about which I have heard many stories of kidnappings. But did I have any other option? Stay at the station in the dark with all these men, knowing about all these rape and assault stories? She starts the motor, the jeep begins to move. "What are you doing? My friend will come here; can't we wait here for him in the car?" "That's too dangerous, we can't stay on this parking space in the bus station, and this parking space is only for short stays, we have to get out of here. I'll drive to the other side of the bus station and we can wait there. You have his number, right?" My mobile phone rings: "I'm already on my way, but it'll take a while, are you okay?" "Yes, I'm with a woman in her car!" Thinking: "Help me!" "If you want, I can talk to him and tell him where we are waiting!" She takes the phone: "Hello, yes, she is with me, come to the parking space at the back of the station!"

We leave the bus station, get on the highway. She is taking me somewhere else! I have to get out of this car; we are *not* driving to the other side of the bus station. She is kidnapping me! I send my friend a text: "Come here as quickly as you can, come!" Shall I jump out of the car? Where are we? This must be a slum, all these street vendors on the street, beggars, if I jump out of the car here, I'd probably be assaulted, or raped, or dead soon. Who is she? She asks me: "What were you doing in Machiques?" "Visiting friends from the [NGO]...." "Oh, I used to work for them!" "So you know the boss there?" "Yes, but I don't remember the name...." Ok, she says she has worked with them, which is good, but she doesn't know their names. That's strange. How can you work for someone without knowing the name? This probably means she does not know them; she's just making it up. "I only brought stuff; I was one of the women who brought clothes." We are getting further away from the bus station. Suddenly she turns right. To a parking space. "Let's wait here. Do you want to give your friend a call again so I can tell him where we are?" Fifteen minutes later he arrives. She just wanted to help me. She is one of the rich Machiques ranchers and knows many people who have been kidnapped. She sent her daughter to France to study. And she probably thought about the chances of her daughter being kidnapped if she had been waiting on her own in the dark at the bus station when she saw me. She saved me.

Generally, the danger of becoming a victim when traveling in violent settings is linked to the necessity of constantly negotiating new trust relationships. Citing David Lewis and Andrew Weigert, Julie Norman differentiates between cognitive and personal or emotional trust. Cognitive trust "is based on a cognitive process which discriminates amongst persons and institutions that are trustworthy, distrusted and unknown."[11] Emotional trust is rooted in personal relationships.[12] These two forms help understand trust relationships in a relatively stable context after having spent some time at a specific research site. As this anecdote illustrates, being on the move in unpredictable violent contexts means that we may find ourselves in situations where trust is not available, where the only option to make a judgement is: intuition. In "normal" circumstances, intuiting wrongly may have the consequence of cheating or betrayal. In conflict zones and other violent contexts, this may cost you your life.

Being exposed directly, even if involuntarily, to the precarious situations that one aims to study is invaluable for understanding people's fear that something *might* happen. Michael Taussig distinguishes between the empirical facts and the experience of violence that inform understandings of violence.[13] I would add the sheer potentiality of violence: having been a potential victim myself shaped how I reflected on the perception of being a "potential victim,"[14] shared by so many borderlanders. Nordstrom and Robben note that "if seduction manipulates ethnographers, then fear, anxiety, and intimidation may paralyze them."[15] Indeed, across sites, this fear became a regular accompanier of my research. It became an eye-opener to the pervasiveness of vulnerability.

And yet, even though I became immersed in these violent contexts, I never was exposed to it in the same way as the borderlanders are. Thus, rather than assuming that experiences are equal, experiencing these risks and uncertainty helped me make sense of clashing levels of vulnerability. My situations of vulnerability were "privileged" ones. Unlike many people I interacted with, I was free to move from and to the borderlands. I was able to decide whether to enter a marginalized region or stay away, whether to proceed with a trip immediately or whether to postpone it. And in many cases, I could rely at least on some institutional support, to name just a few "privileges."

Grappling with various levels of vulnerability led me to more closely examine how vulnerability shapes experiences of insecurity and vice versa. In this regard, one of the major challenges in understanding insecurity I faced was the normalization of violence. Being constantly confronted with violence, like many of my interlocutors, can make it mundane. While this may seem to reduce vulnerability, in fact it often reinforces it. Identifying security-enhancing practices such as coping mechanisms and protection strategies thus became a major component of my endeavor to understand security.

Conclusion

Ultimately, studying insecurity in settings of ongoing violence means experiencing an existential shock. It is a "disorientation about the boundaries between life and death, which appear erratic rather than discrete."[16] Conducting my research in multiple settings meant that this shock was experienced again in each new setting, reshaping my perceptions and capacities to analyze the data in an objective way. It made me come closer to an understanding of how unpredictability, illusoriness, and vulnerability influence experiences of insecurity across the margins.

Reflecting on these existential shocks, on how they shape our own perceptions, and on how they shape locals' perceptions of oneself is crucial both for understanding experiences of insecurity and for carrying out responsible research. Only thanks to the borderlanders' support and help throughout my research across the different research sites was I able to complete my fieldwork successfully, and to write this book. Therefore, I consider it vital to report their perceptions of me and how they have shaped my researcher role—in addition to amplifying their voices—to be fully responsible to those whose lives we study.

Appendix A

FURTHER METHODOLOGICAL NOTES

This appendix outlines the methodological approach I adopted in the research for this book. It includes notes on the research design, my empirical strategy, fieldwork, and data collection methods. In chapter 1, I discuss my ethnographic approach to the subject. The Epilogue highlights the relevance of reflexivity for conducting fieldwork and the research process more broadly. Here, I explain how my fieldwork design supports the epistemological approach of the book pertaining to time, space, and agency, as well as to the transformative goal of tackling security challenges, by making marginalized voices heard.

A.1. Research Design

This book focuses on the Andean borderlands as an extreme case of a complex security landscape, in which multiple violent non-state groups operate in overlapping territory (see chapter 1). I selected the Colombian-Ecuadorian and the Colombian-Venezuelan borderlands as sites for three reasons, with each of them pertaining to one or more of the three analytical foci of this research: violent non-state group interactions, citizen security, and the border effect. First, they constitute "most similar systems," comprising largely the same types of violent non-state groups.[1] This means that I was able to draw on a large number of observations in order to study how violent non-state group interactions impact on citizen security (i.e., more than would be possible with a single site). At the same time, the geographic, cultural, socioeconomic, and historical similarities of these two borderlands allowed me to better isolate these processes from other factors than if I had chosen borderlands from two different parts of the world. Second, the Colombian-Venezuelan and Colombian-Ecuadorian borderlands are the most populated borderlands, compared to Colombia's shared borders with Panama, Brazil, and Peru. These borderlands are also those where both legal and illegal economic cross-border activities are thriving most, including through the involvement of local community members. They are therefore the most suited to analyze the security outcomes of local populations. From a practical point of view, this also makes them the most accessible borderlands. Third, drawing on sites located at two shared borders rather than just one has revelatory power regarding questions of whether and how variation in border and security policies of several states (Ecuador and Venezuela) that adjoin a single state (Colombia) in armed conflict is relevant for the border effect. Such insights arise from comparing the four border zones studied in the case—the Colombian and Ecuadorian border zones, and the Colombian and Venezuelan border zones that share the same border respectively.

Aiming to build novel theory based on an exploratory research strategy rather than testing existing theory, I adopted a "flexible discipline" approach to research design, data collection, and data analysis.[2] This way, I was able to use in my analysis the new insights I gained about the behavioral patterns of violent non-state groups, about the experiences of security, and about "borderlands" as sites of complex security landscapes throughout the research process. The research design was thus developed in an iterative process,[3] informed by the interplay of grounded theory and extant theory on armed actors and their interactions. I started with preliminary propositions about conflict and cooperation among armed groups and, based on data collected in the field, identified more-nuanced types of interactions. Through this process I developed the typology of violent non-state group interactions that comprise eight types and theorized their security repercussions. At the same time, I theorized the border effect.

As a result, this book is based on a comparative case study design with a universe of cases that is constituted by social rather than by spatial configurations, namely, interactions among violent non-state groups, as my independent variable. I based the case selection on the variability of the independent variable in order to study the relationship between these interactions and citizen security in borderlands. The independent variable is thus built from the observations of the empirical data through the iterative research process outlined above.

As the aim of the research was to investigate pathways rather than effects,[4] a case study approach was particularly suitable to acknowledge complexity while creating categories of a parsimonious model to make sense of this complexity. Following John Gerring, I define the case study approach as "the intensive study of a single unit or a small number of units (the cases), for the purpose of understanding a larger class of similar units (a population of cases)."[5] Small-N case studies "preserve the texture and detail of individual cases."[6] This is essential for ensuring the internal validity of my findings within the scope of Colombia's borderlands, including the processes that link the interactions among violent non-state actors to their impacts on security, and to the mechanisms through which the geography of borderlands intensifies these impacts ("the border effect," discussed in chapter 7). The external validity of this research rests in the choice of cases that can be observed not only in the research sites of this book but also across the globe. The discussions in the concluding chapter of the Afghanistan-Pakistan and Congo-Uganda border areas as alternative sites, for example, suggest that the findings from the theory on non-state order and citizen security outcomes—as well as the border effect—are relevant in these different contexts too. Further research would be necessary to reliably test this. Moreover, adopting a borderland lens as an epistemological approach to studying security, the broader argument of this book, provides insights that are relevant beyond the cases studied here.

A.2 Empirical Strategy

My empirical strategy consisted of three steps. Firstly, I identified and mapped observations of violent non-state group interactions. This allowed me to define the categories in my independent variable—the eight types of interactions— that also constitute my cases. Secondly, I traced violent non-state group interactions' impact on citizen security and identified various forms of behavior of community members to cope with or mitigate this impact. Thirdly, I studied the intervening border effect.[7]

Mapping Observations

First, I mapped the presence of violent non-state groups on overlapping territory and identified the hundred most relevant observations of violent non-state group interactions across Colombia's borderlands, in line with the typology of violent non-state groups. This number resulted from an extensive analysis of the data that I collected via interviews, focus groups, observation, risk reports of the Ombudsman's Offices, and other policy documents, and after disregarding some cases for which I did not trust the reliability of the data sources.

In line with the quality and durability of these interactions that are influenced by the availability of distrust-reducing mechanisms to the violent non-state groups (see chapter 2), each of the eight types belongs to one of the three clusters of violent non-state group interactions, the various forms of non-state order (see Figure 2.1). Accordingly, I allocated each of the hundred observations to one specific type in one of the three clusters. Table A.1 summarizes the spread of the observations across the clusters and the two

Table A.1 **Spread of Observations across Clusters and Sites**

	Colombian-Ecuadorian Borderlands	Colombian-Venezuelan Borderlands	Total
"Enmity" Cluster	7	14	21
"Rivalry" Cluster	18	21	39
"Friendship" Cluster	18	22	40
Total	**43**	**57**	**100**

borderlands. Appendix B lists all hundred observations, organized into the eight types of violent non-state group interactions and the respective clusters that comprise them.

All one hundred observations across Colombia's borderlands are presented in chapter 3. On Map 3.5 and Map 3.7, I spatially map the observations (in total 55) that date between 2011 and 2013. This is when I conducted the bulk of my fieldwork and hence I was able to gather data on these interactions and/or their repercussions in real time. Roughly half of the hundred observations, namely 52, are discussed in chapters 4, 5, and 6. They are marked with an asterisk (*) in Table B.1 in appendix B. The selection of these 52 observations was motivated by accounting for varying geographic (e.g., the desert of the Guajira Peninsula, the mountainous Andean zone, or the tropical Amazonas region) and cultural (including indigenous, Afro-Colombian, and farmer cultures) contexts, types of borders (maritime/land), cocaine supply chain stages, and variation in long-standing or recent presence of violent non-state groups.

Tracing Influences on Security

In order to analyze the repercussions of the eight interaction types on citizen security, the second step of the empirical strategy, I focused in more detail on half of the 52 observations discussed in chapters 4, 5, and 6, that is, on 26 observations. They are marked with a dagger (+) in Table B.1 in appendix B. With these 26 observations, I aimed for a relatively balanced selection from both borderland sites and made sure that I had detailed within-case evidence available.[8] Most of these violent non-state group interactions were ongoing while I visited the sub-site (the specific location within the Colombian-Ecuadorian or Colombian-Venezuelan borderlands) where they were taking place or while I interviewed people with first-hand experience of the sub-site in close proximity. Some of them had evolved into another type shortly before (e.g., combat in Arauca and Apure or spot sales and barter agreements in Llorente), which enabled me to compare and contrast differences and commonalities in the security outcomes over time. I chose several observations from all types of violent non-state group interactions in order to avoid potential selection bias, which can result from focusing on only one observation per type. The distribution is presented in Table A.2.

I started by choosing two observations for each interaction type for my in-depth analysis (see Table A.2). In two (absence of arrangements and spot sales/barter agreements) of the eight interaction types, however, I found strong variation in how they took shape empirically. I therefore decided to subdivide them further into subtypes. I chose two observations for each subtype and, in the case of spot sales/barter agreements, added one for spot sales of humans to highlight its distinctiveness. I selected five observations of preponderance. Two of them were selected because they both change over time. The other three are located in Colombia, Ecuador, and Venezuela respectively and thus serve to demonstrate that preponderance contributes to shadow citizenship—a security outcome that defies the state—across the three states, regardless of whether the violent non-state groups explicitly aim to challenge that state's authority.

I conducted three forms of data analysis: first, cross-case analysis of the three clusters; second, within-case analysis of each cluster; and third, within-case analysis of each type of interaction.[9] First, through the cross-case analysis of the three interaction clusters, I demonstrate how the ways in which inter-group distrust is reduced (general distrust, distrust reduced on a particular occasion, or generally reduced distrust) contribute to variation in the security repercussions of the clusters of the absence of an arrangement ("enmity"), of unstable short-term arrangements ("rivalry"), and of stable long-term

Table A.2 **Spread of Selected Observations across Cases**

Type of Violent Non-state Group Interaction	Number of Observations
Absence of an arrangement (combat + armed disputes + tense calm)	2 + 2 + 2
Spot sales/barter agreements (financial + material + human beings)	2 + 2 + 1
Tactical alliances	2
Subcontractual relationships	2
Supply chain relationships	2
Strategic alliances	2
Pacific coexistence	2
Preponderance relations (differing state policies + change over time)	3 + 2

arrangements ("friendship"). Second, the within-case analysis of each cluster highlights intra-cluster variations in citizen security outcomes. Third, the within-case analysis of each type of violent non-state group interaction informed by examples across Colombia's borderlands reveals specific causal mechanisms.[10] Engaging in micro-level process tracing, a "key technique for capturing causal mechanisms in action,"[11] allowed me to demonstrate how the specific types of violent non-state group *interactions* influence security outcomes, rather than to attribute varying levels of physical violence to the *presence* of these groups.

The third form of analysis was an iterative process of deduction and induction to reduce confirmation bias.[12] Deductively, I analyzed whether and how specific interaction types influenced the security of community members. For example, preponderance contributes to shadow citizen security, with one of the causal mechanisms being "exerting social control." Inductively, I examined whether and how security outcomes such as the exposure to violence or uncertainty within a case can be traced back to a specific interaction type.[13] This detailed tracing let me account for complex causality: zooming in on the situation on the ground reveals additional influences on perceived and observed security, in particular, the behavior of community members through which these security impacts can be mitigated. This is reflected in people's avoidance and coping strategies that I discuss in the book.

Establishing the Border Effect

The third step of the empirical strategy, establishing the border effect, involved accounting for the geography of borderlands through a spatial analysis of the violent non-state group interactions and the security repercussions, and through the mapping of illicit flows across both borders. Based on the empirical data, I identified four main causal mechanisms that point to the border effect. Two of them (border as facilitator and border as deterrent) result mainly from the transnationality of borderlands. The other two (border as magnet and border as disguise) result mainly from the borderlands' distance to the centers and their proximity to the borderline. I contrasted data collected in the capital cities, including on border policies, with data collected in the border areas. This served to identify state-centric views on borderlands. It also let me avoid confirmation bias of the relevance of border areas for security more broadly and for the legitimacy of the state. This might have been the case had I collected data in border regions only.

For the data analysis of all three steps of the empirical strategy, I used a provisional list of codes that I defined before starting the coding process. These include, for example, codes representing the characteristic features of borderlands or security outcomes, such as death or fear.[14] Drawing on NVivo10 software,

I engaged in descriptive, structural, process, versus, and emotion coding. Often, the coding was simultaneous: I assigned several codes to the same text sections. I also conducted "In Vivo coding": using phrases from the interviews directly as codes when they were mentioned frequently across different interviews,[15] including "tense calm," "the rule of silence," or "if he's dead, it's because of something." Following Yvonna Lincoln and Egon Guba, throughout the study I filled in additional codes, reconsidered already-coded material in new ways, bridged codes by identifying relationships I had not discovered before, and identified categories emerging from codes.[16]

Spatiality

To highlight the relevance of spatiality for the research, I visualized some of the data through maps. I created all maps in the book with Esri's ArgGIS 10.2 mapping and spatial analysis software. I combined features extracted from satellite images and OpenStreetMap with my own data, for example by geolocating my own photographs. Elevation data were added with SRTM, and national and subnational borders with Natural Earth data. I used reliable additional sources for maps of specific phenomena, for example data from the United Nations Office on Drugs and Crime to map coca cultivation. The maps of border crossings are based on the coordinates of these crossings provided in police, military, and intelligence documents from the three countries that I obtained during my fieldwork and triangulated for robustness.

A.3 Fieldwork

As presented in chapter 1, I collected data by conducting extensive multi-sited ethnographic fieldwork in and on the shared borderlands of Colombia, Ecuador, and Venezuela. My fieldwork design supports the epistemological approach of the book pertaining to (i) time, (ii) space, and (iii) agency.

Time

A longitudinal study carried out between 2008 and 2018, the research is consistent with the study's approach to challenge artificial dichotomies between war and peacetime: I carried out fieldwork during the Colombian government's armed conflict with the FARC, the guerrillas' demobilization process, and in the post-FARC agreement period (in which armed conflict with the ELN persisted) to analytically focus on the changing security dynamics, rather than on binary distinctions.

Space

As the maps of my cross-border fieldwork itineraries show (see appendix C), the fieldwork design is also in line with the epistemological approach to the study that seeks to consider transnational borderlands as one unit of analysis: my itinerary was deliberately of a cross-border nature. Instead of researching either "armed conflict" or "peace" territories, I crossed between conflict and non-conflict territory, which enabled me to shed light on the convergence of conflict and transnational organized crime.

Accordingly, my fieldwork covered a wide range of sub-sites located in the two main fieldwork sites: the Colombian-Ecuadorian and Colombian-Venezuelan borderlands. After a first fieldwork phase in Ecuador in 2009 to study security dynamics in the Ecuadorian northern border zone, I conducted the bulk of the fieldwork between August 2011 and May 2013, in four separate phases that totaled around twelve months. In the first fieldwork phase, I started in Bogotá, from where I conducted a short, exploratory trip to Cúcuta, the capital of Norte de Santander department, which borders Venezuela, and subsequently traveled along the Colombia-Ecuador border. In the second phase, I started in Quito, conducted borderland trips from there, and afterward traveled to the Colombian-Venezuelan borderlands. In the third phase, I started in Caracas and continued along the Colombia-Venezuela border. The fourth phase was a follow-up trip to clarify specific points of the research. Between 2014 and 2018, I carried out more visits to the region, during which I returned to the Colombian border departments again: the Catatumbo region in the Colombian department of Norte de Santander, the departments of Arauca and La Guajira, the department of Nariño and Cúcuta in Norte de Santander, and the departments of Putumayo, Cesar, and La Guajira. I also returned to Venezuelan Táchira. In between and after these visits, I carried out multiple trips to Bogotá to follow the developments of the peace process in the country's power center. Due to the closure of the Colombia-Venezuela border between 2015 and 2016, I had to stay on the Colombian side during some trips, but I mitigated potential bias in the data by interviewing locals on the Colombian side who were crossing the border anyway, including Venezuelan Wayúu, a binational, indigenous people.

Agency

Finally, my fieldwork design is consistent with bringing to the fore non-state agency in influencing security in places defined by the state's absence or weak presence. It is thus conducive to the book's transformative goal of contributing to tackling security challenges by amplifying marginalized voices. Challenging the urban bias that prevails in most conflict and security research, I conducted fieldwork in remote, rural peripheries where no similar research had been carried out previously. As seen on the fieldwork itinerary maps in appendix C, I visited small villages in difficult-to-reach border regions where no police or other state institution was present. Given the lack of road infrastructure, some were accessible only through long walks by foot or via boats on rivers. Far away from urban infrastructure, my accommodation sometimes ranged from tents and outdoor hammocks to simple farmhouses and community centers. I conducted all parts of the fieldwork without an interpreter, to avoid additional "filters" to these voices, and to come as close to local experiences and perceptions as possible.

Data

Both the field of inquiry and the practical and ethical challenges that arise when carrying out fieldwork in conflict settings (see Epilogue) required me to approach fieldwork with openness to what constitute data in the first place. Accordingly, data used in this research include written text, oral data, speech mode (e.g., whispering), gestures, observed power dynamics (e.g., rebel hierarchy), spatial representations (e.g., maps drawn by interviewees), photography, and satellite images (e.g., of informal border crossings). This is crucial to investigate mistrust and people's perceptions of security: nonverbal signals such as lowering one's voice or nervous gazes indicate mistrust and fear and thus capture a broader spectrum of citizen security impacts than verbal data alone would do. Similarly, visual clues such as rebel graffiti on house walls help identify the type of group interaction in contexts where verbal data are not available. Even the absence of data can constitute data in itself. This includes, for example, access denial to a fieldwork site in one specific moment, but not another; the absence of observable measures of insecurity, such as homicides; and the lack of information outflow from a particular territory. These phenomena can indicate strong social control by armed actors (see section 7.4).

Data Collection

Following strict ethical guidelines as per the regulations of my home institution, my main methods of data collection were semi-structured interviews, focus groups, and (participant) observation (see also chapter 1). I also reviewed local and national newspaper articles, Ombudsman's Office reports, and policy documents to explore to what extent the public representation of borderland dynamics differed from the local population's representations. This was complemented by analyzing confidential documents that I was given by my research participants and reviews of the secondary literature. I complemented these qualitative methods with quantitative dimensions, for example by reviewing statistics on homicide rates or surveys on security perceptions. I always kept detailed field notes and wrote more structured analytical fieldwork reports every fortnight to analyze the data collected and their context while the data, especially observations, were still fresh in my mind. Through this initial data analysis carried out while still in the field, I was able to refine my approach and interview questions in line with the preliminary research findings.

Interviews were my main method of recording and of trying to understand marginalized voices. I conducted 606 semi-structured anonymous interviews (433 between 2011 and 2012) based on informed consent in the borderlands and in Bogotá, Caracas, and Quito (see Table A.3). Most of them were in Spanish, some in English, and some in German (my native language). I translated all interview extracts in this book into English. Typically, the interviews lasted between thirty minutes and two hours; the extent to which they were structured depended on the context. Interview questions I asked academics or international organization staff were very specific. For security reasons, questions for interviewees such as ex-combatants or displaced people were more open, in the aim of resembling informal conversations. When the interviewees agreed to the interview, I took notes and/or recorded them with a voice recorder. I later coded the recordings and stored them separately from the coding table. If the interviewee did not want to be recorded, I only took notes. Most interviews were one-to-one interviews; in some cases, several people were present. I conducted most interviews alone; in some I was accompanied by my local trusted contact person, listening next to or behind me.

Table A.3 provides an overview of the distribution of all 606 interviewees across departments of both borderlands and capital cities, as well as across various categories of stakeholders. To ensure anonymity, I list them here only at the departmental level, but as the borderland itinerary maps demonstrate, interviews, focus groups, and observation were carried out not just in the departmental capitals, but also in remote rural areas. I have summarized the interviewees into ten categories, roughly ranging from stakeholders most removed from the state to state representatives themselves:

   i. Guerrillas, paramilitaries, militias
  ii. Displaced persons, victims
 iii. Community leaders, human rights defenders
 iv. Residents, church members, ombudsman's office staff
  v. Non-governmental organization staff
 vi. Associations and private sector representatives
vii. International agency staff

Table A.3 **Spread of Interviews across Stakeholders and Sites**

	Colombian-Ecuadorian Borderlands (203)					Centers (183)			Colombian-Venezuelan Borderlands (219)							
	Colombian Border Zone (120)		Ecuadorian Border Zone (83)						Venezuelan Border Zone (67)			Colombian Border Zone (152)				Total
Stakeholders	Nariño	Putumayo	Esmeraldas	Carchi	Sucumbíos	Quito	Bogotá	Caracas	Apure	Táchira	Zulia	Arauca	N. de Santander	Cesar	La Guajira	
Guerrillas, paramilitaries, militias	7	4	0	0	0	0	0	0	0	0	0	0	1	3	3	**18**
Displaced persons, victims	1	9	2	0	5	0	0	7	3	1	0	0	8	0	1	**37**
Community leaders, human rights defenders	7	12	7	4	12	0	0	0	1	0	2	4	7	0	10	**66**
Residents, church members, ombudsman's office staff	12	10	6	4	5	2	2	3	11	2	5	4	26	2	7	**101**
Non-governmental organization staff	8	2	4	2	0	11	10	6	5	4	13	0	10	0	0	**75**
Associations and private sector representatives	3	3	4	0	0	0	0	0	0	0	0	0	2	0	2	**14**
International agency staff	18	10	4	1	1	11	28	4	1	5	1	6	14	6	1	**111**
Academics, think tank and media staff	1	0	1	1	0	22	23	10	0	4	0	0	4	0	0	**66**
State forces and intelligence officials	0	4	7	2	0	9	8	1	3	1	1	0	3	1	3	**43**
Government officials	5	5	1	4	6	10	14	2	3	0	1	2	17	0	5	**75**
Total	**61**	**59**	**36**	**18**	**29**	**65**	**85**	**33**	**27**	**17**	**23**	**16**	**92**	**12**	**32**	**606**

viii. Academics, think tank and media staff

ix. State forces and intelligence officials

x. Government officials

The category "guerrillas, paramilitaries, militias" includes former combatants. The category "residents, members of the church, ombudsman's office staff" comprises individuals that are generally respected by all stakeholder groups and trusted by local community members. Specific examples include priests (church members), analysts of the early warning system (ombudsman's office staff), and schoolmasters, teachers, and doctors (residents). "International agency staff" include both international and local employees. "Government officials" include both local and national authorities. Where I cite interviewees in the chapters, I characterize them more specifically, but still generally enough to ensure anonymity. I also refrain from citing exact locations to ensure anonymity.

I selected the interviewees mainly using the snowball sampling technique. To avoid selection bias and to balance different sources in each research site,[17] I asked my existing contact persons for references of people from diverse walks of life. Accordingly, in each region, interviews were carried out with individuals from a wide range of different stakeholder groups, and always covering both state and non-state perspectives. This allowed me to triangulate data across a variety of stakeholders. In some cases, I used narratives themselves for my analysis, rather than factual data contained in them. For example, the farmer's memories of violence, shared in chapter 4, offer insights into the long-term harm of being exposed to combat between violent non-state groups, regardless of whether these memories may present a distorted reality.

As Table A.3 shows, the distribution of interviewees across border regions is fairly balanced. Unlike most studies on security in the region that tend to be biased toward a Colombian perspective, during the main fieldwork period (2011–2013), the number of interviews in each border zone was almost equal (Colombian-Ecuadorian borderlands: 90 on the Colombian side, 83 on the Ecuadorian side; Colombian-Venezuelan borderlands: 69 on the Colombian side, 63 on the Venezuelan side). This balance shifted slightly toward the Colombian side only later, due to the major changes taking place in the context of the peace process with the FARC. Interviews carried out in the capital cities served to contrast views from the margins with the perspectives that stakeholders in the power centers have on the borderlands. These also include stakeholders who worked and lived in the borderlands and whose accounts I could compare and contrast with data collection in the borderlands. Some anomalies are due to local conditions or volatile security dynamics (see Epilogue). For example, the presence of international agencies is particularly high in Nariño and Norte de Santander, which explains the relatively high number of interviewees that fall into this category in these two departments. In Arauca, the delicate security situation prevented me from conducting a large number of interviews; I therefore prioritized observation over interviews, complemented with the review of local media reports.

Triangulation and Access

Throughout the process I engaged in thorough triangulation of data collection methods and of data sources, as far as this was possible. Given the complex field sites, the level of access varied and I thus had to mitigate the resulting disparities in data. For example, people tended to be more open when I conducted interviews on my own, whereas the presence of international agency staff sometimes hindered the flow of the conversation (yet increased my own safety). Another example is varying security levels, which made me adapt my data collection methods, as in the case of Arauca mentioned above.

Triangulation was also essential to compensate for incompleteness or incorrectness of data since, after all, my interviewees decided what to tell me and when to tell the truth. I aimed to minimize this incompleteness by establishing solid (albeit often short-term) trust relationships with my interviewees. Given the multi-sited nature of my fieldwork, highlighting particular parts of my identity was a particularly important strategy in this regard. Unlike fieldwork in remote villages over a long period of time common in anthropological studies, or only conducting elite interviews as is often the case in political science research, my fieldwork involved traveling both to remote borderlands and to the capital cities. While I was always perceived as an outsider from Europe, the ways in which my interviewees perceived my specific identity varied across these very different contexts. Awareness of one's own identity is crucial when conducting fieldwork because it can both help and hinder building trust relationships with interviewees and the communities in which one is embedded.[18] "Invoking particular personal characteristics at various times" helps establishing a connection with the persons that often facilitates talking more openly, as Courtney Radsch notes. I therefore highlighted my identity in my interaction with informants, for example, as a woman, a researcher, a former practitioner, or a European.[19] Still, even in solid trust relationships people only provide the information they want to share.

Overall, even though my understanding of personal situations might be incomplete, these shortcomings do not undermine the overall validity of my findings because my objective was not to represent in detail single stories, but to use these accounts to establish a wider understanding of security dynamics in borderlands.

Appendix B

VIOLENT NON-STATE GROUP INTERACTIONS ACROSS THE BORDERLANDS

The following table lists the one hundred observations of the eight types of violent non-state group interactions that I present in chapter 3 (see also appendix A). The 52 observations marked with an asterisk (*) are discussed in chapters 4, 5, and 6. The 26 observations marked with a dagger (†) are the ones used for detailed within-case analysis to trace how the respective interaction type influences citizen security. The observations dated between 2011 and 2013 (55 in total) are presented on Map 3.5 and Map 3.7. Within each type, they are organized geographically, from east to west in the Colombian-Ecuadorian borderlands, and from south to north in the Colombian-Venezuelan borderlands (similar to chapter 3).

Table B.1 **Observations of Violent Non-state Group Interactions**

Interaction Type	Colombian-Ecuadorian Borderlands	Colombian-Venezuelan Borderlands
Combat and armed disputes	1. paramilitaries and guerrillas in Putumayo (COL) and Sucumbíos (ECU), 2000s*†	8. paramilitaries and guerrillas in Arauca (COL), late 1990s/early 2000s
	2. FARC and Rastrojos in Puerto Caicedo (COL), 2009	9. FBL and ELN in Apure (VEN), 2003
	3. Águilas Negras and FARC in Putumayo (COL), 2009	10. FARC, ELN, and FBL in Arauca (COL) and Apure (VEN) between 2006 and 2010*†
	4. post-demobilized groups and guerrillas in Putumayo (COL) and Sucumbíos (ECU), 2010s*†	11. post-demobilized groups and guerrilla militias in Arauca (COL), 2012*†
	5. paramilitaries and guerrillas in Llorente, Nariño (COL), 2002 to 2006*	12. Urabeños and Rastrojos in Cúcuta, Norte de Santander (COL), Ureña and San Antonio de Táchira (VEN), 2011/2012*
	6. FARC and ELN in Nariño (COL), 2006 to 2010	13. Urabeños and Rastrojos in Cúcuta, Norte de Santander (COL), 2011/2012 (tense calm)*†
	7. FARC, Águilas Negras, and Rastrojos in Nariño (COL), 2011	14. paramilitary successors and ELN in Rubio, Táchira (VEN), around 2011*†
		15. Paisas/Urabeños and Águilas Negras in Norte de Santander (COL), 2007/2008
		16. ELN, EPL, FARC, and paramilitaries in Táchira (VEN), after 1999
		17. FARC, ELN, EPL, paramilitary successor groups, and later Rastrojos, Urabeños, and Paisas in Ocaña, Norte de Santander (COL), January to April 2012 (tense calm)*†
		18. paramilitaries and guerrillas in the Catatumbo region, Norte de Santander (COL), mid-1990s to mid-2000s
		19. paramilitaries and guerrillas in Cesar (COL), 1990s
		20. private Wayúu armies and violent non-state groups in La Guajira (COL) and Zulia (VEN), end of 1970s/beginning of 1980s
		21. Paisas/Rastrojos and Urabeños in Cesar and in La Guajira, including Maicao (COL), 2010

Spot sales and barter agreements	

22. FARC Front 48 and Ecuadorian traffickers, near San Miguel between Sucumbíos (ECU) and Putumayo (COL), 2000s
23. Rastrojos and other post-demobilized groups in urban areas along major road in Putumayo (COL), after 2006
24. FARC Front 48, Ecuadorian traffickers, near San Miguel between Sucumbíos (ECU) and Putumayo (COL), 2012*
25. various trafficking groups, Pasto, Nariño (COL), 2011/2012
26. Ecuadorian traffickers and FARC, including Front 29, in rural Carchi and Tulcán, Carchi (ECU) and Ipiales, Nariño (COL), 2011/2012*†
27. various post-demobilized groups and guerrilla militias at the formal border crossing between Ipiales, Nariño (COL) and Tulcán, Carchi (ECU), 2011/2012*
28. FARC and traffickers in Maldonado, Chical, and Tufiño in Carchi (ECU), around 2011/2012
29. Águilas Negras, Mano Negra, Nueva Generación, Rastrojos, and FARC in Llorente, Nariño (COL), around 2007*†
30. Rastrojos and FARC militias in Llorente, Nariño (COL), 2011*
31. paramilitaries and traffickers in Nariño (COL) and Carchi (ECU), 2000s
32. post-demobilized groups, Mexican Zetas, and Sinaloa cartel around Tumaco municipality, Nariño (COL), 2010s
33. Colombian post-demobilized groups in Esmeraldas (ECU), around 2012*

34. post-demobilized groups at border crossings in Arauca including Puerto Lleras and La Playa (COL), around 2011
35. paramilitaries, Mexican cartel members, and Venezuelan criminal groups, San Cristóbal (VEN), 2011/2012*
36. Rastrojos, Urabeños, and post-demobilized groups in Alejandría, Cúcuta, Norte de Santander (COL), 2011*†
37. various post-demobilized groups near Cúcuta, Norte de Santander (COL), 2011–2012
38. Rastrojos and trafficking groups, Puerto Santander (COL) and Boca del Grita (VEN), around 2011/2012
39. guerrillas and criminal groups near Machiques (VEN), 2011/2012*†
40. Rastrojos and Urabeños, La Paz, Cesar (COL), 2011*†
41. FARC and criminal groups, La Guajira (COL) and Zulia (VEN), around 2011/2012

(continued)

Table B.1 Continued

Interaction Type	Colombian-Ecuadorian Borderlands	Colombian-Venezuelan Borderlands
Tactical alliances	42. FARC militias, Rastrojos, Águilas Negras, and other violent non-state groups in Tumaco, Nariño (COL), 2000s	46. various criminal and post-demobilized groups in Maracaibo (VEN), 2012*
	43. Águilas Negras and Rastrojos in Tumaco, Nariño (COL), 2010/2011*	47. Mexican Zeta cartel and Rastrojos in Zulia (VEN), 2011
	44. Rastrojos, FARC militias of mobile column Daniel Aldana, Mexican Sinaloa Cartel, and other criminal groups in Tumaco, Nariño (COL), 2011/2012*†	48. Rastrojos, Urabeños, Paisas, group Alta Guajira, and several private Wayúu armies in Maicao and Riohacha (COL), 2011 and 2012*†
	45. Colombian post-demobilized groups in Esmeraldas (ECU), around 2012	49. drug trafficking/paramilitary group and Wayúu group in La Guajira (COL) and Zulia (VEN), 1990s*
		50. drug trafficking group and Wayúu group in La Guajira (COL) and Zulia (VEN), 2000s*
		51. Counterinsurgent Front Wayúu and Autodefensas Gaitanistas de Colombia in La Guajira (COL), 2008*
		52. Counterinsurgent Front Wayúu (Alta Guajira) and Paisas in La Guajira (COL), 2009*
		53. Paisas and Rastrojos in Cesar and La Guajira (COL), 2010
		54. paramilitary Counterinsurgency Front Wayúu led by "Jorge 40," and Wayúu group led by "Chema Bala" in Bahía Portete, La Guajira (COL), 2004*
Subcontractual relations	55. Mexican Sinaloa Cartel and Águilas Negras in Tumaco, Nariño (COL), 2011	57. post-demobilized groups and local criminal groups in Táchira (VEN), 2009
	56. post-demobilized groups including ERPAC and Águilas Negras in Tumaco, Nariño (COL), and youth gangs in San Lorenzo (ECU), around 2011*†	58. post-demobilized groups and youth gangs in Ocaña, Norte de Santander (COL), 2011/2012*†

		59. Rastrojos, Urabeños, and youth gangs in Maicao, La Guajira (COL), 2011/2012*
		60. Counterinsurgent Front Wayúu (Alta Guajira) and criminal bands in Maicao, Dibulla, and Riohacha, La Guajira (COL), 2008
Supply chain relations	61. guerrillas and other violent non-state groups in Bajo Putumayo (COL) and Sucumbíos (ECU), 2010s*	64. guerrillas and other groups in Arauca (COL) and Apure (VEN), 2012*
	62. ELN's Front Héroes de Sindagua and other groups in Pizarro, Nariño (COL), around 2011/2012	65. FARC, ELN, EPL, and Águilas Negras/Rastrojos in the Catatumbo region, Norte de Santander (COL), 2010s*†
	63. FARC including mobile column Daniel Aldana in Bajo Mira, Rastrojos in Alto Mira and Frontera, and other post-demobilized groups along the River Mira in Nariño (COL) and Esmeraldas and Carchi (ECU), 2011/2012*†	66. guerrillas and other violent non-state groups in Machiques, Zulia (VEN), 2012*
Strategic alliance	67. FARC and ELN in the municipality of Roberto Payán, Nariño (COL), 2011	69. FARC and ELN in Arauca (COL), 2010s
	68. FARC and ELN in parts of Nariño (COL), before 2006*	70. FARC's Front 41 Cacique Upar and Front 33 Mariscal Antonio José de Sucre and ELN's Front Camilo Torres Restrepo in the Catatumbo region, Norte de Santander (COL), around 2011
		71. FARC's Front 59 and ELN in Cesar/Baja Guajira (COL), and Zulia (VEN), around 2011*†
		72. paramilitary group under alias "Pablo" and Wayúu group in La Guajira (COL) and Zulia (VEN), around 2004*†
		73. Paisas and Wayúu groups in La Guajira (COL), 2009*
Pacific coexistence	74. various Colombian violent non-state groups in Sucumbíos (ECU), before 2008†	77. FBL, FARC, and ELN in Alto Apure (VEN), 2010s*†

(continued)

Table B.1 Continued

Interaction Type	Colombian-Ecuadorian Borderlands	Colombian-Venezuelan Borderlands
	75. FARC and ELN in Nariño's mobility corridors that connect the Andean zone with the coastal foothills including municipalities of Santa Cruz, Samaniego, Cumbitara, La Llanada, and Los Andes (COL), around 2011 76. various Colombian violent non-state groups in Esmeraldas (ECU), before 2008*	88. FARC and successors in parts of Arauca (COL) since 1980s 89. ELN in parts of Arauca (COL), 1980s to early 2000s 90. ELN in parts of Arauca (COL), 2012 91. ELN in parts of Apure (VEN) 1990s to early 2000s 92. Rastrojos in urban border areas of Cúcuta, Villa del Rosario, and Los Patios, Norte de Santander (COL), in 2009
Preponderance relations	78. FARC in Putumayo (COL), 1990s*† 79. FARC Front 48 in Putumayo including Puerto Guzmán (COL), and Sucumbíos (ECU), 2011–2012*† 80. post-demobilized groups in Puerto Asís, Putumayo (COL), 2012*† 81. guerrillas in Ipiales, Nariño (COL), 2000s 82. FARC in Cumbal and Samaniego in Nariño (COL), 2007* 83. FARC's mobile column Daniel Aldana in Cumbal, Cuaspud, and Carlosama in Nariño (COL) and Tallambí and Mayasquer in Carchi (ECU), around 2011/2012 84. FARC's mobile column Daniel Aldana in Ricaurte, Nariño (COL) and Carchi villages of Chical, Tufiño, and Maldonado, 2011/2012* 85. guerrillas in Llorente, Nariño (COL), around 2000 86. Rastrojos in Llorente, Nariño (COL), around 2011* 87. FARC Front 29 in Tumaco, Nariño (COL), and Esmeraldas (ECU), around 2010 to 2012*	93. Rastrojos in Puerto Santander, Norte de Santander (COL), 2012 94. guerrillas in Las Mercedes village, Sardinata, Norte de Santander (COL), 2006* 95. FARC and successors, ELN, and a section of EPL, in Catatumbo's rural areas and with militias in urban centres of Norte de Santander (COL), since 1970s 96. Águilas Negras in parts of Norte de Santander (COL), after 2006 97. guerrillas in Sierra de Perijá near Machiques, Zulia (VEN), 2012* 98. FARC's Front 4 and ELN in the Sierra de Perijá, Cesar (COL), after mid-1980s 99. FARC in northern Zulia (VEN), 2012*† 100. post-demobilized groups in Guayabo, Zulia (VEN), 2012*†

Appendix C

BORDERLAND FIELDWORK ITINERARIES

These maps only include the fieldwork that involved travel along and/or across the borders.

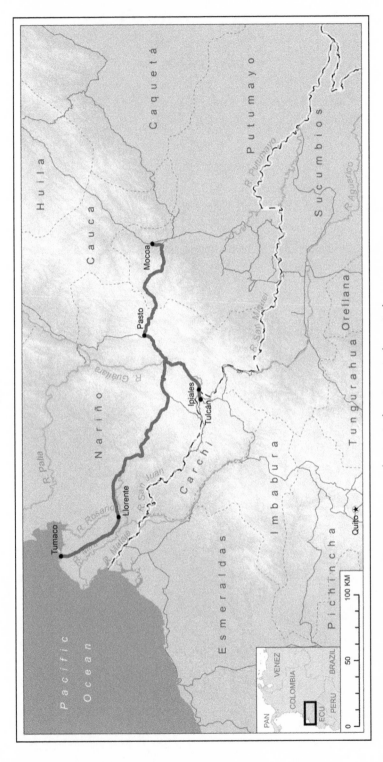

Map C.1 Fieldwork itinerary in Nariño and Putumayo (Colombia) and Carchi (Ecuador). Map created by Author.

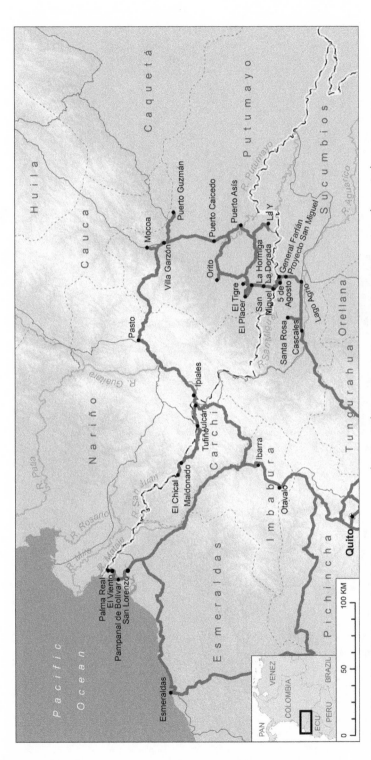

Map C.2 Fieldwork itinerary in Nariño and Putumayo (Colombia) and Esmeraldas, Carchi, and Sucumbíos (Ecuador). Map created by Author.

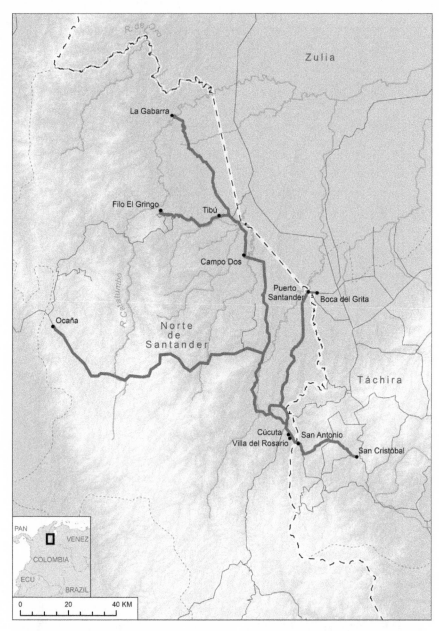

Map C.3 Fieldwork itinerary in Norte de Santander (Colombia) and Táchira (Venezuela). Map created by Author.

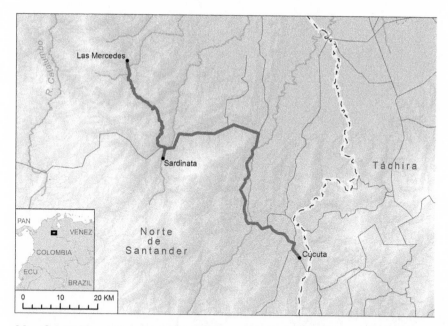

Map C.4 Fieldwork itinerary in Norte de Santander (Colombia). Map created by Author.

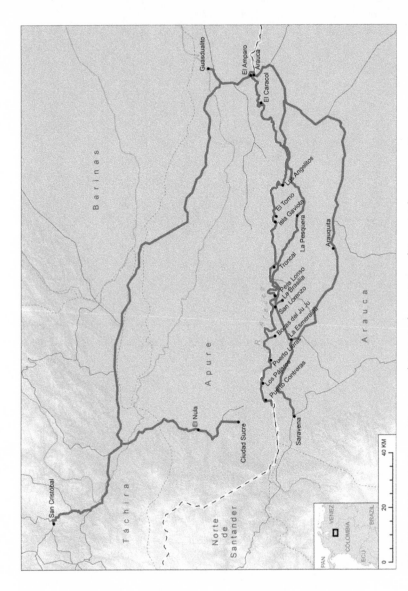

Map C.5 Fieldwork itinerary in Arauca (Colombia) and Apure (Venezuela). Map created by Author.

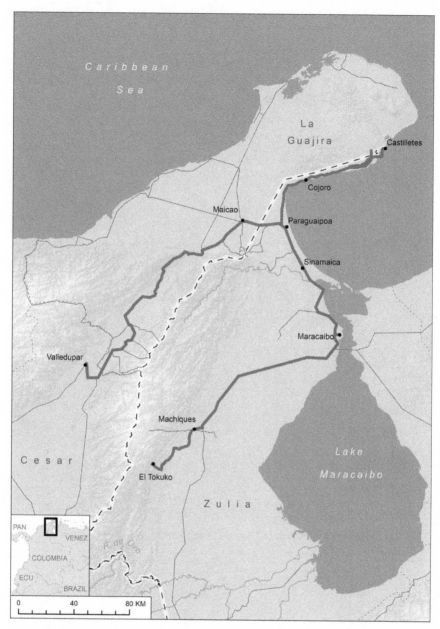

Map C.6 Fieldwork itinerary in Cesar and La Guajira (Colombia) and Zulia (Venezuela). Map created by Author.

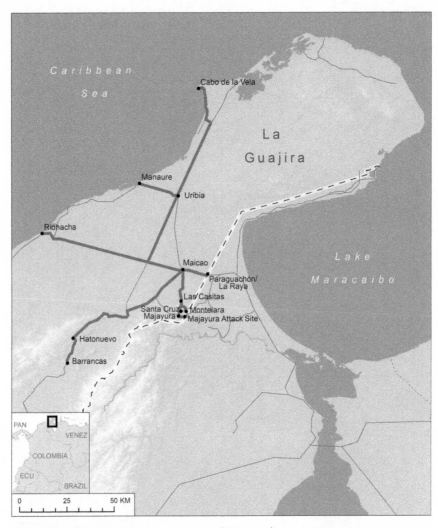

Map C.7 Fieldwork itinerary in La Guajira (Colombia). Map created by Author.

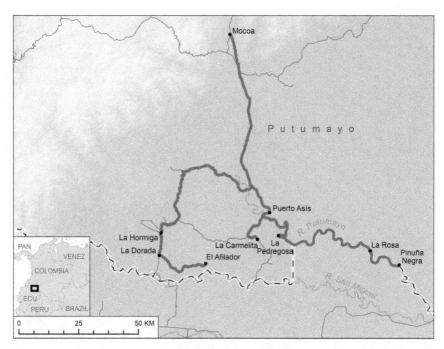

Map C.8 Fieldwork itinerary in Putumayo (Colombia). Map created by Author.

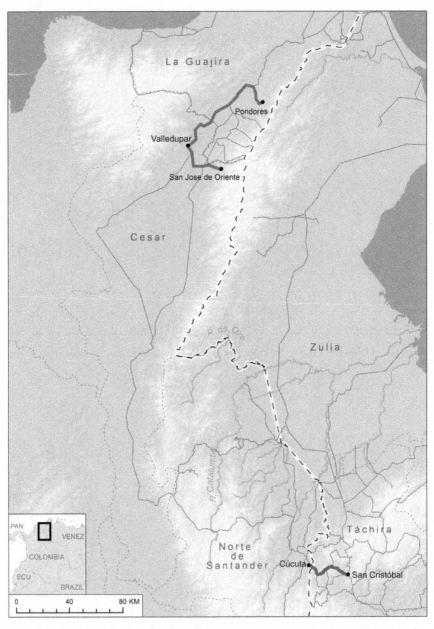

Map C.9 Fieldwork itinerary in Norte de Santander, Cesar and La Guajira (Colombia) and Táchira (Venezuela). Map created by Author.

NOTES

Prologue

1. Although many Colombianists emphasize the importance of the memories of "La Violencia" for understanding present-day violence in the country, no interviewee mentioned that era to me. While historical memories form part of the Colombian debate in the country's political center, their absence in Colombia's most war-torn regions suggests there may be another version of the less recent history at the margins that has lacked attention.

2. See, e.g., Grace Jaramillo, ed., "Las relaciones Ecuador-Colombia desde el incidente de Angostura," in *Construyendo puentes entre Ecuador y Colombia* (Quito: FLACSO OAS UNDP, 2009), 15–34; Gabriel Marcella, *War without Borders: The Colombia-Ecuador Crisis of 2008* (Strategic Studies Institute, 2008); "INTERPOL Rules Prohibit Publication of Blue Notice for Former Colombian Minister of Defence, 10 July 2009," 2009, http://www.interpol.int/Public/ICPO/PressReleases/PR2009/PR200969.asp.

3. Simon Romero, "Manuel Marulanda, Top Commander of Colombia's Largest Guerrilla Group, Is Dead," *New York Times*, May 26, 2008, sec. Americas, https://www.nytimes.com/2008/05/26/world/americas/26marulanda.html.

4. InSight Crime, "Guillermo Leon Saenz Vargas, Alias 'Alfonso Cano,'" *InSight Crime* (blog), March 10, 2017, https://www.insightcrime.org/colombia-organized-crime-news/guillermo-leon-saenz-vargas-alfonso-cano/.

5. This view was expressed to me by various well-regarded peace negotiation experts.

6. Carlos Nasi, "Colombia's Peace Processes, 1982–2002: Conditions, Strategies, and Outcomes," In *Colombia: Building Peace in a Time of War*, ed. Virginia Marie Bouvier, 39–64 (Washington, DC: United States Institute of Peace Press, 2009).

7. The EPL is another often forgotten, yet persistent, violent non-state group. It is considered a criminal group by the Colombian government.

8. *New York Times*, "Colombian Military Kills Warlord of Rural Cocaine Fiefdom," *New York Times*, October 2, 2015; BBC, "Colombia Kills Most Wanted Drug Lord," *BBC News*, October 2, 2015, sec. Latin America & Caribbean, http://www.bbc.co.uk/news/world-latin-america-34430555.

9. Annette Idler, "A Humanitarian and Diplomatic Crisis Is Unfolding on the Colombia-Venezuela Border," *The Conversation* (blog), September 10, 2015, https://theconversation.com/a-humanitarian-and-diplomatic-crisis-is-unfolding-on-the-colombia-venezuela-border-46994.

10. Nobel Prize, "Juan Manuel Santos—Facts," 2016, https://www.nobelprize.org/nobel_prizes/peace/laureates/2016/santos-facts.html.

11. Annette Idler, "Colombia Just Voted No on Its Plebiscite for Peace. Here's Why and What It Means," *Washington Post*, October 3, 2016, sec. Monkey Cage, https://www.washingtonpost.com/news/monkey-cage/wp/2016/10/03/colombia-just-voted-no-on-its-referendum-for-peace-heres-why-and-what-it-means/.

12. Noticias Caracol, "Santos y 'Timochenko' firman el acuerdo de paz definitivo," Noticias Caracol, November 24, 2016, https://noticias.caracoltv.com/acuerdo-final/ delegados-de-gobierno-y-farc-se-reunen-en-bogota-para-firma-del-nuevo-acuerdo; Noticias RCN, "Santos y 'Timochenko' firmaron el nuevo acuerdo en Bogotá," Noticias RCN, November 24, 2016, http://www.noticiasrcn.com/nacional-dialogos-paz/ santos-y-timochenko-firmaron-el-nuevo-acuerdo-bogota.

13. Jineth Prieto, "Las 10 razones por las que el EPL es un problema que se le creció al gobierno," La Silla Vacía, June 30, 2017, http://lasillavacia.com/historia/las-10-razones-por-las-que-el-epl-es-un-problema-que-se-le-crecio-al-gobierno-59861.

14. However, Colombia's presidential elections in 2018 went by without a FARC candidate, and the party performed poorly in Congressional elections.

Chapter 1

1. Interview with a human rights defender, Paraguaipoa, Venezuela, 2012.

2. Interview with a humanitarian organization employee, Cúcuta, Colombia, 2012.

3. Interview with a farmer, General Farfán, Ecuador, 2012.

4. Interview with an ex-guerrilla, Pasto, Colombia, 2011.

5. Borrowing the term from research on natural hazards and environmental change on the one hand, and poverty and development on the other, I define vulnerable regions as regions that are fragile and lack resilience; see Marco A. Janssen and Elinor Ostrom, "Resilience, Vulnerability, and Adaptation: A Cross-Cutting Theme of the International Human Dimensions Programme on Global Environmental Change," in "Resilience, Vulnerability, and Adaptation: A Cross-Cutting Theme of the International Human Dimensions Programme on Global Environmental Change," special issue, *Global Environmental Change* 16, no. 3 (August 1, 2006): 237–39, http://dx.doi.org/10.1016/j.gloenvcha.2006.04.003; Amartya Sen, *Poverty and Famines: An Essay on Entitlement and Deprivation* (Oxford: Clarendon Press, 1981). Regarding vulnerability in the context of natural hazards, Neil Adger, for example, highlights the "stress to which a system is exposed, its sensitivity, and its adaptive capacity." W. Neil Adger, "Vulnerability," in "Resilience, Vulnerability, and Adaptation: A Cross-Cutting Theme of the International Human Dimensions Programme on Global Environmental Change," special issue, *Global Environmental Change* 16, no. 3 (August 1, 2006): 296, https:// www.geos.ed.ac.uk/~nabo/meetings/glthec/materials/simpson/GEC_sdarticle2.pdf. In the context of poverty, Robert Chambers considers vulnerability to be "defencelessness, insecurity, and exposure to risk, shocks and stress" (Robert Chambers, "Vulnerability: How the Poor Cope," *IDS Bulletin* 20, no. 2 (1989)). "Regions" refer to territories at the subnational, supra-national, and transnational level. Contrary to the artificial binary division between Global North and Global South, the term "vulnerable regions" allows accounting for the existence of borderlands as the ones studied in this book across the globe.

6. Justin V. Hastings, *No Man's Land: Globalization, Territory, and Clandestine Groups in Southeast Asia* (Ithaca, NY: Cornell University Press, 2010).

7. Brian Perkins, "Factionalism of the Tehrik-i-Taliban Pakistan: Can the Pakistani Government Correct Past Deficiencies," *Small Wars Journal* (blog), July 19, 2014, http://smallwarsjournal. com/jrnl/art/factionalism-of-the-tehrik-i-taliban-pakistan-can-the-pakistani-government-correct-past-def.

8. Lindsay Scorgie, "Rwenzori Rebels: The Allied Democratic Forces Conflict in the Uganda-Congo Borderland" (University of Cambridge, 2012).

9. Ken Menkhaus and Jacob N. Shapiro, "Non-State Actors and Failed States. Lessons from Al-Qua'ida's Experiences in the Horn of Africa," in *Ungoverned Spaces: Alternatives to State Authority in an Era of Softened Sovereignty*, ed. Anne L. Clunan and Harold A. Trinkunas (Stanford, CA: Stanford University Press, 2010), 77–94; Stig Jarle Hansen, *Al-Shabaab in Somalia: The History and Ideology of a Militant Islamist Group, 2005–2012* (London: C. Hurst & Co. Publishers Ltd., 2013).

10. Rex Hudson, "Terrorist and Organized Crime Groups in the Tri-Border Area (TBA) of South America," a Report Prepared by the Federal Research Division, Library of Congress under an Interagency Agreement with the Crime and Narcotics Center Director of Central

Intelligence (Washington, DC: Library of Congress, 2003); Christine Folch, "Trouble on the Triple Frontier," *Foreign Affairs*, September 6, 2012, http://www.foreignaffairs.com/articles/138096/christine-folch/trouble-on-the-triple-frontier.

11. Shaylih Muehlmann, *When I Wear My Alligator Boots: Narco-Culture in the US-Mexico Borderlands* (Berkeley: University of California Press, 2014).

12. Henry Patterson, *Ireland's Violent Frontier: The Border and Anglo-Irish Relations during the Troubles* (Basingstoke: Palgrave Macmillan, 2013).

13. Carter Center, "Syria. Countrywide Conflict" (Atlanta, GA: Carter Center, 2014), http://www.cartercenter.org/resources/pdfs/peace/conflict_resolution/syria-conflict/NationwideUpdate-Sept-18-2014.pdf.

14. See Angélica Durán-Martínez, "To Kill and Tell? State Power, Criminal Competition, and Drug Violence," *Journal of Conflict Resolution*, June 9, 2015, 1–27, http://journals.sagepub.com/doi/abs/10.1177/0022002715587047; Phil Williams, *Criminals, Militias, and Insurgents: Organized Crime in Iraq* (Carlisle, PA: Strategic Studies Institute, 2009); Dennis Rodgers and Adam Baird, "Understanding Gangs in Contemporary Latin America," in *Handbook of Gangs and Gang Responses*, ed. Scott Decker and David Pyronz (New York: Wiley, 2015); Fotini Christia, *Alliance Formation in Civil Wars* (Cambridge, UK: Cambridge University Press, 2012).

15. For signaling between criminals see Diego Gambetta, *Codes of the Underworld: How Criminals Communicate* (Princeton, NJ: Princeton University Press, 2009).

16. United Nations; World Bank, *Pathways for Peace: Inclusive Approaches to Preventing Violent Conflict* (Washington, DC: World Bank, 2018), 14–19.

17. I consider Colombia a case with ongoing armed conflict due to the active rebel group ELN. The armed conflict between FARC and the government ended with the signing of the peace agreement in 2016 (see Prologue and below).

18. See chapter 2 for how I define violent non-state groups.

19. Hastings Donnan and Thomas M. Wilson, *Border Approaches: Anthropological Perspectives on Frontiers* (Lanham, MD: University Press of America, 1994); M. Baud and W. van Schendel, "Toward a Comparative History of Borderlands," *Journal of World History* 8 (1997): 211–42, https://doi.org/10.1353/jwh.2005.0061.

20. Peter Andreas, *Border Games: Policing the US-Mexico Divide*, 2nd ed. (Ithaca, NY: Cornell University Press, 2009); Willem van Schendel, "Spaces of Engagement: How Borderlands, Illegal Flows, and Territorial States Interlock," in *Illicit Flows and Criminal Things: States, Borders, and the Other Side of Globalization*, ed. Willem van Schendel and Itty Abraham (Bloomington: Indiana University Press, 2005), 38–68.

21. Interview with a member of the church, Ecuadorian northern border zone, Ecuador, 2012.

22. I visited all borderland areas except Venezuelan Amazonas, and Colombian Vichada and Guainía.

23. For a discussion of the research design see appendix A. For the role of reflexivity in research in and on war-torn and violent settings see the Epilogue.

24. See appendix A for the case selection.

25. El País, "7 Infiernos sobre la tierra que jamás deberías visitar," January 22, 2015, http://verne.elpais.com/verne/2015/01/20/articulo/1421773872_248222.html.

26. See, e.g., Phillip McLean, "Colombia: Failed, Failing, or Just Weak?" *Washington Quarterly* 25, no. 3 (2002): 123–34; Juan Manuel Tokatlian, "La construcción de un 'Estado fallido' en la política mundial: El caso de las relaciones entre Estados Unidos y Colombia," *Análisis político* no. 64 (Bogotá, 2008): 67–104.

27. Arlene B. Tickner, Diego García, and Catalina Arrezea, "Actores violentos no estatales y narcotráfico en Colombia," in *Políticas antidroga en Colombia: Éxitos, fracasos, y extravíos* (Bogotá: Universidad de los Andes, 2011), 424.

28. Even though they had entered peace negotiations and agreed to a fragile bilateral ceasefire with the government (see Prologue).

29. Centro Nacional de Memoria Histórica, "Hasta encontrarlos. El drama de la desaparición forzada en Colombia" (Bogotá: Centro Nacional de Memoria Histórica, 2016), 17.

30. United Nations High Commissioner for Refugees, "Colombia Situation Update, December 2016," December 2016, http://www.refworld.org/docid/58627cd24.html.

31. Unidad para las Víctimas, "Registro Único de Víctimas (RUV)," 2018, https://www.
unidadvictimas.gov.co/en/node/37394.

32. This balance shifted again. In addition to leading in processing and trafficking, as of 2015,
Colombia was also the world's principal coca leaf producer; United Nations Office on Drugs
and Crime, "World Drug Report 2017" (Vienna: United Nations Office on Drugs and Crime,
2017), 25.

33. The paramilitaries were groups of armed civilians formed by landowners and traffickers,
with the support of the state, to fight the presence of left-wing guerrillas in the rural areas of
Colombia. See Edgar de Jesús Velásquez Rivera, "Historia del Paramilitarismo en Colombia,"
Historia 26, no. 1 (São Paulo, 2007): 134–53; Otty Patiño, "El Fenómeno Paramilitar en
Colombia: Bajo el Volcán," *Puebla* 3, no. 6 (2003): 71–91; Jacobo Grajales, *Gobernar en Medio
de la Violencia: Estado y Paramilitarismo en Colombia* (Bogotá: Universidad del Rosario, 2017).

34. The destruction of the cartels was a result of various factors, including the conflicts these
cartels had with each other, operations of the Colombian National Police, and the killing of
drug kingpin Pablo Escobar in 1993. For longer discussions see, for example, Adolfo Atehortúa
and Diana Rojas, "El Narcotráfico en Colombia: Pionero y Capos," *Historia y Espacio* 4, no. 31
(2008): 169–207; Camilo Chaparro, *Historia del Cartel de Cali* (Bogotá: Intermedio, 2005).

35. This is an analogy to air being squeezed in a balloon: it does not disappear, but moves to another area of the balloon.

36. The United Self-Defense Forces of Colombia formed near the northern coast of Colombia
in response to the frequent violent acts by left-wing guerrillas. Fidel Castaño started the
formation of the AUC in 1993, followed by his younger brother Carlos, who took control
in 2000. See, for example, Edgar de Jesús Velásquez Rivera, "Historia del Paramilitarismo
en Colombia," *Historia*, 26, no. 1 (São Paulo, 2007): 134–53; Ayala Osorio Germán,
Paramilitarismo en Colombia: Más allá de un fenómeno de violencia política (Cali: Universidad
Autónoma de Occidente, 2011).

37. Winifred Tate, *Drugs, Thugs, and Diplomats: US Policymaking in Colombia*, Anthropology
of Policy (Stanford, CA: Stanford University Press, 2015); Aldo Civico, *The Para-State: An
Ethnography of Colombia's Death Squads* (Oakland: University of California Press, 2016), 209–
10. According to one of the principal paramilitary leaders, Vicente Castaño Gil, more than
35 percent of the members of the Colombian Congress were linked to criminal groups, primarily those involved in the illicit drug trade; "Habla Vicente Castaño," *Revista Semana*, June
5, 2005, http://www.semana.com/portada/articulo/ habla-vicente-castano/72964-3. This
"para-politics" scandal halted Colombia's legislature and triggered extensive investigations;
see Verdad Abierta, "De la curul a la cárcel," August 28, 2013, http://www.verdadabierta.
com/component/content/article/63-nacional/4800-de-la-curul-a-la-carcel. At the height of
the investigations, they concerned more than one-third of the members of Congress. IDEA,
Illicit Networks and Politics in Latin America (Stockholm: International DEA, 2014), 19.

38. Edgar de Jesús Velásquez Rivera, "Historia del Paramilitarismo en Colombia," *Historia* 26, no.
1 (São Paulo, 2007): 139; Ayala Osorio, *Paramilitarismo en Colombia: Más allá de un fenómeno
de violencia Política* (Cali: Universidad Autónoma de Occidente, 2011), 56–60.

39. See chapter 3 for a discussion of how members of the political elite and of the state forces
supported the paramilitary North Bloc in Cesar.

40. For a discussion of the impact of US foreign policy on Colombia see Tate, *Drugs, Thugs,
and Diplomats*; for an analysis of counterinsurgency in Colombia see Dickie Davis, *A Great
Perhaps? Colombia: Conflict and Convergence* (London: Hurst & Company, 2016).

41. Annette Idler, "Preventing Conflict Upstream: Impunity and Illicit Governance across
Colombia's Borders," *Defence Studies* 18, no. 1 (2018): 65.

42. Abigail Poe and Adam Isacson, "Ecuador's Humanitarian Emergency: The Spillover of
Colombia's Conflict" (Washington, DC: Center for International Policy, 2009); Juan Camilo
Molina, "Cooperación internacional al desarrollo y refugio en la frontera norte en Ecuador,"
Ventana a La Cooperación, 2009, 2–19.

43. Zuli Laverde and Edwin Tapia, *Tensión en las fronteras: Un análisis sobre el conflicto armado,
el desplazamiento forzado y el refugio en las fronteras de Colombia con Ecuador, Venezuela, y
Panamá* (Bogotá: Consultoría para los Derechos Humanos y el Desplazamiento Forzado
CODHES, 2009), 95.

44. Soledad Granada, Jorge Restrepo, and Andrés Tobón, "Neoparamilitarismo en Colombia: Una herramienta conceptual para la interpretación de dinámicas recientes del conflicto armado colombiano," in *Guerra y violencias en Colombia. Herramientas e interpretaciones*, ed. J. Restrepo and D. Aponte (Bogotá: Pontificia Universidad Javeriana, 2009); Human Rights Watch, "Paramilitaries' Heirs: The New Face of Violence in Colombia" (New York: Human Rights Watch, 2010). For discussions of whether the term "BACRIM" disguises the real nature of these groups see Pérez-Santiago "Colombia's BACRIM: Common Criminals or Actors in Armed Conflict?," InSight Crime—Organized Crime in the Americas, July 13, 2012, http://www.insightcrime.org/news-analysis/colombias-bacrim-common-criminals-or-actors-in-armed-conflict and Arias Ortiz, "Las BACRIM retan a Santos," *Arcanos*, Corporación Nuevo Arco Iris, 15, no. 17 (2012): 4–35.

45. Consolidación Territorial, "Regiones en Consolidación," 2012, http://www.consolidacion.gov.co/?q=content/regiones-en-consolidaci%C3%B3n.

46. For cross-border false positives see section 7.1. See International Crisis Group, "The Virtuous Twins: Protecting Human Rights and Improving Security in Colombia" (Bogotá Brussels: International Crisis Group, 2009), 8; Alston, "Mission to Colombia of the Special Rapporteur on Extrajudicial, Summary, or Arbitrary Executions," March 31, 2010.

47. See appendix A for the book's research design.

48. *The SAGE Dictionary of Qualitative Inquiry*, 3rd ed. (London: SAGE, 2007), 93.

49. Schwandt, 93–94.

50. Susan L. Woodward, *Balkan Tragedy: Chaos and Dissolution after the Cold War* (Washington, DC Brookings Institution, 1995); Elisabeth Jean Wood, *Insurgent Collective Action and Civil War in El Salvador* (Cambridge, UK: Cambridge University Press, 2003); Séverine Autesserre, *The Trouble with the Congo: Local Violence and the Failure of International Peacebuilding* (Cambridge, UK: Cambridge University Press, 2010).

51. George E. Marcus, "Ethnography in/of the World System: The Emergence of Multi-Sited Ethnography," *Annual Review of Anthropology* 24, no. 1 (1995): 105.

52. Marcus, 106–10.

53. Mark-Anthony Falzon, *Multi-Sited Ethnography: Theory, Praxis, and Locality in Contemporary Research* (Ashgate Publishing, Ltd., 2009), 2.

54. Colombian departments, Ecuadorian provinces, and Venezuelan states are the administrative territorial units that correspond to each other.

55. Orin Starn, *Nightwatch: The Politics of Protest in the Andes* (Durham, NC: Duke University Press, 1999), 15.

56. See Sue Wilkinson, "Focus Group Research," in *Qualitative Research: Theory, Method, and Practice*, ed. David Silverman, 2nd ed. (London; Thousand Oaks, CA: Sage Publications, 2004), 178.

57. Schwandt, *The SAGE Dictionary of Qualitative Inquiry*, 220.

58. Raymond L. Gold, "Roles in Sociological Field Observations," *Social Forces* 36, no. 3 (1958): 217–23, https://doi.org/10.2307/2573808; Buford H. Junker, *Field Work: An Introduction to the Social Sciences* (Chicago: University of Chicago Press, 1960), 35–38; see also Robert G. Burgess, *In the Field: An Introduction to Field Research* (London: Routledge, 1990), 80, 83; Martyn Hammersley and Paul Atkinson, *Ethnography: Principles in Practice* (London: Routledge, 2007), 82.

59. Isabelle Baszanger and Nicolas Dodier, "Ethnography: Relating the Part to the Whole," in *Qualitative Research: Theory, Method, and Practice*, ed. David Silverman, 2nd ed. (London: Sage Publications, 2004), 12.

60. I use "interaction" for all behavioral patterns; "arrangements" include the interactions in the "rivalry" and "friendship" clusters; "relations" include the interactions in the "rivalry" and "friendship" clusters except spot sales and barter agreements.

61. See appendix B for an overview of these hundred observations and appendix A on how I identified them. See Maps 3.5 and 3.7 for the observations dated between 2011 and 2013.

62. Anne L. Clunan and Harold A. Trinkunas, eds., *Ungoverned Spaces: Alternatives to State Authority in an Era of Softened Sovereignty* (Stanford, CA: Stanford University Press, 2010).

63. See, e.g., G. O'Donnell, "Reflections on Contemporary South American Democracies," *Journal of Latin American Studies* 33 (2001): 599–609, https://doi.org/10.1017/

S0022216X01006125; Laurence Whitehead, "On Citizen Security," in *Democratization: Theory and Experience* (Oxford: Oxford University Press, 2002), 165–85.

64. Pinar Bilgin, "Critical Theory," in *Security Studies: An Introduction*, ed. Paul D. Williams, 2nd ed. (London: Routledge, 2013), 103; see also Cynthia Enloe, "Margins, Silences, and Bottom Rungs," in *International Theory: Positivism and Beyond*, ed. Steve Smith, Ken Booth, and Marysia Zalewski (Cambridge, UK: Cambridge University Press, 1996), 186–202.

65. For Europe see Heikki Eskelinen, Ilkka Liikanen, and Jukka Oksa, *Curtains of Iron and Gold: Reconstructing Borders and Scales of Interaction* (Aldershot: Ashgate, 1999); James Anderson, Liam O'Dowd, and Thomas M. Wilson, *New Borders for a Changing Europe: Cross-Border Cooperation and Governance* (London: Frank Cass, 2003); Thomas M. Wilson and Hastings Donnan, *Culture and Power at the Edges of the State: National Support and Subversion in European Border Regions* (Münster: Lit, 2005). For Africa see Dereje Feyissa and Markus Virgil Höhne, *Borders & Borderlands as Resources in the Horn of Africa* (Oxford: James Currey, 2010). For Asia see I. William Zartman, *Understanding Life in the Borderlands: Boundaries in Depth and in Motion* (Athens: University of Georgia Press, 2010); Benedikt Korf and Timothy Raeymaekers, *Violence on the Margins: States, Conflict, and Borderlands* (New York: Palgrave Macmillan, 2013).

66. For the US-Mexico border see Oscar J. Martínez, *Border People: Life and Society in the US-Mexico Borderlands* (Tucson: University of Arizona Press, 1994); Joel Simon, *Endangered Mexico: An Environnment on the Edge* (London: Latin American Bureau, 1998); Andreas, *Border Games*. For the Andean borderlands see Ariel Ávila, ed., *La frontera caliente entre Colombia y Venezuela* (Cota, Colombia: Corporación Nuevo Arco Iris, 2012); Zully Laverde and Edwin Tapia, *Tensión en las fronteras* (Bogotá: CODHES, 2009); Ivan Briscoe, *Trouble on the Borders: Latin America's New Conflict Zones*, Comment (Madrid: FRIDE, 2008); International Crisis Group, "Moving beyond Easy Wins: Colombia's Borders," Latin America Report (Bogotá, Brussels: International Crisis Group, 2011). There are few exceptions such as Bustamante, "The Border Region of North Santander (Colombia)-Táchira (Venezuela): The Border without Walls," *Journal of Borderlands Studies* 23 (2008).

67. See, e.g., Eduardo Pizarro Leongómez, *Una democracia asediada: Balance y perspectivas del conflicto armado en Colombia* (Bogotá: Grupo Editorial Norma, 2004); Daniel Pécaut, *Guerra contra la sociedad* (Bogotá: Espasa, 2001); Frank Safford and Marco Palacios, *Colombia: Fragmented Land, Divided Society* (New York: Oxford University Press, 2002).

68. Angel Rabasa and Peter Chalk, *Colombian Labyrinth: The Synergy of Drugs and Insurgency and Its Implications for Regional Stability* (Santa Monica, CA: Rand, 2001); Carlos Malamud, *The Long Road to Peace in Colombia. Colombia's Difficult Relations with Its Neighbours: Venezuela*, Part 2 (Madrid: Real Instituto Elcano, 2004).

69. Poe and Isacson, "Ecuador's Humanitarian Emergency: The Spillover of Colombia's Conflict"; Richard Millett, *Colombia's Conflicts: The Spillover Effects of a Wider War* (Carlisle, PA: Strategic Studies Institute, 2002); Laura González Carranza, *Peones en un ajedrez militar: Los habitantes de la frontera norte* (Quito: Fundación Regional de Asesoría en Derechos Humanos, 2011); Fernando Carrión and Johanna Espín, *Relaciones fronterizas: Encuentros y conflictos* (Quito: Flacso-Sede Ecuador, 2011).

70. Socorro Ramírez, "Civil Society Peacebuilding on Colombia's Borders," in *Accord. An International Review of Peace Initiatives, Building Peace across Borders*, ed. William Zartman and Alexander Ramsbotham, Accord 22 (London: Conciliation Resources, 2011), 60–61, http://www.c-r.org/accord-article/civil-society-peacebuilding-colombias-borders;   Ana Bustamante, "La frontera colombo-venezolana: De la conflictividad limítrofe a la global," in *Relaciones fronterizas: Encuentros y conflictos*, ed. Fernando Carrión and Johanna Espín (Quito: Flacso-Sede Ecuador, 2011), 203–22.

71. Ann Mason and Arlene B. Tickner, "A Transregional Security Cartography of the Andes," in *State and Society in Conflict: Comparative Perspectives on the Andean Crises*, ed. Paul W. Drake and Eric Hershberg (Pittsburgh: University of Pittsburgh Press, 2006), 74–98; Tickner, García, and Arrezea, "Actores violentos no estatales y narcotráfico en Colombia."

72. Human Rights Watch, "Paramilitaries' Heirs. The New Face of Violence in Colombia."

73. Jonathan Goodhand, "Epilogue: The View from the Border," in *Violence on the Margins: States, Conflict, and Borderlands*, ed. Benedikt Korf and Timothy Raeymaekers (New York: Palgrave

Macmillan, 2013), 247; see also Zartman, *Understanding Life in the Borderlands*; Korf and Raeymaekers, *Violence on the Margins*.

74. Barbara J. Morehouse, Vera Pavlakovich-Kochi, and Doris Wastl-Walter, "Introduction: Perspectives on Borderlands," in *Challenged Borderlands: Transcending Political and Cultural Boundaries*, ed. Barbara J. Morehouse, Vera Pavlakovich-Kochi, and Doris Wastl-Walter (Aldershot: Ashgate, 2004), 28; see also Hastings Donnan and Thomas M. Wilson, *Borderlands: Ethnographic Approaches to Security, Power, and Identity* (Lanham, MD: University Press of America, 2010), http://www.ebrary.com/landing/site/bodleian/index-bodleian.jsp?Docid=10602209.

75. Korf and Raeymaekers, *Violence on the Margins*, 5.

76. I. Salehyan, "Transnational Rebels—Neighboring States as Sanctuary for Rebel Groups," *World Politics* 59 (2007): 217–42, https://doi.org/10.1353/wp.2007.0024.

77. Morehouse, Pavlakovich-Kochi, and Wastl-Walter, "Introduction: Perspectives on Borderlands," 28.

78. Talal Asad, "Where Are the Margins of the State?," in *Anthropology in the Margins of the State*, ed. Veena Das and Deborah Poole (Santa Fe, NM: School for Advanced Research Press; Oxford, 2004), 279–88.

79. Steven Vertovec, *Transnationalism*, Key Ideas (New York: Routledge, 2009); Sanjeev Khagram and Peggy Levitt, *The Transnational Studies Reader: Intersections and Innovations* (New York: Routledge, 2008).

80. Annette Idler and James J. F. Forest, "Behavioral Patterns among (Violent) Non-State Actors: A Study of Complementary Governance" *Stability: International Journal of Security and Development* 4, no. 1 (2015): 1–19, http://dx.doi.org/10.5334/sta.er.

81. For the importance of understanding micro processes in conflict research see, e.g., Stathis N. Kalyvas, *The Logic of Violence in Civil War* (Cambridge, UK: Cambridge University Press, 2006); Zachariah Cherian Mampilly, *Rebel Rulers: Insurgent Governance and Civilian Life during War* (Ithaca, NY: Cornell University Press, 2011); Jeremy M. Weinstein, *Inside Rebellion: The Politics of Insurgent Violence* (Cambridge, UK: Cambridge University Press, 2006).

82. This book discusses coping and avoidance strategies. I analyze more proactive manifestations of agency such as nonviolent resistance elsewhere. See, e.g., Annette Idler, María Belén Garrido, and Cécile Mouly, "Peace Territories in Colombia: Comparing Civil Resistance in Two War-Torn Communities," *Journal of Peacebuilding & Development* 10, no. 3 (September 2, 2015): 1–15, https://doi.org/10.1080/15423166.2015.1082437.

83. See Stathis N. Kalyvas, "The Urban Bias in Research on Civil Wars," *Security Studies* 13, no. 3 (March 1, 2004): 160–90, https://doi.org/10.1080/09636410490914022.

84. See, e.g., Ariel Ávila, *La frontera caliente entre Colombia y Venezuela*.

85. For similar approaches see Douglas Lemke, "Power Politics and Wars without States," *American Journal of Political Science* 52, no. 4 (2008): 774–86, http://onlinelibrary.wiley.com/doi/10.1111/j.1540-5907.2008.00342.x/abstract; Stacie E. Goddard and Daniel H. Nexon, "The Dynamics of Global Power Politics: A Framework for Analysis," *Journal of Global Security Studies* 1, no. 1 (February 1, 2016): 4–18, https://doi.org/10.1093/jogss/ogv007.

86. Kalyvas, *The Logic of Violence in Civil War*; Laia Balcells, "Rivalry and Revenge: Violence against Civilians in Conventional Civil Wars," *International Studies Quarterly* 54, no. 2 (2010): 291–313, http://onlinelibrary.wiley.com/doi/10.1111/j.1468-2478.2010.00588.x/abstract.

87. Navin A. Bapat and Kanisha D. Bond, "Alliances between Militant Groups," *British Journal of Political Science* 42, no. 4 (2012): 793–824, https://doi.org/10.1017/S0007123412000075; Henning Tamm, "The Origins of Transnational Alliances: Rulers, Rebels, and Political Survival in the Congo Wars," *International Security* 41, no. 1 (July 1, 2016): 147–81, http://dx.doi.org/10.1162/ISEC_a_00252; Aisha Ahmad, "The Security Bazaar: Business Interests and Islamist Power in Civil War Somalia," *International Security* 39, no. 3 (January 1, 2015): 89–117, http://dx.doi.org/10.1162/ISEC_a_00187; Phil Williams, "Cooperation among Criminal Organizations," in *Transnational Organized Crime and International Security: Business as Usual?*, ed. Mats R. Berdal (Boulder, CO: Lynne Rienner, 2002), 67–82.

88. See, e.g., Paolo Campana and Federico Varese, "Cooperation in Criminal Organizations: Kinship and Violence as Credible Commitments," *Rationality and Society* 25, no. 3 (August 1, 2013): 263–89, http://journals.sagepub.com/doi/abs/10.1177/1043463113481202; Stathis N. Kalyvas, Ian Shapiro, and Tarek Masoud, eds., *Order, Conflict, and Violence* (Cambridge, UK: Cambridge University Press, 2008). While scholars have highlighted durable cooperation among organized criminals, including a *pax mafiosa* (see, e.g., Claire Sterling, *Crime without Frontiers: The Worldwide Expansion of Organised Crime and the Pax Mafiosa* [London: Warner Books, 1995]), little attention has been given to short-lived alliances (Willem van Schendel, "Spaces of Engagement. How Borderlands, Illegal Flows, and Territorial States Interlock," in *Illicit Flows and Criminal Things: States, Borders, and the Other Side of Globalization*, ed. Willem van Schendel and Itty Abraham [Bloomington: Indiana University Press, 2005], 51, 65).

89. See, e.g., Kristin M. Bakke, Kathleen Gallagher Cunningham, and Lee J. M. Seymour, "A Plague of Initials: Fragmentation, Cohesion, and Infighting in Civil Wars," *Perspectives on Politics* 10, no. 2 (June 2012): 265–83, https://doi.org/10.1017/S1537592712000667; Lee J. M. Seymour, "Why Factions Switch Sides in Civil Wars: Rivalry, Patronage, and Realignment in Sudan," *International Security* 39, no. 2 (October 1, 2014): 92–131, http://dx.doi.org/10.1162/ISEC_a_00179; Wendy Pearlman and Kathleen Gallagher Cunningham, "Nonstate Actors, Fragmentation, and Conflict Processes," *Journal of Conflict Resolution* 56, no. 1 (February 1, 2012): 3–15, https://doi.org/10.1177/0022002711429669; Theodore McLauchlin, Wendy Pearlman, and Kathleen Gallagher Cunningham, "Out-Group Conflict, In-Group Unity?: Exploring the Effect of Repression on Intramovement Cooperation," *Journal of Conflict Resolution* 56, no. 1 (February 1, 2012): 41–66, http://journals.sagepub.com/doi/abs/10.1177/0022002711429707; Reed M. Wood and Jacob D. Kathman, "Competing for the Crown: Inter-Rebel Competition and Civilian Targeting in Civil War," *Political Research Quarterly* 68, no. 1 (2015): 167–79, http://dx.doi.org/10.1177/1065912914563546; Theodore McLauchlin, "Loyalty Strategies and Military Defection in Rebellion," *Comparative Politics* 42, no. 3 (March 31, 2010): 333–50, https://doi.org/10.5129/001041510X12911363509792; David E. Cunningham, Kristian Skrede Gleditsch, and Idean Salehyan, "Non-State Actors in Civil Wars: A New Dataset," *Conflict Management and Peace Science* 30, no. 5 (November 1, 2013): 516–31, https://doi.org/10.1177/0738894213499673.

90. Thomas C. Schelling, *The Strategy of Conflict* (Cambridge, MA: Harvard University Press, 1980); Williams, "Cooperation among Criminal Organizations"; Tamara Makarenko, "The Crime-Terror Continuum: Tracing the Interplay between Transnational Organised Crime and Terrorism," *Global Crime* 6, no. 1 (2004): 129–45, https://doi.org/10.1080/1744057042000297025. See Saab and Taylor, "Criminality and Armed Groups: A Comparative Study of FARC and Paramilitary Groups in Colombia," *Studies in Conflict & Terrorism* 32 (2009): 455–75, https://doi.org/10.1080/10576100902892570. For a discussion of conspiracy theories see Sterling, *Crime without Frontiers: The Worldwide Expansion of Organised Crime and the Pax Mafiosa*; Ehrenfeld, *Narco-Terrorism* and for in-house criminality theories see Chris Dishman, "Terrorism, Crime, and Transformation," *Studies in Conflict & Terrorism* 24 (2001): 43–58.

91. *Criminals, Militias, and Insurgents.* "From the Banality of Violence to Real Terror: The Case of Colombia," in *Societies of Fear: The Legacy of Civil War, Violence, and Terror in Latin America*, ed. Kees Koonings and Dirk Krujit (London: Zed Books, 1999), 144–45.

92. Diego Gambetta, *The Sicilian Mafia: The Business of Private Protection* (Cambridge, MA: Harvard University Press, 1993); Federico Varese, *The Russian Mafia: Private Protection in a New Market Economy* (Oxford: Oxford University Press, 2001); Diego Gambetta, *Codes of the Underworld*.

93. Schelling, *The Strategy of Conflict*; R. Thomas Naylor, *Economic Warfare: Sanctions, Embargo Busting, and Their Human Cost* (Boston: Northeastern University Press, 2001); Campana and Varese, "Cooperation in Criminal Organizations."

94. Peter Andreas, "Criminalized Legacies of War. The Clandestine Political Economy of the Western Balkans," *Problems of Post-Communism* 51, no. 3 (June 2004): 3–9, http://www.tandfonline.com/doi/abs/10.1080/10758216.2004.11052164.

95. Ioan Grillo, *El Narco: The Bloody Rise of Mexican Drug Cartels* (London: Bloomsbury, 2013); Scott Stewart, "Mexico and the Cartel Wars in 2010," Security Weekly (Stratfor. Global Intelligence, 2010), http://www.stratfor.com/weekly/20101215-mexico-and-cartel-wars-2010.

96. Kimberly Marten, "Warlordism in Comparative Perspective," *International Security* 31, no. 3 (January 1, 2007): 41–73, http://dx.doi.org/10.1162/isec.2007.31.3.41.

97. Martha Crenshaw, *Explaining Terrorism: Causes, Processes, and Consequences* (London: Routledge, 2011).

98. Kalyvas, *The Logic of Violence in Civil War*; Weinstein, *Inside Rebellion*; Ana Arjona, "Social Order in Civil War." (PhD diss., Yale University, 2010).

99. Ted Robert Gurr, *Why Men Rebel* (Princeton, NJ Princeton University Press, 1970); James C. Scott, *Weapons of the Weak: Everyday Forms of Peasant Resistance* (New Haven: Yale University Press, 1985).

100. I build on the work of few other scholars with a similar approach, e.g., Andreas, "Criminalized Legacies of War. The Clandestine Political Economy of the Western Balkans"; William Reno, "Crime versus War," in *The Changing Character of War*, ed. Hew Strachan and Sibylle Scheipers, CCW Series (Oxford: Oxford University Press, 2011), 220–40. Stathis N. Kalyvas, "How Civil Wars Help Explain Organized Crime—and How They Do Not," *Journal of Conflict Resolution*, June 4, 2015, 1517–40, http://journals.sagepub.com/doi/abs/10.1177/0022002715587101. For authors who make similar points see Peter Andreas, "International Politics and the Illicit Global Economy," *Perspectives on Politics* 13, no. 3 (September 2015): 782–88, https://doi.org/10.1017/S1537592715001358; Sarah Percy and Anja Shortland, "The Business of Piracy in Somalia," *Journal of Strategic Studies* 36, no. 4 (August 1, 2013): 541–78, https://doi.org/10.1080/01402390.2012.750242.

101. For variation in state-non-state relations see Paul Staniland, "States, Insurgents, and Wartime Political Orders," *Perspectives on Politics* 10, no. 2 (2012): 243–64, https://doi.org/10.1017/S1537592712000655.

102. Amelia Hoover Green, "Repertoires of Violence against Noncombatants: The Role of Armed Group Institutions and Ideologies" (PhD diss., Yale University, 2011).

103. See, e.g., Francisco Gutiérrez Sanín, "Telling the Difference: Guerrillas and Paramilitaries in the Colombian War," *Politics & Society* 36, no. 1 (March 1, 2008): 3–34, http://journals.sagepub.com/doi/abs/10.1177/0032329207312181.

104. Paul Collier, *Breaking the Conflict Trap: Civil War and Development Policy* (Washington, DC; Oxford: World Bank; Oxford University Press, 2003); Kalyvas, *The Logic of Violence in Civil War*; Macartan Humphreys and Jeremy M. Weinstein, "Handling and Manhandling Civilians in Civil War," *American Political Science Review* 100, no. 3 (August 2006); Weinstein, *Inside Rebellion*; Dara Kay Cohen, "Explaining Sexual Violence during Civil War" (PhD diss., Stanford University, 2010); Stathis N. Kalyvas, "Micro-Level Studies of Violence in Civil War: Refining and Extending the Control-Collaboration Model," *Terrorism and Political Violence* 24, no. 4 (2012): 658–68; Human Rights Watch, "Paramilitaries' Heirs. The New Face of Violence in Colombia."

105. C. Hale, "Fear of Crime: A Review of the Literature," *International Review of Victimology* 4, no. 2 (January 1, 1996): 79–150, http://journals.sagepub.com/doi/abs/10.1177/026975809600400201; Murray Lee, "The Genesis of `Fear of Crime'," *Theoretical Criminology* 5, no. 4 (November 1, 2001): 467–85, http://journals.sagepub.com/doi/abs/10.1177/1362480601005004004; Stephen D. Farrall, Jonathan Jackson Jr., and Emily Gray, *Social Order and the Fear of Crime in Contemporary Times* (Oxford: Oxford University Press, 2009).

106. Veena Das, *Life and Words: Violence and the Descent into the Ordinary* (Berkeley: University of California Press, 2007); Nancy Scheper-Hughes, *Death without Weeping: The Violence of Everyday Life in Brazil* (Berkeley: University of California Press, 1993); Michael T. Taussig, *The Nervous System* (New York: Routledge, 1992); Michael T. Taussig, "Culture of Terror—Spaces of Death. Roger Casement's Putumayo Report and the Explanation of Torture," in *Violence: A Reader*, ed. Catherine Lowe Besteman (Basingstoke: Palgrave Macmillan, 2002), 211–43; Nancy Scheper-Hughes and Philippe I. Bourgois, *Violence in War and Peace* (Malden, MA: Blackwell, 2004); Philippe Bourgois, "Recognizing Invisible Violence: A Thirty-Year Ethnographic Retrospective," in *Global Health in Times of Violence*, ed. Barbara

Rylko-Bauer, Linda Whiteford, and Paul Farmer (Santa Fe, NM: School for Advanced Research Press, 2010), 17–40.

107. Susana Rotker, *Citizens of Fear: Urban Violence in Latin America* (New Brunswick, NJ: Rutgers University Press, 2002); Scheper-Hughes and Bourgois, *Violence in War and Peace*; Taussig, "Culture of Terror—Spaces of Death. Roger Casement's Putumayo Report and the Explanation of Torture"; Teresa Pires Do Rio Caldeira, *City of Walls: Crime, Segregation, and Citizenship in São Paulo* (Berkeley: University of California Press, 2000); Kees Koonings and Dirk Krujit, *Societies of Fear: The Legacy of Civil War, Violence, and Terror in Latin America* (London: Zed Books, 1999).

108. Carolyn Nordstrom, "The Tomorrow of Violence," in *Violence*, ed. Neil L. Whitehead, School of American Research Advanced Seminar Series, 223–42 (Santa Fe, NM: School of American Research, 2004). http://catdir.loc.gov/catdir/toc/ecip0420/2004017171.html.

Chapter 2

1. Interview with a humanitarian organization employee, Zulia, Venezuela, 2012.

2. Local orders in contexts of civil war and crime are understood as the informal norms and rules imposed by a violent non-state actor on civilians. See, e.g., Kate Meagher, "The Strength of Weak States? Non-State Security Forces and Hybrid Governance in Africa," Development and Change 43, no. 5 (September 1, 2012): 1073–01, http://onlinelibrary.wiley.com/doi/10.1111/j.1467-7660.2012.01794.x/abstract; Enrique Desmond Arias, "The Dynamics of Criminal Governance: Networks and Social Order in Rio de Janeiro," *Journal of Latin American Studies*, no. 38 (2006): 293–325, https://doi.org/10.1017/S0022216X06000721; Stathis N. Kalyvas, Ian Shapiro, and Tarek Masoud, eds., *Order, Conflict, and Violence* (Cambridge, UK: Cambridge University Press, 2008).

3. I borrow here from James Scott's "Seeing like a State" metaphor. See James C. Scott, *Seeing Like a State: How Certain Schemes to Improve the Human Condition Have Failed*, Yale Agrarian Studies (New Haven: Yale University Press, 1998).

4. This is therefore different to a "world politics" paradigm that focuses on the interactions between states and non-state actors. See, e.g., Joseph S. Nye and Robert O. Keohane, "Transnational Relations and World Politics: An Introduction," *International Organization* 25, no. 3 (1971): 329–49, https://doi.org/10.1017/S0020818300026187. For approaches more similar to mine see Douglas Lemke, "Power Politics and Wars without States," *American Journal of Political Science* 52, no. 4 (2008): 774–86, http://onlinelibrary.wiley.com/doi/10.1111/j.1540-5907.2008.00342.x/abstract; Stacie E. Goddard and Daniel H. Nexon, "The Dynamics of Global Power Politics: A Framework for Analysis," *Journal of Global Security Studies* 1, no. 1 (February 1, 2016): 4–18, https://doi.org/10.1093/jogss/ogv007.

5. Ulrich Schneckener, "Fragile Statehood, Armed Non-State Actors and Security Governance," in *Private Actors and Security Governance*, ed. Alan Bryden and Marina Caparini (Münster: LIT Verlag, 2006), 25; Ulrich Schneckener, "Spoilers or Governance Actors? Engaging Armed Non-State Groups in Areas of Limited Statehood," SFB-Governance Working Paper Series (Berlin: Research Center (SFB) 700, 2009), 8–9.

6. Robert O. Keohane, *After Hegemony: Cooperation and Discord in the World Political Economy* (Princeton, NJ: Princeton University Press, 2005), 75.

7. See, e.g., Alex Schmid, "The Links between Transnational Organized Crime and Terrorist Crimes," *Transnational Organized Crime* 2, no. 4 (Winter 1996): 40–82; Gordon H. McCormick, "Terrorist Decision Making," *Annual Review of Political Science* 6, no. 1 (2003): 473–507, https://doi.org/10.1146/annurev.polisci.6.121901.085601; Bruce Hoffman, *Inside Terrorism* (New York: Columbia University Press, 2006); Martha Crenshaw, "The Logic of Terrorism: Terrorist Behavior as a Product of Strategic Choice," in *Terrorism and Counterterrorism: Understanding the New Security Environment, Readings and Interpretations*, ed. Russell Howard and Bruce Hoffman (Boston: McGraw-Hill Education, 2011), 42–53; James J. F. Forest, *The Terrorism Lectures* (Santa Ana, CA: Nortia Press, 2012); Jacob N. Shapiro, "Terrorist Decision-Making: Insights from Economics and Political Science," *Perspectives on Terrorism* 6, no. 4–5 (September 10, 2012), http://www.terrorismanalysts.com/pt/index.php/pot/article/view/214.

8. This is in reference to the Weberian concept of the state.
9. Throughout the book, I use "armed group" as a subtype of violent non-state groups, for example to refer to the FARC. I also use the term "armed actor" in cases where it is clear that this actor constitutes a violent non-state group.
10. These two are not necessarily the same. A politically motivated group may be economically motivated to cooperate with another one, for example to obtain resources to sustain their fighting.
11. See, e.g., Paul Collier, *Breaking the Conflict Trap: Civil War and Development Policy* (Oxford: World Bank; Oxford University Press, 2003); Mats R. Berdal and David Malone, eds., *Greed & Grievance: Economic Agendas in Civil Wars* (Boulder, CO: Lynne Rienner, 2000); Karen Ballentine and Jake Sherman, *The Political Economy of Armed Conflict: Beyond Greed and Grievance* (Boulder, CO: Lynne Rienner, 2003).
12. The FARC, for example, were referred to as "insurgents" in the 1970s, "drug traffickers" after US president Nixon declared the War on Drugs, and "narco-terrorists" once 9/11 triggered the so-called War on Terror, and only during Santos's presidency, which started in 2008, did the discourse shift back to "guerrillas" or "rebels." On the War on Drugs see Emily Crick, "Drugs as an Existential Threat: An Analysis of the International Securitization of Drugs," *International Journal of Drug Policy* 23, no. 5 (September 2012): 409–11, https://doi.org/ 10.1016/j.drugpo.2012.03.004; on the War on Terror see Annette Idler and Borja Paladini Adell, "When Peace Implies Engaging the 'Terrorist': Peacebuilding in Colombia through Transforming Political Violence and Terrorism," in *The Nexus between Terrorism Studies and Peace and Conflict Studies*, ed. Yannis Tellidis and Harmonie Toros (London: Routledge, 2015).
13. I use the term "violent non-state groups" and "violent non-state actors" mostly interchangeably, with the only difference that "actors" also refers to one or two individuals, for example brokers, in addition to a set of at least three individuals.
14. Andrew Hurrell, *On Global Order: Power, Values, and the Constitution of International Society* (Oxford: Oxford University Press, 2007), 2; see also Jon Elster, *The Cement of Society: A Study of Social Order*, Studies in Rationality and Social Change (Cambridge, UK: Cambridge University Press, 1989); Dennis Hume Wrong, *The Problem of Order: What Unites and Divides Society* (New York: Free Press, 1994); Hedley Bull, *The Anarchical Society: A Study of Order in World Politics*, 4th ed. (New York: Columbia University Press, 2012).
15. Hurrell, *On Global Order*, 2–3; Alexander Wendt, *Social Theory of International Politics* (Cambridge, UK: Cambridge University Press, 1999), 251.
16. Martin Wight, *International Theory: The Three Traditions* (Leicester: Leicester University Press for the Royal Institute of International Affairs, 1991).
17. See Wight; Bull, *The Anarchical Society*, 23. Wendt uses the terms "enmity," "rivalry," and "friendship" to describe roles of states. Wendt, *Social Theory of International Politics*, 257.
18. This does not exclude the existence of authority per se; after all, violent non-state groups operate in state territory and the state is, even if only nominally, the authority.
19. Robert M. Axelrod and Robert O. Keohane, "Achieving Cooperation under Anarchy: Strategies and Institutions," *World Politics* 38, no. 1 (1985): 226; see also Kenneth A. Oye, *Cooperation under Anarchy* (Princeton, NJ: Princeton University Press, 1986).
20. I follow B. Williams's definition of cooperation, according to which "two [or more] agents *cooperate* when they engage in a joint venture for the outcome of which the actions of each are necessary, and where a necessary action by at least one of them is not under the immediate control of the other. [. . .]" (Bernard Williams, "Formal Structures and Social Reality," in *Trust: Making and Breaking Cooperative Relations*, ed. Diego Gambetta, new ed. [Chichester: Wiley-Blackwell, 1990], 5). For the importance of overcoming distrust in inter-organizational cooperation more broadly see, for example, Morton Deutsch, "Cooperation and Trust: Some Theoretical Notes," in *Nebraska Symposium on Motivation*, ed. R. Jones Marshall (Lincoln: University of Nebraska Press, 1962), 275–319; Kenneth Thomas, "Organizational Conflict," in *Organizational Behavior*, ed. Steven Kerr (New York: John Wiley & Sons Inc, 1979), 217; Aneil Mishra, "Organizational Responses to Crisis: The Centrality of Trust," in *Trust in Organizations: Frontiers of Theory and Research*, ed. Roderick M. Kramer and Tom R. Tyler (Thousand Oaks, CA: SAGE, 1996), 261–87.

21. Diego Gambetta, *Codes of the Underworld: How Criminals Communicate* (Princeton, NJ: Princeton University Press, 2009), 33.

22. "The Politics of Drugs and Illicit Trade in the Americas," in *Handbook of Latin American Politics*, ed. Peter Kingstone and Deborah Yashar (New York: Routledge, 2012), 384.

23. For example, Group B takes the son of Group A's leader hostage until it receives the drugs for the money that they paid to Group A. If Group A dishonors the deal, Group B kills the hostage.

24. Gambetta, *Codes of the Underworld*, 35.

25. See ibid., 30–77.

26. Diego Gambetta, "Mafia: The Price of Distrust," in *Trust: Making and Breaking Cooperative Relations*, ed. Diego Gambetta, New edition (Wiley-Blackwell, 1990), 217.

27. Ibid., 219.

28. Karen S. Cook, *Cooperation without Trust?* (New York: Russell Sage Foundation, 2005).

29. See, e.g., Robert M. Axelrod, *The Evolution of Cooperation* (New York: Basic Books, 1984); Elinor Ostrom, *Governing the Commons: The Evolution of Institutions for Collective Action* (Cambridge, UK: Cambridge University Press, 1990); John von Neumann, *Theory of Games and Economic Behavior*, 2nd ed. (Princeton, NJ: Princeton University Press, 1947); Schelling, *The Strategy of Conflict*; Mancur Olson, *The Logic of Collective Action: Public Goods and the Theory of Groups* (Cambridge, MA: Harvard University Press, 1965); Axelrod, *The Evolution of Cooperation*, 1984; Ostrom, *Governing the Commons*.

30. Oye, *Cooperation under Anarchy*. Robert Axelrod and Robert Keohane note that, in addition to institutional factors, actors undertake "deliberate efforts to change the very structure of the situation by changing the context in which each of them would be acting" to incite sustained cooperation ("Achieving Cooperation under Anarchy," 249). Civil war scholars have drawn on game theory and alliance theory to analyze strategies and preferences that make cooperation among violent non-state actors work. On how allegiances shift see, e.g., Stathis N. Kalyvas, "The Ontology of 'Political Violence': Action and Identity in Civil Wars," *Perspectives on Politics* 1, no. 3 (September 2003): 475–94, https://doi.org/10.1017/S1537592703000355). On how rebels overcome commitment problems see Kanisha D. Bond, "Power, Identity, Credibility, and Cooperation: Examining the Cooperative Arrangements among Violent Non-State Actors" (PhD diss., Pennsylvania State University, 2010); Navin A. Bapat and Kanisha D. Bond, "Alliances between Militant Groups," *British Journal of Political Science* 42, no. 4 (2012): 793–824, https://doi.org/10.1017/S0007123412000075. On how the balance of power among fighting factions shapes patterns of alliance formation see Fotini Christia, *Alliance Formation in Civil Wars* (Cambridge, UK: Cambridge University Press, 2012).

31. Bernard Williams, "Formal Structures and Social Reality," in *Trust: Making and Breaking Cooperative Relations*, ed. Diego Gambetta, new ed. (Chichester: Wiley-Blackwell, 1990), 5.

32. Ibid., 7.

33. Axelrod and Keohane, "Achieving Cooperation under Anarchy," 249.

34. Keohane, *After Hegemony*, 75.

35. Williams, "Formal Structures and Social Reality,", 5.

36. Ibid., 10–11; Gambetta, "Mafia: The Price of Distrust," 168. Gambetta refers to "coercion" instead of "power."

37. Williams, "Formal Structures and Social Reality," 10.

38. Michael Barnett and Raymond Duvall, "Power in International Politics," *International Organization* 59, no. 1 (January 1, 2005): 49, https://doi.org/10.1017/S0020818305050010.

39. Williams, "Formal Structures and Social Reality," 10. Since I refer to groups rather than individuals, I do not follow Williams in his categorization into "egoistic" and "non-egoistic."

40. Even though a bond is normally reciprocal, the *perception* of the existence of a bond can be unilateral. Hence, the motive for cooperation serves as a distrust-reducing mechanism only when both or more parties assume the bond to exist, which is what I term "mutual sympathies."

41. This is the case, for example, when motivations change.

42. "Mafia: The Price of Distrust," 168.

43. Carl Schmitt, *Der Begriff des Politischen* (Hamburg: Hanseatische Verlagsanstalt, 1933).

44. Bull, *The Anarchical Society*, 47.

45. Ibid., 47.

46. See, e.g., Staniland, "States, Insurgents, and Wartime Political Orders" on guerrilla disorder.
47. Elinor Ostrom, "Collective Action and the Evolution of Social Norms," *Journal of Economic Perspectives* 14, no. 3 (August 2000): 142, https://doi.org/10.1257/jep.14.3.137.
48. Cook, *Cooperation without Trust?*, 37.
49. Paolo Campana and Federico Varese, "Cooperation in Criminal Organizations: Kinship and Violence as Credible Commitments," *Rationality and Society* 25, no. 3 (August 1, 2013): 281, https://doi.org/10.1177/1043463113481202.
50. Axelrod, *The Evolution of Cooperation*, 1984.
51. Ostrom, "Collective Action and the Evolution of Social Norms," 141–43; Robert M. Axelrod, *The Evolution of Cooperation* (New York: Basic Books, 2006), 6.
52. For private goals and local cleavages, see, e.g., Kalyvas, "The Ontology of 'Political Violence': Action and Identity in Civil Wars"; Nils B. Weidmann, "Micro-Cleavages and Violence in Civil Wars: A Computational Assessment," *Conflict Management and Peace Science* 33, no. 5 (November 1, 2016): 539–58, https://doi.org/10.1177/0738894215570433.
53. On loyalty strategies in the context of military defection see Théodore McLauchlin, "Loyalty Strategies and Military Defection in Rebellion," *Comparative Politics* 42, no. 3 (March 31, 2010): 333–50, https://doi.org/10.5129/001041510X12911363509792.
54. This resonates with Wendt's Lockean logic, or culture of states as self-interested rivals who are guided by a more restrained egoism than enemies: "Unlike enemies, rivals expect each other to act as if they recognize their sovereignty, their 'life and liberty,' as a *right*, and therefore do not try to conquer or dominate them. [...] Unlike friends, however, the recognition among rivals does not extend to the right to be free from violence in disputes." Wendt, 279.
55. See Keohane, *After Hegemony* on instrumental rationality.
56. See "Mafia: The Price of Distrust," 168; "Cooperation in Criminal Organizations." Kinship—cited by Gambetta under personal bonds, and subsumed under hostage-taking by Paolo Campana and Federico Varese—can also fall under "values" if it is shared between groups and thus serves to reduce distrust in a general manner, rather than between individuals.
57. This alludes to Kant's League of Peace but, in this case, it is some sort of "League of the Underworld." See Immanuel Kant, *Zum ewigen Frieden.* (Königsberg, 1795); W. B. Gallie, *Philosophers of Peace and War: Kant, Clausewitz, Marx, Engels, and Tolstoy,* Wiles Lectures; 1976 (Cambridge, UK: Cambridge University Press, 1978), 20.
58. See Sterling, *Crime without Frontiers: The Worldwide Expansion of Organised Crime and the Pax Mafiosa* for "pax mafiosa," a somewhat similar concept.
59. According to Aristotle, there are three types of friendship: the friendship of utility, the friendship of pleasure, and the friendship of virtue. Aristotle, *Nicomachean Ethics*, ed. H. Rackham, Book 8 (Cambridge, MA: Harvard University Press, 1926).
60. Phil Williams, "Cooperation among Criminal Organizations," in *Transnational Organized Crime and International Security: Business as Usual?*, ed. Mats R. Berdal (Boulder, CO: Lynne Rienner, 2002), 68.
61. Phil Williams and Roy Godson, "Anticipating Organized and Transnational Crime," *Crime Law and Social Change* 37 (June 2002): 326–27, https://doi.org/10.1023/A:1016095317864; Manuel Castells, *End of Millennium*, 2nd ed. (Oxford: Wiley-Blackwell, 2010), 174.
62. Castells, *End of Millennium*, 174.
63. See, e.g., Jeffrey H. Dyer and Wujin Chu, "The Determinants of Trust in Supplier-Automaker Relationships in the US, Japan, and Korea," *Journal of International Business Studies* 31, no. 2 (June 2000): 259–85, https://doi.org/10.1057/palgrave.jibs.8490905; Robert Handfield and Christian Bechtel, "The Role of Trust and Relationship Structure in Improving Supply Chain Responsiveness," *Industrial Marketing Management* 31 (2002): 367–82, https://www.researchgate.net/publication/228806675_The_Role_of_Trust_and_Relationship_Structure_in_Improving_Supply_Chain_Responsiveness; David A Johnston et al., "Effects of Supplier Trust on Performance of Cooperative Supplier Relationships," *Journal of Operations Management* 22, no. 1 (February 2004): 23–38, https://doi.org/10.1016/j.jom.2003.12.001.
64. Oxford Dictionaries, "Language Matters," *Oxford Dictionaries* (blog), 2014, http://www.oxforddictionaries.com/definition/english/intuition.

65. Stathis N. Kalyvas, *The Logic of Violence in Civil War* (Cambridge, UK: Cambridge University Press, 2006); Kalyvas, Shapiro, and Masoud, *Order, Conflict, and Violence*; Ana Arjona, "Social Order in Civil War." (PhD diss., Yale University, 2010).

66. Hanne Fjelde and Desirée Nilsson, "Rebels against Rebels: Explaining Violence between Rebel Groups," *Journal of Conflict Resolution* 56, no. 4 (April 24, 2012): 604–28, http://journals.sagepub.com/doi/abs/10.1177/0022002712439496.

67. Staniland, "States, Insurgents, and Wartime Political Orders."

68. Daniel Goldstein, *The Spectacular City: Violence and Performance in Urban Bolivia* (Durham, NC: Duke University Press, 2004), 208.

69. Luis Astorga, *Seguridad, traficantes, y militares: El poder y la sombra* (México, D. F: Tusquets, 2007); Javier Osorio, "Hobbes on Drugs. Understanding Drug Violence in Mexico" (PhD diss., University of Notre Dame, 2013).

70. International Committee of the Red Cross, "International Humanitarian Law and the Challenges of Contemporary Armed Conflicts," *International Review of the Red Cross* 89, no. 867 (2007): 735, https://www.icrc.org/en/document/international-humanitarian-law-and-challenges-contemporary-armed-conflicts.

71. Oliver Juetersonke, Robert Muggah, and Dennis Rodgers, "Gangs and Violence Reduction in Central America," *Security Dialogue* 40, no. 4–5 (2009): 1–25, https://www.oas.org/dsp/documentos/pandillas/2sesion_especial/SMALL%20ARMS%20SURVEY/gangs%20and%20urban%20violence.pdf; Dennis Rodgers, "Living in the Shadow of Death: Gangs, Violence, and Social Order in Urban Nicaragua, 1996–2002," *Journal of Latin American Studies* 38, no. 2 (2006): 267–92, https://doi.org/10.1017/S0022216X0600071X; Max Manwaring, *Street Gangs: The New Urban Insurgency* (Carlisle, PA: Strategic Studies Institute, US Army War College, 2005); Cordula Strocka, "Youth Gangs in Latin America," *SAIS Review of International Affairs* 26, no. 2 (2006): 133–46, https://doi.org/10.1353/sais.2006.0045.

72. See Diego Gambetta, *The Sicilian Mafia: The Business of Private Protection* (Cambridge, MA: Harvard University Press, 1993); Federico Varese, "What Is Organized Crime?," in *Organized Crime*, ed. Federico Varese, Critical Concepts in Criminology (London: Routledge, 2010), 1–35; Misha Glenny, *McMafia: Seriously Organised Crime* (London: Vintage, 2009).

73. This distinction refers mostly to low-intensity conflicts. In high-intensity conflicts, combat in urban areas is more common, as cases such as contemporary Syria attest. In the context of Colombia, Gonzalo Vargas demonstrates how the Colombian town of Barrancabermeja was affected by combat (what he calls urban irregular warfare) in the late 1990s. Gonzalo Vargas, "Urban Irregular Warfare and Violence against Civilians: Evidence from a Colombian City," *Terrorism and Political Violence* 21, no. 1 (2009): 114, https://doi.org/10.1080/09546550802551859.

74. See Kalyvas, *The Logic of Violence in Civil War.*

75. "States, Insurgents, and Wartime Political Orders," 252.

76. Oliver E. Williamson, "Credible Commitments: Using Hostages to Support Exchange," *The American Economic Review* 73, no. 4 (1983): 519–40, http://www.jstor.org/stable/1816557.

77. Williams, "Cooperation among Criminal Organizations," 75.

78. Ariel Ávila and Magda Núñez, "Expansión territorial y alianzas tácticas," *Arcanos*, 2008, 52–61.

79. See Kenneth N Waltz, *Theory of International Politics* (Long Grove, IL: Waveland Press, 2010).

80. See, e.g., Kristin M. Bakke, Kathleen Gallagher Cunningham, and Lee J. M. Seymour, "A Plague of Initials: Fragmentation, Cohesion, and Infighting in Civil Wars," *Perspectives on Politics* 10, no. 2 (June 2012): 265–83, https://doi.org/10.1017/S1537592712000667.

81. See, e.g., Williams, "Cooperation among Criminal Organizations," 70.

82. Diego Gambetta, *The Sicilian Mafia: The Business of Private Protection* (Cambridge, MA; London: Harvard University Press, 1993); Federico Varese, *The Russian Mafia: Private Protection in a New Market Economy* (Oxford: Oxford University Press, 2001).

83. The operational territories of violent non-state groups often coincide with an urban-rural divide. See Arlene B. Tickner, Diego García, and Catalina Arrezea, "Actores violentos no estatales y narcotráfico en Colombia," in *Políticas antidroga en Colombia: Éxitos, fracasos, y extravíos,* (Bogotá: Universidad de los Andes, 2011), 413–45; Zully Laverde and Edwin Tapia, *Tensión en las fronteras* (Bogotá: CODHES, 2009).

84. Duncan Deville, "The Illicit Supply Chain," in *Convergence: Illicit Networks and National Security in the Age of Globalization*, ed. Michael Miklaucic and Jacqueline Brewer (Washington, DC: National Defense University, 2013), 65.

85. Gambetta, *The Sicilian Mafia: The Business of Private Protection*, 17; Vanda Felbab-Brown, "Rules and Regulations in Ungoverned Spaces. Illicit Economies, Criminals, and Belligerents," in *Ungoverned Spaces: Alternatives to State Authority in an Era of Softened Sovereignty*, ed. Anne L. Clunan and Harold A. Trinkunas (Stanford, CA: Stanford University Press, 2010), 179.

86. For the reduction of distrust via brokers see, e.g., Gambetta, *The Sicilian Mafia: The Business of Private Protection*; Felbab-Brown, "Rules and Regulations in Ungoverned Spaces. Illicit Economies, Criminals, and Belligerents." See also Cook, *Cooperation without Trust?*, 37; Douglas Farah, "Fixers, Super Fixers, and Shadow Facilitators: How Networks Connect" (International Assessment and Strategy Center, April 23, 2012); Williams, "Cooperation among Criminal Organizations," 78.

87. For a discussion of brokers ("shadow facilitator") in Liberia and El Salvador see Farah, "Fixers, Super Fixers, and Shadow Facilitators: How Networks Connect."

88. Williams describes brokers as "engineering" cooperation by providing "trusted contacts to facilitate communications and linkages among different criminal organizations." I found that brokers not only initiate but also uphold the arrangement ("Cooperation among Criminal Organizations," 78).

89. Such strategic alliances, as in alliances between ideologically aligned groups, come closest to the Kantian idea of shared values among individuals rather than groups (states or violent non-state groups): individuals act as belonging to one entity.

90. Ariel Ávila and Magda Núñez, "Las dinámicas territoriales del Ejército de Liberación Nacional: Arauca, Cauca y Nariño," *Arcanos*, Corporación Nuevo Arco Iris, no. 15 (2010): 22–33.

91. Ibid.

92. For a somewhat similar view on "friendship" among states see Wendt (*Social Theory of International Politics*, 305).

93. This also applies to states, but while states are based on territorial sovereignty, violent non-state groups at times share territory.

94. W. B. Gallie, "Essentially Contested Concepts," *Proceedings of the Aristotelian Society*, n.s., 56 (January 1, 1955): 167–98, https://doi.org/10.1080/05568641.2010.503465.

95. Paul D. Williams, *Security Studies: An Introduction*, 2nd ed. (London: Routledge, 2012), 2.

96. See, e.g., Keith Krause and Michael Charles Williams, *Critical Security Studies: Concepts and Cases* (London: UCL Press, 1997). See also work by Copenhagen School scholars, e.g., Ole Wæver, "Securitization and Desecuritization," in *On Security*, ed. Ronnie D. Lipschutz (New York: Columbia University Press, 1995), 46–86.

97. Williams, *Security Studies*, 8. It also includes a "widening" of the scope of security threats, encompassing not only the military but also the political, economic, societal, and environmental arenas. Barry Buzan, *People, States, and Fear: An Agenda for International Security Studies in the Post–Cold War Era*, 2nd ed. (Boulder, CO: Lynne Rienner, 1991), 12; Barry Buzan, Ole Wæver, and Jaap de Wilde, *Security: A New Framework for Analysis* (Boulder, CO: Lynne Rienner, 1998), 21–23.

98. Antonius C. G. M. Robben, "The Fear of Indifference: Combatants' Anxieties about the Political Identity of Civilians during Argentina's Dirty War," in *Societies of Fear: The Legacy of Civil War, Violence, and Terror in Latin America*, ed. Kees Koonings and Dirk Krujit (London: Zed Books, 1999), 125.

99. United Nations Development Programme, "Seguridad ciudadana con rostro humano: Diagnóstico y propuestas para América Latina," Human Development Report for Latin America 2013–2014 (New York: United Nations Development Programme, 2013), 8.

100. United Nations Development Programme, 7; World Health Organization, "World Report on Violence and Health. Summary" (Geneva: World Health Organization, 2002), 8, http://www.who.int/violence_injury_prevention/violence/world_report/en/summary_en.pdf.

101. "'Security Traps' and Democratic Governability in Latin America: Dynamics of Crime, Violence, Corruption, Regime, and State," in *Criminality, Public Security, and the Challenge to*

Democracy in Latin America, ed. Marcelo Bergman and Laurence Whitehead (Notre Dame, IN: University of Notre Dame Press, 2009), 274.

102. Charles Tilly, "A Primer on Citizenship," *Theory and Society* 26, no. 4 (August 1, 1997): 599, https://doi.org/10.2307/657863.

103. Kevin Casas-Zamora, *The Besieged Polis: Citizen Insecurity and Democracy in Latin America* (Washington, DC: Latin America Initiative at Brookings, June 2013), 3.

104. Robert Picciotto, Funmi Olonisakin, and Michael Clarke, *Global Development and Human Security* (New Brunswick, NJ: Transaction Publishers, 2007), 12–14.

105. Sam Pizzigati, *Greed and Good: Understanding and Overcoming the Inequality That Limits Our Lives* (New York: Rowman & Littlefield Publishers, 2004), 331.

106. Gabriel Abraham Almond and Sidney Verba, *The Civic Culture: Political Attitudes and Democracy in Five Nations*, New ed. (Newbury Park, CA; London: Sage, 1989).

107. Laurence Whitehead, "On Citizen Security," in *Democratization: Theory and Experience* (Oxford: Oxford University Press, 2002), 166.

108. Robin George Collingwood, *The New Leviathan; or, Man, Society, Civilization, and Barbarism*, edited and introduced by David Boucher (Oxford: Clarendon Press, 1999), 326.

109. Robert D. Putnam, *Making Democracy Work: Civic Traditions in Modern Italy* (Princeton, NJ: Princeton University Press, 1993), 163–85. This is not the case if social capital is only built by certain groups, such as criminal groups.

110. Ronald Inglehart, *Modernization and Postmodernization: Cultural, Economic, and Political Change in 43 Societies* (Princeton, NJ; Chichester: Princeton University Press, 1997); Ronald Inglehart, "Trust, Well-Being, and Democracy," in *Democracy and Trust*, ed. Mark E. Warren (Cambridge, UK: Cambridge University Press, 1999), 88–120.

111. Laura Chinchilla Miranda, "Public Security in Central America," 2002, http://pdba.georgetown.edu/Pubsecurity/ch2.pdf; Laura Chinchilla Miranda, "Experiences with Citizen Participation in Crime Prevention in Central America," in *Crime and Violence in Latin America: Citizen Security, Democracy, and the State*, ed. Joseph S. Tulchin, H. Hugo Frühling, and Heather Golding (Washington, DC: Woodrow Wilson Center Press, 2003), 220–21; José María Rico, *Seguridad ciudadana en Centroamérica: Aspectos teóricos y metodológicos* (San José, Costa Rica: Instituto Interamericano de Derechos Humanos, 1999).

112. James G. March and Johan P. Olsen, *Rediscovering Institutions: The Organizational Basis of Politics* (New York: Free Press, 1989), 17.

113. James G. March and Johan P. Olsen, "The Logic of Appropriateness," in *The Oxford Handbook of Public Policy*, ed. Michael Moran, Martin Rein, and Robert E. Goodin (Oxford: Oxford University Press, 2008). Following authors such as Kjell Goldmann, I consider the logic of appropriateness as overlapping with a logic of consequences. Kjell Goldmann, "Appropriateness and Consequences: The Logic of Neo-Institutionalism," *Governance* 18, no. 1 (January 1, 2005): 35–52, https://doi.org/10.1111/j.1468-0491.2004.00265.x.

114. March and Olsen, "The Logic of Appropriateness,", 689; see also P. Hall and R. C. R. Taylor, "Political Science and the Three New Institutionalisms," *Political Studies* 44 (1996): 939.

115. "On Citizen Security," 166.

116. March and Olsen, "The Logic of Appropriateness," 691.

117. "On Citizen Security," 172.

118. Jaume Curbet, "Inseguridad ciudadana: Víctimas y chivos expiatorios," 2009, http://www.pensamientopenal.com.ar/15082007/curbet.pdf; Luis González Placencia, *Ciudades seguras: Percepción ciudadana de la inseguridad (Política y derecho)* (México D.C.: Fondo de Cultura Económica, 2002); Mauricio Duce and Rogelio Pérez, "Citizen Security and Reform of the Criminal Justice System in Latin America," in *Crime and Violence in Latin America: Citizen Security, Democracy, and the State*, ed. Hugo Fruehling, Joseph S. Tulchin, and Heather A. Golding (Washington, DC: Woodrow Wilson Center Press, 2003), 60–92; Casas-Zamora, "The Besieged Polis. Citizen Insecurity and Democracy in Latin America," 16–37.

119. *Fear and Crime in Latin America: Redefining State-Society Relations* (New York: Routledge, 2012), 1.

120. Dammert, 31–32.

121. *Societies of Fear: The Legacy of Civil War, Violence, and Terror in Latin America* (London: Zed Books, 1999), 15.

122. Dammert, *Fear and Crime in Latin America*, 4.
123. *Encounters with Violence in Latin America: Urban Poor Perceptions from Colombia and Guatemala* (New York; London: Routledge, 2004), 195.
124. Casas-Zamora, "The Besieged Polis: Citizen Insecurity and Democracy in Latin America," 35.
125. "Human Development Report 1994" (New York: United Nations Development Programme, 1994), 24–25.
126. Ibid., 30–31.
127. United Nations Development Programme, "Community Security and Social Cohesion. Towards a UNDP Approach" (New York: United Nations Development Programme, 2009), 18.
128. United Nations Development Programme, "Seguridad ciudadana con rostro humano: Diagnóstico y propuestas para América Latina," 1.
129. United Nations General Assembly, "A/RES/66/290," 2012, http://www.un.org/humansecurity/sites/www.un.org.humansecurity/files/hsu%20documents/GA%20Resolutions.pdf.
130. United Nations Development Programme, "Seguridad ciudadana con rostro humano," 6.
131. Other factors matter too for local security dynamics, including distinct local contexts, differing state policies designed to the situation of armed conflict or to a neighboring country of a conflict state such as the deployment of state forces, and the presence of third parties.
132. Schneckener, "Spoilers or Governance Actors? Engaging Armed Non-State Groups in Areas of Limited Statehood."
133. There is a large body of literature on the contestation between state and non-state actors in civil wars and other fragile settings and, increasingly, on contestation between various non-state actors, exploring how variation in repercussions on security is related to the type, size, organizational structure, and cohesion of the armed actors involved, as well as their level of control in space and over time. See, for example, Andreas and Durán-Martínez, "The Politics of Drugs and Illicit Trade in the Americas," 385; Wendy Pearlman, "Spoiling Inside and Out: Internal Political Contestation and the Middle East Peace Process," *International Security* 33, no. 3 (2008): 79–109, http://www.mitpressjournals.org/doi/pdf/10.1162/isec.2009.33.3.79; Gianluca Fiorentini and Sam Peltzman, *The Economics of Organised Crime* (Cambridge, UK: Cambridge University Press, 1995); Paul Staniland, *Networks of Rebellion: Explaining Insurgent Cohesion and Collapse*, Cornell Studies in Security Affairs (Ithaca, NY: Cornell University Press, 2014); Saab and Taylor, "Criminality and Armed Groups: A Comparative Study of FARC and Paramilitary Groups in Colombia"; Kalyvas, *The Logic of Violence in Civil War*; Laia Balcells, "Rivalry and Revenge: Violence against Civilians in Conventional Civil Wars," *International Studies Quarterly* 54, no. 2 (2010): 291–313, http://onlinelibrary.wiley.com/doi/10.1111/j.1468-2478.2010.00588.x/abstract; Francisco Gutiérrez Sanín, "Telling the Difference: Guerrillas and Paramilitaries in the Colombian War," *Politics & Society* 36, no. 1 (March 1, 2008): 3–34, http://journals.sagepub.com/doi/abs/10.1177/0032329207312181; Francisco Gutiérrez-Sanín and Elisabeth Jean Wood, "What Should We Mean by 'Pattern of Political Violence'? Repertoire, Targeting, Frequency, and Technique," *Perspectives on Politics* 15, no. 1 (March 2017): 20–41, https://doi.org/10.1017/S1537592716004114. For work on the motives that drive insurgent or paramilitary groups to employ violence against civilians see Collier, *Breaking the Conflict Trap: Civil War and Development Policy*; Macartan Humphreys and Jeremy M. Weinstein, "Handling and Manhandling Civilians in Civil War," *American Political Science Review* 100, no. 3 (August 2006), https://doi.org/10.1017/S0003055406062289; Jeremy M. Weinstein, *Inside Rebellion: The Politics of Insurgent Violence* (Cambridge, UK: Cambridge University Press, 2006); Stathis N. Kalyvas, "Micro-Level Studies of Violence in Civil War: Refining and Extending the Control-Collaboration Model," *Terrorism and Political Violence* 24, no. 4 (2012): 658–68, https://doi.org/10.1080/09546553.2012.701986; Nils B. Weidmann, "Violence 'from Above' or 'from Below'? The Role of Ethnicity in Bosnia's Civil War," *The Journal of Politics* 73, no. 4 (2011): 1178–90, https://doi.org/10.1017/S0022381611000831. For a discussion of the variation in the type of violence

(e.g., homicides, torture, kidnappings) in settings of violent contestation between armed groups see "Repertoires of Violence against Noncombatants: The Role of Armed Group Institutions and Ideologies" (PhD diss., Yale University, 2011); Dara Cohen, "Explaining Sexual Violence during Civil War" (PhD diss., Stanford University, 2010); Elisabeth Wood, "Sexual Violence during War: Toward an Understanding of Variation," in *Order, Conflict and Violence*, ed. Ian Shapiro, Stathis N. Kalyvas, and Tarek Masoud (Cambridge, UK: Cambridge University Press, 2008).

134. Nat Colletta and Michelle L. Cullen, "The Nexus between Violent Conflict, Social Capital, and Social Cohesion: Case Studies from Cambodia and Rwanda," Working Paper, Social Capital Initiative (Washington, DC: World Bank, 2000); Moser and McIlwaine, *Encounters with Violence in Latin America*, 157.

135. This does not mean that the armed actors do not seek social, economic, and/or political control over the territory and hence aim to win the community's consent, yet this is hindered by persistent mistrust. The groups still have to resort to violence against communities, making it harder for them to gain consent (rather than rule based on fear).

136. Dennis Rodgers and Adam Baird, "Understanding Gangs in Contemporary Latin America," in *Handbook of Gangs and Gang Responses*, ed. Scott H. Decker and David C. Pyronz (New York: Wiley, 2015), 7.

137. Yoav Bar-Anan, Timothy D. Wilson, and Daniel T. Gilbert, "The Feeling of Uncertainty Intensifies Affective Reactions," *Emotion* 9, no. 1 (n.d.): 123, http://dx.doi.org/10.1037/a0014607; see also Frank H. Knight, *Risk, Uncertainty, and Profit*, Hart, Schaffner & Marx Prize Essays 31 (Boston: Houghton Mifflin, 1921).

138. See Bar-Anan, Wilson, and Gilbert, "The Feeling of Uncertainty Intensifies Affective Reactions"; Ian R. Inglis, "Review: The Central Role of Uncertainty Reduction in Determining Behaviour," *Behaviour* 137, no. 12 (2000): 1567–99, http://psycnet.apa.org/doi/10.1163/156853900502727; Michael A. Hogg, "Subjective Uncertainty Reduction through Self-Categorization: A Motivational Theory of Social Identity Processes," *European Review of Social Psychology* 11, no. 1 (January 1, 2000): 223–55, https://doi.org/10.1080/14792772043000040.

139. Idler and Forest, "Behavioral Patterns among (Violent) Non- State Actors".

140. For governance provided by paramilitaries or insurgents in Colombia see Gustavo Duncan, *Los señores de la guerra: De paramilitares, mafiosos, y autodefensas en Colombia* (Bogotá: Planeta, 2006); Ana Arjona. *Rebelocracy: Social Order in the Colombian Civil War* (New York: Cambridge University Press, 2016). For civil war contexts elsewhere see Timothy P. Wickham-Crowley, "The Rise (and Sometimes Fall) of Guerrilla Governments in Latin America," *Sociological Forum* 2, no. 3 (July 1, 1987): 473–99, https://doi.org/10.2307/684670; Rodney Hall and Thomas J. Biersteker, "Private Authority as Global Governance," in *The Emergence of Private Authority in Global Governance*, ed. Rodney Hall and Thomas J. Biersteker (Cambridge, UK: Cambridge University Press, 2002), 203–22; Kalyvas, Shapiro, and Masoud, *Order, Conflict, and Violence*; Zachariah Cherian Mampilly, *Rebel Rulers: Insurgent Governance and Civilian Life during War* (Ithaca, NY: Cornell University Press, 2011).

141. Arias, "The Dynamics of Criminal Governance: Networks and Social Order in Rio de Janeiro."

142. Idler and Forest, "Behavioral Patterns among (Violent) Non-State Actors"; Mampilly, *Rebel Rulers*, 52–54, http://doi.org/10.5334/sta.er.

143. "Private Authority as Global Governance," 216.

144. Annette Idler, "Espacios invisibilizados: Actores violentos no-estatales y 'Ciudadanía de Sombra' en las zonas fronterizas de Colombia," *Estudios Indiana*, 2014.

145. *Rebel Rulers*.

146. "Private Authority as Global Governance," 216.

147. "Citizenship, Identity, and Social History," *International Review of Social History* 40 (1995): 8.

148. Guillermo O'Donnell, "On the State, Democratization, and Some Conceptual Problems: A Latin American View with Glances at Some Postcommunist Countries," *World Development* 21, no. 8 (1993): 1355–69, https://doi.org/10.1016/0305-750X(93)90048-E.

149. O'Donnell explains how a democratic country can feature "blue areas" characterized by effective institutions and governance, and "brown areas" with ineffective governance and institutions (Guillermo O'Donnell, "Why the Rule of Law Matters," *Journal of Democracy* 15, no. 4 (2004): 41, https://doi.org/10.1353/jod.2004.0076). He argues that "these 'brown areas' are subnational systems of power that have a territorial basis and an informal but quite effective legal system, yet they coexist with a regime that, at least at the national political centre, is democratic." In brown areas, citizens have a low-intensity citizenship rather than "full" citizenship (O'Donnell, "On the State, Democratization, and Some Conceptual Problems: A Latin American View with Glances at Some Postcommunist Countries").

150. *Insurgent Citizenship: Disjunctions of Democracy and Modernity in Brazil* (Princeton, NJ: Princeton University Press, 2008), 9.

151. Barbara Oomen, "Vigilantism or Alternative Citizenship?: The Rise of Mapogo a Mathamaga," *African Studies* 63, no. 2 (2004): 153–71, https://doi.org/10.1080/00020180412331318751.

152. Hall and Biersteker, "Private Authority as Global Governance," 216.

153. Rodney S. Barker, *Political Legitimacy and the State* (Oxford: Clarendon Press, 1990), 25. Against this, normative legitimacy "is the right to rule, understood to mean both that institutional agents are morally justified in making rules and attempting to secure compliance with them and that people subject to those rules have moral, content-independent reasons to follow them and/or to not interfere with others' compliance with them." Allen Buchanan and Robert O. Keohane, "The Legitimacy of Global Governance Institutions," *Ethics & International Affairs*, no. 20 (2006): 411, https://doi.org/doi:10.1111/j.1747-7093.2006.00043.x.

154. Mampilly, *Rebel Rulers*; Gutiérrez Sanín, "Telling the Difference: Guerrillas and Paramilitaries in the Colombian War," 5.

155. Sophia Sabrow, "Local Perceptions of the Legitimacy of Peace Operations by the UN, Regional Organizations, and Individual States—A Case Study of the Mali Conflict," *International Peacekeeping* 24, no. 1 (January 1, 2017): 159–86, https://doi.org/10.1080/13533312.2016.1249365.

156. Duncan, *Los señores de la guerra*.

157. Daniel Pécaut, "From the Banality of Violence to Real Terror: The Case of Colombia," in *Societies of Fear: The Legacy of Civil War, Violence, and Terror in Latin America*, ed. Kees Koonings and Dirk Krujit (London: Zed Books, 1999), 150.

158. Wickham-Crowley, "The Rise (and Sometimes Fall) of Guerrilla Governments in Latin America."

159. Gambetta, *The Sicilian Mafia: The Business of Private Protection*; Varese, "What Is Organized Crime?," 17.

160. See also Annette Idler, "Arrangements of Convenience in Colombia's Borderlands: An Invisible Threat to Citizen Security?," *St Antony's International Review* 7, no. 2 (2012): 93–119, http://www.terrorismanalysts.com/pt/index.php/pot/article/view/217/html.

161. Max Weber, *Politik als Beruf* (Stuttgart: Reclam, Philipp, jun. GmbH, Verlag, 1992).

162. Moser and McIlwaine, *Encounters with Violence in Latin America*, 181; Lars Buur and Steffen Jensen, "Introduction: Vigilantism and the Policing of Everyday Life in South Africa," *African Studies* 63, no. 2 (2004): 144, https://doi.org/10.1080/00020180412331318724; Mario Fumerton and Simone Remijnse, "Civil Defence Forces: Peru's Comites de Autodefensa Civil and Guatemala's Patrullas de Autodefensa Civil in Comparative Perspective," in *Armed Actors: Organised Violence and State Failure in Latin America*, ed. Kees Koonings and Dirk Krujit (London: Zed Books, 2004), 52–72; Koonings and Krujit, *Societies of Fear*; Laurence Whitehead, "Citizen Insecurity and Democracy: Reflections on a Paradoxical Configuration," in *Criminality, Public Security, and the Challenge to Democracy in Latin America*, ed. Marcelo Bergman and Laurence Whitehead (Notre Dame, IN: University of Notre Dame Press, 2009), 282; Daniel M. Goldstein, "Flexible Justice: Neoliberal Violence and 'Self-Help' Security in Bolivia," *Critique of Anthropology* 25, no. 4 (2005): 389–411, http://journals.sagepub.com/doi/abs/10.1177/0308275X05058656; David Pratten, *Global Vigilantes*, ed. David Pratten and Atreyee Sen (London: C. Hurst & Co. Publishers Ltd, 2007).

163. In the context of one non-state group, Kalyvas refers to this as a "countersovereign authority" or a "counter-state." "Wanton and Senseless? The Logic of Massacres in Algeria," *Rationality and Society* 11 (1999): 259.

164. Such rules range from dress codes and employment restrictions to prohibiting contact with state officials.

165. This is the same in the case of the state: the threat of internal rebellion, for example, is deterred by the threat of the intervention of the state forces.

166. See Moser and McIlwaine, *Encounters with Violence in Latin America*, 158; Putnam, *Making Democracy Work*.

167. The rule of silence toward outsiders may be partly appropriate behavior that emerges from shadow citizenship. However, it can also constitute a practice that community members decide to adopt independently. A case in point is a situation in which community members benefit from opportunities in the illicit economy provided by the armed actors and speaking out may have negative security implications due to outside actors' actions or actions by the armed actors themselves.

168. Even though I do not focus explicitly on *interactions* between the state and violent non-state groups, I treat the relations between these two actors in my discussion of how violent non-state groups replace the state in its relationships with communities.

169. As mentioned earlier, cases of cooperation between the Colombian state forces and the paramilitary United Self-Defense Forces of Colombia (Autodefensas Unidas de Colombia— AUC) characterized the conflict until the AUC's demobilization. Similar alliances continued between members of the state forces and post-demobilized groups. Such dynamics can be observed concerning conflict actors, criminals, and mafia groups. Paul Staniland, for example, discusses how different political war orders depend on the civil war actors' relationships with the state (Paul Staniland, "States, Insurgents, and Wartime Political Orders," *Perspectives on Politics* 10, no. 2 [2012]: 243–64, https://doi.org/10.1017/S1537592712000655.). Enrique Desmond Arias considers how collaboration between criminal networks and the state relates to the division of power between levels of government and the electoral system (Enrique Desmond Arias, "Understanding Criminal Networks, Political Order, and Politics in Latin America," in *Ungoverned Spaces: Alternatives to State Authority in an Era of Softened Sovereignty*, ed. Anne L. Clunan and Harold A. Trinkunas [Stanford, CA: Stanford University Press, 2010], 128.). Moisés Naím's "mafia states" build on governments' close relationships with mafia groups. See Moisés Naím, "Mafia States," *Foreign Affairs* 91, no. 3 (June 5, 2012): 100–11.

170. Arlene B. Tickner and Mónica Herz, "No Place for Theory?: Security Studies in Latin America," in *Thinking International Relations Differently*, ed. Arlene B. Tickner and David L. Blaney (Abingdon: Routledge, 2012), 92.

171. Frederic Lane in Charles Tilly, "War Making and State Making as Organized Crime," in *Bringing the State Back in*, ed. Peter B. Evans et al. (Cambridge, UK: Cambridge University Press, 1985), 175.

172. Samuel P Huntington, *The Julian J. Rothbaum Distinguished Lecture Series. Vol. 4, Vol. 4* (Norman: University of Oklahoma Press, 1991), http://search.ebscohost.com/login.aspx ?direct=true&scope=site&db=nlebk&db=nlabk&AN=15342.

173. Inter-American Commission on Human Rights Executive Secretary as cited in OAS/ IACHR, "Report on Citizen Security and Human Rights" (Organization of American States, Inter-American Commission on Human Rights, 2009), 7, Art. 20, http://www.cidh. oas.org/countryrep/Seguridad.eng/CitizenSecurity.II.htm.

174. United Nations Development Programme, "Human Development Report," 2013, 1.

175. This includes North America. United Nations Office on Drugs and Crime, "UNODC Homicide Statistics 2013" (Vienna: United Nations Office on Drugs and Crime, 2013), 18.

176. United Nations Development Programme, "Seguridad ciudadana con rostro humano: Diagnóstico y propuestas para América Latina," 36.

177. See, e.g., Instituto Nacional de Estadística INE, "Encuesta nacional de victimización y percepción de seguridad ciudadana 2009 (ENVPSC-2009). Documento técnico" (Caracas: Instituto Nacional de Estadística, República Bolivariana de Venezuela, May 2010); Plan Seguridad Ciudadana, "Encuesta de victimización y percepción de inseguridad

2008" (Quito: Plan Seguridad Ciudadana, 2008), https://www.oas.org/dsp/Observatorio/
Tablas/Ecuador/encuesta_de_victimizaci%C3%B3n.pdf; Latin American Public
Opinion Project, "Latin American Public Opinion Project," *Latin American Public Opinion
Project 2012. Vanderbilt University* (blog), 2012, http://www.vanderbilt.edu/lapop/;
Latinobarómetro, "Informe 2013" (Santiago de Chile: Corporación Latinobarómetro,
2013); Daniel Ortega and Pablo Sanguinetti, "Citizen Security and Welfare," in *Towards a
Safer Latin America. A New Perspective to Prevent and Control Crime.*, ed. CAF Development
Bank (Bogotá: CAF Development Bank, 2015).

178. "Citizen Security and Justice: Improving Quality Information on Crime and Violence,"
Sistema regional de indicadores estandarizados de convivencia y seguridad ciudadana (blog),
2011, http://www.seguridadyregion.com/en/indicators/citizen-security-indicators.html.

179. United Nations Development Programme, "Seguridad ciudadana con rostro humano:
Diagnóstico y propuestas para América Latina," 36.

180. Stathis N. Kalyvas, "The Urban Bias in Research on Civil Wars," *Security Studies* 13, no. 3
(March 1, 2004): 160–90.

181. See, e.g., Teresa Pires Do Rio Caldeira, *City of Walls: Crime, Segregation, and Citizenship in
São Paulo* (Berkeley: University of California Press, 2000); Dammert, *Fear and Crime in
Latin America*; Mónica Lacarrieu, "La 'insoportable levedad' de lo urbano," *EURE (Santiago)*
33, no. 99 (August 2007): 47–64, https://doi.org/10.4067/S0250-71612007000200005;
Fernando Carrión, ed., *Seguridad ciudadana, ¿espejismo o realidad?"* (Quito: FLACSO Quito,
2007); Alexis Heeb, "Violent Crime, Public Perceptions, and Citizen Security Strategies in
Colombia during the 1990s" (PhD diss., University of Oxford, 2002).

182. The Venezuelan INE "Encuesta nacional de victimización y percepción de seguridad
ciudadana 2009 (ENVPSC-2009). Documento técnico," 160, for example, asked citizens which group they primarily perceive as responsible for insecurity. When people
fear victimization by that group, they are unlikely to state their perceptions in the
questionnaire.

Chapter 3

1. Interview with a community member, San Lorenzo, Ecuador, 2012.

2. Itty Abraham and Willem van Schendel, "Introduction: The Making of Illicitness," in *Illicit
Flows and Criminal Things: States, Borders, and the Other Side of Globalization*, ed. Willem van
and Abraham Schendel (Bloomington: Indiana University Press, 2005), 25.

3. Shulamit Reinharz, *Feminist Methods in Social Research* (New York: Oxford University Press,
1992), 248.

4. I. William Zartman, *Understanding Life in the Borderlands: Boundaries in Depth and in Motion*
(Athens: University of Georgia Press, 2010), 9.

5. Zartman, 11.

6. Peter Andreas, "Redrawing the Line: Borders and Security in the Twenty-First Century,"
International Security 28 (2003): 81.

7. Ibid.

8. See Mladen Klemencic and Clive H. Schofield, "Contested Boundaries and Troubled
Borderlands," in *Challenged Borderlands: Transcending Political and Cultural Boundaries*, ed.
Barbara Jo Morehouse, Vera Pavlakovich-Kochi, and Doris Wastl-Walter (Aldershot: Ashgate,
2004), 63–64.

9. Thomas M. Wilson and Hastings Donnan, "Borders and Border Studies," in *A Companion to
Border Studies*, ed. Thomas M. Wilson and Hastings Donnan (Chichester: Wiley-Blackwell,
2012), 1–3.

10. Barbara J. Morehouse, Vera Pavlakovich-Kochi, and Doris Wastl-Walter, "Introduction:
Perspectives on Borderlands," in *Challenged Borderlands: Transcending Political and Cultural
Boundaries*, ed. Barbara J. Morehouse, Vera Pavlakovich-Kochi, and Doris Wastl-Walter
(Aldershot: Ashgate, 2004), 7; Andreas, "Redrawing the Line: Borders and Security in the
Twenty-First Century," 81. Peter Andreas, *Border Games: Policing the US-Mexico Divide*, 2nd
ed. (Ithaca, NY: Cornell University Press, 2009), vii–viii.

11. Abraham and Schendel, "Introduction: The Making of Illicitness," 5.
12. Kaghram and Levitt, "Constructing Transnational Studies," in *Rethinking Transnationalism: The Meso-Link of Organisations*, ed. Ludger Pries (New York: Routledge, 2008), 24.
13. Peter M. Slowe, "The Geography of Borderlands—The Case of the Quebec—United States Borderlands," *Geographical Journal* 157, no. 2 (1991): 191–98, https://doi.org/10.2307/635276.
14. Anne L. Clunan and Harold A. Trinkunas, eds. *Ungoverned Spaces: Alternatives to State Authority in an Era of Softened Sovereignty* (Stanford, CA: Stanford University Press, 2010), 9.
15. Richard H. Friman and Peter Andreas, eds., "Introduction: International Relations and the Illicit Global Economy," in *The Illicit Global Economy and State Power* (Boulder, CO: Rowman & Littlefield, 1999), 1.
16. Manuel Castells, *End of Millennium*, 2nd ed. (Oxford: Wiley-Blackwell, 2010), 172.
17. Morehouse, Pavlakovich-Kochi, and Wastl-Walter, 7.
18. Neil Brenner, "Beyond State-Centrism? Space, Territoriality, and Geographical Scale in Globalization Studies," *Theory and Society* 28, no. 1 (February 1, 1999): 60–67, https://doi.org/10.1023/A:1006996806674.
19. Ken'ichi Ōmae, *The Borderless World: Power and Strategy in the Interlinked Economy* (London: Collins, 1990).
20. Andreas, "Redrawing the Line: Borders and Security in the Twenty-First Century," 108.
21. Ibid., 83.
22. Abraham and Schendel, "Introduction: The Making of Illicitness," 4.
23. Duncan Deville, "The Illicit Supply Chain," in *Convergence: Illicit Networks and National Security in the Age of Globalization*, ed. Michael Miklaucic and Jacqueline Brewer (Washington, DC: National Defense University, 2013), 63.
24. Andreas, *Border Games*, 15.
25. Ibid., 144.
26. Willem van Schendel, "Spaces of Engagement. How Borderlands, Illegal Flows, and Territorial States Interlock," in *Illicit Flows and Criminal Things: States, Borders, and the Other Side of Globalization*, ed. Willem van Schendel and Itty Abraham (Bloomington: Indiana University Press, 2005), 59; Jonathan Goodhand, "War, Peace and the Places in Between: Why Borderlands Are Central," in *Whose Peace? Critical Perspectives on the Political Economy of Peacebuilding*, ed. Michael Pugh, Neil Cooper, and Mandy Turner (Palgrave Macmillan, 2008), 235; Andreas, *Border Games*, 22–23.
27. Andreas, *Border Games*, 19. The estimated value of drug trafficking alone is 320 billion USD a year. See United Nations Office on Drugs and Crime, "New UNODC Campaign Highlights Transnational Organized Crime as a US$870 Billion a Year Business," United Nations Office on Drugs and Crime (blog), July 16, 2012, http://www.unodc.org/unodc/en/frontpage/2012/July/new-unodc-campaign-highlights-transnational-organized-crime-as-an-us-870-billion-a-year-business.html.
28. Goodhand, "War, Peace and the Places in Between: Why Borderlands Are Central," 236.
29. Daniel Tovar, *Colombia and Venezuela: The Border Dispute over the Gulf*, Military Technology (Bad Neuenahr-Ahrweiler: Mönch Publishing Group, 2016); Semana, "Las claves para entender el lío entre Colombia y Venezuela," *Semana*, June 22, 2015, https://www.semana.com/nacion/articulo/limites-maritimos-entre-colombia-venezuela-entran-de-nuevo-en-disputa/432249-3.
30. Military expenditures of Colombia, Ecuador, and Venezuela were 3.4, 1.7, and 1.4 percent respectively of their GDP in 2013. See Stockholm International Peace Research Institute, "SIPRI Military Expenditure Database" (2014), http://www.sipri.org/research/armaments/milex/milex_database.
31. There are tensions along ethnic boundaries within states though, especially discrimination toward indigenous people.
32. Michael Shifter, "Crisis in the Andes: The Border Dispute between Colombia and Ecuador, and Implications for the Region," *Inter-American Dialogue* (blog), April 10, 2008, http://www.thedialogue.org/page.cfm?pageID=32&pubID=1287. Ideological divides, however, have deepened, especially between Colombia and Venezuela.
33. Gabriel Marcella, *War without Borders: The Colombia-Ecuador Crisis of 2008* (Strategic Studies Institute, 2008), 1; Michael Shifter, "Breakdown in the Andes," *Foreign Affairs*

83 (2004): 126–38; Ivan Briscoe, *Trouble on the Borders: Latin America's New Conflict Zones*, Comment (Madrid: FRIDE, 2008); Scott Mainwaring, Ana María Bejarano, and Eduardo Pizarro Leongómez, *The Crisis of Democratic Representation in the Andes* (Stanford, CA: Stanford University Press, 2006), 1.

34. According to the Táchira police, in 2009, nationally, there were 1,491 detentions for 16,047 homicides, i.e., in 9 percent of cases. In Táchira, for 502 homicides, 30 people were detained, i.e., in only about 6 percent of cases. See Policía de Táchira, "Violencia en el estado de Táchira" (San Cristóbal, Venezuela, 2012). Due to government control, in Venezuela, homicide and impunity rates are difficult to obtain. As of 2011, data gathered by the National Institute of Legal Medicine were managed by the Body of Scientific, Penal and Criminalistics Investigations, appointed by the Venezuelan Ministry of People's Power for Internal Relations and Justice. By withholding the data from the public domain, it is claimed that the Chávez administration and the Maduro administration attempted to cover up the rocketing levels of violence. See, e.g., Juan Diego Restrepo, "'Paras' asesinan en Colombia y arrojan cuerpos en Venezuela," *Verdad Abierta*, August 31, 2011, http://www.verdadabierta.com/index.php?option=com_content&id=2396%3E; Transparencia Venezuela, "Venezuela en el podio de la violencia," February 26, 2015, https://transparencia.org.ve/venezuela-en-el-podio-de-la-violencia/.

35. Marcos Salinas, "Diagnóstico de seguridad ciudadana en el cantón de Sucumbíos. Hacia una política municipal de prevención del delito" (Asociación de Municipalidades del Ecuador, 2012), 21–22; 34. Interview with human rights defender, Lago Agrio, Ecuador, 2012.

36. Nationwide, in 2011, 1 to 3 percent of reported killings in Ecuador resulted in convictions. Since many killings were not reported, less than 1 percent of the overall number of killers were convicted. See Philip Alston, "Report of the Special Rapporteur on Extrajudicial, Summary or Arbitrary Executions, Philip Alston," United Nations General Assembly (Human Rights Council, May 9, 2011), 17.

37. Alta Consejería para la Convivencia y la Seguridad Ciudadana, "Encuesta de convivencia y seguridad ciudadana" (Bogotá: Alta Consejería para la Convivencia y la Seguridad Ciudadana, 2013), http://wsp.presidencia.gov.co/Seguridad-Ciudadana/estrategias-nacionales/Documents/Encuesta-Convivencia-Seguridad-Ciudadana-2013-DANE-comparativo.pdf.

38. Plan Seguridad Ciudadana, "Encuesta de victimización y percepción de inseguridad 2008" (Quito: Plan Seguridad Ciudadana, 2008), 47, https://www.oas.org/dsp/Observatorio/Tablas/Ecuador/encuesta_de_victimizaci%C3%B3n.pdf.

39. "Encuesta nacional de victimización y percepción de seguridad ciudadana 2009 (ENVPSC-2009). Documento técnico" (Caracas: Instituto Nacional de Estadística, República Bolivariana de Venezuela, May 2010), 159.

40. Oscar J. Martínez, *Border People: Life and Society in the US-Mexico Borderlands* (Tucson: University of Arizona Press, 1994), 5–10.

41. Transnational Institute, "Ecuador: 'daños colaterales' por las fumigaciones en la frontera norte," *Transnational Institute* (blog), April 3, 2007, http://www.tni.org/archives/act/16594.

42. El Universo, "Población de la frontera teme que se retomen fumigaciones," August 14, 2014, http://www.eluniverso.com/noticias/2014/08/14/nota/3406196/poblacion-frontera-teme-que-se-retomen-fumigaciones. Colombia banned aerial fumigation in 2015, but in June 2018 it was announced that it would be resumed again, this time with drones (Reuters, "Colombia to Use Drones to Fumigate Coca Leaf with Herbicide," 27 June 2018, https://www.reuters.com/article/us-colombia-drugs/colombia-to-use-drones-to-fumigate-coca-leaf-with-herbicide-idUSKBN1JM368.

43. Marcella, *War without Borders*, v.

44. International Crisis Group, "Improving Security Policy in Colombia," Latin America Briefing (Bogotá, Brussels: International Crisis Group, 2010), 9.

45. Alston, "Report of the Special Rapporteur on Extrajudicial, Summary, or Arbitrary Executions, Philip Alston," 6.

46. Carlos Malamud, *The Long Road to Peace in Colombia. Colombia's Difficult Relations with Its Neighbours: Venezuela*, Part 2 (Madrid: Real Instituto Elcano, 2004).

47. Malamud.

48. Ximena Labrador et al., *Cultura de paz en el Alto Apure y el Táchira: Un reto de frontera*, ed. Rodriguez Villaroel and Arias (Caracas: Universidad Catolica del Tachira, 2009), 234.

49. César Andrés Restrepo, *Colombia: Seguridad y defensa en las fronteras* (Bogotá: Fundación Seguridad y Democracia, 2009), 27.

50. Socorro Ramírez, "Civil Society Peacebuilding on Colombia's Borders," in *Accord. An International Review of Peace Initiatives, Building Peace across Borders,* ed. William Zartman and Alexander Ramsbotham, Accord 22 (London: Conciliation Resources, 2011), 60–61, http://www.c-r.org/accord-article/civil-society-peacebuilding-colombias-borders.

51. In August 2014, Bogotá and Quito announced the formalization of three further border crossings: Chiles/Tufiño, El Carmelo/La Victoria, and Puerto El Carmen/Puerto Ospina Ministerio de Defensa Nacional, "Ecuador y Colombia aúnan esfuerzos para controles en frontera" (Quito: Ministerio de Defensa Nacional de Ecuador, July 24, 2014).

52. Heikki Eskelinen, Ilkka Liikanen, and Jukka Oksa, *Curtains of Iron and Gold: Reconstructing Borders and Scales of Interaction* (Aldershot: Ashgate, 1999), 10.

53. Michel Baud and Willem van Schendel, "Toward a Comparative History of Borderlands," *Journal of World History* 8 (1997): 211–42, http://www.jstor.org/stable/20068594; Abraham and Schendel, "Introduction: The Making of Illicitness"; Willem van Schendel and Itty Abraham, eds., *Illicit Flows and Criminal Things: States, Borders, and the Other Side of Globalization* (Bloomington: Indiana University Press, 2005), 44; Jonathan Goodhand, "Epilogue: The View from the Border," in *Violence on the Margins: States, Conflict, and Borderlands,* ed. Benedikt Korf and Timothy Raeymaekers (New York: Palgrave Macmillan, 2013), 247–64.

54. Benedikt Korf and Timothy Raeymaekers, *Violence on the Margins: States, Conflict, and Borderlands* (New York: Palgrave Macmillan, 2013), 7.

55. Willem van Schendel, *The Bengal Borderland: Beyond State and Nation in South Asia* (London: Anthem, 2005), 385.

56. See Niles M. Hansen, *The Border Economy: Regional Development in the Southwest* (Austin: University of Texas Press, 1981), 19; Zartman, *Understanding Life in the Borderlands,* 1–5; Markus Virgil Höhne and Dereje Feyissa, "Centering Borders and Borderlands: The Evidence from Africa," in *Violence on the Margins: States, Conflict, and Borderlands,* ed. Benedikt Korf and Timothy Raeymaekers (New York: Palgrave Macmillan, 2013), 56.

57. *The Border Economy,* 19.

58. *Curtains of Iron and Gold,* 22.

59. John Robert Victor Prescott, *Political Frontiers and Boundaries* (London: Allen & Unwin, 1987), 13–14.

60. "War, Peace, and the Places in Between: Why Borderlands Are Central," 228.

61. Goodhand, 228; see also Schendel, "Illicit Flows and Criminal Things: States, Borders, and the Other Side of Globalization," 44.

62. For internal borderlands see Jackson "Potential Difference: Internal Borderlands in Africa," in *Whose Peace? Critical Perspectives on the Political Economy of Peacebuilding,* ed. Michael Pugh, Neil Cooper, and Mandy Turner (Basingstoke: Palgrave Macmillan, 2008), 268–88 and Goodhand, "War, Peace and the Places in Between: Why Borderlands Are Central," 228.

63. "Introduction: Perspectives on Borderlands," 29.

64. See Martínez, *Border People: Life and Society in the US-Mexico Borderlands,* xvii–xviii.

65. Raimondo Strassoldo, "Border Studies: The State of the Art in Europe," in *Borderlands in Africa: A Multidisciplinary and Comparative Focus on Nigeria and West Africa,* ed. A. I Asiwaju and P. O. Adeniyi (Lagos: University of Lagos Press, 1989), 393, cited in Zartman 2010, 6.

66. *Violence on the Margins,* 4.

67. See, e.g., David Newman and Anssi Paasi, "Fences and Neighbours in the Postmodern World: Boundary Narratives in Political Geography," *Progress in Human Geography* 22, no. 2 (April 1, 1998): 186–207, https://doi.org/10.1191/030913298666039113; Hastings Donnan and Thomas M. Wilson, *Borders: Frontiers of Identity, Nation, and State* (Oxford: Berg, 1999); Vladimir Kolossov, "Border Studies: Changing Perspectives and Theoretical Approaches," *Geopolitics* 10, no. 4 (2005): 606–32, https://doi.org/10.1080/14650040500318415; David Newman, "The Lines That Continue to Separate Us: Borders in Our 'Borderless' World," *Progress in Human Geography* 30, no. 2 (April 1, 2006): 143–61, https://doi.org/10.1191/0309132506ph599xx; Thomas M. Wilson and Hastings Donnan, *A Companion to Border Studies* (Chichester: Wiley-Blackwell, 2012). I define "heartlands" as

the spaces where the influence of the political and economic centers of the states supersedes the border effect. Schendel and Abraham, *Illicit Flows and Criminal Things: States, Borders, and the Other Side of Globalization*, 49.

68. Baud and van Schendel, "Toward a Comparative History of Borderlands"; Abraham and Schendel, "Introduction: The Making of Illicitness."

69. Goodhand, "War, Peace, and the Places in Between: Why Borderlands Are Central," 230.

70. Goodhand, 228.

71. Schendel, "Illicit Flows and Criminal Things: States, Borders, and the Other Side of Globalization," 46.

72. Zartman, *Understanding Life in the Borderlands*, 2.

73. Ibid., 4.

74. Abraham and Schendel, "Introduction: The Making of Illicitness," 55.

75. United Nations Office on Drugs and Crime, "Transnational Organized Crime: The Globalized Illegal Economy," Transnational Organized Crime: Let's put them out of business, 2017, https://www.unodc.org/toc/en/crimes/organized-crime.html.

76. United Nations Office on Drugs and Crime, "Market Analysis of Plant-Based Drugs. Opiates, Cocaine, Cannabis," in *World Drug Report 2017*, ed. United Nations Office on Drugs and Crime, vol. 3 (Vienna: United Nations Office on Drugs and Crime, 2017), 25–26.

77. United Nations Office on Drugs and Crime and Government of Colombia, "Colombia. Monitoreo de Cultivos de Coca 2017," 24. http://www.unodc.org/documents/colombia/2017/julio/CENSO_2017_WEB_baja.pdf.

78. Various interviews with ex-combatants, Pasto, Colombia, 2012.

79. Bruce Michael Bagley, William O. Walker, and University of Miami. North-South Center, *Drug Trafficking in the Americas* (Coral Gables, FL: University of Miami, North-South Center, 1995); Juan Gabriel Tokatlian, ed., *Narcotráfico en América Latina* (Caracas: Corporación Andina de Fomento—CAF, 2009).

80. While guerrillas dominated rural areas, post-demobilized groups were predominantly present in urban areas.

81. For the Colombian-Venezuelan borderlands see, e.g., Ana Bustamante, "La frontera colombo-venezolana: De la conflictividad limítrofe a la global," in *Relaciones fronterizas: Encuentros y conflictos*, ed. Fernando Carrión and Johanna Espín (Quito: Flacso-Sede Ecuador, 2011), 203–22; for the Colombian-Ecuadorian borderlands see, e.g., Socorro Ramírez, "Dinámicas y problemáticas en la zona fronteriza colombo-ecuatoriana," in *Relaciones fronterizas: Encuentros y conflictos*, ed. Fernando Carrión and Johanna Espín (Quito: Flacso-Sede Ecuador, 2011), 223–34.

82. María Clemencia Ramírez, "Negotiating Peace and Visibility as a Civil Society in Putumayo amid the Armed Conflict and the War on Drugs," in *Colombia: Building Peace in a Time of War*, ed. Virginia Marie Bouvier (Washington, DC: United States Institute of Peace Press, 2009), 312.

83. Alcaldía de Mocoa, "Plan de desarrollo municipal 'Sí hay futuro para Mocoa 2012–2015'" (Mocoa: Alcaldía Municipal de Mocoa, 2012), 25, http://www.putumayo.gov.co/images/documentos/PDMunicipales/PDM_Mocoa2012-2015.pdf.

84. Natalia Lozano-Mancera, "Homicidios de indígenas, 2003–2012: Instrumento de apropiación violenta de la tierra" (Bogotá: Instituto Nacional de Medicina Legal y Ciencias Forenses, 2012), 116. See also María Clemencia Ramírez, *Between the Guerrillas and the State: The Cocalero Movement, Citizenship, and Identity in the Colombian Amazon* (Durham, NC: Duke University Press, 2011).

85. For a detailed account of the role of US foreign policy for Putumayo see Winifred Tate, *Drugs, Thugs, and Diplomats: US Policymaking in Colombia*, Anthropology of Policy (Stanford, CA: Stanford University Press, 2015).

86. Fundación Paz y Reconciliación, "Departamento de Putumayo. Tercera monografía" (Bogotá: Fundación Paz y Reconciliación, February 24, 2014), 13–14.

87. Ramírez, *Between the Guerrillas and the State*.

88. Carla Celi, Molina Camilo, and Weber Gabriela, *Cooperación al desarrollo en la frontera norte: Una mirada desde Sucumbíos 2000–2007* (Quito: Centro de Investigaciones CIUDAD, 2009), 32.

89. I have not detected any strategic alliances and pacific coexistence in this region. This can be explained by the fact that the ELN does not have presence in Putumayo, and other insurgent groups with similar ideological motivations demobilized or exited from the region in previous years.

90. Fundación Paz y Reconciliación, "Departamento de Putumayo. Tercera monografía," 7.

91. Laura González Carranza, *Peones en un ajedrez militar: Los habitantes de la frontera norte* (Quito: Fundación Regional de Asesoría en Derechos Humanos, 2011), 43.

92. Comisión Nacional de Reparación y Reconciliación, "La masacre de El Tigre. Putumayo," (Bogotá: Comisión Nacional de Reparación y Reconciliación, 2011).

93. Office of the High Commissioner for Peace, "Proceso de paz con las autodefensas: Informe ejecutivo" (Bogotá: Presidency of the Republic of Colombia, June 2006), 80.

94. Fundación Paz y Reconciliación, "Departamento de Putumayo. Tercera monografía," 13–14; Sistema de Alertas Tempranas, "Informe de Riesgo N° 026-09," Sistema de Alertas Tempranas. Defensoría del Pueblo de Colombia (Bogotá: Defensoría del Pueblo de Colombia, October 27, 2009).

95. Salinas, "Diagnóstico de seguridad ciudadana en el cantón de Sucumbíos. Hacia una política municipal de prevención del delito," 13.

96. Geoffrey Ramsey, "Mapping Gun Smuggling Routes in Ecuador" (InSight Crime, September 17, 2012), http://www.insightcrime.org/news-briefs/mapping-gun-smuggling-routes-in-ecuador.

97. Salinas, "Diagnóstico de seguridad ciudadana en el cantón de Sucumbíos. Hacia una política municipal de prevención del delito," 13.

98. In 2016, Nariño had the largest coca cultivation area (42,627 hectares) of all Colombian departments, followed by Putumayo with 25,162 hectares. See United Nations Office on Drugs and Crime and Government of Colombia, "Colombia. Monitoreo de Cultivos de Coca 2017," 24.

99. This explains why, in 2013, for example, only one hydrochloride laboratory, part of the second production stage, was destroyed in Putumayo as opposed to twenty-one in Nariño. United Nations Office on Drugs and Crime and Government of Colombia, "Colombia. Monitoreo de Cultivos de Coca 2013," 101.

100. Sander Lauret, *La frontera norte ecuatoriana ante la influencia del conflicto colombiano: Las sorprendentes dimensiones de la dinámica transfronteriza entre la provincia de Carchi y el Departamento de Nariño* (Quito: Abya-Yala, 2009), 124–34, 156.

101. Due to landslides, this road was closed for over six weeks in 2012 when I had intended to return from Mocoa to Pasto. As a result, I traveled from Mocoa to Quito instead.

102. Interviews with farmers, Putumayo, Colombia, and Sucumbíos, Ecuador, 2011 and 2012.

103. Sistema de Alertas Tempranas, "Informe de Riesgo N° 013-10," Sistema de Alertas Tempranas. Defensoría del Pueblo de Colombia (Bogotá: Defensoría del Pueblo de Colombia, 2010).

104. El Espectador, "Puerto Asís, entre la coca y el consumismo," available at: https://colombia2020.elespectador.com/territorio/puerto-asis-entre-la-coca-y-el-consumismo.

105. Interviews with various local residents, Putumayo, Colombia, and Sucumbíos, Ecuador, 2012. See also Fiscalía General del Estado, FLACSO Ecuador, "Control de armas: Propuestas sobre armas de fuego, políticas públicas," *Perfil Criminológico* 17 (July 2015), http://repositorio.flacsoandes.edu.ec/bitstream/10469/7514/2/BFLACSO-PC17.pdf; Dieg Bravo, "Tres sectores se abastecen del tráfico de armas," *El Comercio*, https://www.elcomercio.com/actualidad/seguridad/tres-sectores-se-abastecen-del.html; Maiah Jaskoski, "The Colombian FARC in Northern Ecuador: Borderline and Borderland Dynamics," in *American Crossings: Border Politics in the Western Hemisphere*, ed. Maiah Jaskoski et al., 171–88 (Baltimore: Johns Hopkins University Press, 2015).

106. Sistema de Alertas Tempranas, "Informe de Riesgo N° 026-09," 6.

107. Diaro del Sur, "Evalúan amenazas de 'Águilas Negras,'" January 14, 2009.

108. Office of the High Commissioner for Peace, "Proceso de paz con las autodefensas: Informe ejecutivo," 42.

109. Magda Paola Núñez Gantiva, "ELN-FARC: Ahora sí juntos," *Arcanos* 15, no. 17 (2012): 73.

110. Ariel Ávila and Magda Paola Núñez Gantiva, "Las dinámicas territoriales del Ejército de Liberación Nacional: Arauca, Cauca, y Nariño," *Arcanos* 15 (2010): 29.

111. The FARC are organized hierarchically into Central High Command, the Estado Mayor Central, and into Blocks with several Fronts that include Columns with Companies, Guerrillas, and Squads.

112. Núñez Gantiva, "ELN-FARC: Ahora sí juntos," 72.

113. Interview with an ex-combatant, Pasto, Colombia, 2011.

114. Sistema de Alertas Tempranas, "Nota de Seguimiento N°007-11, Tercera nota al informe de Riesgo N° 029-07," Sistema de Alertas Tempranas. Defensoría del Pueblo de Colombia (Bogotá: Defensoría del Pueblo de Colombia, April 2011), 5.

115. Sistema de Alertas Tempranas, "Nota de Seguimiento N° 017-11. Tercera nota al informe de Riesgo N° 024-08 A.I.," Sistema de Alertas Tempranas. Defensoría del Pueblo de Colombia (Bogotá: Defensoria del Pueblo de Colombia, July 7, 2011).

116. Sistema de Alertas Tempranas, "Nota de Seguimiento N°007-11, Tercera nota al informe de Riesgo N° 029-07," 7–8.

117. Interview with a government official, Pasto, Colombia, 2011.

118. *Elenos* are ELN members.

119. Interview with an ex-guerrilla, Pasto, Colombia, 2011.

120. Diplomatic relations were broken after the Colombian state forces bombed a FARC camp in Ecuador in 2008 (see Prologue).

121. Interview with a civil society representative, Pasto, Colombia, 2011.

122. Interviews and conversations with residents in Chical, Tufiño, and Maldonado, Ecuador, 2012.

123. Opposed to the central government's military approach during the Uribe administration, the successive governments of Nariño implemented development programs to address deficient infrastructure. See Annette Idler and Borja Paladini Adell, "When Peace Implies Engaging the 'Terrorist': Peacebuilding in Colombia through Transforming Political Violence and Terrorism," in *The Nexus between Terrorism Studies and Peace and Conflict Studies*, ed. Yannis Tellidis and Harmonie Toros (London: Routledge, 2015).

124. Interview with a government official, Pasto, Colombia, 2011.

125. Interview with an ex-member of the FARC's financing front, Pasto, Colombia, 2011.

126. United Nations Office on Drugs and Crime and Government of Colombia, "Colombia. Monitoreo de Cultivos de Coca 2017," 11; 90.

127. The River Patia further north plays a similar role.

128. I use the term "twin towns" to refer to towns that are located on opposing sides of an international borderline, typically have close social and/or economic ties with each other, and are relatively similar in size. Isabella Soi and Paul Nugent, "Peripheral Urbanism in Africa: Border Towns and Twin Towns in Africa," *Journal of Borderlands Studies* 32, no. 4 (2017): 535–56, DOI: 10.1080/08865655.2016.1196601.

129. Lauret, *La frontera norte ecuatoriana ante la influencia del conflicto colombiano*, 156.

130. Interview with a local government official, Pasto, Colombia, 2011.

131. Interviews with residents, Tumaco and Pasto, Colombia, 2011.

132. Interview with an international agency staff member, Esmeraldas, Ecuador, 2012. See also El Universo, "Juez ordena prisión de coronel de la policía," September 29, 2011, http://www.eluniverso.com/2011/09/29/1/1422/juez-ordena-prision-coronel-policia.html; La Hora, "Coronel de policía de Esmeraldas condenado a seis años de prisión," June 29, 2012, http://www.lahora.com.ec/index.php/noticias/show/1101354038/-1/Coronel_de_Polic%C3%ADa_de_Esmeraldas_condenado_a_seis_a%C3%B1os_de_prisi%C3%B3n.html#.U_NDuPldWSo.

133. Ana Bustamante, "The Border Region of North Santander (Colombia)-Táchira (Venezuela): The Border without Walls," *Journal of Borderlands Studies* 23 (2008): 9.

134. Semana, "Arauca Saudita," *Semana*, October 27, 1986, http://www.semana.com/especiales/articulo/arauca-saudita/8217-3.

135. Labrador et al., *Cultura de paz en el Alto Apure y el Táchira: Un reto de frontera*, 217.

136. Observación y Solidaridad con Arauca OBSAR, "Arauca: Conflicto armado y problemáticas humanitarias 2011," Arauca, Cultivando Paz en Medio del Conflicto Armado

(Arauca: Secretariado Diocesano de Pastoral Social, Caritas Arauca, 2011); Defensoría del Pueblo de Colombia, "Panorama del conflicto armado en Arauca," PowerPoint presentation (Arauca: Defensoría del Pueblo de Colombia, 2011).

137. Núñez Gantiva, "ELN-FARC: Ahora sí juntos."

138. Defensoría del Pueblo, "Panorama del conflicto armado en Arauca."

139. Jack Sweeney, "Guerras fronterizas: FBL contra el ELN," *VenEconomía Mensual* 22, no. 1 (October 2004), http://www.veneconomy.com/site/files/articulos/artEsp4022_2819.pdf.

140. Supposedly, alias "Grannoble," FARC leader Mono Jojoy's brother, was killed in El Orza Semana, " 'Grannobles', hermano del 'Mono Jojoy': ¿El fin de un 'capo' de las FARC?," September 3, 2012, http://www.semana.com/nacion/articulo/grannobles-hermano-del-mono-jojoy-el-fin-capo-farc/264130-3.

141. Juanita León, "La reconquista de Arauca," *Semana*, January 3, 2003, http://www.semana.com/nacion/articulo/la-reconquista-arauca/56223-3; see also Semana, "Conversación entre corruptos," *Semana*, November 3, 2003, http://www.semana.com/nacion/articulo/conversacion-entre-corruptos/61680-3; Semana, "Vientos de guerra," *Semana*, December 14, 1992, http://www.semana.com/nacion/articulo/vientos-guerra/18844-3.

142. United Nations High Commissioner for Refugees, "Internal Report on Border Mission" (Arauca, Colombia, 2012).

143. Roberto Alexi Rojas Salas, "Cerac evidencia presencia del Clan Úsuga, los Rastrojos, y Águilas Negras en frontera con Venezuela," September 4, 2015, http://lavozdelrioarauca.com/2015/09/cerac-evidencia-presencia-del-clan-usuga-los-rastrojos-y-aguilas-negras-en-frontera-con-venezuela/.

144. Fundación Ideas para la Paz, "El bloque vencedores de Arauca: Documento de la fundación ideas para la paz," *Semana*, April 30, 2008, http://www.semana.com/on-line/articulo/el-bloque-vencedores-arauca/92458-3. According to some reports, the Águilas Negras and the Vencedores are the same group; see, e.g., Rojas Salas, "Cerac evidencia presencia del Clan Úsuga, los Rastrojos, y Águilas Negras en frontera con Venezuela."

145. Interview with a farmer, Norte de Santander, Colombia, October 2014.

146. Interview with various farmers, Norte de Santander, Colombia, October 2014.

147. Fundación Progresar, *Tantas vidas arrebatadas. La desaparición forzada de personas: Una estrategia sistemática de guerra sucia en Norte de Santander*, ed. Wilfredo Cañizares Arévalo (Cúcuta, Colombia, 2010), 38–45.

148. Sistema de Alertas Tempranas, "Informe de Riesgo N° 012-11 A.I.," Defensoría del Pueblo de Colombia (Bogotá, August 18, 2011).

149. See Edgar de Jesús Velásquez Rivera, "Historia del Paramilitarismo en Colombia," *Historia* 26, no. 1 (São Paulo, 2007): 134–53.

150. Fundación Progresar, *Tantas Vidas Arrebatadas*, 38–39.

151. Labrador et al., *Cultura de paz en el Alto Apure y el Táchira: Un reto de frontera*, 221.

152. Sistema de Alertas Tempranas, "Informe de Riesgo N° 012-11 A.I.," 8.

153. See Annette Idler, María Belén Garrido, and Cécile Mouly, "Peace Territories in Colombia: Comparing Civil Resistance in Two War-Torn Communities," *Journal of Peacebuilding & Development* 10, no. 3 (2 September 2015): 1–15, https://doi.org/10.1080/15423166.2015.1082437.

154. Email correspondence with a civil society member in Valledupar, February 2013.

155. Various interviews, Valledupar, Colombia, October 2012. See also Semana, "La nueva estrategia contra las FARC," *Semana*, February 25, 2012, http://www.semana.com//nacion/articulo/la-nueva-estrategia-contra-farc/253985-3.

156. Lia Osório Machado, André Reyes Novaes, and Licio do Rego Monteiro, "Building Walls, Breaking Barriers: Territory, Integration, and the Rule of Law in Frontier Zones," *Journal of Borderlands Studies* 24, no. 3 (2009): 110, https://doi.org/10.1080/08865655.2009.9695742.

157. Various interviews with local community members, Norte de Santander, Colombia, April 2012.

158. Ariel Ávila and Magda Paola Núñez Gantiva, "Expansión territorial y alianzas tácticas," *Arcanos*, 2008, 58.

159. Sistema de Alertas Tempranas, "Informe de Riesgo N° 012-11 A.I.," 8.
160. Ibid.; Francisco E. Thoumi, *Political Economy and Illegal Drugs in Colombia*, Studies on the Impact of the Illegal Drug Trade (Boulder, CO: Lynne Rienner, 1995); Francisco E. Thoumi, *Illegal Drugs, Economy, and Society in the Andes* (London: Woodrow Wilson Center Press; Johns Hopkins University Press, 2003), http://www.loc.gov/catdir/toc/ecip044/2003012400.html.
161. In other cases, this distance may make it hard to consider the place still "borderland." However, the size of borderlands depends on the extent to which cross-border transactions reach into areas distant from the borderline. As Morehouse et al. note, borderlands can be "quite narrow, huddling close to the boundary, or [...] may extend for many miles in one or both directions from the dividing line" (Morehouse, Pavlakovich-Kochi, and Wastl-Walter, "Introduction: Perspectives on Borderlands," 30); see also Vorrath, "On the Margin of Statehood?: State-Society Relations in African Borderlands," 86.
162. Sistema de Alertas Tempranas, "Informe de Riesgo N° 012-11 A.I.," 8.
163. Interview with a community leader, Cúcuta, Colombia, 2011.
164. Interview with a high-ranking police official, Cúcuta, Colombia, 2012.
165. Labrador et al., *Cultura de paz en el Alto Apure y el Táchira: Un reto de frontera*, 221.
166. The M-19 was also present and engaged in kidnappings.
167. Ariel Ávila and Carmen Rosa Guerra Ariza, "Frontera La Guajira y Cesar-Zulia," in *La frontera caliente entre Colombia y Venezuela*, ed. Ariel Ávila (Cota, Colombia: Corporación Nuevo Arco Iris, 2012), 361.
168. United Nations Development Programme, Área de Paz, Desarrollo, y Reconciliación, "Cesar: Análisis de la conflictividad" (United Nations Development Programme, 2010), 32.
169. Ávila and Guerra Ariza, "Frontera La Guajira y Cesar-Zulia," 388; United Nations Development Programme, "Cesar: Análisis de la conflictividad," 40.
170. Juan Francisco "Kiko" Gómez was accused of multiple crimes including several murders and links with the narco-broker Marcos "Marquito" Figueroa García, AUC leaders, and post-demobilized group leaders. Miriam Wells, "Colombia Governor Arrested for Multiple Murders, Crime Links," *InSight Crime—Organized Crime in the Americas* (blog), October 2013, http://www.insightcrime.org/news-briefs/colombia-governor-arrested-for-multiple-murders-crime-links.
171. Ávila and Guerra Ariza, "Frontera La Guajira y Cesar-Zulia," 353.
172. United Nations Development Programme, "Cesar: Análisis de la conflictividad," 17.
173. Cesar is Colombia's second most ethnically and culturally diverse department with seven different indigenous groups and a large Afro-Colombian population. Ibid., 13–14.
174. Ávila and Guerra Ariza, "Frontera La Guajira y Cesar-Zulia," 361.
175. Ibid., 361.
176. Ibid., 357.
177. Ibid., 356–57.
178. Presidencia de la República de Colombia. "Diagnóstico de la situación del pueblo indígena Wayúu" (Bogotá: Observatorio del Programa Presidencial de Derechos Humanos y Derecho Internacional Humanitario de la Presidencia de la República, 2010), 1, http://www.derechoshumanos.gov.co/Observatorio/Documents/2010/DiagnosticoIndigenas/Diagnostico_WAY%C3%9AU.pdf; Milana Peralta et al., "La Guajira en su laberinto: Transformaciones y desafíos de la violencia," Informes FIP (Bogotá: Fundación Ideas para la Paz, August 2011).
179. Peralta et al., "La Guajira en su Laberinto," 7.
180. Lina Britto, "A Trafficker's Paradise: The 'War on Drugs' and the New Cold War in Colombia," *Contemporánea: Historia y problemas del siglo XX* 1, no. 1 (2010): 159; Ávila and Guerra Ariza, "Frontera La Guajira y Cesar-Zulia," 361.
181. Peralta et al., "La Guajira en su laberinto: Transformaciones y desafíos de la violencia."
182. Peralta et al., 9; Ávila and Guerra Ariza, "Frontera La Guajira y Cesar-Zulia," 351.
183. Interview with a Wayúu leader, Maicao, Colombia, 2012.
184. Interview with a Wayúu leader, Paraguaipoa, Venezuela, 2012. Between 18 and 20 April 2004, the paramilitary Counterinsurgency Front Wayúu massacred six Wayúu in Bahía Portete and displaced six hundred people. See Comisión Nacional de Reparación y Reconciliación (Colombia) CNRR, *La masacre de Bahía Portete: Mujeres Wayuu en la mira*, Pensamiento (Bogotá: Taurus, 2010), 29.

185. Interview with an international agency staff member, San Cristóbal, Venezuela, May 2012.
186. Korf and Raeymaekers, *Violence on the Margins*, 5.

Chapter 4

1. Interview with a local resident, Lago Agrio, Ecuador, 2012.
2. Interview with a farmer from Samaniego, Pasto, Colombia, 2012.
3. Paul Staniland, "States, Insurgents, and Wartime Political Orders," *Perspectives on Politics* 10, no. 2 (2012): 243–64, https://www.jstor.org/stable/41479550; Stathis N. Kalyvas, *The Logic of Violence in Civil War* (Cambridge, UK: Cambridge University Press, 2006).
4. "States, Insurgents, and Wartime Political Orders," 252.
5. This situation resembles to some extent Kalyvas' "zone 3" type of territory, which is contested by the parties. See Kalyvas, *The Logic of Violence in Civil War*, 240–43.
6. Stathis N. Kalyvas, "Wanton and Senseless? The Logic of Massacres in Algeria," *Rationality and Society* 11 (1999): 243–85, http://journals.sagepub.com/doi/abs/10.1177/104346399011003001; Kalyvas, *The Logic of Violence in Civil War*.
7. Comisión Nacional de Reparación y Reconciliación, "La masacre de El Tigre. Putumayo," (Bogotá: Comisión Nacional de Reparación y Reconciliación, 2011), 38; Ignacio Martín-Baró, "Prólogo," in *Derechos humanos: Todo es el dolor con que se mira*, ed. Elizabeth Lira and David Becker (Santiago de Chile: Ediciones ILAS, 1989), 9.
8. World Health Organization, "World Report on Violence and Health. Summary" (Geneva: World Health Organization, 2002), 21, http://www.who.int/violence_injury_prevention/violence/world_report/en/summary_en.pdf.
9. Interview with a displaced farmer from Bajo Putumayo, Mocoa, Colombia, 2011.
10. Daniel Pécaut, "From the Banality of Violence to Real Terror: The Case of Colombia," in *Societies of Fear: The Legacy of Civil War, Violence, and Terror in Latin America*, ed. Kees Koonings and Dirk Krujit (London: Zed Books, 1999), 150.
11. Interview with a displaced farmer from Bajo Putumayo, Mocoa, Colombia, 2011.
12. María Clemencia Ramírez, "Negotiating Peace and Visibility as a Civil Society in Putumayo amid the Armed Conflict and the War on Drugs," in *Colombia: Building Peace in a Time of War*, ed. Virginia Marie Bouvier (Washington, DC: United States Institute of Peace Press, 2009), 322.
13. This statement refers to the practice of "false positives" (see chapter 1).
14. Interview with a displaced woman from Bajo Putumayo, Mocoa, Colombia, 2011.
15. "Terror Warfare and the Medicine of Peace," *Medical Anthropology Quarterly*, New Series, 12, no. 1 (March 1, 1998): 107–08, http://statecrime.org/data/2011/10/nordstrom1998a.pdf.
16. Comisión Nacional de Reparación y Reconciliación, "La masacre de El Tigre. Putumayo," 39.
17. Importantly, it is the horrific memories that haunt people and influence their perceived security in the long term, regardless of the factual correctness of their narratives.
18. Laura González Carranza, *Fronteras en el limbo: El Plan Colombia en el Ecuador* (Quito: Fundación Regional de Asesoría en Derechos Humanos, INREDH, 2008), 38–48; Fernando Carrión, "En el límite de la vida: La violencia fronteriza," in *Aproximaciones a la frontera*, ed. Fernando Carrión, Diana Mejía, and Johanna Espín, Colección Fronteras (Quito: FLACSO Ecuador, 2013), 95; Andrés Gómez, "La frontera colombo-ecuatoriana: Desde la ejecución de políticas de seguridad a las consecuencias en seguridad ciudadana," in *Seguridad, planificación y desarrollo de las regiones transfronterizas*, ed. Fernando Carrión, Colección Fronteras (Quito: Ottawa, Canada: FLACSO Ecuador; IDRC-CRDI, 2013), 100.
19. Interview with an employee of a local media outlet, Sucumbíos, Ecuador, January 2012.
20. "Rebels against Rebels: Explaining Violence between Rebel Groups," *Journal of Conflict Resolution* 56, no. 4 (April 24, 2012): 604–28, https://www.jstor.org/stable/23248905.
21. Sistema de Alertas Tempranas, "Informe de Riesgo Nº 018-09," Sistema de Alertas Tempranas. Defensoría del Pueblo de Colombia (Bogotá: Defensoría del Pueblo de Colombia, July 21, 2009), 9.
22. FARC-EP, "Comunicado del décimo frente a la opinión pública colombo-venezolana," September 21, 2004, paras. 3–4.
23. FARC-EP, "Comunicado a la opinión pública," September 30, 2004.

24. Ibid.

25. Sistema de Alertas Tempranas, 9.

26. Observación y Solidaridad con Arauca OBSAR, "Arauca: Conflicto armado y problemáticas humanitarias 2011"; Defensoría del Pueblo, "Panorama del conflicto armado en Arauca," PowerPoint Presentation (Arauca: Defensoría del Pueblo de Colombia, 2011); Núñez Gantiva, "ELN-FARC: Ahora sí juntos," 65.

27. FARC-EP, "Comunicado a la opinión pública," December 20, 2005, para. 3.

28. Ibid., para. 5.

29. FARC-EP, "Comunicado a la opinión pública," December 2007, para. 3; FARC-EP, "Comunicado a la opinión pública nacional e internacional," April 30, 2007, para. 2.

30. Magda Paola Núñez Gantiva, "ELN-FARC: Ahora sí juntos," *Arcanos* 15, no. 17 (2012): 66.

31. Semana, "Cómo el ejército se alió con el ELN en Arauca," January 19, 2009, http://www.semana.com/nacion/como-ejercito-alio-eln-arauca/119765-3.aspx.

32. Ariel Ávila and Sofía León, "Frontera Arauca-Apure," in *La frontera caliente entre Colombia y Venezuela*, ed. Ariel Ávila (Cota, Colombia: Corporación Nuevo Arco Iris, 2012), 81.

33. Ximena Labrador et al., *Cultura de paz en el Alto Apure y el Táchira: Un reto de frontera*, ed. Rodriguez Villaroel and Arias (Caracas: Universidad Catolica del Tachira, 2009), 221.

34. Observación y Solidaridad con Arauca OBSAR, "Arauca: Conflicto armado y problemáticas humanitarias 2011," Arauca, cultivando paz en medio del conflicto armado (Arauca: Secretariado Diocesano de Pastoral Social, Caritas Arauca, 2011), 3.

35. Núñez Gantiva, "ELN-FARC: Ahora sí juntos," 65.

36. Interviews and conversations with local residents, Apure, Venezuela, and Arauca, Colombia, 2012.

37. Interview with a resident, Guasdualito, Venezuela, 2012.

38. Interview with residents, Guasdualito, Venezuela, 2012.

39. Sistema de Alertas Tempranas, "Informe de Riesgo N° 018-09," 3.

40. Núñez Gantiva, "ELN-FARC: Ahora sí juntos," 65.

41. Interviews with residents of border villages, Arauca, Colombia, 2012.

42. Interview with a farmer, Arauca, Colombia, 2012.

43. Interviews with residents of border villages, Arauca, Colombia, 2012. See also United Nations High Commissioner for Refugees, "Internal Report on Border Mission" (Arauca, Colombia, 2012).

44. Risk reports summarize violent incidents, evaluate the threats that arise from the conflict dynamics in a given region, identify vulnerabilities of the affected populations, and provide recommendations to the authorities to prevent and mitigate these risks. See Defensoría del Pueblo de Colombia, "Sistema de Alertas Tempranas," www.defensoria.gov.co/es/public/atencionciudadanoa/1469/Sistema-de-alertas-tempranas---SAT.htm.

45. Observación y Solidaridad con Arauca OBSAR, "Arauca: Conflicto armado y problemáticas humanitarias 2011," 17.

46. Labrador et al., *Cultura de paz en el Alto Apure y el Táchira: Un reto de frontera*, 228, 236–37.

47. Núñez Gantiva, "ELN-FARC: Ahora Sí Juntos."

48. Defensoría del Pueblo, "Panorama del conflicto armado en Arauca"; Sistema de Alertas Tempranas, "Seguimiento a la situación de riesgo por conflicto armado en Arauca," PowerPoint presentation (Defensoría del Pueblo de Colombia, Sistema de Alertas Tempranas, 2010); Ávila and León, 80. In 2010, Arauca was Colombia's third most land mine–affected department. See Sistema de Alertas Tempranas, "Seguimiento a la situación de riesgo por conflicto armado en Arauca," 3.

49. Instituto Nacional de Medicina Legal y Ciencias Forenses, "2016 Forensis, datos para la vida," 18 (Bogotá: Instituto Nacional de Medicina Legal y Ciencias Forenses, 2017), 25, http://www.medicinalegal.gov.co/documents/88730/4023454/Forensis+2016+-+Datos+para+la+Vida.pdf/af636ef3-0e84-46d4-bc1b-a5ec71ac9fc1.

50. Instituto Nacional de Medicina Legal y Ciencias Forenses, "2016 Forensis, datos para la vida"; NoticiasRCN, "Policía confirma que el ELN sí secuestró a 4 arroceros en Arauca," August 18, 2016, http://www.noticiasrcn.com/nacional-pais/policia-confirma-el-eln-si-secuestro-4-arroceros-arauca; El Espectador, "Gaula confirmó que ELN secuestró a cuatro

arroceros en Arauca," August 18, 2016, https://www.elespectador.com/noticias/judicial/gaula-confirmo-eln-secuestro-cuatro-arroceros-arauca-articulo-649746.

51. Nordstrom, "Terror Warfare and the Medicine of Peace," 105.

52. Vaughan Bell et al., "Characteristics of the Colombian Armed Conflict and the Mental Health of Civilians Living in Active Conflict Zones," *Conflict and Health* 6, no. 10 (2012): 6, http://www.conflictandhealth.com/content/pdf/1752-1505-6-10.pdf.

53. Neidi Leonor Macana Tuta, "Comportamiento del suicidio en Colombia, 2011" (Bogotá: National Institute of Legal Medicine and Forensic Sciences of Colombia, 2012), 254–62. This rate dropped subsequently to 5.07 http://www.medicinalegal.gov.co/documents/10180/188820/FORENSIS+2013+3-+suicidio.pdf.

54. La Voz del Cinaruco, "Tres suicidios y el intento de uno más en Arauca en menos de una semana," *La voz del Cinaruco*, September 2012, http://www.lavozdelcinaruco.com/?id=7350.

55. Doris Cardona Arango, Óscar Adolfo Medina-Pérez, and Deisy Viviana Cardona Duque, "Caracterización del suicidio en Colombia, 2000–2010," *Revista colombiana de psicatría* 45, no. 3 (2016): 170–77.

56. Comité Permanente por la Defensa de los Derechos Humanos, "Presencia paramilitar en Arauca. Amenazados líderes sociales" (Colombia, July 12, 2011), http://www.ideaspaz.org/tools/download/54425.

57. Germán De-la-Hoz-Bohórquez, "Colombia. Homicidios 2007" (Bogotá: Instituto Nacional de Medicina Legal y Ciencias Forenses, 2007), 35, http://www.medicinalegal.gov.co/documents/10180/33997/3+Homicidios.pdf/f148f9fe-cafd-4c4a-aafe-16629133821d; Ana Inés Ricaurte-Villota, "Comportamiento del homicidio. Colombia, 2011" (Bogotá: Instituto Nacional de Medicina Legal y Ciencias Forenses, 2011), 83, http://www.medicinalegal.gov.co/documents/10180/34616/2-F-11-Homicidios.pdf/01a6b108-57cd-48bc-9e9b-dcdba0d918a2. Toward the end of 2012, homicide rates rose again. See Natalia Lozano-Mancera, "Homicidios de indígenas, 2003–2012: Instrumento de apropiación violenta de la tierra" (Bogotá: Instituto Nacional de Medicina Legal y Ciencias Forenses, 2012).

58. In Saravena, the Águilas Negras entered already in November 2008. See Sistema de Alertas Tempranas, "Informe de Riesgo N° 018-09," 5. Graffiti appeared; they threatened people with phone calls, text messages, and pamphlets. They were also suspected of extorting phone cards, medicine, arms, and ammunition from traders and ranchers. See Sistema de Alertas Tempranas, 5.

59. Sistema de Alertas Tempranas, "Informe de Riesgo N° 018-09," 3. Stigmatization continued to be a problem in the aftermath of the guerrilla war: in Bocas del Ju Ju, farmers explained that people preferred not to declare themselves as displaced by the FARC because the authorities would accuse them of being ELN collaborators and vice versa.

60. Melvin J. Lerner, *The Belief in a Just World: A Fundamental Delusion* (New York: Plenum Press, 1980). See also Stanley Cohen, *States of Denial: Knowing about Atrocities and Suffering* (Cambridge, UK: Polity Press, 2001), 96.

61. *The Origins of Totalitarianism* (New York: Harcourt Brace & World, 1968), 446.

62. Interview with a displaced farmer, Putumayo, Colombia, 2011.

63. David Keen, *Endless War? Hidden Functions of the "War on Terror"* (London: Pluto Press, 2006), 130–31.

64. Philippe Bourgois, "Recognizing Invisible Violence: A Thirty-Year Ethnographic Retrospective," in *Global Health in Times of Violence*, ed. Barbara Rylko-Bauer, Linda Whiteford, and Paul Farmer (Santa Fe, NM: School for Advanced Research Press, 2010), 19–20.

65. Nancy Scheper-Hughes, *Death without Weeping: The Violence of Everyday Life in Brazil* (Berkeley: University of California Press, 1993).

66. René Girard, *Violence and the Sacred* (London: Bloomsbury Academic, 2013), 90.

67. Núñez Gantiva, "ELN-FARC: Ahora sí juntos," 74.

68. In some areas, guerrilla war *and* combat between insurgent and post-demobilized groups occurred before 2009.

69. Sistema de Alertas Tempranas, "Nota de Seguimiento N°007-11, Tercera nota al informe de Riesgo N° 029-07," Sistema de Alertas Tempranas. Defensoría del Pueblo de Colombia (Bogotá: Defensoría del Pueblo de Colombia, April 2011), 6–9.

70. Interview with an indigenous leader, Pasto, Colombia, November 2011.

71. Caroline Moser and Cathy McIlwaine, *Encounters with Violence in Latin America: Urban Poor Perceptions from Colombia and Guatemala* (New York; London: Routledge, 2004), 179–82.

72. Interview with a non-governmental organization staff member, San Antonio de Táchira, Venezuela, May 2012.

73. Interview with an international agency staff member, Puerto Asís, Colombia, March 2012.

74. "Nota de Seguimiento N°031-09. Segunda al informe de Riesgo N° 020-09 A.I." (Bogotá, December 2009); Sistema de Alertas Tempranas, "Informe de Riesgo N° 018-09," 4.

75. Sistema de Alertas Tempranas, "Informe de Riesgo N° 012-11 A.I.," Sistema de Alertas Tempranas. Defensoría del Pueblo de Colombia (Bogotá August 18, 2011), 8.

76. Hugo Slim, *Killing Civilians: Method, Madness, and Morality in War* (London: Hurst, 2007).

77. Mary Kaldor, *New and Old Wars*, 3rd ed. (Malden, MA: Polity Press, 2012), 6.

78. Susana Rotker, "Cities Written by Violence: An Introduction," in *Citizens of Fear: Urban Violence in Latin America*, ed. Susana Rotker and Katherine Goldman (New Brunswick, NJ: Rutgers University Press, 2002), 16.

79. Elizabeth Niño Ascanio, Edwin Camargo León, and Wilfredo Cañizares Arévalo, "Crímen organizado y grupos ilegales en una frontera en crisis" (Cúcuta, Colombia, 2011), 88.

80. Niño Ascanio, Camargo León, and Cañizares Arévalo, 88; Elizabeth Niño Ascanio, Edwin Camargo León, and Wilfredo Cañizares Arévalo, "Frontera Norte de Santander—Táchira," in *La frontera caliente entre Colombia y Venezuela*, ed. Ariel Ávila (Cota, Colombia: Corporación Nuevo Arco Iris, 2012), 303. In 2009, there was another wave of these pamphlets found on the Colombian side.

81. Niño Ascanio, Camargo León, and Cañizares Arévalo, "Crímen organizado y grupos ilegales en una frontera en crisis," 28.

82. The paramilitary AUC had formally demobilized by that date, but locals commonly still referred to them as "paramilitaries." They claimed these were the same people using the same methods as before the demobilization.

83. *Paracos* are paramilitaries.

84. Interview with a resident of Rubio, Cúcuta, Colombia, 2012.

85. Niño Ascanio, Camargo León, and Cañizares Arévalo, 83.

86. Edelberto Torres-Rivas, "Epilogue: Notes on Terror, Violence, Fear, and Democracy," in *Societies of Fear: The Legacy of Civil War, Violence, and Terror in Latin America*, ed. Kees Koonings and Dirk Krujit (Zed Books, 1999), 293.

87. *The Logic of Violence in Civil War*, 111–243.

88. Kalyvas, 203.

89. Francisco Gutiérrez Sanín, "Telling the Difference: Guerrillas and Paramilitaries in the Colombian War," *Politics & Society* 36, no. 1 (March 1, 2008): 3–34; Gonzalo Vargas, "Urban Irregular Warfare and Violence against Civilians: Evidence from a Colombian City," *Terrorism and Political Violence* 21, no. 1 (2009): 110–32.

90. Interview with a high-ranking police official, Cúcuta, Colombia, April 2012.

91. The police official refers to the division of labor in supply chain relationships in earlier stages of the cocaine production.

92. Interview with a high-ranking police official, Cúcuta, Colombia, April 2012.

93. Ibid.

94. The Hill of the Cross is strategic because of the 360-degree view on Cúcuta from the top.

95. Interview with a civil society leader, Cúcuta, Colombia, 2011.

96. Linda Green, "Fear as a Way of Life," *Cultural Anthropology* 9, no. 2 (1994): 227.

97. See Table A.1 for an overview of the variety of stakeholders I interviewed during my fieldwork.

98. Niño Ascanio, Camargo León, and Cañizares Arévalo, "Frontera Norte de Santander—Táchira," 329–30.

99. Sistema de Alertas Tempranas, "Nota de Seguimiento N° 017-10. Segunda al informe de Riesgo N° 002-09," Sistema de Alertas Tempranas. Defensoría del Pueblo de Colombia (Bogotá: Defensoría del Pueblo de Colombia, July 28, 2010), 4.

100. Interview with a high-ranking police official, Cúcuta, Colombia, April 2012.

101. Ibid.

102. See William Ryan, *Blaming the Victim* (New York: Vintage Books, 1976).
103. Examples of victim blaming during my fieldwork abound: it is careless to drive without locking car doors, with open windows, with a bag on one's lap, or with a phone in one's hands because this attracts thieves. A friend's colleague was assaulted when withdrawing money from a cash machine. My friend expressed disapproval that he unnecessarily exposed himself by going to a public cash machine and not a bank.
104. As mentioned in chapter 1, BACRIM (*bandas criminales emergentes*, emerging criminal bands) is the term the Colombian government used to refer to the groups that I refer to as post-demobilized groups.
105. Carolyn Nordstrom and Antonius C. G. M. Robben, *Fieldwork under Fire: Contemporary Studies of Violence and Survival* (Berkeley: University of California Press, 1995), 16.
106. Fundación Progresar, "Boletín informativo" (Cúcuta, Colombia, July 2011), 1.
107. Interview with a member of the church, Cúcuta, Colombia, 2012.
108. Interview with a senior local government official, Ocaña, Colombia, 2012.
109. Green, "Fear as a Way of Life," 231.
110. Interview with a government official, Ocaña, Colombia, 2012.
111. Interview with a human rights defender, Ocaña, Colombia, 2012.
112. La Opinión, "Panfletos amenazantes en Ocaña," *La Opinión*, May 3, 2012, http://www.laopinion.com.co/demo/index.php?option=com_content&task=view&id=395581&Itemid=28.
113. La Red Independiente Noticias Uno, "Panfleto genera temor en Ocaña. Ya hay 3 muertos," *Noticias uno. La red independiente*, May 6, 2012, http://noticiasunolaredindependiente.com/2012/05/06/noticias/panfleto-genera-temor-en-ocana-ya-hay-3-muertos/.
114. In addition to social cleansing, in May 2012 guerrillas repeatedly attacked the army, resulting in injured and dead police forces and civilians. El Tiempo, "Cinco policías y dos civiles resultaron heridos en ataque en Ocaña," *El Tiempo*, May 7, 2012, http://www.eltiempo.com/archivo/documento/CMS-11732361.
115. See Pécaut, "From the Banality of Violence to Real Terror: The Case of Colombia," 156.

Chapter 5

1. Interview with a civil society leader, Tumaco, Colombia, 2011.
2. Linda Green, "Fear as a Way of Life," *Cultural Anthropology* 9, no. 2 (1994): 230.
3. Stathis N. Kalyvas, *The Logic of Violence in Civil War* (Cambridge, UK: Cambridge University Press, 2006), 89–91.
4. Daniel Pécaut, "From the Banality of Violence to Real Terror: The Case of Colombia," in *Societies of Fear: The Legacy of Civil War, Violence, and Terror in Latin America*, ed. Kees Koonings and Dirk Krujit (London: Zed Books, 1999), 147.
5. Caracol, "Millonarias incautaciones dejan operativos contra el contrabando en varios centros comerciales," *Caracol*, March 18, 2005, http://www.caracol.com.co/noticias/judicial/millonarias-incautaciones-dejan-operativos-contra-el-contrabando-en-varios-centros-comerciales/20050318/nota/162984.aspx; Noticucuta.com, "Operativo especial contra el contrabando en Cúcuta," *Cúcuta Judicial* (blog), December 11, 2007; Omar Elias Laguado Nieto, "Cayó mercancía de contrabando en Alejandría," *Así Es Cúcuta*, August 15, 2012, http://www.asiescucuta.com/portada/2012-08-15/cayo-mercancia-de-contrabando-en-alejandria.html; Contraluz Cúcuta, "'Madrugón' al contrabando en Alejandría," *Contraluz Cúcuta*, August 15, 2012, www.contraluzcucuta.co/articulos/madrugon-al-contrabando-en-alejandria/.
6. Interview with a community leader, Cúcuta, Colombia, 2011. Further interviews with a civil society representative, Cúcuta, Colombia, 2011; and with women's leader, Cúcuta, Colombia, 2012.
7. Interview with a community leader, Cúcuta, Colombia, 2011.
8. Ibid.
9. Veena Das, *Life and Words: Violence and the Descent into the Ordinary* (Berkeley: University of California Press, 2007), 7.
10. Das, 7.

11. La Opinión, "En Alejandría vuelven a sonar las extorsiones," *La Opinión*, August 1, 2013, http://www.laopinion.com.co/demo/index.php?option=com_content&task=view&id=42 5409&Itemid=33.

12. See Caroline Moser and Cathy McIlwaine, *Encounters with Violence in Latin America: Urban Poor Perceptions from Colombia and Guatemala* (New York: Routledge, 2004), 178–80.

13. Verdad Abierta, "La violencia oculta de la costa de Nariño," August 30, 2015, http://www.verdadabierta.com/victimas-seccion/asesinatos-colectivos/5947-la-violencia-oculta-de-la-costa-de-narino.

14. Interview with a Nariño resident, Mocoa, Colombia, 2011.

15. Ibid.

16. Álvaro Sierra, "La coca viajera," *El Tiempo*, October 13, 2002, http://www.eltiempo.com/archivo/documento/MAM-1372034.

17. Interview with a human rights defender, Pasto, Colombia, 2011.

18. Juan Diego Restrepo, "La guerra no abandona a Nariño," *Semana*, May 31, 2006, http://www.semana.com/on-line/articulo/la-guerra-no-abandona-narino/78664-3; Human Rights Watch, "Paramilitaries' Heirs. The New Face of Violence in Colombia" (New York: Human Rights Watch, 2010).

19. Interview with a human rights defender, Pasto, Colombia, 2011.

20. Interview with an international agency staff member, Mocoa, Colombia, 2011. People referred to the successor groups as paramilitaries.

21. Astrubal Guerra, "Capturado jefe de 'Los Rastrojos' en Nariño," *W Radio*, July 17, 2008, http://www.wradio.com.co/noticias/actualidad/capturado-jefe-de-los-rastrojos-en-narino/20080717/nota/634143.aspx; El Tiempo, "Caen nueve integrantes de la banda de los 'Rastrojos' en zona rural de Tumaco," July 17, 2008, http://www.eltiempo.com/archivo/documento/CMS-4381943.

22. Interviews with an international agency staff member and a civil society representative, Pasto, Colombia, 2011; interview with international agency staff, Mocoa, Colombia, 2011.

23. Sistema de Alertas Tempranas, "Informe de Riesgo N° 029-08 A.I.," Sistema de Alertas Tempranas. Defensoría del Pueblo de Colombia (Bogotá: Defensoría del Pueblo de Colombia, December 4, 2008).

24. Two men on a motorbike is a common contract killing practice: the man on the pillion shoots the victim.

25. Veena Das and Arthur Kleinman, "Introduction," in *Violence and Subjectivity*, ed. Veena Das et al. (Berkeley: University of California Press, 2000), 8.

26. FIP, USAID, and OIM, "Dinámicas del conflicto armado en Tumaco y su impacto humanitario," Boletín, Área de Dinámicas del Conflicto y Negociaciones de Paz (Bogotá: Fundación Ideas para la Paz (FIP), February 2014), 27, http://cdn.ideaspaz.org/media/website/document/52f8ecc452239.pdf.

27. Carolyn Nordstrom, "Terror Warfare and the Medicine of Peace," *Medical Anthropology Quarterly*, n.s., 12, no. 1 (March 1, 1998): 103–21.

28. Ana Villarreal, "Fear and Spectacular Drug Violence in Monterrey," in *Violence at the Urban Margins*, ed. Javier Auyero, Philippe I. Bourgois, and Nancy Scheper-Hughes, Global and Comparative Ethnography (New York: Oxford University Press, 2015), 156.

29. Pécaut, "From the Banality of Violence to Real Terror: The Case of Colombia," 156.

30. Interview with a humanitarian organization employee, San Cristóbal, Venezuela, 2012.

31. Interview with a San Cristóbal resident, San Cristóbal, Venezuela, 2012.

32. Pécaut, "From the Banality of Violence to Real Terror: The Case of Colombia," 145.

33. Linda Buckley Green, *Fear as a Way of Life: Mayan Widows in Rural Guatemala* (New York: Columbia University Press, 1999), 69.

34. For the denial of victims see Stanley Cohen, *States of Denial: Knowing about Atrocities and Suffering* (Cambridge, UK: Polity Press, 2001), 110–11.

35. Policía Nacional de Colombia, "Capturado cabecilla de la banda criminal 'Los Rastrojos,'" Noticias y actividades destacadas, April 12, 2011 https://www.policia.gov.co/noticia/capturado-cabecilla-de-la-banda-criminal-los-rastrojos.

36. See Alfredo Rangel Suárez, "Parasites and Predators: Guerrillas and the Insurrection Economy of Colombia," *Journal of International Affairs* 53, no. 2 (Spring 2000): 577.

37. Interview with a civil society representative, Valledupar, Colombia, 2012. See also Ariel Ávila and Carmen Rosa Guerra Ariza, "Frontera La Guajira y Cesar-Zulia," in *La frontera caliente entre Colombia y Venezuela*, ed. Ariel Ávila (Cota, Colombia: Corporación Nuevo Arco Iris, 2012), 503; Milana Peralta et al., "La Guajira en su laberinto: Transformaciones y desafíos de la violencia," Informes FIP (Bogotá: Fundación Ideas para la Paz, August 2011). The FARC charged "taxes" on gasoline smuggled from Venezuela to Colombia.

38. Ávila and Guerra Ariza, 482.

39. Sistema de Alertas Tempranas, "Informe de Riesgo N° 024-12," (Bogotá: Defensoría del Pueblo de Colombia, 2012), 10.

40. Ibid.

41. Ávila and Guerra Ariza, "Frontera La Guajira y Cesar-Zulia," 517.

42. According to Colombia's Ombudsman's Office, for example, in March 2011 the Urabeños threatened a La Paz resident's life by pressuring him to pay back what they had lent him.

43. Sistema de Alertas Tempranas, "Informe de Riesgo N° 024-12."

44. Interview with a human rights defender, Valledupar, Colombia, 2012.

45. See Diego Gambetta, *Codes of the Underworld: How Criminals Communicate* (Princeton, NJ: Princeton University Press, 2009), 35.

46. This is also related to the group type involved (see section 2.2).

47. Milana Peralta et al., "La Guajira en su laberinto: Transformaciones y desafíos de la violencia," Informes FIP (Bogotá: Fundación Ideas para la Paz, August 2011).

48. Interview with a high-ranking police official, Cúcuta, Colombia, 2012.

49. Sistema de Alertas Tempranas, "Informe de Riesgo N° 024-12"; Ávila and Guerra Ariza, "Frontera La Guajira y Cesar-Zulia," 507–10.

50. Sistema de Alertas Tempranas, "Informe de Riesgo N° 024-12."

51. See Pécaut, "From the Banality of Violence to Real Terror: The Case of Colombia," 149.

52. Benedikt Korf and Timothy Raeymaekers, *Violence on the Margins: States, Conflict, and Borderlands* (New York: Palgrave Macmillan, 2013), 5.

53. Judith Vorrath, "On the Margin of Statehood?: State-Society Relations in African Borderlands," in *Understanding Life in the Borderlands: Boundaries in Depth and in Motion*, ed. I. William Zartman (Athens: University of Georgia Press, 2010), 85–87.

54. Peter Andreas, *Border Games: Policing the US-Mexico Divide*, 2nd ed. (Ithaca, NY: Cornell University Press, 2009), 22.

55. "El tráfico de armas vulnera las fronteras norte y sur de Ecuador," *El Comercio*, September 17, 2012, http://www4.elcomercio.com/seguridad/trafico-armas-vulnera-fronteras-Ecuador_0_775122566.html; Geoffrey Ramsey, "Mapping Gun Smuggling Routes in Ecuador" (Insight Crime, September 17, 2012), http://www.insightcrime.org/news-briefs/mapping-gun-smuggling-routes-in-ecuador. Interviews with various military and police officials, Ecuador and Colombia, 2012.

56. Interview with a female ex-combatant, Pasto, Colombia, 2011.

57. Ibid.

58. I removed the name of the villages in this sentence and the previous one to ensure anonymity.

59. Interview with a resident, Carchi, Ecuador, 2012.

60. I removed the name of the village to ensure anonymity.

61. See, e.g., El Comercio, "El tráfico de armas crece en Carchi," December 26, 2009, http://www.elcomercio.com/actualidad/trafico-armas-crece-carchi.html; Hoy, "Indígenas otavaleños, mulas de la guerrilla," September 7, 2008, http://www.hoy.com.ec/noticias-ecuador/indigenas-otavalenos-mulas-de-la-guerrilla-303952.html.

62. El Comercio, "El tráfico de armas vulnera las fronteras norte y sur de Ecuador."

63. United Nations, "Reports Submitted by States Parties under Article 9 of the Convention. Twentieth to Twenty-Second Periodic Reports Due in 2012. Ecuador. CERD/C/ECU/20-22" (United Nations Committee on the Elimination of Racial Discrimination, 2012); Coordinadora Andina de Organizaciones Indígenas, "Informe alternativo presentado por la coordinadora andina de organizaciones indígenas—CAOI ante el Comité para la Eliminación de Todas las Formas de Discriminación Racial—CERD (CERD/C/ECU/20-21)" (Coordinadora Andina de Organizaciones Indígenas, 2012).

64. Robert D. Putnam, *Bowling Alone* (New York: Simon and Schuster, 2001), 23.
65. Roberto Briceño-León, Olga Ávila, and Alberto Camardiel, *Violencia e institucionalidad: Informe del observatorio venezolano de violencia 2012* (Caracas: Editorial Alfa, 2012), 218.
66. See Ana Villarreal, "Secuestrable: Sobre la normalización de la violencia en el México urbano," *Diálogo Global* 3, no. 3 (May 2013): 26–27.
67. Interviews with community members, Machiques, 2012.
68. Interview with a government official, Pasto, Colombia, 2011.
69. Interview with an international agency employee, Tumaco, 2011.
70. Interview with a civil society leader from Tumaco, Quito, 2012.
71. Ibid.
72. See Gambetta, *Codes of the Underworld*, 30–32.
73. Ibid., 33.
74. Interview with a civil society leader from Tumaco, Quito, 2012.
75. Ibid.
76. Ibid.
77. MINGA and INDEPAZ, "En Tumaco: La marcha de la desesperación," Notes (Tumaco: MINGA, INDEPAZ, September 2011), 7.
78. Interview with a government official, Pasto, Colombia, 2012.
79. Various interviews with residents of Tumaco, Colombia, 2011. See also MINGA and INDEPAZ, "En Tumaco: La marcha de la desesperación," Notes (Tumaco: MINGA, INDEPAZ, September 2011), 8.
80. See Pécaut, "From the Banality of Violence to Real Terror: The Case of Colombia," 152.
81. See Susana Rotker, "Cities Written by Violence: An Introduction," in *Citizens of Fear: Urban Violence in Latin America*, ed. Susana Rotker and Katherine Goldman (New Brunswick, NJ: Rutgers University Press, 2002), 16.
82. Asociación MINGA and Instituto de Estudios para el Desarrollo y la Paz, "En Tumaco: La marcha de la desesperación," Notes (Tumaco: MINGA, INDEPAZ, September 2011), 8.
83. Pécaut, "From the Banality of Violence to Real Terror: The Case of Colombia," 152.
84. Interview with a female Tumaco resident, Tumaco, Colombia, 2011.
85. CODHES, "Desplazamiento forzado intraurbano y soluciones duraderas. Vol. II Bogotá, Cúcuta, y Quibdó" (Bogotá: CODHES, 2014), 75.
86. In September 2013, the FARC ousted the Rastrojos from Tumaco. See Ibid.
87. Various interviews with local residents, Tumaco, Colombia, 2016. See also Silla Vacía, "Las Farc mataron a 'Don Y,'" 16 November 2016, http://lasillavacia.com/historia/las-farc-mataron-don-y-58754.
88. Laurence Whitehead, *Democratization: Theory and Experience* (Oxford: Oxford University Press, 2002), 165–85; see also Robin George Collingwood, *The New Leviathan; or, Man, Society, Civilization, and Barbarism*, edited and introduced by David Boucher (Oxford: Clarendon Press, 1999), 326.
89. Whitehead, *Democratization: Theory and Experience*, 74; see also Collingwood, *The New Leviathan: On Man, Society, Civilization, and Barbarism*, 292.
90. Teresa M. Bejan, *Mere Civility: Disagreement and the Limits of Toleration* (Cambridge, MA: Harvard University Press, 2017).
91. Mary Kaldor, *New and Old Wars*, 3rd ed. (Malden, MA: Polity Press, 2012), 6.
92. Asociación MINGA and Instituto de Estudios para el Desarrollo y la Paz, "En Tumaco: La marcha de la desesperación," 8.
93. Interview with a Tumaco resident, Tumaco, Colombia, 2011.
94. Interview with an international agency staff member, Tumaco, Colombia, 2011.
95. Pécaut, "From the Banality of Violence to Real Terror: The Case of Colombia," 148–49.
96. James Gilligan, "Shame, Guilt, and Violence," *Social Research: An International Quarterly* 70, no. 4 (2003): 1149–80.
97. Ibid., 1154.
98. Interview with a civil society leader of Tumaco, Quito, Ecuador, 2012.
99. Hannah Arendt, *On Violence* (New York: Harcourt Brace, 1970), 54.
100. David Keen, *Conflict & Collusion in Sierra Leone* (Oxford: James Currey, 2005), 73.

101. Diana Lary, *Warlord Soldiers: Chinese Common Soldiers, 1911–1937* (Cambridge, UK: Cambridge University Press, 1985); Judith N. Zur, *Violent Memories: Mayan War Widows in Guatemala* (Boulder, CO: Westview Press, 1998).
102. Keen, *Conflict & Collusion in Sierra Leone*, 63.
103. Interview with a local resident, Caracas, Venezuela, 2012.
104. Robert D. Putnam, *Making Democracy Work: Civic Traditions in Modern Italy* (Princeton, NJ: Princeton University Press, 1993), 88–89. To be sure, I do not claim that everyone therefore necessarily manifests such "incivil" behavior. Rather, I argue that the security situation, and everyday life dynamics in Tumaco more broadly, manifest signs of a "lost civility" that can be partly traced back to inter-group dynamics.
105. See Susana Rotker, *Citizens of Fear: Urban Violence in Latin America* (New Brunswick, NJ: Rutgers University Press, 2002); Kees Koonings and Dirk Krujit, *Societies of Fear: The Legacy of Civil War, Violence, and Terror in Latin America* (London: Zed Books, 1999).
106. Interview with a local resident, Tumaco, Colombia, 2012.
107. Green, "Fear as a Way of Life," 1994, 239. See also Marcelo M. Suárez-Orozco, "Speaking of the Unspeakable: Toward a Psychosocial Understanding of Responses to Terror," *Ethos* 18, no. 3 (September 1, 1990): 353–83, https://doi.org/10.1525/eth.1990.18.3.02a00050.
108. Interview with a civil society leader from Tumaco, Quito, Ecuador, 2012.
109. See Cohen, *States of Denial*, 71.
110. Catherine Lowe Besteman, *Violence: A Reader* (Basingstoke: Palgrave Macmillan, 2002).
111. Philippe Bourgois, "Recognizing Invisible Violence: A Thirty-Year Ethnographic Retrospective," in *Global Health in Times of Violence*, ed. Barbara Rylko-Bauer, Linda Whiteford, and Paul Farmer (Santa Fe, NM: School for Advanced Research Press, 2010), 19.
112. Interview with a civil society leader from Tumaco, Quito, Ecuador, 2012.
113. Nordstrom, "Terror Warfare and the Medicine of Peace," 117.
114. See Daniel M. Goldstein, *The Spectacular City: Violence and Performance in Urban Bolivia* (Durham, NC; London: Duke University Press, 2004).
115. Pécaut, "From the Banality of Violence to Real Terror: The Case of Colombia," 142.
116. Interview with a local resident, Tumaco, Colombia, 2011.
117. Das and Kleinman, "Introduction," 8.
118. See section 3.2 for why certain Wayúu clans fall in the analytical category of "violent non-state groups."
119. Primo Levi, "The Gray Zone," in *Violence in War and Peace*, ed. Nancy Scheper-Hughes and Philippe I. Bourgois (Malden, MA: Blackwell, 2004), 83.
120. Ibid.
121. Sistema de Alertas Tempranas, "Informe de Riesgo N° 007-10," (Bogotá: Defensoría del Pueblo de Colombia, June 2010), 3.
122. Diócesis de Riohacha Secretariado de Pastoral Social, "Análisis del contexto del Departamento para Entender la dinámica del conflicto armado en La Guajira" (Rioacha, La Guajira: Pastoral Social, 2008), 9.
123. Sistema de Alertas Tempranas, "Informe de Riesgo N° 007-10," 3. The label "Autodefensas Gaitanistas de Colombia" reappeared in previous years.
124. Juan Carlos Gamboa Martínez, "Una mirada panorámica a la frontera La Guajira–Zulia," internal document (Maicao: PNUD, June 2012), 22.
125. Gamboa Martínez, 24.
126. Sistema de Alertas Tempranas, "Informe de Riesgo N° 007-10," 19.
127. Verdad Abierta, "Gobierno ordena la extradición de alias 'Pablo,'" September 10, 2012, http://www.verdadabierta.com/component/content/article/36-jefes/4213-la-extradicion-de-pablo-el-terror-de-la-guajira.
128. Gamboa Martínez, "Una mirada panorámica a la frontera La Guajira–Zulia."
129. Other interviewees reported that the Paisas, the group Alta Guajira, and several private Wayúu armies continued to be involved in tactical alliances as well around 2011 and 2012, especially in Maicao and Riohacha.
130. Interview with a civil society representative from Riohacha, Valledupar, 2012.

131. Gamboa Martínez, "Una mirada panorámica a la frontera La Guajira–Zulia," 24–25.

132. See Keen, *Conflict & Collusion in Sierra Leone*, 50.

133. Interview with a journalist, Caracas, Venezuela, 2012.

134. Ávila and Guerra Ariza, "Frontera La Guajira y Cesar-Zulia," 415.

135. Sistema de Alertas Tempranas, "Informe de Riesgo N° 007-10," 14.

136. Document shared by an anonymous interviewee.

137. Adam Baird, "Becoming the 'Baddest': Masculine Trajectories of Gang Violence in Medellín," *Journal of Latin American Studies* 50, no. 1 (February 2018): 183–210, https://doi.org/10.1017/S0022216X17000761.

138. Various interviews, Tumaco, Colombia, 2011, 2012, 2016.

139. For Loco Barrera's story see section 6.1.

140. Interview with a Wayúu leader, Maicao, Colombia, October 2012.

141. I changed the real name into "Jairo" to ensure anonymity.

142. I changed the real name into "Carlos" to ensure anonymity.

143. Interview with a Wayúu leader, Maicao, Colombia, October 2012.

144. This was the case in spite of the fact that they threatened the hostile clan to eliminate it.

145. Comisión Nacional de Reparación y Reconciliación (Colombia) CNRR, *La masacre de Bahía Portete: Mujeres Wayuu en la mira*, Pensamiento (Bogotá: Taurus, 2010).

146. Interview with a humanitarian organization employee, Maicao, Colombia, 2012.

147. Sistema de Alertas Tempranas, "Informe de Riesgo N° 007-10," 19.

148. Ibid.

149. Peralta et al., "La Guajira en su laberinto: Transformaciones y desafíos de la violencia," 10; Comisión Nacional de Reparación y Reconciliación, *La masacre de Bahía Portete*, 29.

150. Interview with a Wayúu leader, Riohacha, Colombia, January 2016.

151. Interview with a civil society representative, Valledupar, Colombia, October 2012.

152. For adults, in Colombia the average penalty for homicide is thirteen to twenty-five years in prison. For teenagers between fourteen and eighteen years, the average is two to eight years in detention centers. See Law 599, "Código Penal Colombiano" (Bogotá: Congreso de Colombia, 2000), Art. 103, http://www.alcaldiabogota.gov.co/sisjur/normas/Norma1.jsp?i=6388; Law 1098, "Código de la Infancia y la Adolescencia; Ley 1098 de noviembre 8 de 2006" (Bogotá: Procuraduría General de la Nación, 2006), Art. 187, http://www.procuraduria.gov.co/portal/media/file/Visi%C3%B3n%20Mundial_ Codigo%20de%20 Infancia%202011(1).pdf.

153. Interview with a human rights defender, Ocaña, Colombia, 2012.

154. Interview with a civil society representative from Tumaco, Quito, Ecuador, 2012.

155. Laura González Carranza, *Fronteras en el limbo: El Plan Colombia en el Ecuador* (Quito: Fundación Regional de Asesoría en Derechos Humanos, INREDH, 2008), 221.

156. Das and Kleinman, "Introduction," 1.

157. Pécaut, "From the Banality of Violence to Real Terror: The Case of Colombia," 147.

Chapter 6

1. Interview with a civil society representative from Valledupar, Colombia, 2012.

2. Interview with a resident of the Venezuelan border zone, Venezuela, 2012.

3. See Gurr's *Why Men Rebel* (Princeton, NJ Princeton University Press, 1970). For instances where people engage in non-violent resistance see Adam Roberts and Timothy Garton Ash, *Civil Resistance and Power Politics: The Experience of Non-Violent Action from Gandhi to the Present* (Oxford: Oxford University Press, 2011).

4. Max Weber, *Politik als Beruf* (Stuttgart: Reclam, Philipp, jun. GmbH, Verlag, 1992); see also Rodney Hall and Thomas J. Biersteker, "Private Authority as Global Governance," in *The Emergence of Private Authority in Global Governance*, ed. Rodney Hall and Thomas J. Biersteker (Cambridge, UK: Cambridge University Press, 2002), 203–22.

5. Vanda Felbab-Brown, "Rules and Regulations in Ungoverned Spaces: Illicit Economies, Criminals, and Belligerents," in *Ungoverned Spaces: Alternatives to State Authority in an Era of Softened Sovereignty*, ed. Anne L. Clunan and Harold A. Trinkunas (Stanford, CA: Stanford University Press, 2010), 182.

6. Interview with a female ex-combatant, Pasto, Colombia, 2011.

7. Interview with an ex-guerrilla couple, Pasto, Colombia, 2011.

8. Interviews with community members, Esmeraldas, Ecuador, 2012.

9. Daniel Pécaut, "From the Banality of Violence to Real Terror: The Case of Colombia," in *Societies of Fear: The Legacy of Civil War, Violence, and Terror in Latin America*, ed. Kees Koonings and Dirk Krujit (London: Zed Books, 1999), 154.

10. Interview with a human rights defender, Ocaña, Colombia, 2012.

11. Ibid.

12. Michael T. Taussig, "Talking Terror," in *Violence in War and Peace*, ed. Nancy Scheper-Hughes and Philippe I. Bourgois (Malden, MA: Blackwell, 2004), 171–74.

13. Interview with a member of the church, Ecuadorian northern border zone, Ecuador, 2012.

14. Craig D. Parks and Lorne G. Hulbert, "High and Low Trusters' Responses to Fear in a Payoff Matrix," *The Journal of Conflict Resolution* 39, no. 4 (December 1, 1995): 718–30, https://doi.org/10.2307/174384; Sandra Walklate, "Crime and Community: Fear or Trust?," *The British Journal of Sociology* 49, no. 4 (December 1, 1998): 550–69, https://doi.org/10.2307/591288; Charles Tilly, *Trust and Rule* (Cambridge, UK: Cambridge University Press, 2005).

15. Kees Koonings and Dirk Krujit, *Societies of Fear: The Legacy of Civil War, Violence, and Terror in Latin America* (London: Zed Books, 1999), 19, 2; Edelberto Torres-Rivas, "Epilogue: Notes on Terror, Violence, Fear, and Democracy," in *Societies of Fear*, 288. For discussions of economics and culture as reasons for a violent Colombian society see Peter Waldmann, "Is There a Culture of Violence in Colombia?," *Terrorism and Political Violence* 19, no. 4 (2007): 593–609; Francisco E. Thoumi, *Political Economy and Illegal Drugs in Colombia*, Studies on the Impact of the Illegal Drug Trade 2 (Boulder, CO: Lynne Rienner, 1995).

16. See, e.g., Mark Cohen and Roger Bowles, "Estimating Costs of Crime," in *Handbook of Quantitative Criminology*, ed. Alexis Russell Piquero and David Weisburd (New York; London: Springer, 2010), 143–62.

17. Jenny V. Pearce, "Violence, Power, and Participation: Building Citizenship in Contexts of Chronic Violence," *IDS Working Paper* 274 (2007); Médicos sin Fronteras, Internal document (Colombia, 2011).

18. Interview with a member of the church, Ecuadorian northern border zone, Ecuador, 2012.

19. Koonings and Krujit, *Societies of Fear*; Jean Delumeau, *El miedo: Reflexiones sobre su dimensión social y cultural* (Medellín: Corporación Región, 2002).

20. Michael T. Taussig, "Culture of Terror—Spaces of Death: Roger Casement's Putumayo Report and the Explanation of Torture," in *Violence: A Reader*, ed. Catherine Lowe Besteman (Basingstoke: Palgrave Macmillan, 2002), 223.

21. Interview with a local resident, Tufiño, Ecuador, 2012.

22. Karl Polanyi, *The Great Transformation: The Political and Economic Origins of Our Time*, 2nd pbk. ed. (Boston: Beacon Press, 2001). See also E. P. Thompson, "The Moral Economy of the English Crowd in the Eighteenth Century," *Past & Present* 50, no. 1 (1971): 76–136, https://doi.org/10.1093/past/50.1.76.

23. Interview with a displaced farmer, Mocoa, Colombia, 2011.

24. Interview with an international agency staff member, Mocoa, Colombia, 2011.

25. Interview with a displaced farmer, Mocoa, Colombia, 2011.

26. Interviews with farmers and members of the Ombudsman's Offices, Putumayo and Nariño, Colombia, 2011 and 2012.

27. Interviews with a community leader, General Farfán, and with a human rights defender, Lago Agrio, Ecuador, 2012.

28. Felbab-Brown, "Rules and Regulations in Ungoverned Spaces: Illicit Economies, Criminals, and Belligerents," 178.

29. Winifred Tate, *Drugs, Thugs, and Diplomats: US Policymaking in Colombia*, Anthropology of Policy (Stanford, CA: Stanford University Press, 2015).

30. Ibid., 2011.

31. Ibid.

32. Interview with an international organization employee, Mocoa, Colombia, 2011.

33. Interview with a Colombian farmer, Sucumbíos, Ecuador, 2012.

34. United Nations Office on Drugs and Crime and Government of Colombia, "Colombia: Coca Cultivation Survey 2012." (Bogotá: United Nations Office on Drugs and Crime, Government of Colombia, 2013), 55–57.

35. Various interviews with community members in Putumayo, Colombia, and Sucumbíos, Ecuador, 2011 and 2012. See, e.g., also United Nations Office on Drugs and Crime and Government of Colombia, "Colombia: Coca Cultivation Survey 2012."

36. One *arroba* equals 11.3 kilograms.

37. Interview with a Colombian farmer, Sucumbíos, Ecuador, 2012.

38. I am not aware of any female brokers in the Andean region.

39. See Peter Andreas and Angélica Durán-Martínez, "The Politics of Drugs and Illicit Trade in the Americas," in *Handbook of Latin American Politics*, ed. Peter Kingstone and Deborah Yashar (New York: Routledge, 2012), 385.

40. Annette Idler, "Megateo, the Armed Groups, and the Future of the People of Colombia's Catatumbo," *OpenDemocracy* (blog), October 28, 2015, https://www.opendemocracy.net/democraciaabierta/annette-idler/megateo-armed-groups-and-future-of-people-of-colombia-s-catatumbo.

41. Elizabeth Niño Ascanio, Edwin Camargo León, and Wilfredo Cañizares Arévalo, "Frontera Norte de Santander—Táchira," *La frontera caliente entre Colombia y Venezuela*, ed. Ariel Ávila (Cota, Colombia: Corporación Nuevo Arco Iris, 2012), 268–72.

42. Eric J. Hobsbawm, *Bandits* (Harmondsworth: Penguin Books, 1972).

43. For warlords see Kimberly Marten, "Warlordism in Comparative Perspective," *International Security* 31, no. 3 (January 1, 2007): 41–73; William Reno, *Warlord Politics and African States* (Boulder, CO: Lynne Rienner, 1998); Dipali Mukhopadhyay, *Warlords, Strongman Governors, and the State in Afghanistan* (Cambridge, UK: Cambridge University Press, 2016).

44. Contrary to warlords, brokers also exist in non-conflict countries.

45. Interview with a community leader, Cúcuta, Colombia, 2012.

46. Interview with a high-ranking police official, Cúcuta, Colombia, 2012.

47. Interviews with community leaders, human rights defenders, and civil society representatives, Cúcuta, Colombia, November 2016.

48. Various interviews with civil society representatives, Maicao and Riohacha, Colombia, 2016.

49. Various interviews with community members, Norte de Santander, Colombia, 2012.

50. El País, "¿Captura del Loco Barrera es realmente la caída del último gran capo?," *El País*, September 24, 2012, http://www.elpais.com.co/elpais/judicial/noticias/captura-loco-barrera-significa-realmente-caida-ultimo-gran-capo.

51. Cesar Alarcón Gil, "'El Loco' Barrera: Más allá de la mafia," *Razón pública* (blog), October 2012, http://www.razonpublica.com/index.php/econom-y-sociedad-temas-29/3296-el-loco-barrera-mas-alla-de-la-mafia.html.

52. Insight Crime, "El Loco Barrera," InSight Crime—Organized Crime in the Américas, 2012, http://www.insightcrime.org/personalities-colombia/daniel-barrera-barrera-el-loco-barrera.

53. El Tiempo, "Testaferros llevaron a la policía hasta el 'Loco' Barrera," September 20, 2012, http://www.eltiempo.com/archivo/documento/CMS-12237943.

54. Tribunal Supremo de Justicia, "Solicitud de extradición del ciudadano Walid Makled García" (Caracas: Tribunal Supremo de Justicia de Venezuela, August 20, 2010); Insight Crime, "Walid Makled," 2014, http://www.insightcrime.org/venezuela-organized-crime-news/walid-makled.

55. El Universo, "En campanita empezó la ruta del caso Chauvín," *El Universo*, February 15, 2009, http://www.eluniverso.com/2009/02/15/1/1355/63A74BE0AC1A48CC910D3F121FC770F9.html; El Comercio, "El escándalo del caso Ostaiza," *El Comercio*, 2009, http://www.elcomercio.com/nv_images/especiales/2009/Ostaiza/ostaiza.html Y2 - 25 August 2009; Hoy, "Jooamy EMA, las siglas de los Ostaiza," March 1, 2009, http://www.hoy.com.ec/wphoy-imprimir.php?id=336164.

56. See, e.g., Diego Gambetta, *The Sicilian Mafia: The Business of Private Protection* (Cambridge, MA: Harvard University Press, 1993); Federico Varese, *The Russian Mafia: Private Protection in a New Market Economy* (Oxford: Oxford University Press, 2001); James Cockayne, *Hidden Power* (London: Hurst, 2016), https://global.oup.com/academic/product/hidden-power-9780190627331.

57. Semana, "La nueva estrategia contra las FARC," *Semana*, February 25, 2012, http://www.semana.com//nacion/articulo/la-nueva-estrategia-contra-farc/253985-3; El País, "FARC-ELN, la alianza que tiene en jaque al departamento de Arauca," August 27, 2013, http://www.elpais.com.co/judicial/farc-eln-la-alianza-que-tiene-en-jaque-al-departamento-de-arauca.html; James Bargent, "Discovery of Rebel Cocaine Labs in Colombia Highlight Drug Alliances," Brief, April 26, 2013, https://www.insightcrime.org/news/brief/discovery-of-cocaine-labs-in-colombia-highlights-guerrillas-drug-alliances/.

58. Magda Paola Núñez Gantiva, "ELN-FARC: Ahora sí juntos," *Arcanos* 15, no. 17 (2012): 62.

59. Interviews with various community members, Norte de Santander, Colombia, 2011 and 2012.

60. Ibid.

61. Interview with a civil society representative, Valledupar, Colombia, 2012; interviews with community members, Baja Guajira, Colombia 2016.

62. Interview with a human rights defender and various residents, Valledupar, Colombia, 2012.

63. United Nations Development Programme, "Cesar: Análisis de la conflictividad" (UNDP Área de Paz, Desarrollo, y Reconciliación, 2010), 40.

64. Cases of successful local leadership in the midst of various violent non-state groups are peace territories, for example in Samaniego or Las Mercedes. See, e.g., Annette Idler, María Belén Garrido, and Cécile Mouly, "Peace Territories in Colombia: Comparing Civil Resistance in Two War-Torn Communities," *Journal of Peacebuilding & Development* 10, no. 3 (September 2, 2015): 1–15, https://doi.org/10.1080/15423166.2015.1082437; Cécile Mouly, María Belén Garrido, and Annette Idler, "How Peace Takes Shape Locally: The Experience of Civil Resistance in Samaniego, Colombia," *Peace & Change* 41, no. 2 (April 1, 2016): 129–66, https://doi.org/10.1111/pech.12184; Landon E. Hancock and Christopher R. Mitchell, eds., *Zones of Peace* (Bloomfield, CT: Kumarian Press, 2007).

65. Sistema de Alertas Tempranas, "Informe de Riesgo N° 017-09," (Bogotá: Defensoría del Pueblo de Colombia, July 2009), 5.

66. Verdad Abierta, "'Pablo', Arnulfo Sánchez González," June 20, 2017, http://www.verdadabierta.com/victimarios/3204-alias-pablo-de-funcionario-publico-a-jefe-para.

67. It is plausible that the higher the groom up in the ranks of the paramilitary group and the more hierarchical and disciplined that group, the more stable the alliance.

68. Núñez Gantiva, "ELN-FARC: Ahora sí juntos."

69. Semana, "'Pablito' se equivocó de ruta," November 26, 2010, http://www.semana.com/nacion/articulo/pablito-equivoco-ruta/125089-3.

70. Stathis N. Kalyvas, "Wanton and Senseless?: The Logic of Massacres in Algeria," *Rationality and Society* 11 (1999): 260, http://journals.sagepub.com/doi/abs/10.1177/104346399011003001.

71. Elvira María Restrepo, "The Pursuit of Efficiency and the Colombian Criminal Justice System," in *Criminality, Public Security, and the Challenge to Democracy in Latin America*, ed. Marcelo Bergman and Laurence Whitehead (Notre Dame, IN: University of Notre Dame Press, 2009), 197.

72. Interview with a priest, Apure, Venezuela, 2012.

73. For a condensed version of this example, see Annette Idler and James J. F. Forest, "Behavioral Patterns among (Violent) Non-State Actors: A Study of Complementary Governance," *Stability: International Journal of Security and Development* 4, no. 1 (2015), https://www.stabilityjournal.org/articles/10.5334/sta.er/.

74. Interview with a farmer, Apure, Venezuela, 2012.

75. Ibid.

76. Ibid.

77. Ibid.

78. *Boliches* are FBL members.

79. Interview with a farmer, Apure, Venezuela, 2012.

80. Ibid.

81. Philip Alston, "Report of the Special Rapporteur on Extrajudicial, Summary, or Arbitrary Executions, Philip Alston," United Nations General Assembly (Human Rights Council, May 9, 2011), 6.

82. Diana Mejia, "La política de seguridad en la frontera norte: Modificar las realidades para cambiar las percepciones (entrevista)," Boletín Fronteras (Quito: FLACSO Quito, Programa de Estudios de la Ciudad, 2009).

83. Laura González Carranza, *Peones en un ajedrez militar: Los habitantes de la frontera norte* (Quito: Fundación Regional de Asesoría en Derechos Humanos, 2011).

84. Numerous interviews with ex-combatants and others, Colombia, between 2011 and 2017.

85. Elisabeth Jean Wood, *Insurgent Collective Action and Civil War in El Salvador* (Cambridge, UK: Cambridge University Press, 2003).

86. Interview with a farmer, Bajo Putumayo, Colombia, 2012.

87. Interview with a displaced farmer, Mocoa, Colombia, 2011.

88. González Carranza, *Peones en un ajedrez militar*.

89. Pécaut, "From the Banality of Violence to Real Terror: The Case of Colombia," 149–50.

90. Annette Idler and James J. F. Forest, "Behavioral Patterns among (Violent) Non-State Actors: A Study of Complementary Governance," *Stability: International Journal of Security and Development* 4, no. 1 (2015), https://www.stabilityjournal.org/articles/10.5334/sta.er/.

91. Interviews with community members in Tumaco, Colombia, in 2011 and 2016, and with community members in Esmeraldas, Ecuador, 2012

92. Interviews with community members in Pasto, Colombia, 2011 and 2012, and with community members in Carchi, Ecuador, 2012.

93. Idler and Forest.

94. Colombia's Early Warning System monitors risks to civilians caused by the conflict. Defensoría del Pueblo de Colombia, "Sistema de alertas tempranas," February 5, 2012, http://www.defensoria.org.co/red/?_item=1102&_secc=11&ts=2.

95. Interview with a member of the church, Ecuadorian northern border zone, Ecuador, 2012.

96. The fact that these crimes occurred suggests that the guerrillas did not have fully consolidated their preponderance, tolerated them to avoid state attention, or were involved themselves.

97. Interview with a human rights defender, Paraguaipoa, Venezuela, 2012.

98. Ibid.

99. Nat Colletta and Michelle L. Cullen, "The Nexus between Violent Conflict, Social Capital, and Social Cohesion: Case Studies from Cambodia and Rwanda." Working Paper, Social Capital Initiative (Washington, DC: World Bank, 2000).

100. Interviews with community members, Zulia, Venezuela, 2012.

101. See, e.g., Francisco Gutiérrez Sanín, "Telling the Difference: Guerrillas and Paramilitaries in the Colombian War," *Politics & Society* 36, no. 1 (March 1, 2008): 3–34.

102. Sistema de Alertas Tempranas, "Informe de Riesgo Nº 019-07" (Bogotá: Defensoría del Pueblo de Colombia, July 19, 2007), 2.

103. Sistema de Alertas Tempranas, "Internal Document" (Defensoría del Pueblo de Colombia, 2010).

104. Idler, Garrido, and Mouly, "Peace Territories in Colombia"; Cécile Mouly, Annette Idler, and Belén Garrido, "Zones of Peace in Colombia's Borderlands," *International Journal of Peace Studies* 20, no. 1 (2015), https://doi.org/10.1080/15423166.2015.1082437.

105. Interview with a humanitarian organization staff member, Machiques, Venezuela, 2012.

106. Interview with an ex-guerrilla, Pasto, Colombia, 2011.

107. According to Ávila and Guerra Ariz, in 2011 the paramilitaries also controlled parts of the Zulian Jesús María Semprún municipality up to the southern parts of Machiques. See Ariel Ávila and Carmen Rosa Guerra Ariza, "Frontera La Guajira y Cesar-Zulia," in *La frontera caliente entre Colombia y Venezuela*, ed. Ariel Ávila (Cota, Colombia: Corporación Nuevo Arco Iris, 2012), 347–523.

108. Interview with a humanitarian organization employee, Machiques, Venezuela, 2012.

109. Ariel Ávila, "Colombia's Facebook Hit List: Drug Gangs 2.0," *Corporación Nuevo Arcoiris* (blog), August 27, 2010, http://www.nuevoarcoiris.org.co/sac/?q=node/900.

110. Gutiérrez Sanín, "Telling the Difference: Guerrillas and Paramilitaries in the Colombian War."

111. This does not necessarily apply when violent non-state groups enter a governance vacuum where no other violent non-state group has been present before.

112. Annette Idler, "Espacios invisibilizados: Actores violentos no-estatales y 'Ciudadanía de Sombra' en las zonas fronterizas de Colombia," *Estudios Indiana*, 2014.

113. Note that this does not contradict the mutual exclusivity of the three clusters of violent non-state groups as discussed in chapter 2. Various clusters can exist in the same territory because a multiplicity of different groups can be present there.

114. Interview with a humanitarian organization employee, Zulia, Venezuela, 2012.

115. Interview with a member of the church, Ecuadorian northern border zone, Ecuador, 2012.

116. Anecdotes from my fieldwork illustrate this phenomenon. In 2012 in Guasdualito, I was advised to leave my valuables in the parked car since no one would dare to steal them. In 2012 in Puerto Asís, I was told to leave my laptop in the hotel room because thefts would not occur.

Chapter 7

1. Interview with a local resident, Maicao, Colombia, 2012.

2. Given that I analytically focus on how the border effect influences the group interactions first, which then has consequences for people's security, I do not include rules of appropriate behavior or security-enhancing practices in this overview, as these citizen security elements concern people's security directly. I touch upon these elements in my discussion, though.

3. Paul Nugent and Anthony Ijaola Asiwaju, *African Boundaries: Barriers, Conduits, and Opportunities* (London: Pinter, 1996), 1; Wolfgang Zeller, "Get It While You Can: Building Business and Bureaucracy between Wars in the Uganda-Sudan Borderland," in *Violence on the Margins: States, Conflict, and Borderlands*, ed. Benedikt Korf and Timothy Raeymaekers (New York: Palgrave Macmillan, 2013), 194.

4. Friedrich Ratzel, *Politische Geographie* (Munich: Oldenbourg, 1897).

5. Barbara J. Morehouse, Vera Pavlakovich-Kochi, and Doris Wastl-Walter, "Introduction: Perspectives on Borderlands," in *Challenged Borderlands: Transcending Political and Cultural Boundaries*, ed. Barbara J. Morehouse, Vera Pavlakovich-Kochi, and Doris Wastl-Walter (Aldershot: Ashgate, 2004), 24.

6. Zeller, "Get It While You Can: Building Business and Bureaucracy between Wars in the Uganda-Sudan Borderland," 194.

7. Laura González Carranza, *Peones en un ajedrez militar: Los habitantes de la frontera norte* (Quito: Fundación Regional de Asesoría en Derechos Humanos, 2011), 133–34.

8. Fundación Amazónica Leonidas Proano, "Asesinato de dirigente en Barranca Bermeja," October 8, 2009.

9. Philip Alston, "Report of the Special Rapporteur on Extrajudicial, Summary, or Arbitrary Executions, Philip Alston," United Nations General Assembly (Human Rights Council, May 9, 2011), 6–7.

10. El Universo, "Cancilleres buscarán mejorar relaciones Ecuador-Colombia," *El Universo*, 26 May 2007, http://www.eluniverso.com/2007/05/26/0001/8/0C4EDB477CB249D084A B8D4EFB9619A2.html.

11. So-called false positives across the border by state forces also remain unpunished: in May 2008, members of the Colombian military were accused of crossing the border to Sucumbíos as paramilitaries, taking Ecuadorians to Colombia, shooting them and dressing them up as guerrillas to increase the body count, and to receive additional payments. There also have been investigations into false positives committed by members of the Ecuadorian military. Interview with a human rights defender, Lago Agrio, Ecuador, 2012. See also González Carranza, *Peones en un ajedrez militar*, 93–95; Pablo Jaramillo Viteri, "En las orillas del miedo," *Revista Vanguardia* (blog), 2011, http://web.revistavanguardia.com/index. php?option=com_content&view=article&id=742&Itemid=215; Alberto Rivadeneira Muñoz and Juan Marco Gonzaga, "Acta de inspección al sector de Barranca Bermeja—San Martín, canton Lago Agrio provincia de Sucumbíos." (Lago Agrio, Ecuador: Defensoría del Pueblo de Ecuador, 2008); El Espectador, "Ecuador investiga si hubo 'falsos positivos' en su ejército," May 7, 2010, https://www.elespectador.com/noticias/elmundo/ articulo202064-ecuador-investiga-si-hubo-falsos-positivos-su-ejercito.

12. This was also the case with broker Loco Barrera, FARC's number two Raúl Reyes in Ecuador, and FARC's alias "Timochenko" in Venezuela.
13. Interview with humanitarian organization employee, Cúcuta, Colombia, 2012.
14. Phil Williams, "Lawlessness and Disorder: An Emerging Paradigm for the 21st Century," in *Convergence: Illicit Networks and National Security in the Age of Globalization*, ed. Michael Miklaucic and Jacqueline Brewer (Washington, DC: National Defense University, 2013), 30.
15. Interview with international agency staff, Tumaco, Colombia, 2011.
16. El Colombiano, "Ataque de las FARC dejó 10 policías muertos en Putumayo," *El Colombiano*, 10 September 2010, http://www.elcolombiano.com/BancoConocimiento/A/ataque_de_las_farc_dejo_ocho_policias_muertos_en_putumayo/ataque_de_las_farc_dejo_ocho_policias_muertos_en_putumayo.asp.
17. Interview with police official and others, Puerto Asís, Colombia, 2012. In the same year, various interviewees in Ecuadorian Sucumbíos stated that the Colombian military launched grenades from Colombia against the FARC on the Ecuadorian side.
18. Interviews with international agency staff members, Apure, Venezuela, and Arauca, Colombia, 2012.
19. I changed her name.
20. Interview with a human rights defender, Paraguaipoa, Venezuela, 2012.
21. According to the International Convention for the Protection of All Persons from Enforced Disappearance, "'enforced disappearance' is considered to be the arrest, detention, abduction, or any other form of deprivation of liberty by agents of the State or by persons or groups of persons acting with the authorization, support, or acquiescence of the State, followed by a refusal to acknowledge the deprivation of liberty or by concealment of the fate or whereabouts of the disappeared person, which place such a person outside the protection of the law." United Nations Office of the High Commissioner for Human Rights, "International Convention for the Protection of All Persons from Enforced Disappearance" (United Nations Office of the High Commissioner for Human Rights, n.d.), article 2, http://www.ohchr.org/EN/HRBodies/CED/Pages/ConventionCED.aspx.
22. Edelberto Torres-Rivas, "Epilogue: Notes on Terror, Violence, Fear, and Democracy," in *Societies of Fear: The Legacy of Civil War, Violence, and Terror in Latin America*, ed. Kees Koonings and Dirk Krujit (Zed Books, 1999), 291.
23. Various interviews with local residents, Tumaco, Colombia, 2011.
24. Germán De-la-Hoz-Bohórquez, "Comportamiento del homicidio: Colombia, 2013" (Bogotá: Instituto Nacional de Medicina Legal y Ciencias Forenses, 2013), 106, http://www.medicinalegal.gov.co/documents/10180/34616/2-F-11-Homicidios.pdf/01a6b108-57cd-48bc-9e9b-dcdba0d918a2.
25. Juan Diego Restrepo, "'Paras' asesinan en Colombia y arrojan cuerpos en Venezuela," *Verdad Abierta*, 31 August 2011, http://www.verdadabierta.com/index.php?option=com_content&id=2396%3E. According to Colombia's national register of disappeared people, 947 people were registered as disappeared in Norte Santander between 2000 and 2009. Fundación Progresar, *Tantas vidas arrebatadas. La desaparición forzada de personas: Una estrategia sistemática de guerra sucia en Norte de Santander*, ed. Wilfredo Cañizares Arévalo (Cúcuta, Colombia, 2010), 48.
26. Fundación Progresar, *Tantas vidas arrebatadas. La desaparición forzada de personas: Una estrategia sistemática de guerra sucia en Norte de Santander*, 60; CINEP, "Noche y Niebla: Panorama de derechos humanos y violencia política en Colombia," no. 45 (July 2012).
27. Vicepresidencia de la República, "Algunos indicadores sobre la situación de derechos humanos en la región del Catatumbo." (Bogotá: Programa Presidencial de Derechos Humanos y de Derecho Internacional Humanitario, October 2004); Vicepresidencia, "Diagnostico departamental Norte de Santander" (Bogotá: Observatorio del Programa Presidencial de Derechos Humanos y Derecho Internacional Humanitario, Vicepresidencia de la República, 2007).
28. Fundación Progresar, *Tantas vidas arrebatadas. La desaparición forzada de personas: Una estrategia sistemática de guerra sucia en Norte de Santander*, 51–52.
29. In Cúcuta, in the same period, there were 374 cases of disappearances. Only twenty-five were recorded as enforced disappearances, presumably due to the victims' fear of retaliation.

Fundación Progresar, *Tantas vidas arrebatadas. La desaparición forzada de personas: Una estrategia sistemática de guerra sucia en Norte de Santander*, 51.

30. Ibid., 86–106.
31. Ibid., 92.
32. Programa de Educación—Acción en Derechos Humanos PROVEA, "Situación de los derechos humanos en Venezuela, informe anual octubre 2010 / septiembre 2011" (Caracas: PROVEA, 2012); Programa de Educación—Acción en Derechos Humanos PROVEA, "Situación de los derechos humanos en Venezuelai. Informe anual enero-diciembre 2012" (Caracas: PROVEA, 2013); OVV, "La violencia no se detiene. Informe del OVV—diciembre 2012" (Caracas: Observatorio Venezolano de Violencia, 2012), http://observatoriodeviolencia.org.ve/ws/informe-del-ovv-diciembre-2012/;   OVV, "Las muertes violentas continúan aumentando. Informe del OVV—diciembre 2013" (Caracas: Observatorio Venezolano de Violencia, 2013), http://observatoriodeviolencia. org.ve/ws/informe-del-ovv-diciembre-2013-2/; International Crisis Group, "Violence and Politics in Venezuela," Latin America Report (Bogotá, Brussels: International Crisis Group, 17 August 2011), http://www.crisisgroup.org/en/regions/latin-america-caribbean/andes/ venezuela/038-violence-and-politics-in-venezuela.aspx.
33. Fundación Progresar, *Tantas vidas arrebatadas. La desaparición forzada de personas: Una estrategia sistemática de guerra sucia en Norte de Santander*, 90; Restrepo, " 'Paras' asesinan en Colombia u arrojan cuerpos en Venezuela."
34. United Nations Office for the Coordination of Humanitarian Affairs, "Revisión del mapeo inter-institucional humanitario frontera colombo-venezolana. Norte de Santander," Office for the Coordination of Humanitarian Affairs (OCHA Nororiente, May 2010), 7.
35. Hoy, "Nuevo cierre de frontera colombo-venezolana," *Hoy*, 8 November 2009, http://www. hoy.com.ec/noticias-ecuador/nuevo-cierre-de-frontera-colombo-venezolana-376952. html. According to a resident, one of them survived and claimed that the ELN were the perpetrators.
36. Restrepo, " 'Paras' asesinan en Colombia y arrojan cuerpos en Venezuela."
37. Fundación Progresar, *Tantas vidas arrebatadas*, 87.
38. Torres-Rivas, "Epilogue: Notes on Terror, Violence, Fear, and Democracy," 292.
39. Fundación Progresar, *Tantas Vidas Arrebatadas*, 87.
40. Willem van Schendel, "Spaces of Engagement: How Borderlands, Illegal Flows, and Territorial States Interlock," in *Illicit Flows and Criminal Things: States, Borders, and the Other Side of Globalization*, ed. Willem van Schendel and Itty Abraham (Bloomington: Indiana University Press, 2005), 52–53.
41. Fundación Progresar, 89.
42. Magda Paola Núñez Gantiva, "ELN-FARC: Ahora sí juntos," *Arcanos* 15, no. 17 (2012): 61–62. As of 2010, an estimated 120,000 to 200,000 Colombians in need of international protection were in Venezuela and 135,000 in Ecuador. United Nations High Commissioner for Refugees, "Directrices de elegibilidad del ACNUR para la evaluación de las necesidades de protección internacional de los solicitantes de asilo de Colombia," HCR/EG/COL/10/2 (UNHCR, 27 May 2010), 3–4.
43. 2,700 Colombians were granted refugee status. United Nations High Commissioner for Refugees, "Venezuela" (Caracas, 2010), http://www.acnur.org/t3/uploads/tx_ refugiadosamericas/Ficha_Informativa_de_Venezuela.pdf?view=1.
44. Further reasons are that they do not know how to register as a refugee or prefer anonymity to avoid prosecution.
45. Milana Peralta et al., "La Guajira en su laberinto: Transformaciones y desafíos de la violencia," Informes FIP (Bogotá: Fundación Ideas para la Paz, August 2011), 6.
46. Juan Carlos Gamboa Martínez, "Una mirada panorámica a la frontera La Guajira–Zulia," internal document (Maicao: PNUD, June 2012), 3.
47. Interview with an Awá leader, Pasto, Colombia, 2011.
48. Ministerio del Interior y de Justicia de la República de Colombia, "Ley de víctimas y restitución de tierras" (Bogotá: Ministerio del Interior y de Justicia, 2011).
49. In the first seven months of 2013, 23 percent of the confined population and 73 percent of the displaced were indigenous people and Afro-Colombians, although they constitute only

3 percent and 9 percent of Colombia's population, respectively. United Nations Office for the Coordination of Humanitarian Affairs, "Colombia: Humanitarian Snapshot," Office for the Coordination of Humanitarian Affairs (Bogotá: OCHA Colombia, 14 August 2013).

50. Ministerio del Interior, "Agenda nacional de seguridad ciudadana y gobernabilidad" (Quito: Ministerio del Interior, 2011), 45.

51. Interview with a community leader, Cúcuta, Colombia, 2011. Armed actors also used mobile laboratories in the outskirts of Cúcuta to shift them outside the Metropolitan police forces' range of operation while benefiting from the availability of the labor force.

52. Interview with a humanitarian organization employee, Zulia, Venezuela, 2012.

53. United Nations Office on Drugs and Crime, "World Drug Report 2010" (Vienna: United Nations Office on Drugs and Crime, 2010), 74–75. In 2010, a total of 242 tons were shipped to the United States and Europe from the Caribbean.

54. United Nations Office on Drugs and Crime, "UN Drugs Agency Compliments Ecuador on Seizure of 5.5 Tons of Cocaine" (Vienna: United Nations Office on Drugs and Crime, 2005), https://www.unodc.org/unodc/en/press/releases/press_release_2006-03-17.html.

55. El Universo, "Cronología: Caso huracán de la frontera," El Universo, 23 August 2009, http://www.eluniverso.com/2009/08/23/1/1355/cronologia-caso-huracan-frontera.html.

56. El Universo, "En campanita empezó la ruta del caso Chauvín," El Universo, 15 February 2009, http://www.eluniverso.com/2009/02/15/1/1355/63A74BE0AC1A48CC910D3F121FC770F9.html.

57. William Neuman, "Venezuela is Cocaine Hub despite its Claims," New York Times, 26 July 2012, sec. World/Americas, http://www.nytimes.com/2012/07/27/world/americas/venezuela-is-cocaine-hub-despite-its-claims.html.

58. Ibid.

59. Willem van Schendel, The Bengal Borderland: Beyond State and Nation in South Asia (London: Anthem, 2005), 385.

60. United Nations Office on Drugs and Crime, The Globalization of Crime: A Transnational Organized Crime Threat Assessment (Vienna: United Nations Office on Drugs and Crime, 2010); Mats R. Berdal, Transnational Organized Crime and International Security: Business as Usual? (Boulder, CO: Lynne Rienner, 2002); Rohan Gunaratna, Inside Al Qaeda: Global Network of Terror (New York: Berkley Books, 2003).

61. Zeller, "Get It While You Can: Building Business and Bureaucracy between Wars in the Uganda-Sudan Borderland," 211.

62. See Picciotto, Olonisakin, and Clarke's conceptualization of Hirschman's Exit, Voice and Loyalty: Response to Decline in Firms, Organizations, and States (Cambridge, MA: Harvard University Press, 1972). See Robert Picciotto, Funmi Olonisakin and Michael Clarke, Global Development and Human Security (New Brunswick, NJ: Transaction Publishers, 2007), 12–13.

63. Interview with an international agency staff member, Mocoa, Colombia, 2011. In some cases of confinements, men had to stay while women and children were allowed to leave.

64. Zeller, "Get It While You Can," 193–218; Jonathan Goodhand, "Epilogue: The View from the Border," in Violence on the Margins: States, Conflict, and Borderlands, ed. Benedikt Korf and Timothy Raeymaekers (New York: Palgrave Macmillan, 2013), 247–49.

65. See Anne L. Clunan and Harold A. Trinkunas, eds., Ungoverned Spaces: Alternatives to State Authority in an Era of Softened Sovereignty (Stanford, CA: Stanford University Press, 2010).

66. John Ruggie, "Territoriality and Beyond: Problematizing Modernity in International Relations," International Organization 47, no. 1 (Winter 1993): 139–74.

67. Benedikt Korf and Timothy Raeymaekers, Violence on the Margins, 5.

68. Johanna M. Espín, "Seguridad ciudadana en la frontera norte ecuatoriana," Ventana a la cooperación, 2009, 20–24; Laura González Carranza, Fronteras en el limbo: El Plan Colombia en el Ecuador (Quito: Fundación Regional de Asesoría en Derechos Humanos, INREDH, 2008); Juan Camilo Molina, "Cooperación internacional al desarrollo y refugio en la frontera norte en Ecuador," Ventana a la cooperación, 2009, 2–19.

69. Interview with a border village resident, Carchi, Ecuador, 2012.

70. Interviews with local residents, Carchi, Ecuador, 2012.

71. According to an interviewee from Tufiño, people used to visit the neighboring Colombian village but stopped doing so during fighting between state forces and the guerrillas. Interview with a Tufiño resident, Ecuador, 2012.

72. Interview with a border village resident, Carchi, Ecuador, 2012.

73. See Robert D. Putnam, *Bowling Alone* (New York: Simon and Schuster, 2001), 23.

74. Interview with a politician, Tulcán, Ecuador, 2012.

75. Interview with a member of the church, Carchi, Ecuador, 2012.

76. Interview with an academic, Quito, Ecuador, 2012.

77. Fundación Paz y Reconciliación, "Departamento de Putumayo. Tercera monografía" (Bogotá: Fundación Paz y Reconciliación, 24 February 2014), 58.

78. Interview with a local resident, General Farfán, Ecuador, 2012.

79. Interview with a Colombian woman, General Farfán, Ecuador, 2012.

80. Ibid.

81. Instituto Nacional de Estadística, "Encuesta nacional de victimización y percepción de seguridad ciudadana 2009 (ENVPSC-2009). Documento técnico" (Caracas: Instituto Nacional de Estadística, República Bolivariana de Venezuela, May 2010).

82. Ibid., 183.

83. Ibid., 160.

84. See, e.g., Mónica Serrano and María Celia Toro, "From Drug Trafficking to Transnational Organized Crime in Latin America," in *Transnational Organized Crime and International Security: Business as Usual?*, ed. Mats R. Berdal and M. Serrano (Boulder, CO.: Lynne Rienner, 2002); Willem van Schendel and Itty Abraham, eds., *Illicit Flows and Criminal Things: States, Borders, and the Other Side of Globalization* (Bloomington: Indiana University Press, 2005).

85. Michael Miklaucic and Jacqueline Brewer, "Introduction," in *Convergence: Illicit Networks and National Security in the Age of Globalization*, ed. Michael Miklaucic and Jacqueline Brewer (Washington, DC: National Defense University, 2013), xvii.

86. Similar issues arise across internal borders, where one group has more direct access to intelligence on local authorities and the local population, whereas the outsider groups lacks information. Differing state policies, however, typically reinforce such variations across the border. For a somewhat similar logic concerning the international movements of mafia groups see Federico Varese, *Mafias on the Move: How Organized Crime Conquers New Territories* (Princeton, NJ: Princeton University Press, 2011).

87. Interview with an ex-guerrilla, Pasto, Colombia, 2011.

88. For issue-linkage used by states see Robert M. Axelrod and Robert O. Keohane, "Achieving Cooperation under Anarchy: Strategies and Institutions," *World Politics* 38, no. 1 (1985): 239, http://www.jstor.org/stable/2010357?origin=JSTOR-pdf.

89. Interview with an ex-guerrilla, Pasto, Colombia, 2011.

90. This can be considered an intensified version of the suspicion that arises in settings within the boundaries of a single state, as in the Llorente case (see section 5.1).

91. Molina, "Cooperación internacional al desarrollo y refugio en la frontera norte en Ecuador," 4–5.

92. Zully Laverde and Edwin Tapia, *Tensión en las fronteras* (Bogotá: CODHES, 2009), 65; Programa de Estudios de la Ciudad, "Gobernanza de la seguridad en la frontera norte ecuatoriana," Fronteras (FLACSO Quito, Programa de Estudios de la Ciudad, 2011), 7.

93. Interview with an international agency staff member, Esmeraldas, Ecuador, 2012.

94. Ibid.

95. Note that this is different if the state authorities themselves are complicit in such deals.

96. Interview with a civil society leader of Tumaco, Quito, Ecuador, 2012.

97. Fernando Carrión, "El sicariato: Una realidad ausente," *Ciudad segura*, 2008, 4–9. Interview with Ecuadorian academic, Quito, Ecuador, 2012.

98. González Carranza, *Fronteras en el limbo*, 216–18.

99. Interviews with San Lorenzo residents, Ecuador, 2012.

100. González Carranza, *Fronteras en el limbo*.

101. One resident argued that, thanks to the Colombian conflict's spillover, Quito and the international development agencies had started to pay attention to impoverished San Lorenzo,

which led to asphalting of roads and more presence of the state and international agencies. Interview with a San Lorenzo resident, Ecuador, 2012.

102. Interviews with various community members, San Lorenzo, Ecuador, 2012.

103. Interview with a police official, San Lorenzo, Ecuador, 2012.

104. Daniel Pécaut, *L'ordre et la violence: Évolution socio-politique de la Colombie entre 1930 et 1953* (Paris: École des hautes études en sciences sociales, 1987). Despite locals' claims of feeling safer, in 2013 homicide rates in the canton of San Lorenzo were still soaring, with 96.2 homicides per 100,000 inhabitants. Fiscalía de Ecuador, "Fiscalía liderará reunión en San Lorenzo sobre plan de seguridad ciudadana en zona fronteriza," 8 July 2014, http://www.fiscalia.gob.ec/index.php/sala-de-prensa/2305-fiscal%C3%ADa-liderar%C3%A1-reuni%C3%B3n-en-san-lorenzo-sobre-plan-de-seguridad-ciudadana-en-la-zona-fronteriza.html.

105. Interview with former female and male combatants, Pasto, Colombia, 2011.

106. Scott Stewart, "Mexico and the Cartel Wars in 2010," Security Weekly (Stratfor. Global Intelligence, 2010), http://www.stratfor.com/weekly/20101215-mexico-and-cartel-wars-2010; Paul Gootenberg, *Andean Cocaine: The Making of a Global Drug* (Chapel Hill: University of North Carolina Press, 2008); Patrick Clawson and Rensselaer W. Lee, *The Andean Cocaine Industry* (Basingstoke: Macmillan, 1996).

107. Scott Stewart, "From Colombia to New York City: The Narconomics of Cocaine," Business Insider, 27 June 2016, http://www.businessinsider.com/from-colombia-to-new-york-city-the-economics-of-cocaine-2015-7?IR=T.

108. United Nations Office on Drugs and Crime, "World Drug Report 2014" (Vienna: United Nations Office on Drugs and Crime, 2014); United Nations Office on Drugs and Crime, "World Drug Report 2016" (Vienna: United Nations Office on Drugs and Crime, 2016).

109. Lee J. M. Seymour, "Why Factions Switch Sides in Civil Wars: Rivalry, Patronage, and Realignment in Sudan," *International Security* 39, no. 2 (1 October 2014): 92–131, http://dx.doi.org/10.1162/ISEC_a_00179; Kanisha D. Bond, "Power, Identity, Credibility, and Cooperation: Examining the Cooperative Arrangements among Violent Non-State Actors" (PhD diss., Pennsylvania State University, 2010); Theodore McLauchlin, "Loyalty Strategies and Military Defection in Rebellion," *Comparative Politics* 42, no. 3 (31 March 2010): 333–50, https://doi.org/10.5129/001041510X12911363509792.

110. See, e.g., Eduardo Moncada, "Urban Violence, Political Economy, and Territorial Control: Insights from Medellín," *Latin American Research Review* 61, no. 4 (2016): 234, https://lasa.international.pitt.edu/auth/pub/Larr/CurrentIssue/51-4_225-248_Moncada.pdf.

111. Interview with a government official, Pasto, Colombia, 2011.

112. These advantages are similar to those of cross-border subcontractual relationships. On the same side of the border, however, groups are more interdependent.

113. See, e.g., Robert Gibbons, *Game Theory for Applied Economists* (Princeton, NJ: Princeton University Press, 1992); Avinash K. Dixit, *Games of Strategy*, 3rd ed. (New York: Norton, 2009).

114. Robert M. Axelrod and Robert O. Keohane, "Achieving Cooperation under Anarchy: Strategies and Institutions," *World Politics* 38, no. 1 (1985): 226–54, http://www.jstor.org/stable/2010357?origin=JSTOR-pdf; Kenneth A. Oye, *Cooperation under Anarchy* (Princeton, NJ: Princeton University Press, 1986).

115. Oye, *Cooperation under Anarchy*, 17.

116. Thomas C. Schelling, *The Strategy of Conflict* (Cambridge, MA: Harvard University Press, 1980), 43–46; Robert M. Axelrod, *The Evolution of Cooperation* (New York: Basic Books, 1984), 126–32.

117. See, e.g., Oye, *Cooperation under Anarchy*.

118. See McLauchlin, "Loyalty Strategies and Military Defection in Rebellion."

119. Diego Gambetta, *Codes of the Underworld: How Criminals Communicate* (Princeton, NJ: Princeton University Press, 2009), 35–36.

120. Frank Safford, *Colombia: Fragmented Land, Divided Society* (New York: Oxford University Press, 2002).

121. Korf and Raeymaekers, *Violence on the Margins*, 13.

122. Goodhand, "Epilogue: The View from the Border," 247. "Disconnected" territories also exist for instance in poor neighborhoods in Bogotá, Caracas, and Quito.
123. Sistema de Alertas Tempranas, "Informe de Riesgo N° 017-07 A. I.," Sistema de Alertas Tempranas. Defensoría del Pueblo de Colombia (Bogotá: Defensoria del Pueblo de Colombia, 6 July 2007), 2.
124. This largely correlates with the results of the plebiscite on the peace deal in 2016 in which the "yes" vote prevailed in marginalized regions, affected by the armed conflict, whereas more central regions voted "no."
125. Korf and Raeymaekers, *Violence on the Margins*, 7.
126. Guillermo Herrera, "La realidad sobre la seguridad ciudadana en Carchi," *Observatorio de seguridad ciudadana* 1, no. 1 (2007): 17.
127. Various interviews, Caracas, Venezuela, 2012.
128. René Girard, *Violence and the Sacred* (London: Bloomsbury Academic, 2013).
129. Interview with humanitarian organization employee, Maicao, Colombia, 2012.
130. Interview with a humanitarian organization staff member, Maracaibo, Venezuela, 2012.
131. Interview with a human rights organization employee, Sucumbíos, Ecuador, 2012.
132. Interview with an indigenous leader, Mocoa, Colombia, 2012.
133. Interview with a civil society representative, Sucumbíos, Ecuador, 2012.
134. David Keen, *Conflict & Collusion in Sierra Leone* (Oxford: James Currey, 2005), 57.
135. Policía Nacional de Colombia, "Respuesta derecho de petición S.I.P.Q.R.S 174344-20140910" (Policía Nacional de Colombia, Ministerio de Defensa, September 22, 2014).
136. In 2005 and 2006, FARC ceased armed strikes after communities protested against them. María Clemencia Ramírez, "Negotiating Peace and Visibility as a Civil Society in Putumayo amid the Armed Conflict and the War on Drugs," in *Colombia: Building Peace in a Time of War*, ed. Virginia Marie Bouvier (Washington, DC: United States Institute of Peace Press, 2009), 323. Such resistance was less common in subsequent years.
137. Policía Nacional de Colombia, "Respuesta derecho de petición S.I.P.Q.R.S 174344-20140910."
138. Elizabeth Niño Ascanio, Edwin Camargo León, and Wilfredo Cañizares Arévalo, "Frontera Norte de Santander—Táchira," in *La frontera caliente entre Colombia y Venezuela*, ed. Ariel Ávila (Cota, Colombia: Corporación Nuevo Arco Iris, 2012), 298–99.
139. Supposedly, the National Guard told the paramilitaries to kill their leader after which the border was opened.
140. Instituto Nacional de Estadística, "Encuesta nacional de victimización y percepción de seguridad ciudadana 2009 (ENVPSC-2009). Documento técnico."
141. Crimes in the survey included homicide, personal injury, sexual abuse, robbery, kidnapping, extortion, corruption, theft, fraud, and threat. Instituto Nacional de Estadística, 26; 35.
142. Ibid., 160.
143. Many Venezuelans consider post-demobilized groups criminal groups. This explains why, despite a high homicide rate in Táchira linked to these groups, people do not relate them to paramilitaries.
144. Instituto Nacional de Estadística, "Encuesta nacional de victimización y percepción de seguridad ciudadana 2009 (ENVPSC-2009). Documento técnico," 187–90.
145. United Nations High Commissioner for Refugees Colombia, "Internal Presentation" (Pasto, Colombia, 2011). These municipalities are strategic for international trafficking routes.
146. United Nations High Commissioner for Refugees Colombia. The United Nations High Commissioner for Refugees started to monitor confinements in the region relatively recently.
147. The displacement in La Estrella, Ipiales, resulted from a bombardment of the Colombian state forces against the FARC, supposedly motivated by oil fields in the area.
148. Interview with an international agency staff member, Pasto, Colombia, 2011.
149. Interview with a resident of Puerto Caicedo, Colombia, 2012.
150. United Nations Office for the Coordination of Humanitarian Affairs, "Glossary of Humanitarian Terms. In Relation to the Protection of Civilians in Armed Conflict," Office for the Coordination of Humanitarian Affairs (New York: United Nations, 2003), 27.
151. Hastings Donnan and Thomas M. Wilson, *Border Approaches: Anthropological Perspectives on Frontiers* (Lanham, MD: University Press of America, 1994), 8; M. Baud and W. van

Schendel, "Toward a Comparative History of Borderlands," *Journal of World History* 8 (1997): 219.

152. Oscar J. Martínez, *Border People: Life and Society in the US-Mexico Borderlands* (Tucson: University of Arizona Press, 1994), xviii.

153. Various interviews with government officials, academics, non-governmental organization employees, and others in Bogotá, Caracas, and Quito, 2011 and 2012.

154. With the deepening of the Venezuelan crisis, at the Colombia-Venezuela border this phenomenon exists increasingly in reverse, Venezuelan children attend Colombian schools, for example.

155. Schendel and Abraham, *Illicit Flows and Criminal Things: States, Borders, and the Other Side of Globalization*, 61; Schendel, *The Bengal Borderland*, 384.

156. Korf and Raeymaekers, *Violence on the Margins*, 5.

Chapter 8

1. Interview with a local resident, Baja Guajira, Colombia, 2016.

2. Ibid.

3. Interview with a local resident, San Cristóbal, Venezuela, 2017.

4. Interview with a farmer, Bajo Putumayo, Colombia, 2017.

5. FARC-EP, "Comunicado: FARC-EP declara Cese al fuego unilateral. National Secretariat FARC-EP," July 8, 2015, http://www.pazfarc-ep.org/index.php/comunicadosestadomayorfarc/item/2842-comunicado.

6. Various interviews with community members, La Guajira, Colombia, 2016.

7. Juan David Cárdenas Ruiz, "La crisis fronteriza colombo-venezolana en las pantallas: Análisis desde la comunicación política," *Historia y Comunicación Social* 22, no. 2 (2017): 447–63.

8. Pedro Rafael Sayago Rojas, "Impacto socioeconómico a un año del cierre de la frontera colombo-venezolana: Norte de Santander—Estado Táchira (2015–2016)," *Mundo Fesc* 12 (2016): 92–93.

9. Various interviews with community members and civil society representatives, Arauca and La Guajira, Colombia, 2016.

10. Sayago Rojas, "Impacto socioeconómico a un año del cierre de la frontera colombo-venezolana," 92.

11. Rafael Mathus Ruiz, "La OEA denuncia un auto golpe de estado," *La Nación* (March 30, 2017), https://www.lanacion.com.ar/2001613-venezuela-la-oea-denuncia-un-auto-golpe-de-estado.

12. Conversations with residents of the Colombia-Venezuelan borderlands, 2017. See also Annette Idler, "Venezuela's Instability Has Far Broader Implications: Here's What's at Stake," *Washington Post*, August 10, 2017, sec. Monkey Cage, https://www.washingtonpost.com/news/monkey-cage/wp/2017/08/10/venezuelas-instability-has-far-broader-implications-heres-whats-at-stake/?utm_term=.1beaab715146.

13. Hastings Donnan and Thomas M. Wilson, *Borderlands: Ethnographic Approaches to Security, Power, and Identity* (Lanham, MD: University Press of America, 2010), 7, http://www.ebrary.com/landing/site/bodleian/index-bodleian.jsp?Docid=10602209.

14. Manuel Llorens, "Dolor país, versión Venezuela: Las protestas de 2017 y sus secuelas," *Nueva Sociedad* 274 (2018): 74, 82.

15. El Nacional, "Reporta prostitución de niñas en la Guajira por comida," *El Nacional*, 31 October 2017, http://www.el-nacional.com/noticias/sociedad/reportan-prostitucion-ninas-guaira-por-comida_209904.

16. Interviews with community members, Norte de Santander, Colombia, and Táchira, Venezuela, 2017.

17. Llorens, "Dolor país, versión Venezuela," 74–75.

18. TelesurTV, "Desmantelan campamento paramilitar colombiano en Venezuela," March 22, 2017, https://www.telesurtv.net/news/Desmantelan-campamento-paramilitar-colombiano-en-Venezuela-20170322-0066.html.

19. Various interviews with local residents, San Cristóbal, Venezuela, 2017.

20. See, e.g., Defensoría Delegada para la Prevención de Riesgos de Violaciones a los Derechos Humanos y el DIH, Sistema de Alertas Tempranas, *Grupos Armados Ilegales y nuevos escenarios de riesgo en el posacuerdo* (Bogotá: Defensoría del Pueblo, 2017), http://desarrollos.defensoria. gov.co/desarrollo1/ABCD/bases/marc/documentos/textos/Grupos_Armados_ilegales_ y_nuevos_escenarios_de_riesgo_en_el_posacuerdo.pdf.

21. El Comercio, "Ex FARC forman a redes delictivas de Ecuador," *El Comercio*, 17 April 2017, https://www.elcomercio.com/actualidad/exfarc-redesdelictivas-ecuador-seguridad-sucumbios.html.

22. See, e.g., El Universo, "Habitantes preocupados por un supuesto grupo armado en cantón de Sucumbíos," *El Universo*, August 3, 2016, https://www.eluniverso.com/noticias/2016/ 08/03/nota/5723058/habitantes-preocupados-supuesto-grupo-armado; Mi Putumayo, "Exitosa operación conjunta y coordinada en contra de 'La Constru' en Putumayo," July 31, 2017, http://miputumayo.com.co/2017/07/31/exitosa-operacion-conjunta-y-coordinada-en-contra-de-la-constru-en-putumayo/. Also various interviews with community members, Putumayo, Colombia, 2017.

23. El Tiempo, "Santos realizó visita sorpresa a zona veredal La Carmelita, Putumayo," *El Tiempo*, 18 April 2017, http://www.eltiempo.com/politica/gobierno/santos-visita-zona-veredal-de-la-carmelita-putumayo-79180.

24. Various interviews with community members, Putumayo, Colombia, 2017.

25. Ibid.

26. Ibid.

27. Interview with a farmer, Bajo Putumayo, Colombia, 2017.

28. Such asymmetries also arise within a single state, for example, when a single type of violent non-state group interaction spans various local contexts and societal groups. These and other factors also influence the ways in which the interactions affect citizen security. In territories of marginalized groups such as the indigenous Awá, Otavaleños, or Wayúu, or in territories of Afro-Colombians, for example, these groups can be affected differently by the same type of violent non-state group interaction, if compared to farmer communities in the same territory.

29. State policies also influence the group interactions themselves. They may prompt groups, for example, to forge a strategic alliance to actively fight the government as in Colombian Arauca, or to operate in pacific coexistence to maintain a lower profile, as in Venezuelan Apure (see section 6.2).

30. Christian Lund, "Twilight Institutions: Public Authority and Local Politics in Africa," *Development and Change* 37, no. 4 (2006): 693.

31. Various interviews in several locations in the Catatumbo region with local residents, Colombia, 2011 and 2012.

32. Sistema de Alertas Tempranas, "Nota de Seguimiento N° 002-11. Cuarta al informe de Riesgo N° 006-08A.I." (Bogotá, February 2011), 10.

33. Interviews with local residents, Zulia, 2012.

34. Andrew Hurrell, *On Global Order: Power, Values, and the Constitution of International Society* (Oxford: Oxford University Press, 2007), 26.

35. James C. Scott, *Seeing Like a State: How Certain Schemes to Improve the Human Condition Have Failed*, Yale Agrarian Studies (New Haven: Yale University Press, 1998), 2.

36. Human Security Report Project, "Human Security Report 2009/2010: The Causes of Peace and the Shrinking Costs of War" (New York: Oxford University Press, 2011), 123–31.

37. Jason K. Stearns and Christoph Vogel, "The Landscape of Armed Groups in the Eastern Congo," Congo Research Group (New York: Center on International Cooperation, New York University, 2015), 5.

38. Annette Idler and Lindsay Scorgie, "The Transnationality of Conflict: Lessons Learned from Borderlands," in *Proceedings of the 2010 European Conference of the Association for Borderlands Studies* (Thessaloniki: University of Thessaloniki, 2011), 185–204.

39. "Organized Crime and Instability in Central Africa. A Threat Assessment" (Vienna: United Nations Office on Drugs and Crime, 2011), 9.

40. Lindsay Scorgie-Porter, "Economic Survival and Borderland Rebellion: The Case of the Allied Democratic Forces on the Uganda-Congo Border," *The Journal of the Middle East and Africa* 6, no. 2 (April 3, 2015): 212, https://doi.org/10.1080/21520844.2015.1055452.

41. Kristof Titeca, "The Changing Cross-Border Trade Dynamics between North-Western Uganda, North-Eastern Congo, and Southern Sudan," *Crisis States Research Centre, LSE, Crisis States Working Papers Series* 2 (2009): 2.

42. Wolfgang Zeller, "Illicit Resource Flows in Sugango: Making War and Profit in the Border Triangle of Sudan, Uganda, and Congo-DRC," in *Exploring the Security-Development Nexus—Perspectives from Nepal, Northern Uganda, and Sugango*, ed. Henni Alava (Helsinki: Ministry of Foreign Affairs, 2010), 111–30, https://um.fi/documents/35732/48132/exploring_the_security_development_nexus.

43. Idler and Scorgie, "The Transnationality of Conflict: Lessons Learned from Borderlands."

44. Scorgie-Porter, "Economic Survival and Borderland Rebellion."

45. Oxfam, "Commodities of War. Communities Speak Out on the True Cost of Conflict in Eastern DRC," Oxfam Briefing Paper (Oxford: Oxfam, November 2012), 5, 8.

46. This alliance preceded the deployment of the United Nations Force Intervention Brigade in Lubero and Beni.

47. In 2013, for instance, the M23 engaged in spot sales and barter agreements with the Forces de Résistance Patriotique d'Ituri (FRPI), the FDC, the Mayi-Mayi NDC, the Nyatura Noheri, and Albert Kahasha. Mayi-Mayi Hilaire and Mayi-Mayi Morgan exchanged weapons and ammunition with gold and ivory (S/2013/433, 17).

48. Oxfam, "Commodities of War: Communities Speak Out on the True Cost of Conflict in Eastern DRC," 16.

49. Anthony Kushaba, "M23 Rebels Forge Alliance with Mai Mai Militias," https://ugandaradionetwork.com/story/m23-rebels-forge-alliance-with-mai-mai-militias; Nick Long, "DRC Army, M23 Rebels Compete for Militia Allies," https://www.voanews.com/a/drc-rebels-recruitment/1547636.html.

50. Ferdinand Mushi, "Insecurity and Local Governance in Congo's South Kivu," *Research Report* 74 (2012), http://www.ids.ac.uk/files/dmfile/RR74.pdf.

51. Oxfam, 8.

52. Philip J. Halton, "Core Issues Motivating Afghan Insurgents," *Canadian Army Journal* 14, no. 3 (2012): 51–75; International Crisis Group, "The Insurgency in Afghanistan's Heartland," *Asia Report* 207 (June 27, 2011), http://www.crisisgroup.org/~/media/Files/asia/south-asia/afghanistan/207%20The%20Insurgency%20in%20Afghanistans%20Heartland.pdf.

53. Stanford University, *Mapping Militant Organizations*, August 2012, http://web.stanford.edu/group/mappingmilitants/cgi-bin/groups/view/105?highlight=TEHRIK-E+TALIBAN+PAKISTAN+%28TTP%29.

54. Gretchen Peters and Don Rassler, "Crime and Insurgency in the Tribal Areas of Afghanistan and Pakistan," Combating Terrorism Center, Military Academy, West Point, NY, 2010; Illyvas M. Khan, "The Afghan-Pakistan Militant Nexus," *BBC World News Asia*, 2013, http://www.bbc.com/news/world-asia-21338263.

55. Peters and Rassler, "Crime and Insurgency in the Tribal Areas of Afghanistan and Pakistan."

56. The cases of the indigenous Wayúu across the Colombia-Venezuela border, or the indigenous Awá across the Colombia-Ecuador border, offer useful starting points for comparison (see, e.g., section 5.2).

57. Thomas H. Johnson and M. Chris Mason, "No Sign until the Burst of Fire: Understanding the Pakistan-Afghanistan Frontier," *International Security* 32, no. 4 (April 1, 2008): 41–77, https://doi.org/10.1162/isec.2008.32.4.41.

58. Arabinda Acharya, Syed Adnan Ali Shah Bukhari, and Sadia Sulaiman, "Making Money in the Mayhem: Funding Taliban Insurrection in the Tribal Areas of Pakistan," *Studies in Conflict & Terrorism* 32, no. 2 (2009): 95–108, DOI: 10.1080/10576100802628314.

59. Ibid.

60. United Nations Office on Drugs and Crime, "Afghan Opiate Trafficking through the Southern Route" (Vienna: United Nations Office on Drugs and Crime, 2015), 34.

61. Peters and Rassler, "Crime and Insurgency in the Tribal Areas of Afghanistan and Pakistan."

62. *Ireland's Violent Frontier: The Border and Anglo-Irish Relations during the Troubles* (Basingstoke: Palgrave Macmillan, 2013).
63. Annette Idler and James J. F. Forest, "Behavioral Patterns among (Violent) Non-State Actors: A Study of Complementary Governance," *Stability: International Journal of Security and Development* 4, no. 1 (2015).
64. Charles Tilly, *The Politics of Collective Violence*, Cambridge Studies in Contentious Politics (Cambridge, UK: Cambridge University Press, 2003), 132.
65. United Nations Development Programme, "Seguridad ciudadana con rostro humano: Diagnóstico y propuestas para América Latina," Human Development Report for Latin America 2013–2014 (New York: UNDP, 2013), 111.
66. Latinobarómetro, "Informe 2013" (Santiago de Chile: Corporación Latinobarómetro, 2013), 32.
67. Interview with a FARC member, Tumaco, Colombia, 2016.
68. Interview with a farmer, Putumayo, Colombia, 2017.
69. Benedikt Korf and Timothy Raeymaekers, *Violence on the Margins: States, Conflict, and Borderlands* (New York: Palgrave Macmillan, 2013), 4.
70. Willem van Schendel, "Spaces of Engagement: How Borderlands, Illegal Flows, and Territorial States Interlock," in *Illicit Flows and Criminal Things: States, Borders, and the Other Side of Globalization*, ed. Willem van Schendel and Itty Abraham (Bloomington: Indiana University Press, 2005), 61; Willem van Schendel, *The Bengal Borderland: Beyond State and Nation in South Asia* (London: Anthem, 2005), 385.

Epilogue

1. Lisa Wedeen, "Reflections on Ethnographic Work in Political Science," *Annual Review of Political Science* 13, no. 1 (2010): 258.
2. Stephen Brown, "Dilemmas of Self-Representation and Conduct in the Field," in *Surviving Field Research: Working in Violent and Difficult Situations*, ed. Chandra Lekha Sriram (London: Routledge, 2009), 213–26.
3. Nordstrom and Robben, *Fieldwork under Fire*, 4.
4. Ibid., 16.
5. Chandra Lekha Sriram, *Surviving Field Research: Working in Violent and Difficult Situations* (London: Routledge, 2009), 58.
6. John C. King, "Demystifying Field Research," in *Surviving Field Research: Working in Violent and Difficult Situations*, ed. Chandra Lekha Sriram (London: Routledge, 2009), 16; Amy Ross, "Impact on Research of Security-Seeking Behaviour," in *Surviving Field Research: Working in Violent and Difficult Situations*, ed. Chandra Lekha Sriram (London: Routledge, 2009).
7. Jonathan Goodhand, "Research in Conflict Zones: Ethics and Accountability," *Forced Migration Review*, no. 8 (2000): 3.
8. Carolyn Nordstrom and Antonius C. G. M. Robben, *Fieldwork under Fire: Contemporary Studies of Violence and Survival* (Berkeley: University of California Press, 1995), 19; Maria B. Olujic, in *Fieldwork under Fire: Contemporary Studies of Violence and Survival*, ed. Carolyn Nordstrom and Antonius C. G. M. Robben (Berkeley; London: University of California Press, 1995), 186–205.
9. Hastings Donnan and Dieter Haller, "Liminal No More: The Relevance of Borderland Studies," *Ethnologia Europea* 30, no. 2 (2000): 9.
10. Lindsay Scorgie, "Rwenzori Rebels: The Allied Democratic Forces Conflict in the Uganda-Congo Borderland" (PhD diss., University of Cambridge, 2012).
11. J. David Lewis and Andrew Weigert, "Trust as a Social Reality," *Social Forces* 63, no. 4 (June 1985): 967; Julie M. Norman, "Got Trust? The Challenge of Gaining Access in Conflict Zones," in *Surviving Field Research: Working in Violent and Difficult Situations*, ed. Chandra Lekha Sriram (London: Routledge, 2009), 72–73.
12. Norman, 72–73.
13. Michael T. Taussig, "Culture of Terror—Spaces of Death: Roger Casement's Putumayo Report and the Explanation of Torture," in *Violence: A Reader*, ed. Catherine Lowe Besteman (Basingstoke: Palgrave Macmillan, 2002), 215.

14. Susana Rotker, "Cities Written by Violence: An Introduction," in *Citizens of Fear: Urban Violence in Latin America*, ed. Susana Rotker and Katherine Goldman (New Brunswick, NJ: Rutgers University Press, 2002).

15. *Fieldwork under Fire*, 17.

16. Ibid., 13.

Appendix A

1. Adam Przeworski, *The Logic of Comparative Social Inquiry* (Malabar, FL: Krieger Publishing, 1982), 32.

2. Diana Kapiszewski, Lauren M. MacLean, and Benjamin Lelan Read, *Field Research in Political Science: Practices and Principles, Strategies for Social Inquiry* (Cambridge, UK: Cambridge University Press, 2015), 29.

3. Kathleen M. Eisenhardt, "Building Theories from Case Study Research," *The Academy of Management Review* 14, no. 4 (October 1, 1989): 546, https://doi.org/10.2307/258557.

4. John Gerring, "The Case Study: What It Is and What It Does," in *The Oxford Handbook of Comparative Politics*, ed. Carles Boix and Susan C. Stokes (Oxford University Press, 2009), http://www.oxfordhandbooks.com/view/10.1093/oxfordhb/9780199566020.001.0001/oxfordhb-9780199566020-e-4.

5. Ibid., 9.

6. Ibid., 3.

7. While I list them here as a logical sequence, during the data collection and analysis process I often engaged in these steps concurrently.

8. In the case of strategic alliances, both detailed examples are from the Colombian-Venezuelan borderlands due to insufficient data from the Ecuadorian-Colombian borderlands.

9. Eisenhardt, "Building Theories from Case Study Research."

10. Ibid., 546.

11. Andrew Bennett and Jeffrey T. Checkel, *Process Tracing: From Metaphor to Analytic Tool*, Strategies for Social Inquiry (Cambridge, UK: Cambridge University Press, 2015), 9.

12. Ibid.

13. Ibid.

14. Johnny Saldaña, *The Coding Manual for Qualitative Researchers* (London: SAGE, 2009), 65.

15. Matthew B. Miles and A. M. Huberman, *Qualitative Data Analysis: An Expanded Sourcebook*, 2nd ed. (Thousand Oaks, CA: Sage, 1994), 61; Saldaña, *The Coding Manual for Qualitative Researchers*, 3.

16. Yvonna S. Lincoln, *Naturalistic Inquiry* (Newbury Park, CA: Sage, 1985); see also Miles and Huberman, *Qualitative Data Analysis*.

17. On selection bias, see Gary King, Robert O Keohane, and Sidney Verba, *Designing Social Inquiry: Scientific Inference in Qualitative Research* (Princeton, NJ: Princeton University Press, 1994), 128.

18. Julie M. Norman, "Got Trust? The Challenge of Gaining Access in Conflict Zones," in *Surviving Field Research: Working in Violent and Difficult Situations*, ed. Chandra Lekha Sriram (London: Routledge, 2009), 83.

19. Courtney Radsch, "From Cell Phones to Coffee: Issues of Access in Egypt and Lebanon," in *Surviving Field Research: Working in Violent and Difficult Situations*, ed. Chandra Lekha Sriram (London: Routledge, 2009), 97.

BIBLIOGRAPHY

Abraham, Itty, and Willem van Schendel. "Introduction: The Making of Illicitness." In *Illicit Flows and Criminal Things: States, Borders, and the Other Side of Globalization*, edited by Willem van Schendel and Itty Abraham, 1–37. Bloomington: Indiana University Press, 2005.

Acharya, Arabinda, Syed Adnan Ali Shah Bukhari, and Sadia Sulaiman. "Making Money in the Mayhem: Funding Taliban Insurrection in the Tribal Areas of Pakistan." *Studies in Conflict & Terrorism* 32, no. 2 (2009): 95–108. https://doi.org/10.1080/10576100802628314.

Adger, W. Neil. "Vulnerability." In "Resilience, Vulnerability, and Adaptation: A Cross-Cutting Theme of the International Human Dimensions Programme on Global Environmental Change," edited by Marco A. Janssen and Elinor Ostrom. Special issue, *Global Environmental Change* 16, no. 3 (August 1, 2006): 268–81. https://www.geos.ed.ac.uk/~nabo/meetings/glthec/materials/simpson/GEC_sdarticle2.pdf.

Ahmad, Aisha. "The Security Bazaar: Business Interests and Islamist Power in Civil War Somalia." *International Security* 39, no. 3 (January 1, 2015): 89–117, http://dx.doi.org/10.1162/ISEC_a_00187.

Alarcón Gil, Cesar. "'El Loco' Barrera: Más allá de la mafia." *Razón Pública* (blog), October 2012. http://www.razonpublica.com/index.php/econom-y-sociedad-temas-29/3296-el-loco-barrera-mas-alla-de-la-mafia.html.

Alcaldía de Mocoa. "Plan de desarrollo municipal 'Sí hay futuro para Mocoa 2012–2015.'" Mocoa: Alcaldía Municipal de Mocoa, 2012. http://www.putumayo.gov.co/images/documentos/PDMunicipales/PDM_Mocoa2012-2015.pdf.

Almond, Gabriel Abraham, and Sidney Verba. *The Civic Culture: Political Attitudes and Democracy in Five Nations*. New ed. London: Sage, 1989.

Alston, Philip. "Mission to Colombia of the Special Rapporteur on Extrajudicial, Summary, or Arbitrary Executions," March 31, 2010.

———. "Report of the Special Rapporteur on Extrajudicial, Summary, or Arbitrary Executions, Philip Alston." United Nations General Assembly. Human Rights Council, May 9, 2011.

Alta Consejería para la Convivencia y la Seguridad Ciudadana. "Encuesta de convivencia y seguridad ciudadana." Bogotá: Alta Consejería para la Convivencia y la Seguridad Ciudadana, 2013. http://wsp.presidencia.gov.co/Seguridad-Ciudadana/estrategias-nacionales/Documents/Encuesta-Convivencia-Seguridad-Ciudadana-2013-DANE-comparativo.pdf.

Anderson, James, Liam O'Dowd, and Thomas M. Wilson. *New Borders for a Changing Europe: Cross-Border Cooperation and Governance*. London: Frank Cass, 2003.

Andersson, Ruben. *Illegality, Inc.: Clandestine Migration and the Business of Bordering Europe*. California Series in Public Anthropology 28. Oakland: University of California Press, 2014.

Andreas, Peter. *Border Games: Policing the US-Mexico Divide*. 2nd ed. Ithaca, NY: Cornell University Press, 2009.

————. "Criminalized Legacies of War. The Clandestine Political Economy of the Western Balkans." *Problems of Post-Communism* 51, no. 3 (June 2004): 3–9, http://www.tandfonline.com/doi/abs/10.1080/10758216.2004.11052164?journalCode=mppc20.

————. "International Politics and the Illicit Global Economy." *Perspectives on Politics* 13, no. 3 (September 2015): 782–788. https://doi.org/10.1017/S1537592715001358.

————. *Smuggler Nation: How Illicit Trade Made America.* New York: Oxford University Press, 2014.

————. "Redrawing the Line: Borders and Security in the Twenty-First Century." *International Security* 28 (2003): 78–111. http://dx.doi.org/10.1162/016228803322761973.

Andreas, Peter, and Angélica Durán-Martínez. "The Politics of Drugs and Illicit Trade in the Americas." In *Routledge Handbook of Latin American Politics,* edited by Peter Kingstone and Deborah Yashar, 380–92. New York: Routledge, 2012.

Arendt, Hannah. *On Violence.* New York: Harcourt Brace, 1970.

————. *The Origins of Totalitarianism.* New York: Harcourt Brace & World, 1968.

Arias, Enrique Desmond. *Drugs and Democracy in Rio de Janeiro: Trafficking, Social Networks, and Public Security.* Chapel Hill: University of North Carolina Press, 2006.

————. "The Dynamics of Criminal Governance: Networks and Social Order in Rio de Janeiro." *Journal of Latin American Studies* 38 (2006): 293–325. https://doi.org/10.1017/S0022216X06000721.

————. "Understanding Criminal Networks, Political Order, and Politics in Latin America." In *Ungoverned Spaces: Alternatives to State Authority in an Era of Softened Sovereignty,* edited by Anne L. Clunan and Harold A. Trinkunas, 115–35. Stanford: Stanford University Press, 2010.

Arias Ortiz, Angélica. "Las BACRIM retan a Santos." *Arcanos,* Corporación Nuevo Arco Iris 15, no. 17 (2012): 4–35.

Aristotle, *Nicomachean Ethics.* Translated by H. Rackham. Cambridge, MA: Harvard University Press, 1926.

Arjona, Ana. *Rebelocracy: Social Order in the Colombian Civil War.* New York: Cambridge University Press, 2016.

————. "Social Order in Civil War." PhD diss., Yale University, 2010.

Arjona, Ana, Nelson Kasfir, and Zachariah Cherian Mampilly. *Rebel Governance in Civil War.* Cambridge, UK: Cambridge University Press, 2015.

Asad, Talal. "Where Are the Margins of the State?" In *Anthropology in the Margins of the State,* edited by Veena Das and Deborah Poole, 279–88. Santa Fe, NM: SAR Press; Oxford, 2004.

Asal, Victor, H. Brinton Milward, and Eric W. Schoon. "When Terrorists Go Bad: Analyzing Terrorist Organizations' Involvement in Drug Smuggling." *International Studies Quarterly* 59, no. 1 (March 1, 2015): 112–23. http://dx.doi.org/10.1111/isqu.12162.

Asociación MINGA and Instituto de Estudios para el Desarrollo y la Paz. "En Tumaco: La marcha de la desesperación." Notes. Tumaco: MINGA, INDEPAZ, September 2011.

Astorga, Luis. *Seguridad, traficantes, y militares: El poder y la sombra.* México, D.F: Tusquets, 2007.

Atehortúa, Adolfo, and Rojas, Diana, "El Narcotráfico en Colombia: Pionero y Capos." *Historia y Espacio* 4, no. 31 (2008): 169–207.

Autesserre, Séverine. *The Trouble with the Congo: Local Violence and the Failure of International Peacebuilding.* Cambridge, UK: Cambridge University Press, 2010.

Ávila, Ariel. "Colombia's Facebook Hit List: Drug Gangs 2.0." *Corporación Nuevo Arcoiris* (blog), August 27, 2010. http://www.nuevoarcoiris.org.co/sac/?q=node/900.

————. "Las dinámicas territoriales del ejército de liberación nacional: Arauca, Cauca, y Nariño." *Arcanos,* Corporación Nuevo Arco Iris 15 (2010): 22–33.

Ávila, Ariel, and Carmen Rosa Guerra Ariza. "Frontera La Guajira y Cesar-Zulia." In *La frontera caliente entre Colombia y Venezuela,* edited by Ariel Ávila, 347–523. Cota, Colombia: Corporación Nuevo Arco Iris, 2012.

Ávila, Ariel, and Sofía León. "Frontera Arauca-Apure." In *La frontera caliente entre Colombia y Venezuela*, edited by Ariel Ávila, 75–202. Cota, Colombia: Corporación Nuevo Arco Iris, 2012.

Ávila, Ariel, and Magda Paola Núñez Gativa. "Expansión territorial y alianzas tácticas." *Arcanos*, 2008, 52–61.

Axelrod, Robert M. *The Evolution of Cooperation*. New York: Basic Books, 1984.

Axelrod, Robert M., and Robert O. Keohane. "Achieving Cooperation under Anarchy: Strategies and Institutions." *World Politics* 38, no. 1 (1985): 226–54. http://www.jstor.org/stable/2010357?origin=JSTOR-pdf.

Ayala Osorio, Germán. *Paramilitarismo en Colombia: Más allá de un fenómeno de violencia política*. Cali: Universidad Autónoma de Occidente, 2011.

Bagley, Bruce Michael, William O. Walker, and University of Miami. North-South Center. *Drug Trafficking in the Americas*. Coral Gables, FL: University of Miami, North-South Center, 1995.

Bailey, John. "'Security Traps' and Democratic Governability in Latin America: Dynamics of Crime, Violence, Corruption, Regime, and State." In *Criminality, Public Security, and the Challenge to Democracy in Latin America*, edited by Marcelo Bergman and Laurence Whitehead, 251–76. Notre Dame, IN: University of Notre Dame Press, 2009.

Baird, Adam. "Becoming the 'Baddest': Masculine Trajectories of Gang Violence in Medellín." *Journal of Latin American Studies* 50, no. 1 (February 2018): 183–210., https://doi.org/10.1017/S0022216X17000761.

Bakke, Kristin M., Kathleen Gallagher Cunningham, and Lee J. M. Seymour. "A Plague of Initials: Fragmentation, Cohesion, and Infighting in Civil Wars." *Perspectives on Politics* 10, no. 2 (June 2012): 265–83. https://doi.org/10.1017/S1537592712000667.

Balcells, Laia. "Rivalry and Revenge: Violence against Civilians in Conventional Civil Wars." *International Studies Quarterly* 54, no. 2 (2010): 291–313. https://www.jstor.org/stable/40664168.

Ballentine, Karen, and Jake Sherman. *The Political Economy of Armed Conflict: Beyond Greed and Grievance*. Boulder, CO: Lynne Rienner, 2003.

Bapat, Navin A., and Kanisha D. Bond. "Alliances between Militant Groups." *British Journal of Political Science* 42, no. 4 (2012): 793–824. https://doi.org/10.1017/S0007123412000075.

Bar-Anan, Yoav, Timothy D. Wilson, and Daniel T. Gilbert. "The Feeling of Uncertainty Intensifies Affective Reactions." *Emotion* 9, no. 1 (n.d.): 123–27. http://dx.doi.org/10.1037/a0014607.

Bargent, James. "Discovery of Rebel Cocaine Labs in Colombia Highlight Drug Alliances." Brief, April 26, 2013. https://www.insightcrime.org/news/brief/discovery-of-cocaine-labs-in-colombia-highlights-guerrillas-drug-alliances/.

Barker, Rodney S. *Political Legitimacy and the State*. Oxford: Clarendon Press, 1990.

Barnett, Michael, and Raymond Duvall. "Power in International Politics." *International Organization* 59, no. 1 (January 1, 2005): 39–75. https://doi.org/10.1017/S0020818305050010.

Baszanger, Isabelle, and Nicolas Dodier. "Ethnography: Relating the Part to the Whole." In *Qualitative Research: Theory, Method and Practice*, edited by David Silverman, 9–34. 2nd ed. London: Sage Publications, 2004.

Baud, Michel, and Willem van Schendel. "Toward a Comparative History of Borderlands." *Journal of World History* 8 (1997): 211–42. http://www.jstor.org/stable/20068594?origin=JSTOR-pdf.

BBC. "Colombia Kills Most Wanted Drug Lord." *BBC News*, October 2, 2015, sec. Latin America & Caribbean. http://www.bbc.co.uk/news/world-latin-america-34430555.

Bejan, Teresa M. *Mere Civility: Disagreement and the Limits of Toleration*. Cambridge, MA: Harvard University Press, 2017.

Bell, Vaughan, Fernanda Méndez, Carmen Martínez, Pedro Pablo Palma, and Marc Bosch. "Characteristics of the Colombian Armed Conflict and the Mental Health of Civilians Living in Active Conflict Zones." *Conflict and Health* 6, no. 10 (2012). http://www.conflictandhealth.com/content/pdf/1752-1505-6-10.pdf.

Bennett, Andrew, and Jeffrey T. Checkel. *Process Tracing: From Metaphor to Analytic Tool.* Strategies for Social Inquiry. Cambridge, UK: Cambridge University Press, 2015.

Berdal, Mats R. *Transnational Organized Crime and International Security: Business as Usual?* Boulder, CO: Lynne Rienner, 2002.

Berdal, Mats R., David Malone, and Academy International Peace, eds. *Greed & Grievance: Economic Agendas in Civil Wars.* Boulder, CO: Lynne Rienner, 2000.

Besteman, Catherine Lowe. *Violence: A Reader.* Basingstoke: Palgrave Macmillan, 2002.

Bilgin, Pinar. "Critical Theory." In *Security Studies: An Introduction,* edited by Paul D. Williams, 93–106. 2nd ed. London: Routledge, 2013.

Bond, Kanisha D. "Power, Identity, Credibility, and Cooperation: Examining the Cooperative Arrangements among Violent Non-State Actors." PhD diss., Pennsylvania State University, 2010.

Bourgois, Philippe. "Recognizing Invisible Violence: A Thirty-Year Ethnographic Retrospective." In *Global Health in Times of Violence,* edited by Barbara Rylko-Bauer, Linda Whiteford, and Paul Farmer, 17–40. Santa Fe, NM: School for Advanced Research Press, 2010.

Bravo, Diego, "Tres sectores se abastecen del tráfico de armas." *El Comercio.* N.d. https://www. elcomercio.com/actualidad/seguridad/tres-sectores-se-abastecen-del.html.

Brenner, Neil. "Beyond State-Centrism? Space, Territoriality, and Geographical Scale in Globalization Studies." *Theory and Society* 28, no. 1 (February 1, 1999): 39–78. https://doi. org/10.1023/A:1006996806674.

Briceño-León, Roberto, Olga Ávila, and Alberto Camardiel. *Violencia e institucionalidad: Informe del Observatorio Venezolano de Violencia 2012.* Caracas: Editorial Alfa, 2012.

Briscoe, Ivan. *Trouble on the Borders: Latin America's New Conflict Zones.* Madrid: FRIDE, 2008.

Britto, Lina. "A Trafficker's Paradise: The 'War On Drugs' and the New Cold War in Colombia." *Contemporánea: Historia y problemas del siglo XX* 1, no. 1 (2010): 159–77. https:// www.scholars.northwestern.edu/en/publications/a-traffickers-paradise-the-war-on-drugs-and-the-new-cold-war-in-c.

Brown, Stephen. "Dilemmas of Self-Representation and Conduct in the Field." In *Surviving Field Research: Working in Violent and Difficult Situations,* edited by Chandra Lekha Sriram, 213–26. London: Routledge, 2009.

Buchanan, Allen, and Robert O. Keohane. "The Legitimacy of Global Governance Institutions." *Ethics & International Affairs,* no. 20 (2006): 405–37. https://doi.org/doi:10.1111/ j.1747-7093.2006.00043.x.

Bull, Hedley. *The Anarchical Society: A Study of Order in World Politics.* 4th ed. New York: Columbia University Press, 2012.

Burgess, Robert G. *In the Field: An Introduction to Field Research.* London: Routledge, 1990.

Bustamante, Ana Marleny. "The Border Region of North Santander (Colombia)-Táchira (Venezuela): The Border without Walls." *Journal of Borderlands Studies* 23, no. 3 (2008): 7–18.

———. "La frontera colombo-venezolana: de la conflictividad limítrofe a la global." In *Relaciones fronterizas: Encuentros y conflictos,* edited by Fernando Carrión and Johanna Espín, 203–22. Quito: Flacso-Sede Ecuador, 2011.

Buur, Lars, and Steffen Jensen. "Introduction: Vigilantism and the Policing of Everyday Life in South Africa." *African Studies* 63, no. 2 (2004): 139–152, https://doi.org/10.1080/ 00020180412331318724.

Buzan, Barry. *People, States, and Fear: An Agenda for International Security Studies in the Post–Cold War Era.* 2nd ed. Boulder, CO: Lynne Rienner, 1991.

Buzan, Barry, Ole Wæver, and Jaap de Wilde. *Security: A New Framework for Analysis.* Boulder, CO: Lynne Rienner, 1998.

Caldeira, Teresa Pires Do Rio. *City of Walls: Crime, Segregation, and Citizenship in São Paulo.* Berkeley: University of California Press, 2000.

Campana, Paolo, and Federico Varese. "Cooperation in Criminal Organizations: Kinship and Violence as Credible Commitments." *Rationality and Society* 25, no. 3 (August 1, 2013): 263–89. http://journals.sagepub.com/doi/abs/10.1177/1043463113481202.

Caracol. "Millonarias incautaciones dejan operativos contra el contrabando en varios centros comerciales." *Caracol*, March 18, 2005. http://www.caracol.com.co/noticias/judicial/millonarias-incautaciones-dejan-operativos-contra-el-contrabando-en-varios-centros-comerciales/20050318/nota/162984.aspx.

Cárdenas Ruiz, Juan David. "La crisis fronteriza colombo-venezolana en las pantallas: Análisis desde la comunicación política." *Historia y Comunicación Social* 22, no. 2 (2017): 447–63.

Cardona Arango, Doris, Óscar Adolfo Medina-Pérez, and Deisy Viviana Cardona Duque. "Caracterización del suicidio en Colombia, 2000–2010." *Revista Colombiana de Psicatría* 45, no. 3 (2016): 170–77. http://www.redalyc.org/pdf/806/80648398005.pdf.

Carrión, Fernando. "En el límite de la vida: La violencia fronteriza." In *Aproximaciones a la frontera*, edited by Fernando Carrión, Diana Mejía, and Johanna Espín, 95–105. Colección Fronteras. Quito: FLACSO Ecuador, 2013.

———. "El sicariato: Una realidad ausente." *Ciudad Segura* (2008): 4–9.

Carrión, Fernando, ed. *Seguridad ciudadana, ¿espejismo o realidad?*" Quito: FLACSO Quito, 2007.

Carrión, Fernando, and Johanna Espín. *Relaciones fronterizas: Encuentros y conflictos*. Quito: Flacso-Sede Ecuador, 2011.

Carter Center. "Syria. Countrywide Conflict." Atlanta, GA: Carter Center, 2014. http://www.cartercenter.org/resources/pdfs/peace/conflict_resolution/syria-conflict/NationwideUpdate-Sept-18-2014.pdf.

Casas-Zamora, Kevin. "The Besieged Polis: Citizen Insecurity and Democracy in Latin America." Washington, DC: Latin America Initiative at Brookings, June 2013.

Castells, Manuel. *End of Millennium*. 2nd ed. Chichester: Wiley-Blackwell, 2010.

Celi, Carla, Molina Camilo, and Weber Gabriela. *Cooperación al desarrollo en la frontera norte: Una mirada desde Sucumbíos 2000–2007*. Quito: Centro de Investigaciones CIUDAD, 2009.

Centro Nacional de Memoria Histórica. "Hasta encontrarlos: El drama de la desaparición forzada en Colombia." Bogotá: Centro Nacional de Memoria Histórica, 2016.

Chambers, Robert. "Vulnerability: How the Poor Cope." *IDS Bulletin* 20, no. 2 (1989).

Chaparro, Camilo. *Historia del Cartel de Cali*. Bogotá: Intermedio, 2005.

Chinchilla Miranda, Laura. "Experiences with Citizen Participation in Crime Prevention in Central America." In *Crime and Violence in Latin America: Citizen Security, Democracy, and the State*, edited by Joseph S. Tulchin, H. Hugo Frühling, and Heather Golding, 205–32. Washington, DC: Woodrow Wilson Center Press, 2003.

———. "Public Security in Central America," 2002. http://pdba.georgetown.edu/Pubsecurity/ch2.pdf.

Christia, Fotini. *Alliance Formation in Civil Wars*. Cambridge, UK: Cambridge University Press, 2012.

CINEP. "Noche y niebla: Panorama de derechos humanos y violencia política en Colombia." *Revista noche y niebla* 45 (July 2012).

Civico, Aldo. *The Para-State: An Ethnography of Colombia's Death Squads*. Oakland: University of California Press, 2016.

Clawson, Patrick, and Rensselaer W. Lee. *The Andean Cocaine Industry*. Basingstoke: Macmillan, 1996.

Clunan, Anne L., and Harold A. Trinkunas, eds. *Ungoverned Spaces: Alternatives to State Authority in an Era of Softened Sovereignty*. Stanford, CA: Stanford University Press, 2010.

Comisión Nacional de Reparación y Reconciliación (Colombia). *La masacre de Bahía Portete: Mujeres Wayúu en la mira*. Pensamiento. Bogotá: Taurus, 2010.

———. "La masacre de El Tigre: Putumayo." Bogotá: Comisión Nacional de Reparación y Reconciliación, 2011.

Cockayne, James. *Hidden Power*. London: Hurst, 2016. https://global.oup.com/academic/product/hidden-power-9780190627331.

CODHES. "Desplazamiento forzado intraurbano y soluciones duraderas. Vol. II Bogotá, Cúcuta y Quibdó." Bogotá: CODHES, 2014.

Cohen, Dara Kay. "Explaining Sexual Violence during Civil War." PhD diss., Stanford University, 2010.

Cohen, Mark, and Roger Bowles. "Estimating Costs of Crime." In *Handbook of Quantitative Criminology*, edited by Alexis Russell Piquero and David Weisburd, 143–62. London: Springer, 2010.

Cohen, Stanley. *States of Denial: Knowing about Atrocities and Suffering*. Cambridge, UK: Polity Press, 2001.

Colletta, Nat, and Michelle L. Cullen. "The Nexus between Violent Conflict, Social Capital, and Social Cohesion: Case Studies from Cambodia and Rwanda." Working Paper. Social Capital Initiative. Washington, DC: World Bank, 2000.

Collier, Paul. *Breaking the Conflict Trap: Civil War and Development Policy*. Oxford: Oxford University Press, 2003.

Collingwood, Robin George. *The New Leviathan; or, Man, Society, Civilization, and Barbarism*. Edited and introduced by David Boucher. Oxford: Clarendon Press, 1999.

Comité Permanente por la Defensa de los Derechos Humanos. "Presencia paramilitar en Arauca: Amenazados líderes sociales." Colombia, July 12, 2011. http://www.ideaspaz.org/tools/download/54425.

Consolidación Territorial, "Regiones en Consolidación," 2012. http://www.consolidacion.gov.co/?q=content/regiones-en-consolidaci%C3%B3n.

Contraluz Cúcuta. "'Madrugón' al contrabando en Alejandría." *Contraluz Cúcuta*, August 15, 2012. www.contraluzcucuta.co/articulos/madrugon-al-contrabando-en-alejandria/.

Cook, Karen S. *Cooperation without Trust?* New York: Russell Sage Foundation, 2005.

Coordinadora Andina de Organizaciones Indígenas. "Informe alternativo presentado por la Coordinadora Andina de Organizaciones Indígenas—CAOI ante el Comité para la Eliminación de Todas Las Formas de Discriminación Racial—CERD (CERD/C/ECU/20-21)." Coordinadora Andina de Organizaciones Indígenas, 2012.

Crenshaw, Martha. *Explaining Terrorism: Causes, Processes, and Consequences*. London: Routledge, 2011.

———. "The Logic of Terrorism: Terrorist Behavior as a Product of Strategic Choice." In *Terrorism and Counterterrorism: Understanding the New Security Environment, Readings and Interpretations*, edited by Russell Howard and Bruce Hoffman, 42–53. London: McGraw-Hill Education, 2011.

Crick, Emily. "Drugs as an Existential Threat: An Analysis of the International Securitization of Drugs." *International Journal of Drug Policy* 23, no. 5 (September 2012): 407–14. https://doi.org/10.1016/j.drugpo.2012.03.004.

Cunningham, David E., Kristian Skrede Gleditsch, and Idean Salehyan. "Non-State Actors in Civil Wars: A New Dataset." *Conflict Management and Peace Science* 30, no. 5 (November 1, 2013): 516–31. https://doi.org/10.1177/0738894213499673.

Curbet, Jaume. "Inseguridad ciudadana: Víctimas y chivos expiatorios," 2009. http://www.pensamientopenal.com.ar/15082007/curbet.pdf.

Dammert, Lucía. *Fear and Crime in Latin America: Redefining State-Society Relations*. New York: Routledge, 2012.

Das, Veena. *Life and Words: Violence and the Descent into the Ordinary*. Berkeley: University of California Press, 2007.

Das, Veena, and Arthur Kleinman. "Introduction." In *Violence and Subjectivity*, edited by Veena Das, Arthur Kleinman, Mamphela Ramphele, and Pamela Reynolds, 1–18. Berkeley: University of California Press, 2000.

Davis, Dickie. *A Great Perhaps?: Colombia—Conflict and Convergence*. London: Hurst & Company, 2016.

De Boer, John, and Louise Bosetti. "The Crime-Conflict Nexus: Assessing the Threat and Developing Solutions." Crime-Conflict Nexus Series. United Nations University Centre for Policy Research, May 2017.

Defensoría del Pueblo. "Panorama del conflicto armado en Arauca." PowerPoint presentation. Arauca: Defensoría del Pueblo de Colombia, 2011.

Defensoría del Pueblo de Colombia. "Sistema de alertas tempranas." http://www.defensoria.org. co/red/?_item=1102&_secc=11&ts=2.

Defensoría Delegada para la Prevención de Riesgos de Violaciones a los Derechos Humanos y el DIH, Sistema de Alertas Tempranas. "Grupos armados ilegales y nuevos escenarios de riesgo en el posacuerdo." Bogotá: Defensoría del Pueblo, 2017. http://desarrollos.defensoria.gov. co/desarrollo1/ABCD/bases/marc/documentos/textos/Grupos_Armados_ilegales_y_ nuevos_escenarios_de_riesgo_en_el_posacuerdo.pdf.

De-la-Hoz-Bohórquez, Germán. "Colombia. Homicidios 2007." Bogotá: Instituto Nacional de Medicina Legal y Ciencias Forenses, 2007. http://www.medicinalegal.gov.co/documents/ 10180/33997/3+Homicidios.pdf/f148f9fe-cafd-4c4a-aafe-16629133821d.

———. "Comportamiento del homicidio. Colombia, 2013." Bogotá: Instituto Nacional de Medicina Legal y Ciencias Forenses, 2013. http://www.medicinalegal.gov.co/documents/ 10180/34616/2-F-11-Homicidios.pdf/01a6b108-57cd-48bc-9e9b-dcdba0d918a2.

Delumeau, Jean. *El miedo: Reflexiones sobre su dimensión social y cultural.* Medellín: Corporación Región, 2002.

Deutsch, Morton. "Cooperation and Trust: Some Theoretical Notes." In *Nebraska Symposium on Motivation,* edited by R. Jones Marshall, 275–319. Lincoln: University of Nebraska Press, 1962.

Deville, Duncan. "The Illicit Supply Chain." In *Convergence: Illicit Networks and National Security in the Age of Globalization,* edited by Michael Miklaucic and Jacqueline Brewer, 63–74. Washington, DC: National Defense University, 2013.

Diaro del Sur. "Evalúan amenazas de 'Águilas Negras.'" January 14, 2009.

Dishman, Chris. "Terrorism, Crime, and Transformation." *Studies in Conflict & Terrorism* 24 (2001): 43–58. https://doi.org/10.1080/10576100118878.

Dixit, Avinash K. *Games of Strategy.* 3rd ed. New York: W. W. Norton, 2009.

Donnan, Hastings, and Dieter Haller. "Liminal No More: The Relevance of Borderland Studies." *Ethnologia Europea* 30, no. 2 (2000): 7–22.

Donnan, Hastings, and Thomas M. Wilson. *Border Approaches: Anthropological Perspectives on Frontiers.* Lanham, MD: University Press of America, 1994.

———. *Borderlands: Ethnographic Approaches to Security, Power, and Identity.* Lanham, MD: University Press of America, 2010. http://www.ebrary.com/landing/site/bodleian/ index-bodleian.jsp?Docid=10602209.

———. *Borders: Frontiers of Identity, Nation and State.* Oxford: Berg, 1999.

Dressler, Jeffrey, and Carl Forsberg. "The Quetta Shura Taliban in Southern Afghanistan: Organiza- tion, Operations, and Shadow Governance." *Institute for the Study of War,* 2009. http://www. understandingwar.org/sites/default/files/QuettaShuraTaliban_1.pdf.

Duce, Mauricio, and Rogelio Pérez. "Citizen Security and Reform of the Criminal Justice System in Latin America." In *Crime and Violence in Latin America: Citizen Security, Democracy, and the State,* edited by Hugo Fruehling, Joseph S. Tulchin, and Heather A. Golding, 60–92. Washington, DC: Woodrow Wilson Center Press, 2003.

Duncan, Gustavo. *Los señores de la guerra: De paramilitares, mafiosos, y autodefensas en Colombia.* Bogotá: Planeta, 2006.

Durán-Martínez, Angélica. *The Politics of Drug Violence: Criminals, Cops, and Politicians in Colombia and Mexico.* New York: Oxford University Press, 2018.

———. "To Kill and Tell?: State Power, Criminal Competition, and Drug Violence." *Journal of Conflict Resolution* (June 9, 2015): 1–27.

Dyer, Jeffrey H., and Wujin Chu. "The Determinants of Trust in Supplier-Automaker Relationships in the US, Japan, and Korea." *Journal of International Business Studies* 31, no. 2 (June 2000): 259–85. https://doi.org/10.1057/palgrave.jibs.8490905.

Ehrenfeld, Rachel. *Narco-Terrorism.* New York: Basic Books, 1990.

Eisenhardt, Kathleen M. "Building Theories from Case Study Research." *The Academy of Management Review* 14, no. 4 (October 1, 1989): 532–50. https://doi.org/10.2307/258557.

El Colombiano. "Ataque de las FARC dejó 10 policías muertos en Putumayo." *El Colombiano,* September 10, 2010. http://www.elcolombiano.com/BancoConocimiento/A/ataque_de_ las_farc_dejo_ocho_policias_muertos_en_putumayo/ataque_de_las_farc_dejo_ocho_ policias_muertos_en_putumayo.asp.

El Comercio. "El escándalo del caso Ostaiza." August 25, 2009. http://www.elcomercio.com/nv_ images/especiales/2009/Ostaiza/ostaiza.html.

———. "El tráfico de armas crece en Carchi." December 26, 2009. http://www.elcomercio.com/ actualidad/trafico-armas-crece-carchi.html.

———. "El tráfico de armas vulnera las fronteras norte y sur de Ecuador." September 17, 2012. http://www4.elcomercio.com/seguridad/trafico-armas-vulnera-fronteras-Ecuador_0_ 775122566.html.

———. "Ex FARC forman a redes delictivas de Ecuador." April 17, 2017. https://www.elcomercio. com/actualidad/exfarc-redesdelictivas-ecuador-seguridad-sucumbios.html.

El Espectador. "Ecuador investiga si hubo 'falsos positivos' en su ejército." May 7, 2010. https://www.elespectador.com/noticias/elmundo/articulo202064-ecuador- investiga-si-hubo-falsos-positivos-su-ejercito.

———. "Gaula confirmó que ELN secuestró a cuatro arroceros en Arauca." August 18, 2016. https://www.elespectador.com/noticias/judicial/gaula-confirmo-eln-secuestro-cuatro- arroceros-arauca-articulo-649746.

———. "Puerto Asís, entre la coca y el consumismo." July 16, 2016. https://colombia2020. elespectador.com/territorio/puerto-asis-entre-la-coca-y-el-consumismo.

El Heraldo. "La Paz, emporio de la gasolina de contrabando." May 31, 2011. http://www.elheraldo. co/region/la-paz-emporio-de-la-gasolina-de-contrabando-23569.

El Nacional. "Reporta prostitución de niñas en La Guajira por comida." October 31, 2017. http:// www.el-nacional.com/noticias/sociedad/reportan-prostitucion-ninas-guaira-por-comida_ 209904.

El País. "7 infiernos sobre la tierra que jamás deberías visitar," January 22, 2015. http://verne. elpais.com/verne/2015/01/20/articulo/1421773872_248222.html.

———. "¿Captura del Loco Barrera es realmente la caída del último gran capo?" September 24, 2012. http://www.elpais.com.co/elpais/judicial/noticias/captura-loco-barrera-significa- realmente-caida-ultimo-gran-capo.

———. "FARC-ELN, la alianza que tiene en jaque al departamento de Arauca." August 27, 2013. http://www.elpais.com.co/judicial/farc-eln-la-alianza-que-tiene-en-jaque-al-departamento- de-arauca.html.

El Tiempo. "Caen nueve integrantes de la banda de los "Rastrojos" en zona rural de Tumaco." July 17, 2008. http://www.eltiempo.com/archivo/documento/CMS-4381943.

———. "Cinco policías y dos civiles resultaron heridos en ataque en Ocaña." May 7, 2012. http:// www.eltiempo.com/archivo/documento/CMS-11732361.

———. "Santos realizó visita sorpresa a zona veredal La Carmelita, Putumayo." April 18, 2017. http://www.eltiempo.com/politica/gobierno/santos-visita-zona-veredal-de-la-carmelita- putumayo-79180.

———. "Testaferros llevaron a la policía hasta el 'Loco' Barrera." September 20, 2012. http:// www.eltiempo.com/archivo/documento/CMS-12237943.

El Universo. "Cancilleres buscarán mejorar relaciones Ecuador-Colombia." May 26, 2007. http:// www.eluniverso.com/2007/05/26/0001/8/0C4EDB477CB249D084AB8D4EFB96 19A2.html.

———. "Cronología: Caso Huracán de la frontera." August 23, 2009. http://www.eluniverso. com/2009/08/23/1/1355/cronologia-caso-huracan-frontera.html.

———. "En campanita empezó la ruta del caso Chauvín." February 15, 2009. http://www. eluniverso.com/2009/02/15/1/1355/63A74BE0AC1A48CC910D3F121FC770F9. html.

———. "Habitantes preocupados por un supuesto grupo armado en cantón de Sucumbíos." August 3, 2016. https://www.eluniverso.com/noticias/2016/08/03/nota/5723058/habitantes-preocupados-supuesto-grupo-armado.

———. "Juez ordena prisión de coronel de la policía." September 29, 2011. http://www.eluniverso.com/2011/09/29/1/1422/juez-ordena-prision-coronel-policia.html.

———. "Población de la frontera teme que se retomen fumigaciones." August 14, 2014. http://www.eluniverso.com/noticias/2014/08/14/nota/3406196/poblacion-frontera-teme-que-se-retomen-fumigaciones.

Elster, Jon. *The Cement of Society: A Study of Social Order*. Studies in Rationality and Social Change. Cambridge, UK: Cambridge University Press, 1989.

Enloe, Cynthia. "Margins, Silences, and Bottom Rungs." In *International Theory: Positivism and Beyond*, edited by Steve Smith, Ken Booth, and Marysia Zalewski, 186–202. Cambridge, UK: Cambridge University Press, 1996.

Eskelinen, Heikki, Ilkka Liikanen, and Jukka Oksa. *Curtains of Iron and Gold: Reconstructing Borders and Scales of Interaction*. Aldershot: Ashgate, 1999.

Espín, Johanna M. "Seguridad ciudadana en la frontera norte ecuatoriana." *Ventana a la cooperación* (2009): 20–24.

Falzon, Mark-Anthony. *Multi-Sited Ethnography: Theory, Praxis, and Locality in Contemporary Research*. Farnham: Ashgate Publishing, Ltd., 2009.

Farah, Douglas. "Fixers, Super Fixers, and Shadow Facilitators: How Networks Connect." International Assessment and Strategy Center, April 23, 2012.

FARC-EP. "Comunicado a la opinión pública," September 30, 2004.

———. "Comunicado a la opinión pública," December 20, 2005.

———. "Comunicado a la opinión pública," December 2007.

———. "Comunicado a la opinión pública nacional e internacional," April 30, 2007.

———. "Comunicado del décimo frente a la opinión pública colombo-venezolana," September 21, 2004.

———. "Comunicado: FARC-EP declara cese al fuego unilateral. National Secretariat FARC-EP." July 8, 2015. http://www.pazfarc-ep.org/index.php/comunicadosestadomayorfarc/item/2842-comunicado.

Farrall, Stephen D., Jonathan Jackson Jr., and Emily Gray. *Social Order and the Fear of Crime in Contemporary Times*. Oxford: Oxford University Press, 2009.

Felbab-Brown, Vanda. "Rules and Regulations in Ungoverned Spaces: Illicit Economies, Criminals, and Belligerents." In *Ungoverned Spaces: Alternatives to State Authority in an Era of Softened Sovereignty*, edited by Anne L. Clunan and Harold A. Trinkunas, 175–92. Stanford, CA: Stanford University Press, 2010.

Feyissa, Dereje, and Markus Virgil Höhne. *Borders & Borderlands as Resources in the Horn of Africa*. Oxford: James Currey, 2010.

Fiorentini, Gianluca, and Sam Peltzman. *The Economics of Organised Crime*. Cambridge, UK: Cambridge University Press, 1995.

Fiscalía de Ecuador. "Fiscalía liderará reunión en San Lorenzo sobre plan de seguridad ciudadana en zona fronteriza," July 8, 2014. http://www.fiscalia.gob.ec/index.php/sala-de-prensa/2305-fiscal%C3%ADa-liderar%C3%A1-reuni%C3%B3n-en-san-lorenzo-sobre-plan-de-seguridad-ciudadana-en-la-zona-fronteriza.html.

Fiscalía General del Estado, FLACSO Ecuador. "Control de armas: Propuestas sobre armas de fuego," Políticas Públicas. *Perfil Criminológico* 17 (July 2015). http://repositorio.flacsoandes.edu.ec/bitstream/10469/7514/2/BFLACSO-PC17.pdf.

Fjelde, Hanne, and Desirée Nilsson. "Rebels against Rebels: Explaining Violence between Rebel Groups." *Journal of Conflict Resolution* 56, no. 4 (April 24, 2012): 604–28. http://journals.sagepub.com/doi/abs/10.1177/0022002712439496.

Folch, Christine. "Trouble on the Triple Frontier." *Foreign Affairs*, September 6, 2012. http://www.foreignaffairs.com/articles/138096/christine-folch/trouble-on-the-triple-frontier.

Forest, James J. F. *The Terrorism Lectures*. Santa Ana, CA: Nortia Press, 2012.

Friman, Richard H., and Peter Andreas, eds. "Introduction: International Relations and the Illicit Global Economy." In *The Illicit Global Economy and State Power*, 1–24. Boulder, CO: Rowman & Littlefield, 1999.

Fumerton, Mario, and Simone Remijnse. "Civil Defence Forces: Peru's Comites de Autodefensa Civil and Guatemala's Patrullas de Autodefensa Civil in Comparative Perspective." In *Armed Actors: Organised Violence and State Failure in Latin America*, edited by Kees Koonings and Dirk Kruijt, 52–72. London: Zed Books, 2004.

Fundación Amazónica Leonidas Proano. "Asesinato de dirigente en Barranca Bermeja," October 8, 2009.

Fundación Ideas para la Paz. "El bloque vencedores de Arauca. Documento de La Fundación Ideas para la Paz." *Semana*. April 30, 2008. http://www.semana.com/on-line/articulo/el-bloque-vencedores-arauca/92458-3.

Fundación Ideas para la Paz, United States Agency for International Development, and International Organization for Migration. "Dinámicas del conflicto armado en Tumaco y su impacto humanitario." Boletín. Área de Dinámicas del Conflicto y Negociaciones de Paz. Bogotá: Fundación Ideas para la Paz (FIP), February 2014. http://cdn.ideaspaz.org/media/website/document/52f8ecc452239.pdf.

Fundación Paz y Reconciliación. "Departamento de Putumayo. Tercera monografía." Bogotá: Fundación Paz y Reconciliación, February 24, 2014.

Fundación Progresar. "Boletín informativo." Cúcuta, Colombia, July 2011.

———. *Tantas vidas arrebatadas. La desaparición forzada de personas: Una estrategia sistemática de guerra sucia en Norte de Santander.* Edited by Wilfredo Cañizares Arévalo. Cúcuta, Colombia, 2010.

Gallie, W. B. "Essentially Contested Concepts." *Proceedings of the Aristotelian Society*, n.s., 56 (January 1, 1955): 167–98.

———. *Philosophers of Peace and War: Kant, Clausewitz, Marx, Engels, and Tolstoy.* Wiles Lectures; 1976. Cambridge, UK: Cambridge University Press, 1978.

Gambetta, Diego. *Codes of the Underworld: How Criminals Communicate.* Princeton, NJ: Princeton University Press, 2009.

———. "Mafia: The Price of Distrust." In *Trust: Making and Breaking Cooperative Relations*, edited by Diego Gambetta, new ed., 158–75. Oxford: Blackwell, 1990.

———. *The Sicilian Mafia: The Business of Private Protection.* Cambridge, MA: Harvard University Press, 1993.

Gamboa Martínez, Juan Carlos. "Una mirada panorámica a la frontera La Guajira-Zulia." Internal document. Maicao: PNUD, June 2012.

Gerring, John. "The Case Study: What It Is and What It Does." In *The Oxford Handbook of Comparative Politics*, edited by Carles Boix and Susan C. Stokes. Oxford University Press, 2009. http://www.oxfordhandbooks.com/view/10.1093/oxfordhb/9780199566020.001.0001/oxfordhb-9780199566020-e-4.

Gibbons, Robert. *Game Theory for Applied Economists.* Princeton, NJ: Princeton University Press, 1992.

Gilligan, James. "Shame, Guilt, and Violence." *Social Research: An International Quarterly* 70, no. 4 (2003): 1149–80. https://www.jstor.org/stable/40971965.

Girard, René. *Violence and the Sacred.* London: Bloomsbury Academic, 2013.

Glenny, Misha. *McMafia: Seriously Organised Crime.* London: Vintage, 2009.

Goddard, Stacie E., and Daniel H. Nexon. "The Dynamics of Global Power Politics: A Framework for Analysis." *Journal of Global Security Studies* 1, no. 1 (February 1, 2016): 4–18. https://doi.org/10.1093/jogss/ogv007.

Gold, Raymond L. "Roles in Sociological Field Observations." *Social Forces* 36, no. 3 (1958): 217–23. https://doi.org/10.2307/2573808.

Goldmann, Kjell. "Appropriateness and Consequences: The Logic of Neo-Institutionalism." *Governance* 18, no. 1 (January 1, 2005): 35–52. https://doi.org/10.1111/j.1468-0491.2004.00265.x.

Goldstein, Daniel M. "Flexible Justice: Neoliberal Violence and 'Self-Help' Security in Bolivia." *Critique of Anthropology* 25, no. 4 (2005): 389–411. http://journals.sagepub.com/doi/abs/10.1177/0308275X05058656.

———. *The Spectacular City: Violence and Performance in Urban Bolivia.* Durham, NC; London: Duke University Press, 2004.

Gómez, Andrés. "La frontera colombo-ecuatoriana: Desde la ejecución de políticas de seguridad a las consecuencias en seguridad ciudadana." In *Seguridad, planificación y desarrollo de las regiones transfronterizas,* edited by Fernando Carrión, 88–115. Colección Fronteras. Quito; Ottawa, Canada: FLACSO Ecuador; IDRC-CRDI, 2013.

González Carranza, Laura. *Fronteras en el limbo: El Plan Colombia en el Ecuador.* Quito: Fundación Regional de Asesoría en Derechos Humanos, INREDH, 2008.

———. *Peones en un ajedrez militar: Los habitantes de la frontera norte.* Quito: Fundación Regional de Asesoría en Derechos Humanos, 2011.

González Placencia, Luis. *Ciudades seguras: Percepción ciudadana de la inseguridad (politica y derecho).* México D.C.: Fondo de Cultura Económica, 2002.

Goodhand, Jonathan. "Epilogue: The View from the Border." In *Violence on the Margins: States, Conflict, and Borderlands,* edited by Benedikt Korf and Timothy Raeymaekers, 247–64. New York: Palgrave Macmillan, 2013.

———. "Research in Conflict Zones: Ethics and Accountability." *Forced Migration Review,* no. 8 (2000): 12–15. http://www.fmreview.org/sites/fmr/files/FMRdownloads/en/FMRpdfs/FMR08/fmr8.4.pdf.

———. "War, Peace, and the Places in Between: Why Borderlands Are Central." In *Whose Peace? Critical Perspectives on the Political Economy of Peacebuilding,* edited by Michael Pugh, Neil Cooper, and Mandy Turner, 225–44. New York: Palgrave Macmillan, 2008.

Gootenberg, Paul. *Andean Cocaine: The Making of a Global Drug.* Chapel Hill: University of North Carolina Press, 2008.

Grajales, Jacobo. *Gobernar en Medio de la Violencia: Estado y Paramilitarismo en Colombia.* Bogotá: Universidad del Rosario, 2017.

Granada, Soledad, Jorge Restrepo, and Andrés Tobón. "Neoparamilitarismo en Colombia: Una herramienta conceptual para la interpretación de dinámicas recientes del conflicto armado colombiano." In *Guerra y violencias en Colombia. Herramientas e interpretaciones,* edited by J. Restrepo and D. Aponte. Bogotá: Pontificia Universidad Javeriana, 2009.

Green, Linda. "Fear as a Way of Life." *Cultural Anthropology* 9, no. 2 (1994): 227–56. https://www.jstor.org/stable/656241.

———. *Fear as a Way of Life: Mayan Widows in Rural Guatemala.* New York: Columbia University Press, 1999.

Grillo, Ioan. *El Narco: The Bloody Rise of Mexican Drug Cartels.* London: Bloomsbury, 2013.

Guerra, Astrubal. "Capturado jefe de 'Los Rastrojos' en Nariño." *W Radio.* July 17, 2008. http://www.wradio.com.co/noticias/actualidad/capturado-jefe-de-los-rastrojos-en-narino/20080717/nota/634143.aspx.

Gunaratna, Rohan. *Inside Al Qaeda: Global Network of Terror.* New York: Berkley Books, 2003.

Gurr, Ted Robert. *Why Men Rebel.* Princeton, NJ: Princeton University Press, 1970.

Gutiérrez Sanín, Francisco. "Telling the Difference: Guerrillas and Paramilitaries in the Colombian War." *Politics & Society* 36, no. 1 (March 1, 2008): 3–34. http://journals.sagepub.com/doi/abs/10.1177/0032329207312181.

Gutiérrez-Sanín, Francisco, and Elisabeth Jean Wood. "What Should We Mean by 'Pattern of Political Violence'?: Repertoire, Targeting, Frequency, and Technique." *Perspectives on Politics* 15, no. 1 (March 2017): 20–41. https://doi.org/10.1017/S1537592716004114.

Hale, C. "Fear of Crime: A Review of the Literature." *International Review of Victimology* 4, no. 2 (January 1, 1996): 79–150.

Hall, P., and R. C. R. Taylor. "Political Science and the Three New Institutionalisms." *Political Studies* 44 (1996): 936–57. https://pdfs.semanticscholar.org/8f97/d5d296bcc397c86a37995505bfd9df79dde2.pdf.

Hall, Rodney, and Thomas J. Biersteker. "Private Authority as Global Governance." In *The Emergence of Private Authority in Global Governance*, edited by Rodney Hall and Thomas J. Biersteker, 203–22. Cambridge, UK: Cambridge University Press, 2002.

Halton, Philip J. "Core Issues Motivating Afghan Insurgents." *Canadian Army Journal* 14, no. 3 (2012): 51–75.

Hammersley, Martyn, and Paul Atkinson. *Ethnography: Principles in Practice.* London: Routledge, 2007.

Hancock, Landon E., and Christopher R. Mitchell, eds. *Zones of Peace.* Bloomfield, CT: Kumarian Press, 2007.

Handfield, Robert, and Christian Bechtel. "The Role of Trust and Relationship Structure in Improving Supply Chain Responsiveness." *Industrial Marketing Management* 31 (2002): 367–82. http://www2.nkfust.edu.tw/~percy%20/Report6/TheRoleOfTrrustAndRelation shipStructureInImprovingSupplyChainResponsiveness.pdf.

Hansen, Niles M. *The Border Economy: Regional Development in the Southwest.* Austin: University of Texas Press, 1981.

Hansen, Stig Jarle. *Al-Shabaab in Somalia: The History and Ideology of a Militant Islamist Group, 2005–2012.* London: C. Hurst & Co. Publishers Ltd, 2013.

Hastings, Justin V. *No Man's Land: Globalization, Territory, and Clandestine Groups in Southeast Asia.* Ithaca, NY: Cornell University Press, 2010.

Heeb, Alexis. "Violent Crime, Public Perceptions, and Citizen Security Strategies in Colombia during the 1990s." PhD diss., University of Oxford, 2002.

Herrera, Guillermo. "La realidad sobre la seguridad ciudadana en Carchi." *Observatorio de seguridad ciudadana* 1, no. 1 (2007). http://repositorio.flacsoandes.edu.ec/bitstream/ 10469/1323/1/BFLACSO-SC-01.pdf.

Hirschman, A. O. *Exit, Voice, and Loyalty: Response to Decline in Firms, Organizations, and States.* Cambridge, MA: Harvard University Press, 1972.

Hobsbawm, Eric J. *Bandits.* Harmondsworth: Penguin Books, 1972.

Hoffman, Bruce. *Inside Terrorism.* New York: Columbia University Press, 2006.

Hogg, Michael A. "Subjective Uncertainty Reduction through Self-Categorization: A Motivational Theory of Social Identity Processes." *European Review of Social Psychology* 11, no. 1 (January 1, 2000): 223–55. https://doi.org/10.1080/14792772043000040.

Höhne, Markus Virgil, and Dereje Feyissa. "Centering Borders and Borderlands: The Evidence from Africa." In *Violence on the Margins: States, Conflict, and Borderlands*, edited by Benedikt Korf and Timothy Raeymaekers, 55–86. New York: Palgrave Macmillan, 2013.

Holston, James. *Insurgent Citizenship: Disjunctions of Democracy and Modernity in Brazil.* Princeton, NJ: Princeton University Press, 2008.

Hoover Green, Amelia. "Repertoires of Violence against Noncombatants: The Role of Armed Group Institutions and Ideologies." PhD diss., Yale University, 2011.

Hoy. "Indígenas Otavaleños, mulas de la guerrilla," September 7, 2008. http://www.hoy.com.ec/ noticias-ecuador/indigenas-otavalenos-mulas-de-la-guerrilla-303952.html.

———. "Jooamy EMA, las siglas de los Ostaiza," March 1, 2009. http://www.hoy.com.ec/ wphoy-imprimir.php?id=336164.

———. "Nuevo cierre de frontera colombo-venezolana." *Hoy,* November 8, 2009. http://www. hoy.com.ec/noticias-ecuador/nuevo-cierre-de-frontera-colombo-venezolana-376952. html.

Hudson, Rex. "Terrorist and Organized Crime Groups in the Tri-Border Area (TBA) of South America T." A Report Prepared by the Federal Research Division, Library of Congress under an Interagency Agreement with the Crime and Narcotics Center Director of Central Intelligence. Washington, DC: Library of Congress, 2003.

Human Rights Watch. "Paramilitaries' Heirs. The New Face of Violence in Colombia." New York: Human Rights Watch, 2010.

Human Security Report Project. "Human Security Report 2009/2010: The Causes of Peace and the Shrinking Costs of War." New York: Oxford University Press, 2011.

Humphreys, Macartan, and Jeremy M. Weinstein. "Handling and Manhandling Civilians in Civil War." *American Political Science Review* 100, no. 3 (August 2006): 429–47. https://doi.org/10.1017/S0003055406062289.

Huntington, Samuel P. *The Julian J. Rothbaum Distinguished Lecture Series. Vol. 4.* Norman: University of Oklahoma Press, 1991. http://search.ebscohost.com/login.aspx?direct=true&scope=site&db=nlebk&db=nlabk&AN=15342.

Hurrell, Andrew. *On Global Order: Power, Values, and the Constitution of International Society.* Oxford: Oxford University Press, 2007.

Hutchinson, Steven, and Pat O'Malley. "A Crime-Terror Nexus? Thinking on Some of the Links between Terrorism and Criminality." *Studies in Conflict & Terrorism* 30 (December 2007): 1095–07. https://doi.org/10.1080/10576100701670870.

Idler, Annette. "Arrangements of Convenience in Colombia's Borderlands: An Invisible Threat to Citizen Security?" *St Antony's International Review* 7, no. 2 (2012): 93–119.

———. "Colombia Just Voted No on Its Plebiscite for Peace: Here's Why and What It Means." *Washington Post*, October 3, 2016, sec. Monkey Cage. https://www.washingtonpost.com/news/monkey-cage/wp/2016/10/03/colombia-just-voted-no-on-its-referendum-for-peace-heres-why-and-what-it-means/.

———. "Espacios invisibilizados: Actores violentos no-estatales y 'Ciudadanía de Sombra' en las zonas fronterizas de Colombia." *Estudios Indiana*, 2014.

———. "A Humanitarian and Diplomatic Crisis Is Unfolding on the Colombia-Venezuela Border." *The Conversation* (blog), September 10, 2015. https://theconversation.com/a-humanitarian-and-diplomatic-crisis-is-unfolding-on-the-colombia-venezuela-border-46994.

———. "Megateo, the Armed Groups and the Future of the People of Colombia's Catatumbo." *OpenDemocracy* (blog), October 28, 2015. https://www.opendemocracy.net/democraciaabierta/annette-idler/megateo-armed-groups-and-future-of-people-of-colombia-s-catatumbo.

———. "Preventing Conflict Upstream: Impunity and Illicit Governance across Colombia's Borders." *Defence Studies* 18, no. 1 (2018): 58–75. https://doi.org/10.1080/14702436.2017.1421859.

———. "Venezuela's Instability Has Far Broader Implications. Here's What's at Stake." *Washington Post*, August 10, 2017, sec. Monkey Cage. https://www.washingtonpost.com/news/monkey-cage/wp/2017/08/10/venezuelas-instability-has-far-broader-implications-heres-whats-at-stake/?utm_term=.1beaab715146.

Idler, Annette, and Borja Paladini Adell. "When Peace Implies Engaging the 'Terrorist': Peacebuilding in Colombia through Transforming Political Violence and Terrorism." In *The Nexus between Terrorism Studies and Peace and Conflict Studies*, edited by Yannis Tellidis and Harmonie Toros, 124–45. London: Routledge, 2015.

Idler, Annette, and James J. F. Forest. "Behavioral Patterns among (Violent) Non-State Actors: A Study of Complementary Governance." *Stability: International Journal of Security and Development* 4, no. 1 (2015). https://www.stabilityjournal.org/articles/10.5334/sta.er/.

Idler, Annette, María Belén Garrido, and Cécile Mouly. "Peace Territories in Colombia: Comparing Civil Resistance in Two War-Torn Communities." *Journal of Peacebuilding & Development* 10, no. 3 (September 2, 2015): 1–15. https://doi.org/10.1080/15423166.2015.1082437.

Idler, Annette, and Lindsay Scorgie. "The Transnationality of Conflict: Lessons Learned from Borderlands." In *Proceedings of the 2010 European Conference of the Association for Borderlands Studies*, 185–204. Thessaloniki: University of Thessaloniki, 2011.

Inglehart, Ronald. *Modernization and Postmodernization: Cultural, Economic, and Political Change in 43 Societies.* Princeton, NJ; Chichester: Princeton University Press, 1997.

———. "Trust, Well-Being, and Democracy." In *Democracy and Trust*, edited by Mark E. Warren, 88–120. Cambridge: Cambridge University Press, 1999.

Inglis, Ian R. "Review: The Central Role of Uncertainty Reduction in Determining Behaviour." *Behaviour* 137, no. 12 (2000): 1567–99. https://doi.org/10.1163/156853900502727.

InSight Crime. "El Loco Barrera." InSight Crime—Organized Crime in the Americas, 2012, Last Update November 7, 2016. http://www.insightcrime.org/personalities-colombia/daniel-barrera-barrera-el-loco-barrera.

———. "Guillermo León Sáenz Vargas, Alias 'Alfonso Cano.'" InSight Crime (blog), March 10, 2017. https://www.insightcrime.org/colombia-organized-crime-news/guillermo-leon-saenz-vargas-alfonso-cano/.

———. "Walid Makled," 2014, Last Update October 18, 2016. http://www.insightcrime.org/venezuela-organized-crime-news/walid-makled.

Instituto Nacional de Estadística. "Encuesta Nacional de Victimización y Percepción de Seguridad Ciudadana 2009 (ENVPSC-2009). Documento técnico." Caracas: Instituto Nacional de Estadística, República Bolivariana de Venezuela, May 2010.

Instituto Nacional de Medicina Legal y Ciencias Forenses. "2016 forensis, datos para la vida." 18. Bogotá: Instituto Nacional de Medicina Legal y Ciencias Forenses, 2017. http://www.medicinalegal.gov.co/documents/88730/4023454/Forensis+2016+-+Datos+para+la+Vida.pdf/af636ef3-0e84-46d4-bc1b-a5ec71ac9fc1.

Inter-American Development Bank. "Citizen Security and Justice. Improving Quality Information on Crime and Violence." Sistema regional de indicadores estandarizados de convivencia y seguridad ciudadana (blog), 2011. http://www.seguridadyregion.com/en/indicators/citizen-security-indicators.html.

International Committee of the Red Cross. "International Humanitarian Law and the Challenges of Contemporary Armed Conflicts." International Review of the Red Cross 89, no. 867 (2007): 719–57. https://www.icrc.org/en/document/international-humanitarian-law-and-challenges-contemporary-armed-conflicts.

International Crisis Group. "The Insurgency in Afghanistan's Heartland." Asia Report 207 (June 27, 2011). http://www.crisisgroup.org/~/media/Files/asia/south-asia/afghanistan/207%20The%20Insurgency%20in%20Afghanistans%20Heartland.pdf.

———. "Improving Security Policy in Colombia." Latin America Briefing. Bogotá and Brussels: International Crisis Group, 2010.

———. "Moving beyond Easy Wins: Colombia's Borders." Latin America Report. Bogotá and Brussels: International Crisis Group, 2011.

———. "Violence and Politics in Venezuela." Latin America Report. Bogotá and Brussels: International Crisis Group, August 17, 2011. http://www.crisisgroup.org/en/regions/latin-america-caribbean/andes/venezuela/038-violence-and-politics-in-venezuela.aspx.

———. "The Virtuous Twins: Protecting Human Rights and Improving Security in Colombia." Bogotá and Brussels: International Crisis Group, 2009.

International Institute for Democracy and Electoral Assistance. Illicit Networks and Politics in Latin America. Stockholm: International DEA, 2014.

"INTERPOL Rules Prohibit Publication of Blue Notice for Former Colombian Minister of Defence, July 10, 2009," 2009. http://www.interpol.int/Public/ICPO/PressReleases/PR2009/PR200969.asp.

Jackson, Stephen. "Potential Difference: Internal Borderlands in Africa." In Whose Peace? Critical Perspectives on the Political Economy of Peacebuilding, edited by Michael Pugh, Neil Cooper, and Mandy Turner, 268–88. New York: Palgrave Macmillan, 2008.

Janssen, Marco A., and Elinor Ostrom. "Resilience, Vulnerability, and Adaptation: A Cross-Cutting Theme of the International Human Dimensions Programme on Global Environmental Change." In "Resilience, Vulnerability, and Adaptation: A Cross-Cutting Theme of the International Human Dimensions Programme on Global Environmental Change," edited by Marco A. Janssen and Elinor Ostrom. Special issue, Global Environmental Change 16, no. 3 (August 1, 2006): 237–39. http://dx.doi.org/10.1016/j.gloenvcha.2006.04.003.

Jaramillo, Grace, ed. "Las relaciones Ecuador-Colombia desde el incidente de Angostura." In Construyendo puentes entre Ecuador y Colombia, 15–34. Quito: FLACSO OAS UNDP, 2009.

Jaramillo Viteri, Pablo. "En las orillas del miedo." *Revista Vanguardia* (blog), 2011. http://web. revistavanguardia.com/index.php?option=com_content&view=article&id=742&Ite mid=215.

Jaskoski, Maiah, "The Colombian FARC in Northern Ecuador: Borderline and Borderland Dynamics." In *American Crossings: Border Politics in the Western Hemisphere,* edited by Maiah Jaskoski, Arturo C. Sotomayor, and Harold A. Trinkunas, 171–88. Baltimore: Johns Hopkins University Press, 2015.

Johnson, Thomas H., and M. Chris Mason. "No Sign until the Burst of Fire: Understanding the Pakistan-Afghanistan Frontier." *International Security* 32, no. 4 (April 1, 2008): 41–77. https://doi.org/10.1162/isec.2008.32.4.41.

Johnston, David A, David M. McCutcheon, F. Ian Stuart, and Hazel Kerwood. "Effects of Supplier Trust on Performance of Cooperative Supplier Relationships." *Journal of Operations Management* 22, no. 1 (February 2004): 23–38. https://doi.org/10.1016/j.jom.2003.12.001.

Juetersonke, Oliver, Robert Muggah, and Dennis Rodgers. "Gangs and Violence Reduction in Central America." *Security Dialogue* 40, no. 4–5 (2009): 1–25. https://www.oas.org/dsp/ documentos/pandillas/2sesion_especial/SMALL%20ARMS%20SURVEY/gangs%20 and%20urban%20violence.pdf.

Junker, Buford H. *Field Work: An Introduction to the Social Sciences.* Chicago: University of Chicago Press, 1960.

Kaghram, Sanjeev, and Peggy Levitt. "Constructing Transnational Studies." In *Rethinking Transnationalism: The Meso-Link of Organisations,* edited by Ludger Pries, 21–39. New York: Routledge, 2008.

Kaldor, Mary. *New and Old Wars.* 3rd ed. Cambridge: Polity Press, 2012.

Kalyvas, Stathis N. "How Civil Wars Help Explain Organized Crime—and How They Do Not." *Journal of Conflict Resolution* (June 4, 2015): 1517–40. http://journals.sagepub.com/doi/ abs/10.1177/0022002715587101.

———. *The Logic of Violence in Civil War.* Cambridge, UK: Cambridge University Press, 2006.

———. "Micro-Level Studies of Violence in Civil War: Refining and Extending the Control-Collaboration Model." *Terrorism and Political Violence* 24, no. 4 (2012): 658–68. https://doi. org/10.1080/09546553.2012.701986.

———. "The Ontology of 'Political Violence': Action and Identity in Civil Wars." *Perspectives on Politics* 1, no. 3 (September 2003): 475–94. http://www.jstor.org/stable/3688707.

———. "The Urban Bias in Research on Civil Wars." *Security Studies* 13, no. 3 (March 1, 2004): 160–90. https://doi.org/10.1080/09636410490914022.

———. "Wanton and Senseless? The Logic of Massacres in Algeria." *Rationality and Society* 11 (1999): 243–85. http://journals.sagepub.com/doi/abs/10.1177/104346399011003001.

Kalyvas, Stathis N., Ian Shapiro, and Tarek Masoud, eds. *Order, Conflict, and Violence.* Cambridge, UK: Cambridge University Press, 2008.

Kant, Immanuel. *Zum ewigen Frieden.* 1st ed. Königsberg, 1795.

Kapiszewski, Diana, Lauren M. MacLean, and Benjamin Lelan Read. *Field Research in Political Science: Practices and Principles. Strategies for Social Inquiry.* Cambridge, UK: Cambridge University Press, 2015.

Keen, David. *Conflict & Collusion in Sierra Leone.* Oxford: James Currey, 2005.

———. *Endless War?: Hidden Functions of the "War on Terror."* London: Pluto Press, 2006.

Keohane, Robert O. *After Hegemony: Cooperation and Discord in the World Political Economy.* Princeton, NJ; Chichester: Princeton University Press, 2005.

Khagram, Sanjeev, and Peggy Levitt. *The Transnational Studies Reader: Intersections and Innovations.* New York: Routledge, 2008.

Khan, Illyvas M. "The Afghan-Pakistan Militant Nexus." *BBC World News Asia,* 2013. http://www. bbc.com/news/world-asia-21338263.

King, Gary, Robert O. Keohane, and Sidney Verba. *Designing Social Inquiry: Scientific Inference in Qualitative Research.* Princeton, NJ: Princeton University Press, 1994.

King, John C. "Demystifying Field Research." In *Surviving Field Research: Working in Violent and Difficult Situations*, edited by Chandra Lekha Sriram. London: Routledge, 2009.

Klemencic, Mladen, and Clive H. Schofield. "Contested Boundaries and Troubled Borderlands." In *Challenged Borderlands: Transcending Political and Cultural Boundaries*, edited by Barbara Jo Morehouse, Vera Pavlakovich-Kochi, and Doris Wastl-Walter, 63–74. Aldershot: Ashgate, 2004.

Knight, Frank H. *Risk, Uncertainty, and Profit*. Hart, Schaffner & Marx Prize Essays 31. Boston: Houghton Mifflin, 1921.

Kolossov, Vladimir. "Border Studies: Changing Perspectives and Theoretical Approaches." *Geopolitics* 10, no. 4 (2005): 606–32. https://doi.org/10.1080/14650040500318415.

Koonings, Kees, and Dirk Krujit. *Societies of Fear: The Legacy of Civil War, Violence, and Terror in Latin America*. London: Zed Books, 1999.

Korf, Benedikt, and Timothy Raeymaekers. *Violence on the Margins: States, Conflict, and Borderlands*. New York: Palgrave Macmillan, 2013.

Krause, Keith, and Michael Charles Williams. *Critical Security Studies: Concepts and Cases*. London: UCL Press, 1997.

Kushaba, Anthony. "M23 Rebels Forge Alliance with Mai Mai Militias," November 18, 2012. https://ugandaradionetwork.com/story/m23-rebels-forge-alliance-with-mai-mai-militias.

La Hora. "Coronel de policía de Esmeraldas condenado a seis años de prisión," June 29, 2012. http://www.lahora.com.ec/index.php/noticias/show/1101354038/-1/Coronel_de_Polic%C3%ADa_de_Esmeraldas_condenado_a_seis_a%C3%B1os_de_prisi%C3%B3n.html#.U_NDuPldWSo.

La Opinión. "En Alejandría vuelven a sonar las extorsiones." August 1, 2013. http://www.laopinion.com.co/demo/index.php?option=com_content&task=view&id=425409&Itemid=33.

———. "Panfletos amenazantes en Ocaña." May 3, 2012. http://www.laopinion.com.co/demo/index.php?option=com_content&task=view&id=395581&Itemid=28.

La Silla Vacía, "Las Farc mataron a 'Don Y'," November 16, 2016. http://lasillavacia.com/historia/las-farc-mataron-don-y-58754.

La Voz del Cinaruco. "Tres suicidios y el intento de uno más en Arauca en menos de una semana." *La Voz Del Cinaruco*. September 2012. http://www.lavozdelcinaruco.com/?id=7350.

Labrador, Ximena, Emilio Petrella, Patricia Camacho, Servicio Jesuita de Refugiados, Jesus Rodriguez Villaroel, Rina Arias, and Neida Arias. *Cultura de paz en el Alto Apure y el Táchira: Un reto de frontera*. Edited by Rodriguez Villaroel and Rina Arias. Caracas: Universidad Católica del Táchira, 2009.

Lacarrieu, Mónica. "La 'insoportable levedad' de lo urbano." *EURE (Santiago)* 33, no. 99 (August 2007): 47–64. https://doi.org/10.4067/S0250-71612007000200005.

Laguado Nieto, Omar Elias. "Cayó mercancía de contrabando en Alejandría." *Así es Cúcuta*, August 15, 2012. http://www.asiescucuta.com/portada/2012-08-15/cayo-mercancia-de-contrabando-en-alejandria.html.

Lary, Diana. *Warlord Soldiers: Chinese Common Soldiers, 1911–1937*. Cambridge, UK: Cambridge University Press, 1985.

Latin American Public Opinion Project. "Latin American Public Opinion Project." *Latin American Public Opinion Project 2012. Vanderbilt University* (blog), 2012. http://www.vanderbilt.edu/lapop/.

Latinobarómetro. "Informe 2013." Santiago de Chile: Corporación Latinobarómetro, 2013.

Lauret, Sander. *La frontera norte ecuatoriana ante la influencia del conflicto colombiano: Las sorprendentes dimensiones de la dinámica transfronteriza entre la provincia de Carchi y el departamento de Nariño*. Quito: Abya-Yala, 2009.

Laverde, Zully, and Edwin Tapia. *Tensión en las fronteras: Un análisis sobre el conflicto armado, el desplazamiento forzado, y el refugio en las fronteras de Colombia con Ecuador, Venezuela, y Panamá*. Bogotá: Consultoría para los Derechos Humanos y el Desplazamiento Forzado, 2009.

Law 599. "Código Penal Colombiano." Bogotá: Congreso de Colombia, 2000. http://www. alcaldiabogota.gov.co/sisjur/normas/Norma1.jsp?i=6388.

Law 1098. "Código de la Infancia y la Adolescencia. Ley 1098 de Noviembre 8 de 2006." Bogotá: Procuraduría General de la Nación, 2006. http://www.procuraduria.gov.co/portal/ media/file/Visi%C3%B3n%20Mundial_Codigo%20de%20Infancia%202011(1).pdf.

Lee, Murray. "The Genesis of 'Fear of Crime'." *Theoretical Criminology* 5, no. 4 (November 1, 2001): 467–85. http://journals.sagepub.com/doi/abs/10.1177/1362480601005004004.

Lemke, Douglas. "Power Politics and Wars without States." *American Journal of Political Science* 52, no. 4 (2008): 774–86. http://onlinelibrary.wiley.com/doi/10.1111/j.1540-5907.2008.00342.x/abstract.

León, Juanita. "La reconquista de Arauca." *Semana.* January 3, 2003. http://www.semana.com/ nacion/articulo/la-reconquista-arauca/56223-3.

Lerner, Melvin J. *The Belief in a Just World: A Fundamental Delusion.* New York: Plenum Press, 1980.

Levi, Primo. "The Gray Zone." In *Violence in War and Peace,* edited by Nancy Scheper-Hughes and Philippe I. Bourgois, 83–90. Malden, MA: Blackwell, 2004.

Lewis, J. David, and Andrew Weigert. "Trust as a Social Reality." *Social Forces* 63, no. 4 (June 1985): 967. http://www.jstor.org/stable/2578601.

Lincoln, Yvonna S. *Naturalistic Inquiry.* Newbury Park, CA: Sage, 1985.

Llorens, Manuel. "Dolor país, versión Venezuela: Las protestas de 2017 y sus secuelas." *Nueva Sociedad* 274 (2018): 71–82.

Locke, John. *Of Civil Government: Two Treatises.* Everyman's Library 751. London: Dent, 1924.

Long, Nick. "DRC Army, M23 Rebels Compete for Militia Allies," November 16, 2012. https:// www.voanews.com/a/drc-rebels-recruitment/1547636.html.

Lozano-Mancera, Natalia. *Homicidios de indígenas, 2003–2012: Instrumento de apropiación violenta de la tierra.* Bogotá: Instituto Nacional de Medicina Legal y Ciencias Forenses, 2012.

Lund, Christian. "Twilight Institutions: Public Authority and Local Politics in Africa." *Development and Change* 37, no. 4 (2006): 685–705. http://onlinelibrary.wiley.com/doi/10.1111/ j.1467-7660.2006.00497.x/abstract.

Macana Tuta, Neidi Leonor. "Comportamiento del suicidio en Colombia, 2011." Bogotá: National Institute of Legal Medicine and Forensic Sciences of Colombia, 2012.

Machado, Lia Osório, André Reyes Novaes, and Licio do Rego Monteiro. "Building Walls, Breaking Barriers: Territory, Integration, and the Rule of Law in Frontier Zones." *Journal of Borderlands Studies* 24, no. 3 (2009): 97–114. https://doi.org/10.1080/08865655.2009.9695742.

Mainwaring, Scott, Ana María Bejarano, and Eduardo Pizarro Leongómez. *The Crisis of Democratic Representation in the Andes.* Stanford, CA: Stanford University Press, 2006.

Makarenko, Tamara. "The Crime-Terror Continuum: Tracing the Interplay between Transnational Organised Crime and Terrorism." *Global Crime* 6, no. 1 (2004): 129–45. https://doi.org/ 10.1080/1744057042000297025.

Malamud, Carlos. *The Long Road to Peace in Colombia. Colombia's Difficult Relations with Its Neighbours: Venezuela.* Part 2. Madrid: Real Instituto Elcano, 2004.

Mampilly, Zachariah Cherian. *Rebel Rulers: Insurgent Governance and Civilian Life during War.* Ithaca, NY: Cornell University Press, 2011.

Manwaring, Max. *Street Gangs: The New Urban Insurgency.* Carlisle, PA: Strategic Studies Institute, US Army War College, 2005.

Marcella, Gabriel. *War without Borders: The Colombia-Ecuador Crisis of 2008.* Carlisle, PA: Strategic Studies Institute, 2008.

March, James G., and Johan P. Olsen. *Rediscovering Institutions: The Organizational Basis of Politics.* New York: Free Press, 1989.

———. "The Logic of Appropriateness." In *The Oxford Handbook of Public Policy,* edited by Michael Moran, Martin Rein, and Robert E. Goodin, 691–92. Oxford: Oxford University Press, 2008.

Marcus, George E. "Ethnography in/of the World System: The Emergence of Multi-Sited Ethnography." *Annual Review of Anthropology* 24, no. 1 (1995): 95–117. http://www.annualreviews.org/doi/pdf/10.1146/annurev.an.24.100195.000523.

Marten, Kimberly. "Warlordism in Comparative Perspective." *International Security* 31, no. 3 (January 1, 2007): 41–73. http://dx.doi.org/10.1162/isec.2007.31.3.41.

Martín-Baró, Ignacio. "Prólogo." In *Derechos humanos: Todo es el dolor con que se mira*, edited by Elizabeth Lira and David Becker. Santiago de Chile: Ediciones ILAS, 1989.

Martínez, Oscar J. *Border People: Life and Society in the US-Mexico Borderlands*. Tucson: University of Arizona Press, 1994.

Mason, Ann, and Arlene B. Tickner. "A Transregional Security Cartography of the Andes." In *State and Society in Conflict: Comparative Perspectives on the Andean Crises*, edited by Paul W. Drake and Eric Hershberg, 74–98. Pittsburgh: University of Pittsburgh Press, 2006.

Mathus Ruiz, Rafael. "La OEA denuncia un auto golpe de estado." *La Nación*. March 30, 2017. https://www.lanacion.com.ar/2001613-venezuela-la-oea-denuncia-un-auto-golpe-de-estado.

McCormick, Gordon H. "Terrorist Decision Making." *Annual Review of Political Science* 6, no. 1 (2003): 473–507. https://doi.org/10.1146/annurev.polisci.6.121901.085601.

McLauchlin, Theodore. "Loyalty Strategies and Military Defection in Rebellion." *Comparative Politics* 42, no. 3 (March 31, 2010): 333–50. https://www.jstor.org/stable/27822313.

McLauchlin, Theodore, Wendy Pearlman, and Kathleen Gallagher Cunningham. "Out-Group Conflict, In-Group Unity?: Exploring the Effect of Repression on Intramovement Cooperation." *Journal of Conflict Resolution* 56, no. 1 (February 1, 2012): 41–66. http://journals.sagepub.com/doi/abs/10.1177/0022002711429707.

McLean, Phillip. "Colombia: Failed, Failing, or Just Weak?," *Washington Quarterly* 25, no. 3 (2002): 123–34.

Meagher, Kate. "The Strength of Weak States? Non-State Security Forces and Hybrid Governance in Africa." *Development and Change* 43, no. 5 (September 1, 2012): 1073–1101. http://onlinelibrary.wiley.com/doi/10.1111/j.1467-7660.2012.01794.x/abstract.

Médicos Sin Fronteras. "Internal Document." Colombia, 2011.

Mejia, Diana. "La política de seguridad en la frontera norte: Modificar las realidades para cambiar las percepciones (entrevista)." Boletín Fronteras. Quito: FLACSO Quito, Programa de Estudios de la Ciudad, 2009.

Menkhaus, Ken, and Jacob N. Shapiro. "Non-State Actors and Failed States: Lessons from Al-Qua'ida's Experiences in the Horn of Africa." In *Ungoverned Spaces: Alternatives to State Authority in an Era of Softened Sovereignty*, edited by Anne L. Clunan and Harold A. Trinkunas, 77–94. Stanford, CA: Stanford University Press, 2010.

Mi Putumayo. "Exitosa operación conjunta y coordinada en contra de "La Constru" en Putumayo." July 31, 2017. http://miputumayo.com.co/2017/07/31/exitosa-operacion-conjunta-y-coordinada-en-contra-de-la-constru-en-putumayo/.

Miklaucic, Michael, and Jacqueline Brewer. "Introduction." In *Convergence: Illicit Networks and National Security in the Age of Globalization*, edited by Michael Miklaucic and Jacqueline Brewer, xiii–xxi. Washington, DC: National Defense University, 2013.

Miles, Matthew B., and A. M. Huberman. *Qualitative Data Analysis: An Expanded Sourcebook*. 2nd ed. Thousand Oaks, CA: Sage, 1994.

Millett, Richard. *Colombia's Conflicts: The Spillover Effects of a Wider War*. Carlisle, PA: Strategic Studies Institute, 2002.

Ministerio de Defensa Nacional. "Ecuador y Colombia aúnan esfuerzos para controles en frontera." Quito: Ministerio de Defensa Nacional de Ecuador, July 24, 2014.

Ministerio del Interior. "Agenda nacional de seguridad ciudadana y gobernabilidad." Quito: Ministerio del Interior, 2011.

Ministerio del Interior y de Justicia, República de Colombia. "Ley de víctimas y restitución de tierras." Bogotá: Ministerio del Interior y de Justicia, 2011.

Mishra, Aneil. "Organizational Responses to Crisis: The Centrality of Trust." In *Trust in Organizations: Frontiers of Theory and Research*, edited by Roderick M. Kramer and Tom R. Tyler, 261–87. Thousand Oaks, CA: SAGE, 1996.

Molina, Juan Camilo. "Cooperación internacional al desarrollo y refugio en la frontera norte en Ecuador." *Ventana a la cooperación*, 2009, 2–19.

Moncada, Eduardo. "Urban Violence, Political Economy, and Territorial Control. Insights from Medellín." *Latin American Research Review* 61, no. 4 (2016): 225–48. https://lasa.international.pitt.edu/auth/pub/Larr/CurrentIssue/51-4_225-248_Moncada.pdf.

Morehouse, Barbara J., Vera Pavlakovich-Kochi, and Doris Wastl-Walter. "Introduction: Perspectives on Borderlands." In *Challenged Borderlands: Transcending Political and Cultural Boundaries*, edited by Barbara J. Morehouse, Vera Pavlakovich-Kochi, and Doris Wastl-Walter, 3–11. Aldershot: Ashgate, 2004.

Moser, Caroline, and Cathy McIlwaine. *Encounters with Violence in Latin America: Urban Poor Perceptions from Colombia and Guatemala*. New York: Routledge, 2004.

Mouly, Cécile, María Belén Garrido, and Annette Idler. "How Peace Takes Shape Locally: The Experience of Civil Resistance in Samaniego, Colombia." *Peace & Change* 41, no. 2 (April 1, 2016): 129–66. https://doi.org/10.1111/pech.12184.

Mouly, Cécile, Annette Idler, and Belén Garrido. "Zones of Peace in Colombia's Borderlands." *International Journal of Peace Studies* 20, no. 1 (2015): 51–63.

Muehlmann, Shaylih. *When I Wear My Alligator Boots: Narco-Culture in the US-Mexico Borderlands*. Berkeley: University of California Press, 2014.

Mukhopadhyay, Dipali. *Warlords, Strongman Governors, and the State in Afghanistan*. Cambridge, UK: Cambridge University Press, 2016.

Mushi, Ferdinand, "Insecurity and Local Governance in Congo's South Kivu." *Research Report* 74 (2012). http://www.ids.ac.uk/files/dmfile/RR74.pdf.

Naím, Moisés. "Mafia States." *Foreign Affairs* 91, no. 3 (June 5, 2012): 100–11. https://www.foreignaffairs.com/articles/2012-04-20/mafia-states.

Nasi, Carlos. "Colombia's Peace Processes, 1982–2002: Conditions, Strategies, and Outcomes." In *Colombia: Building Peace in a Time of War*, edited by Virginia Marie Bouvier, 39–64. Washington, DC: United States Institute of Peace Press, 2009.

Naylor, R. Thomas. *Economic Warfare: Sanctions, Embargo Busting, and Their Human Cost*. Boston: Northeastern University Press, 2001.

———. "The Insurgent Economy—Black Market Operations of Guerrilla Organizations." *Crime, Law and Social Change* 20 (July 1993): 13–51. https://link.springer.com/content/pdf/10.1007/BF01308447.pdf.

Neuman, William. "Venezuela Is Cocaine Hub despite Its Claims." *New York Times*, July 26, 2012, sec. World / Americas. http://www.nytimes.com/2012/07/27/world/americas/venezuela-is-cocaine-hub-despite-its-claims.html.

Neumann, John von. *Theory of Games and Economic Behavior*. 2nd ed. Princeton, NJ: Princeton University Press, 1947.

New York Times. "Colombian Military Kills Warlord of Rural Cocaine Fiefdom." *New York Times*, October 2, 2015.

Newman, David. "The Lines That Continue to Separate Us: Borders in Our 'Borderless' World." *Progress in Human Geography* 30, no. 2 (April 1, 2006): 143–61. https://doi.org/10.1191/0309132506ph599xx.

Newman, David, and Anssi Paasi. "Fences and Neighbours in the Postmodern World: Boundary Narratives in Political Geography." *Progress in Human Geography* 22, no. 2 (April 1, 1998): 186–207. https://doi.org/10.1191/030913298666039113.

Niño Ascanio, Elizabeth, Edwin Camargo León, and Wilfredo Cañizares Arévalo. "Crimen organizado y grupos ilegales en una frontera en crisis." Cúcuta, Colombia, 2011.

———. "Frontera Norte de Santander—Táchira." In *La frontera caliente entre Colombia y Venezuela*, edited by Ariel Ávila, 203–346. Cota, Colombia: Corporación Nuevo Arco Iris, 2012.

Nobel Prize. "Juan Manuel Santos—Facts," 2016. https://www.nobelprize.org/nobel_prizes/peace/laureates/2016/santos-facts.html.

Nordstrom, Carolyn. "Terror Warfare and the Medicine of Peace." *Medical Anthropology Quarterly*, n.s., 12, no. 1 (March 1, 1998): 103–21. http://statecrime.org/data/2011/10/nordstrom1998a.pdf.

———. "The Tomorrow of Violence." In *Violence*, edited by Neil L. Whitehead, School of American Research Advanced Seminar Series, 223–42 (Santa Fe, NM: School of American Research, 2004). http://www.loc.gov/catdir/toc/ecip0420/2004017171.html.

Nordstrom, Carolyn, and Antonius C. G. M. Robben. *Fieldwork under Fire: Contemporary Studies of Violence and Survival*. Berkeley: University of California Press, 1995.

Norman, Julie M. "Got Trust? The Challenge of Gaining Access in Conflict Zones." In *Surviving Field Research: Working in Violent and Difficult Situations*, edited by Chandra Lekha Sriram, 71–90. London: Routledge, 2009.

Noticias Caracol. "Santos y 'Timochenko' firman el acuerdo de paz definitivo." November 24, 2016. https://noticias.caracoltv.com/acuerdo-final/delegados-de-gobierno-y-farc-se-reunen-en-bogota-para-firma-del-nuevo-acuerdo.

Noticias RCN. "Policía confirma que el ELN sí secuestró a 4 arroceros en Arauca," August 18, 2016. http://www.noticiasrcn.com/nacional-pais/policia-confirma-el-eln-si-secuestro-4-arroceros-arauca.

———. "Santos y 'Timochenko' firmaron el nuevo acuerdo en Bogotá." November 24, 2016. http://www.noticiasrcn.com/nacional-dialogos-paz/santos-y-timochenko-firmaron-el-nuevo-acuerdo-bogota.

Noticias Uno, La Red Independiente. "Panfleto genera temor en Ocaña. Ya hay 3 muertos." May 6, 2012. http://noticiasunolaredindependiente.com/2012/05/06/noticias/panfleto-genera-temor-en-ocana-ya-hay-3-muertos/.

Noticucuta.com. "Operativo especial contra el contrabando en Cúcuta." *Cúcuta Judicial* (blog), December 11, 2007.

Nugent, Paul, and Anthony Ijaola Asiwaju. *African Boundaries: Barriers, Conduits, and Opportunities*. London: Pinter, 1996.

Núñez Gantiva, Magda Paola. "ELN-FARC: Ahora sí juntos." *Arcanos* 15, no. 17 (2012): 60–75.

Nye, Joseph S., and Robert O. Keohane. "Transnational Relations and World Politics: An Introduction." *International Organization* 25, no. 3 (1971): 329–49. http://www.jstor.org/stable/2706043.

Observación y Solidaridad con Arauca OBSAR. "Arauca: Conflicto armado y problemáticas humanitarias 2011." Arauca, cultivando paz en medio del conflicto armado. Arauca: Secretariado Diocesano de Pastoral Social, Caritas Arauca, 2011.

Observatorio Venezolano de Violencia. "La violencia no se detiene. Informe del OVV—diciembre 2012." Caracas: Observatorio Venezolano de Violencia, 2012. http://observatoriodeviolencia.org.ve/ws/informe-del-ovv-diciembre-2012/.

———. "Las muertes violentas continúan aumentando. Informe del OVV—diciembre 2013." Caracas: Observatorio Venezolano de Violencia, 2013. http://observatoriodeviolencia.org.ve/ws/informe-del-ovv-diciembre-2013-2/.

O'Donnell, Guillermo. "On the State, Democratization, and Some Conceptual Problems: A Latin American View with Glances at Some Postcommunist Countries." *World Development* 21, no. 8 (1993): 1355–69. https://doi.org/10.1016/0305-750X(93)90048-E.

———. "Reflections on Contemporary South American Democracies." *Journal of Latin American Studies* 33 (2001): 599–609. https://doi.org/10.1017/S0022216X01006125.

———. "Why the Rule of Law Matters." *Journal of Democracy* 15, no. 4 (2004): 32–46. https://doi.org/10.1353/jod.2004.0076.

Oficina del Alto Comisionado para la Paz. "Proceso de paz con las autodefensas: Informe ejecutivo." Bogotá: Presidencia de la República de Colombia, June 2006.

Olson, Mancur. *The Logic of Collective Action: Public Goods and the Theory of Groups.* Cambridge, MA: Harvard University Press, 1965.

Olujic, Maria B. In *Fieldwork under Fire: Contemporary Studies of Violence and Survival,* edited by Carolyn Nordstrom and Antonius C. G. M. Robben, 186–205. Berkeley: University of California Press, 1995.

Ōmae, Ken'ichi. *The Borderless World: Power and Strategy in the Interlinked Economy.* London: Collins, 1990.

Oomen, Barbara. "Vigilantism or Alternative Citizenship? The Rise of Mapogo a Mathamaga." *African Studies* 63, no. 2 (2004): 153–71. https://doi.org/10.1080/00020180412331318751.

Organization of American States. "Report on Citizen Security and Human Rights." Organization of American States, Inter-American Commission on Human Rights, 2009. http://www.cidh.oas.org/countryrep/Seguridad.eng/CitizenSecurity.II.htm.

Ortega, Daniel, and Pablo Sanguinetti. "Citizen Security and Welfare." In *Towards a Safer Latin America. A New Perspective to Prevent and Control Crime,* edited by CAF Development Bank. Bogotá: CAF Development Bank, 2015.

Osorio, Javier. "Hobbes on Drugs. Understanding Drug Violence in Mexico." PhD diss., University of Notre Dame, 2013.

Ostrom, Elinor. "Collective Action and the Evolution of Social Norms." *Journal of Economic Perspectives* 14, no. 3 (August 2000): 137–58. https://doi.org/10.1257/jep.14.3.137.

———. *Governing the Commons: The Evolution of Institutions for Collective Action.* Cambridge, UK: Cambridge University Press, 1990.

Oxfam. "Commodities of War. Communities Speak Out on the True Cost of Conflict in Eastern DRC." Oxfam Briefing Paper. Oxford: Oxfam, November 2012.

Oxford Dictionaries. "Language Matters." *Oxford Dictionaries* (blog), 2014. http://www.oxforddictionaries.com/definition/english/intuition.

Oye, Kenneth A. *Cooperation under Anarchy.* Princeton, NJ: Princeton University Press, 1986.

Parks, Craig D., and Lorne G. Hulbert. "High and Low Trusters' Responses to Fear in a Payoff Matrix." *The Journal of Conflict Resolution* 39, no. 4 (December 1, 1995): 718–30. https://doi.org/10.2307/174384.

Patiño, Otty. "El Fenómeno Paramilitar en Colombia. Bajo el Volcán." *Puebla* 3, no. 6 (2003): 71–91.

Patterson, Henry. *Ireland's Violent Frontier: The Border and Anglo-Irish Relations during the Troubles.* Basingstoke: Palgrave Macmillan, 2013.

Pearce, Jenny V. "Violence, Power, and Participation: Building Citizenship in Contexts of Chronic Violence." *IDS Working Paper* 274 (2007).

Pearlman, Wendy. "Spoiling Inside and Out: Internal Political Contestation and the Middle East Peace Process." *International Security* 33, no. 3 (2008): 79–109. http://dx.doi.org/10.1162/isec.2009.33.3.79.

Pearlman, Wendy, and Kathleen Gallagher Cunningham. "Nonstate Actors, Fragmentation, and Conflict Processes." *Journal of Conflict Resolution* 56, no. 1 (February 1, 2012): 3–15. http://journals.sagepub.com/doi/abs/10.1177/0022002711429669.

Pécaut, Daniel. "From the Banality of Violence to Real Terror: The Case of Colombia." In *Societies of Fear: The Legacy of Civil War, Violence, and Terror in Latin America,* edited by Kees Koonings and Dirk Krujit, 141–67. London: Zed Books, 1999.

———. *Guerra contra la sociedad.* Bogotá: Espasa, 2001.

———. *L'ordre et la violence: Évolution socio-politique de la Colombie entre 1930 et 1953.* Paris: École des hautes études en sciences sociales, 1987.

Peralta, Milana, Carolina Serrano, Carlos Prieto, Miguel Ortega, Carol Barajas, and Joana Rojas Roa. "La Guajira en su laberinto: Transformaciones y desafíos de la violencia." Informes FIP. Bogotá: Fundación Ideas para la Paz, August 2011.

Percy, Sarah, and Anja Shortland. "The Business of Piracy in Somalia." *Journal of Strategic Studies* 36, no. 4 (August 1, 2013): 541–78. https://doi.org/10.1080/01402390.2012.750242.

Perez-Santiago, Mariel. "Colombia's BACRIM: Common Criminals or Actors in Armed Conflict?" InSight Crime—Organized Crime in the Americas, July 13, 2012. http://www.insightcrime. org/news-analysis/colombias-bacrim-common-criminals-or-actors-in-armed-conflict.

Perkins, Brian. "Factionalism of the Tehrik-i-Taliban Pakistan: Can the Pakistani Government Correct Past Deficiencies." *Small Wars Journal* (blog), July 19, 2014. http://smallwarsjournal. com/jrnl/art/factionalism-of-the-tehrik-i-taliban-pakistan-can-the-pakistani-government-correct-past-def.

Peters, Gretchen, and Don Rassler. "Crime and Insurgency in the Tribal Areas of Afghanistan and Pakistan." Combating Terrorism Center, Military Academy, West Point, NY, 2010.

Picciotto, Robert, Funmi Olonisakin, and Michael Clarke. *Global Development and Human Security*. New Brunswick, NJ: Transaction Publishers, 2007.

Pizarro Leongómez, Eduardo. *Una democracia asediada: Balance y perspectivas del conflicto armado en Colombia*. Bogotá: Grupo Editorial Norma, 2004.

Pizzigati, Sam. *Greed and Good: Understanding and Overcoming the Inequality That Limits Our Lives.* New York: Rowman & Littlefield, 2004.

Plan Seguridad Ciudadana. "Encuesta de victimización y percepción de inseguridad 2008." Quito: Plan Seguridad Ciudadana, 2008. https://www.oas.org/dsp/Observatorio/Tablas/ Ecuador/encuesta_de_victimizaci%C3%B3n.pdf.

Poe, Abigail, and Adam Isacson. "Ecuador's Humanitarian Emergency: The Spillover of Colombia's Conflict." Washington, DC: Center for International Policy, 2009.

Polanyi, Karl. *The Great Transformation: The Political and Economic Origins of Our Time.* 2nd. ed. Boston, Mass.: Beacon Press, 2001.

Policía de Táchira. "Violencia en el estado de Táchira." San Cristóbal, Venezuela, 2012.

Policía Nacional de Colombia. "Capturado cabecilla de la banda criminal 'Los Rastrojos.'" Noticias y Actividades Destacadas, April 12, 2011. https://www.policia.gov.co/noticia/ capturado-cabecilla-de-la-banda-criminal-los-rastrojos.

Policía Nacional de Colombia. "Respuesta derecho de petición S.I.P.Q.R.S 174344-20140910." Policía Nacional de Colombia, Ministerio de Defensa, September 22, 2014.

Pratten, David. *Global Vigilantes.* Edited by David Pratten and Atreyee Sen. London: C. Hurst & Co., 2007.

Prescott, John Robert Victor. *Political Frontiers and Boundaries.* London: Allen & Unwin, 1987.

Presidencia de la República de Colombia. "Diagnóstico de la situación del pueblo indígena Wayúu." Bogotá: Observatorio del Programa Presidencial de Derechos Humanos y Derecho Internacional Humanitario de la Presidencia de la República, 2010. http://www.derechoshumanos.gov.co/ Observatorio/Documents/2010/DiagnosticoIndigenas/Diagnostico_WAY%C3%9AU.pdf.

Prieto, Jineth. "Las 10 razones por las que el EPL es un problema que se le creció al gobierno." *La Silla Vacía*, February 23, 2017. http://lasillavacia.com/historia/las-10-razones-por-las-que-el-epl-es-un-problema-que-se-le-crecio-al-gobierno-59861.

Programa de Estudios de la Ciudad. "Gobernanza de la seguridad en la frontera norte ecuatoriana." Fronteras. Quito: FLACSO Quito, Programa de Estudios de la Ciudad, 2011.

PROVEA, Programa de Educación—Acción en Derechos Humanos. "Situación de los derechos humanos en Venezuela, informe anual enero–diciembre 2012." Caracas: PROVEA, 2013.

———. "Situación de los derechos humanos en Venezuela, informe anual octubre 2010/ septiembre 2011." Caracas: PROVEA, 2012.

Przeworski, Adam, and Henry Teune. *The Logic of Comparative Social Inquiry.* Malabar, FL: Robert and Krieger Publishing, 1982.

Putnam, Robert D. *Bowling Alone.* New York: Simon and Schuster, 2001.

———. *Making Democracy Work: Civic Traditions in Modern Italy.* Princeton, NJ: Princeton University Press, 1993.

Rabasa, Angel, and Peter Chalk. *Colombian Labyrinth: The Synergy of Drugs and Insurgency and Its Implications for Regional Stability.* Santa Monica, CA: Rand, 2001.

Radsch, Courtney. "From Cell Phones to Coffee: Issues of Access in Egypt and Lebanon." In *Surviving Field Research: Working in Violent and Difficult Situations*, edited by Chandra Lekha Sriram, 91–107. London: Routledge, 2009.

Ramírez, María Clemencia. *Between the Guerrillas and the State: The Cocalero Movement, Citizenship, and Identity in the Colombian Amazon*. Durham, NC: Duke University Press, 2011.

———. "Negotiating Peace and Visibility as a Civil Society in Putumayo amid the Armed Conflict and the War on Drugs." In *Colombia: Building Peace in a Time of War*, edited by Virginia Marie Bouvier, 311–34. Washington, DC: United States Institute of Peace Press, 2009.

Ramírez, Socorro. "Civil Society Peacebuilding on Colombia's Borders." In *Accord. An International Review of Peace Initiatives, Building Peace across Borders*, edited by William Zartman and Alexander Ramsbotham, 60–61. Accord 22. London: Conciliation Resources, 2011. http://www.c-r.org/accord-article/civil-society-peacebuilding-colombias-borders.

———. "Dinámicas y problemáticas en la zona fronteriza colombo-ecuatoriana." In *Relaciones fronterizas: Encuentros y conflictos*, edited by Fernando Carrión and Johanna Espín, 223–34. Quito: Flacso-Sede Ecuador, 2011.

Ramsey, Geoffrey. "Mapping Gun Smuggling Routes in Ecuador." Insight Crime, September 17, 2012. http://www.insightcrime.org/news-briefs/mapping-gun-smuggling-routes-in-ecuador.

Rangel Suárez, Alfredo. "Parasites and Predators: Guerrillas and the Insurrection Economy of Colombia." *Journal of International Affairs* 53, no. 2 (Spring 2000): 577. https://www.jstor.org/stable/24357766.

Ratzel, Friedrich. *Politische Geographie*. Munich: Oldenbourg, 1897.

Reinharz, Shulamit. *Feminist Methods in Social Research*. New York: Oxford University Press, 1992.

Reno, William. "Crime versus War." In *The Changing Character of War*, edited by Hew Strachan and Sibylle Scheipers, 220–40. CCW Series. Oxford: Oxford University Press, 2011.

———. *Warlord Politics and African States*. Boulder, CO: Lynne Rienner, 1998.

Restrepo, César Andrés. *Colombia: Seguridad y defensa en las fronteras*. Bogotá: Fundación Seguridad y Democracia, 2009.

Restrepo, Elvira María. "The Pursuit of Efficiency and the Colombian Criminal Justice System." In *Criminality, Public Security, and the Challenge to Democracy in Latin America*, edited by Marcelo Bergman and Laurence Whitehead, 173–202. Notre Dame, IN: University of Notre Dame Press, 2009.

Restrepo, Juan Diego. "La guerra no abandona a Nariño." *Semana*, May 31, 2006. http://www.semana.com/on-line/articulo/la-guerra-no-abandona-narino/78664-3.

———. "'Paras' asesinan en Colombia y arrojan cuerpos en Venezuela." *Verdad Abierta*, August 31, 2011. http://www.verdadabierta.com/index.php?option=com_content&id=2396%3E.

Reuters, "Colombia to Use Drones to Fumigate Coca Leaf with Herbicide." June 27, 2018. https://www.reuters.com/article/us-colombia-drugs/colombia-to-use-drones-to-fumigate-coca-leaf-with-herbicide-idUSKBN1JM368.

Revista Semana. "Habla Vicente Castaño." *Revista semana*. June 5, 2005. http://www.semana.com/portada/articulo/habla-vicente-castano/72964-3.

Ricaurte-Villota, Ana Inés. "Comportamiento del homicidio. Colombia, 2011." Bogotá: Instituto Nacional de Medicina Legal y Ciencias Forenses, 2011. http://www.medicinalegal.gov.co/documents/10180/34616/2-F-11-Homicidios.pdf/01a6b108-57cd-48bc-9e9b-dcdba0d918a2.

Rico, José María. *Seguridad ciudadana en Centroamérica: Aspectos teóricos y metodológicos*. San José, Costa Rica: Instituto Interamericano de Derechos Humanos, 1999.

Rivadeneira Muñoz, Alberto, and Juan Marco Gonzaga. "Acta de inspección al sector de Barranca Bermeja—San Martin, canton Lago Agrio provincia de Sucumbíos." Lago Agrio, Ecuador: Defensoría del Pueblo de Ecuador, 2008.

Robben, Antonius C. G. M. "The Fear of Indifference: Combatants' Anxieties about the Political Identity of Civilians during Argentina's Dirty War." In *Societies of Fear: The Legacy of Civil War, Violence, and Terror in Latin America*, edited by Kees Koonings and Dirk Krujit, 125–40. London: Zed Books, 1999.

Roberts, Adam, and Timothy Garton Ash. *Civil Resistance and Power Politics: The Experience of Non-Violent Action from Gandhi to the Present.* Oxford: Oxford University Press, 2011.

Rodgers, Dennis. "Living in the Shadow of Death: Gangs, Violence, and Social Order in Urban Nicaragua, 1996–2002." *Journal of Latin American Studies* 38, no. 2 (2006): 267–92. https://doi.org/10.1017/S0022216X0600071X.

Rodgers, Dennis, and Adam Baird. "Understanding Gangs in Contemporary Latin America." In *Handbook of Gangs and Gang Responses,* edited by Scott H. Decker and David C. Pyronz, 478–502. New York: Wiley, 2015.

Rojas Salas, Roberto Alexi. "Cerac evidencia presencia del clan Úsuga, los Rastrojos, y Águilas Negras en frontera con Venezuela," September 4, 2015. http://lavozdelrioarauca.com/2015/09/cerac-evidencia-presencia-del-clan-usuga-los-rastrojos-y-aguilas-negras-en-frontera-con-venezuela/.

Romero, Simon. "Manuel Marulanda, Top Commander of Colombia's Largest Guerrilla Group, Is Dead." *New York Times,* May 26, 2008, sec. Americas. https://www.nytimes.com/2008/05/26/world/americas/26marulanda.html.

Ross, Amy. "Impact on Research of Security-Seeking Behaviour." In *Surviving Field Research: Working in Violent and Difficult Situations,* edited by Chandra Lekha Sriram, 177–88. London: Routledge, 2009.

Rotker, Susana. "Cities Written by Violence: An Introduction." In *Citizens of Fear: Urban Violence in Latin America,* edited by Susana Rotker and Katherine Goldman, 7–24. New Brunswick, NJ: Rutgers University Press, 2002.

Ruggie, John. "Territoriality and Beyond: Problematizing Modernity in International Relations." *International Organization* 47, no. 1 (Winter 1993): 139–74.

Ryan, William. *Blaming the Victim.* New York: Vintage Books, 1976.

Saab, Bilal Y., and Alexandra W. Taylor. "Criminality and Armed Groups: A Comparative Study of FARC and Paramilitary Groups in Colombia." *Studies in Conflict & Terrorism* 32 (2009): 455–75. https://doi.org/10.1080/10576100902892570.

Sabrow, Sophia. "Local Perceptions of the Legitimacy of Peace Operations by the UN, Regional Organizations, and Individual States—A Case Study of the Mali Conflict." *International Peacekeeping* 24, no. 1 (January 1, 2017): 159–86. https://doi.org/10.1080/13533312.2016.1249365.

Safford, Frank, and Marco Palacios. *Colombia: Fragmented Land, Divided Society.* New York: Oxford University Press, 2002.

Saldaña, Johnny. *The Coding Manual for Qualitative Researchers.* London: SAGE, 2009.

Salehyan, I. "Transnational Rebels—Neighboring States as Sanctuary for Rebel Groups." *World Politics* 59, no. 2 (2007): 217–42.

Salinas, Marcos. "Diagnóstico de seguridad ciudadana en el cantón de Sucumbíos. Hacia una política municipal de prevención del delito." Asociación de Municipalidades del Ecuador, 2012.

Sayago Rojas, Pedro Rafael. "Impacto socioeconómico a un año del cierre de la frontera colombo-venezolana: Norte de Santander–Estado Táchira (2015–2016)." *Mundo Fesc* 12 (2016): 86–97.

Schelling, Thomas C. *The Strategy of Conflict.* Cambridge, MA: Harvard University Press, 1980.

Schendel, Willem van. *The Bengal Borderland: Beyond State and Nation in South Asia.* London: Anthem, 2005.

———. "Spaces of Engagement. How Borderlands, Illegal Flows, and Territorial States Interlock." In *Illicit Flows and Criminal Things: States, Borders, and the Other Side of Globalization,* edited by Willem van Schendel and Itty Abraham, 38–68. Bloomington: Indiana University Press, 2005.

Schendel, Willem van, and Itty Abraham, eds. *Illicit Flows and Criminal Things: States, Borders, and the Other Side of Globalization.* Bloomington: Indiana University Press, 2005.

Scheper-Hughes, Nancy. *Death without Weeping: The Violence of Everyday Life in Brazil.* Berkeley: University of California Press, 1993.

Scheper-Hughes, Nancy, and Philippe I. Bourgois. *Violence in War and Peace.* Malden, MA: Blackwell, 2004.

Schmid, Alex. "Links between Transnational Organized Crime and Terrorist Crimes." *Transnational Organized Crime* 2, no. 4 (Winter 1996): 40–82. http://turkishpolicy.com/images/stories/2004-02-globalsecurity/TPQ2004-2-schmid.pdf.

Schmitt, Carl. *Der Begriff des Politischen.* Hamburg: Hanseatische Verlagsanstalt, 1933.

Schneckener, Ulrich. "Fragile Statehood, Armed Non-State Actors, and Security Governance." In *Private Actors and Security Governance,* edited by Alan Bryden and Marina Caparini, 23–40. Münster: LIT Verlag, 2006.

———. "Spoilers or Governance Actors? Engaging Armed Non-State Groups in Areas of Limited Statehood." SFB-Governance Working Paper Series. Berlin: Research Center (SFB) 700, 2009.

Schwandt, Thomas A. *The SAGE Dictionary of Qualitative Inquiry.* 3rd ed. London: SAGE, 2007.

Scorgie, Lindsay. "Rwenzori Rebels: The Allied Democratic Forces Conflict in the Uganda-Congo Borderland." PhD diss., University of Cambridge, 2012.

Scorgie-Porter, Lindsay. "Economic Survival and Borderland Rebellion: The Case of the Allied Democratic Forces on the Uganda-Congo Border." *The Journal of the Middle East and Africa* 6, no. 2 (April 3, 2015): 191–213. https://doi.org/10.1080/21520844.2015.1055452.

Scott, James C. *Seeing Like a State: How Certain Schemes to Improve the Human Condition Have Failed.* Yale Agrarian Studies. New Haven: Yale University Press, 1998.

———. *Weapons of the Weak: Everyday Forms of Peasant Resistance.* New Haven: Yale University Press, 1985.

Secretariado de Pastoral Social, Diócesis de Riohacha. "Análisis del contexto del departamento para entender la dinámica del conflicto armado en La Guajira." Rioacha, La Guajira: Pastoral Social, 2008.

Semana. "Arauca Saudita." October 27, 1986. http://www.semana.com/especiales/articulo/arauca-saudita/8217-3.

———. "Las claves para entender el lío entre Colombia y Venezuela." June 22, 2015. https://www.semana.com/nacion/articulo/limites-maritimos-entre-colombia-venezuela-entran-de-nuevo-en-disputa/432249-3.

———. "Cómo el ejército se alió con el ELN en Arauca." January 19, 2009. http://www.semana.com/nacion/como-ejercito-alio-eln-arauca/119765-3.aspx.

———. "Conversación entre corruptos." November 3, 2003. http://www.semana.com/nacion/articulo/conversacion-entre-corruptos/61680-3.

———. "'Grannobles,' hermano del 'Mono Jojoy': ¿El fin de un 'capo' de las FARC?," September 3, 2012. http://www.semana.com/nacion/articulo/grannobles-hermano-del-mono-jojoy-el-fin-capo-farc/264130-3.

———. "La nueva estrategia contra las FARC." February 25, 2012. http://www.semana.com//nacion/articulo/la-nueva-estrategia-contra-farc/253985-3.

———. "'Pablito' se equivocó de ruta." November 26, 2010. http://www.semana.com/nacion/articulo/pablito-equivoco-ruta/125089-3.

———. "Vientos de guerra." December 14, 1992. http://www.semana.com/nacion/articulo/vientos-guerra/18844-3.

Sen, Amartya. *Poverty and Famines: An Essay on Entitlement and Deprivation.* Oxford: Clarendon Press, 1981.

Serrano, Mónica, and María Celia Toro. "From Drug Trafficking to Transnational Organized Crime in Latin America." In *Transnational Organized Crime and International Security: Business as Usual?,* edited by Mats R. Berdal and Mónica Serrano. Boulder, CO: Lynne Rienner, 2002.

Seymour, Lee J. M. "Why Factions Switch Sides in Civil Wars: Rivalry, Patronage, and Realignment in Sudan." *International Security* 39, no. 2 (October 1, 2014): 92–131. http://dx.doi.org/10.1162/ISEC_a_00179.

Shapiro, Jacob N. "Terrorist Decision-Making: Insights from Economics and Political Science." *Perspectives on Terrorism* 6, no. 4–5 (September 10, 2012). http://www.terrorismanalysts. com/pt/index.php/pot/article/view/214.

Shifter, Michael. "Breakdown in the Andes." *Foreign Affairs* 83 (2004): 126–38.

———. "Crisis in the Andes: The Border Dispute between Colombia and Ecuador, and Implications for the Region." *Inter-American Dialogue* (blog), April 10, 2008. http://www. thedialogue.org/page.cfm?pageID=32&pubID=1287.

Sierra, Álvaro. "La coca viajera." *El Tiempo*, October 13, 2002. http://www.eltiempo.com/ archivo/documento/MAM-1372034.

Simon, Joel. *Endangered Mexico: An Environnment on the Edge*. London: Latin American Bureau, 1998.

Sistema de Alertas Tempranas. Defensoría del Pueblo de Colombia, SAT. "Informe de Riesgo N° 012-11 A.I." Bogotá: Defensoría del Pueblo de Colombia, August 18, 2011.

———. "Informe de Riesgo N° 017-09." Bogotá: Defensoría del Pueblo de Colombia, July 2009.

———. "Informe de Riesgo N° 026-09." Bogotá: Defensoría del Pueblo de Colombia, October 27, 2009.

———. "Informe de Riesgo N° 007-10." Bogotá: Defensoría del Pueblo de Colombia, June 2010.

———. "Informe de Riesgo N° 013-10." Bogotá: Defensoría del Pueblo de Colombia, 2010.

———. "Informe de Riesgo N° 017-07 A. I." Bogotá: Defensoría del Pueblo de Colombia, July 6, 2007.

———. "Informe de Riesgo N° 018-09." Bogotá: Defensoría del Pueblo de Colombia, July 21, 2009.

———. "Informe de Riesgo N° 019-07." Bogotá: Defensoría del Pueblo de Colombia, July 19, 2007.

———. "Informe de Riesgo N° 024-12." Bogotá: Defensoría del Pueblo de Colombia, 2012.

———. "Informe de Riesgo N° 029-08 A.I." Bogotá: Defensoría del Pueblo de Colombia, December 4, 2008.

———. "Internal Document." Sistema de Alertas Tempranas. Defensoría del Pueblo de Colombia, 2010.

———. "Nota de Seguimiento N° 007-11. Tercera nota al informe de Riesgo N° 029-07." Bogotá: Defensoría del Pueblo de Colombia, April 2011.

———. "Nota de Seguimiento N° 002-11. Cuarta nota al informe de Riesgo N° 006-08A.I." Bogotá: Defensoría del Pueblo de Colombia February 2011.

———. "Nota de Seguimiento N° 017-10. Segunda nota al informe de Riesgo N° 002-09." Bogotá: Defensoría del Pueblo de Colombia, July 28, 2010.

———. "Nota de Seguimiento N° 017-11. Tercera nota al informe de Riesgo N° 024-08 A.I." Bogotá: Defensoría del Pueblo de Colombia, July 7, 2011.

———. "Nota de Seguimiento N°031-09. Segunda nota al informe de Riesgo N° 020-09 A.I." Bogotá, December 2009.

———. "Seguimiento a la situación de riesgo por conflicto armado en Arauca." PowerPoint presentation. Arauca, 2010.

Slim, Hugo. *Killing Civilians: Method, Madness, and Morality in War*. London: Hurst, 2007.

Slowe, Peter M. "The Geography of Borderlands—The Case of the Quebec–United States Borderlands." *Geographical Journal* 157, no. 2 (1991): 191–98. https://doi.org/10.2307/635276.

Sriram, Chandra Lekha. *Surviving Field Research: Working in Violent and Difficult Situations*. London: Routledge, 2009.

Stanford University. *Mapping Militant Organizations*, August 2012. http://web.stanford. edu/group/mappingmilitants/cgi-bin/groups/view/105?highlight=TEHRIK-E+ TALIBAN+PAKISTAN+%28TTP%29.

Staniland, Paul. *Networks of Rebellion: Explaining Insurgent Cohesion and Collapse*. Cornell Studies in Security Affairs. Ithaca, NY: Cornell University Press, 2014.

————. "States, Insurgents, and Wartime Political Orders." *Perspectives on Politics* 10, no. 2 (2012): 243–64. https://www.jstor.org/stable/41479550.

Starn, Orin. *Nightwatch: The Politics of Protest in the Andes.* Durham, NC: Duke University Press, 1999.

Stearns, Jason K., and Christoph Vogel. "The Landscape of Armed Groups in the Eastern Congo." Congo Research Group. New York: Center on International Cooperation, New York University, 2015.

Steele, Abbey. *Democracy and Displacement in Colombia's Civil War.* Ithaca, NY: Cornell University Press, 2017.

Sterling, Claire. *Crime without Frontiers: The Worldwide Expansion of Organised Crime and the Pax Mafiosa.* London: Warner Books, 1995.

Stewart, Scott. "From Colombia to New York City: The Narconomics of Cocaine." Business Insider, June 27, 2016. http://www.businessinsider.com/from-colombia-to-new-york-city-the-economics-of-cocaine-2015-7?IR=T.

————. "Mexico and the Cartel Wars in 2010." Security Weekly. Stratfor. Global Intelligence, 2010. http://www.stratfor.com/weekly/20101215-mexico-and-cartel-wars-2010.

Stockholm International Peace Research Institute. "SIPRI Military Expenditure Database." 2014. http://www.sipri.org/research/armaments/milex/milex_database.

Strassoldo, Raimondo. "Border Studies: The State of the Art in Europe." In *Borderlands in Africa: A Multidisciplinary and Comparative Focus on Nigeria and West Africa,* edited by A. I Asiwaju and P. O. Adeniyi. Lagos: University of Lagos Press, 1989.

Strocka, Cordula. "Youth Gangs in Latin America." *SAIS Review of International Affairs* 26, no. 2 (2006): 133–46. https://doi.org/10.1353/sais.2006.0045.

Suárez-Orozco, Marcelo M. "Speaking of the Unspeakable: Toward a Psychosocial Understanding of Responses to Terror." *Ethos* 18, no. 3 (September 1, 1990): 353–83. https://doi.org/10.1525/eth.1990.18.3.02a00050.

Sweeney, Jack. "Guerras fronterizas: FBL contra el ELN," *VenEconomía Mensual* 22, no. 1 (October 2004). http://www.veneconomy.com/site/files/articulos/artEsp4022_2819.pdf.

Tamm, Henning. "The Origins of Transnational Alliances: Rulers, Rebels, and Political Survival in the Congo Wars." *International Security* 41, no. 1 (July 1, 2016): 147–81. http://dx.doi.org/10.1162/ISEC_a_00252.

Tate, Winifred. *Drugs, Thugs, and Diplomats: US Policymaking in Colombia.* Anthropology of Policy. Stanford, CA: Stanford University Press, 2015.

Taussig, Michael T. "Culture of Terror—Spaces of Death. Roger Casement's Putumayo Report and the Explanation of Torture." In *Violence: A Reader,* edited by Catherine Lowe Besteman, 211–43. Basingstoke: Palgrave Macmillan, 2002.

————. *The Nervous System.* New York: Routledge, 1992.

————. "Talking Terror." In *Violence in War and Peace,* edited by Nancy Scheper-Hughes and Philippe I. Bourgois, 171–74. Malden, MA: Blackwell, 2004.

Telesur TV. "Desmantelan campamento paramilitar colombiano en Venezuela." March 22, 2017. https://www.telesurtv.net/news/Desmantelan-campamento-paramilitar-colombiano-en-Venezuela-20170322-0066.html.

Theidon, Kimberly. "'How Was Your Trip?' Self-Care for Researchers Working and Writing on Violence." Drugs, Security, and Democracy (DSD) Program Working Papers on Research Security. Harvard University: Social Science Research Council, 2014.

Thomas, Kenneth. "Organizational Conflict." In *Organizational Behavior,* edited by Steven Kerr, 151–81. New York: John Wiley & Sons Inc, 1979.

Thompson, Charles D. *Border Odyssey: Travels along the US/Mexico Divide.* Austin: University of Texas Press, 2015.

Thompson, E. P. "The Moral Economy of the English Crowd in the Eighteenth Century." *Past & Present* 50, no. 1 (1971): 76–136. https://doi.org/10.1093/past/50.1.76.

Thoumi, Francisco E. *Illegal Drugs, Economy, and Society in the Andes*. London: Woodrow Wilson
    Center Press; Johns Hopkins University Press, 2003. http://www.loc.gov/catdir/toc/
    ecip044/2003012400.html.
———. *Political Economy and Illegal Drugs in Colombia*. Studies on the Impact of the Illegal Drug
    Trade. Boulder, CO: Lynne Rienner, 1995.
Tickner, Arlene B., Diego García, and Catalina Arrezea. "Actores violentos no estatales y
    narcotráfico en Colombia." In *Políticas antidroga en Colombia: Éxitos, fracasos, y extravíos*,
    413–45. Bogotá: Universidad de los Andes, 2011.
Tickner, Arlene B., and Mónica Herz. "No Place for Theory? Security Studies in Latin America." In
    Thinking International Relations Differently, edited by Arlene B. Tickner and David L. Blaney,
    92–114. Abingdon: Routledge, 2012.
Tilly, Charles. "Citizenship, Identity, and Social History." *International Review of Social History* 40
    (1995): 1–17. https://www.cambridge.org/core/services/aop-cambridge-core/content/
    view/S0020859000113586.
———. *The Politics of Collective Violence*. Cambridge Studies in Contentious Politics. Cambridge,
    UK: Cambridge University Press, 2003.
———. "A Primer on Citizenship." *Theory and Society* 26, no. 4 (August 1, 1997): 599–602.
    https://doi.org/10.2307/657863.
———. *Trust and Rule*. Cambridge, UK: Cambridge University Press, 2005.
———. "War Making and State Making as Organized Crime." In *Bringing the State Back in*, edited
    by Peter B. Evans, Dietrich Rueschemeyer, and Theda Skocpol. Structures Social Science
    Research Council. Committee on States and Social, Studies Joint Committee on Latin
    American, and Europe Joint Committee on Western, 169–191. Cambridge, UK: Cambridge
    University Press, 1985.
Titeca, Kristof. "The Changing Cross-Border Trade Dynamics between North-Western Uganda,
    North-Eastern Congo, and Southern Sudan." Crisis States Working Papers Series 2.
    London: Crisis States Research Centre, London School of Economics, 2009.
Tokatlian, Juan Gabriel, ed. *Narcotráfico en América Latina*. Caracas: Corporación Andina de
    Fomento—CAF, 2009.
———. "La construcción de un "Estado fallido" en la política mundial: El caso de las relaciones
    entre Estados Unidos y Colombia." *Análisis político* 64 (Bogotá, 2008): 67–104.
Torres-Rivas, Edelberto. "Epilogue: Notes on Terror, Violence, Fear, and Democracy." In *Societies
    of Fear: The Legacy of Civil War, Violence, and Terror in Latin America*, edited by Kees Koonings
    and Dirk Krujit, 285–300. Zed Books, 1999.
Tovar, Daniel. *Colombia and Venezuela: The Border Dispute over the Gulf*. Military Technology. Bad
    Neuenahr-Ahrweiler: Mönch Publishing Group, 2016.
Transnational Institute. "Ecuador: 'daños colaterales' por las fumigaciones en la frontera
    norte." *Transnational Institute* (blog), April 3, 2007. http://www.tni.org/archives/act/
    16594.
Transparencia Venezuela. "Venezuela en el podio de la violencia," February 26, 2015. https://
    transparencia.org.ve/venezuela-en-el-podio-de-la-violencia/.
Tribunal Supremo de Justicia. "Solicitud de extradición del ciudadano Walid Makled García."
    Caracas: Tribunal Supremo de Justicia de Venezuela, August 20, 2010.
Unidad de Planeación Minero Energética. "PETROLEO–PRECIOS–Precios Históricos de los
    Combustibles Bogotá (DEF)." *Consulta Series de Tiempo*. October 2012. http://www.upme.
    gov.co/generadorconsultas/Consulta_Series.aspx?idModulo=3&tipoSerie=68&grupo=27
    0&fechainicial=01/01/1999&fechafinal=01/10/2012.
Unidad para las Víctimas. "Registro Único de Víctimas (RUV)," July 1, 2018. https://www.
    unidadvictimas.gov.co/en/node/37394.
United Nations. "Reports Submitted by States Parties under Article 9 of the Convention.
    Twentieth to Twenty-Second Periodic Reports Due in 2012. Ecuador. CERD/C/ECU/
    20-22." United Nations Committee on the Elimination of Racial Discrimination, 2012.

United Nations; World Bank. "Pathways for Peace: Inclusive Approaches to Preventing Violent Conflict," Washington, DC: World Bank, 14–19.

United Nations Development Programme. "Cesar: Análisis de la conflictividad." United Nations Development Programme. Área de Paz, Desarrollo y Reconciliación, 2010.

———. "Community Security and Social Cohesion. Towards a UNDP Approach." New York: United Nations Development Programme, 2009.

———. "Human Development Report, 1994." New York: United Nations Development Programme, 1994.

———. "Human Development Report, 2013." New York: United Nations Development Programme, 2013.

———. "Seguridad ciudadana con rostro humano: Diagnóstico y propuestas para América Latina." Human Development Report for Latin America 2013–2014. New York: United Nations Development Programme, 2013.

United Nations General Assembly. "A/RES/66/290," 2012. http://www.un.org/humansecurity/sites/www.un.org.humansecurity/files/hsu%20documents/GA%20Resolutions.pdf.

United Nations High Commissioner for Refugees. "Colombia Situation Update, December 2016," December 2016. http://www.refworld.org/docid/58627cd24.html.

———. "Directrices de eligibilidad del ACNUR para la evaluación de las necesidades de protección internacional de los solicitantes de asilo de Colombia." HCR/EG/COL/10/2. United Nations High Commissioner for Refugees, May 27, 2010.

———. "Internal Report on Border Mission." Arauca, Colombia, 2012.

———. "Venezuela." Caracas, 2010. http://www.acnur.org/t3/uploads/tx_refugiadosamericas/Ficha_Informativa_de_Venezuela.pdf?view=1.

United Nations High Commissioner for Refugees Colombia. "Internal Presentation." Pasto, Colombia, 2011.

United Nations Office of the High Commissioner for Human Rights. "International Convention for the Protection of All Persons from Enforced Disappearance." United Nations Office of the High Commissioner for Human Rights, n.d. http://www.ohchr.org/EN/HRBodies/CED/Pages/ConventionCED.aspx.

United Nations Office for the Coordination of Humanitarian Affairs. "Colombia: Humanitarian Snapshot." Bogotá: OCHA Colombia, August 14, 2013.

———. "Glossary of Humanitarian Terms. In Relation to the Protection of Civilians in Armed Conflict." New York: United Nations, 2003.

———. "Revisión del mapeo inter-institucional humanitario frontera colombo-venezolana. Norte de Santander." United Nations Office for the Coordination of Humanitarian Affairs Nororiente, 2010.

United Nations Office on Drugs and Crime. "Afghan Opiate Trafficking through the Southern Route." Vienna: United Nations Office on Drugs and Crime, 2015.

———. "The Globalization of Crime: A Transnational Organized Crime Threat Assessment." Vienna: United Nations Office on Drugs and Crime, 2010.

———. "Market Analysis of Plant-Based Drugs. Opiates, Cocaine, Cannabis." In *World Drug Report 2017*, edited by UNODC, vol. 3. Vienna: United Nations Office on Drugs and Crime, 2017.

———. "New UNODC Campaign Highlights Transnational Organized Crime as a US$870 Billion a Year Business." United Nations Office on Drugs and Crime (blog), July 16, 2012. http://www.unodc.org/unodc/en/frontpage/2012/July/new-unodc-campaign-highlights-transnational-organized-crime-as-an-us-870-billion-a-year-business.html.

———. "Organized Crime and Instability in Central Africa. A Threat Assessment." Vienna: United Nations Office on Drugs and Crime, 2011.

———. "Transnational Organized Crime: The Globalized Illegal Economy." *Transnational Organized Crime: Let's put them out of business*, 2017. https://www.unodc.org/toc/en/crimes/organized-crime.html.

————. "UN Drugs Agency Compliments Ecuador on Seizure of 5.5 Tons of Cocaine."
    Vienna: United Nations Office on Drugs and Crime, 2005. https://www.unodc.org/unodc/
    en/press/releases/press_release_2006-03-17.html.
————. "UNODC Homicide Statistics 2013." Vienna: United Nations Office on Drugs and
    Crime, 2013.
————. "World Drug Report 2010." Vienna: United Nations Office on Drugs and Crime, 2010.
————. "World Drug Report 2011." Vienna: United Nations Office on Drugs and Crime, 2011.
————. "World Drug Report 2014." Vienna: United Nations Office on Drugs and Crime, 2014.
————. "World Drug Report 2016." Vienna: United Nations Office on Drugs and Crime, 2016.
United Nations Office on Drugs and Crime and Government of Colombia. "Colombia. Coca
    Cultivation Survey 2012." Bogotá: United Nations Office on Drugs and Crime, Government
    of Colombia, June 2013.
————. "Colombia. Monitoreo de Cultivos de Coca 2013." Bogotá: United Nations Office on
    Drugs and Crime, Government of Colombia, 2014.
————. "Colombia. Monitoreo de Cultivos de Coca 2015." Bogotá: United Nations Office on
    Drugs and Crime, Government of Colombia, 2016.
————. "Colombia. Monitoreo de Cultivos de Coca 2017." Bogotá: United Nations Office on
    Drugs and Crime, Government of Colombia, 2017.
Varese, Federico. *Mafias on the Move: How Organized Crime Conquers New Territories*. Princeton,
    NJ: Princeton University Press, 2011.
————. *The Russian Mafia: Private Protection in a New Market Economy*. Oxford: Oxford
    University Press, 2001.
————. "What Is Organized Crime?" In *Organized Crime*, edited by Federico Varese, 1–35.
    Critical Concepts in Criminology. London: Routledge, 2010.
Vargas, Gonzalo. "Urban Irregular Warfare and Violence against Civilians: Evidence from a
    Colombian City." *Terrorism and Political Violence* 21, no. 1 (2009): 110–32.
Velásquez Rivera, Edgar de Jesús. "Historia del Paramilitarismo en Colombia." *Historia* 26, no. 1
    (São Paulo, 2007): 134–53.
Verd Adabierta. "De la curul a la cárcel," August 28, 2013. http://www.verdadabierta.com/
    component/content/article/63-nacional/4800-de-la-curul-a-la-carcel.
————. "Gobierno ordena la extradición de alias 'Pablo,'" September 10, 2012. http://
    www.verdadabierta.com/component/content/article/36-jefes/4213-la-extradicion-
    de-pablo-el-terror-de-la-guajira.
————. "La violencia oculta de la costa de Nariño," August 30, 2015.—http://www.
    verdadabierta.com/victimas-seccion/asesinatos-colectivos/5947-la-violencia-oculta-
    de-la-costa-de-narino.
————. "'Pablo,' Arnulfo Sánchez González." April 19, 2011. http://www.verdadabierta.com/
    victimarios/3204-alias-pablo-de-funcionario-publico-a-jefe-para.
Vertovec, Steven. *Transnationalism*. Key Ideas. London: Routledge, 2009.
Vicepresidencia de la República. "Algunos indicadores sobre la situación de derechos humanos
    en la región del Catatumbo." Bogotá: Programa Presidencial de Derechos Humanos y de
    Derecho Internacional Humanitario, October 2004.
————. "Diagnostico departamental Norte de Santander." Bogotá: Observatorio del Programa
    Presidencial de Derechos Humanos y Derecho Internacional Humanitario, Vicepresidencia
    de la República, 2007.
————. *Diagnóstico Departamental Arauca*. Bogotá, Colombia: Observatorio del Programa
    Presidencial de Derechos Humanos y Derecho Internacional Humanitario, Vicepresidencia
    de la República, 2008.
Villarreal, Ana. "Fear and Spectacular Drug Violence in Monterrey." In *Violence at the Urban
    Margins*, ed. Javier Auyero, Philippe I. Bourgois, and Nancy Scheper-Hughes, 135–61.
    Global and Comparative Ethnography. New York: Oxford University Press, 2015.
————. "Secuestrable: Sobre la normalización de la violencia en el México urbano." *Diálogo
    Global* 3, no. 3 (May 2013): 26–27.

Vorrath, Judith. "On the Margin of Statehood? State-Society Relations in African Borderlands." In *Understanding Life in the Borderlands: Boundaries in Depth and in Motion*, edited by I. William Zartman, 85–104. Athens: University of Georgia Press, 2010.

Wæver, Ole. "Securitization and Desecuritization." In *On Security*, edited by Ronnie D. Lipschutz, 46–86. New York: Columbia University Press, 1995.

Waldmann, Peter. "Is There a Culture of Violence in Colombia?" *Terrorism and Political Violence* 19, no. 4 (2007): 593–609. https://doi.org/10.1080/09546550701626836.

Walklate, Sandra. "Crime and Community: Fear or Trust?" *The British Journal of Sociology* 49, no. 4 (December 1, 1998): 550–69. https://doi.org/10.2307/591288.

Waltz, Kenneth N. *Theory of International Politics*. Long Grove, IL: Waveland Press, 2010.

Weber, Max. *Politik als Beruf*. Stuttgart: Reclam, Philipp, jun. GmbH, Verlag, 1992.

Wedeen, Lisa. "Reflections on Ethnographic Work in Political Science." *Annual Review of Political Science* 13, no. 1 (2010): 255–72.

Weidmann, Nils B. "Micro-Cleavages and Violence in Civil Wars: A Computational Assessment." *Conflict Management and Peace Science* 33, no. 5 (November 1, 2016): 539–58. http://journals.sagepub.com/doi/abs/10.1177/0738894215570433.

———. "Violence 'from above' or "from below"? The Role of Ethnicity in Bosnia's Civil War." *The Journal of Politics* 73, no. 4 (2011): 1178–90. https://doi.org/10.1017/S0022381611000831.

Weinstein, Jeremy M. *Inside Rebellion: The Politics of Insurgent Violence*. Cambridge, UK: Cambridge University Press, 2006.

Wells, Miriam. "Colombia Governor Arrested for Multiple Murders, Crime Links." *InSight Crime—Organized Crime in the Americas* (blog), October 2013. http://www.insightcrime.org/news-briefs/colombia-governor-arrested-for-multiple-murders-crime-links.

Wendt, Alexander. *Social Theory of International Politics*. Cambridge, UK: Cambridge University Press, 1999.

Whitehead, Laurence. "Citizen Insecurity and Democracy. Reflections on a Paradoxical Configuration." In *Criminality, Public Security, and the Challenge to Democracy in Latin America*, edited by Marcelo Bergman and Laurence Whitehead, 277–314. Notre Dame, IN: University of Notre Dame Press, 2009.

———. *Democratization: Theory and Experience*. Oxford: Oxford University Press, 2002.

Wickham-Crowley, Timothy P. "The Rise (and Sometimes Fall) of Guerrilla Governments in Latin America." *Sociological Forum* 2, no. 3 (July 1, 1987): 473–99. https://doi.org/10.2307/684670.

Wight, Martin. *International Theory: The Three Traditions*. Leicester: Leicester University Press for the Royal Institute of International Affairs, 1991.

Wilkinson, Sue. "Focus Group Research." In *Qualitative Research: Theory, Method, and Practice*, ed. David Silverman, 177–99. 2nd ed. London: Sage Publications, 2004.

Williams, Bernard. "Formal Structures and Social Reality." In *Trust: Making and Breaking Cooperative Relations*, edited by Diego Gambetta. New edition, 3–13. Chichester: Wiley-Blackwell, 1990.

Williams, Paul D. *Security Studies: An Introduction*. 2nd ed. London: Routledge, 2012.

Williams, Phil. "Cooperation among Criminal Organizations." In *Transnational Organized Crime and International Security: Business as Usual?*, edited by Mats R. Berdal, 67–82. Boulder, CO: Lynne Rienner, 2002.

———. *Criminals, Militias, and Insurgents: Organized Crime in Iraq*. Carlisle, PA: Strategic Studies Institute, 2009.

———. "Lawlessness and Disorder: An Emerging Paradigm for the 21st Century." In *Convergence: Illicit Networks and National Security in the Age of Globalization*, edited by Michael Miklaucic and Jacqueline Brewer, 15–36. Washington, DC: National Defense University, 2013.

Williams, Phil, and Roy Godson. "Anticipating Organized and Transnational Crime." *Crime Law and Social Change* 37 (June 2002): 311–55. https://link.springer.com/content/pdf/10.1023%2FA%3A1016095317864.pdf.

Williamson, Oliver E. "Credible Commitments: Using Hostages to Support Exchange." *The American Economic Review* 73, no. 4 (1983): 519–40. https://www.jstor.org/stable/1816557.

Wilson, Thomas M., and Hastings Donnan. "Borders and Border Studies." In *A Companion to Border Studies*, edited by Thomas M. Wilson and Hastings Donnan, 1–26. Wiley-Blackwell, 2012.

———. *Culture and Power at the Edges of the State: National Support and Subversion in European Border Regions.* Münster: Lit, 2005.

Wood, Elisabeth Jean. *Insurgent Collective Action and Civil War in El Salvador.* Cambridge, UK: Cambridge University Press, 2003.

———. "Sexual Violence during War: Toward an Understanding of Variation." In *Order, Conflict, and Violence*, edited by Ian Shapiro, Stathis N. Kalyvas, and Tarek Masoud, 321–51. Cambridge, UK: Cambridge University Press, 2008.

Wood, Reed M., and Jacob D. Kathman. "Competing for the Crown: Inter-Rebel Competition and Civilian Targeting in Civil War." *Political Research Quarterly* 68, no. 1 (2015): 167–79. http://dx.doi.org/10.1177/1065912914563546.

Woodward, Susan L. *Balkan Tragedy: Chaos and Dissolution after the Cold War.* Washington, DC: Brookings Institution, 1995.

World Health Organization. "World Report on Violence and Health. Summary." Geneva: World Health Organization, 2002. http://www.who.int/violence_injury_prevention/violence/world_report/en/summary_en.pdf.

Wrong, Dennis Hume. *The Problem of Order: What Unites and Divides Society.* New York: Free Press, 1994.

Zartman, I. William. *Understanding Life in the Borderlands: Boundaries in Depth and in Motion.* Athens: University of Georgia Press, 2010.

Zeller, Wolfgang. "Get It While You Can: Building Business and Bureaucracy between Wars in the Uganda-Sudan Borderland." In *Violence on the Margins: States, Conflict, and Borderlands*, edited by Benedikt Korf and Timothy Raeymaekers, 193–218. New York: Palgrave Macmillan, 2013.

———. "Illicit Resource Flows in Sugango: Making War and Profit in the Border Triangle of Sudan, Uganda and Congo-DRC." In *Exploring the Security-Development Nexus—Perspectives from Nepal, Northern Uganda, and Sugango*, edited by Henni Alava, 111–30. Helsinki: Ministry of Foreign Affairs, 2010. http://formin.finland.fi/public/default.aspx?contentid=193523&nodeid=49542&contentlan=2&culture=en-US.

Zur, Judith N. *Violent Memories: Mayan War Widows in Guatemala.* Boulder, CO: Westview Press, 1998.

INDEX